The Culture of Military Organizati

CW01096166

Culture has an enormous influence on military organizations and their success or failure in war. Cultural biases often result in unstated assumptions that have a deep impact on the making of strategy, operational planning, doctrinal creation, and the organization and training of armed forces. Except in unique circumstances culture grows slowly, embedding so deeply that members often act unconsciously according to its dictates. Of all the factors that are involved in military effectiveness, culture is perhaps the most important. Yet it also remains the most difficult to describe and understand, because it entails so many external factors that impinge, warp, and distort its formation and continuities. The sixteen case studies in this volume examine the culture of armies, navies, and air forces from the American Civil War to the Iraq War and how and why culture affected their performance in the ultimate arbitration of war.

PETER R. MANSOOR, Colonel, US Army (Retired), is the General Raymond E. Mason Jr. Chair of Military History at The Ohio State University. He assumed this position after a twenty-six-year career in the US Army that culminated in his service as the executive officer to General David Petraeus, commanding general of Multi-National Force–Iraq, during the surge of US forces in 2007 and 2008. He is the author of *The GI Offensive in Europe: The Triumph of American Infantry Divisions, 1941–1945; Baghdad at Sunrise: A Brigade Commander's War in Iraq; and Surge: My Journey with General David Petraeus and the Remaking of the Iraq War.*

WILLIAMSON MURRAY is a professor emeritus of history at The Ohio State University. His work over the past fifty years focuses primarily on grand strategy, operations, and airpower. He has published numerous highly acclaimed works, including *The Change in the European Balance of Power, 1938–1939: The Path to Ruin; Luftwaffe; German Military Effectiveness; The Air War in the Persian Gulf; and A War to Be Won: Fighting the Second World War, 1937–1945.*

The Culture of Military Organizations

Edited by

Peter R. Mansoor
The Ohio State University

Williamson Murray
The Ohio State University

CAMBRIDGE
UNIVERSITY PRESS

University Printing House, Cambridge CB2 8BS, United Kingdom

One Liberty Plaza, 20th Floor, New York, NY 10006, USA

477 Williamstown Road, Port Melbourne, VIC 3207, Australia

314–321, 3rd Floor, Plot 3, Splendor Forum, Jasola District Centre,
New Delhi – 110025, India

79 Anson Road, #06–04/06, Singapore 079906

Cambridge University Press is part of the University of Cambridge.

It furthers the University's mission by disseminating knowledge in the pursuit of
education, learning, and research at the highest international levels of excellence.

www.cambridge.org
Information on this title: www.cambridge.org/9781108485739
DOI: 10.1017/9781108622752

© Cambridge University Press 2019

First published 2019
4th printing 2021

Printed in Great Britain by Ashford Colour Press Ltd.

A catalogue record for this publication is available from the British Library.

Library of Congress Cataloging-in-Publication Data
Names: Mansoor, Peter R., 1960– editor. | Murray, Williamson, editor.
Title: The culture of military organizations / edited by Peter R. Mansoor, Ohio
State University ; Williamson Murray, Ohio State University.
Description: New York, NY : Cambridge University Press : Cambridge, [2019] |
Includes index.
Identifiers: LCCN 2019013831 | ISBN 9781108485739
Subjects: LCSH: Sociology, Military. | Armed Forces – Case studies.
Classification: LCC U21.5 .C745 2019 | DDC 306.2/7–dc23
LC record available at https://lccn.loc.gov/2019013831

ISBN 978-1-108-48573-9 Hardback
ISBN 978-1-108-72448-7 Paperback

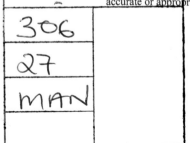

Cambridge University Press has no responsibility for the persistence or accuracy of
URLs for external or third-party internet websites referred to in this publication
and does not guarantee that any content on such websites is, or will remain,
accurate or appropriate.

The editors wish to acknowledge the generous assistance of the Mershon Center for International Security Studies at The Ohio State University, whose grant made possible the conference in September 2017 in Columbus, Ohio, from which this work originated.

Contents

Part III   Maritime Forces

Part IV   Air Forces

Contributors

ROBERT FARLEY, *University of Kentucky*

STEPHEN J. GERRAS, *Strategic Studies Institute*

MARK GRIMSLEY, *The Ohio State University*

WAYNE WEI-SIANG HSIEH, *US Naval Academy*

DAVID HUNTER-CHESTER, *Independent Scholar*

DAVID KILCULLEN, *University of New South Wales*

JOHN T. KUEHN, *US Army Command and General Staff College*

PETER R. MANSOOR, *The Ohio State University*

DANIEL MARSTON, *Australian National University*

ALLAN R. MILLETT, *The Ohio State University (Emeritus) and University of New Orleans*

WILLIAMSON MURRAY, *The Ohio State University (Emeritus)*

REINA PENNINGTON, *Norwich University*

RICHARD HART SINNREICH, *Independent Scholar*

DAVID STUBBS, *Independent Scholar*

GIL-LI VARDI, *Stanford University*

CORBIN WILLIAMSON, *Air War College*

JORIT WINTJES, *Julius Maximilians University of Würzburg*

LEONARD WONG, *Strategic Studies Institute*

KEVIN M. WOODS, *Institute for Defense Analyses*

Introduction

Peter R. Mansoor and Williamson Murray

Culture has an enormous influence on military organizations and institutions and their success or failure in the ultimate arbitration of war. One can broadly define organizational culture as the assumptions, ideas, norms, and beliefs, expressed or reflected in symbols, rituals, myths, and practices, that shape how an organization functions and adapts to external stimuli and that give meaning to its members.[1] Isabel Hull, who has written one of the clearest historical works to date on military culture, defines it as the "habitual practices, default programs, hidden assumptions, and unreflected cognitive frames" that underpin how an organization functions.[2] Except in unique circumstances – in the initial founding of an organization or when it undergoes severe trauma – culture grows slowly over time, embedding itself so deeply into its processes that members often act unconsciously according to its dictates.[3] This may have positive benefits. American service members, for instance, are imbued with the cultural ethic to leave no soldier behind on the battlefield, which undoubtedly enhances morale and willingness to fight rather than flee, knowing that one's comrades will be at one's side if the worst occurs. But culture may also have negative consequences, especially when it locks an organization into dated and inappropriate ways of operating, as occurred with the Royal Navy in the period leading up to the Battle of Jutland in World War I.[4] Culture can also act as a catalyst to increase the brutality of war, and in other cases to decrease it.[5] Because culture lies hidden under more visible organizational doctrine and symbols, one can easily overlook its power. "Nevertheless," writes Hull,

---

[1] For an excellent discussion of organizational culture, see Jeffrey W. Legro, *Cooperation under Fire: Anglo-German Restraint during World War II* (Ithaca, NY, 1995), 19–25, and Mats Alvesson, *Understanding Organizational Culture* (London, 2002), 3–4.

[2] Isabel V. Hull, *Absolute Destruction: Military Culture and the Practices of War in Imperial Germany* (Ithaca, NY, 2006), 2.

[3] For a discussion of the impact of trauma-learning, see ibid., 96.

[4] For an example of how culture influenced the poor performance of the Royal Navy at the Battle of Jutland in 1916, see Andrew Gordon, *The Rules of the Game: Jutland and British Naval Command* (London, 1996).

[5] For an example of culture influencing the ferocity of war, see John W. Dower, *War without Mercy: Race & Power in the Pacific War* (New York, 1986); for examples of culture making war more humane, see Legro, *Cooperation under Fire*.

1

"organizational culture is more likely to determine action than is explicit policy or ideology."[6]

Culture has two major impacts on an organization. First, it creates organizational identity, that is, the distinctive attributes that make the organization different from others. The US Marine Corps, for instance, prides itself on being a flexible expeditionary force capable of rapid deployment at the orders of the president. The US Army has a few units with this same ethos, but the organization as a whole is "America's army" designed to fight and win the nation's wars. Marine leaders expect short, sharp engagements, while Army leaders aim to fight over the long haul. The two cultures sometimes collide, as occurred in the invasion of Saipan in June 1944, when Marine Lt. Gen. Holland "Howlin' Mad" Smith relieved US Army Maj. Gen. Ralph Smith over the latter's perceived lack of aggressiveness in fighting through the mountainous interior of the island.[7] Second, culture establishes expectations of how group members will act in a given situation. The German Army's emphasis on operational maneuver in both world wars, for instance, led senior leaders to ignore more salient aspects of strategy, in particular economic mobilization and logistics. Germany's senior military leaders, imbued with a culture of tactical and operational excellence, believed that maneuver would achieve quick victories over major powers, thus enabling Germany to overcome Great Britain, the Soviet Union, and the United States despite the vast latent industrial power of the Allies.[8] This culture ultimately resulted in the destruction of the Wehrmacht as Allied forces overran Germany in the spring of 1945.

The problem for senior military leaders is not just the difficulty in understanding culture, but in using it to further the goals of the organization. Even harder is changing culture when it becomes antithetical to organizational needs. A highly respected Marine general once commented to one of the editors that "changing culture [is] like trying to turn a large cruise liner" – it can only occur slowly.[9] These problems exist despite the best intentions of leaders and managers to "get" culture. One authority on organizational culture writes, "However, even in those cases where top managers have a strong awareness of the significance of culture, there is often a lack of a deeper understanding of how people and organizations function in terms of culture. Culture is as significant and complex as it is difficult to understand and 'use' in a thoughtful

---

[6] Hull, *Absolute Destruction*, 92.
[7] For the most part, US Army and Marine commanders cooperated with one another during the Pacific War against Japan. For an analysis of the "Smith vs. Smith" controversy, see Sharon Tosi Lacey, *Pacific Blitzkrieg: World War II in the Central Pacific* (Denton, TX, 2013), chapter 4.
[8] For the evolution of German military culture emphasizing operational maneuver and quick victories, see Robert Citino, *The German Way of War: From the Thirty Years' War to the Third Reich* (Lawrence, KS, 2005).
[9] Lt. Gen. Paul van Riper to Williamson Murray, conversation 1996.

way."[10] One of the purposes of this book is to help military leaders understand how organizational culture forms; the influence culture has on organizational functioning and the development of strategy, operations, and tactics; and how culture changes.

Culture is clearly a crucial determinant to the effectiveness of military organizations. It may come as a surprise, then, that perhaps the best study in this genre left out culture as a determinant of military effectiveness. In the three volumes of *Military Effectiveness*, focused on World War I, the interwar period, and World War II, editors Allan R. Millett and Williamson Murray (also the coeditor of this volume) posited a number of factors influencing military effectiveness, defined as "the process by which armed forces convert resources into fighting power."[11] Among these factors are the ability of an armed force to operate within the political milieu to obtain manpower and resources, the fashioning of strategies to achieve political goals, the matching of ways and means to the ends of strategy, the ability to operate within the context of an alliance, the development of doctrine to maximize the capabilities of various arms and services, the willingness of the officer corps to realistically examine the problems confronting an armed force, the reasonable integration of available technology, a coequal emphasis on support elements such as intelligence and logistics, and tactical flexibility and adaptability.[12] To be fair the editors warned that "one must include in the analysis non-quantifiable organizational attitudes, behaviors, and relationships that span a military organization's full activities at the political, strategic, operational, and tactical levels."[13] But organizational culture was not an explicit element of the study and chapter authors for the most part did not address it. The intention of this volume, then, is to revise and expand the discussion of military effectiveness by focusing on the role played by organizational and strategic culture in its development.

Of all the factors involved in military effectiveness, culture is perhaps the most important. Yet it also remains the most difficult to describe and understand, because it involves so many external factors that impinge, warp, and distort its formation and continuities, even in different military organizations within the same nation. These factors explain why it is so difficult for military organizations to change their fundamental, underlying culture.

Thus, even catastrophic military defeat can have relatively little impact on an organization's underlying culture. The performance of the Italian-Piedmontese military in losing or performing badly in a series of wars from the mid-nineteenth century through to its dismal performance during World War II underlines the

---

[10] Alvesson, *Understanding Organizational Culture*, 1.
[11] Allan R. Millett, Williamson Murray, and Kenneth H. Watman, "The Effectiveness of Military Organizations," in Allan R. Millett and Williamson Murray, eds., *Military Effectiveness, vol. I, The First World War* (Boston, 1988), 2.
[12] Ibid., 4–27.   [13] Ibid., 27.

point that military organizations do not necessarily learn from their defeats. As Professor MacGregor Knox has pointed out about the culture of the Italian Army senior leadership, "The fundamental problem was the Italian general staff tradition: Custoza, Lissa, Adua, Caporetto. On those occasions the military ... distinguished itself by the absence of the study, planning, and attention to detail that characterized the Germans, and by a tendency to intrigue and confuse responsibilities among senior officers."[14] In fact, history suggests that largely because of underlying and systemic factors, it has proven extraordinarily difficult to change the basic culture of military organizations.[15]

Despite the foregoing discussion, all too many historians and other commentators argue that military defeat can have a profound impact on the culture of military organizations.[16] More often than not, they cite the example of the German Army in the interwar period as having reacted effectively in response to its disastrous defeat in World War I and thus created modern armored warfare.[17] In fact, the Germans did develop impressive ground forces in the interwar period that had a significant impact in the first two years of World War II. However, those successes rested entirely on the tactical revolution that the Germans had initiated in the last two years of World War I.[18] Moreover, in the larger sense, the German military, and not just the army, failed to learn the more important strategic lessons of the war.[19] Having taken on effectively all of the great powers outside Central Europe between 1914 and 1918, it managed to repeat this same strategic mistake in the next conflict – creating a strategic situation where the Germans to all intents and purposes ended up fighting all of the other major powers in Europe, with the United States again thrown in for good measure.

Yet military cultures do change over time. Horatio Nelson's mantra at Trafalgar summed up the Royal Navy's culture from 1757 to 1815: "No captain can do very wrong if he places his ship alongside that of the enemy."[20] It was a culture that demanded initiative, independent decision-making, and leadership

---

[14] MacGregor Knox, *Mussolini Unleashed, Politics and Strategy in Fascist Italy's Last War* (Cambridge, 1984), 16.

[15] There are, of course, exceptions, as the chapters in this volume on the Army of Northern Virginia (Chapter 4) and the Army of the Tennessee (Chapter 3) point out.

[16] Among others see Barry Posen, *The Sources of Military Doctrine: France, Britain and Germany between the Wars* (Ithaca, NY, 1986).

[17] In fact, what the Germans created was not modern armored warfare, but rather combined-arms tactics into which they folded the tank, which added an element of rapid exploitation to elements already intrinsic in German doctrine.

[18] For the German innovations in armored warfare, see particularly Williamson Murray, "Armored Warfare," in Williamson Murray and Allan R. Millett, eds., *Military Innovation in the Interwar Period* (Cambridge, 1996), chapter 1.

[19] The German Kriegsmarine, having brought the United States into the war in 1917 with disastrous consequences for the Reich, nevertheless was arguing strongly in July 1941 for Hitler to declare war on the United States.

[20] Nelson's memorandum to his captains immediately before the Battle of Trafalgar, October 9, 1805, www.bl.uk/learning/timeline/item106127.html.

at least down to the level of its captains. A century-plus later at Jutland, the captains of Lord Jellicoe's battle fleet exhibited none of these qualities. Over that period, the organizational culture of the Royal Navy had shifted 180 degrees.[21] Significantly, the leaders of the Royal Navy were so humiliated by their performance in 1916 that they instigated major changes in the Navy's culture, so that the performance of the organization improved drastically by the onset of World War II, both in its surface battles in the Mediterranean and in the adaptability of its surface forces to the U-boat threat.[22]

Three important external factors impact military culture: geography, history, and the nature of the environment in which navies, armies, and air forces exist. Geography forms the basic context within which the past has influenced and determined the framework within which armed forces and their leaders view the world. As in real estate, geography is a matter of location, location, location. The events that transpired at Dunkirk in late May and early June 1940 were to a great extent influenced by the fact that the British viewed land's end very differently from the Germans – and the French, for that matter. To the continental militaries, the end of solid ground represented the termination of military operations. To the British, the ocean represented a great highway, an avenue of escape from the vicissitudes of the ground operations that had turned out so badly for them in northern France. Thus the Germans, largely for cultural reasons, bungled the last stages of their campaign that destroyed the French Army, but not that of Great Britain.[23]

Significantly, that sense of the ocean as a great highway has been the basis of British strategy and Britain's military culture since the end of the seventeenth century.[24] Nevertheless, naval power by itself could not win or even influence to a considerable degree the wars of the great continental powers.[25] But

[21] For how this drastic change in culture took place, see particularly Gordon, *The Rules of the Game*.
[22] See Chapter 14 of this volume.
[23] The British had a long history of escapes from impossible military situations that had turned out badly. The most famous of these were the abandonment of Boston in 1776 during the American Revolution, after the Americans had seized and emplaced artillery on Dorchester Heights overlooking the city, and Coruna in Spain in 1808, when the British Army withdrew in the face of Marshal Massena's overwhelming superiority. On the other hand, the failure of British forces to escape from Yorktown in 1781 sealed their fate and with it the outcome of the American Revolutionary War.
[24] That was not B. H. Liddell Hart's argument that the British in the eighteenth and early nineteenth centuries had followed a course of minimum support to the continental wars and maximum support to a blue-water strategy aimed at seizing French colonies. For a rejoinder to this argument, see Williamson Murray, "Grand Strategy, Alliances, and the Anglo-American Way of War," in Peter Mansoor and Williamson Murray, eds., *Grand Strategy and Military Alliances* (Cambridge, 2016), chapter 2.
[25] That has not prevented a significant number of British commentators from early in the eighteenth century onward from arguing in favor of a blue-water school of strategy, in which Britain would not support continental allies, but rather would focus entirely on the naval and mercantile struggle. In this regard, see particularly Jonathan Swift's pamphlet *On the Conduct of the Allies*, a ferocious attack on Marlborough's strategy in the War of Spanish Succession.

Britain's relative invulnerability that resulted from its geography as an island allowed that nation eventually to control the world's oceans.[26] British strategists also provided significant financial and military aid to Britain's allies on the continent to keep them in the fight. Particularly in the wars against Louis XIV and Napoleon, this twofold strategy of providing substantial military aid and financial support to Britain's allies, while dominating the world's oceans, allowed the British to overcome opponents with substantially greater resources. In the great emperor's case, the British confronted a France in control of nearly the entire European continent.[27] This strategy was made possible by a Royal Navy imbued with a culture of independent initiative and aggressiveness that made it feasible for Britain to blockade the continent, ferry British forces to distant battlefields, and keep the British trading economy going even as its continental adversaries controlled much of Europe.

During the Seven Year's War, British Prime Minister William Pitt's strategy of controlling the world's oceans allowed the British to conduct major operations for the control of Canada and the Caribbean islands, while they were at the same time providing substantial ground forces and subsidies to assist Frederick the Great in repelling the combined assaults of France, Austria, and Russia.[28] The one time during the eighteenth century that the British failed to secure firm alliances on the continent, namely during the war against the American revolutionaries, they suffered a major defeat and lost the American colonies in the process.

We should also note that the fact that France, one of Europe's greatest powers, lies immediately across the English Channel has had a profound effect on how the English and then the British have viewed the world. During the Age of Sail, the Low Countries represented a major invasion threat to those directing strategy in London. Elizabeth I took a major risk in supporting the Dutch against the overweening power of Philip II's Spain, because Spanish control of the Low Countries represented an enormous strategic threat to the British Isles. Similarly, the support rendered by English and then British governments to the Second Hundred Years' War against the French from 1688 through 1815 represented a strategic vision that largely determined British strategic culture – a vision rooted in the geography of the English Channel and the North Sea.

In many respects, the strategy followed in the twentieth century by American leaders has reflected the same geographic realities that enabled Britain to succeed in earlier centuries. To all intents and purposes the United States is

---

[26] There were, of course, other significant factors in Britain's rise.

[27] What Liddell Hart entirely ignored was the reality that the British supported a major ground effort on the Iberian Peninsula under the Duke of Wellington that kept the flame of resistance alive and that led Napoleon to describe the war in Spain as his "Iberian ulcer."

[28] Fred Anderson, *Crucible of War: The Seven Year's War and the Fate of Empire in British North America, 1754–1766* (New York, 2001).

an island; its neighbors to the north and south since the War of 1812 and the Mexican-American War of 1847 have never represented a significant threat. Thus, throughout the twentieth century, the Americans have used North America as an economic and military springboard to project military power across the great oceans that separate them from the rest of the world. In World War I, their economic strength kept the Allies in the war, and in 1918, the arrival of great masses of American infantry in France helped to tip the military balance against the Germans and finally made the blockade of the Central Powers effective.[29] In World War II, the United States was truly the "arsenal of democracy," but its success rested on a strategic culture that understood the importance of logistics, economic realities, and the difficulties involved in the projection of power over immense distances.[30] While the Cold War never became hot, the presence of American troops, air forces, and naval power in Europe and Korea kept the balance relatively stable and prevented the disaster of a nuclear war.

For continental powers, the influence of geography on strategic culture is obviously quite different.[31] For the French, the fact that they have always bordered on a major power has had a profound impact on their history. Thus, their efforts against the Spanish in the sixteenth and early seventeenth centuries reflected deep fears about the security of a nation confronted on three sides by Spanish military forces – in the Pyrenees, Italy, and Flanders. And, of course, there was the problem posed by English and later British sea power, which forced the French to divide their military strength between sea power and land power, neither of which they mastered, except when they were led by a Corsican military genius, Napoleon.[32]

The Germans are an interesting case, because for most of their history the Reich was nothing more than a collection of mini-states with no ability to craft anything resembling a common strategy. Prussia emerged in the eighteenth century to provide something resembling a German state, but Prussia's existence depended very much not only on the strength of its army but also on the strategic wisdom of its leadership. The military disaster of 1806 underlined its geographic limitations and was to have a profound impact on the military culture that evolved in the nineteenth century. The Iron Chancellor, Otto von Bismarck, through his brilliant understanding of the weaknesses of Germany's

---

[29] For the extraordinary weakness of the blockade of the Central Powers from 1914 to 1917, see Nicholas Lambert, *Planning Armageddon: British Economic Warfare and the First World War* (Cambridge, MA, 2011).

[30] For the role of economic factors in the American mobilization of its industrial resources, see James Lacey, *Keep from All Thoughtful Men: How U.S. Economists Won World War II* (Annapolis, MD, 2011).

[31] We should note that strategic culture is not the same as organizational culture, although the former exercises considerable influence over the latter, as we point out throughout the book.

[32] Napoleon spoke French with a Corsican-Italian accent.

strategic competitors as well as the milieu in which he was operating, was able to create a unified Germany. But after the "War in Sight Crisis" of 1875, he understood how vulnerable Germany was, surrounded as it was on three sides by great powers.[33]

Despite Bismarck's admonitions, the culture that dominated the German military at the end of the nineteenth century paid no attention to the Reich's strategic position, or to the fact that the only resource that Germany would control in substantial amounts was coal.[34] Thus, Kaiser Wilhelm II disregarded virtually all of Bismarck's policies and in addition created the High Seas Fleet, an explicit threat to the British, thereby driving the British into the arms of the French and their Russian allies. The German nation in the twentieth century would pay a terrible price for ignoring the dictates of geography by embracing a culture that instead emphasized operational, tactical, and technical effectiveness at the expense of sound strategy.

Equally important and to the detriment of German military culture is the fact that the Reich's position in Europe has meant that it has always been located near the center of major wars; consequently, the German military in the wars of German unification had to pay relatively little attention to logistics in its conduct of military operations. By 1914, the development of operational plans ignored any factors that impeded maneuver and the attempt to destroy enemy armies in great *kesselschlachten*, or battles of encirclement. The Schlieffen Plan in 1914 was not just an operational failure but also a logistical one. By the time the Germans approached Paris and the Marne, they were almost out of ammunition, while their food situation had reached such dire straits that officers were issuing the troops wine to keep them going – with obvious results.[35] In World War II, the extraordinary distances over which the Wehrmacht operated – from the North Cape to North Africa and from the Volga to the Atlantic Ocean – meant that logistics was a crucial factor in military operations. And here the Germans proved disastrously inept. The failure of Barbarossa, the invasion of the Soviet Union, was above all a failure of logistics. Even after the war was over, Gen. Franz Halder, the chief of the *Oberkommando des Heeres* (Army) staff from 1938 to 1942, commented that "quartermaster [logisticians] must never hamper operational concepts," a

[33] For Bismarck's strategic policies after the "War in Sight Crisis," see Marcus Jones, "Bismarckian Strategy Policy, 1871–1890," in Williamson Murray and Richard Hart Sinnreich, eds., *Successful Strategies: Triumphing in War and Peace from Antiquity to the Present* (Cambridge, 2014), chapter 8.
[34] For Germany's strategic weaknesses in raw materials, see Williamson Murray, *The Change in the European Balance of Power: The Path to Ruin* (Princeton, NJ, 1984), chapter 1.
[35] For the logistical mess that the Germans had gotten themselves into by early September 1914, see Holger H. Herwig, *The First World War: Germany and Austria-Hungary 1914–1918* (London, 1997), 100–101.

statement that flew in the face of every major campaign in World War II, with the exception perhaps of the 1940 German campaign against France.[36]

The United States makes an interesting contrast to other nations. The first great conflict that the Americans waged as a major power came with the American Civil War. The problem that the North confronted was not just in mobilizing vast military power from a tiny garrison force whose mission had been to keep settlers and Indians separated, but also in fighting a war over continental distances, which would require logistical capabilities unheard of thus far in military history.[37] The vast area of the Confederacy, some 780,000 square miles, was equivalent to the combined territories of Britain, France, the Low Countries, Spain, Germany, and Italy.

The problem for the North then was not just to raise vast armies and mobilize its industry, which was almost completely unprepared to support the needs of a major war, but also to project military power over continental distances – distances that the Europeans had only confronted with Napoleon's invasion of Russia (and then none too successfully). The result was an emphasis on logistics, which has been at the center of US military culture ever since. But then it has to be, because the capabilities of the American military depend on the ability to project power over continental and oceanic distances. Victory in the Pacific and in Europe represented the triumph of American military culture, in which an understanding of logistics was deeply imbedded in its military approach to strategy as well as operations.

If geography is important to the formation of the culture of military organizations, so too are the influences of past military experiences. In some cases, geography and the past are intimately intertwined. In this regard, the experience of Russia is instrumental. It has the greatest land expanse of any major nation, even after the collapse of the Soviet Union. However, unlike the United States, which has no major powers on its borders and has suffered invasions only when it had no significant navy, Russia, despite its vast spaces, has confronted a series of significant invasions beginning with the Mongols in the thirteenth century, whose devastating conquest set Russian civilization far behind that of the rest of Europe. A number of major invasions from the west followed that disaster: the Poles in the seventeenth century, the Swedes in the eighteenth century, Napoleon and the Grand Army in 1812, and finally the Germans in World Wars I and II. The German invasion was the most terrible of all. By the time the Red Army had driven the Wehrmacht off the territory of the Soviet Union, some 27 million Soviet citizens had died. Not surprising, that historical experience has

---

[36] Quoted in Dennis Showalter, *Instruments of War: The German Army 1914–1918* (London, 2016), 188.

[37] For a discussion of the geography of the Confederacy, see Williamson Murray and Wayne Wei-siang Hsieh, *A Savage War: A Military History of the United States* (Princeton, NJ, 2016), 60–62.

given the Russians a strategic culture driven by fear and suspicion of the outsider and an expansionist mentality aiming to incorporate buffer states that lay along its borders, along with a deep suspicion of its neighbors that verges on the paranoiac.[38]

For a specific historical example that underlines the impact of the past on military culture, there are few better examples than the disastrous defeat that the Prussian Army suffered at the hands of Napoleon and his marshals in October 1806 at the double battles of Jena-Auerstadt. In one day, given grossly inept handling at the tactical and operational levels, the Prussian Army collapsed before the Grand Army's onslaught. The collapse of the Prussian state followed soon thereafter. The result was that from the Napoleonic wars onward the Prussian officer corps focused heavily on tactics and military operations. It also developed a military culture that was profoundly anti-intellectual. By 1900, German military writers, largely influenced by the traditions of the Prussian Army, were dismissing concepts of strategy – and even Clausewitz with his emphasis on war as a continuation of politics by other means – as outmoded concepts not worthy of study. As Gen. Geyer von Schweppenburg wrote to Liddell Hart after World War II, "You will be horrified to hear that I have never read Clausewitz or Delbrück or Haushofer. The opinion on Clausewitz in our general staff was that [he was] a theoretician to be read by professors."[39]

The emphasis was now on what the Germans termed "military necessity."[40] In such a strategic culture, the German general staff found it easy to dismiss the consequences of the fact that a violation of Belgium's neutrality during an invasion of France would bring Britain into the war. Similarly, military necessity overrode strategic and political concerns in the German decision to use poison gas in April 1915. Even more disastrous was the decision to resume submarine warfare against the British in January 1917, despite the fact that the Germans knew that doing so would bring the United States into the war. And indeed the Americans did declare war in April 1917 with a strategic impact that sealed the Reich's fate. Underlining the overweening emphasis the Germans placed on tactics is the fact that in developing the plans for the Michael offensive in March 1918, Ludendorff established no operational goals. As he told the army group commander, Crown Prince Rupprecht of Bavaria, who was to command the offensive, "I object to the word 'operation.' We will punch a

---

[38] In dealing with the Russians, it is well to remember that they often talk about the great victories of 1944 and 1945 but rarely of the catastrophic defeats of 1941. But it is the history of 1941 that is burned into their memory.

[39] Geyer von Schweppenburg attended the *Kriegsakademie* immediately before the outbreak of World War I. Letter from Geyer von Schweppenburg to Basil Liddell Hart, 1948, BHLH Archives, King's College Archives, London, 9/24.V/61, 32.

[40] On this see particularly Hull, *Absolute Destruction*.

hole in [their line] and see what turns up."[41] The result was that the Germans conquered only territory that possessed neither strategic nor operational importance and missed a significant chance to seize the main British supply dumps, thereby endangering the British position on the continent.[42]

The third of the great influences on the culture of military organizations has to do with the environment within which they operate. The nature of air power and the fact that aircraft can operate over substantial distances at great speeds provides airmen a freedom that their comrades on the ground and at sea do not possess.[43] It has also created in air forces a highly technical and engineering culture in their approach to war. Moreover, the aircraft and the weapons air forces utilize have created a culture that rests on linear analysis, largely because so much of what air forces do in war and in peace can easily be reduced to statistics: numbers of sorties flown, operational ready rates for aircraft and crews, bombs and tonnage of weapons dropped, availability of parts and munitions, and the number of enemy aircraft destroyed. The list of quantitative metrics for air forces is almost infinite.

However, there is one great problem: these calculations have almost everything to do with efficiency and almost nothing to do with effectiveness. The first raid on the ball bearing plants at Schweinfurt by the US Eighth Air Force underlines this reality in spades. The post-raid photographs indicated that the bombs had wrecked the roofs and walls of much of the factory areas – apparently a major success. But in fact the wreckage of the factories' infrastructure did little damage to the machines that manufactured the ball bearings. The Germans were able then to pull those machines out from the wreckage in relatively undamaged condition and resume production.[44] To sum up, one of the major difficulties in waging a successful air campaign has to do with the fact that in nearly every case, only postwar analysis can indicate how effective air strikes have been.

Air forces' embrace of technology has also caused them to ignore historical realities, however short their histories have been. Strategic bombing culture in the interwar period held as an article of faith that bombers could reach their targets without fighter escort, despite applicable experience from German and Allied bombing campaigns in World War I. Despite even more relevant experience from the great bombing campaigns of World War II, airmen all too often believe that the latest technological gadgets will trump the experience of the past. One air force general, addressing a class at the US Air War College after

---

[41] Crown Prince Rupprecht, *Mein Kriegstagebuch, vol. 2*, ed. by Eugen von Frauenholz (Munich 1929), 372n.

[42] For the strategic and operational imbecility of the German 1918 offensives, see David Zabecki, *The German 1918 Offensives: A Case Study in the Operational Level of War* (London, 2006).

[43] The fact that carriers have allowed navies, and the US Navy in particular, to utilize aircraft has changed the naval equation in this regard as well.

[44] Friedhelm Golücke, *Schweinfurt und die strategische Luftkrieg 1943* (Paderborn, 1980).

the first Gulf War, stated that due to the advent of guided munitions and stealth aircraft, any history before 1991 was irrelevant to air operations in the future.[45] Of course, nothing could be further from the truth, but the anecdote illustrates how the embrace of technology can influence the culture of an organization.

Navies, like air forces, confront the problem that they live in a potentially hostile environment, although air forces have the choice of not flying when the weather is potentially too dangerous. Traditional naval culture has also found itself formed by the fact that once ships leave harbor, their captains have enjoyed the freedom of decision-making because their superiors have had no means of communicating with them. This has given naval captains the ability to take the initiative, but has also subjected them to strict accountability. If a captain runs his ship aground or crashes into another vessel, he is invariably relieved for cause.[46] The inability of higher headquarters to communicate with vessels at sea had changed by the 1930s with increasingly effective radio communications. Nevertheless, the culture of captains displaying initiative was on display in the more effective navies of World War II, the US Navy and the Royal Navy being prime examples. On the other hand, the conduct of the U-boat campaign by the Germans in that conflict witnessed Grand Adm. Dönitz attempting to run everything from shore to the general detriment of operations. The large amount of radio traffic involved created the conditions that allowed British code-breaking efforts to crack the U-boat Enigma cyphers, with a major impact on the conduct of the Battle of the Atlantic.

Armies, however, confront a very different environment from that of navies and air forces. In war, they are almost always in contact with their enemies' ground forces. Moreover, they inevitably have to deal with civilians, not only their own, but, if they are on enemy ground, also those of their opponents. The combat framework is also quite different. In war, they confront the enemy directly in an environment of horror, slaughter, uncertainty and ambiguity that reaches down to the lowest level. Unlike air forces and navies, commanders confront the reality that, as Clausewitz suggests, the lowliest private can disturb, divert, and even compromise the simplest plan: "A battalion is made up of individuals, the least important of whom may chance to delay things or somehow make them go wrong."[47] This makes an enormous difference in the cultures of armies and navies: the captain of an aircraft carrier can order his ship to make a 90 degree turn and all 5,000 sailors will turn with the ship. For an infantry battalion spread out over considerable ground, this quite simply is never going to be the case. Charismatic leadership, therefore, is valued more

---

[45] Anecdote provided to one of the editors by a professor at the Air War College.
[46] The 2017 incidents involving the USS *Fitzgerald* and the USS *John S. McCain*, both of which nearly sank after colliding with a cargo vessel and an oil tanker, respectively, are cases in point.
[47] Carl von Clausewitz, *On War*, trans. and ed. by Michael Howard and Peter Paret (Princeton, NJ, 1976), 119.

highly in army culture than in other services. In addition, the modern battlefield has expanded in distance, so armies have had to develop cultures that emphasize individual decision-making and initiative down to the lowest level.

We should also note that each individual military organization has subcultures that differ in quite substantial ways from that of the larger organization of which they are a part. Those familiar with the US Navy will quite readily recognize that it possesses three subcultures that differ in substantial ways: that of naval aviators, that of the surface navy, and that of the submariners. Moreover, history suggests that these subcultures will adapt to the realities of technological change in substantially different ways. During World War II, US carriers, commanded by naval aviators, adapted to the introduction of radar quite successfully, a factor that played a major role in the American success at Midway. Only a few months later, surface admirals would prove oblivious to the advantage that radar could have provided their ships against the Japanese, who did not possess radar but were expert at night fighting. As a result, in three battles that occurred in the area surrounding Guadalcanal, the surface admirals preferred to use their eyeballs instead of radar, with a resulting heavy loss in US ships.[48]

This volume is organized into four parts: a theory section followed by sections on the organizational culture of armies, navies, and air forces. In the first theory chapter (Chapter 1), social scientists Leonard Wong and Stephen J. Gerras introduce the nine attributes of organizational culture developed by the Global Leadership and Organizational Behavior Effectiveness (GLOBE) Research Program and apply them to military organizations. These attributes are performance orientation, future orientation, assertiveness, institutional collectivism, ingroup collectivism, power distance, humane orientation, uncertainty avoidance, and gender egalitarianism. The editors invited other chapter authors to use the GLOBE attributes in their evaluation of organizational culture, but did not force them to do so.[49] Nevertheless, the GLOBE attributes are included in the volume to help the reader understand the broader aspects of organizational culture. This may assist the reader in understanding organizational culture even in the chapters in which the framework is not used. In the second theory chapter (Chapter 2), anthropologist David Kilcullen discusses strategic culture, a related concept to organizational culture first introduced by RAND researchers in 1977 in the context of strategic nuclear warfare.[50] His findings have direct relevance to the following chapters on the organizational culture of armed services.

---

[48] The most disastrous of these was the night action in the Battle of Savo Island in early August 1942, in which Allied forces lost four heavy cruisers, while the Japanese suffered only one slightly damaged heavy cruiser.

[49] The editors realize that social scientists and historians work according to different disciplinary demands, and did not want to force a model onto chapter authors that might otherwise stifle their creativity.

[50] Jack L. Snyder, *The Soviet Strategic Culture: Implications for Limited Nuclear Operations* (Santa Monica, CA, 1977).

The next sixteen chapters examine the organizational cultures of eleven armies (in the case of the United States and Britain, their armies in different time periods), two navies, a marine corps, and two air forces. The editors believe the salient characteristics and dominant cultures of land, sea, and air services are distinct enough that grouping them thematically is the proper way to organize the volume. Sea and air services are much more reliant on technology than land forces are, and operate in media (water and air) that demand significant technical understanding and respect. On the other hand, land forces operate among people and in the urban areas in which they live. Service cultures are shaped accordingly.

Most of the chapters focus on Western militaries (although chapters also deal with the Indian [Chapter 6], Imperial Japanese [Chapter 9], and Iraqi [Chapter 12] armies), but adding more non-Western case studies would likely require a second volume. We realize that we have left out some obvious cases, among them the French Army from 1871 to 1940, the Italian Army from 1914 to 1945, the Chinese National Army from 1928 to 1948, and the Imperial Japanese Navy. Given the inability to add more material due to the length of the volume, the editors ask for forbearance for their choices.

The importance of culture on military organizations is as vital today as it has been at any other time in history. Everything that military organizations must perform in the pursuit of national security objectives ultimately rests on their cultural foundations. Organizational culture will shape how military organizations respond to the challenges confronting them today and that they will face in the years ahead. The accelerated rate of technological change alone requires military organizations to adapt in order to survive, but as the experience of militaries during the industrial era has shown, their ability to do so is highly dependent on organizational cultures that are willing to accept a certain amount of risk and that study the past as well as the present. Not all do so, to their detriment and potentially to their extinction. The difficulty is that changing military culture represents an extraordinarily difficult task that may require years, if not decades, to accomplish. Perhaps one of the most important enablers to changing military culture during peacetime is the emphasis that military organizations place on professional military education. For example, the contrast between the major emphasis the US military placed on professional military education in the 1920s and 1930s stands in stark contrast to the current situation, with serious implications for the future and for the American military's ability to adapt to the unexpected. It is critical, then, to draw out the insights of history to enable military leaders and policy makers in the present to understand the cultural contexts in which their organizations function. This volume aims to achieve that goal.

Part I

Theoretical Frameworks

1   Culture and Military Organizations

Leonard Wong and Stephen J. Gerras

Explanations for the successes or failures of militaries in both war and peace have traditionally focused on key factors such as technology, leadership, personnel, training, or a combination of all of these. A more recent addition to the list of possible variables contributing to military effectiveness is the concept of *culture* – the sum collection of beliefs, values, attitudes, and learned behavior of a group of people. A military's culture provides the underlying foundation for decisions in strategy, planning, organization, training, and operations. For example, viewing culture as a contributing factor to military effectiveness would suggest that during the American Revolutionary War, the culture of the Continental Army influenced the fledgling army's success and failure on battlefields ranging from Ticonderoga to Trenton.

"Culture," as Raymond Williams has pointed out, however, "is one of the two or three most complicated words in the English language."[1] So while the culture of the Continental Army may have had an impact on its combat effectiveness, defining – and subsequently analyzing – that culture may prove difficult simply because there are multiple levels of analysis of culture. In the case of the Continental Army, many of the troops coming from the New England colonies brought with them their *societal* culture. It was a culture, as Alexis de Tocqueville observed, from a democratic society "containing neither lords nor common people."[2] Unfortunately, this "leveling spirit" of New England egalitarianism often conflicted with the hierarchy and discipline critical to the maneuver and massed fires required of an eighteenth-century army. Part of the eventual success of the Continental Army was George Washington's recognition of this aspect of societal culture and his subsequent (and sometimes draconian) measures to make the distinction between enlisted men and officers more pronounced.[3]

The views expressed in this chapter are those of the authors and do not reflect the official policy or position of the Department of the Army, the Department of Defense, or the US government.

[1] Raymond Williams, *Keywords: A Vocabulary of Culture and Society* (New York, 1983), 87.

[2] Alexis de Tocqueville, *Democracy in America* (New York, 1898), 38.

[3] Mark Edward Lender, *The War for American Independence: A Reference Guide* (Santa Barbara, CA, 2016), 8.

In addition to the culture at the societal level of analysis, there is also the influence of *military* culture. Militaries, regardless of the society they serve, tend to hold some variation of the values and attitudes common to most warriors. Duty, discipline, and selfless service are traits often shared by combatants on both sides of the battlefield. As Barbara Ehrenreich has noted, similarities in military culture often override differences in societal culture:

> The warrior looks out at the enemy and sees men who are, in crucial respects, recognizably like himself. They are warriors, too, and whatever differences they may have, whatever long-standing reasons for hatred, they share the basic tenets of warriordom: a respect for courage, a willingness to stand by one's comrades no matter what, a bold indifference to death. Even when divided by race and vast cultural differences, enemies may admire each other for their conduct as warriors.[4]

To muddy the waters even more, political scientists studying international relations provide yet another cultural level of analysis via the concept of *strategic* culture. A 1977 RAND study examining Soviet reactions to possible US limited nuclear operations defined strategic culture as "the sum total of ideas, conditioned emotional responses, and patterns of habitual behavior that members of a national strategic community have acquired through instruction or imitation and share with each other."[5] According to the study, strategic culture helps to explain how Soviet preoccupation with vulnerability and inferiority led to a fascination with strategies of unilateral damage limitation in the event that deterrence failed.

The focus of the following chapters is not to examine culture at the societal, military, or strategic levels of analysis. Instead, the focus is on *organizational* culture – specifically the pattern of shared assumptions that an organization learns as it solves problems and that has worked well enough to be considered valid and is therefore taught to new members as the correct way to approach those problems. Of course, a military's organizational culture may share similarities with a more universal military culture or reflect aspects of a national strategic culture that is influenced by a larger societal culture. However, the organizational boundaries of a specific military may delimit its organizational culture.

Unfortunately, the existence of subcultures often confounds assessing the impact of organizational culture on military performance. Because individuals tend to gravitate toward those similar to themselves, they also tend to become more cohesive with people they interact with more often. According to one organizational theorist, task interdependence, reporting relationships, and proximity bring members of the organization into contact with each other. This dependence and

---

[4] Barbara Ehrenreich, *Blood Rites: Origins and History of the Passions of War* (Dallas, TX, 1997), 141.
[5] Jack L. Snyder, *The Soviet Strategic Culture: Implications for Limited Nuclear Operations* (Santa Monica, CA, 1977), 8.

interaction serves as a catalyst to subgroup formation and results in the formation of subcultures.[6]

For example, while navies tend to have distinct cultures from those of armies or air forces, the naval aviation subculture is often quite different from the sub-cultures of the naval surface or naval submarine forces. (In the US Navy, they even wear different-colored shoes.) A naval culture clearly serves as a foundation for these subcultures, yet any analysis of a navy culture – or the culture of any complex organization – should include the recognition of subcultures, how they relate to each other, and how they fit together to form the larger culture.

A social psychologist instrumental in introducing the concept of organiza-tional culture proposed that in order to effectively analyze the culture of an organization, it is necessary to examine three components: (a) artifacts, (b) beliefs and values, and (c) underlying basic assumptions.[7] *Artifacts* are the outer layer of a culture that we can see, feel, taste, or smell. These observable facets of a culture can include the design of an army's weaponry, the routine relationships between officers and enlisted, recruiting posters adorning a unit's walls, or even the layout of the barracks. While artifacts are the palpable evidence of a culture, they only reflect the culture, not define it.

Beneath the artifacts, an organization's *beliefs and values* make up the next level of organizational culture. One can detect the espoused beliefs and values of an organization in official sources such as organizational creeds, command philosophies, or doctrinal statements, as well as in unofficial sources such as letters, speeches, or interviews. The stated values of an organization serve the normative function of providing guidance to organizational members concern-ing how to behave or react in key situations or times of uncertainty. While artifacts are the observable clues of a culture, an organization's values reveal more of the motivations and rationale of the organizational culture. Of course, an organization's stated values may not match its demonstrated values. In order to determine the values and beliefs that an organization actually puts into use (as opposed to merely espousing), it is necessary to look deeper into the next level of cultural analysis. Beneath an organization's beliefs and values is the third level of an organizational culture – the *underlying basic assumptions*.

When certain beliefs and values lead to repeated success in addressing problems or dealing with situations, basic assumptions gradually form.[8] The beliefs become taken for granted and shared by nearly all organizational members as the approved way of seeing the world and guiding action. This underlying consensus of unseen and usually unconscious assumptions affects the perceptions, thought processes, and behaviors of an organization. For

[6] Mary Jo Hatch, *Organization Theory* (Oxford, 1997), 229.
[7] Edgar H. Schein, "Organizational Culture," *American Psychologist* 45(2) (1990), 111.
[8] Edgar H. Schein, *Organizational Culture and Leadership*, 5th edn. (Hoboken, NJ, 2017), 21.

example, it is a basic assumption of most Western militaries that in addition to mission accomplishment, preserving the lives of their soldiers is paramount. For those militaries, it is inconceivable to develop a strategy that deliberately sends their soldiers to certain death. Other militaries, however, may not have cultures resting on that assumption and therefore may unhesitatingly deploy suicide bombers.

Edgar Schein proposes five basic assumptions that undergird organizational cultures:

1) assumptions about external adaptation issues,
2) assumptions about managing internal integration,
3) assumptions about the nature of reality and truth,
4) assumptions about the nature of time and space, and
5) assumptions about human nature, activity, and relationships.[9]

While these assumptions are comprehensive, they can be somewhat abstract when used in a military context. For example, Schein states that a central assumption concerning the nature of human activity addresses one's basic orientation to life – what is the appropriate level of activity or passivity? At the organizational level, Schein offers, this assumption concerns questions such as "what is work and what is play?"[10] The utility of this cultural dimension in analyzing organizations such as Google or GEICO that are known for being "fun" places to work is clear. For an army, air force, or navy, however, the efficacy of such questions is not so apparent.

A more relevant set of organizational culture assumptions comes from the work of Geert Hofstede[11] and the follow-on Global Leadership and Organizational Behavior Effectiveness (GLOBE) Research Program.[12] Although focused mainly at the societal level, both the Hofstede and GLOBE research provide an empirically supported assessment of the dimensions that distinguish organizations and societies. Hofstede identified four cultural dimensions – aspects of a culture that one can measure relative to other cultures – by examining employee responses to survey questionnaires from IBM employees in fifty countries. The dimensions were *power distance, collectivism* versus *individualism, femininity* versus *masculinity,* and *uncertainty avoidance*. Hofstede later added another dimension that quantified *long-term* versus *short-term orientation*.[13]

---

[9] Ibid., 87–102.   [10] Ibid., 96.

[11] Geert Hofstede, *Culture's Consequences: International Differences in Work-Related Values* (Los Angeles, CA, 1980).

[12] Robert J. House, Paul J. Hanges, Mansour Javidan, Peter W. Dorfman, and Vipin Gupta, *Culture, Leadership, and Organizations* (Los Angeles, CA, 2004).

[13] Geert Hofstede and Gert Jan Hofstede, *Cultures and Organizations: Software of the Mind* (Boston, MA, 1991).

During the 1990s, Robert House and a team of researchers extended Hofstede's work with the GLOBE project. The GLOBE project collected data from more than 17,000 middle managers in 951 organizations in telecommunications, food processing, and finance industries across sixty-two societies. These data produced a more nuanced understanding of underlying organizational cultural assumptions by using questionnaire responses from the middle managers aggregated to the societal and organizational levels of analysis. Using multiple quantitative and qualitative techniques, GLOBE researchers found the derived scales statistically and conceptually sound.[14]

The GLOBE methodology resulted in the identification of nine major attributes of cultures that serve as good substitutes for the basic assumptions underlying Schein's notions of artifacts and values. These nine dimensions of culture form the foundation of an organization's beliefs and values, which are subsequently reflected in cultural artifacts. The result is a useful framework for analyzing organizational cultures – especially when contrasting organizational cultures across societal boundaries. Of course, some may view a synthesis of multiple theoretical approaches to culture as heretical. Nevertheless, the nine underlying GLOBE dimensions facilitate effective highlighting of the differences between militaries through a cultural lens. The nine dimensions underlying an organization's values are summarized in the following table and are discussed in subsequent paragraphs.[15]

GLOBE dimensions of military organizational culture

Performance Orientation: The degree to which a military encourages and rewards performance improvement and excellence.

Future Orientation: The extent to which a military engages in future-oriented behaviors such as delaying gratification, planning, and investing in the future.

Assertiveness: The degree to which a military encourages individuals to be confrontational and aggressive in relations with others.

Institutional Collectivism: The degree to which a military encourages and rewards the collective distribution of resources.

In-Group Collectivism: The degree to which members of a military express pride, loyalty, and cohesiveness to their military.

Power Distance: The degree to which members of the military expect power to be distributed equally.

Humane Orientation: The degree to which a military encourages and rewards it members to be fair, altruistic, generous, caring, and kind to others.

Uncertainty Avoidance: The extent to which a military relies on procedures and rules to reduce the unpredictability of future events.

Gender Egalitarianism: The degree to which a military minimizes gender inequality.

---

[14] House et al., *Culture, Leadership, and Organizations*, xvi.
[15] Many of the historical examples used to illustrate the GLOBE culture dimensions were graciously provided by Len Fullenkamp.

Performance orientation is the degree to which an organization encourages and rewards members for setting challenging goals, promoting innovation, and striving for excellence. Organizations (and societies) with high performance orientation place great value on education, learning, and exercising initiative. They are comfortable communicating explicitly and directly. Organizations with low performance orientation value social relations, loyalty, tradition, and seniority. They are comfortable with passivity and subtle, indirect communication.[16]

An example of a low performance orientation in a military organizational culture is the Red Army in the late 1930s, when paranoia over allegiance to Stalin, given the massive purges taking place, outweighed concerns for military capabilities. The People's Commissariat for Internal Affairs (NKVD) arrested Marshal M. N. Tukhachevskii, the Red Army's most innovative strategist, in May 1937 with seven other high-ranking generals, and accused him of conspiring with Nazi Germany to overthrow the Soviet regime. Tukhachevskii was tried in secret, found guilty, and shot. The subsequent purge during Stalin's Great Terror eliminated thousands of the Red Army's most experienced officers and reinforced the primacy of loyalty to Stalin at the expense of military innovation and initiative.[17]

Future orientation is the degree to which an organization encourages and rewards forward-looking behaviors such as planning and delayed gratification. It is based on the extent to which organizational members believe their current actions will influence their future. Organizations with a culture of high future orientation have a strategic perspective and tend to be adaptive and flexible. Organizations with a low future orientation focus more on immediate survival and short-term accomplishments. They can be hesitant to explore new methods, since implementing novel ideas might be disruptive to current performance.[18]

A military that exhibited an organizational culture with a high future orientation was the post–World War I Reichswehr, led by Hans von Seeckt. Despite the severe restrictions imposed by the Versailles Treaty (e.g., an army limited to 100,000 men), von Seeckt had the foresight to reorganize the army into a competent, professional force capable of future expansion. His future vision of warfare led to the development of doctrine, tactics, organization, and training that served as the foundation for the Wehrmacht's victories in 1939 and 1940.[19]

Assertiveness is the degree to which organizational members are tough, dominant, and aggressive in their relations with others. Organizations with high assertiveness exhibit a "can do" attitude, value direct and unambiguous communication, and are unafraid to voice their opinions. Organizations with

[16] House et al., *Culture, Leadership, and Organizations*, 277.
[17] Geoffrey Roberts, *Stalin's Wars: From World War to Cold War: 1939–1953* (New Haven, CT, 2006), 15–16.
[18] House et al., *Culture, Leadership, and Organizations*, 289–290.
[19] James S. Corum, *The Roots of Blitzkrieg: Hans von Seeckt and German Military Reform* (Lawrence, KS, 1992), 205.

cultures characterized by low assertiveness prefer communicating indirectly, emphasize "saving face," and value harmony rather than control over the environment.[20] The pre–World War II Japanese military serves as a good example of a military exhibiting an organizational culture high in assertiveness. In the early 1940s, the decision by the Japanese government to go to war was not certain. The emperor wanted to avoid a conflict with the United States and even Tojo, the new prime minister, proposed negotiating accommodations to escape war. But, as Ian Kershaw points out:

> The chiefs of the General Staffs of both armed services, urged on by gung-ho middle-echelon officers in their planning and operational sections, were the most forceful and outspoken advocates of war. By the late summer of 1941, they had pushed through, against no serious opposition, a commitment to military action before the end of the year.[21]

Institutional collectivism is the degree to which an organization practices, encourages, and rewards the collective distribution of resources and action. An organization with high levels of institutional collectivism will emphasize the importance of subjugating wants and desires for the greater good of the organization. An organization low in institutional collectivism will foster an emphasis on individualism and independence, and will cater to the needs of individual organizational members or subordinate units.[22]

An example of a military plagued by a culture low in institutional collectivism is the US military of the early 1980s. With each service subculture looking out for its own interests, the disunity of the US military was evident in highly visible events such as the failed hostage rescue mission in Tehran and the tragedy of the Beirut Marine barracks bombing. By the early 1980s, as one observer has pointed out, "the services wielded their influence more to protect their independence and prerogatives than to develop multiservice commands capable of waging modern warfare."[23] The subsequent military reforms of the Goldwater-Nichols Act of 1986 were a result of congressional dissatisfaction with an American military plagued by a culture of low institutional collectivism.

In-group collectivism reflects the degree to which individuals express pride, loyalty, and cohesiveness in their organization. Organizations with high in-group collectivism pay homage to their lineage, extol the privilege of organizational membership, and enjoy strong bonds between organizational members.[24] Organizations with cultures of low in-group collectivism are more impersonal as connections between organizational members are weak or purely transactional.

[20] House et al., *Culture, Leadership, and Organizations*, 405.
[21] Ian Kershaw, *Fateful Choices: Ten Decisions That Changed the World, 1940–1941* (London, 2008), 280.
[22] House et al., *Culture, Leadership, and Organizations*, 462.
[23] James R. Locher, *Victory on the Potomac* (College Station, TX, 2002), 15.
[24] House et al., *Culture, Leadership, and Organizations*, 463.

In-group collectivism in the military is often manifested as unit cohesion, esprit, or pride. It is a sine qua non for military excellence. It was a key factor in the formation of British commando units in the fall of 1940, the creation of US Army Ranger and Airborne units in 1942, and the establishment of the Green Berets in the 1950s. Of course, not all militaries have cultures with high levels of in-group collectivism. For example, a key factor in the success of the American 2003 invasion of Iraq was the disintegration of the Iraqi Army, including mass surrenders and defections. Captured Iraqi regular army soldiers reported that their decision to surrender was easily made because their loyalties and emotional ties were stronger to their tribe than to their unit. Rather than being motivated by the desire to not let their comrades down, Iraqi regular army soldiers reported that they were driven by fear of retribution by the Ba'ath Party, or Fedayeen Saddam, if they were found avoiding combat.[25]

Power distance is the degree to which an organization is comfortable with the unequal distribution of power. High-power-distance cultures accept large differences in power among the various levels of a hierarchy, while low-power-distance cultures expect a lower level of power differential.[26] Organizations with a high-power-distance culture encourage subordinates to rely on the judgment of superiors and proffer respect to those in higher ranks.

Militaries tend to have organizational cultures with high power distance as deference to those higher in rank is often viewed as a prerequisite to a military organization. Nevertheless, some militaries have deliberately tried to change the power-distance dimension of organizational culture. For example, in an effort to promote closer relations between officers and enlisted soldiers, as well as eliminating the rampant abuse of rank, Mao Zedong abolished all military ranks in the People's Liberation Army (PLA) in 1965. Military reforms and a renewed focus on combat effectiveness, however, led to the eventual restoration of ranks in the PLA in the mid-1980s.[27]

Humane orientation is the degree to which an organization encourages and rewards individuals for being fair, altruistic, generous, and caring. An organization with a high humane orientation promotes the well-being of others while the promotion of self-interest and a lack of consideration of others characterize a culture with a low humane orientation.[28]

It seems unlikely that militaries with the primary mission of fighting their nation's wars would have a culture marked by a high humane orientation. After

---

[25] Leonard Wong, Thomas A. Kolditz, Raymond A. Millen, and Terrence M. Potter, *Why They Fight: Combat Motivation in the Iraq War* (Carlisle, PA, 2003), 7–8.

[26] House et al., *Culture, Leadership, and Organizations*, 529.

[27] Rosita Dellios, *Modern Chinese Defence Strategy: Present Developments, Future Directions* (London, 1990), 76.

[28] House et al., *Culture, Leadership, and Organizations*, 595.

all, "altruistic" and "caring" are not typical descriptors of most armies. And yet modern militaries have been increasingly thrust into a humanitarian role due to famines, earthquakes, civil wars, and tsunamis. Critics, however, question if mere participation in humanitarian missions truly reflects a humane orientation in a military's culture. The executive director of Doctors without Borders has noted that:

> It is simply not possible for a government or military to have the unconditional ambition of only providing humanitarian action … We recognize that aid supplied by military forces can provide relief to people in need as can acts of assistance undertaken by individual soldiers or units moved by a sense of humanity. But this aid is different. It is not humanitarian assistance. It is given to reward, and it can be withheld to punish.[29]

Uncertainty avoidance addresses the extent to which organizational members are comfortable with change and ambiguity. Organizational cultures with high uncertainty avoidance seek consistency, structure, and formalized procedures. They tend to be less tolerant of rule breaking and seek to minimize risk. Cultures with low uncertainty avoidance are comfortable with risk, experimentation, and innovation.[30] While all militaries struggle with the competing tasks of maintaining predictability while embracing uncertainty, the US Army in the late 1990s exhibited a culture marked by high uncertainty avoidance. The lingering effects of training against a predictable Soviet threat, combined with templated Mission Rehearsal Exercises (MREs) for peacekeeping operations, led to a culture where leader development resulted mainly from scripted, formalized training. The resulting culture was, as a US Army War College study has pointed out, marked by "reactive instead of proactive thought, compliance instead of creativity, and adherence instead of audacity." Junior officers, especially company commanders, were "seldom given opportunities to be innovative; to make decisions; or to fail, learn, and try again."[31]

Gender egalitarianism is the degree to which an organization treats both genders equally. An organization with a high level of gender egalitarianism will have many women in positions of authority, accord them higher status, and give them a greater role in decision-making. Militaries, of course, tend to be masculine organizations and thus one might conclude that analysis in this dimension of culture will yield little insight. Recent research in the role of militaries in peacekeeping operations, however, may suggest otherwise. The recent increase in deployments of United Nations peacekeepers throughout the world has resulted in the unintended consequence of sexual exploitation and abuse committed by

---

[29] Nicolas de Torrenté, "Humanitarian NGOs Must Not Ally with Military." MSF USA. May 1, 2006. Accessed November 1, 2017. www.doctorswithoutborders.org/news-stories/op-ed/humanitarian-ngos-must-not-ally-military.

[30] House et al., *Culture, Leadership, and Organizations*, 618–619.

[31] Leonard Wong, *Stifling Innovation: Developing Tomorrow's Leaders Today* (Carlisle, PA, 2002), 3.

peacekeepers on local populations. Human trafficking, prostitution, and sex with minors appear to be disturbing by-products of militaries participating in peace-keeping operations.[32] Interestingly, analysis of mission-level information from 2009 to 2013 shows that units with personnel from countries with better records of gender equality and units with higher proportions of female peacekeepers possess lower levels of sexual exploitation and abuse allegations.[33]

The nine GLOBE dimensions provide a useful framework to analyze a military's organizational culture. Analysis of an organization's culture, however, does not reveal if it is good or bad, right or wrong. Instead, a cultural analysis examines if an organization's culture is properly aligned to its mission and environment. For example, concerning in-group collectivism, it would seem unusual to imagine a mission or environment where a military culture of pride, loyalty, and cohesiveness would not be appropriate. But in-group collectivism can occasionally encourage acts of subversion and rebellion when members believe that group norms will provide anonymity and protection from external authority. The Canadian Airborne Regiment participating in the United Nations humanitarian mission in Somalia in 1992–1993 suffered from in-group collectivism gone awry as the bonds between unit members became a dysfunctional part of a misaligned culture. After a series of scandalous events culminating in the beating death of a Somali teenager and a subsequent cover-up, the Canadian Army disbanded the entire regiment in 1995. As one commentator has concluded in her postmortem analysis of the regiment, "Group bonding is a double-edged sword: What can be functional unit bonding for war can quickly become dysfunctional in an army at peace."[34]

The beliefs, values, and assumptions comprising an organization's culture – regardless if it is aligned or misaligned – are emplaced and perpetuated largely through the actions of organizational leaders. Schein categorizes these actions as *primary embedding mechanisms* and *secondary reinforcement and stabilizing mechanisms*. While these actions play a large role in the genesis and sustainment of an organizational culture, they are also visible artifacts of that culture. Thus, primary embedding and secondary reinforcing mechanisms serve both prescriptive and descriptive roles in the analysis of organizational cultures. They are prescriptive because they are actions that leaders can take if they want to realign a culture. They are descriptive because they are evidence of the assumptions, values, and beliefs held by an organization.

---

[32] Muna Ndulo, "The United Nations Responses to the Sexual Abuse and Exploitation of Women and Girls by Peacekeepers during Peacekeeping Missions," *Berkeley Journal of International Law* 27(1) (2009), 129.

[33] Sabrina Karim and Kyle Beardsley, "Explaining Sexual Exploitation and Abuse in Peacekeeping Missions: The Role of Female Peacekeepers and Gender Equality in Contributing Countries," *Journal of Peace Research* 53(1) (2016), 100.

[34] Donna Winslow, "Rites of Passage and Group Bonding in the Canadian Airborne," in Hank Nuwer, ed., *The Hazing Reader* (Bloomington, IN, 2004), 166.

Schein proposes six primary embedding mechanisms that leaders can use to teach their organizations how to "perceive, think, feel, and behave based on their conscious and unconscious convictions" (see the following table).[35] Primary embedding mechanisms have a direct role in instilling values and assumptions into the culture. While reinforcing mechanisms are often easier to execute, it is embedding mechanisms that give the culture direction and meaning. When leaders are personally involved and engaged, organizational members consciously and subconsciously learn what is truly important to the organization.

Primary embedding mechanisms

What leaders pay attention to, measure, and control on a regular basis
How leaders react to critical incidents and organizational crises
Observed criteria by which leaders allocate scarce resources
Deliberate role modeling, teaching, and coaching
Observed criteria by which leaders recruit, select, promote, retire, and excommunicate organizational members
Observed criteria by which leaders allocate rewards and status

An instructive example of the use of primary embedding mechanisms to effect cultural change lies in the actions of Gen. Maxwell Thurman in the early days of the American all-volunteer army. The US military draft had ended in 1973, but less than a decade later, the viability of the all-volunteer force was in jeopardy. The chorus of complaints concerning the readiness and quality of the force had reached such a volume that many supporters began second-guessing the wisdom of abolishing the draft. Even former president Richard Nixon, who had introduced the all-volunteer army during his campaign for the presidency, wrote in 1980, "I considered the end of the draft in 1973 to be one of the major achievements of my administration. Now seven years later, I have reluctantly concluded that we should reintroduce the draft."[36] In November 1979, with just two weeks' notice, the Army's chief of staff, Gen. Edward Meyer, informed Maj. Gen. Thurman that he was to take over and transform the struggling Army Recruiting Command.

The most potent embedding mechanism available for communicating what leaders believe is important (or unimportant) is *what leaders systematically pay attention to, monitor, or control on a regular basis*. The key to this embedding mechanism is that the action must be systematic. The interest need not be substantial, but it must be consistent. Prior to Thurman taking over the recruiting command, the most important number to an army recruiter was the mission quota, the number of new solders that had to be brought on board. Thurman

---

[35] Schein, *Organizational Culture and Leadership*, 183.
[36] Richard M. Nixon, *The Real War* (New York, 1980), 201.

wanted to change that approach and set out to emphasize quality over quantity. Empirical studies had shown that high-quality soldiers, those with a high school diploma and scoring above the fiftieth percentile in mental aptitude, were more likely to complete their enlistments, have fewer instances of indiscipline, and perform better in training. Thurman directed that each recruiter, as well as his battalion and brigade commander, carry his "mission box," a card specifying not only his monthly targeted number of recruits, but also the quality parameters for each recruit.[37] It became clear to everyone in recruiting command that quality was the goal, not quantity. Thurman's focus on quality soldiers, supported by his continuous monitoring of quality metrics, resulted in demonstrable change. In fiscal year 1980, 54 percent of new recruits had graduated from high school. By 1987, 91 percent were high school graduates. By 1992, only 2 percent of new soldiers did not have a high school diploma.[38]

Schein posits a second embedding mechanism – *how leaders react to critical incidents and organizational crises.* During a time of crisis, anxiety and emotional intensity bring about a heightened sense of learning. The reaction of leaders in dealing with a crisis transmits organizational values that later guide behavior. In the case of the all-volunteer army, it was discovered in 1979 that the Armed Services Vocational Aptitude Battery (ASVAB) was mis-normed and was mistakenly allowing thousands of low-quality personnel into the armed forces. The ASVAB was eventually re-normed and a new test was created. Each of the services, however, had to decide what to do with a large pool of candidates whom the old test had deemed qualified, but who were now disqualified as low quality by the correctly normed test. The decision was critical as thousands of potential recruits were no longer eligible for enlistment according to the new test. The navy reacted by lowering its enlistment standards and permitted about 95 percent of the mis-normed, low-mental-aptitude population to enlist. The army, under Thurman's orders, continued to uphold standards and focused on recruiting high school graduates scoring above the fiftieth percentile in mental aptitude. Even though army recruiters had to scramble to make up the shortfall in numbers, Thurman wanted no part of the unqualified population.[39]

Another embedding mechanism is *how leaders allocate scarce resources.* Budgets, rather than rhetoric, reveal a leader's true priorities. Thurman, encouraged by sociologist Charlie Moskos, was an ardent advocate of a dual market recruiting strategy. Studies showed that young people potentially interested in

---

[37] Gen. Maxwell Thurman, "On Being All You Can Be: A Recruiting Perspective," in J. Eric Fredland, Curtis L. Gilroy, Roger D. Little, and W. S. Sellman, eds., *Professionals on the Front Line: Two Decades of the All-Volunteer Force* (Washington, DC, 1996), 59.

[38] Gen. Alan Ono, quoted in Beth Bailey, *America's Army: Making the All-Volunteer Force* (Cambridge, MA, 2009), 197.

[39] Bernard Rostker, *I Want You! The Evolution of the All-Volunteer Force* (Santa Monica, CA, 2006), 398.

joining the army were generally work-oriented or college-oriented. Higher pay and training appealed to those in the former group who viewed the army as a means to learn a skill. The latter group, however, was attracted to deferred incentives, especially money to attend college. Attracting high-quality, college-bound youth with educational benefits, however, required congressional support for a substantial amount of funding. As a result, Thurman worked closely with Representative Sonny Montgomery to get the GI Bill signed into law in 1984 despite resistance from both the Office of the Secretary of Defense and the Office of Management and Budget.[40]

Deliberate role modeling, teaching, and coaching is a primary embedding mechanism that communicates organizational values and assumptions through the visible behavior of leaders. Thurman realized that part of the struggle in recruiting quality soldiers was the lack of ownership in many parts of recruiting command. He found layers of the bureaucracy merely relaying information without thoroughly comprehending the difficulties and effort involved in recruiting a soldier. For example, a few weeks after taking command, he noticed that leaders, specifically the officers, in recruiting command were isolated from the complexities of the recruiting process experienced by the noncommissioned officers (NCOs) serving as recruiters. Officers were content to manage the process, but often deferred to the NCOs due to a lack of knowledge of the gritty details of recruiting. To eliminate their disengagement from the recruiting process, Thurman mandated that every officer in recruiting command had sixty days to personally recruit a soldier.[41] He also instituted "mission adjudication," quarterly face-to-face meetings between himself and each of his fifty-seven recruiting battalion commanders to specify the quality and numbers of individuals to be recruited. Thurman ensured that the process carried down to the recruiter level and that everyone understood the situation.[42] By involving leaders in the critical aspects of recruiting, he was able to send to the entire command an unmistakable message concerning organizational priorities.

A more subtle embedding mechanism is the *criteria by which leaders select, promote, and separate organizational members*. Thurman firmly believed that the caliber of his recruiting NCOs was critical in attracting quality youth, especially for the combat arms. He maintained that the army's most visible representatives to American society needed to reflect the high-quality soldiers they were trying to recruit. Unfortunately, high-quality combat arms NCOs were not volunteering for duty in recruiting command. At the time, there was an NCO shortage across the army, especially in Europe. Combat arms NCOs were spending three years in units in Germany and then rotating back to the United

[40] Thurman, "Being All You Can Be," 61.
[41] Gen. Maxwell R. Thurman, Oral History, Senior Officer Oral History Program, Military History Institute, 1992, 200–201.
[42] Ibid., 59.

States for a year before getting orders for another tour in Europe. Instead of getting high-quality combat arms NCOs to volunteer for recruiting command, it became obvious that recruiting duty was attracting NCOs who were a) avoiding another Germany tour, or b) looking for an easy job. Thurman corrected the situation with a simple directive: NCOs could no longer volunteer to serve in recruiting command. Instead, the army now selected the best NCOs for a three-year tour as a recruiter and then returned them to the force for the remainder of their careers. The policy, according to Thurman, was essentially saying to NCOs who wanted to be recruiters: "Come and serve in the Recruiting Command for 3 years and then you will get a chance to serve with the people you recruited. Therefore, don't bring us scum bags. Bring us only high quality people."[43]

Another primary embedding mechanism is the *observed criteria by which leaders allocate rewards and status*. Organizational values are transmitted when certain actions or activities receive prestige or honor. For example, Thurman was a strong believer of ensuring policies were supported by empirical analysis. As a result, he relied heavily on the analytical capabilities of four organizations. The first three were RAND, a federally funded research and development center; N. W. Ayer, the advertising agency awarded the army contract for recruiting ads; and the Army Research Institute (ARI), an organization of mostly psychologists and sociologists. But he also stood up the Office of Economic and Manpower Analysis (OEMA) at the US Military Academy and had it report directly to him to serve as a counterweight to the RAND analysis. Direct access to Thurman by each research cell reflected the preeminence of empirically based policy formulation during his tenure.[44]

Once primary embedding mechanisms begin emplacing assumptions and values into an organization's culture, *secondary reinforcement and stabilizing mechanisms* can support and buttress the emerging culture. In order for reinforcing mechanisms to be effective, however, they must be consistent with the organizational beliefs and values transmitted by the primary embedding mechanisms. Schein offers six secondary reinforcement and stabilizing mechanisms:[45]

Secondary reinforcement and stabilizing mechanisms

Organizational systems and procedures
Organization design and structure
Design of physical space, facades, and buildings
Formal statements of organizational philosophy, creeds, and charters
Organizational rites and rituals
Stories, legends, and myths about people and events

[43] Ibid., 222.   [44] Ibid., 212.
[45] Adapted from Schein, *Organizational Culture and Leadership*, 183.

Each reinforcing mechanism is fairly easy to understand and execute compared to the more complex primary embedding mechanisms – which is why leaders sometimes mistakenly rely on reinforcing mechanisms instead of embedding mechanisms to analyze or change a culture. Reinforcing mechanisms alone do not reflect or change a culture. Instead, reinforcing mechanisms only serve in a supporting role to the more difficult and leader-centric work of primary embedding mechanisms. Likewise, reinforcing mechanisms often appear to be obvious cultural artifacts since they tend to be more tangible and well documented than embedding mechanisms. An organization's culture, however, is reflected more in what leaders demonstrate through their behavior than what is written down or inferred from visible structures, systems, rituals, stories, or published doctrine.[46]

Secondary reinforcing and stabilizing mechanisms played a key role in transforming the American draft army organizational culture to one aligned with the notion of a high-quality, all-volunteer army. A number of factors facilitated the effectiveness of the reinforcing mechanisms, especially the continuous oversight of the all-volunteer force as the army promoted Thurman from commanding general of recruiting command to become deputy chief of staff, personnel, and then the US Army vice chief of staff. The extraordinary success of the advertising campaign slogan "Be All You Can Be" underlined the rebound of the all-volunteer army after the near failure in the 1970s. The slogan eventually pushed the army into one of the most recognizable brands in America, but, more important, the slogan was attractive to both potential recruits and serving soldiers. "Be All You Can Be" represented the nascent professional army of the 1980s, a far cry from the "Today's Army Wants to Join You" slogan of the early 1970s. Thurman realized, however, that bringing in high-quality soldiers was only the first step to transforming the army. If soldiers were recruited in hopes of being all they could be, it was imperative that the army deliver on that promise.

It was during this era that the army began introducing changes in *organizational systems and procedures* such as the "training revolution" that focused on more deliberate planning, measurable outcomes, and continual evaluation. The renewed emphasis on training culminated in new *organizational design and structures* such as the establishment of the National Training Center at Fort Irwin, California. With more than 1,000 square miles (2,590 km²) for maneuvering large units and operating ranges, an unrestrictive electromagnetic spectrum, open airspace for military use, and isolation from the local populace, Fort Irwin became the model for large-scale, force-on-force, instrumented training.

In addition to the transformed emphasis on training, the army introduced much-needed improvements to key acquisition programs. The "Big Five"

---

[46] Ibid., 196.

weapons system programs were initiated in the 1970s, but arrived in the 1980s to a force desperate for modernization. The Abrams main battle tank, Bradley infantry fighting vehicle, Patriot missile system, Blackhawk helicopter, and Apache attack helicopter gave the army a much improved combat capability that helped fuel the increasing professionalism of the force. The all-volunteer army had marketed itself as an increasingly high-tech organization and the introduction of the Big Five weapon systems confirmed that claim.

By the early 1980s, the army realized that a key component to retaining high-quality NCOs and officers in an all-volunteer force was their families. Recognizing that the *design of physical space* could support the cultural change sweeping through the force, army posts underwent extensive renovation as part of the emphasis on improving the living and working conditions for soldiers and their families. In 1983, funding for family housing increased 57 percent due largely to an additional $74 million in the housing budget.[47] In that same year, the army signed the Army Family White Paper, which was a *formal statement of organizational philosophy* expressing the army's commitment to wellness and the sense of community within the army.

The renewed attention on the families and the emphasis on raising the overall quality of life for soldiers were part of a gradual departure from a conscription-based belief that soldiers were a "free good." The draft had created an organizational culture that valued the service of soldiers, yet the army acted as if soldiers were replaceable at zero cost. From senior leaders to drill sergeants, a gradual realization emerged that if soldiers did not feel valued or respected, especially the high-quality troops, they would leave. The all-volunteer force required a realignment of the army's organizational culture that was accomplished through the leader-centric actions of primary embedding mechanisms and then supported by secondary reinforcing and stabilizing mechanisms.

This chapter has presented a framework to understand and assess organizational culture. Comprehending the deep assumptions that influence the decision-making logic for most human behaviors in a large, complex organization whose main purpose is to kill its nation's foes is a messy endeavor full of inferences, contradictions, and inconsistencies. Few take on this task, yet the efficacy of having an organizational culture aligned with the challenges of the organization's mission and environment may be the most underrated variable in war and strategy.

---

[47] Department of the Army, *Department of the Army Historical Summary: Fiscal Year 1983* (Center for Military History), 81.

2   Strategic Culture

David Kilcullen

In May 2011, as the Arab Spring roiled the Middle East and America and its allies intervened in Libya and continued their surge in Afghanistan, I was teaching at the North Atlantic Treaty Organization (NATO) Defense College in Rome. In my group of twelve students, alongside US military leaders, were European officers from all services and an army officer from the Russian Federation.[1] I asked what the group thought of the ongoing cascade of revolutions, and what role NATO military forces should or should not play in stabilizing the situation.

To a man (they were all men) the Western Europeans shook their heads and spoke of overstretch: too many troops in Afghanistan, resources strained by the 2008 global financial crisis, publics weary of conflict and unsure of the purpose of involvement. Was dealing with revolution in Africa and Arabia really an appropriate role for Europe's militaries? The age of empire was over, after all. Eastern European students, on average, framed the situation differently: not as an optional out-of-area operation like Afghanistan, but as a mandatory defensive action to stabilize NATO's southern flank and defend Europe from external threat. I saw one American officer roll his eyes slightly, perhaps contrasting European weariness over Afghanistan with his country's much larger effort in Iraq, Afghanistan, and the broader war on terror – a war to protect the very Western civilizational order that its inheritors seemed reluctant to defend.

But the strongest reaction was from the Russian officer. Our visitor looked slowly around the room, and then said, "I was a Soviet officer in the Cold War. Back then, we thought NATO was like this." He raised a clenched fist on an erect forearm. "But now I realize, it is like *this*" – and let his arm droop flaccidly to the table.

National stereotypes were all too clearly on display in this conversation: Western Europeans, languid and scarred by postcolonial guilt; Americans carrying the burden for their allies, the New World saving the Old once again, with a combined sense of resignation, entitlement, and pride; Eastern Europeans

---

[1] This being before the Russian covert invasion and annexation of Crimea, when Russian students were still welcomed at NATO educational institutions.

determined to defend a civilizational frontier against the barbarians at the gate; and a Russian seeing military power as a crudely sexual contest of manly prowess. If this seems like a cliché-driven joke ("An American, a European, and a Russian officer walk into a bar … "), it might be because such stereotypes, though clearly reductionist, do contain a kernel of truth about the nations they depict, and the way political leaders and military commanders view the use of force.

Organizational versus Strategic Culture

In a broad sense (that is to say, purely as a matter of statistical averages and despite a wide range of individual differences), members of ethnic groups demonstrably hold similar, unspoken assumptions about what is normal, share expectations as to what is or is not appropriate, and adopt common framing constructs – ways of categorizing events to make sense of their experience.[2] Like the fish in David Foster Wallace's *This Is Water* (an older fish asks two young-sters how the water is today, and after a pause one of the younger ones turns to the other and asks, "What the hell is water?"), such perceptual frameworks and pervasive assumptions may be so unexamined that group members are unaware of their existence.[3] We call this phenomenon, of shared sense-making and norm creation within an ethnic group, *culture* (or rather, this is one of many things for which English speakers confusingly use that term).

In a book on military organizational culture, the relevance of such norms seems axiomatic. Recruits to military organizations are acculturated, through tools like boot camp, barracks life, training exercises, and war colleges, into common ways of perceiving the world, shared frameworks for making sense of it, and similar purpose-driven (*teleological*) behaviors – many unconscious – that support the organization's reason for being.

At the operational level of war, the apotheosis of this approach was the great German General Staff of the nineteenth and early twentieth centuries, with its notion that any officer, schooled from earliest adulthood in a particular way of thinking, and internalizing a single cultural outlook, would – if confronted by a given set of circumstances – interpret them in an identical manner, to reach a "staff solution" that his peers would recognize as correct. One officer could, ideally, predict the decision another would reach, provided he knew the situation his peer faced. At the tactical level, the imperial German system of mission command

---

[2] Throughout this chapter, I use the term *ethnicity* in its nonacademic sense, relating to groups of people with common national, tribal, religious, linguistic, regional, or cultural origins. Ethnicity is a matter of self-identity, ascribed identity, and acceptance within a community defined by common culture. It is often contrasted with race, which is a genetically determined set of physiological characteristics that can exist independent of ethnicity. In this sense, ethnicity may be considered somewhat akin to gender, while race is similar to biological sex, though the analogy is not perfect.

[3] David Foster Wallace, *This Is Water*, 2005, 1, www.metastatic.org/text/This%20is%20Water.pdf.

(*auftragstaktik*) was grounded in this notion: subordinates could be implicitly trusted to execute missions without oversight, or chiefs of staff to issue orders in the name of the commander without checking first, precisely because their superiors could count on them to interpret situations in a predictable manner.

The trust engendered by common culture meant orders could be abbreviated to the absolute minimum, enabling the rapid maneuver and decentralized command required by infiltration tactics – famously illustrated by the Storm Troop commander captured on the first day of Germany's 1918 Spring Offensive, who revealed under interrogation that his orders were simply "the further, the better."[4] He had penetrated as far as a British brigade headquarters, part of the biggest breakthrough of the entire war until the Australians and Americans broke the Hindenburg Line six months later.

Americans returning from World War I criticized this "theory of a composite directive mind, 'a theoretical single mind' composed of a General and a selected group of staff officers," arguing in overtly ethnic terms that this approach "is German, is discredited by the German debacle [and] the results require no comment."[5] But by the 1980s, beginning in the US Marine Corps and spreading first to the US Army and then to other services and allied militaries, an appreciation of mission-type command and directive control – the foundations of maneuver warfare – spread through the armed services. Some ridiculed the Germanophile tendencies of a force that had defeated the Germans twice in a generation, while others critiqued the "hive mind" that seemed to result as the expression of a particular organizational culture. Yet the advantages of this approach, from the 100-hour war in the Gulf in 1991 to the rapid overthrow of Saddam Hussein in 2003, soon became clear. (Its disadvantages took longer to emerge.)

But the term *strategic culture* usually denotes something different from, and more contested than, military organizational culture. The notion of strategic culture typically refers to nationally or ethnically defined, rather than institutionally modulated, cultural norms. Individuals and subgroups within ethnic groups are presumed to self-ascribe to a certain identity, absorb distinctive attitudes about the use of force, and thus adopt a national "way of war," whatever their institutional home and despite their organizational differences.

For example, American flyers, sailors, soldiers, and Marines all exhibit subtly different organizational cultures – in Afghanistan, we used to say, "Army are campers, Marines are hikers," as a way of getting at these differences – but at a broader national level, all Americans, irrespective of service, or indeed whether they are service members or civilian decision-makers, are

---

[4] Jim Storr, "A Command Philosophy for the Information Age," *Defence Studies* 3(3) (Autumn 2003), 122.

[5] John H. Parker, Col. A.E.F., "Staff Organization and the Theoretical Single Mind," *Military Engineer* XII(66) (December 1920), 565–566.

presumed to share a strategic culture, an American way of war that influences how situations are interpreted and decisions are made.

Attitudes, norms, and expectations around the use of force – in defense of family, clan, tribe, or nation – are fundamental to social organization. Indeed, anthropologist Harry Turney-High suggested in 1981 that the organization of all known societies has been so heavily influenced, since earliest antiquity, by the need to prepare for and conduct organized violence against other human social groups that "warfare *is* social organization."[6] Likewise, historian Philip Bobbitt considers warfare one of three key influencers (along with law and commerce) on the shape of the state through history.[7] Lawrence Keeley, another anthropologist, argues that "a society's demography, economy, and social system provide the means for, and impose limits on, military technique."[8]

As I wrote in an earlier book, "if we accept this, along with the fact that war has been endemic in roughly 95 per cent of all known human societies throughout history and pre-history, it follows that warfare is a central and probably a permanent human social institution."[9] Given the centrality – and, more important, the utter normality – of war in virtually all known societies, it would be surprising indeed if the same factors that give rise to distinct cultures within ethnic groups did not also create national strategic cultures.

Strategic Culture Precedes Organizational Culture

Organizational and ethnic cultures coexist, of course, in any one military unit, and there may be multiple subcultures – snipers, drone operators, and EOD personnel, for example, are famous for their clannishness, and every rifle company believes itself uniquely different from (and better than) every other. But more than this: strategic culture, since it derives from enduring ethnic and national characteristics, precedes and supersedes organizational culture. An incident from Somalia illustrates this.

In mid-2012, I had the opportunity to accompany a battalion of the Somali National Army (SNA) during operations against the jihadist group Al-Shabaab around Afgoye, a town in the lower Shebelle river valley, about fifteen miles – an hour's drive in normal times, but six months' hard fighting in 2012 – from

[6] Harry Holbert Turney-High, *The Military: The Theory of Land Warfare As Behavioral Science* (North Quincy, MA, 1981), 34, quoted in Lawrence H. Keeley, *War before Civilization: The Myth of the Peaceful Savage* (New York, 1997), 47–48.

[7] See Philip Bobbitt, *The Shield of Achilles: War, Peace and the Course of History* (New York, 2002).

[8] Keeley's groundbreaking 1997 study integrates research from several different statistical sources to suggest that 90–95 percent of all known societies throughout history have regularly engaged in organized warfare. Keeley, *War before Civilization*, chapters 2 and 3.

[9] David Kilcullen, *Out of the Mountains: The Coming Age of the Urban Guerrilla* (New York, 2013), 27.

Somalia's capital city, Mogadishu. This particular unit had been recruited from members of warlord Mohammed Farah Aideed's Somali National Alliance, who fought Task Force Ranger in the 1993 Battle of Mogadishu depicted in the book and film *Black Hawk Down*. As such, this battalion fought according to traditional, informal norms – folkways of warfare – that they had learned on the job over more than two decades of fighting. I have described their dynamic swarm tactics elsewhere, but the culture underpinning these tactics is worth noting. As I wrote at the time:

> [A]ny professional soldier in the world would be proud to command troops with this kind of tactical initiative. Indeed, I found only one slight issue on which to fault the SNA tactics: the fact that the squad leader stayed in the vehicle while his troops dismounted to assault. Western tactics would call for the leader to dismount with the troops, carrying a radio to talk back to the vehicle and direct its fire, and leaving a trusted subordinate, as vehicle commander, to maneuver the gun truck. But as soon as this thought entered my head, I realized I was looking at the Somali squad in completely the wrong way: I was misapplying the social and economic framework of a professional state-run military to an organization that had evolved from an irregular militia. In the Somali environment of fragmented, semi-anarchic clan organizations in which these tactics had emerged, the way someone became a squad leader in the first place was to own the [armed SUV known as a] Technical, an extremely substantial piece of capital equipment. The squad leader became the squad leader precisely because it was his vehicle, so it would have been the height of stupidity for him to dismount and thereby cede control of the gun truck to someone else – let alone to leave someone behind him with a machine gun. He might not have remained the squad leader for long! Moreover, dismounted fighters are cheap and replaceable, but the vehicle is a precious investment that is decidedly not expendable. Seen from this perspective, the SNA's "mounted swarm" tactics have (like any tactical system) an economic, political, and social logic, as well as a military grammar.[10]

Here we see a strategic culture (the way of war and combat style of a clan-based, non-state militia) influencing the organizational culture of a national military unit a generation later, with ethnic and historical factors setting the cultural parameters within which organizational culture and individual initiative operate. In this case, as in other examples, strategic culture can be clearly seen to precede and shape military organizational culture.

We ignore this culture at our peril, particularly in situations (like Afghanistan, Libya, Iraq, or Somalia) where Western trainers and advisors work with indigenous forces. Books have been written on the tendency of US advisors to produce partner military forces in their own image, generating local military allies burdened with lavish equipment but systematically stripped of their naturally acquired ways of war, of the sort these Somalis clearly retained. In fact, this critique could be made of almost any military force in foreign

[10] Ibid., 81–86.

internal defense (FID) or security force assistance – or indeed, of any intervening outsider in a crisis situation (including nongovernmental organizations
and aid agencies in development and humanitarian programs) – so that it is less
a US military failing than a generic problem.[11]

Still, imagine how different today's Afghan army (for example) would look, if
instead of taking a group that knew how to fight, had been fighting the Taliban for a
decade, and had a self-organizing tactical system superbly adapted to its own
environment and giving it complicated heavy weapons, vehicles that bound it to
roads, and an enduring dependence on Western air support, we had left its fighting
style as undisturbed as possible, while inserting niche capabilities only, and improving human capital through education, health care, ethics, and civics programs led by
Afghans. To even verbalize such a fantasy is to tag myself as a member of a
particular "tribe" within the Western way of war, of course. But the key point is
that ethnic culture frames strategic culture (that subset of culture dealing with the
use of force) which in turn interacts with organizational structure, institutional form,
and individual incentives to create military organizational culture.

Subnational Strategic Cultures

It is worth noting that the strategic culture at play in the Somali example is not
national but subnational (relating to a regionally prominent subclan, the Habar
Gidir of the Hawiye clan, which dominates the Mogadishu region). The
existence of subnational strategic cultures is largely absent from the literature
on comparative strategic culture, which tends to focus at the national level, yet
is readily observable.[12] Within the British Raj, for example, colonial administrators in India after 1857 overtly designated some ethnic groups as "martial
races" and others as non-martial. "Martial races" included Sikhs, Gurkhas,
Baluch, Pathans (Pashtuns), and Rajputs, ethnic groups whose outlook, religion, material culture, and regional environments were deemed – by British
officials, but also by these groups themselves and by others – to confer a
particular aptitude for warfare.[13] It is worth pointing out that the imputation
of military skills to racial rather than ethnic characteristics (see note 2) was
common among administrators and scholars alike up until the mid-twentieth

---

[11] For a comprehensive and sophisticated historical analysis of pathologies in international
advisory missions to Afghanistan since the 1920s, see Antonio Giustozzi and Artemy
Kalinovsky, *Missionaries of Modernity: Advisory Missions and the Struggle for Hegemony in
Afghanistan and Beyond* (London, 2016). The pathologies Giustozzi and Kalinovsky identify
clearly cut across time, space, and national identity, so that British and European advisors in the
early twentieth century, Soviets and Americans in the Cold War, and NATO and the US-led
coalition in Afghanistan in the twenty-first century can all be seen experiencing similar issues.
[12] See, for example, Colin S. Gray, "Comparative Strategic Culture," *Parameters* (Winter 1984), 26–33.
[13] Rajit K. Mazumder, *The Indian Army and the Making of Punjab* (London, 2003), 99–105.

century. Many members of the so-called martial races ended up in Pakistan after Partition in 1947. Arguably, by internalizing a racialized self-ascription of military prowess (and denigrating as "non-martial" the ethnic groups that mostly found themselves in India after 1947), Pakistanis went into the Indo-Pakistan conflicts of 1965 and 1971 with unjustified confidence in their ability to defeat numerically superior Indian and Bangladeshi forces.[14]

In Africa and Australasia, similar racialized notions of military prowess were at work during the British Empire – for British colonial administrators, Zulus, Maori, Dayaks, and Matabele were "martial," while Australian aborigines, Chinese "coolies," and Egyptian *fellaheen* were not. Even at home in the British Isles, imperial administrators designated some ethnic groups – in particular, Scots Highlanders and Ulstermen – as "believed to possess a biological or cultural disposition to the racial and masculine qualities necessary for the arts of war."[15] Likewise, Scots-Irish immigrants to the United States were described as "born fighting" and having a higher participation rate in America's wars.[16]

In the American case, these immigrants have been variously believed to have inherited martial characteristics from their Scottish and Irish forebears (perhaps a spillover from the nineteenth-century British stereotype), to maintain greater military skill because of the harsh mountain environment of Appalachia where many settled, or to have been motivated to join the service by a culture of honor and by bitter hardship after the Confederacy's defeat in the American Civil War.[17] The same environmental determinism – hardy mountain tribes fighting off invaders – was applied to other ethnic groups in different contexts (think of Albanians, Kurds, and Pashtuns), while honor culture is believed by some Hispanics to account for their overrepresentation in the Marine Corps and in combat units generally. Thus, even in nation-state military forces, or imperial domains like the British or Ottoman empires, subnational – regional or ethnic – cultures can impact strategic culture at the national level, as well as influencing military organizational culture by helping shape self-identity. (As an exchange officer with the British Army in the 1990s, I was struck by the thoroughly English, lowland origins of many officers in Scottish Highland regiments, and yet at the same time by how thoroughly they had absorbed a conception of themselves as "Highlanders.")

Indeed, to borrow a term from feminist theory, an individual within a given armed service may experience a high degree of intersectionality – where

---

[14] Agha Humayun Amin, "Ethnicity, Religion, Military Performance: British Recruitment Policy and the Indian Army, 1757–1947," *Defence Journal* (December 2000), www.defencejournal.com/2000/dec/ethnicity.htm.

[15] See Heather Streets, *Martial Races: The Military, Race and Masculinity in British Imperial Culture, 1857–1914* (Birmingham, 2004).

[16] Jim Webb, *Born Fighting: How the Scots-Irish Shaped America* (New York, 2004).

[17] For examples of several of these ideas, see ibid.

national and subnational strategic culture, ethnicity and gender identity, biological factors such as race and sex, unit- or formation-level organizational cultures, and "niche" subcultures overlap. Anthropologists speak of multivalent and contingent identities as a way to explain how individuals and groups react to these cultural, genetic, and environmental overlaps.

Actual data on Hispanic (and Scots-Irish) participation rates in combat units, let alone on the combat performance of "martial" versus "non-martial" ethnic groups, are far more complex than this discussion would suggest, a fact that highlights another element of strategic culture, and of culture generally – that identity may be based on fictive (imagined) kinship with related groups, or on self-conceptions that may be remarkably at variance from observable fact.[18] As for the Highland Regiment officers just mentioned, these fictive aspects of identity may in turn become elements of a national myth that influences national-level strategic culture. This is perhaps the case in the Pakistani example noted earlier, but an even more prominent instance is that of Australia's "Anzac legend," partly founded on the belief that the country's all-volunteer force in World War I was mostly drawn from hardy, rural, outdoorsy stock whose physical fitness and ability to shoot and ride made them natural soldiers. This myth was debunked more than forty years ago, but persists as an element of self-perceived national character that arguably affects Australian strategic decision-making to this day.[19]

Before moving to the strategic level of analysis, it is worth summarizing some key observations. Strategic culture, as defined here, is distinct from military institutional and organizational culture per se, though influencing it and tending to supersede and precede it. It is ethnically and nationally driven, derived from a combination of racial, religious, regional, geographical, and historical factors. It may be national or subnational, and it may be based on real or imagined traits. It tends to be both enduring and unexamined, or even unconscious, chugging along in the background without being noticed and despite changing circumstances. It involves intersectionality between national, subnational, and organizational cultures, and may invoke aspects of fictive and contingent identity. It manifests itself in

---

[18] For data on Hispanic participation in US forces, see Mady Wechsler Segal and David R. Segal, "Latinos Claim Larger Share of U.S. Military Personnel," Population Reference Bureau (2007), www.prb.org/Publications/Articles/2007/HispanicsUSMilitary.aspx; and Office of the Under Secretary of Defense for Personnel and Readiness, *Population Representation in the Military Services: Fiscal Year 2014 Summary Report* at www.people.mil/Portals/56/Documents/2014% 20Summary.pdf?ver=2016-09-14-154051-563. See also Mackubbin T. Owens, *The Color of Combat: The Minority-Disproportion Myth* (2002), http://ashbrook.org/publications/oped-ow ens-02-combat/.

[19] For a prominent example of such myth-making, see C. E. W. Bean, *Official History of Australia in the War of 1914–18, vol. I: The Story of ANZAC: From the Outbreak of War to the End of the First Phase of the Gallipoli Campaign, May 4, 1915* (Canberra, 1921). For a statistical analysis debunking the "rural Anzac" myth, see Leslie Lloyd Robson, "The Origin and Character of the First A.I.F., 1914–1918: Some Statistical Evidence," *Historical Studies* 15(61) (1973), 737–749.

the ways individuals and organizations make sense of reality, in noticing and not noticing, selecting experiences to be remembered or forgotten, determining what attributes an organization values or scorns, framing and defining situations, and in the inclusion or exclusion of events from categories such as "war."

Evolutionary anthropologists might argue – as in the case of German *auf-tragstaktik* discussed earlier – that the development of a common cultural outlook can be considered an adaptive trait (i.e., one that increases the survivability of a military organism) when it produces bonds of trust that facilitate rapid and dynamic maneuver, simplifies command and control, or generates (even through fictive aspects such as the Anzac myth) motivating ideas that help mobilize and energize a force. At the institutional level, such a culture can also help preserve corporate memory, ensure effective transmission of complex concepts and plans, and generate a self-healing command climate.

But clearly, as military capabilities, technologies, adversaries, and environments evolve, once-adaptive traits can become maladaptive, ultimately undermining their (conscious or unconscious) purpose. Herbert Simon's notion of "bounded rationality" – in which actors respond to stimuli in a rational manner within certain environmental bounds, but act nonrationally once they reach the limits of cognition or situational interpretation – is helpful here.[20] It is only a slight extension of Simon's theory to include group norms, expectations, and sense-making frameworks as cultural elements of the "cognitive limits" and "structures of the environment" that he argues define the bounds of rational decision-making.

Again, a Somali example is useful. Consider the tactical situation of Task Force Ranger in Mogadishu at precisely 1620 hours on October 3, 1993 – the moment when the first Blackhawk downed, Super 61, crashed in the city. At that moment, the raid's objective had already been achieved: the SNA safe house near Bakara Market had been assaulted and the Somali militia leaders who were the raid's targets had been captured and loaded in trucks for extraction, and were awaiting departure for the Task Force's base at the Mogadishu airport. Commanders knew that time was critical, as swarms of militia were already closing in to block the convoy's route back to the airport. Yet after waiting a full six minutes under increasing fire, at 1626, the convoy began moving – not toward the airport, but toward Super 61's crash site, attempting to locate and extract survivors, even though aircraft were already overhead and another quick reaction force had already been dispatched to the site. By 1628, two minutes after the convoy began moving, aircraft orbiting overhead confirmed that Super 61's pilot and copilot were dead, and that the Delta Force sniper pair assigned to the aircraft was nowhere in sight. Yet the convoy kept fighting to the crash site for another twenty-

---

[20] Herbert A. Simon, "Bounded Rationality and Organizational Learning," *Organization Science* 2 (1) (1991), 125–134; see also Daniel Kahnemann, "A Perspective on Judgment and Choice: Mapping Bounded Rationality," *American Psychologist* 58(9) (September 2003), 697–720.

six minutes – an eternity in an urban firefight of that intensity – running a gauntlet of multiple ambushes, losing its route back to the airport, and suffering 50 percent casualties (wounded or killed in action) in the process.[21]

Clearly, rational military decision-making is not a sufficient explanation for behavior in what was later dubbed the "lost convoy." Cultural factors – in particular, the unbreakable rule of "no man left behind" – played a decisive role. Commanders knew their mission required them to extract the high-value targets to their base, but they moved to the crash site anyway, in response to cultural imperatives, or what we might call "combat norms," rather than fully rational judgments. In Simon's terms, the loss of Super 61 had pushed them beyond the bounds of rational decision-making by changing their cognitive frameworks (from raid to rescue) and their perceived structure of the environment (from the end of a successful "capture" mission to the beginning of an urban battle to recover the downed aircrew). Within two minutes of starting the move, they knew the crew members were almost certainly dead and that another convoy was heading for the site, yet they continued – driving through ambush after ambush with their valuable Somali captives in the back of the trucks. Without in any way second-guessing commanders on the ground, this incident illustrates clearly that cultural norms that were once adaptive traits – units that leave nobody behind can count on higher morale, especially in dangerous light infantry missions – became maladaptive in the special circumstances of Bakara Market in the late afternoon on that fateful day.

Strategic Culture, Statecraft, and Strategy

With this as background, it is now appropriate to lift our analysis to the strategic level and consider how strategic culture interacts with statecraft and strategic decision-making.[22] In this context, an established model in strategic theory holds that strategic culture drives patterns of national statecraft, which in turn drive military strategy. Like other forms of culture, strategic culture changes slowly, if at all. Therefore, even a perfect defense policy or military strategy "is likely to fail if it does not align with strategic culture. A policy that lies outside the boundaries of culturally normative strategic behavior will simply not be followed."[23] Strategic culture, as we've seen in the examples already discussed, consists of "the traditional cultural, historical, political and societal factors that help shape the defense policies and strategic behavior of

---

[21] *Timeline of the Battle of Mogadishu*, https://en.wikipedia.org/wiki/Timeline_of_the_1993_Battle_of_Mogadishu.

[22] Portions of the next section, in an earlier form, were previously published as David Kilcullen, "Australian Statecraft: The Challenge of Aligning Policy with Strategic Culture," *Security Challenges* 4(3) (November 2007), 45–65.

[23] Ibid., 46.

countries."[24] Numerous theorists have argued that, over time, grand strategy derives from strategic culture, which emerges from enduring geographical, economic, and historical circumstances rather than from leaders' conscious decisions.[25] Inherent in the notion of strategic culture is the idea that a nation's enduring circumstances give rise to a distinctive manner of perceiving and using national power – including military force.[26]

Grand strategy, in the generic sense of national security strategy, seeks to "coordinate and direct the resources of a nation, or a band of nations, towards the attainment of … goals defined by fundamental policy."[27] Some nations, for example the United States, Australia, the United Kingdom, and the Russian Federation, express their national security strategy formally, through official government documents.[28] More commonly, grand strategy may simply be an observable pattern of behavior enacted in pursuit of long-term goals. Thus, grand strategy occupies the same mental space as strategic culture, often chugging along unexamined in the background, rarely or never consciously articulated. One characteristic of grand-strategic behavior, however, is that it tends to be independent of the political orientation of a particular administration. This can be illustrated diagrammatically (see Figure 1).[29]

In this model, enduring strategic circumstances inform national culture, a subset of which is strategic culture – which, as we have defined it, is in turn that subset of ethnic or national culture relating to the use of force. According to theorists like Adda Bozeman and Edward N. Luttwak, an underlying strategic culture, in turn, drives patterns of statecraft, which inform broad policy settings, which in turn drive specific policy decisions.[30] Each level of this cognitive model tends to change more slowly than the levels above: enduring circumstances may last millennia; national culture changes over centuries, and strategic culture over decades. Policies change with each administration over years and months, while decisions occur in days and minutes. Thus, patterns of statecraft tend to be more enduring than the (often short-lived) policies and decisions that flow from them.

---

[24] Ken Booth and Russell Trood, *Strategic Cultures in the Asia-Pacific Region* (Auckland, NZ, 2004).

[25] See, for example, Bobbitt, *The Shield of Achilles*; Michael Evans, *The Tyranny of Dissonance: Australia's Strategic Culture and Way of War 1901–2005*, LWSC Study Paper No. 306 (Canberra, February 2005); Victor Davis Hanson, *Why the West Has Won: Carnage and Culture from Salamis to Vietnam* (New York, 2001).

[26] Gray, "Comparative Strategic Culture."

[27] Basil H. Liddell Hart, *Strategy* (New York, 1967), 322.

[28] For the 2015 US National Security Strategy, see www.g8.army.mil/pdf/National_Security_Str ategy_6Feb2015.pdf. The Russian equivalent is available in English translation at www.ieee.es/ Galerias/fichero/OtrasPublicaciones/Internacional/2016/Russian-National-Security-Strategy-3 1Dec2015.pdf, or in the original Russian at http://static.kremlin.ru/media/acts/files/00012015 12310038.pdf.

[29] Kilcullen, "Australian Statecraft," 46.

[30] See Adda B. Bozeman, *Politics and Culture in International History* (Princeton, NJ, 1960); Edward N. Luttwak, *The Grand Strategy of the Roman Empire* (Baltimore, 1976).

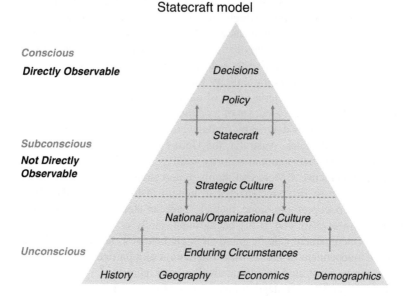

Figure 1 Relationship between strategic culture, statecraft, and policy

Note too that only decisions and policy choices (the top two layers of the model) are directly observable, whereas the remaining two-thirds of the model are unobservable – below the waterline, as it were. Like an iceberg, the observable elements of strategic behavior move in accordance with inertia, drift, and the influence of environmental currents on an underlying, unobservable cultural substructure. From this, as from our previous observation that strategic culture precedes and supersedes military organizational culture, it follows that policies that are misaligned with strategic culture are never, or at least very seldom, enacted in practice: real decisions follow behavioral patterns driven by underlying strategic culture, just as the above-water parts of an iceberg move with the much larger submerged portion. Several case studies illustrate this model.

Australian Strategic Culture

As a nation with a vast territory and a relatively small population, separated by intercontinental distances from trading partners, allies, and markets, and with virtually all its major population centers located on its coastline, Australia has the key characteristics of a "trade-dependent maritime state,"[31] one that cannot

---

[31] Dennis Rumley, *The Geopolitics of Australia's International Relations* (Dordrecht, 1999), 274; quoted in Michael Evans, *The Continental School of Strategy*, LWSC (Canberra, 2004), 113.

be secure in an insecure global or regional environment. This applies particularly to Southeast Asia, where internal turmoil, refugee flows, terrorism, economic instability, or state-on-state conflict could undermine the country's security and prosperity. But Australia is not solely part of the Southeast Asian regional system. Rather, Australia holds a central position in Halford Mackinder's classic geopolitical "outer or insular crescent" of sea-based power.[32] Hence, Australia is simultaneously a Pacific Ocean power, an Indian Ocean power, and a major player in Antarctica and the Southern Ocean. This "three-ocean dynamic" is an enduring feature of Australia's strategic circumstances, meaning that Australia's interests depend upon the security, stability, and economic viability of a vast portion of the earth's surface – an area well beyond Australia's national capacity to secure on its own.

Almost certainly because of these enduring circumstances, policy decisions by successive Australian leaders ever since independence in 1901 have indicated a consistent strategic culture of "forward engagement." Australian strategic culture values expeditionary power projection, ideally in cooperation with allies. This strategic culture values engagement with culturally compatible, like-minded worldwide powers, coalitions, or multilateral institutions. It appears to be the reason for a clearly observable pattern wherein Australian defense policy is designed to contribute to global and regional security, with the expectation that this will result in a safer world, bringing flow-on benefits for Australia's interests. This pattern has been a consistent feature of policy for well over a century, under Australian governments of almost every political character.

But the "forward school" is not the only school of Australian statecraft. A rival tradition, the "continental school," seeks to opt out of global engagement in favor of a continental, or at most regional, exceptionalism. This tradition views Australia as an island continent that, thanks to unique geographical and historical circumstances, can stand aside from Northern Hemisphere great-power politics, and pursue its unique interests through self-reliance. The continental school has a long and distinguished pedigree in Australian strategic thought; it values Australia's egalitarian origins, free of the British class system, sees offshore military engagements as adventurism ("other people's wars"), and finds alliances distasteful. Like isolationists in the United States, members of the continental school see armed forces as dangerous, since military power is believed to be unnecessary for a remote, unthreatened country like Australia, and military forces are believed to divert funds from the pursuit of a prosperous, socially just, classless society.

---

[32] See Halford Mackinder, "The Geographical Pivot of History," *Geographical Journal* 23 (1904), 421–444. For a detailed analysis of Mackinder's geopolitics, see *Geographical Journal* 170(4) (December 2004), a special issue on Mackinder's ideas and influence.

But whereas the continental school of thought has been prominent in the domestic dimension of statecraft, in foreign and defense policy it has largely been a theoretical construct – Australia's actual behavior has consistently reflected "forward school" statecraft, even when governments have talked exceptionalism. The model suggests that this is because Australia's enduring circumstances give rise to a strategic culture that favors forward engagement in practice, whatever the stated policy of the day may be.

Indonesian Strategic Culture

Across the so-called sea-air gap from Australia – the term itself a somewhat anachronistic holdover from the way that continental strategists of the twentieth century talked about the planet's most populous continent – several countries in Southeast Asia offer useful illustrations of the combination between enduring circumstances and historical experience in forming strategic cultures.

The Indonesian archipelago emerged from colonialism in 1945, after 350 years of occupation by multiple European powers and state-like corporations – the Dutch East India Company, Britain and its network of commercial and local proxies, Portugal, and Spain. The European presence not only defined the boundaries of today's nation-states, but also prompted the formation of nationalist and identity movements in opposition to foreign occupation that eventually came to supersede the fragmented and competing political power structures (competing hereditary monarchies, ethnic and tribal groupings, and religious sects, for the most part) that had enabled colonialism in the first place.

The Republic of Indonesia, shaped by this historical experience, developed a strategic culture in the 1950s and 1960s that was heavily influenced by anti-imperialism and Cold War "neutralism." But two other factors, revealingly, drove Indonesian strategic culture. The first was the geographically distributed nature of power within the country's archipelago of more than 17,000 islands and twenty-seven major ethnic groups (which forced Indonesian strategists to focus primarily on national cohesion and internal, rather than external, power projection – albeit over distances that would have been considered expeditionary in almost any other country). The second was the historically driven factional makeup of Indonesia's armed forces, whose founding leadership groups were drawn from the Dutch colonial military, as well as from the PETA irregular force raised by the Imperial Japanese military during Japan's relatively brief but bloody occupation of the region during World War II, and from a collection of ethnic, religious, and political militias and guerrilla groups.

For the first generation after Indonesia's independence, these circumstances drove a mismatch between rhetoric and action in Indonesian strategy. The founding generation of independence leaders – led by Ahmed Sukarno – came to be seen as a Cold War threat by Western powers concerned by his fiery anti-imperialist rhetoric and embrace of Communist Bloc assistance. But at the level of action, Indonesian military engagements focused solely on gaining control of the country's territory, crushing a series of regional rebellions, creating an internal power-projection capability, and completing a process (started under the Dutch) of annexing and controlling neighboring territories (notably, West Papua) that were geographically part of the archipelago into the Indonesian state.

Likewise, after the overthrow of Sukarno, despite the far more pro-Western rhetoric under the regime of his successor, Soeharto, Indonesia continued – in the invasion and occupation of East Timor – with the implementation of a long-standing strategic agenda of territorial consolidation and state control that went back to the colonial period. Even after Indonesia's transition to democracy in 1998 and the professionalization and modernization of its armed forces under succeeding elected leaders, the nation's strategic culture – shaped by geographical and national circumstances, but mediated through the political structures of the day and the organizational antecedents of its armed forces – endured.

German Strategic Culture

Like Australia and Indonesia, Germany's enduring circumstances have given rise to a distinct strategic culture, one that has also been heavily influenced by the country's historical experience (since unification in 1871) of two world wars, the Cold War, occupation and partition, and reunification. German strategy has tended to seesaw between two poles, characterized by Chancellor Helmut Kohl as the pursuit of a "European Germany" versus a "German Europe." Modern German politicians have faced a choice among rival strategies of *Ostpolitik* (rapprochement with the East, principally Russia), *Westbindung* (deepening of ties with the West), and *Sonderweg* (the neutralist or exceptionalist notion of Germany pursuing its own "special path").[33]

Much as Australia has all the characteristics of a maritime trading nation and Indonesia of an archipelagic one, Germany exhibits those of a continental power. Germany is Europe's largest country in terms of population (at 82 million inhabitants in 2016, followed by France as a distant second at 64 million). It holds a central strategic position at the heart of the continent, giving it the military advantage of interior lines and the economic benefit of a central trading position astride Europe's river, road, rail, and (more recently) oil and gas pipeline networks. As Europe's largest, most industrialized economy, Germany's manufacturing and export sectors drive its relations with other states. Its population – until the mid-1950s – was also relatively homogenous in cultural terms, though with distinct regional subcultures and sizeable (though comparatively well-integrated) ethnic minorities.

---

[33] James Kirchick, *The End of Europe: Dictators, Demagogues, and the Coming Dark Age* (New Haven, CT, 2017).

Indeed, since unification in 1871, Germany's size, strength, and location, along with its economic and military importance, created an imbalance at the heart of continental Europe – the so-called German problem – that shaped much of European and world history in the twentieth century. Other powers, principally France and Russia in the nineteenth century, joined by Britain and the United States beginning with World War I, were forced to shape their diplomatic and military policies around either coopting or containing Germany's rise to the global eminence many Germans considered theirs by right, which Imperial Foreign Secretary Bernhard von Bülow articulated most clearly in 1897: "We wish to throw nobody into the shade, but we demand our own place in the sun."[34] The problem was not that this desire was illegitimate, but that Germany's size and strength rendered it a threat to others and led to a series of confrontations. German strategic culture, influenced by enduring circumstances and national culture, and modulated through this series of wars and crises, initially took a revisionist, militaristic bent that favored the use of force as a primary tool to resolve political disputes, an approach that persisted right up until the country's occupation and partition in 1945.

Germany, however, offers an example of how a radical transformation in underlying circumstances can alter a country's strategic culture. Beginning in 1945, the country was divided and placed under military occupation for two generations. The entire structure of German militarism and self-identity was systematically dismantled, NATO was created, in the words of its first secretary-general, to "keep the Russians out, the Americans in and the Germans down," and the European Union (EU) emerged as a means to link Germany and France in an interdependent partnership and so prevent a recurrence of conflict. Moreover, Germany's demographic makeup began to change significantly with the influx, from the mid-1950s, of very large numbers of non-European (principally Turkish) migrants. At the same time, Germans were forced to reckon with their history – in particular, with the Nazi period and the Holocaust – leaving many with a sense that previous generations had been uniquely evil, and that Germans today have a responsibility to apply a highly moral, humanitarian approach in all aspects of foreign policy and defense.[35]

The impact on German strategic culture since reunification in 1990 has been profound. The "German problem" still exists (since the underlying reality of German size and strength persists), but in its current form it is a nonmilitary one: a question of trade imbalances, of dominance of Europe's single currency and banking system, and of an export-driven economy whose needs are not always those of other EU nations. German use of military force has been extremely tentative, despite Germany boasting one of the continent's most capable

---

[34] For the original German text of von Bülow's speech, see *Deutschlands Platz an der Sonne*, https://de.wikisource.org/wiki/Deutschlands_Platz_an_der_Sonne.

[35] Richard J. Evans, "From Nazism to Never Again: How Germany Came to Terms with Its Past," *Foreign Affairs* 97(1) (January–February 2018), 8–15.

militaries. Germany did not intervene in the Balkan Wars until 1999, and then only in a humanitarian capacity to stop the Kosovo genocide. It sat out the Iraq War entirely, and it intervened in Afghanistan with a focus on peacekeeping and reconstruction in the country's safest (at that time) northern provinces. It did not become involved in Libya in 2011, not only not participating in NATO's military intervention but also abstaining from the UN Security Council Resolution that authorized it. And in responding to Russian aggression in Crimea in 2014 and in eastern Ukraine since, German leaders have been some of the strongest voices arguing for a measured, nonmilitary response.

But perhaps the most significant sign of a changed German strategic culture was in the country's response to the 2015 mass migration crisis prompted by the Syrian civil war. By temporarily suspending entry controls in the late summer of 2015 and declaring that any refugee, economic migrant, or asylum seeker making it to German territory would be granted EU residence, German Chancellor Angela Merkel staked out a uniquely welcoming position on non-European migration. She arguably also triggered a much greater flow of migrants (from Africa, Afghanistan, and other parts of the Middle East, not just Syria) than would otherwise have been the case. For a country whose earlier leaders had spoken of *lebensraum* in the east, of expelling ethnic and religious minorities, and of "blood and soil," and who had of course enacted the worst genocide in history, this was a remarkable departure from previous policy – one that can only be understood in light of the tremendous transformation undergone by Germany since 1945. The degree of demographic and economic change caused by these decisions, not only in Germany but also in Europe at large, is only beginning to appear, but the political impact is already clear – including populist and right-wing backlash against immigrants, a sharp rise in migrant-related crime, the emergence of a sustained pattern of low-grade Islamist terrorism in Europe, and increasing strain on EU structures. Germany's attitude has also alienated some NATO allies further to its east (notably Hungary, Poland, and the Czech Republic), who see the influx as a deeply destabilizing threat to European culture and security. If the theory of strategic culture described earlier is valid, this is likely to lead to a profound shift in European grand strategy and military posture in the future.

Russian Strategic Culture

Finally, the reaction of the Russian officer in my NATO Defense College classroom invites discussion of one last case study in strategic culture. Just as von Bülow in 1897 called for Germany's "place in the sun" while claiming no desire to push others into the shade, Russian President Vladimir Putin has spoken about how Russia seeks respect from the international community and the right to pursue its sovereign interests without interference in its own sphere of influence. "Respect for [sovereignty] and its consolidation will help underwrite peace and stability both at the national and international levels ... But we do not seek global domination, expansion or confrontation with anyone."[36]

Russian strategic culture, like that of the other countries discussed in this chapter, derives ultimately from enduring circumstances. Russia straddles Europe and Asia, has a vast territory and a relatively small population, has historically experienced population decline and deindustrialization, and feels itself both threatened and disrespected by outside powers while claiming a protective responsibility for the "Russian World," defined expansively as all areas of the world with populations who speak Russian, identify as Russian, have Russian ethnicities, or follow Orthodox Christianity. Russia faces an encroaching NATO to its west, extremist Islam to its south, and the rising global and regional power of China to its east. Russia has a centuries-old history, driven by these enduring circumstances, of frequent recourse to military force as a means to dominate its neighbors, deter or prevent attack, expand its territory, crush unruly ethnic groups that challenge its central government, and further its policies worldwide.

Like that of Germany (and, in a different way, Indonesia), Russian strategic culture is also hugely influenced by a set of searing twentieth-century experiences – the Russian Revolution, Communist oppression, the massive bloodletting of World War II, the fall of the Soviet Union (which left 25 million Russians outside the country's new borders), post-Soviet chaos and decline, the humiliating loss of global influence in the 1990s, and the reemergence of authoritarian rule under Putin since 2000. Perhaps the strongest impact of the fall of Communism has been a sense of injured pride, a desire to re-litigate the outcome of the Cold War, to reestablish Russia as a great power, and to assuage the humiliations of the post-Soviet generation. Whereas its general industrial capacity suffered significantly in the 1990s, Russia remains a major oil and gas exporter, a fact that allowed it to garner significant oil revenue in the early 2000s during a period of high global oil prices, as well as to control (and thereby weaponize) oil and gas supplies to its neighbors. It also retains a powerful nuclear arsenal and a capable military-industrial base. Russia's Cold War-era arms supply networks also gave it a ready-made network for weapons export and power projection through military sales.

Combined with Soviet-era military concepts emphasizing deception, ambiguity, forms of political and economic warfare involving the "combination of all forms of struggle," and a willingness to raise local proxy and surrogate forces (and to tolerate a high degree of chaos and error in the process), these circumstances give rise to a distinctive contemporary Russian way of war. As characterized by Chief of the Russian General Staff Valeriy Gerasimov in 2013, this includes the seamless use of political, diplomatic, and "other nonmilitary

---

[36] President of Russia, speech at the meeting of the Valdai International Discussion Club, October 27, 2016, http://en.kremlin.ru/events/president/news/53151.

measures" (including criminal activities and cyberwarfare) combined with military force, the initiation of military operations in peacetime, the conduct of highly maneuverable noncontact operations by interagency or joint combat groups, and the reduction of an enemy's military-economic potential through rapid destruction of critical military and civilian infrastructure. Gerasimov emphasized the mass use of precision weapons, the large-scale use of special operations forces, robotics, weapons based on "novel physical principles," and simultaneous effects on an enemy's civil and military forces and facilities throughout the entire depth of its territories. All this amounts to a focus on simultaneous operations in all physical domains as well as in the information space, asymmetric and indirect operations, and a propensity to create and exploit "frozen conflicts" to further political objectives by using military means that stay just under the threshold of open conflict.[37]

The details of this approach – currently on full display in Ukraine, Syria, and the frozen conflicts of Russia's borderlands, as well as in the Baltic, Arctic, and North Seas and in the aerospace and cyberspace domains (not to mention in the guise of political interference by Russian military intelligence in democratic processes in the United States and elsewhere) – are hugely important in themselves. But in the context of the present book, focused on military organizations and strategic culture, one final point is worth making.

Conclusion: The Dangers of Cultural Asymmetry

Whatever else it might be, the Russian conception of warfare – influenced, as we have seen, by enduring circumstances and a strategic culture founded on reversing a generation of injured pride by any means necessary – is a far broader concept than that of powers like the United States and its allies, who define war much more narrowly and tend to focus on battlefield success by force of arms as the primary goal. In cultural terms, this matters a lot, since, as we have seen, one of the functions of strategic culture is to frame and define reality, fitting events and patterns into recognized categories (such as "war," "peace," "crime," "international," or "domestic").

If Americans and their allies, with a narrowly defined cultural norm for what is and is not war, confront an adversary with a vastly broader cultural understanding of conflict, then two equally dangerous things can arise. First, we can be engaged in conflict with an adversary who considers himself to be at war with us, and yet not realize that fact. (This is arguably part of what happened in the US election of 2016.) Second, an equal and opposite danger is that we can be engaged in activities that seem innocuous or peaceful to us – exercises,

---

[37] For a detailed analysis of Gerasimov's seminal article, see Charles K. Bartles, "Getting Gerasimov Right," *Military Review* (January–February 2016), 30–37.

routine deployments, support for peaceful democracy movements, expansion of military alliances, assertion of what we regard as universal norms – and our adversaries can perceive these as acts of war and respond accordingly.

This is perhaps already happening: in any case, it represents one of the key risks when actors with a high degree of what we might call "cultural asymmetry" engage each other. The examples in this book illustrate this point neatly, as well as exploring the specific military organizational cultures that emerge from the intersection of strategic culture, organizational structure, the changing character of the environment, and the dynamic evolution of highly adaptive enemies.

Part II

Land Forces

3 Ulysses S. Grant and the Culture of the Union Army of the Tennessee

Wayne Wei-siang Hsieh

Most military cultures value continuity and tradition, even if that tradition ends up more a product of self-conscious artifice than organic change over long stretches of time. But even if a military organization hopes to escape the past, prior practice tends to constrain radical change. Armies have powerful reasons to avoid departing too far from tried and true methods, and military organizations that embark on major changes run the risk of triggering irreparable failure in wartime. The American Civil War presented an exceptional state of affairs in modern warfare, however, because strong personalities could embed their own command philosophies into field armies, due to the miniscule size of the American military establishment at the war's outbreak. The effectiveness of the Union Army of the Tennessee stemmed in large part from the strong influence of Ulysses S. Grant, who as early as the fall of 1861 imbued in its commanders and soldiers an aggressive mind-set. However, Grant's command culture went beyond simple aggressiveness – it included most importantly an emphasis on suppressing internal rivalries among sometimes prideful officers for the sake of winning victories – a rare feat in a war that saw its fair share of interpersonal and interservice bickering.

In 1860, when the American Civil War broke out, the US Army numbered approximately 16,000 officers and men. Antebellum West Point classes numbered in the forties and fifties, so even when including those officers (like Grant) who had left the service, officers with professional training remained a rare and precious resource. West Pointers' virtual monopoly on military expertise in antebellum America meant that they could and did have an outsized influence on the organization and training of the war's field armies. Furthermore, most Southern graduates followed their states into the Confederate army, further reducing the pool of trained officers in the Union. Worse yet, West Point–trained professionals had no experience in or training for commanding large field armies. Winfield Scott's army during the decisive Vera Cruz campaign in Mexico (the closest historical antecedent to the American Civil War) numbered fewer than

10,000 men, while in contrast Irvin McDowell's undersized field army at First Bull Run, during the initial and chaotic months of Union mobilization, numbered 35,000 men.

While the US Army provided both sections' military forces a coherent and expansible professional model, the sectional conflict presented an essentially unprecedented problem in American history. The collapse of the militia system meant that only West Pointers and a smattering of veterans from the regular army and Mexican War volunteer regiments had any substantive military experience at the start of the war. Former regular army officers such as Grant were thus in high demand as drillmasters, commanders, and organizers during the early days of the conflict. Indeed, Grant's departure from the army under a cloud of suspicion and his less than distinguished civilian career hardly recommended him for command at the war's outbreak. But the fact that he was West Point trained, combined with his strong combat record in Mexico and some helpful political influence, gave him an opportunity to command that he probably would not have had in a war with a less frantic and disorganized period of mobilization.[1]

Grant's academy credentials helped provide him the opportunity to command, but few of his fellow alumni would aid him in his early military efforts. Grant's first field army, based at Cairo, Illinois, which he would lead into battle during the Belmont campaign, had a single fellow West Pointer in its ranks. In contrast, Irvin McDowell's army at First Bull Run had eight West Pointers among its brigade and division commanders, albeit in the hothouse environment of Washington, DC, where the North's political leaders kept a close eye on the major Union army in Virginia. In contrast, Grant had a far freer hand with his own troops and with subordinates, who certainly possessed healthy egos, but also had none of his claims to professional military expertise. He also had the benefit of commanding a smaller force than McClellan's Army of the Potomac – three divisions during the Forts Henry and Donelson campaign, compared to the five infantry corps McClellan brought to the Peninsula.[2] Nevertheless, even a commander such as McClellan, who inherited a high proportion of regulars as subordinates, could still put a powerful stamp on his army's institutional culture, because by appointing the initial set of brigade and division commanders, he could both further a specific command style and

---

[1] For coverage of these issues, see Wayne Wei-siang Hsieh, *West Pointers and the Civil War* (Chapel Hill, 2009).

[2] Biographical data of the officers in the high commands of the Army of the Potomac, the Army of the Tennessee, and the Army of the Ohio are drawn from Frank Welcher, *The Union Army, 1861–1865*, 2 vols. (Bloomington, IN, 1989–1993), Ezra J. Warner, *Generals in Blue: Lives of the Union Commanders* (Baton Rouge, LA, 1964), and George W. Cullum, *Biographical Register of the Officers and Graduates of the U.S. Military Academy at West Point, N.Y.*, 3rd edn., 3 vols. (Boston, MA, 1891), and F. B. Heitman, *Historical Register of the U.S. Army: From Its Organization, September 29, 1789, to March 2, 1903*, 2 vols. (Washington, DC, 1903).

determine future candidates for promotion to division and corps command. In a significantly smaller army, and one less exposed to political interference, Grant's influence was likely to have been all the more important.

Grant also exposed his troops from an early date to aggressive operations in the field. In November, he struck a Confederate force at Belmont. Officers whom Grant led at Belmont included future corps commanders John McClernand and John Logan and future division commander Jacob Lauman. Even though Grant had not presided over the initial brigading of C. F. Smith's regiments at Paducah, he also immediately moved those forces into offensive operations for the important Forts Henry and Donelson campaign in February 1862. What would become the Army of the Tennessee continued to add units to its organization until the Battle of Shiloh, which led to a brief interlude during which Grant was essentially shelved. When the army reunited under Grant's command, it would go through various periods of reorganization, including the important creation of corps commands at the end of 1862. But it was in the period between the winter of 1861 and the spring of 1862 that the Army of the Tennessee, as historians know it, was organized and consolidated into a single force. The singular trait of that period was that Grant kept his army in the field for aggressive operations, establishing important precedents for both his soldiers and officers that would resonate even after Grant's eventual departure to the east. The capture of Vicksburg the following summer represented the culminating triumph of that army, cementing the self-confident force that would help capture Atlanta and form the backbone of Sherman's March to the Sea.

In contrast, the Army of the Potomac spent most of that period organizing, training, and drilling. That army had in many ways a superior training regimen than Grant's forces, with probably the most extensive and organized program of target practice, bayonet drill, and large unit maneuvers of any major US Civil War field army.[3] Moreover, McClellan's collection of brigade and division commanders had far more experience than Grant's. The majority were regular army veterans, and in many ways represented the cream of American military talent. Historians can find much important information in the collective biographies of the commanders of the infantry brigades and divisions McClellan organized in August 1861, shortly after he replaced McDowell as the primary Union field army commander in the east.[4]

Among McClellan's first set of eight division commanders between their organization and the move to the Peninsula, each had served at some point as an

---

[3] Hsieh, *West Pointers and the Civil War*, 146–147.

[4] For the purposes of this chapter, I have excluded from my analysis three divisions (commanded by non–West Pointers Nathaniel Banks, Louis Blenker, and Frederick Lander), which did not deploy to the Peninsula between the York and James Rivers in the spring 1862 campaign against Richmond and did not become part of the core of the Army of the Potomac (i.e., Corps I–VI).

officer in the Old Army and only two were not West Pointers (Edwin V. Sumner and Philip Kearny). Of the fifty-eight different brigade and division commanders McClellan assigned during this period, only sixteen had not served in the regular army. Forty (or 69 percent) had graduated from West Point and three others had served in the regular army as officers. In contrast, of the fifty-one regimental, brigade, and division commanders in the forces Grant organized for the Forts Henry and Donelson campaign, only three (or 6 percent) were West Point graduates. Of these three, two were regimental commanders, leaving C. F. Smith as the lone West Point–trained division commander.

Don Carlos Buell's Army of the Ohio, which eventually became the Army of the Cumberland, also serves as another useful point of comparison to Grant's army. On December 2, 1861, Buell organized the Army of the Ohio into six divisions. He added a seventh division in March, and while the bulk of the assignments dated from the winter, there was some churn among unit and command assignments until the spring. Looking at this entire period, out of the thirty-six total division and infantry brigade commanders appointed in the Army of the Ohio, thirteen (or 36 percent) were graduates from West Point, and another two were professional naval officers.[5] In sum, while Buell did not enjoy as strong a stable of regular officers as McClellan, he had far more military experience among his senior subordinates than did Grant. Of the three commanders, Grant had by far the least access to trained military talent, but he eventually proved the most successful.

McClellan's cautious style has sometimes been linked to his background as an engineer in the Old Army. The engineers certainly held a disproportionate share of senior command positions, but by no means possessed a monopoly on high rank in the army. During this period, McClellan appointed engineers (either Corps of Engineers or Topographical Engineer officers) as commanders for three of his divisions at one point or the other – Rufus King, William B. Franklin, George W. Morell, and William F. Smith. Considering the miniscule size of the engineering branches in the Old Army, this was a striking share of senior command positions. One other division commander, Charles P. Stone, was an ordnance officer, a staff bureau that inhabited the second rung of West Point's academic elite, but that by definition did not serve in the line. Thus, McClellan's selection of brigade and division commanders reflected a strong preference not only for Old Army men, but also for the technical elite created by West Point's engineering-heavy curriculum. Moreover, ten out of the forty-three regular army veterans among these brigade and division commanders had served at West Point as a faculty member, which again testifies to the important role the army's professional elite played in the Army of the Potomac, which tended to hail from the gray-clad Corps of Cadets on the Hudson.

[5] Welcher, *The Union Army*, 2:192–196.

McClellan by no means had complete freedom of action in choosing his subordinates. In addition to the army's strong respect for seniority, Lincoln also imposed a corps organization on McClellan before the latter moved on Richmond, and the president cited seniority in his appointments. Nevertheless, as the commander in the field, McClellan retained some freedom of action. He organized two provisional corps in May 1862 – what later became the Army of the Potomac's V and VI Corps – with his own hand-picked commanders. Due to their later organization, not all of these officers are included in the earlier census of commanders appointed in the summer 1861 organization. Among the corps and division commanders in this organization, three came from the army's engineering branches – William B. Franklin commanding the VI Corps had been a topographical engineer in the Old Army, along with one of his two division commanders, William F. Smith. In the V Corps, George W. Morell, commissioned like McClellan into the Corps of Engineers out of West Point, commanded a division. The V Corps also included a new division of regular regiments, headed by George Sykes (an infantry officer), who had started the war commanding a regular army battalion in First Bull Run. All the corps and division commanders in the two organizations had graduated from West Point.

These handpicked subordinates of McClellan had decidedly mixed combat records, reflecting the larger flaws in the Army of the Potomac's command culture. Franklin proved a poor corps commander and contributed much to the Union disaster at Fredericksburg. Fitz-John Porter fought splendidly during the Seven Days battles, and if he had commanded the army, the Union might very well have captured Richmond during that campaign. Unfortunately, he wore his conservative Democratic politics even more conspicuously on his sleeve than did McClellan, and he refused to cooperate with John Pope at Second Bull Run. While by no means fully responsible for that disaster, Porter's political indiscretions and unwillingness to overcome military tribalism for the larger Union cause led to his relief, depriving the Army of the Potomac of one of its better corps commanders.

Of the division commanders in V Corps, Sykes would eventually prove a competent corps commander, although perhaps not an exceptional one. Morell, the former engineer, would top out at division command. In the VI Corps, Henry W. Slocum, an artillery officer, would rise to corps command but would prove unworthy of that responsibility. William F. Smith would prove a fine senior engineering officer who helped Grant open the cracker line to relieve Chattanooga in the fall of 1863, but a mediocre corps commander in the summer of 1864. In this respect, he was similar to Gouverneur Warren, one of the V Corps' brigade commanders, who had not commanded one of the brigades during the late summer 1861 reorganization, but who later did fine service as an engineering officer at Gettysburg. Unfortunately for both him and the Union

Army, Warren would falter as VI Corps commander in the campaigns of 1864 and beyond, leading eventually to his controversial relief by Philip Sheridan just before Lee's surrender at Appomattox.

Nevertheless, it would be a mistake to underplay the merits of McClellan's subordinates. Not only did they reflect the antebellum army's focus on technical and scientific competence – a product of the Thayer system at West Point – the group as a whole also possessed strong operational records. If we restrict our examination to the forty-three regular army veterans among the brigade and division commanders during McClellan's summer 1861 organization, the only striking commonality is significant operational experience. Twenty-eight had not only served during the active campaigns of the Mexican War but also had distinguished themselves well enough to win brevet promotions (the army's then-primary method for commending exemplary service). Thirteen of the twenty-eight who were old enough to have fought in the Second Seminole War (1837–1842) – the most important (and controversial) of the antebellum era's Indian Wars – did so. In contrast, out of the relatively few West Pointers who served in Grant's armies between Belmont and Shiloh, few had much operational experience outside of C. F. Smith and Sherman, and even Sherman had essentially missed the major combat operations of the Mexican War.

It is a truism bordering almost on cliché among historians of the American Civil War that the Army of the Potomac had chronic command problems, but we should not underestimate the qualifications of the subordinates McClellan collected and put in place. Those officers, under McClellan's astute direction, trained the army's citizen-soldier volunteers and created a tactically proficient and cohesive force. While mocked by outsiders, McClellan's program of parades also encouraged a powerful *esprit de corps* in the Army of the Potomac, whose rank and file bore an affection for Little Mac that Grant would never enjoy from any of his troops. Nevertheless, despite the willingness of its members to take fearsome combat losses year after year between 1862 and 1865, this hard-luck military force won only two unambiguous victories – the three-day battle at Gettysburg in 1863 and the Appomattox campaign in 1865 that finally resulted in the surrender of the Confederate Army of Northern Virginia. However, even these battles revealed serious problems in the Army of the Potomac's military effectiveness. At Gettysburg, it benefited from fighting a defensive battle on favorable terrain deep behind Union lines in the heart of Pennsylvania. At Appomattox, this army's only offensive victory came after a grinding siege had already left the Army of Northern Virginia a half-starved shell of its former self. Even then, much of that triumph came to fruition due to the involvement of cavalry forces under the command of Philip Sheridan, a general who rose to division command in the west, and who had continuous clashes with the Army of the Potomac's senior generals after his transfer east.

Moreover, his cavalry troopers had not been a part of McClellan's core organization.

In short, most historians have rightly portrayed the Army of the Potomac as institutionally sluggish, passive, and incapable of the aggressive decisiveness needed for success in offensive military operations. With the army's rank-and-file record of bravery in combat, and an officer corps far better qualified than its more successful Western counterpart, the historian's attention rightly turns to the man at the head of the army during its early campaigns – George B. McClellan. The Army of the Potomac never seemed to escape entirely the cautious ethos of its first commander, which the army's repeated drubbings at the hands of Robert E. Lee's Army of Northern Virginia – including defeats at Fredericksburg and Chancellorsville where McClellan was no longer in command – only served to exacerbate.

In contrast, while McClellan refused to move his forces, Grant's small army, led by a far less impressive collection of subordinates in terms of their experience, went on the offensive on the Mississippi River at Belmont, Missouri, on November 7, 1861. In making the attack on the Confederate camp commanded by Gideon Pillow, Grant actually exceeded his orders from his departmental commander, John C. Fremont, who only envisioned a demonstration that would deter the Confederates from reinforcing southeastern Missouri. Grant moved his forces via transports down the Mississippi River from Cairo, Illinois, bringing along two supporting gunboats. The battle's course and outcome reflected the inexperience of the troops engaged. Grant's forces scored an initial tactical success, although Grant himself showed his own inexperience as a commander by doing little to control the battle. This lack of control became problematic when his men lost discipline after the capture of the Confederate camp and disintegrated into a mob preoccupied with looting Confederate possessions. One of Grant's brigade commanders, political general John McClernand, who also represented southern Illinois in Congress, even resorted to speechifying, although he had at least done well on the battlefield beforehand. During this confused interlude, the Confederates rallied and counterattacked, forcing Grant to retreat to his transports. They inflicted significant casualties on his small expeditionary force – upward of 600 casualties out of a force of just over 3,100 men engaged. The Confederates suffered, in comparison, 641 casualties out of roughly 5,000 men engaged.[6]

Belmont was hardly an unmitigated success. In some ways, it was near disaster, leading even to some special pleading in Grant's memoirs on the whole affair. Nevertheless, his leadership established important precedents.

---

[6] Nathaniel Cheairs Hughes Jr., *The Battle of Belmont: Grant Strikes South* (Chapel Hill, NC, 1991).

The most important was that, as always, Grant pushed his troops to take the initiative and remain on the offensive. Even Charles W. Wills, an Illinois soldier, who bluntly declared that "Grant got whipped," also asserted that "the boys are not the least discouraged and they all want to go back and try it again."[7] Wills had not actually fought at the battle, but talked with members of regiments who did, and if he had seen a mounted Grant clamber aboard a gangway onto a departing transport – literally the last Federal to board the boat – he might have had a more positive view of Grant's leadership.[8] Regardless, even if many of Grant's men had come away from the battle not terribly impressed with Grant himself, they at least felt proud of their own performance under fire and confident in their martial abilities. In contrast, while the Army of the Potomac was by no means demoralized by the fiasco at Ball's Bluff in October, Belmont was obviously a far preferable first engagement for a field army.

Grant's subordinates also showed ample willingness to follow his lead in waging an aggressive style of warfare. Even the controversial McClernand showed his abilities as a battlefield commander. As early as Belmont, this most controversial of the political generals in the Army of the Tennessee showed both his virtues and his faults. John Logan, still a regimental commander at this point, also displayed his merits as a battlefield commander in this early battle, along with Jacob Lauman, who would do fine service as a brigade commander at Fort Donelson. Henry Dougherty, Grant's other brigade commander and another volunteer officer, excelled in the battle but suffered such grievous wounds he would never see field service again during the war. Despite their nonregular army backgrounds, Grant would support all these officers' promotions, although he would eventually break with McClernand after Shiloh when the latter became increasingly insubordinate. In contrast, Grant would give only lukewarm support to his only West Point–trained regimental commander at Belmont, Napoleon Buford, who defied orders and imperiled both his own regiment and the larger army during its retreat after the Confederate counterattack. Buford would eventually gain a general's star, but he would do his best service to the Union not as a combat commander, but as a garrison administrator in Arkansas dealing with cotton speculators and the various challenges of occupation duty.[9]

Grant's assault on Belmont also presaged his excellent relations with naval officers. Union gunboats at Belmont had covered the landing point for his troops, and the navy would prove invaluable to Grant in his most famous campaigns. Grant had an excellent working relationship with Flag Officer

[7] Charles W. Wills, *Army Life of an Illinois Soldier, Including a Day by Day Record of Sherman's March to the Sea* (Washington, DC, 1906), 43.
[8] Hughes, *The Battle of Belmont*, 171.   [9] Ibid., 203; Warner, *Generals in Blue*, 54.

Andrew Hull Foote.[10] He would also enjoy a similar rapport with David Dixon Porter during the Vicksburg campaign.[11] Historians should not assume such good relations. Interservice rivalry could and did cause serious problems for combined army-navy operations in places such as Charleston and Wilmington. Porter, for example, would sharply clash with Benjamin Butler during the campaign to take Fort Fisher near Wilmington during the war's last year. Even when army and navy commanders were not openly hostile to one another, they could still miss the opportunities provided by the capabilities of the other service. This certainly was the failing of Henry Halleck, who as the senior Union commander in the western theater, did not support David Glasgow Farragut's strike at Vicksburg in the summer of 1862, which failed in large part due to the absence of supporting ground forces.[12] In contrast to Halleck, the Army of the Tennessee would prove comfortable working with the navy throughout its entire history. This strong working relationship with the navy originated in many ways with Grant's own indifference to perquisites and the trappings of rank, which also applied to his dealings with subordinates. Grant thus also set an example of collegiality and cohesiveness for his senior sub-ordinates, helping to lead to an army with a relatively harmonious leadership cadre.

Such organizational harmony should in no ways be assumed. In many ways, mid-nineteenth-century America provided poor terrain for the order and discipline we usually associate with effective military organizations. The citizen-soldier volunteers who filled the ranks of US Civil War armies valued independence and freedom from exterior restraint, which they strongly associated with their era's conceptions of manhood. They had inherited from their Revolutionary predecessors a distaste and contempt for the professional standing armies of Europe, comprised in their view of the dregs of society and led by arrogant aristocrats. The underfunded US Army of the antebellum period, which filled its enlisted ranks in large part from immigrants and the urban poor at the bottom of the American social ladder, only further supported these cultural presumptions. Moreover, the volunteers who joined the armies to put down the rebellion also saw themselves as exemplars of republican virtue who deserved better treatment than the harsh discipline associated with the whiskey- and desertion-plagued regular army. Their belief that they were fighting to put down a tyrannical slave power only furthered their hostility to regular army

---

[10] Benjamin Franklin Cooling, "The Forging of Joint Army-Navy Operations: Andrew Hull Foote and Grant," in Steven E. Woodworth, ed., *Grant's Lieutenants: From Cairo to Vicksburg* (Lawrence, KS, 2001), 91–108.

[11] R. Blake Dunnavent, "'We Had Lively Times up the Yazoo': Admiral David Dixon Porter," in Steven E. Woodworth, ed., *Grant's Lieutenants: From Cairo to Vicksburg* (Lawrence, KS, 2001), 169–182.

[12] Williamson Murray and Wayne Wei-siang Hsieh, *A Savage War: A Military History of the Civil War* (Princeton, NJ, 2016), 163.

notions of discipline, which borrowed some of its corporal punishments from slavery.[13]

Despite their ideological and cultural hostility to many forms of military discipline, effective US Civil War armies obviously could not survive without at least some measure of coercion. As a new colonel of volunteers, Grant found that necessary balance. He knew the necessity of using the rod, but he also had a self-effacing personality uncharacteristic among his fellow officers, which helped him balance regular army discipline with the volunteers' distaste for restraint. Challenging combat service in the Indian and Mexican Wars had bred among some Old Army officers a contempt for civilian society. Grant, in contrast, related a story in his *Memoirs* of his return home as a young lieutenant after graduation from West Point, proudly displaying his new uniform. A street urchin promptly put him back in his place; the urchin's derision stemmed from the army's penurious practice of selling off used uniforms, which then became the garments of beggars and vagabonds, further highlighting the dubious social status of soldering in antebellum America. Whether right or wrong, Grant had learned a hard lesson about Americans' views of America's professional soldiers, and like another regular army general who knew how to handle volunteers, Zachary Taylor, Grant would famously eschew dress uniform finery. In contrast, commanders such as Don Carlos Buell and Braxton Bragg inspired hostility from their enlisted ranks that could rise to the level of outright hatred.[14] While their collective failures as commanders stemmed from a wide variety of faults, low morale among their troops and a lack of confidence in their commander hardly helped their causes.

Perhaps even more serious than enlisted soldiers' resistance to discipline was the fractious temperament of *officers*, both regular army and volunteer. Both groups of officers shared broad similarities in outlook as middle-class Victorians, with their own class-based notions of status, individual honor, and social standing. Both could be sensitive toward perceived slights, and the history of the American Civil War is filled with generals bickering over their relative standing, with little regards at times for their formal positions in their military hierarchies. The Army of the Tennessee was by no means invulnerable to rivalry among its senior leaders. Grant proved capable of not only containing those conflicts but also managing his political capital sufficiently well with his own superiors to first contain and even eventually expel John McClernand, the greatest source of discord within the army.

McClernand's trouble-making did not indicate, however, that West Pointers were as a group more harmonious in their behavior. In the Confederate army,

[13] Steven J. Ramold, *Baring the Iron Hand: Discipline in the Union Army* (DeKalb, IL, 2010).
[14] Ulysses S. Grant, *Personal Memoirs of U.S. Grant*, 2 vols. (New York, 1892), 1:43–44; Murray and Hsieh, *A Savage War*, 95, 208–210.

for example, Joseph Johnston and Jefferson Davis (both West Point graduates) waged a bitter war of words over Johnston's relative standing among his general officer peers. Before the war, when Davis had served as a vigorous and reformist secretary of war, he had a similar feud with General in Chief Winfield Scott, the greatest American soldier of the first half of the nineteenth century, and perhaps America's brightest professional exemplar.[15] Infighting and backstabbing among senior commanders in both the Union Army of the Potomac and the Confederate Army of Tennessee are other well-known examples of armies where commanders failed to enforce a common sense of purpose and mission among senior subordinates – problems that were by no means exclusive to officers drawn from civilian life.

On the presence or absence of internal harmony in an army, Buell's contentious tenure at the head of the Army of the Ohio provides a useful counterpoint to Grant's Army of the Tennessee. Buell himself had a notorious reputation as a martinet and tyrant, leading to much rancor in the ranks. Grant may have never received much genuine affection from his men, but they certainly never *hated* him the way some of Buell's men despised their commander.[16] Buell also had a penchant for picking senior subordinates who sowed strife and dissension. He appointed William Nelson a corps commander and included in his forces a substantial number of Indiana regiments despite the ferocious dislike Indiana troops especially held for Nelson. Nelson also ran afoul of Jefferson Davis, a Union division commander (not to be confused with the Confederate president). After several heated arguments, Davis murdered Nelson, his prospective corps commander. So hated was Nelson that the 105th Ohio Regiment and Indiana troops cheered the deed.

Nelson was a complex character who inspired both hatred and affection, and many officers were deeply outraged by Davis's offense. Davis's reputation never entirely recovered from the episode, but due to a mix of political influence and the confused circumstances surrounding the Perryville campaign and Buell's eventual relief, Davis escaped direct punishment and even achieved de facto corps command under Sherman during the March to the Sea.[17] Buell also appointed another controversial corps commander, Charles Gilbert, who in addition to having insufficient rank would also inspire more than his fair share of genuine hate from his troops.[18] In the end, Buell never overcame the bitterly divided command culture he both found and to some degree encouraged in the

[15] William J. Cooper Jr., *Jefferson Davis, American* (New York, 2000), 363–364, 252–254.

[16] Kenneth W. Noe, *Perryville: This Grand Havoc of Battle* (Lexington, KY, 2001), 10–12, 78–79.

[17] Nathaniel Cheairs Hughes Jr. and Gordon D. Whitney, *Jefferson Davis in Blue: The Life of Sherman's Relentless Warrior* (Baton Rouge, LA, 2002), 102–126. Davis's career was also marked by the controversy surrounding his abandonment of African-American refugees to Confederate cavalry at Ebenezer Creek during the March to the Sea.

[18] Noe, *Perryville*, 97–98, 122–123.

Army of the Ohio. And while that army included as fine a combat commander as George Thomas, it would never achieve the aggressive efficiency seen in the Army of the Tennessee.[19]

The experience of George W. Morgan's division helps illuminate the differences between the Army of the Ohio and the Army of the Tennessee, because it served in both organizations. Morgan had attended West Point but failed to graduate due to academic deficiencies; he nevertheless served with distinction in the Mexican War. Morgan successfully took Cumberland Gap in June 1862, holding it until the fall, and by virtue of his detached service, avoided many of the controversies in Buell's Army of the Ohio. Nevertheless, he would perform poorly during the assault at Chickasaw and clash again with Sherman during the Arkansas Post Expedition. An opponent of emancipation and the use of African American troops, he resigned before Vicksburg's fall in 1863.[20] However, Morgan's division did fine service under the command of Peter J. Osterhaus during the Vicksburg campaign, compiling a strong combat record before it was consolidated with another division in late summer.[21]

In contrast to the laurels Morgan's division earned in the Army of the Tennessee, its parent unit would have a much more mixed battlefield record. Buell's career came to a close after the Battle of Perryville, where he showed himself as incapable of effective tactical leadership as he was at creating a productive command environment. His replacement, William Rosecrans, now at the head of the Army of the Cumberland, proved a more capable general, but his notorious temper, which led in large part to his falling out with Grant after the Iuka and Corinth campaigns, produced a poisonous command environment that led to catastrophe at Chickamauga. In that battle, Rosecrans had so sharply rebuked Thomas J. Wood, a division commander with a strong wartime record of service up to that point, for not obeying orders with sufficient alacrity that Wood later chose to obey a clearly erroneous order. That, in turn, opened a major gap in the Federal line, through which James Longstreet hurled an entire Confederate corps.[22] George Thomas's splendid performance at Chickamauga would save the Army of the Cumberland, and he later proved a solid commander of the army, but his organization never quite seemed to break completely free of the problems that had plagued its earlier history.

---

[19] Steven E. Woodworth, "'Old Slow Trot': George H. Thomas," in Steven E. Woodworth, ed., *Grant's Lieutenants from Chattanooga to Appomattox* (Lawrence, KS, 2008), 23–46.

[20] Warner, *Generals in Blue*, 333–334; Steven E. Woodworth, *Nothing but Victory: The Army of the Tennessee, 1861–1865* (New York, 2005), 280.

[21] Warner, *Generals in Blue*, 352–353; Welcher, *The Union Army*, 2:259–261.

[22] Mark Grimsley, "Success and Failure in Civil War Armies: Clues from Organizational Culture," in Wayne Lee, ed., *Warfare and Culture in World History* (New York, 2011), 115–116.

Grant was by no means as retiring and unambitious as he portrayed himself to be. In this sense, he had some similarities to his commander in chief, who also masked a good deal of ambition behind a self-deprecating demeanor. But unlike so many of his peers, Grant acted as if he was indifferent to public signs of rank and status. As long as a commander could further his primary goal, winning victories on the battlefield, Grant was generally willing to overlook perceived personal slights toward himself or self-serving gestures on the part of others. In the case of interacting with naval officers, who came from a rival service, this was an invaluable character trait. But Grant's interaction with two key subordinates, C. F. Smith and William T. Sherman, also exemplified this style of command, where both superiors and subordinates committed to a common purpose and refrained from backbiting and scheming for personal advantage.

Because of Grant's superior political connections, Smith was Grant's subordinate during the war, despite the fact that the former had actually been Grant's commandant at West Point and had had a far more impressive antebellum military career. Grant remained a great admirer of Smith, who in turn excelled as a division commander during the Forts Henry and Donelson campaign and helped implement Grant's aggressive style of command. While many other generals would have grumbled at the situation and waged campaigns of influence via newspapers and politicians to undermine a superior to their own advantage, Smith did none of these things and went to great pains to make clear to Grant that the latter was in fact the commanding general. Smith would perish in the spring after an untimely accident disabled him shortly after the Donelson campaign, which unintentionally helped set the stage for Sherman's rise as Grant's most important lieutenant and a great commander in his own right.[23]

After Belmont, Grant continued his aggressive style of campaigning and scored a major victory for the Union with the capture of Forts Henry and Donelson in February 1862. In many ways, the Confederate military position in the west never recovered from this blow, which allowed the Union to use the Tennessee and Cumberland Rivers as secure invasion routes into the Confederate heartland. Grant moved his forces farther south, and he was now joined by two divisions commanded by William T. Sherman and Benjamin Prentiss. Flush from victory, Grant did not pay as much attention as he should have to possible Confederate responses, while Sherman was attempting to rehabilitate his reputation from a near nervous breakdown in Kentucky, where he had been unable to manage the psychological burdens of command. This primed the situation for a near Federal disaster, when Confederates struck the Federal camps at Pittsburgh Landing on April 6 with an army laboriously

---

[23] Brooks Simpson, *Ulysses S. Grant: Triumph over Adversity* (Boston, MA, 2000), 138–140.

concentrated via rail from all across the Confederate states. Both Grant and Sherman were caught by surprise, although a higher burden of responsibility fell on the latter for ignoring clear warning signs of an imminent Confederate attack. Nevertheless, Sherman redeemed himself to some degree by organizing a spirited defense, and the Union troops fought tenaciously enough to survive the first day. On the second day, Grant ordered a counterattack that drove the Confederates back.

As at Belmont, but on a much larger scale, Grant's generalship at Shiloh was (and is to this day) still questioned. Three of Grant's divisions, moreover, had not been at Donelson with him, so those men had few attachments to him from his earlier triumphs. But even for those soldiers who felt their commander had mishandled the first day, they emerged from the battle confident in their own fighting abilities, as seen in the army's survival and subsequent counterattack. They had moved deep into the heart of the Confederacy, fought a great battle when the Confederates mustered a powerful counter-stroke, and held their ground with expectations of further advances south. Contrast to this the outcome of the Seven Days in the East, where despite winning a series of tactical victories, McClellan ceded ground near Richmond and chose to retreat to the James River. Worse yet, the Army of the Potomac had to then scramble back north to respond to Lee's aggressive moves, culminating in a major battle in Maryland. The bloodbath at Shiloh, along with his constant demands for hard fighting, might have been one reason Grant never seemed to inspire the sort of affection from his rank and file McClellan possessed, but what his army gained from it was more militarily important – a faith in its own fighting abilities and indomitable spirit on the battlefield.

One participant, S. D. Thompson, later said, "after the first onset of the enemy, which was to the whole army, if not General Grant himself, a complete surprise, the field was contested by our troops with a heroism which will forever redound to their honor." Whatever Grant's failings that day, it was the rank and file's battlefield courage that truly counted. "Divisions, brigades, regiments, men, fought recklessly, but no one could tell how; such was the tumult without and within."[24] Indeed, Seymour bluntly stated that the battle "diminished our confidence in General Grant" because "he had allowed an immense army to march upon him and surprise him, and that surprise had entailed upon us defeat, and, to a certain degree, dishonor."[25] Furthermore, according to Seymour, his division criticized Grant for not mounting a vigorous pursuit after the battle, another sign of the fighting spirit of the Army of the Tennessee's rank and file.[26] Seymour believed that Shiloh "changed materially the *morale* of the army. It had diminished our inclination to boast. If it had not

[24] S. D. Thompson, *Recollections with the Third Iowa Regiment* (Cincinnati, OH, 1864), 209.
[25] Ibid., 249.   [26] Ibid., 241.

taught us to respect ourselves less, it had taught us to respect our enemies more." As with Belmont, some of Grant's men raised questions about the quality of their leadership at Shiloh, and some "believed that this battle had demonstrated the superiority of the enemy's generals; but at least the equal bravery of our own troops."[27] That trust in their own courage would serve the army well until the end of the war.

Despite his criticism of Grant, Seymour displayed no rancor in his account of his regiment's encounter with Grant on the battlefield: "The General's countenance wore an anxious look, yet bore no evidence of excitement or trepidation. He rode leisurely to the front line."[28] Like his army, Grant had reaped the whirlwind of overconfidence, but unlike many of his panicked troops, he remained calm and collected. When a dispirited Sherman found Grant after nightfall on the first day of fighting, he initially thought of suggesting a retreat across the river, but as Sherman himself later recalled, "some wise and sudden instinct impelled me to a more cautious and less impulsive proposition than at first intended." Sherman instead remarked, with more than a little understatement, "Well, Grant, we've had the devil's own day, haven't we?" Grant replied, "Yes, lick 'em tomorrow, though."[29]

The heavy losses among Grant's most effective subordinates at Shiloh further highlighted the importance of self-confidence among his rank and file. C. F. Smith, already disabled and sorely missed at the battle, would finally succumb on April 25 to the complicated infection created by his earlier injury.[30] Confederate forces captured Prentiss, and he would not be exchanged until that October. He would then be assigned to the controversial court-martial case trying Fitz-John Porter for his actions at Second Manassas, presumably not only for his gallantry at Shiloh, but for his political reliability as a Republican.[31] The court-martial found Porter guilty and dismissed him from the army in January, after which Prentiss took command of the District of Eastern Arkansas.[32] The highly capable W. H. L. Wallace also suffered a mortal wound at Shiloh, while gallantly leading his division alongside Prentiss's during the critical portion of the battle's first day.

Wallace's all-too-short career (from the Union's perspective) should be compared to that of John Logan. They were two excellent combat commanders whose merits Grant recognized early on in the war despite their civilian backgrounds. The leading current authority on the Army of the Tennessee cites Wallace as an example of how while Grant generally preferred military professionals as his senior subordinates, "he was also unusual among professional officers in his relative willingness to promote and rely on capable citizen-

[27] Ibid., 249–250.   [28] Ibid., 215–216.
[29] Dan Macauley, "Chestnut Grove," *Washington Post*, December 17, 1893.
[30] Simpson, *Triumph over Adversity*, 138.   [31] Warner, *Generals in Blue*, 386.
[32] Welcher, *The Union Army*, 2:96.

generals."[33] Grant singled out both Wallace and Logan for promotion to brigadier general after the Donelson campaign, writing that while they came "from civil pursuits ... they have fully earned the position on the field of battle." Grant's two other recommendations for promotion in Donelson's after-math also spoke well to his eye for talent: Morgan L. Smith, who would go on to a distinguished career limited only by a severe wound later in the war, and J. D. Webster, one of Grant's and Sherman's best staff officers throughout the war. Grant called both "old soldiers," but Smith had served as an enlisted man (an important distinction in the class-conscious Old Army) and while Webster had held a commission as a topographical engineer, he had not graduated from West Point.[34]

Grant also proved willing to support the promotions of volunteer officers without regular army backgrounds, even if they lacked political influence. In early July 1862, he wrote Senator Henry Wilson of Massachusetts to endorse Morgan L. Smith's nomination once again for a general's star, along with J. M. Thayer, a brigade commander in Lew Wallace's division, and Calvin C. Marsh, a brigade commander in McClernand's division. Marsh never received his star, testifying to his lack of political influence.[35] In sum, Grant paid far less heed to the West Point elite of the regular army than most of his peers. And in Wallace's case, Grant furthered the career of an officer who had no great fondness for his commander, although unlike McClernand, he had the good sense of keeping his doubts private.[36] Grant's support for officers drawn from civil life also bears comparison to Sherman's strong preference for West Pointers, which led to the latter's controversial decision after McPherson's death to put O. O. Howard, a justly maligned failed corps commander exiled from the east, at the head of the Army of the Tennessee, as opposed to the combat-tested John Logan. In contrast, Grant nearly replaced West Point graduate George Thomas with Logan for the former's sluggish performance before the Battle of Nashville in December 1864.[37]

Sherman emerged from Shiloh chastened by his overconfidence before the battle, but also empowered by his strong battlefield performance. Grant rightly chose to focus on the latter, and while he could have easily used Sherman as a scapegoat for the surprise on the first day, he chose not to. Sherman never forgot that fact, and he would be Grant's loyal subordinate to the end. Moreover, Grant's willingness to bear in full the burden of responsibility that came with command freed Sherman from the inner demons that had nearly destroyed his

[33] Steven E. Woodworth, "'Earned on the Field of Battle': William H. L. Wallace," in Steven E. Woodworth, ed., *Grant's Lieutenants: From Cairo to Vicksburg* (Lawrence, KS, 2001), 41.
[34] John Y. Simon, ed., *The Papers of Ulysses S. Grant*, 32 vols. (Carbondale, IL, 1967–2012), 4:356–367 (henceforth cited as *PUSG*); Warner, *Generals in Blue*, 460–461, 546–547.
[35] *PUSG*, 1:184–185.   [36] Woodworth, "William H. L. Wallace," 32, 35.
[37] Murray and Hsieh, *A Savage War*, 438.

military career in Kentucky. Even after Grant went east, Sherman could take solace that Grant remained the Union's most senior general, and the one most responsible for its victories and defeats. As Sherman himself later put it to an aide, "I am a damned sight smarter man than Grant ... but I'll tell you where he beats me and where he beats the world. He don't care a damn for what the enemy does out of his sight, but it scares me like hell!"[38] The counterpoint to Sherman was McClernand, who sensed a turn in the political winds against Grant after the controversial battle at Shiloh.[39]

In Shiloh's immediate aftermath, the survival of Grant's career was questionable, and the thought that he would eventually lead a crucial campaign against Vicksburg unthinkable. Halleck had long mistrusted Grant, and even before Shiloh, he had intended to concentrate the armies of the western theater under his own immediate command to move on Corinth. This new, reorganized force, comprised of elements from Grant's Army of the Tennessee, Buell's Army of the Ohio, and John Pope's Army of the Mississippi, exhibited Halleck's skepticism in both Grant and his subordinates. Halleck even moved George Thomas's division from the Army of the Ohio into a newly organized right wing composed mostly of Army of the Tennessee units in order to place Thomas at the head of the wing, as opposed to Sherman and Stephen Hurlbut, Grant's ranking division commanders. Halleck mitigated McClernand's seniority by placing him and his division at the head of the new army's reserve. As for Grant himself, Halleck made his future superior the second in command of the new army, a position with no defined responsibilities.[40] Halleck's estimate of Thomas's worth, placing the competent Virginian ahead of both Grant and Sherman, looks all the more striking in light of both Grant's and Sherman's later frustrations with Thomas as a sluggish, if otherwise competent subordinate.

Halleck slowly and methodically advanced toward Corinth, so lethargically that by the time Halleck reached it in late May, the Confederates had evacuated the city and saved their field army.[41] Halleck showed that if Grant and Sherman had suffered from serious overconfidence at Pittsburgh Landing, his own solution of excessive caution would never have brought the war to a victorious conclusion. After Corinth's capture, Grant seriously considered leaving the army for at least a lengthy leave of absence and perhaps for much longer, but Sherman's intercession and Halleck's decision to put Grant back in command of the Army of the Tennessee kept him in the field.[42] Grant established a new headquarters in Memphis, where he found himself subject to more hectoring from Halleck, reflecting no real change in the latter's opinion of Grant's

---

[38] James Harrison Wilson, *Under the Old Flag: Recollections of Military Operations in the War for the Union, the Spanish War, the Boxer Rebellion, Etc.*, 2 vols. (New York, 1912), 2:17.
[39] Simpson, *Triumph over Adversity*, 140.   [40] Woodworth, *Nothing but Victory*, 205–206.
[41] Ibid., 208–209.   [42] Ibid., 207–208; Simpson, *Triumph over Adversity*, 143.

capabilities. Only Halleck's recall to Washington on July 11 to take over as general in chief of all the Union armies saved Grant from further overbearing supervision.[43]

For his advance into Mississippi in November 1862, essentially the beginning of the Vicksburg campaign, Grant organized his forces into three wings, essentially informal corps, before the Lincoln administration imposed a formal corps organization on Grant at the end of the year. As his wing commanders, Grant selected Sherman, who commanded three divisions, Charles S. Hamilton, who commanded another three divisions, and James B. McPherson, who commanded two divisions.[44] Sherman's selection was obvious, but the other two deserve comment. McPherson had the sort of résumé McClellan would have esteemed: first in the West Point class of 1853 and an engineer. He served Grant in that technical capacity during the Forts Henry and Donelson campaign, and he impressed his commander so much that he was given a division in October after a brief trial run as a brigade commander during the Corinth campaign.

After Grant's promotion and departure for the east, McPherson would take command of the Army of the Tennessee under Sherman. He would be killed in action near Atlanta in 1864.[45] Grant and Sherman would grieve over his death as if he was their fallen son. McPherson's impeccable West Point credentials showed that Grant had no animus against the elite of the antebellum Old Army, and McPherson's youth showed Grant's indifference toward the prerogatives attached to seniority and time in rank. However, Grant's elevation of McPherson above Logan despite the latter's superior combat record showed that he may have had a real preference for regular army officers, especially in senior positions that required administrative capacity in addition to battlefield courage.

The last wing commander, Charles S. Hamilton, was a relative newcomer to the Army of the Tennessee. He had served as a division commander in the Army of the Mississippi under William Rosecrans, which in the shifting of forces following Halleck's departure from the west merged into Grant's command. Rosecrans would go on to become the commander of the Army of the Cumberland after Buell's relief in the wake of the Perryville campaign in October 1862.[46] Hamilton was a classmate of Grant's and a fellow infantry officer who earned a brevet for valor in Mexico. He had served as a division commander under McClellan, but was relieved by the latter after the siege of Yorktown. He then redeemed his reputation in the west during the Iuka and

[43] Simpson, *Triumph over Adversity*, 145–146.   [44] Woodworth, *Nothing but Victory*, 253.
[45] Warner, *Generals in Blue*, 307; Cullum, *Biographical Register*, 2:515–516.
[46] Welcher, *The Union Army*, 2:191.

Corinth campaign, and Grant rewarded his classmate accordingly, advocating for his promotion.[47]

Hamilton, however, would prove another intriguer like McClernand – shortly after Grant's strong endorsement, he even claimed to Senator James R. Doolittle of Wisconsin the following January that "*Grant is a drunkard.*" In general, Hamilton made a pest of himself as he sought higher rank, leading Stephen Hurlbut at one point to bluntly ask Grant that he be transferred out of the department.[48] Grant would effectively shelve Hamilton in early 1863, and he resigned in April of that year without having participated in the active parts of the Vicksburg campaign.[49] Once again, Grant showed how much he valued prowess in the field, but that he was more than willing to dismiss officers unwilling to work in harmony with their superiors and colleagues.

Grant could not deal so expeditiously with the ambitious McClernand, however, due to the latter's powerful political connections. The latter personally lobbied Lincoln for command of an army to take Vicksburg, and after much wrangling involving him, Lincoln, and Halleck, the president finally ordered Grant to appoint corps commanders in December, with McClernand at the head of the riverine force to strike at Vicksburg, albeit under Grant's overall command (the crucial concession Halleck successfully extracted out of the administration, perhaps his most important contribution to the Union war effort).[50] In line with the numbering of the corps in the Union's eastern armies, the new organizational table included the XIII Corps led by McClernand, the XV Corps commanded by Sherman, the XVI Corps under Stephen A. Hurlbut, and the newly promoted James McPherson at the head of the XVII Corps.

Three of the four appointments reflected Grant's preferences: Sherman and McPherson had already commanded informal wing or corps organizations, while Hurlbut had fought well at Shiloh as a division commander and deserved his subsequent promotion to corps command.[51] He had also performed well during Grant's Corinth campaign in October. Nevertheless, Grant obviously thought more highly of Sherman and McPherson, and Hurlbut would spend most of the rest of the war commanding garrisons in western Tennessee, unglamorous but important duties. Hurlbut's eventual disgrace for corruption after his transfer to the Department of the Gulf vindicated Grant's promotion of other generals ahead of him.[52] In sum, Grant had a strong stable of corps commanders, and even his most problematic one, John McClernand, was still a competent battlefield commander if disloyal in his overweening ambition.

Like Lee, Grant also proved adept at transferring out of his department commanders he found unsatisfactory. One of the reasons he pushed the

[47] *PUSG*, 7:29.   [48] Ibid., 7:308.
[49] Cullum, *Biographical Register*, 2:181; Warner, *Generals in Blue*, 198–199.
[50] Woodworth, *Nothing but Victory*, 248–253, 264–265; Welcher, *The Union Army*, 2:258.
[51] Welcher, *The Union Army*, 2:125–126, 198.   [52] Warner, *Generals in Blue*, 245.

promotion of McPherson to major general in December 1862 was that without McPherson, Brig. Gen. Thomas J. McKean would have been next in line to command a corps. McKean had had a curious record. While a West Point graduate, his relatively advanced age (he was born in 1810) relegated him to mostly administrative duties during the war.[53] The heavy losses at Shiloh in Prentiss's 6th Division, however, led to his appointment as Prentiss's replacement (Prentiss's two brigade commanders had also been captured).[54] McKean performed reasonably well at Corinth.[55] Nevertheless, Grant seemed to find his performance afterward wanting and McKean returned to administrative duties in January after being relieved of his duties as a division commander the previous month.[56]

Grant's division commanders also deserve notice.[57] Shortly before the administration imposed both McClernand and the formal corps organization on him, Grant wrote Halleck that "I am now better situated with regard to wing and division commanders than I have ever been before and hope no officers will be sent into the Department who rank those who are now with me."[58] In Grant's wing organization before McClernand's return, McPherson commanded three divisions. Two of the three division commanders had long and distinguished service in the Army of the Tennessee, the famed John Logan and the generally competent Jacob G. Lauman, who had commanded the 7th Iowa back at Belmont. Lauman later did fine service at Fort Donelson as a brigade commander and as a division commander at Shiloh. While he would eventually be relieved for mishandling his division at Jackson in July 1863, he had a strong résumé for division command at this point in the war.[59] The third division commander was James W. Denver, namesake of the Colorado city and a political appointee, who served as a brigade commander under Sherman during the Corinth campaign, but had served in mostly administrative posts beforehand. He would not surprisingly find himself relegated to garrison duties, as opposed to his more distinguished colleagues.[60]

Two of Hamilton's three division commanders were also veterans of the Army of the Tennessee, John McArthur and Leonard Ross, while the third, Isaac F. Quinby, was an old friend of Grant's and a West Point graduate. John McArthur served as a brigade commander under C. F. Smith during the Forts Henry and Donelson campaign, and he was promoted to division commander after W. H. L. Wallace's mortal wounding at Shiloh. He would finish the war with a distinguished career as a division commander in multiple campaigns.[61] Leonard Ross was a political general and a brigade commander under

[53] Ibid., 301.   [54] Welcher, *The Union Army*, 2:233.
[55] Woodworth, *Nothing but Victory*, 226–227.
[56] *PUSG*, 7:32–33; Warner, *Generals in Blue*, 256.   [57] Welcher, *The Union Army*, 2:256–258.
[58] *PUSG*, 7:29.   [59] Warner, *Generals in Blue*, 275–276.   [60] Ibid., 120–121.
[61] Ibid., 288–289.

McClernand at Donelson. He would serve as division commander during the active parts of the Vicksburg campaign, until resigning shortly after Vicksburg's fall.[62] Quinby was a classmate of Grant's, and his career included a stint as an instructor at West Point. He had left the army to teach math and science at the University of Rochester. He commanded a volunteer regiment under Sherman at First Manassas, after which he left the army. He returned to the service in the spring of 1862 and was given a division in Grant's army in September. He would serve in the decisive portions of Grant's Vicksburg campaign but would resign due to illness at the end of 1863.[63]

In Sherman's subordinate command tasked to move on Vicksburg via the Mississippi, three of the four divisions had been transferred to Grant from other departments.[64] Two of these divisions would later be assigned to McClernand after his return, symbolizing to some degree his ostracism from Grant's larger command structure. After that reorganization, Sherman would retain the services of the aforementioned Morgan L. Smith, a former enlisted soldier in the Old Army and brigade commander at Fort Donelson. He fought splendidly at Shiloh and would be grievously wounded during Sherman's assault at Chickasaw Bluffs. Although he would do good service as a division commander in the Chattanooga and Atlanta campaigns (he even commanded the XV Corps temporarily, when Logan briefly commanded the Army of the Tennessee in between McPherson's death and Howard's promotion), he would return to garrison duty due to his prior wounds at the end of the war.[65] While not tabbed as a division commander in this reorganization, Smith's replacement, David Stuart, also deserves mention here. Stuart was a political general who fought splendidly at Shiloh in Sherman's division, and who took over Smith's division after the latter was wounded at Chickasaw Bluffs. Sherman and Grant preferred him to stay in division command. The Senate, however, refused to ratify his nomination for promotion in the spring of 1863 due to a prewar scandal involving accusations of him having an affair with a married woman, after which he left the service.[66] Sherman's other division commander in the newly organized XV Corps, Frederick Steele, brought with him a division from Arkansas. Steele was another classmate of Grant's, and like Grant, he won brevets for valor as an infantry officer in the Mexican War. The two had been close friends at West Point. Unlike Grant, he never left the army and had commanded a battalion of regulars at Wilson's Creek. He would command his division in the XV Corps for the active portions of the Vicksburg campaign,

---

[62] Ibid., 411–412.   [63] Ibid., 387–388.   [64] Welcher, *The Union Army*, 2:853.
[65] Warner, *Generals in Blue*, 460–461.
[66] Ibid., 484–485; *PUSG*, 8:164–165. The divorce case gained notoriety and would have been known to Lincoln, although the jury actually exonerated Stuart. See Theodore Calvin Pease and James G. Randall, eds., *The Diary of Orville Hickman Browning* (Springfield, IL, 1925), 1:435–441. Special thanks to Eric M. Burke for highlighting Stuart's significance to me.

returning to Arkansas to deal with the Confederates there after Vicksburg's fall.[67]

The other division commanders who served under McClernand were the aforementioned George W. Morgan, whose division had originally been a part of the Army of the Ohio, and A. J. Smith, who led a unit of mostly new regiments that had been organized in Kentucky.[68] Smith had graduated from West Point in 1838 and served in the dragoons for the entire antebellum period. He commanded Halleck's cavalry until the Union capture of Corinth, and he did not take command of the division he would lead under Sherman until October. Unlike Morgan, he would go on to a successful career that included service in the active components of the Vicksburg campaign, command of his own corps, and a triumph over Nathan Bedford Forrest at Tupelo in July 1864.[69]

McClernand's return did not disturb Grant's stable of division commanders, and of the ten, five had strong records of service in the Army of the Tennessee – dating in the case of Logan all the way back to Belmont. The remaining five generals all had credible records, and four had substantial prewar military experience. The only true political general of the five, Denver, was tasked with mostly garrison duties. In sum, even the three division commanders Grant brought in from outside his department had credible records, and two would go on to successful careers during the rest of the war. Only one, Morgan, would prove an outright failure. Grant further maximized his chances for success by moving his best division commanders to the front, while leaving behind competent commanders to protect his logistical apparatus in the rear. He thus transferred McArthur's and Quinby's divisions to McPherson's XVII Corps the following January, while Hurlbut received in exchange Denver's and Lauman's divisions.[70]

Whatever McClernand's virtues as a leader of men on the battlefield, he continued to scheme against Grant behind the scenes, and it is fortunate for the Union war effort that his accusations of Grant's drunkenness and incompetence failed. Nevertheless, Grant still entrusted McClernand with leading the advance down the west bank of the Mississippi that would kick off the decisive phase of the Vicksburg campaign, as Grant positioned his troops to cross the river and assault Vicksburg from the south and east after breaking loose from his own lines of communication. McClernand's performance during the campaign was mostly a mixed bag. He proved somewhat tardy and negligent in his efforts to move his divisions across the river, was dangerously late at Champion's Hill, but also proved sufficiently competent in the important early engagement at Port Gibson on May 1.[71]

[67] Pease and Randall, *Diary of Orville Hickman*, 474; Simpson, *Ulysses S. Grant*, 14.
[68] Welcher, *The Union Army*, 2:196, 181–182.   [69] Warner, *Generals in Blue*, 454.
[70] Welcher, *The Union Army*, 2:258.
[71] Woodworth, *Nothing but Victory*, 317, 321, 333, 338, 345–346, 382, 387.

In general, Grant successfully adapted his organizational arrangements to his circumstances. For example, he attached two more divisions to the XIII Corps under seasoned commanders, Alvin P. Hovey, who had fought well at Shiloh and who later commanded a division in Arkansas, and Eugene A. Carr, a West Pointer with a strong combat record in Missouri. Hovey in particular distinguished himself at Champion's Hill. Grant also found a worthy replacement for Morgan L. Smith for command of a division in Sherman's XV Corps in Frank P. Blair Jr., a well-connected political general who proved a successful corps commander during Sherman's March to the Sea.[72]

Whatever creativity Grant could use in appointing and apportioning qualified division commanders, however, could not fully solve the problem of McClernand, which came to a head when that ambitious corps commander's erroneous dispatch regarding a supposed breakthrough on his front led to bloody and futile assaults during a failed attempt to storm Vicksburg's defensive works on May 22.[73] McClernand then compounded this error by sending an unauthorized dispatch to Northern newspapers claiming false credit for his own corps and casting incorrect aspersions on the rest of the army, which infuriated his colleagues outside of the XIII Corps, including the politically powerful Frank Blair. Taking advantage of the moral capital created by his triumphs near Vicksburg and that city's impending fall, Grant relieved McClernand and replaced him with Edward O. C. Ord, whom Grant had previously worked with during the Corinth campaign, and who would justify Grant's confidence with a distinguished career as a corps commander during the rest of the war.[74]

Historians have chronicled at great length the magnificence of the Vicksburg campaign, and there is no need here for yet another account of that justly famous campaign. It suffices for our purposes to underline that Grant could not have won this signal triumph for Union arms without a veteran army led by battle-tested and competent subordinates. Vicksburg would only cement the Army of the Tennessee's self-confidence, helping to set the stage for future triumphs during the Atlanta campaign and in the Carolinas, after Grant himself had departed for the Virginia theater. The army's rank and file might not have always had complete confidence in their commanders, but they would learn even from their commanders' missteps supreme self-confidence. Meanwhile, not only did Grant himself mature as a commander but he also slowly but surely found the subordinate corps and division commanders who could create an organizational culture capable of aggressive and decisive military action, even after he departed the army. In addition to competence and aggressiveness, that

---

[72] Welcher, *The Union Army*, 2:260–262, 282; Warner, *Generals in Blue*, 235, 70–71, 36; Woodworth, *Nothing but Victory*, 379.

[73] Woodworth, *Nothing but Victory*, 419–420.

[74] Ibid., 430–434; Warner, *Generals in Blue*, 349–350.

culture would value mutual cooperation and trust and remove officers such as McClernand, who lacked that crucial character trait. Grant did not possess the resources and trained military professionals available to other commanders such as Buell and McClellan, but he could still play a crucial role in creating the Army of the Tennessee's successful military culture – a testament to his professionalism, judgment, and insight into the character of others.

4   "Playing a Very Bold Game"
The Organizational Culture of the Army of Northern
Virginia, 1862–1865

Mark Grimsley

Nothing had gone right on that rain-soaked day just east of Richmond, Virginia, on May 31, 1862. Confederate Gen. Joseph E. Johnston did not mind the rain itself, though it had fallen pitilessly on his 50,000 troops. In fact, he had welcomed it: the rain would sweep away the rickety bridges of the nearby Chickahominy River, cutting off the main body of his rival's army – the Army of the Potomac under Maj. Gen. George B. McClellan – from the exposed Union corps, centered on the sleepy crossroads of Seven Pines, which formed the objective of his surprise attack.

Decidedly less welcome was the unending series of frustrations that this vexed day had visited on the fifty-five-year-old Johnston. Troop movements had been delayed. Whole divisions had taken wrong roads and even gotten in each other's way. By a freak of atmospheric conditions, a so-called acoustic shadow had muffled the rattle of musketry so much that for more than an hour Johnston did not even know his attack had begun. Although Johnston would not know all the details until many days later, only two-thirds of the troops committed to the attack actually went into action. But at 6:30 PM, with sunset only an hour away, he told his staff officers to send the word: the army's regiments must remain in place that night wherever they happened to be, in hopes of renewing the battle the next morning.

Johnston gave the order while sitting on horseback atop a knoll from which he could observe the fighting. He and his staff were well within range of enemy fire, and he retained enough of his jaunty demeanor to chuckle at a staff officer who ducked whenever a Minié ball whizzed by. "Colonel," he laughed, "there is no use dodging: when you hear them they have passed."[1] So presumably Johnston did not hear the bullet that struck his right shoulder a few moments later, and certainly not the heavy shell fragment that struck him full in the chest

---

[1] Drury L. Armistead, "The Battle in Which General Johnston Was Wounded, Described by His Courier," *Southern Historical Society Papers*, 18:187.

and knocked him to the ground unconscious. When he regained consciousness some minutes later, he soon saw the grave faces of President Jefferson Davis and Davis's military advisor, Gen. Robert E. Lee. Both men spoke gently to Johnston about their concern for him and their hopes for his recovery. But it was obvious to everyone that Johnston's ten-month tenure in command of the army had come to an end.

It was just as obvious, Davis and Lee soon discovered, that Johnston's second in command, Maj. Gen. Gustavus W. Smith, was completely out of his depth. During their brief interview with him, Smith clearly knew almost nothing of the military situation; worse, he seemed almost on the verge of nervous collapse. As the two men turned their horses back toward the Confederate capital, the president informed his general that he, Lee, would immediately assume permanent command of the army. Lee received a written order the next day and soon announced the news to his troops, calling them the "Army of Northern Virginia." Thus began the memorable partnership between one of the great captains in the American military experience and one of its most famous field armies.

Social psychologists Kim S. Cameron and Robert E. Quinn have argued that one can place organizations somewhere on a quadrant with two scales of "competing values": on the vertical scale, flexibility versus control, and on the horizontal scale, an internal focus on maintenance and integration versus an external focus on positioning and differentiation. This scheme results in four types of culture, of which two are relevant to US Civil War armies: *hierarchy* and *clan*.

The *hierarchy* culture corresponds to the traditional corporate model of strong, top-down control. It best fits US Civil War armies when assessing the interactions of the high command. The *clan* is more flexible. "Rather than strict rules and procedures," the authors explain, "people are driven through vision, shared goals, outputs and outcomes." Rules do exist, "but are often communicated and instilled socially to reinforce [an organization's] commitment to its people."[2] The clan model works well when assessing the organizational culture of the regiment, the fundamental building block of US Civil War armies.

Thinking in terms of two, not one, organizational cultures is imperative because organizations in the US Civil War era differed from their modern counterparts in one crucial respect. Modern organizations have the ability to exert their norms and values from the company president all the way down to the lowliest clerk. Their ability to do so hinges on a high degree of what business historian Alfred D. Chandler terms *administrative coordination*. In 1860s America, however, this attribute had not yet emerged, although the first

---

[2] Kim S. Cameron and Robert Quinn, *Diagnosing and Changing Organizational Culture* (Reading, PA, 1999).

modern enterprises – the railroad and the telegraph – were beginning to develop it.[3] Exerting norms and values would have been problematic in any case, since neither the Union nor the Confederate armies had any official doctrine beyond the tactical manuals utilized at the regimental and company levels.

This helps explain why this chapter focuses on Lee's army as opposed to the Confederate Army in general. It is simple: the Confederate Army as a whole did not have an organizational culture. How could it? Aside from a tiny regular army, the Confederate Army was actually the *Provisional* Army of the Confederate States, and it sprang up in an ad hoc fashion. In the weeks after the firing on Fort Sumter, communities across the South organized companies of 100 men and state governments then gathered them into regiments of approximately 1,000. The fledgling Confederate government then accepted the regiments and soldiers into service and dispatched them individually to points scattered along the South's military frontier. There local commanders organized them into brigades and later, if the total force on hand justified it, divisions. Initially, an organizational culture in any meaningful sense existed at no level higher than that of a regiment. It took time before one could speak meaningfully of an organizational culture at the level of a field army, and at no point during the Confederacy's four-year life could one could speak sensibly about an organizational culture that encompassed the entire Confederate Army.

Lee's Army of Northern Virginia was the first field army that the Confederacy created, it was usually the largest, and it defended the most critical sector – the 100-mile corridor between Richmond and Washington, DC. It was unquestionably the best Confederate field army and arguably the best field army on either side of the conflict. Certainly the fortunes of its parent nation rested upon this army more than any other, North or South. One might go further and argue, as has historian Gary W. Gallagher, that the Army of Northern Virginia was the beating heart of Confederate nationalism. "Robert E. Lee and his soldiers functioned as the principal focus of Confederate nationalism for much of the war," Gallagher notes. "Through battlefield victories, reenlistments, and letters to the home front, the officers and men of Lee's army served as an engine propelling national loyalty among civilians and soldiers throughout the Confederacy." For many Confederates, Gallagher believes, the Army of Northern Virginia's surrender at Appomattox was synonymous with the death of their four-year-old republic.[4] If Gallagher is correct, then except for George Washington's Continental Army, the Army of Northern Virginia has no analog in the entire American military experience.

[3] Alfred D. Chandler Jr., *The Visible Hand: The Managerial Revolution in American Business* (Cambridge, MA, 1977).

[4] Gary W. Gallagher, *The Confederate War: How Popular Will, Nationalism, and Military Strategy Could Not Stave Off Defeat* (Cambridge, MA, 1997), 63–111. The quotation is on page 63.

It has no analog, that is, if one considers the army as it existed after June 1, 1862, the day that Lee's adjutant issued Special Orders No. 22, announcing to the army that Lee had assumed command and declaring that Lee "feels assured that every man has resolved to maintain the ancient fame of the Army of Northern Virginia and the reputation of its general [Johnston] and to conquer or die in the approaching contest."[5] This is true in two senses. First and most important, as Gallagher notes, it was "Lee and his soldiers" who served as a focus for Confederate nationalism. Second, not until Lee took the helm was the army habitually called the Army of Northern Virginia. Up to that point it was most commonly called the "Army of the Potomac" – somewhat confusingly since its main opponent bore the same name.

What's in a name? Conceivably a great deal, because the change could have been Lee's way of indicating that a new sheriff was in town. This probably was not the case, for reasons given shortly. Nonetheless, it serves as a reminder that the army had been in existence for twelve months, serving under two previous commanders. Consequently that first year deserves a look. Edwin H. Schein, who pioneered the concept of organizational culture, has argued that the founders of organizations almost invariably create their cultures. This poses the question: Did Lee create, or did he recreate, the organizational culture of the Army of Northern Virginia?

It was Gen. P. G. T. Beauregard who bestowed the title "Army of the Potomac" on the regiments that the Confederate War Department had channeled to Manassas Junction, a key position where the Orange & Alexandria Railroad, the obvious supply line for any Union army seeking to invade Virginia, joined the Manassas Gap Railroad, which ran westward to the Shenandoah Valley, a fertile region that soon would be known as the "Breadbasket of the Confederacy" because of the wheat, corn, and livestock that abounded there. Beauregard had organized the regiments into eight brigades totaling 20,000 men. Another 12,000 men, five brigades under Joe Johnston, shielded the lower Shenandoah Valley.

On July 21, 1861, a Union army, dispatched at President Abraham Lincoln's insistence, launched an attack upon Beauregard's army, which was deployed behind a sluggish stream called Bull Run. The Federals might have won the battle – known in the North as First Bull Run and in the South as First Manassas – but for the arrival of Johnston's army, which had sped down the Manassas Gap Railroad to reinforce Beauregard's beleaguered troops just in the nick of time. The combined force transformed the Union's near victory into a humiliating rout that dismayed the North, thrilled the South, and guaranteed that the war

---

[5] Special Orders No. 22, June 1, 1862, *War of the Rebellion: A Compilation of the Official Records of the Union and Confederate Armies*, 128 vols. (Washington, DC, 1880–1901), Series I, *vol.* 11, Pt. 3, p. 569. Cited hereafter as *OR*. All citations are to Series I.

would not end quickly. Because Johnston was senior in rank to Beauregard, he thereafter commanded the combined force, which Confederates continued to call the Army of the Potomac.

Because Beauregard's tenure as sole commander was brief, and because after First Manassas, the Army of the Potomac truly merited its name – its 35,000 men soon grew to 45,000 – if anyone might be called the army's founder, it was Johnston. The question is whether Johnston imbued the army with a distinctive culture or whether he presided over a force where no organizational culture existed in any meaningful sense except at the regimental level: an amalgamation of clans.

The second answer is the most plausible. During the same period in which Johnston's opposite number, Maj. Gen. George B. McClellan, created and placed his indelible stamp on the Union Army of the Potomac, Johnston spent his time bickering with President Jefferson Davis, whom he loathed, and aside from organizing his brigades into divisions and conducting obligatory military reviews, interacted primarily with his senior leadership. The Confederate rank and file had great confidence in Johnston and basked in the glory of the army's triumph at Manassas, but the individual soldiers identified mainly with their regiments. The principal exception were the five Virginia regiments under Brig. Gen. Thomas J. Jackson, who earned the enduring sobriquet "Stonewall" for his unyielding stand during the most critical moment at First Manassas. They called themselves the Stonewall Brigade – and after Jackson's death in 1863 would successfully petition the government to make the name official.

One might argue that the army Lee inherited had actually come into being only on April 12, 1862, the day that Jefferson Davis merged the Department of Norfolk and the Department of the Peninsula with Johnston's Army of the Potomac. Lee relayed the news in Special Orders No. 6, which, significant in view of the name game, termed Johnston's force the "Army of Northern Virginia" but only because it had originated in the geographical Department of Northern Virginia.[6] In correspondence, Lee habitually referred to the "Army of Northern Virginia." But almost no one else did. The name did not take hold until Lee took hold of the reins. Lee, of course, eventually *did* create a distinctive organizational culture at the army level, but not in a single day. It took a period of at least sixteen weeks. But his method was simple. He baptized the army in blood, fighting three major campaigns in less than four months. And because this was how he did it, the campaigns deserve attention.

On the day that Lee took command, the Confederacy's strategic situation was on the verge of disaster. By this point in time, Union armies had secured control of the border states; established an effective blockade of the

<hr />

[6] Special Orders No. 6, April 12, 1862, *OR, vol.* 11, Pt. 3, p. 438.

Confederate coast; captured or neutralized several important Southern inlets and harbors; captured New Orleans, the Confederacy's largest city; sent gunboats up the Mississippi River as far as Vicksburg; driven down the Mississippi River almost to Memphis (the city would fall on June 6); captured the forts that guarded the Tennessee and Cumberland Rivers; won a major if blood-drenched victory at Shiloh; and seized the strategic railroad junction at Corinth, Mississippi, where the Confederacy's main north-to-south and east-to-west trunk lines intersected. Johnston's attack at Seven Pines had been a costly failure. The advanced elements of McClellan's army could see the church spires of Richmond, just five miles distant.

The "official" Confederate strategy was what Davis called the "offensive-defensive." By this Davis meant that the Confederate forces would remain on the defensive until the enemy axis of advance became apparent, then concentrate, counterattack, and defeat the attacking army. This is what the Confederates attempted at Shiloh, and it nearly worked. But the strategy had two main drawbacks. First, the Federals seldom attacked in only one place at a time. By concentrating at Shiloh, for example, the Confederates had denuded New Orleans of troops, with the result that once the Union fleet had passed the two forts guarding the city, its warships placed the city under their guns and forced it to surrender. Thus, there was no land battle for New Orleans. The second problem, at least as far as Lee was concerned, was that the "offensive-defensive" was reactive. For his part, he consistently favored taking the strategic as well as the operational offensive.

In June 1862, the chance of ever assuming the strategic offensive may have seemed remote. But the sort of counterthrust contemplated by the "offensive-defensive" was imperative. "McClellan," Lee informed Davis on June 5, "will make this a battle of Posts. He will take position from position, under cover of his heavy guns & we cannot get at him without storming his works, which with our new troops is extremely hazardous." Lee, therefore, began "preparing a line that I can hold with part of our forces in front, while with the rest I will endeavour to make a diversion to bring McClellan out" – in other words, he aimed to force McClellan to fight a battle of maneuver.[7]

To accomplish this, Lee would have to work within the organizational structure and senior leadership already in place. Both were faulty. The merging of the Departments of Northern Virginia, Norfolk, and the Peninsula had resulted in an unbalanced force whose top-level components varied widely in size. Lee knew from observation that some of his generals were mediocrities, but he could not yet afford to remove them, and he had others who were

---

[7] Lee to Davis, June 5, 1862, in Douglas Southall Freeman, ed., *Lee's Dispatches: Unpublished Letters of General Robert E. Lee, C.S.A., to Jefferson Davis and the War Department of the Confederate States of America, 1862–1865* (1915; reprint, Baton Rouge, LA, 1994), 7.

question marks. All he could do was craft the plan for a counteroffensive and trust that the army's organization and senior leadership were adequate.

Lee's officers and men could wonder, with good reason, whether Lee was adequate. In the war thus far, he had fought only one engagement: the so-called Battle of Cheat Mountain in September 1861, in which fewer than 200 men had become casualties, largely because Lee's planned attack had been a fiasco. Col. E. P. Alexander thus had excellent grounds for asking Col. Joseph Ives, a member of Davis's staff, whether Lee possessed the audacity the moment required. He never forgot Ives's answer. "Alexander," the staff officer replied, "if there is one man in either army, Confederate or Federal, head and shoulders above every other in audacity, it is Gen. Lee. His name might be Audacity. He will take more desperate chances, and take them quicker than any other general, North or South; and you will live to see it, too."[8]

Ives could make this declaration because he had already witnessed the daring of Lee's strategic vision. During his time as Davis's military advisor, Lee had no power to command, but he could certainly suggest, and in a series of mid-April dispatches to Stonewall Jackson, Lee had masterminded the bold counter-thrust that made Jackson's Valley Campaign one of the most legendary in American military history. Jackson's movement was a strategic diversion that fully served its purpose, robbing McClellan of 30,000 men that might have made the Peninsula offensive unstoppable. Jackson's execution of the plan had been flawless, but the plan itself was Lee's.[9]

In the first days after taking command, Lee ordered the construction of earthen fieldworks in front of Richmond, a defensive move that earned him the derisive sobriquet "Granny Lee." But Ives was correct. Lee never considered fighting on the defensive. Instead he wanted to convert a campaign of regular approaches, at which McClellan excelled, into a campaign of maneuver, which McClellan had consistently avoided. After the war, a former Confederate colonel, William Allen, interviewed Lee on several occasions. During Allen's final interview with Lee, the Confederate chieftain talked at length about the Battle of Gettysburg, the culmination of Lee's second strategic

---

[8] E. P. Alexander, *Military Memoirs of a Confederate: A Critical Narrative* (New York, 1907), 111. The quote seems too good to be true, but Alexander discusses his conversation with Ives at length in a memoir written primarily for his children and unpublished until 1989. See Gary W. Gallagher, ed., *Fighting for the Confederacy: The Personal Memoirs of General Edward Porter Alexander* (Chapel Hill, NC, 1989), 91–93. In it Alexander shows that he too was surprised by the force and eloquence of Ives's reply, and his account has the ring of truth.

[9] Among most US Civil War historians there is a kind of mindless derision of McClellan and a wholly unwarranted admiration for Lincoln's attempt to trap Jackson's force, an attempt that played directly into Confederate hands. See Mark Grimsley, "The Lincoln-McClellan Relationship in Myth and Memory," *Journal of the Abraham Lincoln Association* 38(2) (Summer 2017), 63–81; and Grimsley, "Lincoln As Commander in Chief: Forays into Generalship," in Stephen D. Engle, ed., *The War Worth Fighting: Abraham Lincoln's Presidency and Civil War America* (Gainesville, FL, 2015), 62–87.

offensive, and explained why he had chosen an aggressive strategy for fighting the war, selecting the offensive as often as possible despite the fact that his assignment, protecting the Confederacy's de facto independence, was essentially defensive. "Spoke feelingly of Gettysburg," Allen recorded, "said much was said [by critics] about risky movements – Everything was risky in our war. He knew oftentimes that he was playing a very bold game, but it was the only possible one."[10] The game began the moment Lee took command.

Lee inherited an army that had fought primarily on the defensive. First Manassas had been a defensive victory, as were the repulse of an ill-advised Union probe at Ball's Bluff (October 21, 1861), a successful rear guard fight at Williamsburg (May 5, 1862), and the containment of a Federal lodgment at Eltham's Landing on the York River (May 7, 1862). Rather than fight near Manassas, Johnston had withdrawn some sixty miles to a position behind the Rapidan River. During the Peninsula campaign, he had withdrawn another fifty miles. Seven Pines, the army's only major attack, had been botched completely. It was far from clear that the army could successfully undertake a major counteroffensive, much less one with the ambitious objective not just of repelling McClellan army's, but of destroying it.

Within that army, however, there were a few aggressive commanders. At Williamsburg, Maj. Gen. James Longstreet had organized a counterattack that stopped a Union division dead in its tracks and briefly threatened to overwhelm it. Brig. Gen. Jubal A. Early launched a local counterattack with two regiments that went badly, to say the least, but he too had chosen to counterattack. At Eltham's Landing, Brig. Gen. John B. Hood's Texas Brigade had struck a Union division so fiercely that the division's commander had congratulated himself on simply maintaining his position. Johnston, who had instructed Hood merely to "feel the enemy gently and then fall back," sharply questioned Hood's judgment and asked what Hood's Texans would have done if he had actually received an order to attack. Hood thought for a moment and replied, "I suppose, General, they would have driven them into the river, and tried to swim out to capture the gunboats."[11] Lee had one other aggressive commander as well: Stonewall Jackson in the Shenandoah Valley. After outmaneuvering the Union forces that had vainly tried to catch him, Jackson parried their final efforts at Cross Keys (June 8) and Port Republic (June 9), and then took his 17,000 men to join the Army of Northern Virginia. Lee gave the key assignment to Jackson in his plan of attack.

[10] William Allan, "Memoranda of Conversations with Robert E. Lee," in Gary W. Gallagher, ed., *Lee the Soldier* (Lincoln, NE, 1996), 17. The fact that Allen recorded each interview on the same day that it occurred is in ibid., 18, note 1. The interview took place on February 19, 1870, seven months before Lee's death.

[11] J. H. L., "Hood 'Feeling the Enemy,'" in Clarence C. Buel and Robert U. Johnson, eds., *Battles and Leaders of the Civil War*, 4 vols. (New York, 1886), 2:276.

In mid-June, McClellan's army was astride the Chickahominy River, a sluggish stream with marshlands on either side that made it a much greater military obstacle than its watercourse alone would suggest. McClellan had deployed four of his five corps south of the Chickahominy. The V Corps was north of the river, primarily because McClellan expected (in vain, it turned out) the arrival of a sixth corps by an overland route from Fredericksburg fifty-five miles to the north, but also because it shielded the Union supply line, consisting of a single-track railroad that ran from Richmond to the hamlet of West Point at the head of the York River. When a cavalry reconnaissance discerned that the V Corps' right flank was "in the air" – that is to say, anchored to no natural obstacle – Lee decided to strike this corps and destroy it, a move that would fatally compromise the Union supply line and force McClellan to retreat. Lee expected that the remaining Union corps would be vulnerable enough, and his own force aggressive enough, to destroy McClellan's army. (Contrary to the assertions of many military historians, this was the only time in the war when Lee explicitly said that his objective was the enemy army's outright destruction.)

Jackson had the key assignment: striking the V Corps in the flank and rear and rolling it up. This potentially was a risky move, since most of Jackson's troops could arrive from the Valley literally only on the eve of the attack. But Lee had confidence in Jackson and unhesitatingly made the gamble. An over-sized division under Maj. Gen. A. P. Hill, whose orders were to attack as soon as he heard the sound of Jackson's guns, would support the attack. Lee set June 26 as the day the offensive would begin.

On that day, Hill waited intently for Jackson's arrival but heard nothing. At mid-afternoon, he decided to launch his attack anyway. The ensuing battle of Mechanicsville gained the Confederates nothing but casualties. Worse, it alerted the V Corps to the potential danger and caused it to fall back to a stronger position around Gaines's Mill. In his after-action report, Lee called Hill's decision "courageous and impetuous, but exceedingly imprudent." But as later events would demonstrate, he cared mainly about the courageous and impetuous part, and dismissed the imprudence.

The following day, Jackson's force belatedly reached the battlefield. Hill's division launched a second attack that fixed the V Corps in place until Jackson slammed into its right flank in late afternoon. Simultaneously, Longstreet's division menaced the V Corps' left. While the assault did not destroy the V Corps outright, it forced the corps into a swift retreat across the Chickahominy, exposing McClellan's vulnerable supply line and compelling him to begin what he euphemistically called a "change of base" to an as-yet nonexistent supply base on the James River. After that everything went wrong for the Confederates; not with Lee's plan, which was excellent, but with its execution, which was mediocre at best. Lee launched three attacks against

McClellan's retreating army, but in a series of strong rear guard actions the Union army escaped. Lee had nevertheless wrecked the enemy's campaign and forced it away from the gates of Richmond to a hastily prepared base at Harrison's Landing on the James.

The Seven Days, as Lee's counteroffensive became known, caused jubilation in the South and dismay in the North, which saw imminent triumph dissolve into stalemate. But Lee himself was unhappy. "Under ordinary circumstances," he fumed, "the Federal Army should have been destroyed."[12] The counteroffensive's disappointing outcome was due to several factors, but among them were weak performances by several subordinates (including, surprisingly, Jackson himself). Lee relieved none of them outright, but – as would repeatedly prove the case – subordinates who displeased Lee had a way of being transferred elsewhere. A number of generals who had botched their assignments or proven too cautious disappeared. Jackson remained. Lee forgave his substandard performance because Jackson was ordinarily as aggressive as Lee could ever wish. The disappearance of commanders without the killer instinct made clear that Lee sought an organizational culture built upon aggressiveness and a willingness to take calculated risks.

The sequel to the Seven Days can quickly be told. While McClellan's Army of the Potomac licked its wounds at Harrison's Landing, a new threat materialized some seventy miles to the north, in the form of a newly created "Army of Virginia" under Maj. Gen. John Pope. As soon as Lee became convinced that McClellan would not advance anytime soon, he sent Jackson northward to block Pope's advance southward. When it became obvious to Lee that McClellan's army was being withdrawn from the Peninsula altogether – Lincoln had lost confidence in McClellan's Peninsula scheme, about which he had had misgivings from the start – Lee took almost his entire army to join Jackson. During this period, Lee was able to improve the army's organization by dividing it into two "wings" of roughly equal strength, commanded respectively by Jackson and Longstreet. The ensuing Second Manassas campaign, a masterpiece of deception and maneuver, brought Pope to ruin.

Lee then had three choices. He could stand on the defensive, an option he rejected out of hand. He could attack nearby Washington, but its forbidding belt of fortifications offered a strong disincentive. Or he could cross the Potomac and invade Maryland, with the intention of continuing into Pennsylvania unless President Davis objected "upon political or other grounds."[13] Lee confessed that the army was "not properly equipped for an invasion of an enemy's territory." The army lacked supply wagons, most of its horses were worn out,

---

[12]   Lee's final report on the Seven Days, March 6, 1863, in Clifford Dowdey and Louis H. Manarin, eds., *The Wartime Papers of R. E. Lee* (Boston, MA, 1961), 221.
[13]   Lee to Davis, September 3, 1862, in ibid., 294.

"the men are poorly provided with clothes, and in thousands of instances are destitute of shoes," Lee informed Davis. But his army could not afford to be idle, Lee continued, "and though weaker than our opponents in men and equipment, must endeavor to harass, if we cannot destroy them."[14] Lee also reasoned that the operation might conceivably bring the slaveholding state of Maryland into the Confederacy.

The resulting Maryland campaign lasted barely two weeks. McClellan, now back in Washington, reorganized his own army, augmented it with Pope's, and incorporated dozens of raw, recently arrived volunteer regiments. It was an astonishing performance. On September 7, just three days after Lee crossed the Potomac, McClellan put this revitalized army in motion to drive Lee back into Virginia. Lee had no idea that McClellan would move this promptly and therefore did not hesitate about dividing his army into five parts in order to capture a Union garrison of 12,500 men at Harpers Ferry at the confluence of the Potomac and Shenandoah Rivers. This risky operation was still unfinished, when, on September 14, three Union corps attacked the badly outnumbered forces that Lee had left to guard South Mountain, a long wooded ridge that bisected Maryland. The attack was far too cautious, and the Confederates fended it off for most of the day, but by evening, Lee realized that he had lost. With McClellan in his front and the Harpers Ferry garrison still intact, he saw no choice but to abandon the campaign and recross the Potomac into Virginia. But news from Jackson, predicting that the fall of Harpers Ferry was imminent, caused Lee to reconsider his course of action. Instead of retreating, his army would make a stand on the ridgeline that rose from the west bank of Antietam Creek near the little village of Sharpsburg, Maryland.

It was the single most controversial decision of Lee's military career. The Army of Northern Virginia remained divided, with much of it still committed to the Harpers Ferry operation, and it was numerically inferior to the Army of the Potomac. Worse, it would have to fight with its back to the Potomac River, with only one ford available by which to escape. Defeat would therefore involve the likely annihilation of the army.[15] "On the face of it," perceptive Civil War historian Bruce Catton observed,

---

[14] Ibid., 293.
[15] Nowadays it is so fashionable to sneer at McClellan's generalship that historians not closely acquainted with the facts tend to underestimate just how dangerous this course of action was. Lee did not share their opinion. After the war, when asked to name his most formidable opponent, Lee responded emphatically, "McClellan, by all odds." Cazenove Lee memorandum, undated, printed in Robert E. Lee [Jr.], *Recollections and Letters of General Robert E. Lee* (New York, 1904), 416. For the case against Lee's decision, see Robert K. Krick, "The Army of Northern Virginia in September 1862: Its Circumstances, Its Opportunities, and Why It Should Not Have Been at Sharpsburg," in Gary W. Gallagher, ed., *Antietam: Essays on the 1862 Maryland Campaign* (Kent, OH, 1989), 35–55.

there was every reason for a quiet departure without a fight and hardly any reason for remaining and defying the Army of the Potomac to do its worst. And yet ... And yet Lee stayed when he did not have to stay and fought when he did not have to fight, and since he was not out of his mind the only conceivable answer is that he believed he could win.[16]

But win what? Lee had no ability to attack McClellan outright or any realistic way to maneuver so as to continue his offensive foray. He could only hope that when McClellan attacked, he would attack so rashly as to give Lee an opening for a decisive riposte – and no one has ever accused McClellan of being rash. Further, in order to thwart Lee, McClellan did not even need to attack. Once he sent two corps across Antietam Creek, as he did on September 16, to block the only road by which Lee could conceivably have continued north, Lee ultimately had little choice but to retreat back into Virginia. It was simply a question of whether he would do so before or after fighting a major battle.

Lee chose to fight the battle. It remains the bloodiest single day in American military history. About 87,000 Federals under McClellan faced off against fewer than 40,000 Confederates. Lee was fortunate in that McClellan's Army of the Potomac attacked him in piecemeal fashion and held far too many troops in reserve, but at several points during the day, his army was on the verge of being overwhelmed. By most accounts, only the last-minute arrival of A. P. Hill's division, after a seventeen-mile forced march from Harpers Ferry, saved the Army of Northern Virginia from outright disaster. Darkness fell with both armies still confronting one another.

Yet, in spite of this near debacle, Lee's aggressiveness remained undiminished. That evening, he met with his senior leaders to consider whether a counteroffensive was possible. Reluctantly convinced of the need to withdraw, he nonetheless stood his ground on the following day, *seemingly* daring the Union army to hit him again, which it completely failed to do. Lee then withdrew in what *seemed* to be his own good time.

The qualifications are necessary because it is unrealistic to believe that Lee could assess his options, order a retreat, organize it, and execute it, all in one night. He could do the first two, but he had to remain at Sharpsburg a second day before he could actually carry out the retreat. This recognition does not alter how the stand on September 18 *appeared*. To the troops on both sides – McClellan's as well as his own – it looked as if Lee were defying McClellan and daring him to renew the attack.

Nothing disappears more quickly in history than people's actual motives, but it is not unlikely that Lee understood that what he chose to do after the reversal at South Mountain would define both himself and the army he led. Certainly this was the effect. Lee's stand at Sharpsburg consolidated the Army of

---

[16] Bruce Catton, *Terrible Swift Sword* (Garden City, NY, 1963), 451–452.

Northern Virginia's reputation as a mortally dangerous opponent, and the fact that the army held the field at the end of the battle was a source of enormous pride to Lee's soldiers. Dozens of letters from officers and men written in the days after the campaign attest to this, leading historian Gary W. Gallagher to conclude that "many historians, myself included, have taken Lee to task for remaining on the battlefield at Sharpsburg through the 18th after nearly suffering disaster the previous day. ... But testimony from soldiers proud of holding the field in the face of a powerful enemy suggests that Lee might have known better than his critics in this instance."[17] This observation becomes even stronger when one shifts the issue to Lee's decision to fight at Sharpsburg in the first place. What would his soldiers have thought if he had taken them on a foray into Maryland and then tamely withdrawn into Virginia after suffering a clear loss at South Mountain?

During October, while the Army of Northern Virginia rested and received sufficient reinforcements to offset the losses of the Second Manassas and Maryland campaigns, Lee took advantage of this first clear opportunity to organize the army to his liking. Lee had inherited a whopper-jawed organization on June 1. The arrival of Jackson's force from the Shenandoah Valley was a welcome addition to Lee's strength but made the army even more organizationally unbalanced. After the Seven Days, several of Lee's weaker subordinates departed from the Army of Northern Virginia, and Lee created the two "wings" under Longstreet and Jackson, but a fully coherent organization did not occur until October, when the Confederate Congress formally authorized the creation of corps as well as the rank of lieutenant general. Longstreet and Jackson were promoted to that rank; Lee created the I Corps (under Longstreet) and the II Corps (under Jackson), and shifted around his infantry divisions until for the first time he had a balanced force.

A second major reorganization took place in May 1863, after Lee won the Battle of Chancellorsville but lost Jackson, who died of complications from gunshot wounds accidentally inflicted by his own men. Lee had come to believe that in the wooded country of Virginia, no commander could keep track of more than 20,000 men, so reorganization might have occurred in any event. Jackson's death made it imperative: Lee had no one who could fill his shoes. Lee retained Longstreet in command of the I Corps, gave the II Corps to Lt. Gen. Richard S. Ewell, who replaced the fallen Jackson, and created the III Corps under newly promoted Lt. Gen. A. P. Hill. Each corps had three infantry divisions. Lee also abolished the army's large Artillery Reserve and distributed its battalions evenly over the three corps.

---

[17] Gary W. Gallagher, "'The Result of the Campaign Was in Our Favor': Confederate Reaction to the Maryland Campaign," in Gary W. Gallagher, ed., *The Antietam Campaign* (Chapel Hill, NC, 1999), 20.

Thus, in October 1862, Lee created the army's organization the way he wanted it. In May 1863, he refined it in light of what he had learned during the intervening months. During the ensuing Gettysburg campaign, Maj. Gen. Jeb Stuart's cavalry remained a single, oversized division of about 10,000 men, but afterward it too became a corps, with its brigades folded into divisions and Stuart given the rank of lieutenant general.[18]

Lee handpicked his subordinates at the corps and division levels. Always mindful that he might lose senior officers to wounds or death, he frequently selected subordinates at the brigade level too. Lee looked for two attributes: first, the administrative ability to handle the job and second, a pronounced willingness to take calculated risks, to play the "very bold game" that Lee believed the Confederates had to play. A well-known anecdote illustrates Lee's dissatisfaction with anything less than squeezing every ounce of advantage out of a victory. Chancellorsville is usually considered Lee's greatest triumph. Although outnumbered two to one, he and Jackson took advantage of Maj. Gen. Joseph Hooker's decision to divide the Army of the Potomac and rolled up the main body in a brilliant flank attack. For three days, Hooker fought on the defensive just to get his army safely back north of the Rappahannock River. On the fourth day, Confederate brigade commander Brig. Gen. Dorsey Pender sent forward skirmishers who discerned that the Federals had completed the cross-ing. Lee was furious. "Why, General Pender!" he snapped. "That is what you young men always do. You allow these people to get away. I tell you what to do, but you don't do it." Then, with an impatient wave of the hand, he ordered Pender: "Go after them and damage them all you can."[19]

Lee was perhaps all the more disappointed because he had already identified Pender as a candidate for division command – and his reprimand did not prevent Lee from soon promoting Pender to that position. But regimental leaders who aspired to higher rank could not help but note that cautious brigade and division commanders tended to disappear from the army. Lee sometimes relieved them outright. At other times he did not object when the War Department sought to transfer them elsewhere. And it is unprovable, but likely, that, given the Davis administration's full confidence in him, Lee could quietly arrange the transfer of a general who disappointed him.

Perhaps the most striking example of Lee's bias in favor of aggressiveness was the different treatment he accorded two of his corps commanders, Ewell and Hill, during the Overland campaign (May 4–June 12, 1864). As comman-der of the II Corps, Ewell inevitably provoked comparisons with his dead predecessor and initially they were flattering. During the Gettysburg campaign,

---

[18] Late in the war, Lee would create a IV Corps, but largely to rebalance his army after the II Corps departed for an extended period of independent operations in the Shenandoah Valley.
[19] Jedediah Hotchkiss, *Confederate Military History: Virginia* (Atlanta, GA, 1899), 392.

he wrecked a Union division at Winchester (June 15, 1863), clearing the path for the Army of Northern Virginia to cross the Potomac into Maryland and Pennsylvania. On the first day at Gettysburg (July 1, 1863), Ewell's corps broke the Union right and forced every Federal unit on the field to fall back on Cemetery Hill, where the Union commander had placed a division as a hedge against just such an eventuality. Ewell was roundly criticized for his failure to capture the hill, which proved the keystone of the position that the Army of the Potomac occupied for the rest of the three-day battle. Lee ordered him to take the hill "if practicable." Ewell thought it wasn't (he was correct), and Lee accepted his decision. During the Battle of the Wilderness in May 1864, Ewell handled his troops well and fought the Federals in his sector to a standstill.

In contrast, Hill had great days – his counterattack at Antietam, for example – and bad ones, such as his "exceedingly imprudent" attack at Mechanicsville. His worst day came at Bristoe Station (October 14, 1863), when he led his troops into a trap and suffered fearful casualties as a result. Afterward, he confessed to Lee that the blunder was entirely his own fault. Lee agreed with him and told him with brutal candor exactly what he had done wrong. "Well, well, general," he concluded, "bury these poor men and let us say no more about it."[20]

Although Ewell showed much greater competence in the Wilderness fight, neither he nor Hill distinguished themselves in the remaining battles of the Overland campaign. Eventually both men became seriously ill and temporarily relinquished command, in each case to Maj. Gen. Jubal A. Early, an officer whose aggressiveness as a brigade and division commander Lee had long admired. When both officers reported themselves fit to resume duty, Lee disingenuously insisted that Ewell was sicker than Ewell believed – despite Ewell's fervent assertions to the contrary – and flatly refused to let him return to corps command. Instead, he made Early the permanent commander of the corps. In contrast, despite deficiencies in Hill's subsequent performance, Lee restored him to corps command and retained him until Hill's death a week before the surrender at Appomattox. The reason for Lee's differential treatment of Hill and Ewell is obvious: whatever Hill's shortcomings, Lee could count on his aggressiveness; in Ewell's case, he had lost that confidence.

Lee wanted generals who could play the bold game, but how did he expect to win it? Critics frequently assert that Lee expected to win by destroying the Union Army in an American Austerlitz, but except for the Seven Days, Lee acknowledged no such aim. The enemy's real center of gravity, he believed,

---

[20] The quotation is in A. L. Long, *Memoirs of Robert E. Lee: His Military and Personal History* (New York, 1886), 311. The incident is recounted in greater detail in the diary of a Confederate captain who was present. Entry for October 15, 1863, in Terry L. Jones, ed., *The Civil War Memoirs of Captain William J. Seymour: Reminiscences of a Louisiana Tiger* (Baton Rouge, LA, 1991), 89.

was Northern public opinion, and on *this* matter Lee is on record more than once. For example, during the initial moves of the Gettysburg campaign, he penned Davis a lengthy letter in which he complained that the rhetorical insistence of fire-eating Southern newspaper editors on no outcome but complete independence was undercutting the North's Peace Democrats – who were at that moment running candidates for governor in both Ohio and Pennsylvania. Lee thought they should cut it out, particularly since the material strength of the North was growing over time. The next passage is so politically astute that it is worth quoting at length:

> Under these circumstances we should neglect no honorable means of dividing and weakening our enemies that they may feel some of the difficulties experienced by ourselves. It seems to me that the most effectual mode of accomplishing this object, now within our reach, is to give all the encouragement we can, consistently with truth, to the rising peace party of the North.
>
> Nor do I think we should, in this connection, make nice distinction between those who declare for peace unconditionally and those who advocate it as a means of restoring the Union, however much we may prefer the former.
>
> We should bear in mind that the friends of peace at the North must make concessions to the earnest desire that exists in the minds of their countrymen for a restoration of the Union, and that to hold out such a result as an inducement is essential to the success of their party.
>
> Should the belief that peace will bring back the Union become general, the war would no longer be supported, and that, after all, is what we are interested in bringing about. When peace is proposed to us, it will be time enough to discuss its terms, and it is not the part of prudence to spurn the proposition in advance.

Lee was careful to conclude: "If the views I have indicated meet the approval of Your Excellency, you will best know how to give effect to them. Should you deem them inexpedient or impracticable, I think you will nevertheless agree with me that we should at least carefully abstain from measures or expressions that tend to discourage any party whose purpose is peace."[21] This gets at another element that strengthened the Army of Northern Virginia: unlike Joe Johnston, who could not get along at all with the Confederate president, Lee knew exactly how to talk to the prickly Davis.

He also understood one central reality: he commanded an army of citizen-soldiers, not professionals. During the Overland campaign, Brig. Gen. Ambrose R. Wright botched an assignment so badly that his corps commander, A. P. Hill, demanded a court of inquiry. Lee dissuaded him:

> These men are not an army; they are citizens defending their country. General Wright is not a soldier; he's a lawyer. I cannot do many things that I could do with a trained army. The soldiers know their duties better than the general officers do,

---

[21] Lee to Davis, June 10, 1863, in Dowdey and Manarin, eds., *The Wartime Papers of R. E. Lee*, 507–509.

and they have fought magnificently. Sometimes I would like to mask troops and then deploy them, but if I were to give the proper order, the general officers would not understand it; so I have to make the best of what I have and lose much time in making dispositions. You understand all this, but if you humiliated General Wright, the people of Georgia would not understand. Besides, whom would you put in his place? You have to do what I do: When a man makes a mistake, I call him to my tent, talk to him, and use the authority of my position to make him do the right thing the next time.[22]

For every Jackson, Longstreet, or Hill, Lee had a dozen Ambrose Wrights, so it's worth taking a moment to explore Wright's background. Born in 1826, Ambrose Ransom "Rans" Wright made his living as a lawyer, just as Lee said, but he had also scratched persistently at the door of politics. He held no public office of consequence but was nevertheless a prominent figure thanks to his brother-in-law, Herschel V. Johnson, who had been a US senator from Georgia, then governor of the state, and then a member of the Confederate Senate from 1862 until the war's end. When the war broke out, Wright enlisted as a private in the Georgia militia, but soon became colonel of the 3rd Georgia Volunteer Infantry Regiment. This was not as unlikely as it might seem. During the US Civil War, soldiers of both North and South frequently elected their own officers, sometimes – as with Wright – all the way up to the rank of colonel. While the practice of electing regimental commanders was understandably curtailed, in many units, soldiers continued throughout the war to elect their noncommissioned officers, lieutenants, and captains.

The 3rd Georgia was part of a brigade initially commanded by Brig. Gen. Albert G. Blanchard. Blanchard was a professional soldier who had graduated from West Point in 1829, the same class that included Robert E. Lee. But after Seven Pines, Blanchard found himself reassigned – because of advancing age, some said, because of poor performance, said others – and Wright took over. He led gallantly and well, commanding the brigade in every engagement from June 1862 until November 1864, when he was sent to Georgia to defend his home state. He was seriously wounded at Antietam. At Gettysburg, his brigade briefly broke the Union line and captured twenty cannon before being forced back for lack of support.[23]

Wright was among 1,954 colonels who served in the Army of Northern Virginia at some point. Of these, 75 were Mexican War veterans (3.8 percent), 22 were veterans of volunteer service in other wars (1.1 percent), and 70 were professional soldiers (3.5 percent). Of the remaining, 1,487 (76.1 percent) were without prewar military experience of any kind. Of these, the top five prewar

---

[22] Col. William H. Palmer to Douglas Southall Freeman, June 25, 1920, in Douglas Southall Freeman, *R. E. Lee: A Biography*, 4 vols. (New York, 1934–1935), 3:331fn.

[23] Ezra J. Warner, *Generals in Gray: Lives of the Confederate Commanders* (Baton Rouge, LA, 1959), 345–346.

occupations were judges and lawyers like Wright (170), state-level politicians (137), planters/farmers (105), teachers (82), and medical doctors (73).[24]

At lower ranks, the percentage of men without prewar military experience was even higher. Moreover, the social distance between the leaders and the led was small. Although the median income of officers was about three times that of enlisted men ($3,305/year versus $1,125/year), there was considerable overlap. One in every three enlisted men or their families owned three or more slaves. About 20 percent of officers owned property worth less than $800; 55.5 percent of enlisted men owned more than $800 in property. On average, officers were only four years older than their enlisted counterparts.[25] The practice of election made it difficult for officers to impose discipline, and, although soldiers fought well, it was frequently a different story in camp life. Junior officers also came from the same communities as their soldiers, and if familiarity did not breed contempt, it did breed disdain for officers who tried to throw their weight around.

The practice of election seemingly guaranteed trouble. One junior officer observed, "One telling point in favor of a candidate was that he would not 'expose his men' as they called it; namely, would not make them fight." He considered the system of "reorganization," as elections were called, "an injury to the morale of the troops which they never got over." Officers who insisted upon discipline frequently lost their positions during the next "reorganization." The lesson, he wrote, was crystal clear: "*Keep in with your men, whatever the consequences, if you don't want to be turned out some day.*"[26] A journalist who spent much time observing the Army of Northern Virginia believed that "once elected, [officers] did their duty faithfully in the field" – an assertion the fighting quality of the army's soldiers amply justified – "but they were either too weak, or too inexperienced, to keep the strict rules of discipline applied during the trying inactivity of camp; and they were too conscious of the social and mental equality of their men to enforce the distinction between officer and private."[27]

Needless to say, this is not a system that Lee would have tolerated if he had possessed the authority to end it. But he did not, and the practice of election remained one of several ways in which the "clannish" organizational culture at the regimental level remained outside the hierarchical culture of the senior leadership. Confederate field armies sometimes established examination boards to weed out the least competent junior officers, but the sheer number

---

[24] Robert K. Krick, *Lee's Colonels: A Biographical Register of the Field Officers of the Army of Northern Virginia* (Dayton, OH, 1979), xvi, xviii.

[25] Joseph T. Glatthaar, *General Lee's Army: From Victory to Collapse* (New York, 2008), 188.

[26] W. W. Blackford, *War Years with Jeb Stuart* (1945; reprint, Baton Rouge, LA, 1993), 62. Emphasis in the original.

[27] Thomas Cooper DeLeon, *Four Years in Rebel Capitals* (Mobile, AL, 1890), 133–134.

of officers, coupled with the operational tempo, meant that the use of these boards was inconsistent at best. Nonetheless, taken on the whole this system worked better than one might suppose. The Army of Northern Virginia fought as well as, if not better than, other US Civil War armies. Mistakes, when they occurred, were made by senior officers and no more than the fog of war would have made likely.

In some US Civil War armies, the soldiers continued to identify mainly with their regiments or brigades. But soldiers in Lee's army soon took pride in being members of the Army of Northern Virginia, thanks largely to their idolization of its leader. In a letter home just after the Antietam campaign, Lt. John Hampden Chamberlayne elegantly expressed what most soldiers said in more earthy ways. "When by accident I at any time see Gen. Lee, or when I think of him, whether I will or no, there looms up to me some king-of-men, superior by the head, a Gigantic figure, on whom rests the world, With Atlantean shoulder, fit to bear The weight of Empire."[28] Lee's soldiers frequently referred to him as "Marse Robert," a telling phrase in a slaveholding society. White Southerners liked to imagine slaves as simple and faithful, and in calling Lee "Marse Robert" his soldiers implicitly imagined themselves as his faithful servants.

Why did these soldiers fight? Confederate soldiers were familiar with slavery, and a prominent motivation was its preservation. While only one Southern family in four owned any slaves at all, many aspired to ownership and many more viewed slavery as the only reliable mechanism for racial control. There was also a common political view among white Southerners that societies are inherently unequal: Democracy, went the argument, was possible only because slaves provided a "mudsill" at the bottom. The mudsill reduced the social distance between wealthy whites and poor whites enough to permit something close to equality. Without slavery, poor whites would join free blacks at the bottom of Southern society, and their participation in democracy would be compromised.[29]

The Army of Northern Virginia fought entirely in the war's eastern theater, that is to say, Virginia and (briefly) Maryland and Pennsylvania. There is a canard to the effect that Lee was Virginia-centric and thought only about the defense of that state, but careful examination of his correspondence shows that he was well aware of what was going on in other theaters. When Davis transferred two divisions of Longstreet's I Corps, as well as Longstreet, to Bragg's Army of Tennessee, Lee did not complain about the decision, neither did he demand the return of the divisions as soon as possible. On the contrary, when Bragg sent Longstreet on an independent mission to recover Knoxville,

---

[28] John Hampden Chamberlayne to Lucy Park Chamberlayne, October 13, 1862, in C. G. Chamberlayne, ed., *Ham Chamberlayne – Virginian: Letters and Papers of an Artillery Officer in the War for Southern Independence, 1861–1865* (Richmond, VA, 1932), 126.

[29] James M. McPherson, *What They Fought For, 1861–1865* (Baton Rouge, LA, 1994), 9–26.

and Longstreet ended up northeast of Knoxville with a direct railroad line back to Lee's main army, Lee did not demand the return of Longstreet's corps even then. Instead, when Longstreet hatched a plan to invade Kentucky, Lee accompanied Longstreet to Richmond to help convince Davis to implement the plan. Longstreet returned to Lee's army only on the eve of the 1864 spring campaign, and then only after it had become apparent that he would be most useful there.[30]

In June 1864, Lee detached his II Corps, now under Jubal Early, to the Shenandoah Valley, where it remained for several months. Even with the bulk of his army pinned to the defense of Richmond-Petersburg, he wanted to retain a capacity for offensive action. Early supplied just that, first clearing the Valley of Union troops, and then crossing the Potomac into Maryland and swinging southeast to threaten Washington's fortifications. This forced Grant to detach the Union VI Corps, one of the best in the Army of the Potomac, to stop the Confederate advance, and then to mount a major effort in the Valley to defeat Early. Early usually fought at a 2:3 numerical disadvantage, and yet remained a significant threat until March 1865, when Sheridan finally defeated him decisively at the Battle of Waynesboro. Put simply, Lee never minded running serious risks by sending troops elsewhere whenever he thought it would be advantageous to the Confederacy do so.

Lee, of course, believed that if the Confederacy were to win the war, it had to do so on a short clock, and thus he committed his army to offensive action whenever possible. Victories like Fredericksburg, which were won on the defensive, left him dissatisfied because they merely humiliated the Federals but offered no scope for him to take the initiative. Although Lee could not have destroyed the Union Army, he could have defeated Northern public opinion. He came close to doing so in the summer of 1864, when the protracted stalemate at Richmond-Petersburg, coupled with Early's raid on Washington, nearly cost Lincoln the election.

What saved Lincoln was not what happened in Maryland and Virginia but rather the capture of Atlanta on September 3. Furthermore, it was Sherman's advance through the Carolinas to join Grant in early 1865, rather than anything Grant did, that impelled Lee to retreat from Richmond-Petersburg. The operational concept was to link up with the remnants of the Army of Tennessee somewhere near the Virginia-North Carolina state line. The combined armies would then withdraw into northern Alabama, which was all but unoccupied by Federal troops. The gambit failed. The pursuing Army of the Potomac finally cornered the Army of Northern Virginia at Appomattox Court-House. With his army surrounded, Lee met Grant in the parlor of a local home and surrendered.

---

[30] Steven E. Woodworth, *Davis and Lee at War* (Lawrence, KS, 1995), 262–270.

Despite this severe reversal, the Davis administration intended to continue resistance in the same way that Washington's Continental Army had done – maintain a force in being and tie itself to no city or other strategic point.[31] But the surrender at Appomattox began a cascade of surrenders by the Confederacy's remaining armies, and by the end of May 1865, the war was over. Few but US Civil War specialists recall those other surrenders. By 1865, the Army of Northern Virginia was regarded as the beating heart of the Confederacy. When that heart ceased to beat, the embryonic nation it sustained perished.

---

[31] Historians frequently misinterpret Davis as advocating guerrilla warfare. This idea is exploded in William B. Feis, "Jefferson Davis and the 'Guerrilla Option': A Reexamination," in Mark Grimsley and Brooks D. Simpson, eds., *The Collapse of the Confederacy* (Lincoln, NE, 2002), 104–128.

5   German Army Culture, 1871–1945

Jorit Wintjes

Introduction: Birth of an Army

The end of World War I saw a revolution in Germany that swept away much of the old order. Between November 7 and November 23, 1918, all dynastic rulers in Germany either fled or abdicated. In Bavaria, the Freie Volksstaat Bayern proclaimed by its first *Premierminister*, Kurt Eisner, initially replaced the monarchy. Yet, barely four months later, on February 21, 1919, rightists assassinated Eisner after he had lost the first democratic election in January, and Bavaria plunged into chaos. On April 7, 1919, radical leftists proclaimed a soviet republic in Munich, and the legitimate government under Johannes Hoffmann fled to Bamberg.[1] Although Munich was back under government control within a month, with the Bavarian soviet republic defeated by a force of loyal army units and several *Freikorps*, the Hoffmann government stayed in Bamberg for several months, preparing a proposal for a new constitution that the Bavarian parliament accepted on August 14, 1919, the so-called Bamberg Constitution.[2] Apart from declaring the Bavarian state a republic, it also stated that "Bavarian forces are part of the German Wehrmacht," a force whose commander in chief, according to the Weimar constitution, was the *Reichspräsident*, who also had the power to commission and dismiss officers.[3] While the Bamberg constitution also stated that Bavarian forces were not to be dispersed among the army of the new Weimar Republic, the days of the Bavarian *Wehrhoheit*, an autonomy in military matters guaranteeing the existence of a Bavarian army recruited from Bavaria, led by Bavarian-trained officers, and serving under Bavarian military law, were over.[4]

---

[1] Wolfgang Zorn, *Bayerns Geschichte im 20. Jahrhundert* (München, 1986), 145–148, 168–185.
[2] For an in-depth discussion, see Christian Georg Ruf, *Die Bayerische Verfassung vom 14. August 1919* (Baden-Baden, 2015).
[3] See Bamberg Constitution, section 9, § 87: "Die bayerischen Truppen bilden einen Teil der Wehrmacht des Deutschen Reiches"; Weimar Constitution, part 1, section 3, § 46: "Der Reichspräsident ernennt und entläßt die Reichsbeamten und die Offiziere, soweit nicht durch Gesetz etwas anderes bestimmtist ... " and § 47: "Der Reichspräsident hat den Oberbefehl über die gesamte Wehrmacht des Reiches."
[4] See section 9, § 87: "Die [bayerischen Streitkräfte] sind ein geschlossener Truppenverband."

However, the decision of the Bavarian government to give up Bavaria's military autonomy also marks the true beginning of the history of a "German Army" – after the end of World War I and more than forty years after the creation of the German Empire in the wake of the Prusso-German victory over France in 1870–1871. While this episode is nowadays often overlooked, it serves particularly well to highlight a key aspect of German military history in the 1871–1945 period. Instead of one monolithic "German Army," the forces usually bound together by that description were of a surprisingly varied character and cultural background, and for all the cultural continuity that historians often regarded as one major element in German military history, linking the wars of the Grand Elector with the Second World War, for much of the 1871–1945 period at least, the "German Army" – or the "German armies," to be more precise – was a force in transition.

During the two world wars, the Germany Army displayed significant operational capabilities repeatedly offset by glaring strategic weaknesses; indeed, one could argue that those in charge of the army that entered the Second World War lacked any sound strategic thinking at all, surrendering the strategic decision-making process to an increasingly erratic political leader. Yet although a focus on operational and strategic thinking is without doubt useful for understanding the German Army's failure to avoid a war of attrition by a bold strike in 1914 – which ended with the army fighting and losing the very war of attrition it had tried to avoid – and its misguided and mismanaged invasion into the Soviet Union in the Second World War eventually resulting in the worst defeat in German military history, it serves less well for understanding how the cultural background of the German Army shaped both its organizational and operational cultures. While the interdependence between operational and strategic thinking has attracted considerable attention, the relationship between the cultural background of the German Army and its operational culture has received less attention.

This chapter therefore takes a slightly unorthodox approach to German military history and leaves out any in-depth discussion of German strategic thinking – or rather the significant lack thereof. Instead, it explores the cultural background of the forces associated with the German nation-state from its establishment in 1871 to the end of World War II in 1945 and examines the operational consequences of that background. It explores how a rather heterogeneous collection of different forces under the leadership of Prussia developed first into a homogenous army that understood itself as standing in the direct tradition of the Prussian army of the nineteenth century and then further into a force ultimately evolving beyond the framework of a national army, before then analyzing how this process was accompanied by developments in doctrine and tactics.

分析

Historical Background: Confederation to Empire, 1815–1871

Few expressions serve better to describe nineteenth-century German military history than "diversity." After Napoleon's final defeat in 1815, thirty-eight states formed the German Confederation at the Vienna Congress (with a thirty-ninth joining two years later), and as they had done for centuries in the context of the former Holy Roman Empire, the smaller states looked to one of the leading German-speaking powers at the time for protection.[5] Any contemporary observer would have had little difficulty in identifying which was the most important German-speaking power (Austria) or the second most important one (Prussia).[6]

The ranking of the lesser powers was slightly more difficult, particularly as some had been allied with France for a fairly long period. Even so, to contemporaries, the kingdoms of Bavaria, Hanover, Saxony, and Württemberg, as well as the Grand Duchy of Baden, constituted in one way or another the third rank of German powers, each fielding an army of its own with an institutional history going back well into the seventeenth century. In the German Confederation, all these forces – as well as more than thirty smaller ones – contributed to the confederation's army according to the military potential of the respective members, from Austria providing more than 90,000 men down to the Principality of Liechtenstein, which contributed an undoubtedly spirited but nevertheless somewhat smaller contingent of 55 men.[7]

While most of these armies nowadays appear to have been second- or even third-rate, taken together, they made up more than 40 percent of the army of the German Confederation. The larger ones could not only look back on a long tradition, they also had an active history in the nineteenth century beyond providing cannon fodder for Napoleon's ill-fated march on Moscow. The decades following the Napoleonic Wars were characterized by technological progress and military reform, with the latter usually associated with Prussian reformers led by Gerhard von Scharnhorst. Yet the smaller German armies also produced military theoreticians and reformers – such as Hessian officer Wilhelm von Plönnies, a small-arms expert of international renown around the middle of the nineteenth century – who were widely respected by their contemporaries, even if they are nowadays mostly forgotten.[8] While historians often argue that the reforms Scharnhorst instigated set Prussia on a path at the end of which lay Sedan and Napoleon

---

[5] Michael Kotulla, *Deutsches Verfassungsrecht 1806–1918, 1. Band* (Heidelberg, 2006), 48–51.
[6] Their relative importance is mirrored by the number of troops they were supposed to provide for the Bundesarmee (see later in this chapter).
[7] Georg Ortenburg, *Das deutsche Bundesheer. Nach dem Uniformwerk aus den Jahren 1835 bis 1843* (Dortmund, 1990), 16.
[8] Friedrich Knöpp and Karl Esselborn, *Hessische Lebensläufe, 2. Aufl.* (Darmstadt, 1979), 364–380.

III's handing over of his sword to Bismarck, in fact, other German states also tried to find solutions to the military challenges they faced. Thus, facing the need of reequipping their infantry with rifled guns after the middle of the century, the armies of Württemberg, Baden, and Hesse, which together formed an army corps in the army of the German Confederation, joined forces to develop a common rifled musket, the *Vereinsgewehr*, which entered service with all three armies in 1857.[9] A year later, the Bavarian Army introduced a new rifled musket of its own, the *Podewils-Gewehr*, which already was one of the most advanced muzzle-loading rifles of the time, even if the development of breech-loading rifles less than a decade later quickly made them obsolete.[10] The Bavarian Army could also pride itself on being the first German force to field an early machine gun in combat, the four-barreled *Feldl-Geschütz*, which saw limited action in the Franco-Prussian War.[11] Beyond being mere technological curiosities, these examples indicate not only that the smaller German armies were actively looking for technological solutions to the challenges of the mid-nineteenth century but also that they were keeping pace with technological developments in Prussia and Austria.

Despite these activities of the smaller German armies, which form part of a rich and still to a surprising extent largely unexplored military history, one cannot deny the overall importance of the Prussian Army. As a result, historians often regard it as the logical predecessor of the German armies of the twentieth century. Thus, the first mass mobilization in 1812, Scharnhorst's reforms, and Clausewitz's new approach to military theory appear as part of a long line of development ultimately leading to German prewar planning and the First World War. According to this line of thought, German military history is essentially an extension of the "Prussification" not only of German military affairs but also of German society. As a consequence, from the theoretical understanding of war to operational concepts and to the relationship between the army and society, scholarship has usually focused on the Prussian Army. This scholarship has focused on the reactionary elements in Prussian and later German society, which were staunch opponents of those supporting liberal and democratic reform.[12] While such an approach to Prussian military history is perfectly valid, if applied to the forces of the German Empire between 1871 and 1914, it somewhat obscures a much richer and more varied cultural background to German military history, in which the Prussian Army played an important

---

[9] Hans-Dieter Götz, *Militärgewehre und Pistolen der deutschen Staaten 1800–1870* (Stuttgart, 1978), 265–271.

[10] Wilhelm von Plönnies, *Neue Studien ueber die Gezogene Feuerwaffe der Infanterie* (Darmstadt, 1861), 145–173.

[11] Richard Wille, *Über Kartätschgeschütze* (Berlin, 1871), 131–137.

[12] Hans-Ulrich Wehler, *Deutsche Gesellschaftsgeschichte, vol. 3, 1849–1914* (München, 1995), 873–885.

but not exclusive part. Although it is hard to argue against Prussian attempts to gain control over all forces of the German Empire, this "Prussification" did not meet with universal enthusiasm. There was, in fact, considerable opposition to ever-increasing Prussian influence within the German Empire, indicated, for example, by repeated Bavarian attempts well into 1915 to claim additional territories in an expanded postwar Germany in order to offset any Prussian territorial acquisitions.[13]

German Armies, 1871–1945

This complex background is reflected by the history of what eventually became known as the German Army in the 1871–1945 period. From 1871 onward, the history of the German Army – or rather, the "German armies" – falls into five phases, each of quite different character.

Initially, the forces of the newly founded German Empire, while dominated by the Prussian military, were anything but the army of a German nation-state. In times of peace, the German Army technically did not have one army, but four, with the *Reservatrechte* guaranteeing the armies of Saxony and Württemberg an independent structure.[14] They were under the overall command of the German emperor, though, who, according to the empire's constitution, served as the commander in chief of all German forces, or rather of all but one. In peacetime, the Bavarian Army enjoyed complete independence, only coming under control of the German emperor in times of war, when it was to serve as a separate army.

This independence was originally not only evident in the organization of the army, with Bavaria having its own ministry of war, as had Saxony and Württemberg, and with its own military penal code and regimental numbering system, but was also obvious for even the most casual observers, as Bavarian soldiers continued to wear the *Raupenhelm*, a rather conspicuous piece of headgear, for more than a decade after the foundation of the German Empire. Only after the turn of the century with a new uniform in *Feldgrau* (field grey) assigned to all German forces did Bavarian infantrymen finally look similar to Prussian ones – at least superficially, as closer inspection would still have revealed subtle variations such as different cockades and buttons. Apart from the uniform, the Bavarian Army initially also continued to use its own equipment with the Werder rifle, introduced only in 1869 and soldiering on after it

---

[13] On Bavarian war aims, see Dieter Albrecht, "Bayern im Ersten Weltkrieg 1914–1918," in Max Spindler and Alois Schmid, eds., *Handbuch der bayerischen Geschichte. Bd. IV: Das neue Bayern. Von 1800 bis zur Gegenwart. Teilbd. 1: Staat und Politik* (München, 2003), 417–425.
[14] Ernst Rudolf Huber, *Deutsche Verfassungsgeschichte seit 1789: Struktur und Krisen des Kaiserreichs* (Stuttgart, 1982), 1052; see also Kotulla, *Deutsches Verfassungsrecht*, 231–232 (on Baden) and 232–239 (on Bavaria).

was rechambered to the Prussian M/71 cartridge until the end of the century, being the most prominent example.[15]

Beneath these outward differences lay a deeper cultural divide, even after the Bavarian Army had been reorganized on the Prussian model after its defeat in 1866. Not only was the Bavarian Army a predominantly Catholic force, whereas the Prussian Army, despite having a fairly diverse recruiting base due to the acquisition of Catholic territories throughout the nineteenth century, had a distinct Protestant tradition, the social composition of the two armies was also markedly different. In the Prussian officer corps, a considerable number of officers were members of the aristocracy. In the Bavarian Army, the proportion of officers with an aristocratic background fell from around a third in the early 1860s to less than 15 percent in 1914.[16] Although differences in organization and equipment were gradually overcome during the decades before World War I, the cultural gap between the Prussian Army and the other armies remained, with Bavaria, Saxony, and Württemberg in particular keen on preserving their independence. Therefore, one can best understand the history of the pre–First World War forces of the German Empire as a struggle between the Prussian military establishment trying to integrate all other armies in the German Empire as fully as possible, and those armies putting up considerable resistance to assimilation.

The outbreak of the First World War marks the beginning of the second phase of German military history between 1871 and 1945. While the forces of the German Empire initially went to war in the way prescribed by the *Militärkonvention* of 1870, the Bavarian Army forming the Sixth Army under the command of Crown Prince Rupprecht of Bavaria, it took but a few weeks for the realities of war to lead to Bavarian units being assigned to other armies and integrating replacements from outside Bavaria.[17] Only during the initial battles in Lorraine did the Bavarian Army fight as a single and separate force.[18] The armies of Saxony and Württemberg, which each formed an army corps, had a similar experience.

In general, the war caused the "German armies" increasingly to lose the independence they had enjoyed before 1914, even if their institutional framework (i.e., the war ministries) continued to exist. Moreover, mass mobilization in combination with the huge losses suffered during the early stages of the war also narrowed the cultural gap between the Prussian and the other armies.

[15] Hans Dieter-Götz, *Die deutschen Militärgewehre und Maschinenpistolen 1871–1945* (Stuttgart, 1994), 10–19.

[16] Heinz Reif, *Adel im 19. und 20. Jahrhundert* (München, 2012), 79–80.

[17] Dieter Storz, "Kronprinz Rupprecht von Bayern – dynastische Heerführung im Massenkrieg," in Winfried Heinemann and Markus Pöhlmann, eds., *Monarchen und ihr Militär* (Potsdam, 2010), 47–48.

[18] Bayerisches Kriegsarchiv, ed., *Die Bayern im Großen Kriege 1914–1918* (München, 1923), 2.

Regiments were still nominally tied to their local recruiting base. Yet a steady influx of new recruits from various sources changed the previously regional character of units. Also, as losses among the officers mounted, the number of aristocrats in the officer corps fell. In general, the unifying impact of the war was considerable; it effectively forged the forces of the German Empire together into a true "German Army," which by 1918 was already fairly homogenous both in outward appearance and in inward nature.

The end of the First World War, the revolution, and the flight of the dynastic rulers in Germany stand at the beginning of the third phase of German military history between 1871 and 1945. Discounting the failed attempt at establishing a *Reichsheer* in 1848–1849, the newly established Reichswehr was the first true German Army. Although Bavarian Reichswehr units retained some token independence, as only Bavarian citizens were supposed to serve in the 7th Division and the 17th Cavalry Regiment, which together formed what in the early 1920s was known as the "Bavarian Reichswehr," Bavaria as well as Saxony and Württemberg had finally surrendered their military autonomy.[19] For some years thereafter, the position of a special Bavarian *Landeskommandant* remained, but from 1924 onward, the Bavarian units found themselves fully integrated into the command structure of the Reichswehr. In some way, then, the establishment of the Reichswehr represented the final success of the assimilation attempts by the Prussian military establishment that had characterized the four decades between the Franco-Prussian War and World War I.

In terms of its character and its self-understanding, the Reichswehr was far from a successor to the forces of the German Empire, which were still rooted in the army of the German Confederation. Rather, the Reichswehr saw itself mostly as the direct successor to the Prussian Army, and while its second commander in chief, Hans von Seeckt, who had a formative influence on the character of the force, put great emphasis on military tradition, it was mostly the Prussian military tradition with which the Reichswehr connected.[20]

Ironically, the Versailles Treaty, which limited Germany to an army of only 100,000 men led by 4,000 carefully selected officers, made this "Prussification" of the German Army considerably easier.[21] William Mulligan has shown that Walter Reinhardt, the Reichswehr's first commander in chief, favored former front officers for the new army, while his eventual successor Seeckt preferred former staff officers for the highest positions and the new Reichswehr

---

[19] Kai Uwe Tapken, *Die Reichswehr in Bayern von 1919 bis 1924* (Hamburg, 2002), 47–48.

[20] Hans-Ulrich Wehler, *Deutsche Gesellschaftsgeschichte, vol. 4, 1914–1949* (München, 2003), 418–419.

[21] In July 1920, 34,000 officers remained active in the Reichswehr; by the end of the year, the number had fallen to 4,000 (ibid., 418).

ministerium, not least so they could preserve the spirit of the old, i.e. Prussian, army.[22] Seeckt, who himself had served with the General Staff from 1897 onward, prevailed, and while he did not discount front-line officers, his position on the respective qualities of staff officers and front officers is quite obvious. During a discussion in July 1920, he stated that the army should choose future officers from both those who had held front and staff positions, but added: "From the best only the very best can be chosen; only the elite can join the new ministry." There can be little doubt whom he thought to belong to the elite, as former staff officers dominated the ministry.[23] Both his preference for former staff officers and his emphasis on a distinctly Prussian character of the Reichswehr were to have a significant impact on German military history beyond the existence of the force or the state it supposedly protected. As most of the Wehrmacht's general officers had a Reichswehr background, the army of the Third Reich, at least during the years leading up to the Second World War, retained both its homogeneity and its Prussian character.

Seeckt also shaped the character of the Reichswehr with regard to its relationship to the new republic in particular and to politics in general. Initially, as one historian has suggested, one can discern three different groups within the officer corps: adherents of the old monarchy, supporters of the new state, and those preferring to keep the army clear of any political struggles.[24] As Seeckt led the last group, the Reichswehr from 1920 onward understood itself as "apolitical" and beyond the politics of the day, distancing itself so much from the new republic that it eventually developed into a "state within a state." The precise nature of the civil-military relationship of the Reichswehr and its consequences for the eventual fate of the Weimar Republic has attracted considerable scholarship, usually focusing on the question to what extent, or whether at all, it had destabilized the new republic.[25] While Seeckt's decision to keep the Reichswehr as "apolitical" as possible was probably less detrimental to the existence of the Weimar Republic than some interpreters have argued, it resulted in a relationship to the political decision makers that was problematic at best.[26] One cannot but wonder how the cooperation between Seeckt and his Reichswehr on one hand and the political leadership of the Weimar Republic on

---

[22] William Mulligan, *The Creation of the Modern German Army: General Walther Reinhardt and the Weimar Republic, 1914–1930* (New York, 2005), 132.

[23] Ibid., 133.

[24] Wolfgang Sauer, "Die Reichswehr," in Karl Dietrich Bracher, ed., *Die Auflösung der Weimarer Republik. Eine Studie zum Problem des Machtverfalls in der Demokratie* (Düsseldorf, 1984), 205–253.

[25] For a concise overview, see Mulligan, *Creation of the Modern German Army*, 5–9.

[26] Even Hans-Ulrich Wehler, while highly critical of Seeckt and the way he shaped the Reichswehr as a conservative force, noted that it served "in a highly critical situation, it has to be conceded, several times as an effective brace for state unity" (Wehler, *Gesellschaftsgeschichte*, 4:419).

the other might have worked out in the case of a national emergency, or whether there would have been any in the first place.

In the case of such an emergency, Seeckt planned to use the Reichswehr as a core cadre around which to build a much larger army. In 1923, he ordered the *Truppenamt* (Troop Office) to plan for an army of 102 divisions, with which the army would fight a war of movement against any invader, presumed to be France or Poland, or both.[27] At the same time, the head of the army department in the *Truppenamt*, Col. Joachim von Stülpnagel, published an alternative concept of resisting an invader by what amounted to guerrilla warfare by the population, or *Volkskrieg*, which found several supporters.[28] Whether in an emergency this concept, which, as Andreas Dietz rightly stresses, dangerously blurred the distinction between combatants and noncombatants, would have been met with enthusiasm by the political leadership is questionable.[29] Apart from displaying a disturbing readiness to accept the direct, active participation of civilians in military action, the *Volkskrieg* concept again showed how the Reichswehr had distanced itself from the political decision makers of the Weimar Republic.

Given the "apolitical" character of the Reichswehr, it is mildly surprising that an eminently political demonstration of commitment to the state marks the beginning of the fourth phase of German military history between 1871 and 1945. Immediately after the death of President Paul von Hindenburg in August 1934, Defense Minister Werner von Blomberg and Maj. Gen. Walther von Reichenau had every member of the Reichswehr take an oath of personal loyalty to Hitler, thereby tying the fate of the army directly to that of the political leadership.[30] Earlier in February of the same year, Blomberg had summarily given all Jewish Reichswehr personnel a dishonorable discharge.[31] Reichenau best illustrates the readiness with which the Reichswehr leadership embraced the new regime; he claimed that the army had to move "into the new state and occupy its proper position."[32] This seems to have echoed Seeckt's position, according to which the Reichswehr should wait until a favorable political constellation had come about, and then act. Indeed, historians often stress that the Wehrmacht that went to war in 1939 was basically the army formed by Seeckt, with much of its tactical and operational doctrine already developed in the 1920s.

---

[27] Andreas Dietz, *Das Primat der Politik in kaiserlicher Armee, Reichswehr, Wehrmacht und Bundeswehr* (Tübingen, 2011), 235; by comparison, the forces of the German Empire had entered the war in 1914 with 92 divisions, to which 36 divisions were added by the end of the year; by 1918, this number had increased to 212 divisions.

[28] Mulligan, *Creation of the Modern German Army*, 203–207.

[29] Dietz, *Primat der Politik*, 236.   [30] For an overview, see ibid., 357–361.

[31] Ibid., 377–378.

[32] Klaus-Jürgen Müller, *Das Heer und Hitler. Armee und Nationalsozialistisches Regime 1933–1940* (Stuttgart, 1969), 54.

Yet despite its attempts at gaining political advantages through early displays of loyalty, and although the German rearmament program, which from 1935 onward included conscription, brought a massive increase in numbers in the army, the newly renamed Wehrmacht found itself in fact in a very different situation from that of the Reichswehr in the old Weimar Republic. The situation did not compare entirely favorably, for three reasons. First, while the Reichswehr was small, too small for the ambitions of some, its diminutive size had at the same time allowed its leadership to form an army that saw itself as an elite within an otherwise civilian society, an elite that was conservative, committed to the tradition of the Prussian Army, and largely looked back on wartime experience. It carefully vetted its officers and trained its noncommissioned officers intensively to become the core of a much larger army. However, with the reintroduction of conscription in 1935, the character of the army changed significantly. A large influx of young men without any combat experience rapidly turned the Wehrmacht into a mass army whose connection to the past, to Prussian history in general, and to the German Empire in particular was much more tenuous.

Second, the new Wehrmacht, while getting the opportunity to significantly enlarge itself and to adopt modern technology, now was no longer the only armed and uniformed force in society. Instead, particularly as a result of the rise of paramilitary forces, the Wehrmacht had to compete for the attention of political decision makers and of society in general. Once the war began, competition for attention soon turned into competition for resources, and one cannot help but wonder how much the existence of parallel organizations such as the Heereswaffenamt and the SS Waffenamt actually hampered the German war effort. Moreover, any special recognition the Reichswehr might have enjoyed as the only armed and uniformed force of the Weimar Republic dissipated quickly in a state where the citizens spent a significant time of their childhood and early adult years in uniform.

Finally, although the Wehrmacht remained at the forefront of tactical, technological, and operational developments, its complete subordination under the political leadership of the new state resulted in anything but a fruitful relationship between the political and the military leadership once the war began. Instead, Hitler exerted complete control not only in theory but also in practice, regularly intervening in the planning and execution of operations, while the Wehrmacht was unable to find efficient ways of cooperating with the political leadership, let alone of exerting some modicum of control. Despite these issues, the army that went to war in 1939 was initially outstandingly successful, though already operations in France brought to the surface a disturbing tendency of the political leadership to interfere with the execution of military operations.

Most of the developments sketched out earlier in this chapter continued throughout the war; thus the SS gained considerably in importance, in turn increasing the importance of the Waffen-SS, which competed with the Wehrmacht for the best equipment, while direct interference by Hitler would steadily increase and eventually become a significant hindrance to German operational planning. However, the German attack on the Soviet Union also brought about another important change in the character of the German Army and thus stands at the beginning of the last phase of German military history between 1871 and 1945.

While the wars against Poland and France initially aimed at the revision of the Versailles Treaty and at territorial expansion, National Socialist propaganda presented the war against the Soviet Union as a massive struggle against Bolshevism. Thus, the war took on a decidedly political character, which would set the Wehrmacht on a road toward active participation in some of the worst atrocities of the Second World War. At the same time, the Wehrmacht transformed from a purely German force into one in which significant numbers of foreigners from all over Europe served as volunteers, either in combat or in noncombat roles. Thus, approximately 1 million non-Germans served mostly on the Eastern Front in the Wehrmacht, while another 500,000 served in the foreign volunteer units of the Waffen-SS.[33] Both in terms of the propaganda accompanying it and in terms of the participants, the war in the east had turned from a war for territorial expansion into both an internationalist crusade against Bolshevism and a race war against Slavic *untermenschen*. The war retained this character right up to the end, when the French members of the SS Waffen Grenadier Division "Charlemagne" were among the last defenders of Berlin.[34] Seeckt, who had built up the Reichswehr to defend Germany against French aggression, would have been profoundly irritated.

A "German" Way of Waging War?

The foregoing brief overview of German military history between 1871 and 1945 suggests that the German Army – or "armies" – had a rather checkered background and that a number of important turning points, each changing the nature of the force considerably, marked its history. Rooted in the heterogeneous forces of the German Confederation, the German military during the decades before the First World War became dominated by the Prussian Army. The smaller German states, however, put up determined resistance against total "Prussification" and tried to keep their own military establishments as independent as possible. This continued into the war, although the realities of the conflict had a significant unifying effect on the armed forces of the German

---

[33] George Stein, *The Waffen SS: Hitler's Elite Guard at War, 1939–1945* (Ithaca, NY, 1984), 133.
[34] Philippe Carrard, *The French Who Fought for Hitler: Memories from the Outcasts* (Cambridge, 2010), 54–57.

Empire. The establishment of the Reichswehr then brought about a dramatic change. Seeckt modelled the new force on the Prussian Army and its traditions. The Reichswehr claimed for itself a prominent position in the new state. In 1933, its leadership embraced the new regime in order to improve its position, although in the end, the Wehrmacht failed even to retain the prominence the Reichswehr had enjoyed in the Weimar Republic, let alone increase its importance in society. Moreover, the effects of conscription had a negative impact on the army's specific Prussian character. Finally, during the latter half of World War II, the Wehrmacht moved even further away from the traditions of the Prussian Army and in some respects even from a purely "German" one.

Yet, despite these remarkable changes in the character of the German Army, the operational culture, so to speak, displayed an equally remarkable constancy from the middle of the nineteenth century onward. It is due to this constancy in what the German Army was *doing*, as opposed to its character and cultural background, that leads military historians to see the army's history as a continuation of Prussian military history, even if more recent trends in scholarship have focused not only on Prussia and to a lesser degree on Austria but on other German states as well.[35] Any specific "German" way of war is therefore generally considered to have emerged from Prussian traditions. Although it would be wrong to discount the influence of non-Prussian military tradition on the forces with which the German Empire entered the First World War, one can hardly deny the Prussian dominance in German military history of the latter half of the nineteenth century and the early decades of the twentieth.

In fact, it was Prussia's military successes that after the middle of the nineteenth century set in motion a wave of *imitatio Borussiae*, which saw other nations copying key elements of the Prussian military establishment.[36] Moreover, the Prussians set trends in military fashion, with spiked helmets suddenly enjoying an enormous popularity. Thus, it is hard to argue against a widespread Prussian military influence, when suddenly even the papal guardsmen were wearing *Pickelhaube* helmets.[37] As a consequence, the contemporaries of the German Empire interpreted its forces as essentially being extensions of the Prussian Army, a view that modern scholarship continues to emulate. Robert Citino shows how what is usually seen as characteristic for German military operations – rapid mobilization in times of war and the equally rapid movement of forces to outmaneuver the enemy, achieve a crushing victory, and thus pave the way for a favorable peace settlement – had its roots in a Prussian military tradition that went back to the seventeenth century.

---

[35] For an overview, see Abigail Green, "The Federal Alternative? A New View of Modern German History," *Historical Journal* 46 (2003), 187–202.

[36] See, for example, Trevor N. Dupuy, *A Genius for War: The German Army and General Staff, 1807–1945* (Upper Saddle River, NJ, 1977), 113–144.

[37] Paul Krieg, *Die Schweizergarde in Rom* (Luzern, 1960), 440.

That tradition had resulted originally from a specific set of circumstances – a lack of natural resources, a small recruiting base, vulnerable borders, and limited financial means – which affected the Electorate of Brandenburg.[38]

By the middle of the nineteenth century, Prussia had changed from a small, impoverished, rural, and predominantly Protestant yet fairly homogenous state into something quite different. The acquisition of territories in the eighteenth century, and even more so in the aftermath of the Napoleonic Wars, had resulted in Prussia turning into both a large and comparatively wealthy power and at the same time into a rather heterogeneous state with a significant Catholic population, particularly in its western provinces with their large cities. It still, however, shared long and vulnerable borders with Austria and Russia, two neighboring powers with whom it also shared a long history of conflict. It is not particularly surprising, then, that the idea of striking quickly (preferably first), hard, and decisively had firmly embedded itself in the Prussian military mind in the nineteenth century.

Although Prussia had been among Europe's premier military powers in 1815, only a generation later, budgetary constraints and a general lack of attention toward the army had turned it into a second-rate power, the army of which was fairly small and lacking in training. In 1835, Prussian artillery officer Karl von Decker, who was one of the leading tacticians of his time, complained that he had been "a brigadier for eight years, and I never commanded artillery in person during a peace manoeuvre, so I am lacking any practical experience."[39] That Prussia rose again around the middle of the century, eventually becoming continental Europe's premier land power in 1870, is inseparably connected with the career of Prussia's greatest general, Helmuth von Moltke. Appointed chief of Prussia's general staff in 1857, Moltke instigated a series of reforms that turned the Prussian Army into a formidable instrument of war. Moltke's attempts at reforming the army focused on three areas. First, in order to overcome the command and control problems caused by attempting to move large forces, he developed the concept of a war of movement, in which one large army did not move together, but rather several smaller forces, initially moving independently, outmaneuvered the enemy. Second, in order to make this war of movement possible, he reformed not only the army's organizational framework but also its mobilization process. After running Prussia's first railway exercise in 1858, he put great effort into improving and reorganizing the Prussian railway network to facilitate both easier mobilization and the rapid and efficient movement of forces across Prussia.[40] Third, in order to equip the newly reformed army, and in particular

[38] Robert M. Citino, *The German Way of War* (Lawrence, KS, 2005), xiii–xiv.
[39] Hermann von Müller, *Die Entwickelung der Feld-Artillerie in Bezug auf Material, Organisation und Taktik, von 1815 bis 1870* (Berlin, 1873), 88.
[40] Geoffrey Wawro, *Warfare and Society in Europe 1792–1914* (London, 2000), 83.

to enable it to cause maximum destruction, Moltke readily adopted modern military technology, even if untried. Thus the Prussian Army was one of the first larger armies to introduce a breech-loading rifle, the Dreyse *Zündnadelgewehr* (needle gun), and was also among the earliest users of breech-loading artillery, beginning with first experiments as early as 1851 and introducing a first breech-loading gun, the 6pdr C/61, in 1860.[41]

In addition to these three areas, Moltke placed great emphasis on the training of both staff and front officers, particularly trying to prepare them for the frictions that would invariably occur on the battlefield; that Prussian officers accepted friction as a fact of war and were prepared to deal with its consequences was quite possibly one of the main reasons for Prusso-German forces' successes in the nineteenth century. A key instrument in exposing officers to friction was the *Kriegsspiel*, with war games specifically designed to replicate the uncertainties one was likely to encounter on the battlefield.[42] Until 1871, the Prussian Army was the only military establishment in the world using war gaming as a regular training instrument. After the victory over France, war gaming spread rapidly throughout Europe and beyond, becoming what is probably Prussia's longest-lasting legacy.[43]

Moltke's reforms faced the test of reality in the wars of 1866 and 1870–1871. On the surface, they represented an outstanding success, which stunned contemporary observers. Prussian Army operations in these conflicts displayed a specific mind-set of many Prussian officers who saw, in addition to the importance of Clausewitz's theoretical approach as well as the study of the development of military doctrine, aggressive action as the key to operational success on the battlefield.[44] It was this aggressiveness that made many Prussian commanders instinctively turn toward an enemy and attack even against unfavorable odds. Traditionally, historians and military analysts have seen this approach as a positive element in Prussian command culture, an approach that would eventually develop into the fabled *Auftragstaktik* that was instrumental in bringing about Prussian and German success on the battlefield.[45] However, more recent scholarship has challenged the effectiveness of the aggressive and independent mind-set of Prussian officers, highlighting instead the operational dangers that such a command culture brought about.[46] Even in 1870, there was a thin line between independent action conducive to the plans of higher

---

[41] Müller, *Die Entwickelung der Feld-Artillerie*, 167–170.
[42] Jorit Wintjes, "When a Spiel Is Not a Game: The Prussian Kriegsspiel from 1824 to 1871," *Vulcan* 5(1) (2015), 5–28, 9–12.
[43] Ibid., 23–24.   [44] Citino, *German Way of War*, 138–141.
[45] For an example of independent action by noncommissioned officers, see Geoffrey Wawro, *The Franco-Prussian War* (Cambridge, 2003), 12; at present, it is unclear whether this was an exceptional case. See Marco Sigg, *Der Unterführer als Feldherr im Taschenformat. Theorie und Praxis der Auftragstaktik im deutschen Heer 1869–1945* (Paderborn, 2014), 180.
[46] Sigg, *Der Unterführer als Feldherr*, 177–252.

command and unauthorized action threatening them and jeopardizing the outcome of the battle.[47]

Moltke's concept of *Bewegungskrieg* possibly made matters worse; while it required commanders to act on their own, at the same time, they had to adhere to an overall plan that not only was complex but possibly was also beyond what an individual field commander could understand. As a result, commanders acting on their own initiative could cause entire campaign plans to unravel. For example, in 1866, Moltke had planned to have the Army of the Main under Vogel von Falckenstein surround the Hanoverian Army in order to prevent it from fully mobilizing and from joining forces with allies in southern Germany. Yet Falckenstein not only failed to encircle the Hanoverian Army, he also broke off the pursuit and turned toward Frankfurt instead, thereby endangering the entire operational plan.[48]

The "Prussian mind-set" also highlighted another rather serious problem: aggressiveness combined with independent-mindedness made the already thorny issue of command and control infinitely worse. Even without subordinates acting on their own initiative, Moltke and anyone else trying to fight a complex war of movement faced serious challenges. While weapons technology had made dramatic progress between 1848 and 1871, vastly increasing not only fighting capability but also the geographical extent of the battlefield, and while mass mobilization provided commanders with armies of unprecedented size, command and control capabilities had not developed at the same pace.

For example, field telegraphy was only introduced to the Prussian Army in 1870 and initially caused a rather less than enthusiastic response. Many officers paid little attention to the specific needs of communications personnel, such as keeping ordinary soldiers from turning poles into firewood.[49] Indeed, Moltke had already felt a distinct uneasiness about his actual capability of controlling what happened on a battlefield where half a million men fought each other. A closer look at some of the actions of the Austro-Prussian and Franco-Prussian wars suggests that far from being well-orchestrated pieces of *Bewegungskrieg*, they were in fact pretty chaotic engagements, with the overall commander in his headquarters getting information that was either outdated or wrong, and with subordinate commanders unable either to understand or to act on his orders, or simply unwilling to do so and openly questioning the authority of the overall commander instead. An outstanding example of the latter is Prussian general Albrecht von Manstein, who at the Battle of Königgrätz is said to have commented on an order by stating, "This is all very good, but who is General Moltke?"[50]

[47] Ibid., 180–181.   [48] Ibid., 185–186.
[49] Felix Buchholtz, *Ueber die Thätigkeit der Feldtelegraphen in den jüngsten Kriegen* (Berlin, 1880), 6.
[50] Citino, *German Way of War*, 171–172.

Simply put, the Prussian Army had a serious command and control problem, and as much as the capability of coming up with brilliant operational plans may have been "typically Prussian," the incapability of putting them into action as planned was not atypical for Prussian military operations. While by the outbreak of the First World War communications technology had slightly improved, with wireless telegraphy having entered service a few years earlier, the size of the armies had further increased, and exerting control over a large army was as much a problematic issue as it had been in 1866.

The Prussian successes in the Austro-Prussian and Franco-Prussian wars had two wide-reaching consequences for the Prussian Army as well as for Prussian society, and therefore to a significant extent on the German Empire, which came into being in 1871. For Prussian society, success resulted in the army gaining considerably in prestige. In the newly established German Empire, the army served as an important instrument of national unity, and the decades between 1871 and the outbreak of the First World War saw an increasing "militarization" of society. As far as the army was concerned, the war initiated discussions, which after 1871, initially concentrated, not unexpectedly, on the reasons for the Prussian success, and to some extent on what had not worked. Having been at the receiving end of rapid technological progress, with an infantry rifle capable of hitting targets at barely half the distance of their opponents, Prussian officers became increasingly aware of how technological progress continued to change the combat environment. Discussions in the military literature of the time focused more and more on how the seemingly ever-increasing firepower of the infantry made movement on the battlefield difficult. Apart from technological issues, reviewing the command and control problems revealed by operations in the Franco-Prussian War eventually resulted in attempts to formalize *Auftragstaktik* and to reign in commanders' tendency to act on their own. These attempts culminated in the 1887 *Felddienstordnung* (*FO*), sketching out general leadership requirements for officers, specific rules for giving and communicating orders, and general tactical as well as operational guidelines.[51] The 1887 *FO* underwent two revisions in 1890 and 1894 before being replaced in 1908 by a new *FO*, which remained in use until the end of the First World War.[52] While the latter

---

[51] Stephan Leistenschneider, *Auftragstaktik im preußisch-deutschen Heer 1871 bis 1914* (Hamburg, 2002), 69–72; Sigg, *Der Unterführer als Feldherr*, 60–61.

[52] On the 1890 and 1894 revisions, see Hans Peter Stein, "Zur Geschichte der Gefechtsarten: Angriff, Verteidigung, Verzögerung," in Hans-Martin Ottmer and Heiger Ostertag, eds., *Ausgewählte Operationen und ihre militärhistorischen Grundlagen* (Bonn, 1993), 106–248, at 160; on the 1908 *FO*, see Ralf Raths, *Vom Massensturm zur Stoßtrupptaktik. Die Deutsche Landkriegtaktik im Spiegel von Dienstvorschriften und Publizistik 1906–1918* (Freiburg, 2009), 68.

was a milestone in the development of tactics in the German Army, it still stressed decisive action as crucial for military success.[53]

The forces with which the German Empire entered the war in 1914 were, as discussed earlier in this chapter, quite different from the Prussian Army of the 1860s and 1870s. In addition, the nature of warfare had changed due to continuing technological progress, but even more so as the result of a significant increase in the numerical size of the armies. Simply put, whereas moving around about 220,000 men in Bohemia had been just possible in 1866, if already a command and control nightmare, trying to break into northern France with nearly seven times as many men resulted in problems on a scale unforeseen by the military thinkers of the nineteenth century.

Prussian officers, however, had not changed much, or so it seems. The initial battles on the Western Front brought remarkable successes and resulted not only in German forces beating back the initial French forays into Lorraine and overrunning large parts of Belgium, but also in eventually pushing the British Expeditionary Force and the French Fifth Army back to the Marne in an episode aptly named the Great Retreat. Nevertheless, there were still cases of local commanders acting out of their own initiative and without any regard for their orders, instances that were as stunning as Manstein's reply to Moltke's order at Königgrätz. An example from the Eastern Front underlines this all too clearly. In August 1914, Maximilian von Prittwitz, commander of the Eighth Army in East Prussia, faced a potentially massive onslaught of two Russian armies. As a consequence he decided to allow the Russian forces to cross the border with the Eighth Army fighting a series of defensive battles within East Prussia. He intended first to defeat the First Russian Army and then to turn on the Second Russian Army by leveraging East Prussia's railway network. While the events that followed would eventually prove Prittwitz right, one of his corps commanders, Hermann von Francois, commanding the I Army Corps, protested against what he believed was a fundamentally flawed plan.[54]

Realizing he went nowhere with his protests, Francois then blatantly decided to ignore his orders to retreat and moved his corps against the enemy, ending up forty kilometers in front of the Eighth Army. He also attempted to mask his actions by leaving his corps headquarters back in Insterburg. Francois then attacked the Russians at Stallupönen on August 17, and while the battle was a tactical victory, the movements of I Corps had cost the Eighth Army so much time that the whole operational plan nearly became unhinged.[55] Francois, one is tempted to say, carried on the tradition of

---

[53] *FO* 1908, § 38 (p. 16): "So bleibt entschlossenes Handeln das erste Erfordernis im Kriege."

[54] Dennis Showalter, *Tannenberg: Clash of Empires* (Hamden, 1991), 155.

[55] Friedrich-August Schack, "Operative Führungsprobleme in Vergangenheit und Gegenwart," *Deutsche Wehr* 46 (1942), 670–672, at 672.

Prussian corps and divisional commanders wrecking their superiors' plans by acting out of their own initiative and the belief that engaging the enemy was the first duty of an officer.

Conversely, the German high command, the Oberste Heeresleitung (OHL), was not beyond shrinking from giving operational guidance where necessary. Marco Sigg has pointed to a particularly striking example involving the Bavarian Army, which at the beginning of the war, had formed the Sixth Army commanded by Crown Prince Rupprecht, who also had the Seventh Army under his command. Rupprecht was originally supposed to guard Lorraine and the left German flank against any French incursion. When, however, his forces defeated the initial probing attacks by the French, Rupprecht intended to commence offensive operations of his own. The OHL opposed any such operations. Nevertheless, instead of setting out clear orders for the Sixth and Seventh Armies, the *Generalquartiermeister* at the OHL, Hermann von Stein, suggested to the Sixth Army command that "the responsibility was theirs," a statement that is more than only mildly surprising given that the main responsibility of the OHL was guiding the conduct of the overall Schlieffen Plan.[56]

On the whole, the German command effort at the beginning of the war clearly left something to be desired, and control problems caused by large armies and insufficient means of communications meant the German campaign in 1914 ultimately failed. After trench warfare had set in, the German high command looked for tactical solutions to the impasse and from 1915 onward developed new tactics stressing the independence of decision makers down to the company level. Later in the war, this would gain fame as *Stoßtrupptaktik*, which many historians believe was responsible for the initial successes in the German spring offensives of 1918. Nevertheless, while on the surface the *Stoßtrupptaktik* appeared as the 1918 equivalent of the *Auftragstaktik* of the preceding century, reality was somewhat different. By the latter half of the war, company and battalion commanders often lacked the necessary training required for successfully applying mission tactics, and higher-ranking officers were fully aware of this weakness.[57] At any rate, German high command was not exactly enthusiastic about keeping forces on a long leash. In fact, already in October 1917, during the Battle of Passchendaele, Crown Prince Rupprecht complained about the constant meddling of Ludendorff and the OHL in the running of his operations: "General Ludendorff ... is on the phone every moment asking questions. The constant stream of tactical orders is distracting." It obviously did not require real-time imagery for

---

[56] Sigg, *Der Unterführer als Feldherr*, 212.   [57] Ibid., 217–218.

high-ranking officers to succumb to the temptation of micromanagement. A simple telephone could prove a powerful tool as well.[58]

After the war, the Reichswehr, while required to cut nearly all ties to the army of the German Empire, was consciously built up by Seeckt around a core of Prussian traditions. It is hardly surprising, then, that when in 1921 a new doctrinal publication (*Führung und Gefecht der verbundenen Waffen*) finally replaced the 1908 *Felddienstordnung*, it not only covered the lessons learned with regard to the challenge of technology but also connected directly to the concept of *Auftragstaktik* as originally envisioned in the latter half of the nineteenth century. For Seeckt, who intended to fight a war of movement inside Germany in case of a French or Polish invasion, field commanders who were capable of acting on their own without jeopardizing the overall plan were as important as they had been for Moltke half a century earlier. With an officer corps of only 4,000 men, Seeckt stood a much better chance of preparing his officers for such a challenge.

Indeed, one could argue that for the 1871–1945 period, the officer corps reached its highest level of training and came closest to being capable of putting *Auftragstaktik* into practice in the years between 1921 and 1933. From an operational point of view, it was Seeckt's Reichswehr that embodied every-thing that is often identified as "Prussian" or even "German" leadership culture. However, for all its quality and high standard of training, the Reichswehr faced a problem that was essentially unsolvable. While producing what was probably the most professional army Germany had ever possessed, it was at the same time supposed to form the cadre of a much larger army to be mobilized in time of war. This would have meant not only swelling the ranks with ordinary soldiers but also adding considerable numbers of officers who did not have the same level of training and the same capability of acting independently as the Reichswehr officers. The overall level of competence was, therefore, bound to fall in case of a mobilization, calling into question whether Seeckt's operational concepts would have worked in case of a war.

While the Truppenamt was aware of this problem as early as 1927, the Reichswehr planning of the 1920s was never put into practice.[59] This changed rather suddenly with the reorganization of the army and the rapid increase of the 1933–1939 years through the introduction of general conscription. Now

---

[58] Stefan Kaufmann, "Telefon und Krieg – oder: Von der Macht der Liebe zur Schlacht ums Netz," in Jürgen Bräunlein and Bernd Flesner, eds., *Der sprechende Knochen: Perspektiven von Telefonkulturen* (Würzburg, 2000), 10–28, at 11–12; already in 1911 Prussian military theore-tician Hugo von Freytag-Loringhoven, who held a number of divisional commands during the war, ending it as deputy chief of the general staff, was highly critical of the constant use of the telephone by the OHL. See Hugo von Freytag-Loringhoven, *Die Macht der Persönlichkeit im Kriege. Studien nach Clausewitz* (Berlin, 1905), 179–180.

[59] Jürgen Förster, *Die Wehrmacht im NS-Staat. Eine strukturgeschichtliche Analyse* (München, 2007), 14.

large numbers of officers and men had to be accommodated into the army, and as a result the training, particularly of younger officers, suffered to the point that in the late 1930s, there were increased warnings to pay closer attention to the quality of officer training.[60] This offers some insights into the problems the Reichswehr would have faced when trying to form a larger army by mobilizing in an even shorter period of time. Even so, the army that entered the Second World War still had former Reichswehr personnel in strength, displaying in the Polish and Norwegian campaigns as well as in the attack on France a high level of training.

At the same time, the issue of independent action by officers again raised its head, the campaign against France providing examples that are not too dissimilar from what had happened in East Prussia in autumn 1914. To take but one occurrence, when the XIX Army Corps under the command of Heinz Guderian reached the Meuse River near Sedan on May 12, 1940, its commander decided to force a river crossing there and then, even though his superior, Heinrich von Kleist, had explicitly ordered him to move further west before trying to cross. In planning his attack on Sedan, Guderian wanted to rely on constant close air support by dive bombers (*Stukas*), a tactical concept he had developed together with the commander of II Fliegerkorps, Bruno Loerzer. However, Loerzer's superior, Hugo Sperrle, who commanded Luftflotte 3, had agreed to a request by Kleist to support the attack by an area bombardment and had ordered Loerzer to do so. This order reached Loerzer probably on May 12, 1940, yet he simply ignored it, confessing later to Guderian that he did not forward the order to the units under his command.[61]

Throughout the whole campaign, Guderian would repeatedly ignore orders not only by Kleist, but, in the aftermath of the forcing of the Meuse, also by the army high command and even by Hitler himself. Guderian clearly saw the plans of his superiors as a hindrance to his own operational planning, saying so quite openly in his memoirs.[62] His superiors tolerated his actions up to a point, as they ended in operational successes, although they caused immense friction within the German command structure, culminating in Kleist briefly removing Guderian from his post on May 17, 1940.[63] In general, it should not come as a surprise that not only Guderian but also other panzer corps commanders as well had a tendency to act on their own; their behavior had its roots in the mission tactics culture of the Prussian Army. By the time of the outbreak of the Second World War, the new technology of fast-moving tanks had lent considerable

---

[60] Sigg, *Der Unterführer als Feldherr*, 230–231.
[61] Karl-Heinz Frieser, *Blitzkrieg-Legende. Der Westfeldzug 1940* (München, 1995), 187–190.
[62] Heinz Guderian, *Erinnerungen eines Soldaten* (Heidelberg, 1951), 80.
[63] Frieser, *Blitzkrieg-Legende*, 316–319; Guderian, *Erinnerungen*, 98.

support to those advocating independent action, and as a consequence, some commanders went so far as to ignore direct orders.[64]

Conclusion

This brief review of German operational thinking from the mid-nineteenth century makes obvious that German military affairs were to a large degree dominated throughout the period by Prussian military thinking. And while some of the examples discussed earlier in this chapter suggest that Prusso-German mastery of the art of operational warfare was not quite as total as some have assumed, one could nevertheless argue that from an operational point of view, German military history of the 1871–1945 period was indeed a direct continuation of Prussian military history. Therefore, approaches that focus on the continuing lines of development linking Prussian military history with the post-1871 period are fully justified and can serve well to improve the understanding of what lay at the core of Prusso-German operational thinking.

However, an examination looking beyond the level of operations, as well as strategy not covered in this chapter, reveals that there is more to German military history than just operational thinking. German military forces had a cultural background that was as varied as their operational thinking was unified. Even after more than forty years of existence, the army of the German Empire, while outwardly uniform at the beginning of the First World War, still reflected the history of the empire. The army had evolved from the German Confederation and some states were guarding their remaining authority, which in the case of Bavaria included full military autonomy, with considerable vigilance. During the decades after the First World War, the German Army turned first into a small, elite force embodying the traditions of the old Prussian Army, then into a mass army, and finally into a force transcending the boundaries of the nation-state.

These rather significant changes in character, however, had apparently little impact on the development of operational thinking within the German forces. The discrepancy between its cultural background on one hand and its operational thinking on the other has attracted fairly little scholarly attention, if compared with other aspects of German military history. Even so, whatever their operational capabilities, it may in fact be this discrepancy between the cultural background of German armed forces and their operational thinking that is more typically German than anything else.

---

[64] Frieser, *Blitzkrieg-Legende*, 426–427.

6   The Culture of the Indian Army, 1900–1947

An Evolving Identity

Daniel Marston

Attempting to define military culture is a difficult task. Don Snider has defined it as comprising various elements including discipline, professional ethos, etiquette, cohesion, and *esprit de corps*.[1] Williamson Murray describes military culture as representing "the ethos and professional attributes, both in terms of experience and intellectual study, that contribute to a common core under-standing of the nature of war within military organizations."[2] This chapter attempts to identify and assess the culture and climate of the British Indian Army in the first half of the twentieth century through three core themes: recruitment, "Indianization" of the officer corps, and the ability of the army to adapt to the spectrum of conflict. These elements came to define a culture in the Indian Army that was distinct from that of its cousin, the British Army, or of other Dominion forces during the same period. The culture of the Indian Army rested on a firm foundation of its history and ethos, but it was also adaptable enough to deal with the changing environment that occurred outside its domains. The Indian soldier of 1945 would have been well imbued with the history and ethos of his great-grandfather, but he would also have understood that the army of 1945 looked and differed considerably from that of the army of 1880, particularly in the types of people who served and commanded.

    The Indian Army faced fundamental changes to its identity in the first half of the twentieth century, from those who served in its ranks to how they were recruited to who ended up in command within it. Unlike many other armies of the same era, it also faced challenging operations across the spectrum of conflict, from internal security operations to high-end conventional war against peer enemies. The Indian Army faced significant challenges and experienced setbacks; however, with independence on the horizon during the Second World War, the army reformed and performed at the highest levels of professionalism,

---

[1] Don Snider, "An Uniformed Debate on Military Culture," *Orbis* (Winter 1999), 14–18.
[2] Williamson Murray, "Does Military Culture Matter?" *Orbis* (Winter 1999), 27.

especially in 1944 and 1945. In fact, its performance in the Second World War was the high-water mark of the largest all-volunteer army in history.

Another subtheme that runs through this period of time is that of the role of the British Indian Army's final commander in chief, Field Marshal Sir Claude Auchinleck.[3] Murray writes that "another major factor in military culture is the generational change that occurs in military organizations as the collective experience of the senior officer corps evolve[s] with the passage of time."[4] Auchinleck was a core element of the Indian Army's evolving cultural identity. His career spanned the years focused on here, and he came to be affectionately known, by soldiers and officers alike, as the father of the Indian Army. His direction and influence steered the army onto paths that would secure its professional reputation for years to come.

A British Indian Army officer, John Masters, in an anecdote from his memoirs captures best the changes that the organization experienced during this period, and the cultural identity that grew out of them:

> As the tanks burst away down the road to Rangoon … it took possession of the empire we had built … Twenty races, a dozen religions, a score of languages passed in those trucks and tanks. When my great-great-grandfather first went to India there had been as many nations; now there was one – India … It was all summed up in the voice of an Indian colonel of artillery. Now the Indian, bending close to an English colonel over a map, straightened and said with a smile, "O.K., George. Thanks. I've got it. We'll take over all tasks at 1800. What about a beer?"[5]

Recruitment

The recruitment structure of the old English East India Company (EIC) Army (later the Indian Army) during the eighteenth and early nineteenth centuries was drastically different from that of the twentieth-century Indian Army.[6] The

---

[3] Auchinleck served with the 62nd Punjab Regiment, later the 1/1st Punjab Regiment, and won a Distinguished Service Order in the First World War. He served as an instructor at the Indian Staff College, Quetta, and commanded the Peshawar Brigade during the Mohmand operations of 1935. He later became commander in chief of the Indian Army on two occasions during the Second World War, and is considered a man of "reforming ideals" by many ex-Indian officers and men. He was a champion of the Indian officer and so-called non-martial races. He disliked the prewar segregation system and was not inclined to believe that there were only specific martial races in the country. He is a large figure in this work for his ability, his desire to reform the army, and his position as commander in chief, India, from mid-1943 until the end of the Raj in August 1947. See John Connell, *Auchinleck: A Critical Biography* (London, 1959) for a definitive study of this very important military commander.

[4] Murray, "Does Military Culture Matter?" 30.

[5] John Masters, *The Road Past Mandalay: A Personal Narrative* (London, 1961), 312–313.

[6] See the following works for more detail on this period of the EIC: Douglas Peers,*Between Mars and Mammon: Colonial Armies and the Garrison State in Early 19th Century India* (London, 1995); Channa Wickremesekera, *Best Black Troops in the World: British Perceptions and the*

EIC was divided into the three presidencies of Bombay, Bengal, and Madras, each of which fielded its own units. By the late 1750s, the British had adopted the French practice of recruiting local Indians as sepoys and training them in "continental" or traditional European linear warfare style.[7] However, as the nineteenth century progressed and the British EIC became dominant, the recruiting practices of the various presidencies changed. Madras tended to recruit from the Madras region, from all classes, which meant that no one class dominated its army. The Bombay Army followed a similar process.[8] The army of the Bengal presidency was different. At the beginning of the 1760s, many of its soldiers came from the Rajput and Brahmin castes. Over the next fifty years, however, the Bengal Army chose to recruit almost exclusively from the high-caste members of the Awadh region.[9] By the early 1800s, the Bengal Army was the dominant force of the three presidencies, but some felt that it had become too segregated.

After the First and Second Anglo-Sikh Wars of the 1840s, the Bengal Army began to recruit from the Punjab region.[10] The Sikhs had created a reputable army of Muslims, Hindus, and Sikhs drilled in the European fashion. After the wars ended, the British recruited some of the defeated army into the Punjab Irregular Force (later the Punjab Frontier Force) and allowed recruitment within the Bengal infantry units stationed in the Punjab.[11] For the most part, however, opposition to opening up the regular regiments of the Bengal Army to former soldiers of the Sikh army persisted for a variety of reasons, including

Making of the Sepoy, 1746–1805 (New Delhi, 2002); Raymond Callahan, *The East India Company and Army Reform* (Cambridge, MA, 1972); Amiya Barat, *The Bengal Native Infantry: Its Organisation and Discipline, 1796–1852* (Calcutta, 1962); V. Longer, *Red Coats to Olive Green: A History of the Indian Army, 1600–1974* (Bombay, 1974); Kaushik Roy, ed., *War and Society in Colonial India* (New Delhi, 2006); Kaushik Roy, "The Armed Expansion of the English East India Company: 1740s–1849," in Daniel Marston and Chandar Sundaram, eds., *A Military History of India and South Asia* (Westport, CT, 2007); Nile Green, *Islam and the Army in Colonial India: Sepoy Religion in the Service of Empire* (Cambridge, 2009); and Seema Alavi, *Sepoys and the Company* (New Delhi, 1995).

[7] From the Persian word *sipah*, meaning army.

[8] See Heather Streets, *Martial Races: The Military, Race, and Masculinity in the British Imperial Culture, 1857–1914* (Manchester, 2004); Tan Tai Yong, *The Garrison State: The Military, Government and Society in Colonial Punjab, 1849–1947* (New Delhi, 2005); Susan Bayly, "Caste and Race in the Colonial Ethnography of India," in Peter Robb, ed., *The Concept of Race in South Asia* (Oxford, 1995); Stephen Cohen, "The Untouchable Soldier: Caste, Politics, and the Indian Army," *Journal of Asian Studies*, 28 (1969); Douglas Peers, "The Martial Races and the Indian Army in the Victorian Era," in Daniel Marston and Chandar Sundaram, eds., *A Military History of India and South Asia*; and David Omissi, *The Sepoy and the Raj: The Indian Army 1860–1940* (Basingstoke, 1994). It is interesting to compare their definitions and discussions of classes, castes, martial races, and the central role of the Punjab in recruitment with Lt. Gen. Sir George MacMunn, *Martial Races of India* (London, 1933).

[9] Alavi, *Sepoys and the Company*, 292–295.

[10] See Tan, *The Garrison State*, for a detailed description of the role of the Punjab in recruitment for the Indian Army.

[11] Close to 14,000 men.

professional jealousy, suspicion of Sikhs, and ongoing assertions from British authorities on the necessity of demilitarizing the Punjab.[12]

The reluctance to recruit from the Punjab changed with the Indian Mutiny of 1857.[13] During the Mutiny, eighteen new regiments raised from the Punjab remained loyal throughout the crisis. With the Punjab Irregular Force and the new regiments, this meant more than 50,000 men under arms in the Punjab who were loyal to the British suppression of the mutinous Bengal army regiments in northern India.[14]

The threat presented by Russia and the Second Afghan War (1879–1881) further reinforced recruitment for the Indian Army toward the northern and northwestern regions.[15] The reinforcement began with the report of the 1879 Eden Commission, which recommended significant reforms. Among these were the creation of an army corps that would fall under the command of a single commander in chief, which would obviate the need for the three separate commander in chief positions in existence at that time. Other suggestions included formally bringing the Punjab Frontier Force under army command, further recruitment of troops from the Punjab region, and downsizing the Madras Army.

Field Marshal Lord Roberts of Kandahar was appointed commander in chief, India, in 1885.[16] Lord Roberts stated: "I have no hesitation myself in stating that except Gurkhas, Dogras, Sikhs, the pick of Punjabi Muhammadans, Hindustanis of the Jat and Ranghur casts … certain classes of Pathans, there are no Native soldiers in our service whom we could venture with safety to place in the field against the Russians."[17] The recruitment drive to bring more northern Indians into the Bengal Army, later expanded to the army as a whole,

---

[12] Tan, *The Garrison State*, 37–39.

[13] The Indian Mutiny has been the topic of hundreds of books and articles since 1857. The following works are a good starting point for understanding its complexities: G. B. Malleson, ed., *Kaye's and Malleson's History of the Indian Mutiny of 1857–8*, 6 vols. (London: 1898); Philip Mason, *A Matter of Honour: An Account of the Indian Army, Its Officers and Men* (London, 1974); S. N. Sen, *Eighteen Fifty-Seven* (New Delhi, 1957); C. A. Bayly and Eric Stokes, *The Peasant Armed: The Indian Revolt of 1857* (Oxford, 1986); Saul David, *The Indian Mutiny: 1857* (London, 2002); J. A. B. Palmer, *Mutiny Outbreak at Meerut* (Cambridge, 1966); Rudrangshu Mukherjee, *Mangal Pandy: Brave Martyr or Accidental Hero?* (New Delhi, 2005); Peter Stanley, *The White Mutiny: British Military Culture in India 1825–1875* (New York, 1998); and Raymond Callahan, "The Great Sepoy Mutiny," in Daniel Marston and Chandar Sundaram, eds., *A Military History of India and South Asia* (Westport, CT, 2007).

[14] Tan, *The Garrison State*, 48.

[15] The recruitment of Gurkhas from Nepal was also expanded, in recognition of their perceived loyalty and performance during the same period. The Bengal Army in 1870 had forty-nine infantry regiments, of which the Gurkhas and other "hill people" made up four and the Punjab sixteen; the rest came from outside the Punjab and Nepal. Ibid., 54–55.

[16] Commander in chief of the Madras Army, 1880–1885; commander in chief of the Bengal Army (hence unofficial commander in chief of all three presidencies), 1885–1893.

[17] See C. H. Philips, ed., *Select Documents on the History of India and Pakistan, vol. 4, The Evolution of India and Pakistan, 1858–1947* (London, 1964), 517. See also Gen. Roberts's comments in his book *Forty-One Years in India* (London, 1898), 531–532, for an interesting perspective.

was the product of what became known as the martial race theory.[18] This assertion – that some groups were martial and others were non-martial – was to have lasting repercussions in India. Thus, the British deemed many classes of Indians, such as Bengalis and numerous groups from southern India, "non-martial" and, as a result, excluded them from the army.[19] The British now favored the northern areas of India, especially the Punjab, as their main recruiting grounds. Even so, not all northern classes or peoples were acceptable. People who lived in cities and towns were not considered to be of the correct stock – only those from the countryside. By 1893, 44 percent of the Indian Army was drawing recruits from the martial races.[20]

On the eve of the First World War, of the 552 infantry companies in the Indian Army as a whole, 211 were composed of men from the Punjab, 121 were from the Frontier region, 80 companies were Gurkhas, and the remaining troops came from the other regions of acceptable classes.[21] Overall, by 1914, 75 percent of the Indian Army was recruited from the martial races.[22]

During the First World War, the traditional system of recruitment, with heavy emphasis on the Punjab, continued for at least the first years.[23] As the war

---

[18] Between the circumstances of the Mutiny and the influence of opinions of officers who had served in the Punjab, races such as the Bengalis and Madrassis came to be widely considered non-martial. As Thomas Metcalf noted, "whether defined by race, climate, or personality, martial races were those who most closely resembled what the British imagined themselves to be ... they were what the Bengali was not." Thomas Metcalf, *Ideologies of the Raj* (Cambridge, 1995), 127. See also Omissi, *The Sepoy and the Raj*; Streets, *Martial Races*; MacMunn, *Martial Races of India*; Tan, *The Garrison State*; and Roberts, *Forty-One Years in India* for more discussion of the concept of "martial races."

[19] "Class" was used to denote a given tribe or ethnic grouping within the army.

[20] Streets, *Martial Races*, 100.

[21] The reason for the breakdown in the companies list is that most infantry battalions and cavalry regiments were composed of various class companies or squadrons. This practice, which had been started before the Mutiny, was reinforced afterward, in the belief that if a battalion had a three- or four-company mixture of classes, it would be more difficult for the unit to unify in a common revolt. However, during the Mutiny, whole units of Muslims and Hindus did join together in open revolt. Not all regiments followed the practice of creating different class companies (the 14th and 15th Sikh were entirely composed of Jat Sikhs and the Gurkha regiments were all Hindu). Omissi, *The Sepoy and the Raj*, 19.

[22] Streets, *Martial Races*, 100. See also the chapter "Recruiting in the Punjab: 'Martial Races' and the Military Districts," in Tan, *The Garrison State*, for more detail on the specific recruiting grounds, as well as motivating factors for the various recruits and the beginning of the "garrison state" concept in the Punjab.

[23] For detail on the professional performance of the Indian Army in the First World War, see Charles Chenevix-Trench, *The Indian Army and the King's Enemies, 1901–1947* (London, 1996); George Morton-Jack, *Indian Army on the Western Front* (Cambridge, 2014); G. Corrigan, *Sepoys in the Trenches: The Indian Corps on the Western Front: 1914–1915* (London, 1996); and specific chapters in Kaushik Roy, ed., *The Indian Army in the Two World Wars* (Amsterdam, 2011). An important perspective from the "ranks" is available in David Omissi, *Indian Voices of the Great War: Soldiers' Letters, 1914–1918* (London, 1994); and Nikolas Gardner, *Trial by Fire: Command and Control and the British Expeditionary Force in 1914* (Westport, CT, 2003).

expanded and there was more need for Indian troops, the structure suffered increasing strain, reaching a crisis point in 1915.[24] As a result, the army abandoned much of the prewar class recruitment system, and in the Punjab opened up other areas. It added twenty-two new classes to the recruitment list, and in 1917, a new system of territorial recruitment began.[25] Regimental officers and depots were established in regions where no recruitment had ever happened before. Numerous classes were discovered who had not previously been recruited and who were suitable candidates for army service. As one Indian civil servant noted: "there was also considerable exclusiveness on the part of the army; certain tribes capable of providing excellent material were barred by reason of some real or fancied social objection."[26] Whole regions of the Punjab opened up to recruitment from a variety of regiments, not just steered into specific units. By the end of the First World War, the Punjab had supplied more than 40 percent of all recruits for the combatant arms of the Indian Army. It came down to one soldier out of every 26 men, compared to the rest of India, which provided one soldier of every 150 men mobilized.[27] Three-fourths of all Indian Army recruits in this period came from the Punjab and the recruiting grounds of the United Province.[28] Even with this dominance, other peoples from across India who had previously been dropped from the Army List were once again considered eligible.[29] The performance of some of the "non-martial races" in the First World War sparked debate and attempts to bolster support for them, but the controversy was short-lived.

Recruitment for the Indian Army in the interwar period followed pre–First World War practices. Initially, the Government of India wished for a large postwar standing army that would encompass many of the newly raised units and expanded classes of people. The idea behind this was that it would be easy to recruit and keep up reserves for any future conflict. Unfortunately, the Government of India had to cut back due to the financial constraints of the 1920s and 1930s, and when the axe fell, the first units to suffer were the newly raised. Under pressure, the government followed the old line of sticking to prewar martial race theory.[30]

[24] Indian Army formations served on the Western Front and in East Africa, Gallipoli, Mesopotamia, and Palestine, as well as in normal internal security duties in India.
[25] Tan, *The Garrison State*, 108–117.
[26] M. S. Leigh, *The Punjab and the War* (Lahore, 1922), 34.
[27] Ibid., 41. See also pages 59–62 for complete lists of the recruits from the different districts in the Punjab.
[28] "The Simon Commission on Army Recruitment, 1930," in C. H. Philips, ed., *Select Documents on the History of India and Pakistan, vol. 4, The Evolution of India and Pakistan, 1858–1947* (London, 1964), 533.
[29] Coorgs, Mahars, Mappilas, and 51,000 men from Madras. Omissi, *The Sepoy and the Raj*, 38.
[30] Within other units, the class compositions were streamlined, with an overwhelming focus on the Punjab and northern India. The 2/1st Punjab Regiment was designated to have two companies of Punjabi Musalmans, one of Jat Sikhs, and one of Rajputs. The Jats who had been part of the

The findings of the Simon Commission on Army Recruitment in 1930 further reinforced the bias toward the martial race recruitment practice. It openly stated that "broadly speaking, one may say that those races [martial] which furnish the best sepoys are emphatically not those which exhibit the greatest accomplishments of mind in an examination."[31] It also highlighted that in 1930, the Punjab provided 54 percent of all recruits for the army (and if one did not include the Gurkha regiments, this number rose to 62 percent). The report went on to elaborate that, due to economic conditions, it was best to recruit from the traditional groups to ensure professionalism and fighting ability. It also stated that, while Indian politicians wished for more Indian unity as embodied in the army, the politicians did not understand the role of the army and that such a vision would take years to achieve due to the competing religions and ongoing racial tensions. It clearly stated that defense problems in India were quite complex, and that the political push for self-government did not fully comprehend this complexity.[32]

By 1939, the composition of the Indian Army was similar to its 1914 counterpart, relying heavily on a select group of classes and martial races of Indians, mostly from the Punjab, for all of its recruitment needs. As had occurred in the First World War, the exhaustion of the limited recruiting pool also became a problem early in the Second World War, especially in the Punjab.

The Second World War precipitated a period of unprecedented expansion for the Indian Army. Between 1939 and 1945, the Army expanded from 200,000 to more than 2.5 million men and officers, even though the government never imposed conscription. The Indian Army began the war as the "Imperial Reserve" for the British government, and by its end had lost 24,000 killed, 64,000 wounded, 60,000 captured,[33] and 11,000 missing on active service.[34]

Throughout the Second World War, the Indian Army also faced fundamental questions about its existence, size, and composition.[35] Recruitment expanded, as it had in the First World War, to include South Asian ethnic groups long dismissed as

battalion were sent to other regiments or were disbanded. The other two prewar battalions followed their previous rules. The 1/11th Sikh recruited only Jat Sikhs and the 4/12th FFR and 2/13th FFR all had one company each of PMs, Sikhs, Dogras, and Pathans. No. A-8552-1 L/MIL/7/5483 Oriental and India Office Collection (OIOC), British Library (BL) and Indian Army List 1930.

[31] Simon Commission, 532.

[32] Ibid. See the Indian Statutory Commission, Cmd 3568 (1930), *vol.* I for more details.

[33] Most of these men were captured early in the war in the Malayan and First Burma campaigns of 1941–1942.

[34] S. L. Menezes, *Fidelity & Honour: The Indian Army from the Seventeenth to the Twenty-First Century* (New Delhi, 1993), 370.

[35] Questions were raised in certain quarters about whether the Indian Army needed to be expanded. Prime Minister Winston Churchill in particular denigrated the Indian Army's efforts throughout the war, even after it had undertaken significant reforms, conclusively defeated the Imperial Japanese Army, and played an important supporting role in the successful East African, North African, and Italian campaigns. See Raymond Callahan's work in *Churchill and His*

"non-martial." The rapid expansion of the Indian Army placed a significant strain on the areas from which recruits were traditionally drawn, especially in the Punjab, which by 1943 was providing 36 percent of all soldiers recruited into the army.[36] Rapid expansion placed noticeable strain on the resources of the traditional recruitment areas, and GHQ India headquarters realized that it had to broaden recruitment to other areas and groups. It undertook this decision tentatively at first, by taking Madrassis and others into the expanding service corps of the army. Following Gen. Sir Claude Auchinleck's appointment as commander in chief, recruitment reform became more decisive. Auchinleck stated that "as regards to recruitment of the rank and file I have no doubt at all that apart from political considerations we must broaden our basis and this was already in hand before I arrived. I propose to continue and hasten the process. There is plenty of good untouched material which we can and should use."[37]

Neither did Auchinleck intend to confine recruitment from non-martial races to the service corps. He specifically suggested that new infantry units should be raised to represent the other provinces.[38] He asserted that these units were not to be for show only, but would be used alongside other units in fighting the war. He recognized the political dimensions of this move, stating that "it will greatly help in meeting the political demand for the wider representation in the army."[39] Leo Amery, as secretary of state for India, recognized and accepted these proposals, and was disappointed when Churchill appointed Auchinleck commander in chief of the Middle East in June 1941, taking him away from the opportunity to implement them personally.[40]

The recruitment of non-martial races had been stepped up from 1940 to 1942, but there was still a faction in GHQ India that doubted their potential as fighting troops. Many of the new recruits were sent to non-infantry or cavalry services within the army, as well as to the Indian Army Service Corps, signals, engineers, and artillery.[41] A report published in February 1942 documents

Generals (Lawrence, KS, 2007) for a detailed discussion of the tensions between Churchill and his Indian Army commanders, chiefly Gens. Claude Auchinleck and William Slim.

[36] Tan, *The Garrison State*, 290–291.
[37] Auchinleck to Amery, March 17, 1941, Auchinleck Papers, University of Manchester.
[38] When he was commander in chief, Middle East, the Assam, Bihar, Chamar, and Afidi regiments were raised.
[39] Auchinleck to Amery, March 17, 1941, Auchinleck Papers, University of Manchester.
[40] Amery stated that he was sad to lose him due to his great work for the Indian war effort and his point of view on certain issues relevant to the army. Amery to Auchinleck, June 25, 1941, Auchinleck Papers, University of Manchester.
[41] Infantry units besides the Sikh Light Infantry and the Madras Regiment were raised from the new classes: four battalions of the Bihar Regiment, of which the 1st Battalion saw active service in Burma; three battalions of the Assam Regiment, of which the 1st Battalion saw service in Burma; five battalions of the Mahar Regiment, although none saw active service; four battalions of the Ajmer Regiment; and two battalions of the Chamar Regiment, of which one served in Burma. None of these units saw active service until 1944 and 1945; prior to this, they were all held in reserve.

38,000 recruits from non-martial races enlisted, of whom 33,000 were stationed in India. Meanwhile, "martial races" such as Jat Sikhs and Punjabi Musalmans (PMs) reported numbers at 50 percent stationed in India and 50 percent overseas.[42] A report by the adjutant general's office in late 1942 argued for recruitment from non-martial races by making the claim that the performance of PMs, Dogras, and Jat Sikhs in the field was declining. The report also documented how many of the new units were lacking in junior leaders, and recommended that this be remedied quickly – noting, however, that "foreign" Viceroy Commissioned Officers (VCOs) or British noncommissioned officers (NCOs) were not the answer.[43] In a war staff communiqué to London, GHQ India formally announced that "the former distinction of martial and non-martial race has been removed."[44] By mid-1943, there were still those within the Indian Army who were willing to concede that the recruitment of non-martial races was necessary, but who continued to assert that it should not be done too quickly.

The return of Auchinleck as commander in chief, India, for a second stint in late June 1943 brought a strong supporter of expanding recruitment and training of non-martial race troops for battle. His arrival coincided with the aftermath of the First Arakan defeat in Burma, when the British government was calling for the Indian Army to be downsized. Churchill stated clearly what he felt the problems were, but he failed to recognize the significance of the tactical errors those in command had committed in battle, which were subsequently rectified. He was also apparently unaware that non-martial race units had not seen active service in the campaigns.[45] They had all been stationed in India or near the front on lines of communication duties. During the summer of 1943, the British government called upon the Indian Army to reduce the numbers of units and formations. Auchinleck viewed this as a signal that the British government had lost confidence in the Indian Army and that this loss was partly due to the expanded recruitment of non-martial races. In a letter of response to the viceroy, Field Marshal Wavell, Auchinleck described in some detail his thoughts and feelings on the topic of non-martial races and the government's attitude. "The idea underlying the demand for reduction seems to be based upon the idea that the Indian Army is now composed to a large

---

[42] 1/2/42 L/WS/1/456 Class Composition of the Army in India OIOC, BL.
[43] 3/11/42 L/WS/968 OIOC, BL.   [44] 17/2/43L/WS/1/136 OIOC, BL
[45] Even Leo Amery stated, in a letter to Linlithgow on August 27, 1942, the following point: "Congress has nothing in common with the fighting races of India of whom well over a million have volunteered for the Army during the present war." Nicholas Mansergh and E. W. R. Lumby, eds., *Transfer of Power: 1942–7*, 14 vols. (London, 1970–1984), 2:830. Hereafter cited as *TOP*.

extent of men who because they belong to classes previously untried as soldiers are unreliable and unsuitable."[46]

By the end of the war, the recruitment totals indicate a preference for the prewar classes, but this is partly attributable to the recruitment bias that was still extant during the early part of the war. The numbers of the new class recruits rose steadily toward the end of the war,[47] although the Punjab was still heavily represented.[48]

Transformation of the Officer Corps

A system of British officers and Native (later Viceroy) Commissioned Officers officered the EIC Army and the Indian Army for more than 100 years.[49] Indians could not receive commissions from Addiscombe, the EIC officer training academy, or, later, from the Royal Military College, Sandhurst, or the Royal Military Academy, Woolwich, until the 1920s.[50] Only white British officers were put in charge of battalions or regiments until the Second World War. The reasons for these decisions were fear of a lack of loyalty, and that Indians were not considered capable of leading battalions or regiments in the field, a myth perpetuated for many years.[51]

[46] Auchinleck to Wavell, "Size and Composition of the India Army," August 2, 1943, Auchinleck Papers, University of Manchester.
[47] "New class" implies units raised during the Second World War. Many of the peoples had served in either the EIC Army or the Indian Army but had fallen out of favor at different periods.
[48] Jat Sikhs 88 percent; Kumaonis 50 percent; Pathans 50 percent; Jats (Hindus) 46 percent; Sikhs (others, including Mazbhi and Ramdasia) 40 percent; Garwhalis 38 percent; Dogras 32 percent; Punjabi Musalmans 30 percent; Ranghars 27 percent; Gujars 24 percent; Brahmins 23 percent; Rajputs 22 percent; Rajputana Musalmans 18 percent; Maharrattas 16 percent; Coorgs 15 percent; Madrassis 14 percent; Baluchis 10 percent; Mahars 8 percent; Ahirs 7 percent; Assamese 3 percent; and Chamars 3 percent. Recruitment of the Indian Army 1939–1945, L/MIL/17/5/2153, OIOC, BL. See also Stephen Cohen's article "'The Untouchable Soldier'" for more details.
[49] Native and later Viceroy Commissioned Officers were Indian sepoys who had risen through the ranks of a unit based on seniority instead of merit. The ranks of the Native officers were Jemadar, Subedar, and Subedar Major (infantry), and Jemadar, Risaldar, and Risaldar Major (cavalry). A senior Indian VCO, Subedar Major, or Risaldar Major most likely had served for twenty years before attaining the rank. However, a Subedar Major still had to accept orders from a young British subaltern just out from Addiscombe or Sandhurst. There is no exact rank equivalent in the British Army: VCOs commanded platoons, as did lieutenants. For a wider discussion of the debates of the nineteenth century, see Chandar Sundraham, "Grudging Concessions: The Officer Corps and Indianization," in Daniel Marston and Chandar Sundraham, eds., *A Military History of India and South Asia* (Westport, CT, 2007).
[50] Officers for the infantry and cavalry regiments of the British Army and later the Indian Army trained at Sandhurst, while officers for the artillery and engineers trained at Woolwich.
[51] See the work of Chandar Sundaram, "Reviving a Dead Letter: Military Indianization and the Ideology of Anglo-India, 1885–1891," in P. S. Gupta and A. Deshpande, eds., *The British Raj and Its Armed Forces, 1857–1939* (Delhi, 2002) and "Grudging Concessions: The Officer Corps and Its Indianization, 1817–1940," in Daniel Marston and Chandar Sundaram, eds., *A Military History of India and South Asia* (Westport, CT, 2007).

Even in the nineteenth century, this position sparked debate and discussion, most of which fell on deaf ears, especially during the tenure of Gen. Sir Frederick Roberts as commander in chief of the Bengal Army.[52] He was against any proposal that allowed the possibility of Native officers having command over their British counterparts, and the system aimed to ensure that Indian officers would not command British officers, no matter how junior in age or experience they might be. This was all tied to the central plank of the British rule in India and racial interpretations of power. British officers were considered able to command many different classes of Indians without getting caught up in the men's religious or class issues,[53] but Native officers were considered incapable of rising above these controversies.[54]

Despite these prejudices, in reality Native officers regularly commanded companies of men during the days of the EIC and the early years of the British government control of India, because the numbers of British officers were quite low in any given unit, especially in the Irregular Corps.[55] The performance of Native officers serving with irregular units during the Mutiny of 1857 demonstrated that Indians, when given the responsibility, could perform well in the field and remain loyal.[56] Many in the army believed that Native officers should rise through the ranks on the basis of merit, but conservative elements decided that men would be awarded VCO ranks by seniority instead. This system ensured that VCOs were old and trusted soldiers. By 1914, the number of British officers had risen to twelve to fifteen men per infantry battalion or cavalry regiment, while VCOs numbered approximately eighteen to twenty men. The VCOs were in command of platoons, while the British officers served as company commanders and company officers.

[52] Many Anglo-Indians, people of mixed race, served with distinction in the old EIC Army. James Skinner raised one of the most famous cavalry regiments, Skinner's Horse. He was the son of a Scottish EIC Army officer and a Rajput princess.

[53] This was an issue with the VCOs. The VCOs were of the same class as the company to which they were assigned. The VCOs from a Sikh or Pathan company commanded platoons of the same class. The idea was that sepoys would follow the orders and commands of VCOs due to the fact they were of the same class. This system led to preferential treatment in certain companies, as the VCO would favor men from his own village.

[54] This eventually proved false. Indian Commissioned Officers were found generally not to prefer any one class over another even if one of the classes was their own. Sepoys also did not have difficulty in following the commands of Indian Commissioned Officers even if they were not of the same class or if the officer originated from a non-martial race class.

[55] The irregular forces were mostly cavalry regiments. The units raised during the Indian Mutiny, such as Hodson's Horse and Fane's Horse, are examples of these. The Punjab Irregular Force also had different officering levels due to the fact it was seen as an irregular force for a number of years.

[56] See Henry Lawrence, "Military Defence of Our Empire in the East," *Calcutta Review* 2(3) (1844) and the efforts of Gen. Sir George Chesney as a member of the Viceroy's Executive Council.

The First World War and the sacrifices made by the Indian Army finally opened the door for Indian commissions, but only slightly.[57] A select few VCOs were given King's Commissions; the majority had served most of their lives and would shortly retire before they reached higher ranks. In 1918, the Indian Cadet College was established in Indorein to give commissions to men who had served in the war.[58] Many were men of the VCO rank, but few of them had received any significant level of education.

The attempt to broaden commission eligibility was part of an overall British reform policy in India, which included devolution of far greater power to elected Indian politicians, particularly at the provincial level, through the Montagu-Chelmsford Reforms of 1918, and more rapid Indianization of a broad range of civilian services.[59] The Government of India Act of 1919 created the Legislative Assembly for India, composed of both elected and appointed officials at the provincial level.[60] The assembly debated issues such as recruitment and further Indianization of the officer corps and forwarded relevant questions to the Government of India.

Beginning in 1920, ten places at Sandhurst were reserved for Indians. At first, most of those selected came from the martial races, and were either themselves VCOs or the sons of VCOs; university-educated men were also chosen. The first cadets from both Sandhurst and Indore received King's Commissions, which meant that in theory they held the same powers of command and punishment as any white officer in the Indian Army, and underwent the same training process as white officers had done since the Mutiny.[61] They were posted for a year as platoon commanders with a British battalion in India; after that, they were posted to any regiment they chose, provided a vacancy was available.[62] At first there appeared to be no issues of racial discrimination, although some senior officers expressed reservations, fearing

---

[57] Indians had received commissions as medical officers during the war. An estimated 700 men were commissioned into the Indian Medical Services, but not as fighting soldiers. Chenevix-Trench, *The Indian Army and the King's Enemies*, 116.

[58] It was closed in 1919 and cadets were then sent to Sandhurst.

[59] Sir Edwin Montagu, the India secretary, had stated in 1917: "The Government have decided that the bar which has hitherto precluded the admission of Indians to commissioned rank in His Majesty's Army should be removed." Quoted in Sundaram, "Grudging Concessions," p. 94.

[60] Reforms originating in the Montagu-Chelmsford Report of 1918 were published within this act.

[61] Only one feature differentiated British King's Commissioned Officers from King's Commissioned Indian Officers, and this would later affect the Indian Commissioned Officers from Dehra Dun. British officers, upon appointment to the Indian Army, were paid an extra wage due to the fact they were serving far from home. As the Indian cadets graduated, they were not granted this extra wage since they were serving at home. While the Government of India had imposed this as a cost-saving measure, it caused bitter resentment among the Indian cadets, who felt that they had been shunted aside in some way and were not considered of the same quality. This issue would not be properly addressed until 1945.

[62] Gurkha regiments were not part of the process. They were still only open to British cadets. This would not change until Indian independence in 1947.

that junior British officers might end up serving under an Indian. For many British officers in the Indian Army, this possibility was still inconceivable.[63]

Field Marshal Henry Rawlinson, commander in chief of the Indian Army, announced an eight-unit scheme in 1923 that earmarked designated units for Indianization.[64] Only those British officers already serving would continue to do so and complete their time, so that there would be no possibility of an Indian commanding a British officer. The eight-unit scheme was a scaled-back version of an earlier proposal (which had called for twenty units); this was necessary because the failure rate of Indian cadets at Sandhurst at this time was about 30 percent.[65] Rawlinson apparently feared it would prove difficult to get the required number of Indian officers to implement the first proposal.[66]

Over the course of the 1920s, the number of Indian men seeking officers' commissions dropped. Sandhurst was one stumbling block; the amount of money required for fees, and the distance that most cadets would be required to travel, were daunting for many prospective candidates.[67] According to the Indian Sandhurst Committee's Report from 1927, the limiting "eight-unit scheme" was another reason why the number of applicants had not increased.[68] As they stated: "it is necessary to widen the field of opportunity."

The Indian Military Academy

Following the demand by the Indian legislature for the commissioning of more Indians at Sandhurst, and the subsequent lack of response from potential cadets,

[63] Mason, *A Matter of Honour*, 454.
[64] He had actually envisioned a different Indianization process, where 25 percent of all Indian Army commissions would go to Indians, allowing the Indianization of the officer corps to occur much more quickly. Omissi, *The Sepoy and the Raj*, 166–172.
[65] One reason for the failure rate was the intense discipline of the regime at Sandhurst. Many British cadets had some experience of this sort of discipline from having attended public schools, but the Indians sent to Sandhurst had not previously experienced it. The Prince of Wales Royal Military College was founded in 1922 to rectify this and to prepare Indian cadets for Sandhurst. Another important issue was the distance Indian cadets traveled from home to attend.
[66] Interesting, most of the eight units selected for Indianization were not so-called elite units. The scheme called for cadets to be sought from all over India, but the feeling persisted that only cadets from the martial races were suitable. This prejudice was propagated by the belief that the martial race troops – such as Sikhs, PMs, and Dogras – would not consent to being led by officers who were Bengali or Madrassi. Recruiting cadets from the preferred martial races initially posed problems, as candidates often lacked the educational requirements stipulated by the selection process, forcing the army to recruit from other classes as well. To complicate matters still further, the establishment was also concerned that VCOs would not respect newly commissioned Indian officers.
[67] Omissi, *The Sepoy and the Raj*, 172–176.
[68] See "The Indian Sandhurst Committee's Report, November 1926," in C. H. Philips, ed., *Select Documents on the History of India and Pakistan, vol. 4, The Evolution of India and Pakistan, 1858–1947* (London, 1964), 531–532.

the decision was made to create the Indian Military Academy (IMA) at Dehra Dun. The academy formally opened on December 10, 1932; cadets who completed the required course of training would henceforth achieve the designation of Indian Commissioned Officer (ICO), and they would only be eligible to command Indian soldiers,[69] unlike their predecessors, the King's Commissioned Indian Officers (KCIOs), who had been eligible for positions of command over both British and Indian troops.[70] A precedent for this decision did already exist, in that Dominion officers experienced a similar fate. This decision was to cause bitter resentment among the officers and to create significant friction between KCIOs and ICOs.[71]

The 1920s and 1930s had marked slow progress for Indianization, but the foundations for the future had been laid. The myth that men and VCOs of the martial classes would not want to be led or commanded by Indian officers (of either the martial or non-martial classes) was in the process of being dispelled as Indian officers and men served together in operations on the frontier and during Aid to the Civil Power exercises. The growing numbers of Indian officers, as well as their performance, helped to enhance their reputation to some degree with British officers serving outside the Indianized units.

The Second World War ended the interwar Indianization process. With the expansion of the Indian Army in the spring of 1940, Indianization of the officer corps took on a new importance, since the army would need more officers to make up the war establishment.[72] By 1945, 7,546 Indian officers served in the combatant arms of the Indian Army. Counting the noncombatant arms, the number was closer to 13,000 officers. The total, British and Indian, for the Indian Army, including all arms and services, was close to 40,000 officers. Indian officers in the combatant arms represented 25 percent of the number, compared with just 10 percent in 1939.[73]

When Auchinleck was commander in chief in 1941, the order ending the old Indianized system was formally listed.[74] The last group of regular ICOs graduated in June 1941, and the Indian Military Academy, Dehra Dun,

---

[69] This was similar to the graduates of the Canadian and Australian military academies (Kingston and Duntroon), who only held commissions within their own Dominion forces.

[70] Realistically, the possibility of a KCIO commanding a British officer had been limited by the eight-unit scheme.

[71] This perception of ICOs as "second class" was considered a contributing factor to the decision by some ICO prisoners of war to switch sides and participate in the formation of the Indian National Army (INA). Capt. Mohan Singh, an ICO who graduated from the IMA, was one of the first officers to join the INA.

[72] In cavalry units, the establishment was doubled. British and Indian Officers (ECOs and EICOs) would command troops. In infantry battalions, the numbers also doubled; extra officers were not platoon leaders but extra company officers. All units retained VCOs.

[73] Bisheswar Prasad, *Official History of the Indian Armed Forces: Expansion of the Armed Forces and Defence Organisation* (Calcutta, 1956), 182.

[74] Army Instruction (India) No. 76 of 1941 L/MIL/17/5/531 OIOC, BL.

reopened as an "emergency" Officer Training School (OTS), initially for Indian cadets. Auchinleck also tried to deal with the differences of pay of Indian and British officers within the first few months of his taking command.

Many Indian officers felt that three important changes had brought about the smooth transformation of interwar bias.[75] First, the vast majority of Emergency Commissioned Officers (ECOs) came from the United Kingdom, and so had no preconceived notions about what relations between Indians and Britons should be. Moreover, most knew nothing of the prewar Indianized system, so did not consider the idea of serving with or under the command of Indians foreign or unacceptable. Second, by 1943, Indians and Emergency Indian Commissioned Officers (EICOs) had proven themselves in battle alongside their British counterparts, and this was widely acknowledged and commended. Third, during Auchinleck's second tenure as commander in chief, many ECOs and regular officers looked to him as a leader and shared his views.[76] Many Indian officers, from both the prewar and war years, expressed the opinion that it was the commanding officer who set the tone, either negative or positive, within the regiment or battalion. It appears that a majority of them sought to emulate Auchinleck, and as a result a majority of units accepted Indianization.[77]

In December 1944, Auchinleck laid out his intentions for the future of the Indian Army: "I propose as a principle that the three services [Indian Army, Air Force, and Navy] after the war shall be officered entirely by Indian officers so far as this is possible and that the number of European officers shall be limited to that required to fill positions which cannot be held by Indians owing to their lack of experience or training."[78] To attain Auchinleck's goals of an Indianized army, many EICOs would need to receive regular (postwar) commissions. The Government of India began the final process of Indianization with this document.[79]

The War Cabinet, as well as others, was aware that British officers would need to remain in some positions, especially at the highest levels, due to the lack of Indian officers at or above the brigadier rank. Estimates were that it would take a decade for the Indian Army to educate and train enough senior Indian officers to assume the higher levels of command from British officers

---

[75] Interviews and correspondence with retired Indian officers, from 1999 to 2009.

[76] See comments by Christopher Bayley and Tim Harper in *Forgotten Armies: The Fall of British Asia, 1941–1945* (Cambridge, MA, 2005), 74.

[77] I have interviewed more than 200 officers since 1999, and this was the majority sentiment that came across.

[78] Auchinleck to Wavell, December 19, 1944, L/WS/1/924 OIOC, BL, Post-war Officering of the Indian Army.

[79] Wavell to Amery, March 5, 1945, *TOP*, 5:297. See also page 298, which highlights the initial debates, but also reinforces the notion that the army performed well during the war, even during the Quit India movement.

and twenty years for complete Indianization to occur.[80] By early April, Leo Amery, secretary of state for India, and Auchinleck were moving to end the entry of any British officers to the army at the lowest levels.[81] This move caused much political tension for the coalition government in London. Following deliberations, the War Cabinet and the India Committee released their findings on the proposal on April 25. Two days later, the War Cabinet formally agreed to them, with Churchill's acquiescence.[82]

Auchinleck reinforced the trend toward complete Indianization throughout the summer of 1945. The notes of the Army Commanders Conference in 1945 confirm his interest: "Relationships between British and Indian officers must be kept constantly in mind by Army commanders. He had laid down the policy of complete integration between the two types and Cos and others (Indian as well as British) who did not do all they could to complete that policy would be removed."[83]

Adaptation to the Spectrum of Conflict

The three chief roles of the Indian Army during the period between 1903 and the end of the Second World War were providing Aid to the Civil Power (internal security);[84] carrying out policing duties on the North-West Frontier (covering troops);[85] and conventional warfare (field army).[86] As one author stated, "[the] Indian Army must be organized and equipped for a minor and a major danger."[87] The Indian Army, due to the shifting requirements of internal and external security missions, found its units called upon to deal with the "spectrum of conflict," especially in the twentieth century. It was in the first half of that century that the Indian Army demonstrated its ability to learn and adapt

[80] War Cabinet, March 27, 1945, *TOP*, 5:346; see pages 775–776 for specific numbers. Although in a later memo the time period was decreased to ten to fifteen years; see War Cabinet, April 23, 1945, *TOP*, 5:405, 933.
[81] War Cabinet, April 2, 1945, *TOP*, 5:363, paragraph 10.
[82] See War Cabinet, April 27, 1945, *TOP*, 5:423, 983.
[83] L/WS/1/1523 Army Commanders Conference, August 1945, OIOC, BL.
[84] To many in the army as well as in the Government of India, this was the most important mission. Aid to the Civil Power was defined by minimum use of force, civil-military cooperation, and deterrence of unrest. Many accounts by British and Indian Army officers relate difficult experiences with internal security. One of the best and most accessible is by Field Marshal Sir William Slim, *Unofficial History* (London, 1959), 75–98.
[85] Units of the Indian Army had been carrying out countless small- and large-scale campaigns in the North-West Frontier region since the mid-1800s. The tribes (commonly referred to as the Pathans) living in the region periodically came down from the hills to attack civil and military outposts in the region for various reasons.
[86] Field army units trained and organized for conventional defense of any invasion by a neighboring country (chiefly Afghanistan), while the covering troops were stationed in the North-West Frontier Province and Baluchistan on frontier duties. L/MIL/17/5/1793 OIOC, BL.
[87] Chenevix-Trench, *The Indian Army and the King's Enemies*, 14.

to the various missions it was required to carry out.[88] Along with British Army and other Empire forces, the Indian Army would find itself tested and found wanting in the early stages of conventional warfare against peer enemies. As with the British and Empire forces over the course of both the First and Second World Wars, the Indian Army would also prove it could learn on the battlefield and reverse its losses against those same enemies.

Internal Security Garrison

At the start of the twentieth century, the Indian and British army units of the Army in India were known as the "Sword of the Raj." They participated in the difficult task of providing Aid to the Civil Power. The reasons for deployment in this task lay in the inability of the Indian Police (IP) and the Indian Civil Service (ICS) to deal with some political, domestic, labor, communal, or civil unrest. Between 1860 and 1878, the Army in India was called out on internal security duties forty-six times, and between 1899 and 1901, at least sixty-six times.[89] With the rise of various Indian nationalist groups in the early twentieth century, the British Raj came to rely more on British units in carrying out internal security duties, as some within the administration feared using Indian troops against nationalists.[90] Contemporary reports, investigations, and memoirs indicate that internal security was a duty that many Indian and British soldiers, NCOs, VCOs, and officers detested.

As a result of the Amritsar Massacre of 1919,[91] the Indian and British Army units received clear instructions and training to deal with internal security.[92] Success in internal security rested in the ability of the ICS, IP, and Indian Army to cooperate on many levels to create true civil-military cooperation and to

---

[88] See the recent work by Alan Jeffreys in his new book *Approach to Battle: Training the Indian Army during the Second World War* (Solihull, UK, 2017) for an exhaustive description of training in the interwar and Second World War Indian Army.

[89] Omissi, *The Sepoy and the Raj*, 216.   [90] Ibid., graph on page 210.

[91] See Report of the Committee appointed by the Government of India to investigate the disturbances in the Punjab, OIOC L/MIL/17/1/12/42, as well as "Statement by Brigadier R. E. Dyer," in Evidence Taken before the Disorders Inquiry Committee, *vol.* 3: Amritsar, OIOC V/26/262/5, as well as N. A. Collet, *The Butcher of Amritsar: General Reginald Dyer* (London, 2005); Alfred Draper, *Amritsar: The Massacre That Ended the Raj* (London, 1981); and Charles Gwynn, *Imperial Policing* (London, 1934), for more information.

[92] L/MIL/17/5/4252 Internal Security Instructions 1937. OIOC, BL. For an account of the development of the internal security doctrine for the Indian Army during the interwar period, see Srinath Raghaven, "Protecting the Raj: The Army in India and Internal Security, 1919–1939," *Small Wars and Insurgencies* 16(3) (December 2005), and for more details, see Gyanesh Kudaisya, "In the Aid of the Civil Power: The Colonial Army in Northern India, 1919–42," *Journal of Imperial and Commonwealth History* 32(1) (January 2004), plus the internal security chapters from Roy, *The Indian Army in the Two World Wars*.

make sure that all individuals involved worked within the confines of civil and military law and with correct and actionable intelligence.[93]

The Indian Army found itself called out many times during the 1920s and 1930s as an aid to the civil power. David Omissi notes that over a four-month period in 1922, the army was called out on sixty-two occasions.[94] Usually it was summoned to disperse crowds engaged in communal violence, political agitation, trade union protests, and general *dacoit* behavior.[95] There was only one serious incident involving the army in a major episode of civil unrest; this took place in the North-West Frontier in the city of Peshawar in 1930.[96]

Future field marshal Sir William Slim noted in his discussion of Aid to the Civil Power that instructions such as the Indian Army's I. A. F. D. 908 (Instructions to Officers Acting in the Aid of the Civil Power for Dispersal of Unlawful Assemblies) "[were] a useful thing to have about."[97] This formalized structure during the interwar period worked well in containing communal violence, as well as political agitation that sometimes became violent. Troops were called out regularly, but frequently did not have to use force to dispel crowds. The ability of the ICS and the IP to provide accurate intelligence and other important information allowed the troops to quell disturbances quite easily. For the interwar period, one commentator has noted: "Though the 'in the aid to the civil power' function experienced routinisation in the 1920 contraction and partial withdrawal in the late 1930s ... the internal security troops remained extraordinarily effective."[98]

During the Second World War, the need for internal security duties did not diminish. During the Quit India Movement of 1942, the government called out just under sixty battalions to quell communal and political violence.[99] Troops also mobilized in 1943 to support aid distribution during the Bengal Famine. This was at the same time that the Indian Army was expanding and waging war in North Africa and Burma. The army had to still contend with the spectrum of warfare in the midst of a global war.

---

[93] Raghaven, "Protecting the Raj," 262.   [94] Omissi, *The Sepoy and the Raj*, 219.

[95] *Dacoit* behavior, defined legally, referred to an armed robbery involving five or more people. The British authorities expanded the definition to include any civil or guerrilla activity. Ibid., 220.

[96] See Francis Ingall's chapter "Red Shirts and Afridis," in *The Last of the Bengal Lancers* (London, 1988) for another practitioner's view of the aid to the civil power.

[97] Slim, *Unofficial History*, 77–81. The chapter "Aid to the Civil" provides a succinct understanding of the tensions and the issues that can arise in this role.

[98] Kudaisya, "In the Aid of the Civil Power," 63.

[99] See Daniel Marston, *The Indian Army and the End of the Raj* (Cambridge, 2014), 104–109, for more detail.

Punitive Operations on the North-West Frontier

The Indian Army had to contend with the "troublesome" area of the North-West Frontier of India (present-day northwest Pakistan) after annexing the Punjab in the Second Anglo-Sikh War of 1849.[100] The British administration adopted multiple policies, including "closed-border" and "forward" policies, in an attempt to contain the Pathan or Pashtun tribal groups in the region. The Indian Army carried out a series of punitive or small wars in the region that ranged from battalion- and brigade- to corps-level activities. The British administration, first in Calcutta and later in New Delhi, focused on the incessant problem, as many of the deployments of the Indian Army occurred in the region. As noted earlier, the Bengal Army and the specialized Punjab Irregular Force (later the Punjab Frontier Force) spent much of their time on various operations in the region and in Afghanistan. The army continuously maintained troops in the area as a buffer between the tribal regions and the plains of the Punjab below. Units were regularly called upon to "open" tracks or roads to relieve pressure on a post under tribal attack. Between 1849 and 1914, more than fifty-two punitive operations took place in the North-West Frontier.

The key theme that emerged from all this fighting, related to the performance of the Indian Army in the two great wars, was the professionalization, learning, and adaptation that occurred and became embedded in the minds of many officers. Over the course of years, the Indian Army developed various tactics, doctrines, and training to deal with these operations. While some historians feel that these "small wars" inhibited the Indian Army in the First and Second World Wars, the historical record partially proves otherwise. Many of the officers who were at the forefront of the reform movements in both world wars had served multiple times on the frontier, and had debated and developed ideas based upon their experiences. Patrick Rose highlights some of the issues with "frontier experience" that would pop up in the Second World War. "Indian Army officers were willing and able to effectively utilize a decentralised approach to command … [T]he mindset and experience this developed proved highly valuable to a generation of Indian Army officers destined to lead large formations in the major British campaigns fought between 1940–1945 … [It also] led to certain negative practices [which] were ruthlessly exposed

---

[100] For a very detailed analysis of the doctrine and various major actions of the time and region, see T. R. Moreman's *The Army in India and the Development of Frontier Warfare, 1849–1947* (Basingstoke, 1998). His chapter "Passing It On: The Army in India and Frontier Warfare, 1914–1939," in Kaushik Roy, ed., *War and Society in Colonial India* (New Delhi, 2006), gives a short synopsis of his key arguments. For specific details of operations in the interwar period, see "Report on the Mohmand Operations," 18–19. L/MIL/7/16968 Frontier Operations Mohmand Operations August to October, 1935 OIOC, BL; "Report of the 1st Phase of Operations," L/MIL/7/16971 Frontier Operations Waziristan 1937 OIOC, BL; and the various official histories written in the interwar period and during the Second World War covering these operations.

fighting against the well trained, well equipped and highly motivated opponents Indian Army formations faced on the battlefield during the early years of
the Second World War."[101]

Between 1900 and 1945, the Indian Army carried out multiple division-level
operations in the region: the 1908 Zakka Khel and Mohmand expedition, the
1919 Third Afghan War, the 1919–1920 Waziristan campaign, the 1935
Mohmand campaign, the 1936–1937 Waziristan campaign, and operations in
the Second World War. In the Second World War, even as the Indian Army was
fighting in campaigns against German, Italian, Vichy French, and Japanese
troops, it still deployed forces to the region to maintain "the peace." Over this
period of time, officers constantly debated "lessons" from their experiences.
They updated manuals and professional journals, and published numerous
articles discussing ideas regarding operations in the region. Training was
enhanced for all units heading to the frontier. Many of these themes would
reoccur in the Second World War as manuals were created after the initial
defeats in North Africa and Asia. Indian Army formations created specialized
training centers and schools for their units as they headed to the front. This was
a continuous learning process that had its roots in preparing for operations on
the frontier.[102]

The Field Army

The Russian threat to India through Afghanistan had not dissipated by the start
of the twentieth century. Gen. Horatio Herbert Kitchener, fresh from success in
the Second Anglo-Boer War, arrived in India and set about reorganizing the
army to deal with a "peer" threat. He set out to streamline all the bureaucratic
command structures, logistics, training, and financial austerity. Much of his
effort was tied to major debates and political fights with Viceroy Lord
Curzon.[103] Kitchener also set about creating division-level headquarters and
organizations. These divisions were to serve in the Field Army or to be used in
internal security if need be. He rationalized the numbers of military stations and
barracks to cut costs. Units were called upon to carry out higher-level training
exercises in the coming years.[104] While the Russian threat appeared to recede
with the Anglo-Russian Convention of 1907, in 1910, Lt. Gen. Douglas Haig

[101] Patrick Rose, "Indian Army Command Culture and the North-West Frontier, 1919–1939," in
Alan Jeffreys, ed., *The Indian Army, 1939–1947: Experience and Development* (Farnham,
Surrey, 2012), 55.
[102] See the recent work done by Alan Jeffreys in "Training the Indian Army, 1939–1945," in
Jeffreys, *The Indian Army*, and in Jeffreys, *Approach to Battle* for a wider discussion of the
links within training across the Indian Army in the Second World War.
[103] See Hew Strachan, *The Politics of the British Army* (Oxford, 1997), chapter 5, for a detailed
discussion of the political battles.
[104] Omissi, *The Sepoy and the Raj*, 206–207.

was appointed as the first commander general staff India. Haig had done quite a bit of work in the United Kingdom to prepare the future British Expeditionary Force (BEF) for operations.[105] He saw the need for the Indian Army to provide an Imperial Reserve for the United Kingdom, possibly in the Persian Gulf, against the Ottomans. As with Kitchener and Curzon, Haig and Viceroy Lord Hardinge disagreed about the potential threats to India. Most of these debates centered on costs. The viceroy perceived the chief issues for the Indian Army were the North-West Frontier Province and internal security duties. The First World War changed his opinion, as the Indian Army provided many expeditionary groups to fight as far away as France. In 1914, six divisions and six cavalry brigades were fully equipped for mobilization. However, there were no corps-level organizations, and the divisions had not carried out division-level training.[106]

Much of what people may know about the Indian Army in the First World War centers around a perceived lackluster performance – a perception that is not correct. The Indian Army, along with the ANZACS, Canadians, and other armies that served in the BEF on the Western Front and in other theaters had to deal with major issues of rapid and over-expansion of forces, fighting a long, drawn-out industrial war, and learning and adaptation on the battlefield. The Indian Army, along with its British and Empire counterparts, achieved victory in 1918 – much more than a lackluster performance. By instituting a culture of learning and adaptation on the battlefield, the Indian Army went through a series of significant organizational, tactical, and operational reforms that enabled it to not only hold its own but also to emerge from battle in 1918 as a victorious and modern institution.[107] By the end of the war, the Indian Army could rightly be proud of its performance when compared with other forces in the Empire. Notably, it served as the strategic reserve for the British Empire, especially in the campaigns against the Ottoman Empire.

When the First World War broke out in 1914, the Indian Army was an all-volunteer force, comprising around 159,000 officers, VCOs, NCOs, and *jawans* organized into 138 battalions of infantry, 39 regiments of cavalry, and 12 mountain batteries. The army remained an all-volunteer force throughout

---

[105] See J. P. Harris, *Douglas Haig and the First World War* (Cambridge, 2012), for an in-depth understanding of Haig.

[106] Ross Anderson, "Logistics of the Indian Expeditionary Force D in Mesopotamia," in Kaushik Roy, ed., *The Indian Army in the Two World Wars* (Amsterdam, 2011), 109.

[107] See Paddy Griffith, *Battle Tactics on the Western Front* (New Haven, CT, 1994); Bill Rawlins, *Surviving Trench Warfare: Technology and the Canadian Corps, 1914–1918* (Toronto, 1992); Tim Travers, *The Killing Ground* (London, 1987); Tim Travers, *How the War Was Won* (London, 1992); Mark Grotelueschen, *The AEF Way of War: The American Army and Combat in World War One* (Cambridge, 2007); and Jonathan Boff, *Winning and Losing on the Western Front: The British Third Army and the Defeat of Germany in 1918* (Cambridge, 2012) for in-depth discussion of the learning curve for British Empire and US forces.

the war and at its peak numbered 1 million troops. As with the Second World War, the Indian Army encountered major issues with its expansion. The BEF and other Dominion forces would face the same challenges in the first years of the war.

Following their deployment to France and Belgium, the 3rd Lahore and 7th Meerut (Regular) Divisions went into the line in and around Ypres in late October and early November 1914. The Indian Corps helped relieve the British II Corps that had been fighting since August, and by the end of 1914, it represented nearly one-third of the BEF. British authorities in London and New Delhi had not anticipated the level of violence associated with combat in 1914. On arrival in France, the Indian Corps had been reequipped with the newest rifles and equipment. Despite this, by the end of November, many Indian Army battalions had suffered close to 50 percent casualties, as had the BEF's professional battalions. One Indian battalion, the 57th Wilde's Rifles, Frontier Force, had landed in France in August with 14 British officers and 788 VCOs, NCOs, and men. After a year of more or less continuous combat, the unit reported 10 officers killed, 8 wounded, 16 Indian officers killed or wounded, and 800 men killed or wounded.[108]

The Indian Corps gained numerous battle honors in France during this period, including Ypres, Neuvelle Chappelle, Aubers Ridge, Festubert, and Loos. Five Indian soldiers won the Victoria Cross. As with British units before them and Canadians after, Indian units and formations struggled to come to grips with the brutality of the Western Front. The Indian Army, similar to some regular BEF formations, had a solid core of officers, VCOs, NCOs, and men who had active duty experience. It may have been on the North-West Frontier or in China, but it was still useful, and many of these veterans attempted to adapt their knowledge to the unique environment of the Western Front. They used skirmish tactics learned on the frontier, just as their British counterparts adapted tactics from the Boer War to trench raids and control of no-man's land. The Indian Frontier Force units succeeded so well that they were commended in 1915 for their successes in scouting and dominating no-man's land.[109]

Throughout 1914 and 1915, Indian units honed their skills on the battlefields of the Western Front. They learned from veteran formations, consumed the various circulars developed by senior commands, and carried out their own focused in-theater training for replacements arriving from India. As with their

[108] W. E. H. Condon, *Frontier Force Rifles* (Aldershot, 1953), 57.
[109] See Morton-Jack, *Indian Army on the Western Front*, specifically the chapter "Old Tactics," for a much more detailed examination and discussion of the adaptability of the Indian Army to the new environment. See page 203 for a humorous description of a scouting mission.

British and Canadian allies, not all Indian Corps units performed at the same level, but the desire to learn and adapt was evident.[110] As one historian notes:

> Up to the end of 1915, the British Army had adapted to the western front like the Indian Army. From August to December 1914, its pre-war regular battalions learned lessons much as the Indian troops did about how to hold trenches. Whether they were drawn from the Home Army or the Army in India, they frequently made the same mistakes overexposing themselves to German fire, before they improved through common sense, discussion with more experienced officers and men, and tactical circulars.[111]

While the Indian Army came to support the Empire in France, it was in the Middle East, chiefly Mesopotamia and Palestine, where the bulk of the army – 600,000 alone in Mesopotamia – served, and in the end achieved its greatest victories during the First World War. The Indian Army landed troops in the Gulf region in the autumn of 1914 to protect British interests in the region. This force received the title of the Indian Expeditionary Force D (IEFD), and by the end of November, its troops had seized the Gulf region and Basra in Mesopotamia.[112] The campaign expanded in April 1915 when the Turks attacked Indian Army positions in southern Mesopotamia. The Indian Army was able to repulse and follow up the attack with an advance north to Kut-al Amara.[113]

The Indian Army had achieved its initial goal of securing British interests in the Gulf region. It had successfully occupied Basra and defended and extended its line of control to the north. The advance further up the Tigris River to Kut-al Amara resulted in the seizure of that city by September 29.

At this juncture, the planning and strategy started to fall apart. Plans were formed and supported by London for a continued advance toward Baghdad, a further 300 miles upriver. Despite serious questions regarding logistical support and reinforcement policies, the army continued to advance and succeeded in destroying various Turkish formations. The force was thirty miles south of Baghdad by early November, stretched to the logistical breaking point and short of reinforcements, while now confronting veteran Turkish troops from the Gallipoli campaign. November 22–24, the two armies met at Ctesiphon and the

---

[110] Ibid.; see the chapter "New Tactics" for a thorough discussion of the learning and adaptation that took place on the battlefield.

[111] Ibid., 242.

[112] See Anderson, "Logistics of the Indian Expeditionary Force D in Mesopotamia," as well as R. Evans, *A Brief Outline of the Campaign in Mesopotamia: 1914–1918* (London, 1926); Nickolas Gardner, "Sepoys and the Siege of Kut-al-Amara," *War in History* 11 (2004); Ronald Millar, *Kut: Death of an Army* (London, 1969); and F. J. Moberly, *Official History of the Great War: The Campaign in Mesopotamia*, 4 vols. (London, 1923–1927) for much more detail regarding the campaign.

[113] See the work done by Andrew Syk, "Command in the Indian Expeditionary Force D: Mesopotamia, 1915–16," in Kaushik Roy, ed., *The Indian Army in the Two World Wars* (Amsterdam, 2011), for more detailed descriptions.

Turks defeated the Indian troops. The army withdrew to Kut, where Turkish forces surrounded it.

Three attempts to lift the siege at Kut failed. Facing starvation, the British commander surrendered his garrison to the Turks in late April. This disaster, following on that of Gallipoli, sparked calls in London for inquiries into the causes of the defeats. Yet again, a core issue was a lack of properly trained British officers for the various formations and units, as the Indian Army rapidly expanded in 1914 and 1915, similar to the BEF in 1915 and 1916. Another key issue was the inability to fill staff positions within the various division and corps headquarters with appropriately trained officers. Experienced officers from the Indian Corps, which had served in France, were not present in the higher-level headquarters attempting to lift the siege of Kut.

After the debacle at Kut, the British overhauled the entire military situation in Mesopotamia. Lt. Gen. Sir Stanley Maude took command in July 1916. Maude set out to reform the army. He created a stronger logistical and sustainment system. Replacements arrived to fill the ranks. The quality of British officers also began to improve, although this issue was never entirely resolved.[114] Corps, divisions, brigades, battalions, and regiments all rested and retrained. The army disseminated battlefield experience and lessons from the fighting in Mesopotamia, as well as from other theaters, throughout the force. Battalion records highlight these improvements: the 45th Rattray Sikhs noted repeatedly in their histories "a period of intensive training. Company training … carried out in the morning with the Battalion drill in the afternoons. The Brigade worked together … practicing attack, retirement and night operations."[115]

Equally important, better equipment and more artillery arrived in the IEFD to deal with the lack of fire support that had plagued earlier phases of the campaign. The IEFD, with more than 150,000 men, was ready by the end of 1916 to carry out a counteroffensive toward Baghdad. It recaptured Kut in February 1917 and Baghdad in March. Maude noted that "the men are tremendously pleased with themselves as well they may be, for their conduct has been splendid."[116] For his part, Maude had shown that he was more than just a solid administrator and reformer; he was also a sound commander in the field. After the seizure of Baghdad, the IEFD stopped its advance and restored the fighting condition of its forces. The lessons and training transformation continued; in

[114] Specifically see Morton-Jack, *Indian Army on the Western Front*, 221–222, where a veteran Sikh soldier describes the officer issues in his battalion by late 1915. Many veteran officers had been killed or wounded in France, Mesopotamia, and elsewhere. Many young officers had only minimal time in theater as well as inadequate language skills, leadership abilities, and experience. This was an issue that would occur again in the Second World War.

[115] R. H. Anderson, *Regimental History of the 45th Rattray's Sikhs: During the Great War and After* (London, 1925), 43.

[116] Quoted in Morton-Jack, *Indian Army on the Western Front*, 253.

April 1917, the 45th Sikhs recorded that the month had passed in "quiet training and re-organisation … [T]raining in all branches was carried on."[117] Other units carried out similar efforts. In November 1917, Maude died of cholera, but the army moved on to defeat the Ottomans.

In 1918, in response to German offensives on the Western Front, the War Office in London began shifting forces between fronts. In an effort to support the final offensives in Palestine, IEFD units redeployed from Mesopotamia and Indian cavalry units from France. These forces stiffened the Palestine campaign and spread the lessons identified from the fighting in Mesopotamia and on the Western Front.

While the IEFD was successful in Mesopotamia, the final act in the Palestine campaign probably represented the high-water mark of the Indian Army's performance throughout the war.[118] Gen. Sir Edmund Allenby had reformed his army, as Maude had done in Mesopotamia, and had advanced as far as Jerusalem by December 1917. However, due to the need to reinforce British troops fighting against the German spring offensives on the Western Front, Allenby had to delay his final offensive, receiving Indian cavalry divisions in exchange for British troops. By the end of the campaign in October 1918, only two of the ten divisions, the 54th Division and the Australian and New Zealand Mounted Divisions, had no Indian troops.

The Egyptian Expeditionary Force had been Indianized for the final offensive. Indian battalions deployed inside various British divisions to fill the spaces left by British battalions, which had moved to the Western Front. This massive reorganization took months to complete as units and formations settled into their new roles. This process ran smoothly as Indian and British battalions worked hard to distill lessons and orient their men to the coming campaign. The units implemented in numerous training programs lessons from the Western Front, captured in doctrinal pamphlets such as *Training and Employment of a Platoon, 1918* and *Training and Deployment of Divisions, 1918.*

Allenby and his staff turned their focus to the last major objectives in the Palestine campaign: the destruction of the Turkish armies to the north. The offensive began in September, with the Battle of Megiddo taking place September 19–25. Damascus fell on October 1, Beirut on October 8, and Aleppo soon afterward. James Kitchen suggests that "Megiddo thus stands alongside 14th Army's [Second World War] Burma operations … [a]s evidence

---

[117] Anderson, *Regimental History of the 45th Rattray's Sikhs*, 84–85.

[118] See Dennis Showalter, "The Indianization of the Egyptian Expeditionary Force, 1917–1918: An Imperial Turning Point" and James Kitchen, "The Indianization of the Egyptian Expeditionary Force: Palestine 1918," in Kaushik Roy, ed., *The Indian Army in the Two World Wars* (Amsterdam, 2011) for a more detailed discussion.

that the twentieth century British led Indian Army was capable of organizing, fighting and winning a modern military campaign."[119]

The interwar period for the Indian Army followed traditional patterns. The army found its units frequently occupied with duties on the North-West Frontier, as well as dealing with civil unrest in internal security duties. Due to the lessons of the First World War, the various regiments were amalgamated into large regiments, with five regular battalions and one training battalion. The cavalry regiments were streamlined as well into larger regiments and training groups. Modernization took time; as in the United Kingdom, costs were the driving factor. With the rise in tensions in both Europe and Asia, the senior command of the Indian Army started to look toward modernization and mobilization with more seriousness in the late 1930s. A series of reorganization committees formed in both India and the United Kingdom in the late 1930s. Maj. Gen. Claude Auchinleck was made deputy chief of the general staff, India, in 1936. The commander in chief of the Indian Army at this time was Gen. Sir Robert Cassels, and he instructed Auchinleck to form a committee to assess the capability of the Indian Army to modernize for war.[120] The specific roles of the army were to be clearly defined for all to understand. Auchinleck's findings outlined several roles for the army. Cassels accepted all of his recommendations without changes.[121]

The British government formed a committee to assess how to bring about the modernization of the Indian armed forces and report on the overall expenditures required to achieve the necessary improvements.[122] Adm. of the Fleet Lord Chatfield chaired the committee, which included other senior officers of the services.[123] Due to the fact that Auchinleck had recently completed his own report, he became a member of the committee, which held seventy-eight meetings and consulted sixty-three witnesses.[124] It convened in London in January 1939 to finalize the report, which reached almost the same conclusions as Auchinleck's earlier report. The frontier, internal security, and coastal defense troops remained the top three priorities. The general reserve became a fifth role for the Indian Army, which received the mission to deal with unforeseen emergencies. In peacetime, the largest unit formation would be the brigade.[125]

While Auchinleck was a member of the Chatfield Committee, he did not fully agree with its final report. His two major criticisms concerned proposals to

[119] Kitchen, "The Indianization of the Egyptian Expeditionary Force," 190.
[120] Known as the Modernisation Committee.
[121] Mason, *A Matter of Honour*, 467, and Connell, *Auchinleck*, 68–69.
[122] The Expert Committee on the Defence of India, 1938–1939.
[123] It was subsequently referred to as the Chatfield Committee, OIOC/L/MIL/5/886.
[124] Letter from India Office, Whitehall to Auchinleck, No. 2, October 24, 1938, Auchinleck Papers, University of Manchester.
[125] Brigade HQ, three infantry battalions and one cavalry regiment. L/MIL/17/5/1805 OIOC, BL.

disband units and to deploy troops in Western Command. The Chatfield report proposed to disband two Indian cavalry regiments and fourteen infantry battalions and withdraw two British cavalry regiments and six battalions of infantry. Auchinleck felt that this would cause major disruption in India.[126] The report went further in terms of internal security. It called for a major reduction of both British and Indian Army forces to support the mission of internal security.[127] Auchinleck believed that, with growing tensions in Europe, there was likely to be a need for Indian Army regiments and battalions. Thus troops would have to possess the capabilities to contend with any modern European power, not just Pathan tribesmen.

The outbreak of the Second World War proved that Gen. Auchinleck and his committee were correct. In the first months of the war, the government in London did not expect to use the Indian Army. Neville Chamberlain and his government, which considered Indian troops unnecessary in a European war (apparently forgetting the Indian troops who had served with the British Army in the First World War), declined their use.[128] Initially, the British government expected the Indian Army to focus on potential threats to the North-West Frontier Province, as well as to deal with any specific internal security duties that might arise.[129]

The defeat of France in 1940, along with Italy's entry into the war, changed the strategic situation, and the British government reversed its earlier decision of not expanding the Indian Army. The subsequent rapid expansion of the Indian Army was driven by the need to have an Imperial Reserve, as highlighted by the deployments of 1941. Six new divisions were raised from summer 1940 to summer 1941.[130] Another six had formed by the end of 1941.[131] Thus, the Indian Army expanded from about 200,000 officers and men to more than 1 million in just two years. As a result of this rapid growth, many units lacked properly trained officers and soldiers. Not surprising, this

---

[126] Due to the fact that the Second World War broke out soon after the report was submitted, no units were disbanded.

[127] British units were to be reduced from twenty-six to twenty-one and Indian Army units were to be reduced from twenty to eleven. See Kudaisya, "In the Aid of the Civil Power," 58, and IOL/L/MIL/5/886.

[128] Lord Linlithgow to Haig (Governor of the Punjab), L/WS/1/136 Recruitment in India OIOC, BL.

[129] Two major formations, the 5th and 11th Brigade Groups (which formed the basis of the 4th Indian Division), that had enough modern equipment and weapons had been shipped to Egypt in August/September 1939 as a strategic Imperial Reserve to the area. Chenevix-Trench, *The Indian Army and the King's Enemies*, 138.

[130] The divisional structure was to follow the British system: three brigades, with three battalions of infantry. However, over the course of the next two years, each brigade was restructured to have two Indian battalions and one British battalion. The British battalion was there as the "backbone" for the brigade. As subsequent events demonstrated, the perceived need for a British backbone was outdated.

[131] Prasad, *Official History of the Indian Armed Forces*, 212–230.

shortcoming was to have a major impact on the formations and units that deployed to North Africa and the Far East, chiefly in Malaya and Burma.[132]

A brief overview of the various deployments in North and East Africa, Iraq, Iran, and Italy demonstrates that the Indian Army was seriously overstretched.[133] The units and formations that followed in 1941 were untried and needed to learn at the front, as their First World War brethren had done. As the war progressed, the Indian Army learned its trade, and its increasing professionalism and successes[134] in the North and East African as well as the Italian campaigns were duly noted by Allied commanders.[135]

The Far East campaigns came to represent the main Indian Army effort and the greatest performance on the battlefield in its 200-year history. Along with their counterparts in the Middle East and Africa, the formations in the Far East went through significant growing pains. As with the army as a whole, these units were recruited from ethnic and religious groups from across India, who consistently performed well and contributed to the army's success and growth. The formations in the Far East also benefited from the expansion of the officer corps to include more Indians, who proved themselves in combat and were in some cases leading battalions in battle by 1945.

The campaign in Burma in 1942 was also a resounding defeat – the longest retreat in British military history, more than 900 miles. The one saving grace was that the Japanese failed to completely destroy Burma Corps. Unlike Malaya, many veterans from the Burma campaign escaped to Assam, bringing with them valuable experiences and lessons.[136] None of the units and formations that served in the Malaya and Burma campaigns was prepared for the sort of warfare the Japanese unleashed. It is a tribute to both Indian and British units

[132] Interview with Brig. Randle, April 10, 2000; Lt. Coubrough, March 27, 2000, 7/10th Baluch; and Maj. Kirkwood, March 15, 2000 1/11th Sikh.
[133] For more detail, see "The Performance of the Indian Army in the Second World War," chapter 2 in Marston, *The Indian Army and the End of the Raj*; Tim Moreman, "From the Desert to the Sands to the Burmese Jungle: The Indian Army and the Lessons of North Africa, September 1939–November 1942," in Kaushik Roy, ed., *The Indian Army in the Two World Wars* (Amsterdam, 2011); Jeffreys, *Approach to Battle*; and Callahan, *Churchill and His Generals*.
[134] As noted previously, Indian units were used at times to back up other Allied units, including British units. One example was noted by a British officer from the Rifle Brigade. He stated, "a private told me [about] an unfortunate county battalion ... brigaded with Indian troops. The whole battalion had cut and run from a German tank attack. The Indians recaptured the ground. The brigadier formed both battalions into a square, the Indians on the outside with their weapons, the county regiment on the inside, without their weapons. He then told them what he thought of them." Quoted in Callahan, *Churchill and His Generals*, 291, n. 23.
[135] See Tuker papers in the Imperial War Museum (IWM) and Holworthy MSS, 91/40/1, IWM, letters of September 9 and 29 and October 5, 1944.
[136] Some Malaya veterans were able to escape from the debacle as well, but many more men and officers from the Burma campaign escaped to influence subsequent reforms. *Fighting Cock: The 23rd Indian Division*, by Lt. Col. A. J. R. Doulton, as well as works by Randle, Slim, and Lunt, offer very interesting insights into the arrival of the retreating BURCORPS, as the 23rd was shipped into Assam to receive the survivors of BURCORPS and prepare area defenses.

that they learned from their defeats, using them as a tool to retrain and eventually to inflict a far worse defeat on the Japanese.

As with previous efforts in the First World War and in the North and East African campaigns, the Indian Army carried out a major reform process, based on a deep analysis of its defeats.[137] The findings of the Infantry Committee in June 1943 set out to rectify the mistakes and to professionalize the force. The training of the army was streamlined. Doctrine, in the form of the *Jungle Book*, was created and disseminated to enable officers and men to understand the tactics of jungle warfare. Initiatives and practices relevant to training, operational lessons, and constant performance assessment began to permeate the whole of the army from mid-1943 onward. The army's war in the Far East was also reorganized with the creation of South East Asia Command[138] under the command of Adm. Lord Louis Mountbatten.[139] The Fourteenth Army became the land component, led by Gen. Slim, while Auchinleck took over as commander in chief, India, for a second stint.[140]

Slim considered Gen. Auchinleck's appointment to India Command as one of the most important contributors to the Indian Army's progress toward eventual victory in Burma. He commented that:

> [L]uckily, General Auchinleck was the man to do it. There was a considerable and prompt injection of ginger into the Indian administrative machine, military and civil. Even at the beginning of 1944 the results of Auchinleck's drive began to show ... It was a good for us when he took command of India ... [W]ithout him and what he and the Army in India did for us we could not have existed, let alone conquered.[141]

The Indian Army's training transformation was under way by the end of 1943 with the 17th and 23rd Indian Divisions, both of whom had instituted assessment and jungle warfare programs, holding the line in the Imphal region

[137] See Daniel Marston, *Phoenix from the Ashes: The Indian Army in the Burma Campaign* (Westport, CT, 2003), and Jeffreys, *Approach to Battle*, for a detailed description of this reform process.

[138] See Earl Mountbatten's *Report to the Combined Chiefs of Staff by the Supreme Allied Commander: South East Asia* (London, 1951) report for details on the history and the setup of this command as well as a general narrative of the campaign in Burma and Malaya.

[139] He served as the last viceroy of India and played a prominent role in the decisions made in 1947.

[140] Auchinleck became commander in chief of the Indian Army on June 20, 1943. See Callahan, *Churchill and His Generals*, 194–198, as well.

[141] William Slim, *Defeat into Victory* (London, 1956), 175–176; see also Linlithgow's letter of June 1, 1943, *TOP*, 3:755, 1034, "My own judgment is that so far as India and the training and improvement of morale of the Indian Army is concerned, Auchinleck is much the best man we can get ... [H]is excellent qualities are primarily the qualities of the fighting soldier, and a soldier's general." Note also Linlithgow's letter to Amery on June 10, 1943, *TOP*, 3:769, 1053: "His [Auchinleck's] value, as you and I both recognize, is in terms of the effects of his employment on Indian Army morale, and our being able to use his great experience with the Indian soldier in connection with training, etc."

of Assam.[142] The 5th and 7th Indian Divisions[143] were sent to the Arakan region to start another offensive along the Mayu Range.[144] The Imperial Japanese Army, for its part, failed to notice that the forces arrayed against it in late 1943 and 1944 were not the same as those it had faced in the past.

By 1944, the formations that fought in the Fourteenth Army had been transformed. In early 1944, the Japanese decided to launch Operation Ha-Go in the Arakan to offset British advances in the area and distract attention from their major offensive in the Imphal region. By early February, the Japanese 55th Division was on the move, intending to destroy the 5th and 7th Indian Divisions. But these British and Indian units did not break and run as their predecessors had. They stood their ground. This was a transformed army, ensconced in its new box formations and patrol bases and refusing to budge.

Around the same time, Slim began to receive reports that the Japanese were on the move in the Assam region. IV Corps – the 17th, 20th, and 23rd Indian Divisions and various brigades – were stationed in and around the Imphal region. The Japanese had concentrated more than three divisions with orders to destroy IV Corps and seize the important supply depots in the area. Operation U-Go began on March 9, when the 17th Indian Division made contact with Japanese forces along the Tiddim Road.[145] The fight for Imphal and Kohima became a battle of attrition as British and Indian units held their ground against countless Japanese attacks. Air-dropped and air-landed supplies and troops reinforced the Fourteenth Army units.[146] The British-Indian counteroffensive began from the north, as elements of the 5th and 7th Indian Divisions (recently flown in from the fighting in the Arakan), along with the 2nd British Division, fought and destroyed the Japanese forces in and around Kohima, linking up with the Imphal garrison on June 22. The Japanese refused to accept defeat until July 9, when they ordered a withdrawal to Burma. By that time, however, it was

---

[142] See WO 172/1960, 17 Ind. Div., 1943, NA, as well as Marston, *Phoenix from the Ashes*.

[143] The 5th was a veteran division, having served in East and North Africa; however, it had undergone further training in jungle warfare. See Antony Brett-James, *Ball of Fire: The Fifth Indian Division in the Second World War* (Aldershot, 1951) for more details.

[144] The Mayu Range was a line of mountains that ran north to south, almost equally dividing the Mayu peninsula. The mountains were jungle clad and thought impenetrable, as there were not many tracks. See WO 172/1936, 5 Ind. Div., and WO 172/1943, 7th Ind. Div., 1943, NA. See also Lt. Gen. Frank Messervy Papers, MSS (7 Ind. Div.) and Maj. Gen. Sir Douglas Gracey Papers, MSS (20th Indian Division) for more evidence of training and lessons work being done by the units. They are located at the Liddell Hart Centre for Military Archives, King's College, London. See also Marston, *Phoenix from the Ashes*; Tim Moreman, *The Jungle: Japanese and the British Commonwealth Armies at War, 1941–1945* (New York, 2014); and Jeffreys, *Approach to Battle*.

[145] Some units became so adept at jungle warfare and patrolling that they were able to cause considerable damage to the Japanese advance. See 14/13th Frontier Force Rifles fighting in Marston, *Phoenix from the Ashes*, 142–145.

[146] Both the 5th and 7th Indian Divisions were flown into the fighting in Kohima and Imphal to reinforce the garrisons.

too late, and IV Corps, seizing the advantage, carried on with a counteroffensive that started to destroy the Japanese forces in the region and pushed south toward the Chindwin River.

The rest of the Fourteenth Army had not been idle. As the 5th Indian and 11th East African Divisions continued the advance to destroy the Japanese forces as they withdrew during the monsoon season, other formations assessed lessons from the operations of 1944 and made improvements in training and deployment accordingly. Assessment also identified the fact that, as the army advanced into Burma, the terrain would change, offering new challenges that would need to be examined and discussed. The divisional commanders, as their counterparts in North Africa and Italy had done, expected officers and men to write down experiences, identify lessons, and assess mistakes. These assessments were incorporated in divisional lessons and training exercises, as well as in the official doctrine written by GHQ India and embodied in the Army in India Training Memorandum (AITM) and military training pamphlets, with lessons shared among the various theaters of operation.[147]

Operations Capital and Extended Capital brought about the final destruction of the Imperial Japanese Burma Area Army.[148] Slim and his commanders began the advance into Burma in November 1944. The offensive began in earnest in early December, when the 19th and 20th Indian Divisions crossed the Chindwin River and advanced on Japanese forces stationed on the other side, hoping to trap them on the Shwebo Plain. However, most Japanese forces had withdrawn to the east and south, back across the far side of the Irrawaddy River. Slim theorized that "if we took Meiktila while Kimura [the Japanese commander] was deeply engaged along the Irrawaddy about Mandalay, he would be compelled to detach large forces to clear his vital communications. This would give me not only the major battle I desired, but the chance to repeat the hammer and anvil tactics [used previously at Imphal and Kohima] ... [with] XXXIII Corps the hammer from the north against the anvil of IV Corps at Meiktila and the Japanese between."[149]

---

[147] See Marston, *Phoenix from the Ashes*, 170–179; Moreman, *The Jungle*, 146–160; Jeffreys, *Approach to Battle*, 148–180; and Ray Callahan, *Triumph at Kohima-Imphal: How the Indian Army Finally Stopped the Japanese Juggernaut* (Lawrence, KS, 2017), as well as the countless military training pamphlets and AITM available at the British Library, National Army Museum and IWM.

[148] The XV Corps, 25th, 26th Indian, 81st, and 82nd West African Divisions continued their advance down the Arakan region of Burma and were successful in tying down Japanese forces in the area. Ramree Island was seized by February 1945. Airfields were seized on the island that would prove pivotal to support the campaign in central Burma.

[149] Slim, *Defeat into Victory*, 327.

Fierce fighting ensued in and around Mandalay and Meiktila and along the Irrawaddy River. The Japanese began to withdraw from the Irrawaddy River positions, Mandalay, and Meiktila on March 24, unable to hold their positions against the aggressive British and Indian forces. With the area firmly under British and Indian control, the race to Rangoon began. The Indian Army demonstrated its professionalism as its units quickly adapted to new conditions; some units executed open-style and mechanized warfare, while others reverted to jungle tactics as they systematically destroyed the Japanese along the banks of the southern reaches of the Irrawaddy River and along the road to Rangoon. The army that marched to Rangoon was in all important respects the Indian Army.[150] Rangoon fell to an amphibious and airborne assault on May 3, ending the war in Burma for all intents and purposes.

The Burma campaign, which had begun as the longest retreat in British military history, ended as the Imperial Japanese Army's conclusive defeat, with the Indian Army playing the central role. It was a spectacular reversal of the events of 1942. The main engine for such radical changes was ultimately senior Indian Army leadership, led by officers such as Auchinleck, Slim, and Savory. As one historian has noted:

> The rebuilding of the Indian Army and Slim's Arakan and Imphal victories were demonstrations of the aggressive determination and imaginative leadership ... [The Indian Army] had remade itself by 1944 and 1945, perhaps in some ways aided by the quasi autonomy that allowed Auchinleck, Savory, Slim, and many others to get on with the business of forging a battleworthy weapon, with few interventions from above ... [T]he war in Burma was the war the Indian Army had, and it got on with preparing to win it, accepting whatever new structures or doctrines were necessary.[151]

Assessment

It would be difficult to overstate how far-reaching and fundamental were the changes that the Indian Army had gone through in the Second World War. In 1945, it was a highly professional and modern force. It had played the leading role in the destruction of the Imperial Japanese Army in Burma, as well as significant supporting roles in the defeats of Italian and German forces in

[150] See Raymond Callahan, "The Indian Army, Total War, and the Dog That Didn't Bark in the Night," in Jane Hathaway, ed., *Rebellion, Repression, Reinvention: Mutiny in Comparative Perspective* (Westport, CT, 2002), 126.
[151] Callahan, *Churchill and His Generals*, 211 and 239; see also Raymond Callahan, "Were the Sepoy Generals Any Good? A Re-appraisal of the British-Indian Army's High-Command in the Second World War," in Kaushik Roy, ed., *War and Society in Colonial India* (New Delhi, 2006).

North and East Africa and Italy. Throughout all of these engagements, the Indian Army also continued to maintain its traditional duties of frontier defense on the North-West Frontier and Aid to the Civil Power in India. In almost every way, the Indian Army of 1945 – battle-seasoned, imbued with regimental *esprit de corps*, and above all victorious – was a different force from the one that suffered crippling defeats in the difficult early days of the Second World War.

Through the upheaval of the war years, the Indian Army's officers and men kept focused on the need to learn from the mistakes that were inevitable for any force finding itself in new situations and environments with inexperienced personnel. The army had a number of teething troubles as it grew in strength and experience, but it was always able to point with pride to its ability to learn from mistakes and adapt to conditions. The Indian Army's successes in Africa, the Middle East, Italy, and particularly the Far East could not have occurred without fundamental reforms, notably expanding recruitment of ethnic groups and classes far beyond traditional limitations, restructuring the officer corps to admit more ICOs, and allowing Indians to command and sit on courts-martial of white soldiers and officers. These reforms went hand in hand with the tactical and operational level reforms that occurred on the battlefields of the Second World War. By the beginning of 1944, the Indian Army had reached a level of performance characterized by consistent and reliable professionalism.[152] Its success, particularly in contrast to earlier defeats in Malaya and Burma, reinforced the army's perceptions of itself as a truly professional force, and bolstered *esprit de corps* throughout the war and into the postwar period, even in the face of impending national independence and change.[153] Gen. Archibald Wavell, speaking as viceroy in 1945, stated that "the Indian Army had done splendidly during the war and had enhanced its own and India's reputation."[154]

Changes in recruitment, "Indianization" of the officer corps, and the ability of the army to adapt to the spectrum of conflict came to define a culture in the Indian Army that was distinct from that of its cousin, the British Army, or of other Dominion forces. Indian Army culture rested on the firm foundation of its history and ethos, but it was also adaptable enough to deal with the changing environment that occurred outside its domains. The Indian Army faced fundamental changes to its identity in the first half of the twentieth century, from who served in its ranks to how they were recruited to who ended up commanding its formations. Unlike many

---

[152] The performance of the Indian divisions in the North African campaign remains largely unexamined. A comparative analysis with other Commonwealth forces is needed.

[153] This image of the Indian Army in Indian society had significant political weight, as even members of the Indian National Congress came to recognize.

[154] Cabinet Paper, July 18, 1945, *TOP*, 5:624, 1272.

other armies of the same era, it also faced challenging operations across the spectrum of conflict, from internal security operations to high-end conventional war against peer enemies. The Indian Army faced significant challenges and experienced setbacks; however, during the Second World War the army reformed and performed at the highest levels of professionalism, especially in 1944 and 1945. Its performance in that conflict was the high-water mark of the largest all-volunteer army in history.

7   An Army Apart

The Influence of Culture on the Victorian British Army

Richard Hart Sinnreich

True military history does not begin with the armies; nor in the council chamber or legislative halls. It begins with the people – the culture if you wish ... Battles are not fought in vacuo but by products of a certain system of life. The task of the military historian is to show this connection.[1]

During the six decades from the end of the Crimean War to the dispatch of the British Expeditionary Force to France in August 1914 – an era called by some contemporaries "the long peace" – British soldiers and their locally recruited European and indigenous adjuncts fought in more than seventy campaigns from Abyssinia to Zululand.[2] Most of these were relatively obscure affairs, fought "by the orders of the Great White Queen" to preserve, and frequently to enlarge, a colonial empire that by the close of the nineteenth century encompassed nearly a quarter of the earth's land surface and population.[3]

Romanticized by writers from Rudyard Kipling to George MacDonald Fraser and in motion pictures like Zoltan Korda's *The Four Feathers* and Cy Endfield's *Zulu*, what Byron Farwell called "Queen Victoria's Little Wars" typically reflected little or no strategic premeditation. As one author has noted, "There was certainly not any grand design underpinning the 'forward policies'" of Disraeli or the annexations Lord Salisbury reluctantly contemplated in the 1890s."[4] British soldiers were dispatched abroad for purposes ranging from putting down native outlawry and suppressing revolts against British dominion to what soldiers of the era, untrammeled by political correctness, called "nigger-smashing" – punitive expeditions undertaken in response to perceived

---

[1] Maj. John H. Burns, "What about Military History?" *Coast Artillery Journal* (July–August 1938), 292.
[2] Gwyn Harries-Jenkins, *The Army in Victorian Society* (Toronto, 1977), 35.
[3] Reply by Capt. R. Duncombe of the Natal Native Contingent on being challenged to state on whose orders he and his comrades were invading Zululand, January 11, 1879. Quoted in Ian Knight, ed., *"By the Orders of the Great White Queen"* (London, 1992), 11.
[4] Edward M. Spiers, *The Late Victorian Army, 1868–1902* (Manchester, 1992), 272.

provocations ranging from diplomatic insult to mistreatment of British nationals.[5] The soldiers involved improvised not a few of these campaigns on the spot, with little or no prior consultation with a distant and often disengaged home government.

The army that conducted them was "born of paradox, forged in adversity, often betrayed by the government it obeyed and usually poorly understood by the nation it served."[6] It was an army manned largely by the most disadvantaged members of British society and officered largely by its most advantaged, serving as a convenient depository for lower-class Britain's unemployed and as an outlet for its restless upper-class youth as much as an instrument of foreign policy. And yet, although rarely exceeding 200,000 regulars, operating in some of the world's most challenging geography, and despite suffering more than one embarrassing debacle at the hands of less well-armed and disciplined enemies, the Victorian army was on the whole astonishingly successful. Reflected historian Richard Holmes almost bemusedly, "It had a certain something that flickers out across two centuries like an electric current."[7]

Holmes's "certain something" was an institutional culture almost perfectly adapted to Victorian soldiers' social origins, the kinds of tasks that they were called upon to perform, and the colonial arenas in which they were asked to perform them, but also a culture that found itself increasingly out of step with its own society and evolving military technologies, methods, and challenges. Instead, fortified by the army's success at its colonial tasks, and despite repeated efforts by politicians and even some of the army's own brightest intellectual lights, it survived – one might almost say defied – one institutional reform after another, until in South Africa in 1899, a string of calamitous defeats at the hands of what amounted to well-armed Boer farmers upended both the army's confidence and that of the British people in its professional competence. "The army that landed at the Cape [of Good Hope] was the same army as that which had fought in the Crimea. Certainly there had been changes in weapons ... But the ethos of the Victorian army remain unchanged."[8] In the Second South African War, that ethos, or at least, significant aspects of it, proved dysfunctional in ways that no longer could be ignored.

The political and institutional soul-searching that followed finally succeeded, at least to some extent, in transforming the British Army from what had become in many ways a military anachronism into a modern fighting force. The transformation came just in time to enable it to survive the bloody opening

---

[5] Unlike European wars, wrote one contemporary with no sense of irony, "ours have almost always been wars for the purpose of extending social improvement and good government." J. H. Stocqueler, *The Old Field Officer* (Edinburgh, 1853), 145.

[6] Richard Holmes, *Redcoat: The British Soldier in the Age of Horse and Musket* (London, 2001), xv.

[7] Ibid., xvi.   [8] Harries-Jenkins, *The Army in Victorian Society*, 275.

engagements of World War I and, in the process, to play a pivotal role in averting the rapid and decisive defeat of the Allied armies in France.

Not One Army, But Many

Before examining the culture of that army, we should recognize that, far from a unitary organization like today's US Army (or today's British Army, for that matter), the Victorian army instead comprised several different armies, each organizationally distinct and with its own cultural peculiarities. For starters, it comprised both units in the British Isles and others stationed more or less permanently throughout Britain's enlarging colonial empire. These tended to develop somewhat different cultural attitudes, not least because, while forces at home saw active service only episodically, many of those abroad found themselves in action more frequently. At the same time, distance from the homeland relieved soldiers and especially officers in overseas posts of some of British society's social constraints and obligations and their associated costs and expectations. Service in India in particular tended to attract soldiers and especially officers who lacked the financial means required to serve in more expensive home regiments, preferred the subcontinent's greater opportunities for active combat experience, or simply sought a more exotic lifestyle.

At home and abroad, the strength of the regular army resided in its infantry and cavalry regiments. Historically, both had been numbered according to the seniority of their creation, with no particular territorial association. In the early 1870s, however, pursuant to the Cardwell and Childers reforms, a new Localisation Bill divided the United Kingdom into brigade districts, each with a depot hosting two regiments, with the intention, never completely realized, that these would alternate overseas assignments.[9] Subsequently, single-battalion infantry regiments, by far the majority, were further amalgamated into multi-battalion regiments named for the locations in which their depots were situated, losing their historical numerical designations altogether. Thus, for example, the 71st and 74th Regiments of Foot were amalgamated into the Highland Light Infantry, and the 67th with the 37th to form the Hampshire Regiment.[10]

---

[9] These reforms included a series of institutional and organizational reforms introduced in 1868 by Secretary of State for War Edward Cardwell, belatedly correcting institutional weaknesses revealed by the Crimean War, but resisted by Conservative politicians and senior army officers until election of a reform-minded Liberal government. Temporarily curtailed by the Liberals' electoral loss in 1874, the reforms resumed on Gladstone's return to office in 1881 by Cardwell's successor, Secretary of State for War Hugh Childers.

[10] Whence much wailing and gnashing of teeth by officers and other ranks alike, many of whom continued stubbornly to refer to their former numerical designations in defiance of amalgamation. See Erik W. Flint, "Queen Victoria's Army and the Road to Reform, 1815–1872" (www .academia.edu/10656762/Queen Victoria's Army and the Road to Reform, 1815–1872), 18.

Reserve forces comprised the militia (including the yeomanry) and local volunteers, typically former regular soldiers. Until the Childers reforms, these had no direct connection with the regular army. Instead, they effectively were controlled by the lord lieutenants of the counties from which they were recruited and in which they resided. Under Childers, they were brought like the regular forces under control of the War Office. Later still, amalgamated into a Territorial Army, they were affiliated with the army's regular regiments, becoming in effect their third or higher-numbered battalions, though available for overseas deployment only in special circumstances.

After the Crimean War, driven by concern that more regular troops were needed to defend the homeland, but unwilling to increase the size of the army, the government drew down many colonial garrisons.[11] The exception was India, in which the British had stationed regulars since the days of Clive, supplementing locally recruited forces.[12] Until the Sepoy Mutiny of 1856–1857, they were for all intents and purposes leased to a private corporation, the Honorable East India Company, thence farmed out to its three semiautonomous presidencies of Bombay, Madras, and Bengal. After the Mutiny and subsequent nationalization of "John" Company in 1858, both the regular regiments of the British Army in India and the homegrown "Company" regiments of the Indian Army were subordinated to the Crown under the commander in chief, East Indies.[13]

Needless to say, given their different locations, tasks, and organizational arrangements, the cultures of these organizations differed. But while the differences between regulars and reserves and between British forces at home and those stationed overseas, especially in India, prompted occasional squabbles over matters from precedence to professionalization, their cultural differences in the end were less important than their commonalities.[14]

An Army of Tribes

Still more was that true of an even more important manifestation of Victorian army diversity. One cannot discuss British military culture in the Victorian era, or even today, for that matter, without recognizing the cultural centrality of the regiment. Historically an artifact of the feudal era when landowners/rulers

[11] Though as late as the Zulu War of 1879, 82 of the army's 141 battalions remained abroad.
[12] Richard Holmes, *Sahib: The British Soldier in India, 1750–1914* (London, 2005), 44–51.
[13] Interesting, the presidencies retained their separately manned and led armies until 1895, when they finally were amalgamated into a unified Indian army. Philip Mason, *A Matter of Honour* (New York, 1974), 25.
[14] Farwell notes that "the British officers in India had their own long-established customs and way of life, but they were not those of the regular establishment." Byron Farwell, *Queen Victoria's Little Wars* (New York, 1972), 91. That was more true of "Company" officers, however, than of those in deployed Crown regiments.

raised proprietary military units, the regiment was a communal as well as an administrative and tactical organization, and in the case of elite formations such as the Guards and Household Cavalry Regiments, maintained as much for social and ceremonial functions as for potential combat operations.[15] Throughout the Victorian era, officers and other ranks alike typically volunteered, not for "the army," but instead for service in a specific regiment, with which they were likely to remain affiliated for as long as they wore the uniform, even when actually serving elsewhere or, in the case of officers, temporarily inactive on half pay.[16]

For soldiers, the regiment was a source of identity, authority, and nurture. Recruited as they were from Britain's economically poorest classes, many found in the regiment the first economic stability they had ever known. For officers, "the regiment was a private, exclusive club, a fitting home for gentlemen," and, together with the church, a socially approved field of endeavor for non-inheriting "second sons."[17] For both officers and other ranks, and especially those on active service, the regiment was home and hearth, virtually an extended if artificial family. Indeed, regiments during the Victorian era often were extended families in more than an artificial sense, officers and other ranks following generation after generation into the same regiments. The Northcott family, for example, sent four successive generations into the Rifle Brigade (a single regiment despite its name) from Waterloo through the Crimean and Boer Wars to the First World War.[18] In Scottish, Irish, and Welsh regiments especially, soldiering was for many virtually a family business. The family of Lt. Gonville Bromhead, commanding B Company of the 24th Foot (South Wales Borderers) at Rorke's Drift, had served in the regiment for more than 120 years.[19]

From a cultural perspective, the vital importance of the regiment was its socializing influence. Its compactness, insularity, and hierarchical character alone would have exerted a powerful cultural discipline, requiring adherence to relatively strict standards of dress, deportment, and behavior. Those demands tended to be more rigorous in home regiments, especially those routinely involved in ceremonial duties, and less stringent among overseas units, especially those actually in the field, but they were nowhere entirely absent.

For other ranks, enforced intimacy and the regiment's chain of authority tended to suppress any impulse to individuality. Still more was that true for

[15] The oldest, though not senior, of the regular regiments was the 3rd Regiment of Foot, later the Royal East Kents, raised in 1572 by the London Guilds. Byron Farwell, *Mr. Kipling's Army* (New York, 1981), 24.
[16] Notes J. W. Fortescue, "So powerful were the traditions of the old proprietary system that soldiers still thought of themselves as belonging to this or that regiment rather than to the Army at large." J. W. Fortescue, *A History of the British Army, Book XVI* (London, 1930), 598.
[17] Farwell, *Mr. Kipling's Army*, 25. [18] Ibid., 26.
[19] Farwell, *Queen Victoria's Little Wars*, 231.

officers, for whom the regiment was not only a society in its own right but also a token of membership in, and for many an entree into, the larger society of upper-class Britain. "Military service could confirm social status," Spiers notes, "because it had already become a traditional and highly regarded career for the sons of many landed families."[20] The more socially exclusive the regiment, the more stringent its entry prerequisites and the less room for discordant attitudes or behavior. Usefully from a political perspective, the regimental system thus "thwarted the emergence of a cohesive officers corps, with a common sense of identity, interests and grievances ... inhibiting any disposition to intervene politically."[21]

The power of tradition reinforced formal authority and peer pressure. Regiments had histories, and these affected everything from their memorabilia and mascots to whether certain regiments could safely be brigaded together. "Officers and men alike took tremendous pride in their regiment, in its battle honours, its traditions, the distinctiveness of its uniform, and, in the case of infantry regiments, in their regional and local associations."[22] The effect of that pride and of regimental socialization generally was by no means merely superficial. "Battlefield performance was in great measure a product of long and close association in barrack-room and bivouac, grog-shop and brothel, with the creation of a small and introspective world with rules of its own ... In good regiments the process became a virtuous spiral, and a collective fighting spirit, which neither depended on discipline nor required strong leadership, took over."[23]

In return for that undoubted contribution to discipline and unit cohesion, service in the regiment imposed what could become an almost stifling and militarily dysfunctional conformity. Eccentricity could be and was tolerated, but only in proportion to seniority, and even then, only within strict limits. Nevertheless, efforts over the years to break the hold of the regimental system on the army's culture, and especially on the attitudinal uniformity of the officer corps, met with persistent resistance. Even Gen. Sir Garnet Wolseley, among the most admired Victorian army commanders and a vocal proponent of efforts to reform it, warned politicians to "keep your hands off the regiment."[24] The young Winston Churchill, himself a one-time regimental officer, echoed that

---

[20] Spiers, *The Late Victorian Army*, 95–96.   [21] Ibid., 158.

[22] Valerie B. Parkhouse, *Memorializing the Anglo-Boer War of 1899–1902* (Leicester, 2015), 7. The distinctiveness of British regimental uniforms has not changed over the years. During the author's service at NATO's military headquarters in the 1970s, it was a standing joke among Americans that if one saw two British officers in the same uniform, one of them probably was a spy.

[23] Holmes, *Redcoat*, 400–401.

[24] Wolseley was allegedly the model for the "Modern Major General" in Gilbert and Sullivan's *Pirates of Penzance*. Reflecting the admiration soldiers held for him, the phrase "All Sir Garnet" became shorthand for everything in order.

warning, when in 1904, he cautioned the House of Commons, as it contemplated post–Boer War reforms, that "regiments are not like houses. They cannot
be pulled down and altered structurally to suit the convenience of the occupier
or the caprice of the owner. They are more like plants; they grow slowly if they
are to grow strong ... and if they are blighted or transplanted they are apt to
wither."[25]

Class and Cromwell: Soldiers

In any discussion of Victorian military culture, the starting point must be the
culture of nineteenth-century British society and the class structure that it
reflected. Although by the middle of the century, the growth of Britain's middle
class had begun to erode the stark division between landowning and laboring
classes, that change was much slower to affect the army. In part, that was
because cultural change in British society lagged economic development. In a
social sense, middle-class Britons continued to take their cultural cues from the
landowning elites that many aspired to join and that continued to furnish most
of the army's commissioned officers. Meanwhile, as industrialization replaced
agriculture as the nation's dominant economic activity, the army's other ranks
began increasingly to reflect not the rural counties from which they historically
had been recruited, especially in Ireland and Scotland, but instead the slums of
Britain's urbanizing industrial centers.

Officer and enlisted recruitment also were a product of Britain's political
history, and especially of the English Civil War, which – in addition to depriving Charles I of both his crown and the head to which it was attached – also
afflicted Britain's governing classes with an enduring fear of standing armies
and distrust of professional soldiers.[26] "Since Cromwell's rule by the Major
Generals," one writer noted, "parliament was terrified of officers who were
professional military adventurers dependent on soldiering for a living, and with
no stake in the land."[27] Agreed another, "No sentiment is more firmly rooted in
the English national character than a hatred of militarism and military
dictatorship."[28]

One response to that distrust was a profound resistance to conscription.
Insistence on manning the army entirely from voluntary enlistment conditioned
everything from soldiers' geographical origins and class complexion to terms
of service and methods of discipline. Until industrialization and urbanization
began to shift recruitment from the agricultural countryside to the cities, even

---

[25] Winston Churchill to the House of Commons, August 8, 1904. Quoted in Parkhouse,
Memorializing the Anglo-Boer War of 1899–1902, 8.
[26] Harries-Jenkins, *The Army in Victorian Society*, 6.
[27] Mark Adkin, *The Charge* (London, 1996), 35–36.
[28] Cecil Woodham-Smith, *The Reason Why* (New York, 1954), 30–31.

nominally English regiments tended to overfill with non-English recruits. Economically, the army perforce tended to recruit from among the nation's most deprived. Richard Holmes noted, "Most of those who enlisted were unemployed, driven into the army by what one senior officer called 'the compulsion of destitution.'"[29] Even then, few families even among the nation's poorest were eager to see their sons in uniform. Writes Spiers, "The army never eroded the stigma which was attached to enlistment," quoting Lord Wavell's recollection that "there was in the minds of the ordinary God-fearing citizen no such thing as a good soldier; to have a member who had gone for a soldier was for many families a crowning disgrace."[30]

In return for societal disdain, harsh discipline ranging from fines and incarceration to flogging and hanging, and the ever-present possibility of death or injury far from home at the hands of an enlarging number of inhospitable natives, service in the ranks could offer only comradeship, enough money for women and drink, and, for the more conscientious, a chance at noncommissioned rank.[31] Making it even less attractive, a twenty-one-year term of service effectively committed the volunteer to a lifetime in uniform. Together, those disincentives made filling the ranks challenging. The army's growing reliance on enlistment from among the urban proletariat made it even more difficult. Such recruits tended simply as a result of their economic circumstances to be less healthy and hardy than their rural predecessors, and by mid-century, medical fitness was becoming a serious obstacle to recruitment.[32]

In an effort to overcome those challenges, in 1870, the Gladstone government introduced short-service enlistment, allowing the recruit to enlist for twelve years rather than twenty-one, and to serve only half of that enlistment on active service, the remainder in the reserves. Together with other reforms such as the abolition of flogging and payment of a modest stipend for service in the reserves, short service had an immediate beneficial impact on enlistment.[33] But it had little impact on the quality of the average recruit. As late as the outbreak of World War I, nearly three-quarters of the army's other ranks still came from the least skilled among the working classes.[34]

Together, the almost instinctive deference to superiors characteristic of his lower-class origins, the hothouse conformity imposed by life in the regiment, and the harshness of military discipline tended to produce a steady, obedient,

[29] Holmes, *Redcoat*, 149.   [30] Spiers, *The Late Victorian Army*, 135.
[31] Or even, for a fortunate few, commissions. Perhaps the most famous was Field Marshal Sir William Robertson, who rose from ranker to chief of the Imperial General Staff. Another was Colour-Sergeant Frank Bourne, hero of Rorke's Drift, who retired as a lieutenant colonel commanding.
[32] A problem with which today's US military sadly has become all too familiar.
[33] In garrisons, flogging remained legal on campaign until 1881, and in military prisons until 1907. Holmes, *Sahib*, 430–432.
[34] Farwell, Mr. *Kipling's Army*, 85. See also Spiers, *The Late Victorian Army*, 21.

and courageous soldier. But while they undoubtedly helped stiffen the line when confronted by Dervish spears or Zulu assegais, those same cultural pressures also tended to stifle subordinate initiative and to breed a tactical rigidity ill equipped to deal with more modern and sophisticated enemies.

Class and Cromwell: Officers

For officers before 1871, the clearest manifestation of both social class distinctions and political distrust of military professionalism was the purchase system, which, until abolished as one of Cardwell's reforms, required most infantry and cavalry officers to buy their initial commissions and every subsequent promotion through lieutenant colonel.[35] Today's soldiers doubtless would agree with Farwell that "the notion that an individual could purchase military rank up to and including that of lieutenant colonel, which could involve the command of a regiment in wartime, seems wholly bizarre."[36] In Britain, however, conservative and even some liberal politicians and soldiers insisted on its contribution to important economic, social, and political interests, as a result of which, despite the egregious leadership failures of the Crimean War, purchase endured for more than a decade thereafter.

The requirement that officers have independent financial means to enter and rise in the army's commissioned ranks made it unnecessary for the government to pay them a living wage, let alone a salary sufficient to sustain the lifestyle expected of a regimental officer. The cost of that lifestyle could be substantial. The minimum annual income required to serve in one of the tonier cavalry regiments appears to have been between £600 and £700 – roughly $60,000 to $70,000 in today's currency – this, at a time when a newly commissioned ensign's annual pay and allowances amounted to less than £100.[37] Service in a line infantry regiment (though not in the Rifle Brigade or one of the Guards regiments) was less costly, but only in degree. Unsurprising, then, "it was generally accepted that at no time and in no place could the British officer in those years depend on his pay as his only means of subsistence."[38]

At the same time, the considerable sums changing hands as officers bought their way up the promotion ladder, typically from a more senior officer doing the same thing or choosing to retire or go on half pay, in effect doubled as a

---

[35] Artillery and engineer officers obtained their commissions by matriculating at the Royal Military Academy, Woolwich, and thereafter were promoted by seniority. During combat operations, both commissions and promotions often were awarded for heroic behavior and to fill casualty-produced vacancies.

[36] Holmes, *Redcoat*, 158–159.   [37] Harries-Jenkins, *The Army in Victorian Society*, 97.

[38] That cost was among the major reasons driving many officers to apply to less expensive Indian army regiments, a situation that persisted as late as 1914, long after purchase had been abolished. Spiers, *The Late Victorian Army*, 105. See also Holmes, *Sahib*, 243.

pension fund, obviating the need for the government to provide one.[39] While theoretically regulated by the War Office, the prices actually paid for each such purchase, especially in the more exclusive and expensive Guards and Household Cavalry Regiments, tended to be much higher, and often required side payments. Senior officers thus could accumulate a considerable retirement nest egg.[40]

That accumulation, moreover, served still another argued value of the system: the powerful disciplinary constraint associated with the financial investment involved. Men with the private means to purchase commissions and promotions were judged to be less likely in the first place to abuse their positions by looting, embezzling, or profiteering. At the same time, military and political leaders could rely on the recognition that cashierment could deprive an officer not only of his commission but also of all the money cumulatively invested in it, to deter both military misconduct and resistance to political authority.

Above all, restricting commissions and promotions to those with significant financial means kept the army's leadership in the hands of those social and economic classes felt to have a vested interest in political stability and thus believed least likely to succumb to revolutionary impulses, a concern only the greater after 1848 given the upheavals roiling continental Europe. Declared Prime Minister Henry Palmerston to a parliamentary commission in 1857: "If the connection between the Army and the higher class of society were dissolved, then the Army would present a dangerous and unconstitutional appearance. It was only when the Army was unconnected with those whose property gave them an interest in the country, and was commanded by unprincipled military adventurers, that it ever became formidable to the liberties of the nation."[41]

Not surprising, most senior officers and especially the Duke of Cambridge, the queen's cousin and the army's commander in chief for nearly forty years, shared that view.[42] He and other conservative officers, including a group of senior retired officers known as "the colonels," lobbied strenuously against efforts to abolish purchase, arguing that replacing it with merit-based accession and promotion risked politicizing the officer ranks and turning them over to men of inferior breeding and social standing. Many parliamentarians, meanwhile, objected to the estimated £8 million cost to the exchequer involved in

[39] Harries-Jenkins notes that it was this practice, more than the purchase of initial commissions, that prompted the greatest controversy. Harries-Jenkins, *The Army in Victorian Society*, 72.

[40] To the point where some colonels actually chose to resign rather than accept promotion at the price of losing their investments. Ibid., 68–72.

[41] Henry Lord Palmerston to the Commission on Purchase, 1857, quoted in Woodham-Smith, *The Reason Why*, 32.

[42] From 1856 to 1895. Comments Holmes: "He set his face firmly against military reform, fearing that tradition would be undermined." Holmes, *Redcoat*, 83–84.

buying back officers' commissions at the inflated values accrued over their lifetimes. Risking legislative defeat in the face of parliamentary opposition, the Gladstone government instead resorted to abolition by royal warrant.[43]

For all the angst that it prompted, however, abolition in the end had little real effect on the social structure and cultural attitudes of the officer corps. "Despite the abolition of purchase, officers came predominantly from the same groups in society, with their social homogeneity increasingly reflecting a public school education and the possession of private means."[44] The largest share, remaining virtually constant from 1830 to 1912, continued to represent the landed gentry.[45] Among senior officers in particular, colonels and generals, the proportion furnished by the landowning class changed scarcely at all between 1868 and 1914. Looked at another way, even as Britain's urban proletariat increasingly replaced its rural peasantry as the major source of the army's enlisted strength, no fewer than two-thirds of its officers continued to be drawn from agricultural counties.[46] Of the remainder, a majority were themselves the offspring of career soldiers, commissioned through the Royal Military College Sandhurst, the Addiscombe Military Seminary, or the Royal Military Academy Woolwich for aspirants to the "scientific" branches, gunners and engineers.[47] In any case, "even officers whose background was not that of the landed interest were induced through their assimilation and socialization into the privileged world of the regiment to accept [its] social values."[48]

The army's enlisted composition and its continued leadership largely by the scions of the nation's landed interests combined to perpetuate a nearly feudal relationship between officers and other ranks long after it had begun to erode in British society at large, a relationship marked on one side by an unembarrassed conviction of intrinsic superiority and paternalism, and on the other by a near-instinctive deference to it.[49] Together, they produced a powerful set of shared behavioral expectations, as well as a mutual confidence that today's more egalitarian soldiers might find surprising. "The common soldiers' faith in the superiority of their gentlemen-officers as leaders and commanders promoted a steadiness in the ranks that was often commented upon ... It was faith in the type of man occupying positions of leadership, despite deficiencies in technical

---

[43] Spiers, *The Late Victorian Army*, 16–18. A circumvention made possible by the fact that commissions legally were the gift of the monarch, not of Parliament.

[44] Ibid., 114. Cardwell himself disclaimed any intention to level the class playing field.

[45] Harries-Jenkins, *The Army in Victorian Society*, 44.

[46] Spiers, *The Late Victorian Army*, 94–97.

[47] Addiscombe was the Indian army counterpart of Sandhurst until it was disestablished in 1861.

[48] Harries-Jenkins, *The Army in Victorian Society*, 278.

[49] Although elements of it still linger. A recent article describes the relationship between English barristers – litigating lawyers – and their clerks as "an enduring example of a classic British phenomenon: professional interaction across a chasmic class divide." Simon Akam, "The Exquisitely English (and Amazingly Lucrative) World of London Clerks," *Bloomberg Businessweek*, May 22, 2017.

and tactical skill, that encouraged British soldiers to stand their ground in the face of horrendous punishment and mounting losses."[50]

Only Gentlemen Need Apply

As the preceding quotation suggests, the preeminent requirement of Victorian officership, in the view of leaders and led alike, was that the commissioned officer be a gentleman. In Victorian Britain, that term carried much heavier personal and associational baggage than today's more superficial meaning. "[A]n officer had either to be born and bred and educated as a gentleman, or be prepared to act and behave like a 'natural' gentleman within the confines of regimental society. Embodied in the norms of gentlemanly behaviour were requirements of dress and deportment, an emphasis on honour and integrity, and a conformity with the manners and etiquette of polite society. Upholding these standards of behaviour was deemed necessary for maintaining the harmony and concord of the officers' mess."[51]

It also was believed essential to leading British soldiers, a view famously expressed by Wellington, echoed by Wolseley, and shared not only by most officers but also by many ordinary soldiers.[52] Wrote one, "Whatever folks may say upon the matter, I know from experience, that in our army the men like best to be officered by gentlemen, men whose education has rendered them more kind in manners than your coarse officer, sprung from obscure origin, and whose style is brutal and overbearing," adding, "[m]y observation has often led me to remark amongst men, that those whose birth and station might reasonably have made them fastidious under hardship and toil, have generally borne their miseries without a murmur; whilst those whose previous life, one would have thought, might have better prepared them for the toils of war, have been the first to cry out and complain of their hard fate."[53] His opinion was far from unique, and notably contrary to that of contemporary, mostly civilian critics who charged that the upper-class pretensions of the Victorian officer were wholly self-indulgent.

Some of the gentlemanly attributes believed essential to officership certainly may have been vulnerable to complaints of affectation, but others were much more consequential for military effectiveness, both positively and negatively.

---

[50] James A. Shaw, "Officers and Gentlemen: Gentlemanly Mystique and Military Effectiveness in the Nineteenth-Century British Army" (www.militaryhistoryonline.com/general/articles/offi cersandgentlemen.aspx#), 17.

[51] Edward M. Spiers, *The Army and Society, 1815–1914* (London, 1980), 1.

[52] "The British officer is a gentleman. We require that he should be one, and above all that he should conduct himself as such – and most particularly in reference to the soldier, and in his intercourse with the non-commissioned officers and privates." Quoted in "Military Education," *Tait's Edinburgh Magazine* (January–December 1856), 350.

[53] Henry Curling, ed., *Recollections of Rifleman Harris* (London, 1848), 60–61.

Far and away the most important were demonstrated physical courage and a studied indifference to discomfort. "Courage came first," noted one writer, "and without that nothing else counted."[54] Contemporary observers and later historians alike confirm that British officers of all ranks routinely displayed almost suicidal bravery under fire. To display "funk," even when the funk in question was no more than militarily sensible prudence, risked subjecting the offender to penalties ranging from mere contempt to outright ostracism or worse. Recalled one Crimea veteran about his officers, "More than half did not know how to maneuver a company … but it would be impossible to dispute their bravery for they were brave unto madness."[55]

Courage of course is by no means a gratuitous quality in a military leader, and Victorian officers' habitual contempt for danger undoubtedly helped inspire the stolid steadiness that Wellington's red-coated "articles" had made famous. But it also tended to breed tactical foolhardiness that occasionally approached culpable negligence. On January 22, 1879, for example, an entire British battalion and its native auxiliaries were annihilated by Zulu warriors at Isandlwana when the British commander declined to laager his encampment, though forewarned of the presence of enemies in overwhelming strength.[56] At Omdurman in the Sudan on September 2, 1898, replaying in miniature the Crimea's charge of the light brigade, the 400 troopers of the 21st Lancers, accompanied by a young Winston Churchill, lost nearly a fifth of their number recklessly attacking 2,000-odd Dervish warriors who might easily have been dispersed with gunfire.[57] While some uniformed contemporaries criticized the episode, most civilians praised it, including the queen, who awarded three of the participants Victoria Crosses and the regiment the right to style itself "Empress of India's." In these cases and others, the engrained cultural reluctance to be perceived as fainthearted merely reinforced a uniform belief in the innate superiority of the British soldier and a rigid adherence to tactical formalism, along with disdain approaching contempt for the fighting qualities of most (though not all) colonial enemies.[58]

---

[54] Mason, *A Matter of Honour*, 366.
[55] Timothy Gowing, quoted in Holmes, *Redcoat*, 123. Overall, officers received nearly half of all the Victoria Crosses awarded during the nineteenth century. Melvin Charles Smith, *Awarded for Valor: A History of the Victoria Cross and the Evolution of British Heroism* (London, 2008),139.
[56] Knight, *"By the Orders of the Great White Queen,"* 63–86. See also James O. Gump, *The Dust Rose Like Smoke* (Lincoln, NE, 1994), 15–18.
[57] Harries-Jenkins, *The Army in Victorian Society*, 174. Churchill's presence was gratuitous; he was not a member of the regiment. As Farwell points out, however, "joining a cavalry charge for the fun of it was not particularly unusual for officers." Farwell, *Queen Victoria's Little Wars*, 131.
[58] Farwell, *Mr. Kipling's Army*, 110. As Farwell noted, some "martial" races, e.g. Pathans (Afghans), Dervishes, and Gurkhas, were excepted, typically after demonstrating their ferocity in battle to British soldiers' discomfiture.

Closely associated with courage was an astonishing indifference to physical injury and impairment. In the award-winning motion picture *Lawrence of Arabia*, Peter O'Toole, playing a young T. E. Lawrence, extinguishes a lit match with his fingers. When his corporal attempts the same trick, he burns his fingers and complains that it hurts. "What's the trick then?" he asks. "The trick, William Potter," Lawrence replies, "is not minding that it hurts." During the Victorian era's "savage wars of peace," in Kipling's phrase, even senior officers routinely ignored injuries that today would compel their evacuation from the battlefield and that in many cases debar them from further combat or even from military service altogether. Apart from contemporary commentaries, one can find evidence of this trait not only in the high officer-to-enlisted casualty rates that characterized the wars of the late Victorian era (and that, moreover, carried over into the early days of World War I) but also in the extraordinary extent to which injured and disabled officers continued to serve.[59] To cite only the most famous example, having lost an arm at Waterloo, FitzRoy Somerset Lord Raglan served another thirty years, ending by commanding British forces in the Crimea. Gonville Bromhead, hero of Rorke's Drift, was virtually deaf. Less well known, Maj. Gen. Andrew Wauchope, commissioned in the Black Watch in 1864, was twice seriously wounded in 1873 in the Second Ashanti War, again in 1884 in the Sudan, once more a year later on the Nile Expedition, and finally was killed in 1899 in the opening minutes of the Battle of Magersfontein.[60] And his experience was far from unique.[61]

After courage and disdain for injury, whatever its cost in effectiveness, perhaps the next most expected quality associated with being a gentleman was a willingness to participate in sport, initially field sports such as hunting, fishing, and horse racing, but increasingly, under the influence of the public schools through which nearly all officers ultimately matriculated, coming to include team sports from cricket to polo. "With the officer corps firmly rooted in the social and cultural traditions of the rural upper class, it would naturally follow that the values and pastimes of that class would dominate the British officer corps, and they did. One of these class characteristics that dominated the life of the British officer was a passion for sport – mainly field sports and competitive games ... The average officer spent the vast majority of his time occupied with sport, more so than any other single activity, to include his

---

[59] In which nearly half of all officers became casualties during the first year. See Harold E. Raugh, *The Victorians at War, 1815–1914: An Encyclopedia of British Military History* (Westport, CT, 2004), 21.

[60] William Wright, *Warriors of the Queen: Fighting Generals of the Victorian Age* (Charleston, SC, 2014).

[61] The astonishing exemplar probably was the late Sir Adrian Carton de Wiart, wounded twice in the Boer War, nine more times in World War I, and once more in World War II.

military duties."[62] Indeed, not the least of the attractions of service in India, in addition to its lower living costs and greater chance of active campaigning, were its opportunities to pursue sports ranging from polo, pig-sticking, and spear hunting from horseback to big-game hunting.

Far from being viewed by superiors as detracting from an officer's military diligence, sporting activity was instead encouraged as a contributor to hardiness and aggressiveness. A scene in George MacDonald Fraser's satirical novel *Flashman*, in which fictional Lt. Harry Flashman finds his way onto (nonfictional) Maj. Gen. Sir William Elphinstone's staff, thence into the middle of the First Afghan War, by lancing a stray dog under the eye of another senior general, is an accurate reflection of the attitude of most if not all Victorian commanders. In his widely read vade mecum *The Soldier's Pocketbook*, then-Col. Wolseley wrote that "being a good sportsman, a good cricketer, good at rackets or any other manly game, is no mean recommendation for staff employments. Such a man, without book lore, is preferable to the most deeply-read one of lethargic habits."[63] Nor did increasing rank alter his attitude. "I hope the officers of Her Majesty's Army may never degenerate into bookworms," he wrote in 1897 as army commander in chief, adding, "I am glad to say this generation is as fond of danger, adventure, and all manly out-of-door sports as its forefathers were."[64]

The preoccupation with "all manly out-of-door sports" certainly contributed to the health and fitness of the Victorian officer and over time contributed in a useful way to bonding officers and other ranks more closely.[65] But it came at a price. Sporting activities were much more likely to fill Victorian army officers' plentiful leisure time than professional study or exercise. An officer who chose to "swot" rather than participate in sports was apt to be rebuked, if not worse, not only by his peers but also, as Wolseley's comment implies, by his superiors.[66] In fact, many including Wolseley considered participation in sports

---

[62] James Dunbar Campbell, "'The Army Isn't All Work': Physical Culture in the Evolution of the British Army, 1860–1920," *Electronic Theses and Dissertations*, Paper 185, 2003, 10–12.

[63] Col. Sir Garnett J. Wolseley, *The Soldier's Pocket-Book for Field Service*, 2nd edn. (London, 1871), 153. Victorian soldiers were not unique in that view. A bronze plaque at West Point's Michie Stadium displays a quotation attributed, possibly apocryphally, to Gen. George C. Marshall: "I want an officer for a secret and dangerous mission. I want a West Point football player."

[64] Tim Travers, *The Killing Ground: The British Army, The Western Front and the Emergence of Modern Warfare, 1900–1918* (London, 1982), 39.

[65] "The passion for sports came to be shared by all ranks, and it brought an almost egalitarian spirit into the army. It was to be sure, a very particular kind of egalitarianism, for the two castes remained distinct, but at least it gave the gentlemen-officers and the peasant-proletarian other ranks a common interest beside the spirit of the regiment." Farwell, *Mr. Kipling's Army*, 203. See also Fortescue, *A History of the British Army*, 599.

[66] "The few officers, who took a professional interest in the arts and sciences of war, were regarded as slightly eccentric. Only a few had any conception of, or interest in, logistics or administration of any kind." Farwell, *Queen Victoria's Little Wars*, 71.

an ideal preparation for combat. Not surprising, then, "the distinction between sport and war became blurred in the minds of officers who went from public schools to Sandhurst to regiments. More and more used the language of games and hunting when speaking of war, which came to be regarded as the greatest game of all."[67]

The Amateur Ideal

If war was sport, it is unsurprising that, like sport, it was viewed by upper-class Britons as preferentially the preoccupation of amateurs. In the 1981 motion picture *Chariots of Fire*, the master of Cambridge University's Trinity College reproves future Olympian gold medalist Harold Abrahams for employing a personal trainer, accusing him of adopting a "professional" attitude: "We've always believed that our games are indispensable in helping to complete the education of an Englishman," he declares. "[But] this university believes that the way of the amateur is the only one to provide satisfactory results." The scene of course takes place in the 1920s, long after the period examined here. But the implied distaste bordering on contempt for anything smacking of studied professionalism was common in upper-class British society throughout the Victorian period, and its effects inevitably pervaded an officer corps largely drawn from or aspiring to join that society. "The British officer felt only encouragement in his freedom from serious professional obligations. He could remain indifferent to technical or practical knowledge, even to the details of routine administration ... There was, in fact, a marked suspicion of 'scientific' (i.e. professional) officers among their more conventional fellows."[68]

Contributing to that predisposition, ironically, was the army's growing reliance throughout the late Victorian era on Britain's public schools as sources of officer accession. With purchase abolished, by far the most common route to a commission became the public school, either by direct commission or via Sandhurst and Woolwich.[69] "The gentlemanly ideal, which army officers were expected to embody, was transmitted from generation to generation most perfectly through the medium of Britain's greater and lesser public schools, from which many officers graduated."[70] The academic curricula of these institutions, heavily biased toward the classics, were viewed even by their own faculty as less important than inculcating the traits of character and "muscular Christianity" considered essential to sustaining Britain's empire and furthering its civilizing mission. "The essential objectives of the public

---

[67] Farwell, *Mr. Kipling's Army*, 206.   [68] Shaw, "Officers and Gentlemen," 7.
[69] By 1900, public schools were furnishing more than 50 percent of Sandhurst's entrants and nearly 80 percent of Woolwich's. Harries-Jenkins, *The Army in Victorian Society*, 141. Addiscombe closed in 1861 following the amalgamation of the Indian with the Royal Army.
[70] Shaw, "Officers and Gentlemen," 6.

school and the university were thus the transmission of a body of central cultural values, to the total exclusion of considerations about vocational or professional needs."[71]

The effect of this was most marked in the debates that raged throughout the later Victorian period concerning the need for and value of professional military education. Even as developments on the continent, especially Prussia's decisive victories in 1866 and 1870–1871, revealed the mounting impact of technology on the battlefield and the associated increase in tactical complexity, efforts to improve officer education and to increase its impact on career advancement encountered bitter resistance. "[T]he army itself was not certain whether a formal professional training was entirely necessary. The force of the 'amateur ideal' continued to be very pronounced. It was a notion that manners, signifying virtue, and classical culture, signifying a well-turned mind, were better credentials for leadership than any amount of expert practical training."[72] Sandhurst's and Woolwich's eligibility, curricula, and graduation standards changed repeatedly throughout the 1870s and 1880s, and while officers post-purchase had to sit examinations to become eligible for promotion, promotion itself continued to rest on seniority. Examinations accordingly remained undemanding and *pro forma*, and the commander in chief resolutely opposed efforts to make them competitive.[73]

The Staff College at Camberley fared little better. Established in 1858, it initially had little impact. Few junior officers were eager to sacrifice the pleasures of the regimental mess for its two-year course of instruction, and those who were willing to do so received little encouragement from peers and superiors.[74] Gradually, the reputation of the course and the value of a "PSC" (Passed Staff College) credential improved, especially after Wolseley began including graduates in his "Wolseley ring" of favored staff officers and encouraging ambitious young officers to compete for Camberley's limited spaces. By the time of his 1882 Egyptian campaign, Camberley graduates filled thirty-four of his staff appointments, many such as Evelyn Wood and Redvers Buller destined to achieve high rank themselves.[75]

[71] Harries-Jenkins, *The Army in Victorian Society*, 112. See also Lawrence James, *The Rise and Fall of the British Empire* (London, 1994),206.
[72] Harries-Jenkins, *The Army in Victorian Society*, 147.
[73] Spiers, *The Late Victorian Army*, 109.
[74] Wrote one graduate, "For a considerable number of years after it was opened the staff college was looked on with some disfavor, by the old officers because it was a newfangled notion, and by the young officers as a 'mug's game.'" Maj. Gen. Sir George Younghusband, *A Soldier's Memories in Peace and War* (London, 1917), 115. See also David Stubbs, "A Perspective on Military Education and Leadership: Past, Present and Future," *Journal of the Royal Air Force College* (May 2013), 20.
[75] Spiers, *The Late Victorian Army*, 111.

Notwithstanding, the college continued to be viewed with disdain by many regimental officers, who considered the course itself elitist in character and attendance by their peers a means of evading their share of more prosaic regimental duties. For all his encouragement of officer professionalization, Wolseley himself assigned more importance in selecting his own acolytes to family background, congeniality, and love of sport than to formal schooling, ranking the latter well below field experience as a desirable subordinate attribute. Accordingly, even though the academic reputation of the college and its curriculum improved materially over the second half of the century, grooming several of the army's best thinkers, its overall impact on the professionalization of the officer corps languished, remaining far behind that of continental counterparts such as Prussia's *Kriegsakademie*. Complained one contemporary journal, "Whether an army ought to be a profession or a plaything, seems a question which in England, but in England alone, is still a matter of indecision and perplexity."[76]

Tactical Inertia

Conviction in the intrinsic superiority of British manhood and the resistance of the army's leadership to professionalization and institutional change combined to retard tactical adaptation where it did not stifle it entirely. The half-century between the Crimean and the Second South African Wars was one of unprecedentedly rapid change in military technology and method. While the British Army adopted a rifled musket in 1851, for example, a majority of the troops deployed to the Crimea still carried the 1842 smoothbore. It took another twenty years to design and issue a purpose-built single-shot breechloader, the Martini-Henry, and that rifle still was in general service when the Zulus attacked Rorke's Drift in December 1879. A magazine-fed rifle finally reached the hands of the troops ten years later. By that time, French and German armies already were fielding lighter, harder-hitting, second-generation bolt-action rifles firing smokeless cartridges.

Artillery development was even more glacial. The army actually fielded its first rifled breechloader in 1859, only to revert a few years later to cheaper and less complicated muzzle-loaders. Not until 1885 would the army belatedly reissue breech-loading field artillery. As a result, in 1899, British artillerymen would find themselves outgunned and outranged by Boer "pom-poms" and 75 mm guns from Krupp and Creusot. The army was somewhat quicker to adapt to the machinegun, adopting its first Gatling guns in 1871 and using those and other crank-operated rapid-firers in several colonial campaigns down to and including the Gordon Relief Expedition of 1884–1885. By the Battle of

---

[76] *Tait's Edinburgh Magazine*, January–December 1856, 354.

Omdurman on September 2, 1898, the army had replaced them with more reliable and effective belt-fed Maxim guns.[77] Nevertheless, they still were treated essentially as artillery, adjuncts to, but no replacement for, massed musketry.

Tactics witnessed a similar inertia. The strength of the British Army long had resided in the close-order formations and disciplined volley fire of its infantry. Despite the occasional debacle such as Isandlwana and Maiwand, those tactics continued throughout the Victorian period to succeed more often than not against less well-armed and disciplined indigenous enemies. But they were becoming increasingly hazardous with the emergence of breech-loading rifles, powerful smokeless cartridges, and quick-firing long-range artillery.

British leaders were not ignorant of the changes taking place in foreign armies. The US Civil War, the Franco-Prussian War, and the Russo-Turkish War of 1877–1878 all were closely observed. But cultural hubris and colonial preoccupation combined to limit their impact. As one writer notes, "[F]orms of technology such as the breech-loading rifle and machine gun were not simply passive objects. Their use, their reception and their representation were not value neutral."[78] Where their employment clashed with traditional infantry, cavalry, and artillery practices, the latter were apt to prevail.

Efforts to adopt infantry tactics relying on independent fire and dispersed maneuver, for example, met with determined resistance. As late as the early 1890s, authoritative military experts such as Col. G. F. R. Henderson, a professor of military art and history at Camberley and the author of a widely praised biography of Stonewall Jackson, continued to insist on the decisive role of the frontal attack with the bayonet.[79] Even Wolseley was loath to abandon tactics that had served the army well for so long, and the tactical manuals issued during his term of office as adjutant general continued to stress the close formations, linear tactics, and fire-by-volley that had been the hallmarks of the British infantry since Wellington.[80] Cavalry tactics suffered from similar inertia. While the mobility afforded by the horse would not be challenged by any army until long after the advent of mechanization, mounted formations were becoming even more vulnerable than infantry to magazine-fed rifles and quick-firing artillery. Nevertheless, British cavalry regiments continued through the 1880s to issue and train their troopers in the use of lance and saber, and the mounted charge remained a staple of British cavalry tactics.[81]

---

[77] Whence Hilaire Belloc's satirical jingle, "Whatever happens we have got the Maxim gun, and they have not." H. B. and B. T. B., *The Modern Traveler* (London, 1898), 41.

[78] Michael Brown, "Cold Steel, Weak Flesh: Mechanism, Masculinity and the Anxieties of Late Victorian Empire," *Cultural and Social History: The Journal of the Social History Society* (2016), 176.

[79] Spiers, *The Late Victorian Army*, 250.   [80] Ibid., 251.   [81] Ibid., 259.

Finally, for all the regimental system's undoubted contribution to unit cohesion and *esprit de corps*, one less helpful by-product, reinforced by the colonial policing tasks to which the Victorian army largely found itself committed, was a disinclination to plan for or practice larger unit operations. Even the example of the Franco-Prussian War of 1870–1871 proved insufficient to compel political and military leaders to think in terms of and to resource permanent organizations above the regimental level. "The British army was basically a mere collection of regiments which were assembled in any order a general saw fit when the need arose."[82] Regiments typically assembled in brigades and divisions only in preparation for or even after deployment. As a result, "Whenever a crisis arose, the appointed field commander had to improvise in his preparatory planning, choice of staff, and logistical and transport arrangements."[83] In the Abyssinian campaign of 1868, for example, launched to punish Ethiopian Emperor Theodore II for imprisoning several missionaries and two British government representatives, the army required nearly five months to assemble and deploy 13,000 British and Indian soldiers, 26,000 camp followers, and more than 40,000 animals, including 44 elephants. One result was that an expedition expected to last only a few months and to cost no more than £4 million ended instead lasting nearly a year and costing more than £9 million.[84]

An Army for What?

That sort of improvisation reflected the disinclination of British governments and the army's leadership to conduct what we would call strategic planning. Even the army's core missions remained formally undefined until 1888, when, under pressure from Wolseley, Secretary of State for War Edward Stanhope finally issued what became known as the Stanhope Memorandum, defining five army priorities. Reflecting Victorian Britain's strategic insularity, however, Stanhope relegated to last priority preparation for major overseas commitment against a peer adversary, on the argument that "the employment of an Army Corps in the field in any European war is sufficiently improbable to make it the primary duty of the military authorities to organise our forces efficiently for the defence of this country."[85] Which might explain why, as late as 1903, St John Brodrick, Stanhope's successor several times removed, was still complaining

---

[82] Farwell, *Mr. Kipling's Army*, 21.   [83] Spiers, *The Late Victorian Army*, 67–68.

[84] Farwell, *Queen Victoria's Little Wars*, 169–175. See also Harries-Jenkins, *The Army in Victorian Society*, 178. It was, however, astonishingly successful, both operationally and as a logistical achievement, and the latter capability repeated itself in South Africa, confirming the high art to which Victorian logisticians raised "muddling through."

[85] Spiers, *The Late Victorian Army*, 337. First priority, tellingly, was support of the civil authority, in effect suppression of domestic unrest.

to Prime Minister Arthur Balfour that "I do not find that any definite instruction exists as to what is the exact purpose for which the army exists and what duties it is supposed to perform."[86]

In part, of course, that omission reflected the strategic and institutional primacy of the Royal Navy, reflected in Viscount Edward Grey's famous comment to the effect that "the British army should be a projectile to be fired by the British navy." But it was even more an almost inevitable result of the Victorian army's colonial preoccupations. "Since these were the actions in which, with the solitary exception of the Crimea, the British Army had been involved from Waterloo onward, [they] had a profound effect on the development of military professionalism."[87] What Harries-Jenkins calls a "small war mentality" particularly affected the officer corps, the senior leaders of which, having enjoyed almost unbroken success in those contests, saw little reason to alter methods that had served the army so well.[88] Further encouraging that self-satisfied complacency was the genuine fear among more senior officers, including even reformists such as Wolseley, that introducing new tactical methods would undermine the cohesion and steadiness that made British infantry so formidable, and the audacity and "dash" believed essential to the effectiveness of British cavalry.[89] As one officer admitted in the wake of the army's early defeats in South Africa, service in small colonial wars "had developed physical and personal qualities which would always be vital in combat, but it had also produced a dangerous narrowing of the intellectual vision" essential to managing large forces in modern warfare.[90]

South African Wake-Up

In his magisterial *A History of the British Army*, J. W. Fortescue commented wryly that "in any serious war, it is always the fate of the existing British army to be destroyed within three months."[91] While the British Army in South Africa was not destroyed in the first three months of the Second Boer War, it certainly was humiliated. Invading Cape Colony and Natal at the outset of hostilities, fast-moving Boer commandos quickly besieged British garrisons in Ladysmith, Kimberley, and Mafeking, and during the "Black Week" of December 10–15, 1899, at Stormberg, Magersfontein, and Colenso, inflicted

---

[86] Farwell, *Mr. Kipling's Army.*   [87] Harries-Jenkins, *The Army in Victorian Society*, 84.
[88] Notes Harries-Jenkins, "in itself, this was not unreasonable," adding in words that resonate today, "if it could be guaranteed by the civil power that the military would not be used against any other kind of opponent, then the use of outmoded tactics by the army or the reluctance of the officer corps to consider more critically wider strategical issues, were unimportant factors." Ibid., 211.
[89] Spiers, *The Late Victorian Army*, 299.   [90] Ibid., 299–300.
[91] Fortescue, *A History of the British Army*, 261.

stinging open-field defeats on the British forces attempting to relieve the besieged.

More British embarrassment followed at Spion Kop on January 23–24, Vaal Krantz on February 5–7, and Paardeberg on February 18. In the last named battle, Gen. Herbert Kitchener, commanding in place of an indisposed Gen. Frederick Roberts, ordered his Highlanders and Canadians to charge straight at enemy trenches across nearly 1,000 yards of open ground. The Boers held their fire until the British closed to within a few hundred yards, then slaughtered them. All told, the day's fighting cost the British more than 1,000 casualties, the worst one-day loss of the entire war.

For the British public, the rare drubbing by Pathans, Dervishes, or Zulus could be blamed on unlucky commanders, feckless native troops, or numerically superior if less well-armed enemies. Not so the debacle that afflicted British forces in South Africa in the last three months of 1899 and the first two months of 1900. British regulars, including storied regiments, repeatedly were outgeneraled, outmaneuvered, and outfought by South Africa's indifferently organized but well-armed and determined Boer militias. Eventually, of course, under the leadership of Roberts and a chastened Kitchener, and after receiving significant reinforcements from home, the army recovered from its early defeats, crushing the last regular Boer force in August 1900. What followed was not peace, however, but rather a bitter insurgency that dragged on for two more years. In the end, to defeat it, the British had to employ methods the harshness of which exacted a terrible toll on the civilian population, outraged liberals in and out of government, and earned the nation widespread international condemnation.[92]

At home, the duration and difficulty of the struggle shattered the confidence of both government leaders and ordinary Britons in the nation's military competence. The war had lasted more than twice as long as anyone had expected, and cost Britain heavily in lives and treasure.[93] Wrote one historian, "The army had been so thoroughly humiliated by its long-suffering attempts to deal with what at first was called by the press 'a tea-time war' that Whitehall feared that some essential élan had disappeared from the English race and that some weaknesses had been exposed which other countries were eager to exploit."[94]

---

[92] It was in South Africa that the concentration camp was born, in an effective but also widely condemned effort to separate the insurgents from the civilian population. See Denis Judd and Keith Surridge, *The Boer War* (London, 2003), chapter 12.

[93] "Expected to be over by Christmas 1899, it lasted for another twenty-nine months and cost the British taxpayer some £201,000,000" – an enormous sum for the day. Spiers, *The Late Victorian Army*, 312.

[94] Cecil D. Eby, *The Road to Armageddon* (Durham, NC, 1987), 28. Another writer put it more epigrammatically: "The Boer War," he declared, "knocked the gilt off the Victorian Age." J. A.

The *Schadenfreude* with which the continental powers observed Britain's military embarrassment, and the recognition that a war against any of them would invite even worse humiliation, only intensified the resulting national paranoia. Even before the war, Prime Minister Salisbury had warned the queen that "as land forces go in these days, we have no army capable of meeting even a second-class Continental Power."[95] South Africa hammered that reality home with stunning brutality. In turn, that humiliation finally spurred the organizational and institutional reform efforts that so many had resisted for so long.[96] In a postmortem report covering four dense volumes, a Royal Commission under the chairmanship of the Earl of Elgin indicted organizational and institutional deficiencies ranging from the inadequate training of officers and a lack of subordinate initiative to poor marksmanship and inadequate use of entrenchment.[97]

The Elgin report focused more on shortcomings than on remedies, but one immediate result was the establishment of Britain's first permanent cabinet-level civil-military coordinating body, the Committee of Imperial Defence. Subsequently, a subcommittee of that body chaired by Lord Esher, a member of the Commission, undertook the more onerous task of proposing reforms to correct the deficiencies identified in the report. The most important of those recommendations found policy expression in the reforms undertaken by Secretary of State for War Richard Haldane between 1905 and 1912.[98] Although concentrated largely on the senior management of the army and its preparation for large-scale expeditionary operations, the Haldane reforms also required the army to address tactical shortcomings that the Second Boer War had thrown into sharp relief.[99] It was in the controversies that resulted that culture and adaptation clashed most directly.

S. Grenville, *Lord Salisbury and Foreign Policy: The Close of the Nineteenth Century* (London, 1970), 268.

[95] John Charmley, *Splendid Isolation? Britain, the Balance of Power, and the Origins of the First World War* (London, 1999), 207.

[96] Noted one critic, "'Something business-like' would have to replace the 'smartness, gilt braid, and gallantry' which had hitherto characterized the army." James, *The Rise and Fall of the British Empire*, 321.

[97] The Royal Commission, *Report on the War in South Africa* (London, 1903). Tellingly, many of the Commission's criticisms mirrored similar indictments following the Crimean War.

[98] For a useful treatment, see Simon Giles Higgens, "How Was Richard Haldane Able to Reform the British Army? An Historical Assessment Using a Contemporary Change Management Model," Master's thesis, University of Birmingham, 2010. Higgens concluded that "lasting [army] reform required the technical and social dimensions of it to be addressed simultaneously and as an organic whole."

[99] Maj. Andrew J. Risio, "Building the Old Contemptibles: British Military Transformation and Tactical Development from the Boer War to the Great War, 1899–1914" (US Army Command and General Staff College, 2005), 28.

Culture and Adaptation

Examining the evolution of the British Army between 1902 and 1914, one writer notes, "In the twelve years between the end of the Boer War and the outbreak of the First World War, the army underwent vast and important organizational and tactical reforms that ultimately produced, in the words of official historian John Edmonds, 'incomparably the best trained, best organised, and best equipped British Army which ever went forth to war.'"[100]

Some might quibble with Edmond's appraisal, but there's no doubt that the army that deployed to France in August 1914 looked very different from the one that landed in Cape Town in November 1899. Changes ranged from the establishment of the first army general staff to doctrinal changes in every branch of the service (infantry, cavalry, artillery, and engineers) and at every command level from company to brigade. Bitter debates preceded those changes, however, and the ultimate results were by no means universally applauded in or out of the army. "A consensus on clear-cut lessons did not immediately emerge, and interservice rivalry, social snobbery, and the continuing struggle between cliques within the officer corps confused the issues still further."[101] The Russo-Japanese War of 1904–1905 only compounded the confusion. While the war confirmed many of the tactical lessons learned in South Africa, it obscured others. Confronted with the war's evidence, one recent analyst commented, "Partisans of particular doctrinal approaches tended to find what they wanted to suit their own arguments."[102]

The challenge is not to critique those arguments or their eventual results, but rather to try to understand to what extent they reflected the Victorian army's underlying culture, and, as important, what additional proposed changes, whether urged by the army's own South African experience, that of the Russo-Japanese War, or both, proved unable to overcome engrained cultural resistance. Three issues in particular help to illuminate the conflict between culture and adaptation.

The first was the question how to respond tactically to the enormous increase in range and lethality associated with introduction of the magazine-fed rifle and machine gun. South Africa had made abundantly clear the vulnerability to such weapons of the compact linear formations that had been British infantry's predominant tactical method throughout the Victorian era. Against the rush of more numerous but undisciplined and ill-armed native tribesmen, such formations gave soldiers a comforting sense of solidarity and allowed close

---

[100] Spencer Jones, *From Boer War to World War: Tactical Reform of the British Army, 1902–1914* (Kindle Edition) (Norman, OK, 2012), 9–10. This section relies heavily on his work.

[101] Ibid., 35.

[102] Jonathan B. A. Bailey, "Military History and the Pathology of Lessons Learned," in Williamson Murray and Richard Hart Sinnreich, eds., *The Past As Prologue: The Importance of History to the Military Profession* (Cambridge, 2006), 185.

control of fire discipline. But they virtually precluded the effective use of cover in the attack and forfeited all the advantages of concealment afforded by breech-loading weapons and smokeless propellants in the defense.

The obvious solution was to abandon close formations in favor of the extended and dispersed formations long associated with skirmishing, and after the disasters of Spion Kop and Paardeberg, Lord Roberts issued guidance directing such formations. Even then, however, many units were slow to comply. "Taking cover during the attack was a controversial subject within the pre–Boer War British Army, and it was not widely practiced in peacetime. The army was proud of its reputation for 'dash,' and there was a spirit of resistance to any tactical method that threatened to reduce this much-prized attribute."[103]

After the war, peacetime training continued to preach respect for enemy fire, the need to avoid tactical rigidity, and the need to adapt movement and positioning to the terrain. But not all agreed with the abandonment of close-order formations. "Although a return to close-order shoulder-to-shoulder formations was never seriously advocated, a number of officers questioned the lessons of extension derived from South Africa."[104] Skeptics argued that both the enemy and the battlefield environment of the South African War were unique. "The extreme extension we adopted was justified by results, but it would be a very unsound generalisation to assume that similar extensions would answer against an active European drilled army."[105] Unlike Boer units, which rarely held their positions under close assault, such skeptics believed that more disciplined European soldiers would have to be overwhelmed by concentrated firepower and the bayonet. The success of dense Japanese attacks against entrenched Russian positions, albeit at ruinous cost, gave them additional ammunition. So did the French Army's emerging obsession with *élan vital* as the decisive factor in tactical success, especially in the offensive. Fortunately, such skeptics were in the minority, and while debate about how to reconcile open order with shock in the attack never entirely subsided, by 1914, the army had largely internalized dispersal and exploitation of the terrain in both offensive and defensive operations.

But abandonment of close-order tactics would be unachievable without a fundamental change in the battlefield behavior of the soldier, and derivatively in the relationship between soldiers and leaders. "Cherished concepts such as strict discipline and unthinking obedience to orders [would be] of limited value in a conflict where officers and men were often widely separated and forced to

---

[103] Jones, *From Boer War to World War*, 78.   [104] Ibid., 81.
[105] Lt.-Col. F. N. Maude, "Continental versus South African Tactics: A Comparison and Reply to Some Critics," *Journal of the Royal United Services Institute* 46(1) (1902), 324. Quoted in Jones, *From Boer War to World War*, 81–82.

rely on their own initiative to an unprecedented degree."[106] To a considerable extent, resistance to adoption of open-order tactics reflected an inbred distrust of the individual soldier. Many officers feared that, deprived of the stiffening proximity of comrades and close officer supervision, he might neither advance nor stand, and that absent close control of the firing line, most ammunition would be wasted.[107] But dispersed tactics would render those conditions infeasible. Soldiers advancing or defending in extended order and using the terrain for cover and concealment would be less vulnerable to enemy fire, but also more alone. Directing their movements would be more difficult, and controlling their fire virtually impossible.

To the last concern, the obvious answer was improved marksmanship training, and to that reform, few objected. "The quality of individual musketry and the seriousness that was now attached to it was the most striking change in the British infantry in the aftermath of the Boer War."[108] Although debate persisted about the range at which soldiers should be trained to fire independently and how much training ammunition would be necessary to achieve desired skill levels, virtually everyone agreed on the need for better shooting. By 1914, British soldiers were uniformly better marksmen than their foreign peers, a superiority acknowledged by friend and foe alike. At the First Battle of Ypres, British rifle fire was so rapid and accurate that the Germans attributed it to machine gun fire.[109]

Requiring greater initiative from individual soldiers and noncommissioned officers (NCOs) proved more problematic. Doing so confronted deep-seated obstacles. Many doubted that soldiers recruited from Britain's lowest and least educated social class could be trained to the necessary standard. "The contradictory factors of lingering mistrust of the social class from which much of the army was drawn and a desire to encourage skill and initiative among the men caused the British Army to undergo what M. A. Ramsay termed 'a paradigmatic crisis' as it searched for tactical solutions to the problems of modern warfare."[110] The solution once again was improved individual and small unit training, and for that purpose, the presence during the run-up to 1914 of so many Boer War veterans in the ranks was the most important single factor in overcoming the cultural obstacles.

The problem remained of adjusting the attitudes and behavior of officers, far and away those culturally most affected by and resistant to fundamental tactical change. Part of the job had been done by the Boers, who were quick to take advantage of British officers' studied indifference to risk and conviction in the

[106] Jones, *From Boer War to World War*, 37.
[107] A not unreasonable concern, as a later war confirmed. See S. L. A. Marshall, *Men against Fire: The Problem of Battle Command* (New York, 1947). Though later criticized, Marshall's work had a positive effect on US Army marksmanship training.
[108] Jones, *From Boer War to World War*, 93.   [109] Ibid., 100.   [110] Ibid., 46.

necessity of leading visibly from the front. One account reported that "by late October 1899, British forces in Natal had lost seventy-three officers and three commanding officers, proportionally twice as many casualties as the men."[111] Officers soon divested themselves of sabers and insignia, and by the Battle of Spion Kop, were indistinguishable from their soldiers.

Less easy was inducing them to relegate to NCOs the close supervision of fire and maneuver previously believed solely manageable by commissioned officers. "Social status remained an important aspect to command, with one prize-winning essay published in 1914 arguing, 'The "habit to command" is largely hereditary,' while another officer felt that it would be impossible to expect NCOs to be capable of the same intellectual standards expected from officers unless they were drawn from the same social class."[112]

Between greater formation dispersal and officers' self-imposed visual anonymity, however, and in the absence of the tactical communications available to today's small units, battalion and company-grade officers during the Boer War had had little choice but to empower their noncommissioned subordinates. Reflecting that experience, and in response to the Elgin commission's critique of the army's tactical rigidity and lack of subordinate initiative, in 1904, the army established its first formal NCO academy at Salisbury Plain, the army's principal training ground, aimed squarely at improving NCOs' ability and willingness to assume tactical command responsibility. Only two years later, however, it was disestablished, allegedly for budgetary reasons, but more plausibly a casualty of the continuing cultural reluctance to delegate authority to members of a lower social class.[113] In the end, perforce, practicality overruled culture: "Although social prejudice created certain tensions and limited the development of the tactical role played by NCOs, it did not stop overall improvements taking place in training for all ranks during the 1902–1914 period."[114]

If British infantry eventually succeeded in overcoming cultural resistance to tactical change, however, other arms were less successful. After scrapping sword and lance in favor of firearms in South Africa, for example, the cavalry reintroduced both a few years after the war, and the mounted charge continued to resist all efforts to abandon it. The 1907 edition of the *Cavalry Manual* declared that "the rifle, effective as it is, cannot replace the effect produced by the speed of the horse, the magnetism of the charge, and the terror of cold

---

[111] Thomas Pakenham, *The Boer War* (London, 1997), 151. Quoted in Jones, *From Boer War to World War*, 79.

[112] Jones, *From Boer War to World War*, 47.

[113] M. A. Ramsay, *Command and Cohesion: The Citizen Soldier and Minor Tactics in the British Army, 1870–1918* (London, 2002), 56 and 64.

[114] Jones, *From Boer War to World War*, 48.

steel."[115] The field artillery similarly resisted moving guns into defilade, insisting that relying on new indirect fire techniques would reduce artillery's effectiveness, have a deleterious moral effect on supported infantry, and expose gunners to charges of unmanliness. South Africa's lesson on the importance of entrenchment also tended to fade from view, victim of the increasing preoccupation with the offensive that the Edwardian British Army shared with its continental counterparts. All of these syndromes would perish expensively in the waning months of 1914 at places with names like Mons, Le Cateau, and Ypres.

An Army Apart

The experience of the British Army between Crimea and World War I confirms the pervasive influence of cultural attitudes on military behavior, and their durability even in the face of countervailing pressures for institutional reform. The culture of the Victorian army proved throughout Britain's late nineteenth-century colonial expansion to be a powerful contributor to unit cohesion and combat effectiveness, enabling often outnumbered British soldiers operating far from home in hostile climates and difficult terrain to achieve remarkably consistent battlefield success against less sophisticated and disciplined enemies. But that same culture acted as a troublesome brake on tactical and technical progress, at best unduly delaying needed change, and at worst obstructing it outright. Even the chastening experience of the Boer War and the reinforcing evidence of the Russo-Japanese War could not altogether overcome prejudices reflecting decades of relative cultural stasis and, in the view of those sharing them, the confirming confidence resulting from a history of nearly unbroken colonial victories.

Perhaps the most perplexing aspect of that cultural stasis was its survival during a period when the culture of the larger society was changing significantly. By the turn of the century, the binary class division of preindustrial British society had virtually disappeared. Although the burgeoning middle class continued to take many of its attitudinal cues from the upper classes, even among the latter, cultural attitudes and expectations had begun to dissipate under the pressure of economic progress and political liberalization. How, then, were increasingly archaic cultural attitudes and expectations able to survive in the Victorian army in the face of mounting challenges to their political acceptability and military utility?

Almost certainly, the most important single answer is that it was a self-selected army, and moreover, given its composition, public attitudes, and the tasks to which it was applied, a physically and psychologically remote army.

---

[115] Quoted by Bailey in "Military History and the Pathology of Lessons Learned," 188.

Recruited and officered from a narrow and increasingly unrepresentative societal base and serving in distant places for purposes often obscure to ordinary citizens, Victoria's soldiers became for many Britons little more than military cardboard cutouts, to be ignored or disdained between overhyped triumphs and embarrassing defeats. "The little wars in Asia and Africa seldom seriously engaged the mind of the average Briton. He was aware that fighting was going on more or less continuously on the ever-expanding fringes of the Empire, but except for the officers and a few politicians and merchants very few Britons were interested."[116] As a result, until the Boer War, those who took the queen's shilling became increasingly alien to and alienated from their fellow citizens. Even late nineteenth-century social Darwinism and the British public's ardent embrace of the empire's "civilizing mission" couldn't entirely dissipate the cynical ambivalence captured in Kipling's "Tommy":

> "Oh, it's Tommy this, an' Tommy that, an' 'Tommy, go away';
> But it's 'Thank you, Mister Atkins', when the band begins to play."[117]

The experience of the Victorian British Army thus prefigured a challenge with which today's US military has become unhappily familiar: a volunteer military, especially one committed serially to distant wars against obscure enemies for ill-understood purposes, purchases internal cohesion and durability only at the risk of societal disconnection and cultural stasis. As one recent commentator wrote not long ago, echoing Farwell, "[Our] reverent but disengaged attitude toward the military – we love the troops, but we'd rather not think about them – has become so familiar that we assume it is the American norm."[118] Meanwhile, like its Victorian British predecessor and for analogous reasons, today's US military is having trouble deciding what it should look like. Notes columnist George Will, "[C]hanging the trajectory of military thinking … often requires changing a service's viscous culture."[119]

Both problems can be overcome, but doing so requires vigorous political and military leadership to keep the force engaged with civil society and vice versa, and to ensure that today's commitments will not eat tomorrow's capabilities.

---

[116] Farwell, *Queen Victoria's Little Wars*, 66.

[117] Rudyard Kipling, *Barrack-Room Ballads and Other Verses* (London, 1892). Wrote one puzzled foreign observer, "How this blind glorification and worship of the Army continues to coexist with the contemptuous dislike felt toward the members of it, must remain a problem in the national psychology." Spiers, *The Late Victorian Army*, 202. See also Edward Peter Joshua Gosling, "Tommy Atkins, War Office Reform and the Social and Cultural Presence of the Late-Victorian Army in Britain, C.1868–1899" (PhD thesis, Plymouth University, 2015), 353.

[118] James Fallows, "The Tragedy of the American Military," *Atlantic* (January–February 2015). See also Maj. Gen. Jeffrey Snow, "Army Recruiting Needs Your Support," *Army Echoes* (https://sol dierforlife.army.mil/sites/default/files/echoes_issues/Army_Echoes_Oct_2017.pdf), 6.

[119] George F. Will, "In Search of a Higher-Altitude Air Force," *Washington Post*, July 20, 2017, A19.

Even with the benefit of post–Boer War reforms, the British Army paid a steep price for its prolonged resistance to change. And while the BEF in 1914 was successful in staving off both Britain's precipitate defeat and that of its French ally, it managed that feat only at the cost of its own near annihilation.

At least, therefore, the Victorian military experience should furnish a cautionary tale. Americans will not thank political and military leaders who invite a similar sacrifice through failure to keep America's military connected with its parent society and relevant to a changing battlefield landscape.

8   The Culture of the British Army, 1914–1945

Williamson Murray

A number of factors affect the culture of armies, navies, and air forces. The most obvious of these has to do with the geographic and strategic framework as well as the domains – ground, sea, and air – within which military forces operate.[1] Equally important are the political imperatives that their masters impose on them. But the unseen baggage of their history over the decades and centuries may have as much impact on their cultural understanding of the world as the more obvious influences. Moreover, military institutions, as Michael Howard has pointed out, confront the distinct problem that they rarely find themselves employed in war: the task of fighting that is their main justification.[2] Exacerbating that difficulty is the fact that they can replicate in peacetime few of the chaotic and terrifying circumstances that make up war at the sharp end. And finally, at the heart of military effectiveness is the fact that the increasing pace of technological change since the last decades of the nineteenth century has altered the character of war and made innovation and adaptation both more difficult and uncertain.

The first and most difficult challenge that armies confront is that of persuading young men to place their lives in jeopardy in situations where common sense dictates that they should depart as rapidly as possible. They do this through establishing a culture that emphasizes a combination of discipline, traditions, and depictions of the enemy as representing an existential threat to the polity as well as to their own lives. Organizational culture is essential in transmitting those qualities throughout the officer and noncommissioned officer (NCO) corps.[3] As Lord Moran described it in his superb study on human

---

[1] Air forces, navies, and armies all operate in very different physical environments, against very different kinds of enemies. These environments exercise important influences and constraints on how they view war and the world. As a marine general once commented to me, a carrier captain orders his ship to turn 90 degrees and all 5,000 sailors turn at the same time. On the other hand, a regimental commander may order his 3,000 men to turn 90 degrees to outflank an opponent, but substantial numbers may not get the order, or may be in combat and therefore may not be able to disengage.

[2] For a wonderful discussion of this fundamental truth, see Michael Howard, "The Use and Abuse of Military History," *Royal United Services Journal* 138(1).

[3] The transmission of that culture throughout the ranks in the British Army stands in stark contrast with that of the Italian Army. As Marshal Rodolpho Graziani commented immediately before Italy's entrance into the Second World War, "[w]hen the cannon sounds everything will fall into

courage, armies must provide "the capacity to frame plans that will succeed and the faculty for persuading others to carry them out in the face of death."[4] Interesting, at a time when war was far simpler for the common soldier, Clausewitz pointed out that it represents as much an intellectual challenge as a physical one.[5] How well military institutions respond to the complex issues that war raises plays a major role in their effectiveness.[6] Clausewitz's point was to prove of even greater significance over the course of the twentieth century.[7]

Unfortunately, the nature of the British Army and its regimental system created a culture that was deeply hostile to book learning. This was the essential conundrum of the British Army: it was outstanding in persuading young men to fight with stubbornness, courage, and tenacity at the sharp end, but the intellectual preparation of its officers, on which innovation in peacetime and adaptation in war depended, was less than impressive. Part of the problem was that even after the reforms of the Boer War, its officer corps remained intimately tied to the upper classes. The Duke of Cambridge underlined that point in the nineteenth century: "The British officer should be a gentleman first and an officer second."[8]

In the period from 1914 to 1945, the army drew most of its officers from a narrow segment of British upper-class society – a factor that only began to break down during the Second World War. Throughout the two world wars, those regimental officers proved exceptionally able at leading their men unflinchingly into the cauldron of modern combat. Yet the army's performance in supplying the brains and imagination required to develop the plans, doctrine, and execution at the operational level required in the two great world wars was not entirely satisfactory. That failure at the higher levels was responsible for increasing the terrible casualties that the nature of combat on the Western Front from 1914 to 1918 imposed on those fighting in the British Expeditionary Force (BEF). Only the collapse of the French Army in the debacle of May 1940 prevented the British Army and nation from suffering a similar bloodbath on the Western Front in the second great German war.[9]

---

place automatically." Quoted in MacGregor Knox, *Mussolini Unleashed, 1939–1941, Politics and Strategy in Fascist Italy's Last War* (Cambridge, 1982), 121.

[4] Lord Moran, *The Anatomy of Courage*, 2nd edn. (London, 1966), 180.

[5] As Clausewitz notes in Book 1: "[I]n our view even junior positions of command require outstanding intellectual qualities for outstanding achievement." Carl von Clausewitz, *On War*, trans. and ed. by Michael Howard and Peter Paret (Princeton, NJ, 1976), 111.

[6] On military effectiveness, see Allan R. Millett and Williamson Murray, *Military Effectiveness, vol. 1, The First World War, vol. 2, The Interwar Period, and vol. 3, The Second World War* (London, 1988, and 2nd edn., Cambridge, 2010).

[7] Clausewitz notes the following: "Since in our view even junior positions of command require outstanding intellectual qualities for outstanding achievement, and since the standard rises with every step, it follows that we recognize the abilities that are needed." Clausewitz, *On War*, 111.

[8] Quoted in Brian Bond, *The Victorian Army and the Staff College, 1854–1914* (London, 1978), 17.

[9] Of course, the fighting in France in 1944 and then onto the north German plain in 1945 did involve considerable casualties, but nothing close to those suffered in the First World War.

Historical legacy as well as the nation's strategic position dominated the culture of the British Army that went to war in August 1914. While substantial reforms had occurred in the period after the Crimean and Boer Wars, none was sufficient to alter the army's basic *Weltanschauung*. In the distant past, the memory of Cromwell's military dictatorship in the mid-seventeenth century continued to haunt civilian and political thinking in Britain about military affairs. Even more important was the fact that in the wars against France in the eighteenth and early nineteenth centuries, Britain not only won uncontested dominion over the seas, but a great global empire, the security requirements of which required the nation to deploy major portions of the army abroad.[10] But Britain's successes in the wars for empire also depended on the commitment of substantial ground forces on the European continent to support her allies.[11] The only war in which that had not been the case had been the American Revolution, and that had been the only war the British lost in the eighteenth century.

The destruction of the Napoleonic empire at Waterloo then allowed the British, as well as Europe, a substantial period of peace lasting almost a century. In effect, with the exception of the Crimean War, the army found itself committed to garrison duty and small wars across the wide expanse of what had become a global empire. Through to the end of the nineteenth century, the British were able to pursue a period of what they termed "splendid isolation." After the Franco-Prussian War, the new German state, under Otto von Bismarck, had kept the continent relatively stable and peaceable, largely because the "Iron Chancellor" recognized that Germany had the most to lose in a major European conflict.[12] For the army, that meant that it confronted no major continental threats, at least until the new German Kaiser replaced Bismarck and drove the Reich's strategy and foreign policy in dangerous and aggressive new directions.

Despite the creation of a staff college in 1858, the army remained tied to a regimental system that created an organization of separate tribes, the soldiers of which did not even wear common uniforms.[13] The system as it existed created

---

[10] The Seven Years' War against the French saw Britain eliminate France as a peer competitor for global supremacy. For a brilliant account of that conflict, see Fred Anderson, *Crucible of War: The Seven Years' War and the Fate of Empire in British North America, 1754–1766* (New York, 2001).

[11] In this regard, see particularly Williamson Murray, "Grand Strategy, Alliances, and the Anglo-American Way of War," in Peter Mansoor and Williamson Murray, eds., *Grand Strategy and Military Alliances* (Cambridge, 2016), chapter 2.

[12] For Bismarck's strategy after the "War in Sight Crisis" of 1875, see Marcus Jones, "Bismarckian Strategic Policy, 1871–1890," in Williamson Murray and Richard Hart Sinnreich, eds., *Successful Strategies: Triumphing in War and Peace from Antiquity to the Present* (Cambridge, 2014).

[13] An American officer, who had spent considerable time with the British Army, once commented to me that a mess night that included a number of officers from different regiments resembled a gathering of officers from a large number of foreign countries rather than officers from the same army.

regiments that trained their soldiers rigorously and effectively. But the humiliating failures of the Boer War underlined how ineffective the system was in the face of competent opponents who possessed a degree of modern equipment. Yet, even after the army had absorbed the more obvious lessons of the Boer War, it remained an army of regiments, tied to them in terms of culture, values, traditions, and histories.

In some respects, regiments, at least among their officers, resembled a grown-up version of English public schools. They were certainly not organizations that encouraged a serious study of war. Given the fact that after Waterloo the army had spent much of the next century in garrison duty and in fighting small wars, there was little opportunity or need for serious study. Nevertheless, these regiments were particularly good at producing officers who learned the local languages and the nature of the people among whom they were garrisoned or fighting. In other words, the regimental system produced an army effective at fighting small wars.

However, with the coming of World War I in August 1914, as with most British institutions of the Victorian and Edwardian eras, the army confronted a set of extraordinarily new challenges, for which past solutions and preparations proved less than satisfactory. The problems that the army's culture would create are, thus, the subject of this chapter and cover three distinct periods from 1914 through 1945: the First World War, the interwar period, and the Second World War.

The First World War

The First World War broke over Europe with a shattering impact, destroying in its wake the comfortable illusions and assumptions of Western civilization. What was true for society at large proved true as well for Europe's military organizations. In their search for those responsible for the slaughter in the trenches, historians have simplified the enormously difficult problems military institutions confronted in World War I. The First World War, as with the American Civil War, saw the two great social-military revolutions of the late eighteenth century, the French Revolution and the Industrial Revolution, come together to provide the opposing powers with an almost inexhaustible supply of manpower and weapons.[14]

Exacerbating the difficulties confronting Europe's military leaders was the fact that the Industrial Revolution had produced a massive wave of technological and scientific developments in the nineteenth and early twentieth

---

[14] For an extended discussion of the series of social-military revolutions and their accompanying revolutions in military affairs that have accompanied Western military history, see Williamson Murray, *America and the Future of War: The Past As Prologue* (Stanford, CA, 2017), chapter 2.

centuries, the implications of which in terms of their impact on the battlefield were not clear, but that would significantly impact the battlefields of the First World War.[15] About the only way the armies could learn in this period of rapid change was by sacrificing their soldiers in an environment in which both sides were adapting their tactics as the war progressed. The result was that it was not until 1917 and 1918 that the armies on the Western Front began to develop what we would today call "combined arms tactics."

As Paul Kennedy has suggested, the difficulties at the tactical level had considerable implications at the operational and strategic levels:

> [I]t was at the *tactical* level in this war … that the critical problems occurred. The argument, very crudely, would run as follows: because soldiers simply could not break through a trench system, then generals' plans for campaign successes were stalemated on each side; these operational failures in turn impacted on the strategic debate at the highest level and thus upon the strategic options being considered by national policy makers, the changing nature of civil-military relations, and the allocation of national resources.[16]

Moreover, tragically for a whole generation of British youth, there was no strategic alternative to a massive continental commitment to fight the Germans on the Western Front, other than Britain's outright surrender of European hegemony to the Reich.[17]

The BEF that deployed to France in early August 1914 was undoubtedly the best trained of the European armies at the sharp end.[18] It played a role out of all proportion to its strength in the vicious fighting in which it found itself engaged from August through November 1914. Unfortunately, its leadership at the top fell short of the competence and bravery displayed by its riflemen and junior officers. Nevertheless, in the strategic sense, its mere presence on the far left of the Allied line in northern France prevented the German First Army from outflanking and then rolling up the badly deployed French armies. The flight from Mons after the first clash with the Germans was not one of the great moments in British military history, nor was the overly cautious British effort in

---

[15] Even the development of barbed wire, a simple method to keep animals corralled, was to have huge consequences in the fighting on the Western Front.

[16] Paul Kennedy, "Military Effectiveness in the First World War," in Millett and Williamson, eds., *Military Effectiveness, vol. 1,* 330.

[17] And that is what makes Naill Ferguson's argument that Britain should never have participated in the First World War so perniciously misguided. See Naill Ferguson, *The Pity of War: Explaining World War I* (New York, 2000).

[18] The traditional picture of the British Army in the First World War is one of "lions led by donkeys." For an example of the genre, see Alan Clark, *The Donkeys* (New York, 1965), or C. S. Forester, *The General* (Baltimore, MD, 1982). For the most careful and nuanced study of the British Army in the First World War, but highly critical, see Timothy Travers, *The Killing Ground: The British Army, the Western Front, and the Emergence of Modern War, 1900–1918* (London, 1987).

the First Battle of the Marne, which allowed the Germans to escape the dangerous situation into which their First Army had fallen.

The BEF's finest moments, however, came in fall 1914 in the fighting in Flanders, when heavily outnumbered and facing massive infantry attacks, it held off the Germans and prevented them from capturing the Channel ports. So impressive was the volume and aimed fire of British infantry that the Germans came to the conclusion that the British organizational complement of machine guns was much higher than that of German units. As a result, the Germans considerably increased the number of machine guns allocated to their infantry, with a direct impact on the effectiveness of their defenses on the Western Front in 1915 and throughout the remainder of the war. Nevertheless, the British success came at a heavy price. Quite rightly, British general Anthony Farrar-Hockley titled his study of the BEF's 1914 campaign *Death of an Army.*

The implications of the huge losses the BEF suffered in the 1914 battles were considerable. To begin with its deployment to France in August 1914, the BEF had swept up virtually all the staff officers in the War Office and throughout the United Kingdom – a substantial number of whom took command positions and suffered heavy losses. As Michael Howard has pointed out:

> By autumn 1915 the original highly trained British Expeditionary Force had disap-peared and in the New Armies which replaced it all ranks from the Commander in Chief to private soldiers were learning, from the beginning and at hideous cost, a new kind of war which baffled even experienced armies. It was only in 1918 that even the Germans developed effective techniques of attack under conditions of trench war.[19]

One of the most important factors confronting the British Army was that, like the other European armies, it had calculated on a short war. However, the other European armies possessed large training establishments to handle the massive intakes of conscripted civilians that occurred every year. Thus, they were able to rebuild their shattered divisions and their armies quickly after the huge losses suffered in late summer and fall 1914. That was not the case in the United Kingdom, where the professional army had a smaller training establishment to handle fewer new soldiers every year.

How, then, would the army train the massive numbers of civilians volunteer-ing in the first months of the war? That represented a major problem. The British did have a reserve force, the Territorial Army, but the new head of the War Office, Field Marshal Lord Kitchener, had little use for the Territorials. Therefore, the new armies found themselves desperately short of a training establishment. With its heavy losses in NCOs and officers, the BEF was hardly in a position to provide training cadres. There was one saving grace in the recruitment and training of the Kitchener volunteers. The War Office organized

---

[19] Michael Howard, *The Continental Commitment* (London, 1972), 57–58.

them along local lines, such as the London Rifle Brigade or the Tyneside Irish, which made for a natural cohesion among the troops, at least as long as they survived. Adding to the losses suffered by the BEF was the fact that the fighting in 1914 had killed off significant numbers of staff officers and potential staff officers. And here was the one great disadvantage the British suffered when compared to their German opponents. The German general staff system did send general staff officers to serve in combat positions, but then only for relatively short periods of time. Not so in the case of the British.

Future Field Marshal Bernard Law Montgomery represents an interesting exception to the rule. Wounded so badly in the Flanders fighting that he was almost left for dead, Montgomery was characterized by the army's doctors as not fit for combat duty. His first assignment after his recovery was to serve as second in command in one of the new Kitchener brigades, where his commanding officer gave him great latitude to set the training regimen; thereafter he found himself in a number of staff positions. His experience in 1917 as the GSO 2 (general staff officer training) for the IX Corps was particularly useful for his long-term growth, because the Second Army commander, Gen. Herbert Plummer, was well known for his meticulous planning.

The result of the British Army's approach to the assigning of staff officers was that the army was never able to create a staff organization with a culture similar to that of the Great General Staff that the Germans possessed. That complicated the problem of developing effective tactics on the Western Front, which lay at the heart of the problems the armies confronted throughout the war.[20] The culture of the high command exacerbated this issue. For the British, the culture of leadership that the BEF's commander, Field Marshal Douglas Haig, exhibited, a style in which he brooked no disagreement with his views or those of his headquarters, created many of the BEF's difficulties.[21] Haig was clearly not the most suitable officer in the army for his appointment to the position, but the social and political framework of Edwardian Britain made his appointment inevitable.

As one of the foremost historians of the British Army in the First World War has noted: "In retrospect the means of selecting officers for the top command appointments, depending as it did, so much on seniority, and influenced, as it still could be, by royal patronage, appears [to have been] completely inadequate."[22] While Haig proved to have quite exceptional talents in

---

[20] For a discussions of these problems, see Williamson Murray, *Military Adaptation in War: With Fear of Change* (Cambridge, 2011), chapter 3.

[21] J. P. Harris, *Douglas Haig and the First World War* (Cambridge, 2008), 537. Harris's biography of Haig is by far and away the fairest and most perceptive of all the biographies about the field marshal. What makes Harris's work so useful and important is that he has carefully analyzed where it is clear that Haig actually was involved in the crucial decision-making processes.

[22] Ibid., 546.

organizing the BEF's logistical and administrative structure, he exhibited little interest in the tactical problems the war raised. His staff and the staffs of his subordinate commanders were there to execute his conceptions without challenging his assumptions or providing unwarranted advice. It was top-down leadership with little information flowing upward, and certainly little that might make general headquarters uncomfortable about its assumptions.

Here the difference between the British staff system and the German general staff system could not be clearer. In the latter case, senior general staff officers as well as specially selected experts were in the position to overrule army commanders. This was particularly the case with Colonel Fritz von Lossberg, the defensive expert on the Western Front, and Georg Bruckmüller, the army's artillery expert.[23] Moreover, the German general staff system allowed an alternative and relatively smooth-flowing system to provide clear reports on what was actually happening at the front. The result was that Ludendorff was able to divine the defensive problems on the Somme in fall 1916.

By early winter 1916–1917, the Germans had developed a doctrine for a system of defense-in-depth that they thoroughly integrated into their defensive system on the Western Front before the Allied spring offensives began. The German system encouraged the upward and downward flow of information about the tactical situation. On his arrival on the Western Front in fall 1916, Ludendorff demanded that officers and soldiers speak their minds, not something "made to order."[24] The result of the opening of information channels from below was the creation of modern defensive tactics. On the other hand, the British proved far less able to identify and create a defense system over the winter of 1917–1918 in spite of their experience in fighting against the German system. Their staffs proved incapable of transmitting doctrine into practice and so all too many units simply muddled through.

Ironically, as early as 1915, several senior British officers had come to the conclusion that only limited success was possible on the Western Front. Even then it would require a massive use of artillery to break through the hard crust of German defenses. But if the lesson was clear to a significant number of generals, it was not clear to Haig. His whole design for the great Somme offensive of July 1, 1916, displayed a willful ignorance of the BEF's tactical experiences in the 1915 battles. The Fourth Army Commander, Gen. Henry Rawlinson, tried to make clear to Haig initially that there needed to be a heavier emphasis on the artillery preparation, particularly counter-battery fire, but he then relapsed into accepting the commander in chief's faulty assumptions.

---

[23] For Lossberg, see the recently translated volume of his memoirs: Fritz von Lossberg, *Lossberg's War: The World War I Memoirs of a German Chief of Staff*, trans. and ed. by David T. Zabecki and Dieter J. Biedekarken (Lexington, KY, 2017). For Bruckmüller, see David Zabecki, *Steel Wind: Colonel Georg Bruckmüller and the Birth of Modern Artillery* (New York, 1994).
[24] Erich Ludendorff, *Memoirs*, vol. *1* (New York, 1919), 24.

Thus, "counter-battery fire activity, which Rawlinson in the light of the Battle of Loos [in 1915] had characterized as a prerequisite for victory, degenerated under Fourth Army's [the controlling headquarters for the July 1, 1916 offensive] preparation into a matter wholly at the whim of the individual corps commanders."[25]

Rawlinson also seems to have grasped the possibility of using a creeping barrage before the disastrous attack of July 1, 1916. But the British system had no culture of analysis with which to take such insights and pass them throughout the various levels of command. Rawlinson, certainly, made no effort to do so, while Haig had no interest in such matters. To make matters worse, Haig extended the attacking frontage to the point where it drastically watered down the artillery support available for the attacking troops. The result was the catastrophic casualty bill of 57,000 on the first day of the battle.[26] Simply put, the tactical disaster had nothing to do with good or bad infantry tactics on that grim day. It did not matter one way or the other. If the artillery were sufficiently heavy and effective, then the infantry gained some measure of success; if it were not, then the attack failed, however well trained the infantry.[27]

The pieces were there for the British Army to launch a more effective offensive, but the cultural milieu among senior leaders resulted in a lack of the kind of analytic framework required to provide insights into how to handle the tactical problems that conditions on the Western Front raised. "Only an abundance of guns and shells on the Western Front could create the conditions whereby rank and file infantry might operate on the battlefield with any degree of success."[28] In fairness to the British, while the Germans possessed a general staff system capable of disseminating tactical lessons, they would not utilize that system effectively until Ludendorff took over in September 1916. By that time, the German defenders on the Somme had suffered almost as many casualties as the British and French attackers.[29]

Slightly less than two weeks after the disastrous first day, two corps of Rawlinson's Fourth Army launched a concentrated night attack on German positions. The weight of artillery support was five times that of the support per kilometer on the first day. Moreover, the artillery focused on the enemy front-

---

[25] Robin Prior and Trevor Wilson, *The Somme* (New Haven, CT, 2005), 56.

[26] John Keegan's chapter on the first day on the Somme remains a classic. See John Keegan, *The Face of Battle: A Study of Agincourt, Waterloo, and the Somme* (London, 1978).

[27] Robin Prior and Trevor Wilson have carefully worked this out by analyzing the artillery support and the infantry tactics (few of which were similar) used by the different divisions. Prior and Wilson, *The Somme*, 114–116.

[28] Ibid., 118.

[29] One must not forget that the French Army was a major participant in the Allied assault on German positions on the Somme. In this regard, see particularly William Philpott, *Three Armies on the Somme: The First Battle of the Twentieth Century* (London, 2011).

line positions, where the Germans had concentrated the great bulk of their defending troops. In the sense that the BEF, or any of the armies, including the German, were capable of achieving a significant breach into an enemy's position, the Fourth Army's attack was a considerable success.[30] But from Haig's uncompromising belief that a great breakthrough battle was possible, it was a failure. The Somme campaign then degenerated into a series of attacks that occasioned heavy losses on both sides; ironically, the failure of Haig and his system to learn more effectively from their experiences resulted in attrition warfare. By mid-July, the BEF was using rolling (also called creeping) barrages against the German defenders. Despite the narrative that the Somme represented an unmitigated disaster for British arms, the fighting after the first day hurt the Germans severely in what they termed a *Materielschlacht* (battle of material).[31] Some Germans commented after the war that their army never fully recovered from its experiences on the Somme, but the inability of the British to develop a coherent tactical doctrine resulted in a failure to hurt their opponents as effectively as they might have done otherwise.

The following year represented the grimmest for British and Allied fortunes. Once again, the BEF's top-down style of leadership failed to challenge the basic assumptions on which Haig was approaching the fighting on the Western Front. Once again he focused on creating a great breakthrough.[32] Haig even seems to have believed that there would be a role for the cavalry in the exploitation phase of his offensive. There were tactical possibilities but only in a rather limited fashion, and they demanded a careful, ruthless examination of the realities. Given the cultural framework of the officer corps within which the Kitchener volunteers and then the vast numbers of conscripted had been poured, there was little possibility of innovation bubbling up from below. It was certainly not an army that valued input from those of lower rank.

Nevertheless, despite the fact that it offered no evidence that a major breakthrough operation was possible, that was precisely what Haig planned for in 1917 – this time in Flanders, where a great swamp had once existed during the Middle Ages. Initially, Haig asked Rawlinson and Plummer to draw up plans, but he replaced both after they came up with limited proposals that failed to seek distant objectives. Haig then settled on Gen. Herbert Gough, whose only claim to high command was that he was a cavalry officer and the fact that he, like Haig, "was a devotee of the 'hurroosh' – the rapid advance."[33] Matters at least began rather well. On June 7, 1917, after a massive bombardment, the

[30] Prior and Wilson, *The Somme*, 131–140.
[31] For the German view of the Somme, see Christopher Duffy, *Through German Eyes: The British and the Somme, 1916* (London, 1916).
[32] For the origins, planning, and course of the fighting in Flanders in 1917, see Robin Prior and Trevor Wilson, *Passchendaele: The Untold Story* (New Haven, CT, 1996).
[33] Ibid., 51.

British exploded a series of massive mines underneath the main German defenses along Messines Ridge. In terms of the bite-and-hold approach that some generals were urging, the Messines operation represented a considerable success.[34]

If the first day of the Flanders offensive was a partial success, what followed was a nightmare. Massive amounts of rain deluged the Flanders plain and with the artillery bombardment, the ground soon turned into the swamp that it had once been. Perhaps not surprising in an army without a coherent approach to lessons learned was the fact that there was no means to pass best practices between the BEF's various armies. As the two foremost commentators on the Battle of Passchendaele note: "It is a sorry comment on the dissemination of information by the higher commands on the Western Front that the methods used to achieve success by one army commander might be completely unknown to another."[35] A larger fault lay in the fact that "while changes in operational and tactical methods could be tried out [in the BEF], they would be on a piecemeal basis, [but] the army as a whole did not encourage open discussion and reassessment, since that would have threatened the service's cultural norms of loyalty, deference, and unthinking courage."[36] In the end, Passchendaele disintegrated into a slugging match in a sea of mud, a result that has given it a justified reputation as having had the worst conditions of any battle in the First World War.

There were other possibilities. In November, a British attack at Cambrai that utilized tanks, artillery, and infantry effectively for the first time caused a major disruption of German front-line positions. Significantly, Haig, to his credit, had been a major supporter of the development of armored fighting vehicles. After the war, the military pundits, J. F. C. Fuller and B. H. Liddell Hart in particular, would argue that the Cambrai success was largely due to tanks. They were wrong; the success was the result of combined arms: a sudden and effective artillery bombardment that took out much of the German defenses and then suppressed German artillery with counter-battery fire, followed by tanks and infantry working closely together to break through the German defenses. But as the Germans were to discover the following spring, no ability yet existed to exploit a tactical success at the operational level.

The government in London, which bore full responsibility for allowing Haig to continue the Flanders offensive, then hit on the dubious method of forcing Haig to halt the BEF's offensive operations on the Western Front in late fall by holding potential reinforcements in Britain. That fact has led some historians to suggest the collapse of Gough's Fifth Army in March 1918 before Ludendorff's

[34] For an excellent description of the Messines operation, see ibid., 55–66.   [35] Ibid., 27.
[36] Paul Kennedy, "Britain in the First World War," in Millett and Murray, eds., *Military Effectiveness, vol. 1*, 53–54.

"Michael" offensive resulted from the London government's failure to provide the reinforcements Haig required. That shortage of reserves may have played a role, but there was a more important factor. The BEF confronted a distinct offensive threat because the collapse of Russia allowed the Germans to concentrate on the Western Front. In response, the BEF's leadership attempted to copy the German system of defense in depth. Gough, as a cavalryman "brilliant to the top of his boots," to use Lloyd George's *bon mot*, was simply not up to the task. Other army commanders did better, but what was lacking was the ability to inculcate the whole BEF in a new tactical system. In the end, the German "Michael" offensive, which collapsed Gough's Fifth Army, came perilously close to splitting the BEF from its French allies and capturing the main British supply depots at Amiens. But German incompetence at the operational level and desperate British resistance then stopped the Germans from gaining any significant operational success.[37]

The BEF then would fight the most impressive series of battles in its history in summer and fall 1918 in a campaign that played the major role in the breaking of the German army.[38] Tanks played a major role in the successful attack on August 5, 1918 – a reflection not only of the military's support for the weapon's development but also of support from the civilian side as well. But by now, the BEF had learned how to use its forces in what today would be recognized as combined-arms tactics. Unlike the Germans, who had developed a doctrinal framework and then instituted that framework throughout their army, the British approach was very much ad hoc, with each of the BEF's armies working out its own approach. In other words, they were learning by themselves, with the result that the survivors would learn and apply the lessons of combat in their next battle. In the end, the approach worked, but at terrible cost.

The Interwar Period

The massive demobilization the army underwent after November 1918 saw the service return almost immediately to the posture that had marked its prewar organizational and cultural framework. As one brigadier supposedly exclaimed at the war's end, "now we can get back to the real business of soldiering." The only difference between the army of 1913 and that of 1920 was that the former

---

[37] For a brilliant assessment of the German offensives, see David Zabecki, *The German 1918 Offensives: A Case Study in the Operational Level of War* (London, 2006).

[38] The most outstanding work on the BEF in this period of the war is J. P. Harris, *Amiens to the Armistice: The BEF in the Hundred Days' Campaign, 8 August–11 November 1918* (London, 2003). The extent to which Allied offensives and four years of sustained attrition had finally broken the German Army by fall 1918 is suggested by the fact that by that point, the army had no fewer than 700,000 deserters.

confronted a major threat to British interests in Europe that demanded a significant continental commitment. That was certainly how the army viewed Britain's strategic situation before the war, and there was no quarrel on the part of the politicians. However, with Germany now defeated, that was no longer the case. Throughout the interwar period, not only did the army receive the least resources of all the services, but the Royal Air Force was a new contestant for defense dollars. Not until February 1939 would the Chamberlain government agree to a commitment of the British Army to the defense of France and authorize a major expansion as well to its force structure – the latter now to focus on fighting against a first-class enemy.[39]

Some historians have used that lack of funding as an excuse to explain the army's appallingly bad preparation for the war that broke out in September 1939. There is a certain amount of truth to that argument, but it excuses the army's lackadaisical intellectual preparations throughout the interwar period.[40] The Germans make a sharp comparison to what was occurring in Britain. Once matters had settled down in the Reich, the Reichsheer, under the leadership of Gen. Hans von Seeckt, ordered a massive study of what had actually occurred in the fighting in the First World War. Seeckt authorized no fewer than fifty-seven different committees to examine the lessons of that war.[41] On the other hand, the British failed to establish a study group to study the lessons of World War I until 1932. The Chief of the Imperial General Staff (CIGS) at the time, Lord Milne, gave the committee members broad powers and requested that they "study the lessons of the last war … and to report whether the lessons are being correctly and adequately applied in our manuals and in our training generally."[42] However, the next CIGS, Field Marshal Archibald Montgomery-Massingberd, was unhappy with the resulting study because it was overly critical and ordered that the army issue only a watered-down version.[43] Thus, the British study, far too late as it was, had no discernable impact on the army's preparation for war.

At the same time that much of the officer corps was dealing with small wars such as Irish unrest and fighting on the North-West Frontier, the British carried out a number of impressive experiments with the tank. In the previous war, the British Army had led in the development of armored fighting vehicles. The

---

[39] For the arguments that took place in the Chamberlain government, see particularly Williamson Murray, *The Change in the European Balance of Power, 1938–1939* (Princeton, NJ, 1984), 276–278.

[40] The contrast with the US Army's major emphasis on professional military education could not be more graphic.

[41] For the Seeckt reforms, see particularly James S. Corum, *The Roots of Blitzkrieg: Hans von Seeckt and German Military Reform* (Lawrence, KS, 1992).

[42] Quoted in Harold R. Winton, *To Change an Army: General Sir John Burnett-Stuart and British Army Doctrine, 1927–1938* (Lexington, KY, 1988), 127.

[43] Ibid., 131.

results of interwar experimentation were both positive and negative. From the outside, Liddell Hart and Fuller launched a series of attacks on the army's leadership and its supposedly conservative unwillingness to innovate with the tank.[44] To a considerable extent, such attacks were unjustified, since the governments of the interwar period provided the army with minuscule budgets to accomplish its main mission of protecting the empire. Nevertheless, the experiments with tanks on the Salisbury Plain in 1927, 1928, and 1934 suggested a great deal about the future of the armored fighting vehicle. Unfortunately, the Germans appear to have learned the most from these British efforts, not so much from their intelligence efforts, but ironically from the reports in British newspapers, especially those by Liddell Hart.[45]

The failure of these experiments to push the army toward coherent development of a doctrine for mechanized warfare lay in the fact that, because of the army's failure to examine carefully the lessons of the Western Front in 1918, it lacked a combined-arms conception of future ground war. Thus, the maneuvers in which the tanks participated saw each branch operating separately with little emphasis on working in a combined-arms environment. Moreover, throughout their writings in this period, Fuller and Liddell Hart emphasized that tanks should operate by themselves in massed formations. That emphasis fit in well with the army's culture, while the creation of the Royal Tank Corps added one more player to the separation of infantry, artillery, and cavalry. Not surprising, with the approach of war, the Royal Tank Corps expanded into battalions and then regiments, further adding to the army's tribalization. Thus, the British Army remained tied up within its regiments and separate constituencies of infantry, cavalry, and artillery, with the tankers now having their own regimental force.

In the late 1930s, with cavalry appearing to have a less significant role, the army leadership determined to have a number of the cavalry regiments give up their horses and replace them with light tanks and armored cars. The decision caused enormous angst throughout the cavalry regiments, all of which had close ties to the higher levels of the British establishment. Representing such views, Secretary of State for War Alfred Duff Cooper announced in the House of Commons in 1935 that asking the cavalry to give up horses for tanks "was like asking a great musical performer to throw away his violin and devote himself in the future to the gramophone."[46] The regiments were to maintain their old badges and traditions, while the Royal Tank Corps would only train

---

[44] Liddell Hart's attacks came from columns in the newspapers and utilized his position as their military correspondent. Fuller, for his part, enraged army generals after his retirement with books such as *Generalship: Its Diseases and Their Cures.*

[45] See in particular Williamson Murray, "Armored Warfare," in Williamson Murray and Allan R. Millett, eds., *Military Innovation in the Interwar Period* (Cambridge, 1996), 40, fn. 127.

[46] B. H. Liddell Hart, *Memoirs, vol. 1* (London, 1966), 227.

them. In April 1937, the War Office explained the rationale behind this decision:

> Various proposals were considered including one for an army of a more highly mechanized nature than that decided for the regular army ... The Chiefs of Staff have stated that in their opinion the present would be a most unfortunate moment to disturb an organization which has valuable traditions and has survived the lean years through which it has passed since the war.[47]

One cannot think of a worse choice, because the cavalry and its officers had had virtually no experience fighting on the Western Front in 1918 and therefore had not even the slightest idea of what combined-arms tactics involved. Tank innovator Percy Hobart, at the time in 1939 commander of the armored division in Egypt, wrote his wife about his experiences in trying to bring his "cavalry" regiments, now equipped with tanks, up to the standards of modern mechanized warfare:

> I had the cavalry CO's in and laid my cards on the table. They are such nice chaps socially. That's what makes it so difficult. But they're so conservative of their spurs and swords and regimental tradition, etc., and so certain that the good old Umpteenth will be all right ..., so easily satisfied with an excuse if things aren't right, so prone to blame the machine or machinery. And unless someone upsets their polo, etc., for which they have paid heavily – it's so hard to get anything more into them or any more work out of them. Three days a week they come in six miles to Gezirah Club for polo. At 5 pm it's getting dark; they are sweaty and tired. Not fit for much and most of them full up of socials in Cairo.[48]

The army budgets of the late 1930s suggest a great deal about where the army's priorities lay. In 1937, the equitation school at Weedon had a budget of £20,000 to train 38 students, while the tank corps school of 550 students had to exist on a budget of £46,000.[49] The 1938 army budget provided £772,000 for petroleum and £400,000 for forage.[50]

In 1914, one could at least say that on the tactical level, soldier for soldier the BEF was more than an equal to its German opponent, while the military leadership on both sides miscalculated on the potential for a long war. In World War II, that was clearly not the case. It was not a matter of personal bravery, because British soldiers proved themselves as doggedly brave in the coming war as their predecessors in the previous conflict. But on the tactical and operational levels, the army's leaders and the tactical framework within which the army was to fight proved distinctly inferior to that of the

---

[47] PRO CAB 24/269, C.P. 115 (37), 23.4.37., "The Organization, Armament, and Equipment of the Army," Memorandum by the Secretary of War, 138.

[48] K. MacKesy, *Armored Crusader* (London, 1967), 159.

[49] B. H. Liddell Hart, *Europe in Arms* (London, 1937), 234–235.

[50] Michael Howard, "The Liddell Hart Memoirs," *Journal of the Royal United Services Institute* (February 1966), 60.

Wehrmacht's ground forces. In Malaya and Burma, that was also to prove the case against the Japanese, at least until that extraordinary soldier William Slim was able to sort matters out and fundamentally alter the basic culture and training under which the Fourteenth Army fought the last years of the war in Burma.

The Second World War

As suggested earlier, the army that went to war in 1939 was distinctly unprepared to meet the challenges it confronted. It possessed no combined-arms doctrine, neither did it possess the analytic systems necessary to understand how the enemy fought and then pass the lessons learned along to those in the field or those about to engage the enemy on the sharp end. Underlying these obvious faults was a culture that prized games, parades, and hunting. In reviewing Liddell Hart's *Memoirs*, the great historian Michael Howard noted the following about the army that went to war in September 1939: "The evidence is strong that the Army was still as firmly geared to the pace and perspective of regimental soldiering as it had been before 1914; that to many of its members looked on soldiering as an agreeable and honorable profession rather than a profession demanding no less intellectual dedication than that of the doctor, lawyer or the engineer."[51]

Unlike the First World War, much of the army spent the first four years confined to the British Isles. The incompetence of British forces in meeting the German attack on Norway served to underline just how unprepared both the Royal Navy and the army were for any kind of amphibious operations.[52] The failure is explicable by the British underestimation of Hitler's willingness to take risks, as well as the disinterest the services, especially the army, had exhibited in such operations before the war.[53] Nevertheless, the disaster in France quickly overshadowed events in Norway once the war in the west began. It also served to cover up the gross incompetence that Churchill had displayed throughout the Scandinavian campaign.[54]

Despite the French collapse, the British Army's escape at Dunkirk provided the British with sufficient ground forces to rebuild the army, while the Royal Air Force's Fighter Command prevented the Germans from launching

[51] Ibid., 61.
[52] For the most recent and brilliant account of the British debacle, see John Kiszely, *Anatomy of a Campaign: The British Fiasco in Norway, 1940* (Cambridge, 2017).
[53] In 1939, Lord Gort, at the time the chief of the Imperial General Staff, announced in a meeting of the Chiefs of Staff that railroads would always allow land-based power to concentrate more rapidly than sea power. Thus, the strategic mobility conferred by sea power, although politically an attractive idea, no longer worked in favor of sea power. PRO CAB 53/10, COS/268th Meeting, January 18, 1939, 83.
[54] Kiszely, *Anatomy of a Campaign*, conclusion.

Operation Sealion.[55] Thereafter, the British Army trained throughout the next four years to provide reinforcements for the campaigns in the Mediterranean and Burma. Unfortunately, outside of Bernard Montgomery, the generals responsible for much of the training in the United Kingdom were unimaginative and appear to have had little sense of how necessary combined-arms training was to build an effective fighting force. Typical of the officers responsible for training the army in the United Kingdom was Gen. Frederick Paget, commander in chief of Home Forces in the period before Montgomery took over in early 1944. He once commented, "Anyone can handle armored forces. No special knowledge is needed!"[56] Exacerbating the difficulties involved in training and morale was the fact that during much of the four years in the United Kingdom, it was clear to the ground troops that they were not going to fight anytime soon.

In December 1941, Gen., later Field Marshal, Alan Brooke became the chief of the Imperial General Staff. He would hold that position through to the end of the war. As such, he became Prime Minister Winston Churchill's chief strategic advisor. That duty alone consumed much of his time and most of his energy, and he played a key role in deflecting the prime minister's many hair-brained schemes. As the head of the army, he proved less successful. In 1942, he bemoaned the state of generalship in the British Army in a diary entry:

> Furthermore it [the military performance of the army] is made worse by the lack of good military commanders. Half our Corps and Division Commanders are totally unfit for their appointments, and yet if I were to sack them, I could find no better! They lack character, imagination, drive, and power of leadership.[57]

It was a dismal portrait, yet Brooke seems not to have done much to bring a change in the army's culture. In fact, he picked Gen. Frederick "Boy" Browning to head the 1st Airborne Division, a position that would eventually lead him by September 1944 to the command of the First Allied Airborne Army that launched the airborne portion of Operation Market Garden. Browning

---

[55] An unlikely possibility, since the Kriegsmarine had only a few cruisers and destroyers left after the Norwegian campaign.

[56] B. H. Liddell Hart, "The 'New' Doctrine," June 1942, Liddell Hart Papers, 11/1942/55. Centre for Military Archives, King's College, University of London.

[57] Quoted in David Fraser, *Alanbrooke* (New York, 1982), 297. One of the explanations for the less than impressive performance lies in the heavy losses British officers suffered in the First World War. Yet the Germans also suffered very heavy losses. The explanation seems to lie in the fact that the graduates of the *Kriegsakadamie* immediately before the war included Erich von Manstein, Heinz Guderian, and virtually every field marshal except for Rommel. While these officers spent some time in the trenches, much more of their time was spent in staff positions. Interesting, Rommel, after his spectacular combat performance in 1917 at Caporetto, spent 1918 in a staff position in a third-class division. My suspicion is that the army assignments branch pulled him out of another combat assignment precisely to keep him around for the next war.

would make a hash of that operation.[58] His claim to fame largely rested on the fact that he married novelist Daphne du Maurier and on his assignment as a disciplinarian adjutant at Sandhurst. Apparently, Brooke assigned him to the airborne position because the "Guards" regiments needed representation among the general officer corps.

The results in the fighting against the Afrika Korps underline the inadequacy of troop training back in the United Kingdom. The army had apparently forgotten how to conduct the type of combined-arms fighting that had characterized the BEF's battles in the last six months of the war on the Western Front in 1918. Moreover, those at home appear to have paid little, if any, attention to the combat reports coming back from Libya and Egypt. RAF Marshal Lord Tedder noted that in North Africa, the army suffered from "an excess of bravery and a shortage of brains."[59] But it was not just a matter of brains. From the time that the Germans arrived to save their Italian allies in February 1941, through to Montgomery's arrival at Eighth Army in August 1942, British armored units fought with a minimum of cooperation from other branches.

The problem was twofold. On one hand, the British troops in the desert confronted the most outstanding tactical and operational commander of the war, Field Marshal Erwin Rommel. But Rommel's presence on the battlefield only served to exacerbate the performance of British mobile forces in a war where mobility counted for a great deal more than in the European theater. Hiding behind a screen of 88s, other antitank guns, and infantry and supported by artillery, the Germans made mincemeat of British armor that was fighting alone and then mopped up what failed to escape. One of the experienced armor officers in the desert characterized the slaughter of newly arrived armored cavalry units from the United Kingdom in the following terms:

> Other officers told me how they had seen the Hussars charging into the Jerry tanks, sitting on top of their turrets more or less with their whips out. "It looked like the run-up to the first fence at a point-to-point," the adjutant described it. This first action was very typical of these early encounters involving cavalry regiments. They had incredible enthusiasm and dash, and sheer exciting courage which was only curbed by the rapidly decreasing stock of dashing officers and tanks.[60]

Unfortunately for British forces in the desert, the lack of professionalism that Professor Howard alluded to was all too typical. Lord Carver, a future chief of

---

[58] Among his appalling mistakes was to place the inexperienced British 1st Airborne Division on the farthest drop zone, pay no attention to the Dutch underground warnings about Waffen SS units positioned in the area around Arnhem, allocate thirty-four precious gliders to his headquarters staff, and then blame failure on the Poles.
[59] Lord Tedder, *With Prejudice* (London, 1966), 217.
[60] Robert Crisp, *Brazen Chariots* (New York, 1960), 32.

the Imperial General Staff and a veteran of the fighting in both North Africa and Europe, commented after the war:

> Our real weakness was the failure to develop tactics for a concentrated attack employing tanks, artillery, and infantry in depth on a narrow front. Time and again the tanks motored or charged at the enemy on a broad front until the leading troops were knocked out by the enemy tanks or anti-tank guns; the momentum of the attack immediately failed. Such artillery as was supporting the tanks indulged in some splattering of the enemy ... after which the tanks motored about or charged again with the same results as before ... the infantry not taking part, their task being to follow up and occupy the objective after it had been captured by the tanks.[61]

German reports from the fighting in Italy again provide a picture of a military culture that failed to develop the requisite professionalism, especially against an opponent who took the training and tactical preparation of troops with the utmost seriousness:

> British attacking formations were split up into large numbers of assault squads commanded by officers. NCOs were rarely in the "big picture," so that if officers became a casualty, they were unable to act in accordance with the main plan. The result was that in a quickly changing situation, *the junior commanders showed insufficient flexibility.* For instance, when an objective was reached, the enemy would fail to exploit and dig in for defense. The conclusion is: as far as possible *go for the enemy officers.* Then seize the initiative yourself.[62]

As Rommel noted about the Guards Brigade, "it was almost the living embodiment of the virtues and faults of the British soldier – tremendous courage and tenacity combined with a rigid lack of mobility."[63]

Montgomery certainly recognized the weaknesses in the army, and much of how he conducted the large-scale battles against the Germans in North Africa, Sicily, and France reflected that knowledge. His report on the condition of the army when he assumed command underlines how inadequately trained the Eighth Army remained after two years of fighting in the desert. "The condition of the Eighth Army ... was almost unbelievable ... Gross mismanagement, faulty command, and bad staff work ... Divisions were split into pieces all over the desert; the armor was not concentrated; the gunners had forgotten the art of employing artillery in a concentrated form."[64] It was not a pretty picture.

Immediately on assuming command, he made clear how different his approach was from that of his predecessors. To begin with, there would be no more retreating. He informed the troops defending Alam Hafa Ridge that they

---

[61] Quoted in Shelford Bidwell and Dominick Graham, *Fire-Power: British Army Weapons and Theories of War, 1904–1945* (London, 1982), 228.

[62] Quoted in Max Hastings, *D-Day and the Battle for Normandy* (New York, 1984), 147. Italics in the original.

[63] Erwin Rommel, *The Rommel Papers*, ed. by B. H. Liddell Hart (New York, 1953), 222.

[64] Quoted in Fraser, *Alanbrooke*, 289.

would stay there alive, or they would stay there dead. Constantly badgered by Churchill in London to attack, he ended up with only three months to repair the major deficiencies in leadership, training, and culture that characterized British forces in Egypt. In the end, he had to settle on a battle that involved careful, methodical planning and closely controlled conduct of operations. At the Battle of El Alamein, using the considerable superiority in armor, infantry, and artillery that the Eighth Army enjoyed, he broke the back of the Afrika Korps in a massive battle of attrition. It was not a thing of operational beauty, and victory masked the cultural and professional weaknesses of the force under him. A general unwillingness to display initiative also marked the pursuit to Tunisia after the Afrika Korps collapsed, but Montgomery understood that any kind of mobile battle was bound to get his troops in trouble.

Similarly, Montgomery fought the Battle of Normandy in a fashion that maximized the strength of the forces available to him. He had arrived back in the United Kingdom in January 1944 and had a bare four months to get the army's units ready for the taxing business of fighting the Germans on their home turf. As in North Africa in July 1942, Montgomery did not have sufficient time to repair the training of the inadequately prepared ground forces. Moreover, the extraordinary demands the war had made on a British empire already in political and economic decline severely limited the manpower available for the British units that would have to fight in France. Thus, Montgomery chose a cautious, attrition-based approach that drove his American counterparts crazy.

The one time he attempted to move with speed to take advantage of what appeared to be a German collapse in the west was in late August and early to mid-September 1944, the result being a military defeat in Operation Market Garden that guaranteed the Western Allies would not break into Germany until spring 1945. Operation Market Garden depended on the speed with which British XXX Corps could reinforce the British and American paratroopers on the road to Arnhem. But the tankers proved more interested in brewing up tea than in relieving the hard-pressed British 1st Airborne Division at Arnhem. Montgomery's reputation must rest on the caution that fully took account of the weaknesses in the armies he led. That cautious approach has led to considerable criticism by historians unwilling to recognize that he was not leading the Wehrmacht.[65]

The other exception to the army's culture came in fighting in distant Burma with the extraordinary leadership of Gen., later Field Marshal, William Slim. Slim assumed command of the remnants of the troops the Japanese had smashed in Burma. It was a rotten command. The officers had shown scant

---

[65] Montgomery did not help his postwar reputation by writing one of the more dishonest memoirs about the war, his dishonesty exceeded perhaps only by the memoirs of the German generals.

leadership; the troops had not trained to fight in Burma's jungle; and all took away from the defeat that the Japanese were inherently superior as fighters. At the end of an immensely long logistical line with the empire engaged in desperate fights elsewhere, Slim's corps and the eventually expanded Fourteenth Army received the leavings. And, of course, the British Army's culture permeated the forces for which Slim was now responsible. But the one thing Slim had was time, something Montgomery had never possessed in either North Africa or in France.

Slim almost missed his opportunity. In early 1943, the British launched an offensive down the Arakan Peninsula. Slim had a clear idea of what needed to be done, but his immediate superior, Noel Irwin, took over command of the operation and left Slim out of the picture. Irwin apparently had it in for Slim, who had relieved one of Irwin's friends from battalion command for incompetence. Irwin was also an officer cut in the Haig model, who had no intention of listening to his subordinates. Having made a hash of the campaign – he had stuffed no less than nine brigades into the inadequate command and control of the 14th Indian Division – Irwin brought Slim into the battle when it was clear that the effort had failed with the obvious intention of blaming Slim for the failure. He then fired Slim, but was himself relieved of command and replaced by Slim.[66]

What Slim set about to do was not just to retrain beaten and dispirited troops and restore their morale but also to change the Fourteenth Army's culture from top to bottom. He first set about analyzing what had gone wrong in the Burma campaign and what he needed to fix. It was the second problem that required the real work, because it demanded a fundamental change in the culture of command. Moreover, Slim led an army that consisted of units drawn from all parts of the empire. The nature of the fighting in Burma's jungles demanded units that could operate on their own, but at the same time could come together and cooperate under extraordinarily difficult circumstances. As he put it in his memoirs:

> My corps and divisions were called upon to act with at least as much freedom as armies and corps in other theaters. Commanders at all levels had to act more on their own; they were given greater latitude to work out their own plans to achieve what they knew was the Army Commander's intention. In time they developed to a marked degree a flexibility of mind and a firmness of decision that enabled them to act swiftly to take advantage of sudden information or changing circumstances without reference to their superiors.[67]

---

[66] Raymond Callahan, *Triumph at Imphal-Kohima: How the Indian Army Finally Stopped the Japanese Juggernaut* (Lawrence, KS, 2017), 31, 40–43.
[67] Field Marshal Sir William Slim, *Defeat into Victory* (London, 1956), 541–542.

The results that Slim achieved in terms of operational capabilities were indeed outstanding, and the performance of the Fourteenth Army in the pursuit of Japanese forces in Burma in 1945 was wholly different from that of British forces in other parts of the world. The 300-mile race from Meiktila to Rangoon in April 1945, accomplished in a little more than a week, stands in stark contrast to the Guards Armored Division brewing up tea on the road to Arnhem.

Conclusion

Slim's performance in changing the culture of the Fourteenth Army over the three-year period of his leadership certainly suggests that the British Army was not a hopeless case. But as a senior marine general pointed out to the author in the mid-1990s, it is extraordinarily difficult to change the organizational culture of a military organization, much like trying to change the direction of an ocean liner that is not moving.[68]

Because they were outsiders, the careers of both Montgomery and Slim are instructive about how crucial the education, career progression, and cultural framework within which they work are for the creation of intuitive and imaginative senior officers who really can think outside the box. Montgomery's service throughout the First World War in training positions and then in staff positions provided him with a wide perspective on the various pieces necessary to put together effective combined-arms operations. This inclination and the fact that he had significant teaching experience in the interwar period added to his understanding of what would prove to be essential components in guiding British military operations both in North Africa and Northwest Europe. With Montgomery's considerable interest in military history, his teaching experience at the staff college further deepened his understanding of war. His brilliance in his profession allowed him to escape the fact that he was widely despised by substantial numbers of his contemporaries. One fellow officer described Montgomery as that "little shit." In that respect, he was much like the American chief of naval operations, Adm. Ernest King.

In considerable contrast, "Bill" Slim was well liked by his peers, respected by his subordinates, and beloved by the soldiers who served under him.[69] Yet he had a hard road. With the wrong accent, from the wrong class, and with no outside funds to support him in an army career, Slim's only choice was to opt for the Indian Army and even there he had to write detective stories to support his family. But like Montgomery, Slim was an avid reader of history, and his performance at the staff college at Quetta was so outstanding that he then had a

---

[68] The individual was Lt. Gen. Paul K. van Riper, one of the truly innovative senior officers in the American military in the last two decades of the twentieth century.

[69] For the last case, see particularly the superb memoir by George MacDonald Fraser, *Quartered Safe Out Here* (London, 2014).

three-year tour teaching at Camberley. Throughout the interwar period, Slim used his time to expand his knowledge of war and to prepare himself for what proved to be a brilliant career in turning the Fourteenth Army into an exceptional instrument for killing Japanese.

What is particularly noteworthy about both generals in their preparation for the coming war was that they stood outside of the British Army's (and the Indian Army's) culture. They were students of their profession, not only of its present demands but also of the past and what the past suggested about war. The similarities in their preparation for the future demands of war suggest how important intellectual preparation of the officer corps must be in developing a military culture that can adapt to the realities of war. Slim had time to change the culture of the Fourteenth Army; Montgomery had only time to work around the edges of the Eighth Army and the forces he commanded in Europe. But the story was the same. Not until both had made great efforts to change the culture of the armies they led were British arms able to triumph.

The message would seem clear to us today. If US military leaders fail to emphasize the intellectual side of military professionalism in their military services as well as the technological and administrative business of running multibillion-dollar businesses, they will achieve the same results as in Vietnam and in American failures in Iraq between 2003 and 2006. If US military leaders continue to remain ignorant of the past, they will only learn on the battlefields of the future, as Gen. Jim Mattis has suggested, "by filling body bags."

9   Imperial Japanese Army Culture, 1918–1945

Duty Heavier than a Mountain, Death Lighter than a Feather

David Hunter-Chester

By 1918, Japan had achieved many of the goals conceived more than fifty years previously by those known in the West as oligarchs, and in Japan as *genrō* (elder statesmen). Japan was a rich, creditor nation, reckoned among the global powers. Its soldiers, soon to be known as the Imperial Japanese Army (IJA), had been victorious in three wars and several smaller actions, and they were respected around the world for their decorum and courage. Having sided with the Entente Powers in World War I, Japan had gained strategically important Pacific islands that Imperial Germany had previously controlled, with relatively little fighting. No doubt Japan's leaders expected to share in other spoils as they prepared for the Versailles Peace Conference. But 1918 proved pivotal, and from this point forward Yamato's fighting men lost much of their luster, both at home and abroad, while the wider society began to fracture. Parts of the IJA became radicalized by the 1930s. Soldiers who often intoned the Rescript to Soldiers and Sailors, promulgated by the emperor in 1882, which read, in part, "do your utmost for the protection of the state ... neither be led astray by current opinions nor meddle in politics," ignored the latter injunction, rationalizing that to protect the state, the army must control it.[1] The IJA then led Japan into a war with China it could not win.

   The organizational culture of the IJA can be traced back to the founding in Tokyo of its first important unit, the Imperial Guard, in 1871. An army ministry had preceded this by two years, and this ministry, headed by one of the most powerful oligarchs, Yamagata Aritomo, considered the father of the Japanese army, had orchestrated the Guard's founding, as well as that of three more garrisons in Osaka, Kumamoto, and Sendai, and of smaller detachments at several other locations. The troops were mostly infantry, with some artillery

---

[1] Gary D. Allison, *The Columbia Guide to Modern Japanese History* (New York, 1999), 227.

and engineers.[2] From its beginning, foundational factors of Japan's wider culture shaped the IJA's organizational culture.

Two important artifacts[3] of Japan's culture concern the place and role of the emperor: historically, closeness to the emperor has bestowed power, but the emperor has not ruled.[4] Instead, this "empty center," the emperor, was "primarily an emotional point of reference," capable of legitimizing all manner of widely varying beliefs.[5] As well, underlying assumptions[6] of Japan's culture privilege group social action, and give rise to organizing such groups along ie-type or familial lines. Groups' "major features … are … strong collective goals, functional hierarchy, and a very high degree of autonomy of the organizational units."[7] The IJA was one such group, and Yamagata took steps to ensure its centrality and autonomy.

In 1874, the government appointed the home minister to lead an army contingent to quell a samurai uprising in Kyushu. Yamagata, at this point the army minister and imperial advisor to the army's Tokyo headquarters, "was so annoyed by civilian command he reorganized the army ministry's sixth bureau into a small prototype general staff to exercise control over military operations."[8] Yamagata then resigned as minister, and appointed himself both director of this new operations staff and commander of the Imperial Guard, which he led to crush the uprising. The fighting had ended by the time the Guard arrived, but this established an important precedent: the army would ignore civilian authority and claim to rely solely on the supreme command of the emperor.

The oligarchy used the symbolic and legitimizing authority of the emperor to further their conviction that preserving Japan's independence and dignity required "'catching up and surpassing' the West."[9] But in the pell-mell rush to form a Westphalian-style state, following the Meiji Restoration of 1868, powerful, autonomous groups proliferated and the oligarchs had to compete with these groups for influence. One such group led what became known as the popular rights movement. As education and an awareness of the wider world spread throughout Japanese society in the Meiji era, this movement led a call for representative assemblies, like those in other countries. The government established prefectural assemblies in 1878, hoping to assuage the movement, but this only increased calls for a national assembly and a constitution. In 1881,

---

[2] Edward J. Drea, *Japan's Imperial Army* (Lincoln, NE, 2009), 24.
[3] Using Edgar Schein's terminology, as described by Wong and Gerras in Chapter 1 of this volume.
[4] Toshio Iritani, *Group Psychology of the Japanese in Wartime* (New York, 1991), 1.
[5] Shmuel N. Eisenstadt, *Japanese Civilization: A Comparative View* (Chicago, 1996), 357.
[6] Schein's third, innermost, and often unconscious layer of culture. See Wong and Gerras, Chapter 1 of this volume.
[7] Eisenstadt, *Japanese Civilization*, 12.   [8] Drea, *Japan's Imperial Army*, 37.
[9] Richard J. Samuels, *Securing Japan: Tokyo's Grand Strategy and the Future of East Asia* (Ithaca, NY, 2007), 15.

the emperor promised a constitution and a national assembly by 1890. That same year, Japan's first political party formed, with another formed the following year.

The constitution codified many beliefs and values,[10] investing all sovereignty in the person of the emperor, but limiting the monarch. Though he could issue decrees (written by others), those had to be cosigned by ministers to go into effect. His prime minister could not select ministers, but could "suspend or reprimand them"; executive power remained divided between "the cabinet, the privy council, the imperial household ministry and the military high command."[11]

The national assembly, known as the Diet, gave the political parties a bully pulpit to "attack oligarchic leadership free from police harassment and unhindered by press or libel laws," while "the Diet's right of appeal to the emperor" allowed them "to pass resolutions impeaching government ministers. Although these had no legal standing, they were profoundly embarrassing."[12] Tradition and mounting precedents appended other de facto limits to executive power, while a developing professional bureaucracy added another body jostling for influence. Control over budget approval gave the Diet, and thus the new political parties, more power than Ito Hirobumi, the primary author of the constitution and another of the most powerful oligarchs, had probably intended. Ito insisted, at first, on "transcendental cabinets," ones dominated by the *genrō* and thus above political parties, but then, bowing to what he perceived as inevitable, he formed one himself in 1900.[13]

Yamagata remained opposed to political parties. At his instigation, the Meiji Constitution had codified the supreme command of the emperor with this command exercised through the general staff (which an army reorganization had provided). The constitution also granted "direct access" to the emperor by "both the general staff and the service ministers."[14] As prime minister, Yamagata further tilted the complicated influence structure in favor of the military by passing an ordinance in 1899 requiring that service ministers be active-duty "generals or admirals."[15] This, paired with "the tradition of cabinet unity,"[16] allowed the army to veto cabinet policy, since the resignation of a service minister could bring a cabinet down.[17]

The lineaments of the IJA's organizational culture were thus formed by 1900. Subsequent wars reinforced those features and shaped new ones. Victory in the

---

[10] Used in Schein's sense as the middle layer of culture. See Wong and Gerras, Chapter 1 of this volume.
[11] Peter Duus, *Modern Japan*, 2nd edn. (Boston, MA, 1998), 126.   [12] Ibid., 172.
[13] Ibid., 172–174.
[14] Paul E. Dunscomb, *Japan's Siberian Intervention, 1918–1922* (Lanham, MD, 2011), 13.
[15] Duus, *Modern Japan*, 173.   [16] Dunscomb, *Japan's Siberian Intervention*, 13.
[17] Ibid.; Duus, *Modern Japan*, 174.

First Sino-Japanese War in 1895 made Japan a regional power, while triumph in the Russo-Japanese War in 1905 granted the country standing as a Great Power – a status coveted since the beginning of the Meiji era. The impacts on the IJA's organizational culture were less sanguine and ultimately more sanguinary: the myths (in Schein's terms, secondary reinforcing and stabilizing mechanisms)[18] that came out of the victory in the Russo-Japanese War reinforced the IJA's growing "ritualiz[ation of] death" and strengthened the "informal taboo against being taken captive."[19] Another important legacy of the conflict was a strengthening and wider dissemination of the myth of Japan's superior spiritual strength, which would grant inevitable victory, no matter the foe.

In reality, the Russo-Japanese War had been a near-run thing. Though Third Army commander Lt. Gen. Nogi Maresuke was apotheosized after accepting the Russian commander of Port Arthur's surrender, many of the troops and commanders who served in the war considered him incompetent. Nogi could not even read a map, and his "victory" only came after three major offensives and at a cost of 59,000 casualties. But the IJA was more concerned about its reputation than the truth, and ensured negative reports were not made public. Instead, when Adm. Tōgō Heihachirō's naval victory over Russia's Baltic Fleet exacerbated Russia's domestic tension and led Russia to negotiate a war settlement, the Japanese public thrilled to stories of the unique effectiveness of the Japanese soldier, always attacking, courageous, selfless, and victorious.[20]

By 1918, the IJA basked in contrived glory, while in the larger society, nationalism grew apace. Economically, Japan prosecuted its most successful war as one of the Entente Powers in World War I: "The developed economies of the West were fully occupied in mutual destruction, unable even to exploit the colonial markets from which Japan had been excluded. Japan's modern sector was prepared to fill the gap."[21] Japan transformed itself from a debtor to a creditor nation, its gross domestic product growing more than 40 percent during the war years.[22]

But an economic crash followed this high point when Westerners returned to dominate trade in the Pacific after the war. In addition, although Japan was one of the five Great Powers accorded a seat on the Council of the League of Nations, many of Japan's leaders, both civilian and military, began to feel, as Prince Konoe Fumimaro, who accompanied Japan's representative to the Versailles Peace Conference, expressed it, that World War I had really been about "'have' and 'have not' powers." Konoe expressed sympathy for Germany, like Japan a late-organizing state that had become a Great Power,

---

[18] Wong and Gerras, Chapter 1 of this volume. [19] Drea, *Japan's Imperial Army*, 119.
[20] Ibid., 107–121.
[21] Marius B. Jansen, *The Making of Modern Japan* (Cambridge, 2000), 531. [22] Ibid.

and voiced antipathy toward the other Western powers who now wanted to protect their prerogatives.[23] Anger toward the West grew in wider society as the economic crash became Japan's deepest depression since the beginning of industrialization. Resentment grew further as the United States outlawed Japanese immigration. In 1922, Japan was granted a smaller ratio of naval tonnage than either the United States or the United Kingdom at the naval arms limitation talks in Washington, which led many Japanese to view the resulting treaty as yet more proof of Western discrimination.[24]

At this point, Japanese society began to fracture. More widespread education brought a new awareness of "haves" and "have nots" not only internationally but domestically. Zaibatsu, that is, Japan's new conglomerates, and some industrialized sectors had either weathered the depression or recovered relatively quickly, but the farming sector and those engaged in traditional crafts – still the majority of the population – suffered. The *genrō* were proving ultimately mortal and without their extraconstitutional guidance, party governments during this so-called Taishō Democracy period (which began in 1912) tried to seize the reins, but the constitutional system and government institutions proved inadequate and the leadership weak.[25] The army grew concerned.

After World War I, two main factions grew in the IJA, displacing groupings originally based on regions of birth. The new factions grew from IJA soldiers having taken divergent lessons from World War I: one segment believed World War I demonstrated future wars would be prolonged and total, requiring the mobilization of all a nation's people and resources to prevail. Another segment believed Japan, insufficient in terms of the necessary natural resources, could not fight a prolonged war, and must instead aim for a short war, preferably against a single opponent, the results then safeguarded by diplomacy from a position of strength after victory.

The proponents of a short war argued for a large standing army, ready to overwhelm any opponent. Realizing Japan's deficiencies in size and resources compared to likely enemies such as the United States and the Soviet Union, these short-war advocates, harkening back to a mythologized effectiveness of the samurai in the Satsuma Rebellion (the last and largest of the samurai insurrections) and the equally mythologized effectiveness of the IJA in the Russo-Japanese War, doubled down on the belief that Japan's distinctive family state, under the divine emperor, granted its people and especially its soldiers a unique spiritual strength no enemy could ultimately withstand. They also stressed the army's role as the direct extension of the emperor's divine will. Many in this group eventually coalesced into what was called the Kōdōha, or

---

[23] Ibid., 519. Also Herbert P. Bix, *Hirohito and the Making of Modern Japan* (New York, 2000), 176–177.

[24] Jansen, *The Making of Modern Japan*, 520–522.   [25] Ibid., 519–575.

Imperial Way Faction. The Imperial Way Faction's faith predated World War I. In 1909, the army had put forward what "became the bedrock of future Japanese tactical doctrine ... Japan's unique history and culture (*kokutai*), combined with national characteristics and geographical setting, determined the nature of the army ... Infantry was the decisive arm in combat, the spirit of attack the basis of warfare, and hand-to-hand combat the decisive factor in battle."[26]

The second group, whose adherents considered prolonged, total war inevitable, became concerned about gaining control of Japan's economy in order to expand its heavy industries; they desired control of society as a whole in order to enforce mobilization of all of Japan's people when it became necessary. Many in this group became known as the Tōseiha, or Control Faction. The Tōseiha was willing to sacrifice some force structure – that is, numbers of troops and amount of equipment – for money to invest in industrial infrastructure.[27] Later developing, one can trace the origins of this faction to the "Provisional Military Research Committee" established in 1915, the findings of which led the general staff to direct formation of another committee, chaired by Vice Chief of Staff Lt. Gen. Tanaka Giichi, who became a leading proponent of total-war theory to revise Japan's defense strategy.[28]

Using the Global Leadership and Organizational Behavior Effectiveness (GLOBE) dimensions, it is clear the IJA after World War I stood at a crossroads, ready to embrace an organizational culture whose future orientation was strong, in the case of the careful planners of the Control Faction, or weak, in the case of the zealots of the Imperial Way Faction.[29]

Regarding another GLOBE dimension, Institutional Collectivism, Japan's Imperial forces were weak. The Japanese norm empowering autonomous groups and the absence of effective civilian control had exacerbated this weakness. The army and navy had been unable to agree on a single strategy in the first national military strategy published in 1907. That document had identified Russia as the army's main enemy, but the United States as the navy's primary opponent. While exhibiting low institutional collectivism, both organizations were abiding by a strong cultural norm in Japan, a preference for harmony in decision-making bodies.[30] These norms were evident as well in the revised national defense strategy, published in 1918.

The new strategy "posited Japan fighting against a coalition, likely composed of the United States, the Soviet Union, and China." In this instance,

---

[26] Drea, *Japan's Imperial Army*, 133.
[27] Ibid., 150–169. See also Samuels, *Securing Japan*, 15–21.
[28] Drea, *Japan's Imperial Army*, 138.
[29] All references to GLOBE dimensions are according to the definitions listed by Wong and Gerras, Chapter 1 of this volume.
[30] Eisenstadt, *Japanese Civilization*, 320.

instead of the two services, the two main factions of the IJA were accommodated. The strategy called for quick offensive operations leading to a "decisive
victory … because early battlefield success would ensure self-sufficiency,
which in turn would enable Japan to fight a protracted struggle." The document
also called for Japan to deploy troops into China to protect "Japanese interests
and residents," and for Japan to occupy "strategic locations east of Lake Baikal
and in joint operations with the navy, occupy Luzon, Philippines."[31]

Some officers noted the inherent contradictions involved, but the need for
harmony had prevailed, at least while Japan was flush with wartime prosperity.
When boom turned to bust immediately afterward, enough comity remained
between competing power structures for the army and navy to agree to a budget
in 1920, the only time the two organizations so agreed. The strategy projected a
naval buildup through 1927, which then would have been followed by army
expansion. But worsening economic conditions, new ideologies, and public
dissatisfaction with the IJA's ill-fated Siberian Expedition turned many
Japanese against military spending.[32]

The Siberian Expedition began in 1918. The Entente Powers had asked
Japan to intervene in Europe during World War I a few times, but the IJA
general staff, concerned about the number of troops required and the expense,
as well as the escalating instability in the traditional enemy, Russia, had fended
off such requests. After the Bolshevik Revolution in 1917 with the formation of
the new Union of Soviet Socialist Republics, the IJA intervened in Vladivostok
to restore order and began to examine establishing a buffer zone against the
Soviets east of Lake Baikal. Long-war advocates saw this as a way to better
ensure Japan's access to the resources of China and Manchuria, while short-war
advocates saw it as a way "to rid Japan permanently" of the Russia threat.[33] In
April 1918, the Soviets signed a peace treaty with Germany and "demanded
that Czech army units then in Russia disarm." The Czechs, who had been
fighting for the Entente, instead "occupied sections of the Trans-Siberian
Railroad,"[34] consolidated east of Lake Baikal and began moving west, "becoming the spearhead of the counter-revolutionary army."[35] At the urging of the
British and French, the United States, which had been hesitant to intervene,
asked Japan to deploy troops with the Americans in a combined force, not to
exceed 7,000 soldiers, to aid the Czechs. In addition to the pacification efforts
in Vladivostok, the Japanese had already been secretly supplying anti-Soviet
forces in northern Manchuria. Japan agreed to the combined force, but sowed
distrust with the Americans and other Entente forces by quickly exceeding both

[31] Drea, *Japan's Imperial Army*, 140.   [32] Ibid., 141.
[33] Ibid., 142. Also Dunscomb, *Japan's Siberian Intervention*, 109.
[34] Ibid.; Drea, *Japan's Imperial Army*.   [35] Dunscomb, *Japan's Siberian Intervention*, 50.

the initially agreed-upon troop total, and a subsequently agreed-upon revised total of 12,000 soldiers.[36]

Japanese soldiers, like many conventional troops, were unprepared for guerilla warfare. There were no front lines, and the enemy, a mixture of partisans and bandits, was indistinguishable from noncombatants. As the Soviets consolidated, most Entente forces left Siberia within little more than a year and the Czech forces by 1920. But Japanese forces remained. Suffering through the cold, the massacre of an isolated IJA battalion, an arms scandal involving Chinese warlord troops in Manchuria, and increasingly bad press at home, army morale plummeted and the IJA's reputation in Japan steadily worsened. Under these clouds, Japanese troops withdrew from the mainland in 1922, though some troops remained on Sakhalin Island until 1925.[37]

Defeat in Siberia gave the army a chance to absorb the lessons. But instead of realizing, for instance, the necessity of centralized, non-factional control, the major lesson the army embraced was the need to protect its public reputation. The army strongly exhibited the GLOBE dimension In-Group Collectivism: soldiers were extremely proud of being in the army. Special emissaries of the emperor, they would not allow any shame to accrue to the organization. This unwillingness to admit fault to the public left a number of critical dysfunctions unaddressed.

The Taishō era gave way in 1925 to the Shōwa era under the young emperor, Hirohito. The agrarian sector of the economy, still the largest, remained acutely distressed, and right-leaning groups started calling for a Shōwa Restoration, ahistorically projecting onto the empty emperor a golden age under his direct, divine rule. Some IJA soldiers converted to this new faith, but the wider institution became more concerned with how to restore continence to Japanese society.

As a result, generals and admirals became more powerful political actors. From 1885 until 1945, half of the thirty prime ministers were active duty or retired military. Though this percentage had dipped in the 1920s, it rose again in the 1930s as Japan reeled from crisis to crisis, both domestic and international.[38] Both short-war and total-war advocates ascended to leadership. As the war minister in 1925, IJA Gen. Ugaki Kazushige, a protégé of Tanaka Giichi and a long-war advocate, was able to push through a reduction of force of about 40,000 soldiers in order to fund equipment modernization, but what he did with these displaced soldiers was more significant in the long run. Placing "officers from inactivated units into positions as military instructors in elementary and middle schools as drill instructors, extending the

[36] Drea, *Japan's Imperial Army*, 142–143.
[37] Though I have relied upon Drea's *Japan's Imperial Army* for troop movements, Dunscomb, *Japan's Siberian Intervention*, is the best source for an overall, holistic view of the conflict.
[38] Jansen, *The Making of Modern Japan*, 590–591.

army's influence in the education system [to] indoctrinate youth with accepted military values and patriotism," Ugaki strove to both better prepare imperial subjects for conscription and address the perceived need for discipline in the civilian populace.[39]

In 1926, Ugaki furthered these goals by establishing the Young Men's Military Training Corps, "a voluntary organization that offered civics education and military training under the auspices of members of the Reservists Association to youths age 16 to 20 who had completed their education," with the incentive that those who completed the training and were drafted could shorten their conscription period by six months.[40] In 1910, at the inauguration ceremony for the Imperial Military Reserve Association, Yamagata had enjoined, "We reservists ... must carry out our organizations' primary aims and fulfill the ideal that all citizens are soldiers."[41] With the reforms in the 1920s, Yamagata's goal had marched forward.

Yet the high command's design to instill discipline in the wider society – always secondary to a goal of gaining the general population's approval of and support for the army – lagged. The Great Depression worsened the already acute situation in the countryside; lawlessness and terror in the population spread and began infecting the army: "Between 1930 and 1935, there were twenty major domestic terrorist incidents, four political assassinations, five planned assassinations and four attempted coups."[42] In the so-called 2.26 incident, on February 26, 1936, a group of radicalized young army officers and civilian right-wing terrorists murdered the lord privy seal (a retired admiral), the inspector general of military education (an active-duty army general), and the finance minister (a civilian) while they slept in their bedrooms. The prime minister escaped the attempt on his life, but others were wounded. The goal of the insurrectionists was a Shōwa Restoration, and they wanted to name one prominent Imperial Way general to be prime minister and another, Araki Sadao, to the post of home minister to "carry out" the restoration. The extremists were captured, the radical officers were executed or imprisoned, and the influence of the Imperial Way Faction was curtailed, at least at the highest levels.[43]

By 1936, the IJA had been involved in a low-intensity war in Manchuria for almost five years. How the conflict had begun and why it continued illustrates some of the dysfunctions of the IJA's organizational culture. A contract for training and advice by the Prussian Army, in 1880, had fatefully brought Maj. Gen. Klemens Wilhelm Jakob Meckel to teach at Japan's Army Staff College. Meckel's focus, like Prussia's, was continental, and he warned Japan's army

[39] Drea, *Japan's Imperial Army*, 154.   [40] Ibid.
[41] Richard J. Smethurst, *A Social Basis for Prewar Japanese Militarism: The Army and the Rural Community* (Berkeley, 1974), 2.
[42] Drea, *Japan's Imperial Army*, 181.   [43] Jansen, *The Making of Modern Japan*, 597–598.

that the Korean peninsula was a dagger pointed at the heart of Japan. Subsequently, in 1890, in his first speech to the Diet as prime minister, Yamagata steered Japan's strategic culture from its traditional, maritime or insular (in both senses of the term) orientation, to a continental one, when he proclaimed the empire's need to secure a "line of sovereignty" that included all Japanese territory proper, and a "line of interests," which included Korea.[44]

After two wars over control of the peninsula, Japan formally annexed Korea in 1910, thereby extending Japanese territory onto the continent. Thus the line of Japanese interests had extended into Siberia to the north and China to the west. An operational doctrine that continued to stress victory hinged on independent, offensive-minded action by army units at all levels, as well as the total-war leanings of a key IJA staff officer, led to the so-called Manchurian Incident and the beginning of what some Japanese call the Fifteen-Year War. The seizure of Manchuria in 1931 had been independently planned and executed by the Kantōgun, usually Romanized as the Kwantung Army in English, a constabulary force already in the area to protect the South Manchurian Railway.[45] In addition to the weak Institutional Collectivism both within the army and within Japan's overall governing apparatus, two other GLOBE dimensions, Power Distance and Assertiveness, were important.

In Japan's hierarchical culture, Power Distance is strong throughout society. In the IJA, this norm had been reinforced. The army had taught officers, in particular, that they represented the emperor in all they did, and there was no higher symbol for legitimate action. Brutal penalties up to and including death were meted out to those of lesser rank who questioned officers, commissioned or noncommissioned. In addition, in the 1920s through the 1930s and 1940s, commanders and key staff officers were all graduates of the Army Staff College, which had reinforced their belief that they were the elite. They were "supremely self-assured, uncompromising and impatient toward any modification of their plans or actions by higher headquarters."[46] This was Power Distance buttressed and given a brutal twist, found in few other organizations, which, in turn, bolstered the Assertiveness of IJA officers, while undermining their effectiveness and professionalism. The graduates of the staff college, in short, had begun to believe their own press, with ultimately disastrous results.

In September 1931, members of the Kwantung Army exploded a bomb on the South Manchurian Railroad. Blaming the act on Chinese bandits, the emperor's soldiers used the incident to extend their control throughout Manchuria. The spark for, planning of, and leadership of the Manchurian Incident was provided by a charismatic lieutenant colonel, Ishiwara Kanji,

---

[44] Drea, *Japan's Imperial Army*, 74–75.   [45] Ibid.
[46] Mark R. Peattie, *Ishiwara Kanji and Japan's Confrontation with the West* (Princeton, NJ, 1975), 19.

who had both graduated from and taught at the Army Staff College. Ishiwara had long believed that Japan must prepare for total war. When he joined the Kwantung Army, he saw an opportunity to bring Manchuria's resources under Japan's aegis. With his supreme confidence and his decisions supported by a doctrine that continued to stress independent initiative, Ishiwara illustrated yet another key belief basic to the IJA's organizational culture: confidence in inevitable victory. When he returned to Japan in 1932, he boasted that "[e]ven if Japan has to face the entire world she can't be beaten."[47]

Albeit grudgingly, the weak central government accepted the Manchurian Incident, valuing harmony, a "principle ... that admits no distinction between good and bad as operating in ... Japan," more highly than other considerations.[48] Still another cultural factor that encouraged the Japanese government and the Japanese people to accept Ishiwara's fait accompli was the fact that they judged him and his accomplices to have possessed pure or sincere intentions, sincerity being a quality that trumps many sins in Japanese culture.[49]

On July 7, 1937, at the Marco Polo Bridge near Beijing, a Japanese colonel, keeping the ideal of offensive-minded initiative foremost, led his troops into what could have been a fairly minor skirmish between Japanese and Chinese forces. Instead, it became Japan's next step in a long war. A familiar saga of hastily dispatched reinforcements meeting continued resistance, leading to more reinforcements, unfolded as Japan's war extended into what would become the quagmire of the Second Sino-Japanese War.[50]

Domestically, Prince Konoe became prime minister. Konoe brought Araki back into government as the education minister. Previously, as the war minister beginning in December 1931, Araki had been instrumental in strengthening the artifact of the IJA's organizational culture that emphasized the unique and super-ior spiritual strength of the Japanese people, emanating from the emperor. He referred to Japan as an "imperial nation (*kōkoku*)" and to the army as the Imperial Army (*kōgun*). He forbade the use of the terms *retreat* and *surrender* as "detri-mental to army spirit and morale."[51] As education minister, Araki then dissemi-nated these ideas about Japan's unique *seishin*, or spirit, and the *kokutai*, the semi-mystical family state under the benevolent and divine guidance of the emperor, throughout the educational system, thus further propagating these fundamental IJA cultural precepts throughout Japanese society.[52]

Konoe had been convinced of a coming "race war" with the West since at least 1918.[53] Believing Japan had a mission to civilize and lead the rest of Asia, as prime minister, he declared a New Order in Asia, predominantly focused on the perceived rights of Japan on the continent. After a break, returning to

---

[47] Ibid., 136.   [48] Eisenstadt, *Japanese Civilization*, 320.   [49] Ibid., 319–320, 326–327.
[50] Drea, *Japan's Imperial Army*, 191.   [51] Ibid., 176.
[52] Jansen, *The Making of Modern Japan*, 620.   [53] Samuels, *Securing Japan*, 27.

become premier when it became clear Japan would extend its war into the Pacific, Konoe expanded this notion into the Greater East Asia Co-Prosperity Sphere in August 1940.[54] Japan occupied northern Indochina and signed the Axis alliance with Germany and Italy in Berlin the following month.[55]

The Anglo-Americans then imposed sanctions. Its need for resources more acute than ever, Japan invaded southern Indochina in July 1941. America "froze all of Japan's assets" and embargoed oil.[56] The army estimated Japan had enough fuel to fight until autumn without securing more resources. Konoe engaged in negotiations with the United States, but resigned in October. His replacement was the war minister, Tōseiha member Tōjō Hideki. The army's perceived deadline to either acquiesce to Western demands or to attack to carve out autarky in the western Pacific[57] was extended twice, into December.[58]

By the time Japan attacked Pearl Harbor, the IJA was suffering from disastrous dysfunction, especially at the strategic level. Yet much was still laudable about the emperor's soldiers. Foreign military observers remarked on the excellent discipline of Japanese troops from their participation in the Boxer Rebellion up through the Siberian Expedition. Brutal punishments and hazing administered by officers and noncommissioned officers had enforced this discipline. But culturally, discipline was also facilitated by a focus on *bun*, the necessity of fulfilling role expectations and on *kata*, the breaking down of almost any conceivable action into component parts, the sequence of which is then to be mastered. The soldiers thus were acculturated to embody the role of soldier, while individually and collectively they strove to master doctrinal tactics, techniques, and procedures, systematized as *kata*. This mastery was evident, for instance, in the "tactical brilliance" displayed by the IJA in its march through Malaya.[59]

Though the IJA often focused more on burnishing a pristine reputation than honestly reporting to the public, internally, the army could be professionally, brutally honest. After the debacle at Nomonhan, for instance, where a woefully underequipped Kwantung Army had taken on a modernized, mechanized Soviet force in northern Manchuria in 1939 and was thoroughly defeated, the IJA had drawn extremely detailed and unsparing lessons. The Kwantung Army, confident of inevitable victory, had used traditional infantry doctrine and attempted an encirclement of the enemy. But the Soviet mechanized forces that it encountered had overmatched the Japanese forces. In the initial

---

[54] Ibid., 28.   [55] Drea, *Japan's Imperial Army*, 213.

[56] Jansen, *The Making of Modern Japan*, 636.

[57] For the Control Faction's drive for autarky, see Michael A. Barnhart, *Japan Prepares for Total War: The Search for Economic Security, 1919–1941* (Ithaca, NY, 1987).

[58] Jansen, *The Making of Modern Japan*, 639–642. Also see David Hunter-Chester, *Creating Japan's Ground Self-Defense Force, 1945–2015: A Sword Well Made* (Lanham, MD, 2016), 14–23.

[59] Francis Pike, *Hirohito's War: The Pacific War, 1941–1945* (London, 2015), 239.

encounter, in May 1939, the Kwantung Army's light infantry forces met Red Army combined arms units, which included light tanks. After two days of fighting and a 63 percent casualty rate, the Japanese broke off the encounter, not only having failed their attempted encirclement, but having had to break out of the successful encirclement of their own position by the Soviets.[60]

The Kwantung Army then received reinforcements, including "the entire 23rd Division, two tank regiments (seventy-three tanks total), and one infantry battalion detached from the Seventh Infantry Division," but the Japanese forces remained unprepared in terms of overall mechanization, antitank weapons, doctrine, and expectations. When the Japanese tried to encircle and dislodge the Soviet forces again in July, the Soviets flanked them in the north and attacked Japanese forces with armored cars and tanks, forcing a withdrawal, while stopping Japanese forces in the south with "antitank guns and entrenched infantry." Instead of employing combined-arms tactics, the Japanese used their armor in "piecemeal attacks." Meanwhile, the Soviets "riddled Japanese tanks, leaving half of them smoldering wrecks." Both sides then reinforced and settled into prolonged, daily artillery exchanges. On August 20, the Soviets surprised the Japanese when their "armored formations raced around or smashed through the Japanese flanks and surrounded the 23rd Division." By the time a ceasefire was negotiated on September 16, the Japanese had suffered 73 percent casualties.[61]

Even before the ceasefire, the IJA officers began assiduously studying Japan's disastrous encounter with Soviet combined-arms warfare. By the end of September, they had submitted a seventy-four-page report, later expanded with commentary from officers and soldiers who had participated in the fight into a 262-page document. The report was an honest, accurate postmortem with recommendations for transforming the IJA into a modern combined-arms force. While "these documents provide a striking example of an army's ability to criticize itself," in the end, it failed to implement widely the report's recommendations.[62] By 1941, the IJA had only managed to motorize three divisions (the three that then produced the "tactical brilliance" in the Malaya campaign).[63] The reasons for this failure to further mechanize have to do with dysfunctions at the strategic level, but were also due to a lack of resources and industrial capacity and to the fact that the ongoing operations in China and elsewhere were absorbing the IJA's attention.

This failure must have been particularly galling to combined arms advocates in the IJA. While being strong in the GLOBE dimension of Uncertainty Avoidance meant IJA troops often did not deviate from traditional tactics, the

[60] Edward J. Drea, *In the Service of the Emperor: Essays on Japan's Imperial Army* (Lincoln, NE, 1998), 1–3.
[61] Ibid., 2–4.   [62] Ibid., 5.   [63] Ibid., 10.

army could be innovative. The Japanese had used tanks both in its earliest Manchurian operations and in its subsequent pacification operation in Shanghai in the early 1930s. In Manchuria, resistance was ineffective and the tanks did not come into play, while in Shanghai, the urban setting had demonstrated the platforms' limits; Chinese soldiers easily blocked the machines on constricted streets. But the army did not abandon tanks. Two years later, trying to shore up its control of Manchuria, the IJA "unleashed a major offensive, the Battle of Rehe, aimed at capturing the Inner Mongolian province just north of Beijing."[64] The Chinese warlord that Japan's 8th Division battled was on the run, but the division commander "Lieutenant General Yoshikazu Nishi ... realized his traditional infantry would not be able to chase down and rout the Chinese before they established a new line of defense. At his disposal, however, was the now-experienced 1st Tank Company, consisting of 11 Type 89 tanks and two Type 92 heavy armored cars, along with 100 or so trucks and armored cars from the Kwantung Army Automobile Group ... [H]e ordered Major General Tadashi Kawahara and his Battle Group Kawahara – an ad-hoc formation consisting of the 1st Tank Company, a mountain artillery company, an engineer company, a radio communications squad, and two infantry battalions – to exploit the initial breakthrough and advance ahead of the main Japanese force toward Chengde, the provincial capital, to disrupt Chinese defenses."[65]

Battle Group Kawahara covered 200 miles in four days. Catching the Chinese completely off guard, the warlord's troops abandoned their positions and the combined-arms force rolled into Chengde unopposed. Significantly, this combined arms maneuver occurred years before Germany's Wehrmacht stunned the world with its blitzkrieg tactics. Based on the lessons learned, Japan formed the 1st Independent Mixed Brigade in 1934. However, the chance to embrace combined-arms warfare as doctrine suffered when, deployed to northern China at the beginning of the Second Sino-Japanese War in 1937, the brigade's higher commander disregarded the earlier success in the Battle of Rehe. Lt. Gen. Tōjō Hideki, commanding the Expeditionary Force with his narrow, traditionalist mind-set, ignored protests from the brigade's commander and broke up the formation, consigning the tanks and other vehicles to support infantry commanders, who, in turn, did not know how to use the armor effectively.[66]

Thus, again, a failure of leadership – this time at the operational level – thwarted opportunities for the army to become a more effective fighting force. But the foregoing account highlights the fact that, disastrously dysfunctional as

[64] Jiaxin "Jesse" Du, "Pride before the Fall: Why Japan Failed at Tank Warfare," *World War II Magazine*, Historynet, February 27, 2017, www.historynet.com/why-japan-armored-warfare-failed.htm.
[65] Ibid.   [66] Ibid.

it proved to be at the strategic level, at the tactical level and sometimes even at the operational level, Japan's army could be innovative. As another example of innovation, in the 1920s the IJA had been a leader in amphibious operations developments. Having conducted landing operations in its first three wars (Sino-Japanese War, Russo-Japanese War, and World War I), the army began experimenting with amphibious operations. Particularly seeking to improve ship-to-shore platforms, "the Japanese were world leaders in the design of landing craft in 1929."[67] But it is also true that the Japanese did not, then, continue to innovate and were less prepared for contested amphibious landings, especially after Nomonhan, when they refocused on continental warfare. Finally, though less than salutary, IJA pilots were the first to conduct strategic bombing over China in 1938.[68]

Brilliant and innovative though they could be, the IJA soldiers in the Pacific leave an image in the minds of Western readers of suicidal fanatics, capable of the basest atrocities. The Battle of Saipan is both emblematic of this image and of the failures arising from the IJA's organizational culture. Japan had taken Saipan from German control in World War I. One of the largest of the Marianas Islands, Saipan has a varied topography "with beaches, jungles, swamps, mountains, hills, valleys, caves and dense sugarcane fields."[69] More than 30,000 civilians, both Japanese and native Chamorros, lived and worked on Saipan in 1944.[70] The US aim was to use Saipan as a forward air base from which to fly bombing runs against Japan. The Japanese realized the danger and began to try to bolster their small garrison in the spring of 1944, but American submarines sank many of the ships transporting reinforcements. The Japanese navy rescued many of these soldiers, but they often arrived on Saipan without weapons or other equipment. Still, the troop strength on Saipan increased from about 1,500 early in 1944 to approximately 30,000 immediately before the American invasion. This was about twice the number American intelligence expected at the time.[71]

The American invasion began on June 15 after a three-day naval barrage. The IJA defenders, though they had not built fortifications or installed heavy weapons to the degree they had planned (having not expected the Americans until November), skillfully used the terrain and camouflage to endure the barrage with few casualties. The shelling severed numerous Japanese communication lines, however, making subsequent tactical coordination difficult and demoralizing many Japanese soldiers who endured the constant pounding of

[67] Drea, *In the Service of the Emperor*, 24.
[68] Harno Tohmatsu and H. P. Willmott, *A Gathering Darkness: The Coming of War in the Far East and the Pacific, 1921–1942* (Lanham, MD, 2004), xvii.
[69] Harold J. Goldberg, *D-Day in the Pacific: The Battle of Saipan* (Bloomington, IN, 2007), 30.
[70] Francis A. O'Brien, *Battling for Saipan* (New York, 2003), 67.
[71] Goldberg, *D-Day in the Pacific*, 34.

the naval guns. The Japanese attempted to defend at the water's edge to prevent the Americans from gaining a toehold ashore. When the marines of the 4th and 2nd Divisions began landing on the beaches, they met withering fire. By the end of the first day, the marines had suffered more than 2,000 casualties in order to occupy a position 10,000 yards wide by 1,500 yards deep.[72] That evening, Japanese counterattacks were limited and piecemeal, though they probed the 2nd Division's left flank persistently throughout the first night. But the issue was never in doubt. An American bomber attack on June 11 had "destroyed or damaged 147 enemy planes" on Saipan and that, along with the Great Marianas Turkey Shoot, had guaranteed American air supremacy.[73] Furthermore, the Battle of the Philippine Sea had crippled the Japanese fleet. Already under-equipped, the Japanese could hope for neither reinforcements nor resupply.[74]

Still the IJA continued to resist. The Americans decided to land the army's 27th Infantry Division, the designated reserve, on the second day, and the joint force made its painful way north and east against the Japanese, the fierceness of the fight indicated by the names the Americans gave landmarks, such as Death Valley and Purple Heart Ridge. The Japanese withdrew to a point just north of Mount Tapotchau near the center of the island in an area the Americans called Paradise Valley. The Japanese called it the Valley of Hell. More difficult and of longer duration than the Americans had planned, that battle was nearing its end by July 4. The commander of Japan's ground forces (which included Naval Landing Forces members and a Naval Guard Force), Lt. Gen. Saito Yoshitsugu, had also determined the end was near. He and the Imperial Navy commanding officer, Vice Adm. Nagumo Chuichi, met on July 5 for a ceremonial dinner. Afterward, Saito transmitted a final order:

> I am addressing the men of the Imperial Army on Saipan. For more than twenty days since the American Devils attacked, the officers, men and civilian employees of the Imperial Army and Navy on this island have fought well and bravely. Everywhere they have demonstrated the honor and glory of the Imperial forces. I expected that every man would do his duty.
>
> Heaven has not given us an opportunity ... Our comrades have fallen one after another. Despite the bitterness of defeat we pledge "seven lives to repay our country" ...
>
> As it says in the *Senjinkun [Battle Ethics]*, "I will never suffer the disgrace of being taken alive" and "I will offer up the courage of my soul and calmly rejoice in living by the eternal principle."
>
> Here I pray for the eternal life of the Emperor and the welfare of the country and I advance to seek out the enemy. Follow me![75]

Apparently Saito meant he would lead in spirit, since he committed ritual suicide soon after directing the message be sent to all remaining units.

[72] Ibid., 39–89; O'Brien, *Battling for Saipan*, 81.   [73] Goldberg, *D-Day in the Pacific*, 53.
[74] Ibid., 90–102.   [75] Ibid., 172. Brackets in the original.

In the early morning hours of July 6, thousands of Japanese poured into, around, and through American lines in the largest Banzai attack of the war. Americans saw enemy armed with "rifles or pistols ... knives, swords, grenades, pikes, bamboo poles, and even limbs with bayonets attached."[76] Two army battalions were overrun and fighting continued through the end of the next day. Afterward, the Americans counted more than 4,300 Japanese bodies, though some unknown number of those had probably been killed prior to the Banzai charge. After this charge, the Americans continued clearing the island up to Marpi Point in the north. When Saipan was declared secure on July 9, the Americans next tried to urge noncombatants still sheltering in caves to come out, using Japanese prisoners with bullhorns to persuade their countrymen. In many cases, in a "final act of horror" Americans saw Japanese troops shooting civilians who tried to leave the caves, while also witnessing civilians who flung themselves, sometimes with their children, off a steep cliff or into the ocean, committing suicide rather than surrendering.[77]

The object of this volume is to explore the impact of organizational culture on the effectiveness of militaries. In the case of the IJA, the organizational culture, in some ways, was propagated throughout the larger population. Yamagata had intended to spread soldiers' values and beliefs throughout society to cultivate patriotism; veteran groups and army domination of education had furthered this goal. So most Japanese were familiar with the Imperial Rescript to Soldiers and Sailors, which says in part, "Duty is weightier than a mountain, while death is lighter than a feather."[78] And when the government described the first of what became known in the West as Banzai charges, the fight to the death of all 2,600 IJA troops on the Aleutian island of Attu, as a *gyokusai* (literally, a broken jewel), many thus-acculturated Japanese were "electrified."[79] But the tragic consequences of propagating such a twisted version of Japan's culture of honor was clear on Saipan, as it was in many other places.

Finally, one needs to comment about Japanese atrocities. Having rationalized away the Rescript's prohibition against "meddl[ing] in politics," the army had increasingly dominated, until "instead of the Army serving the interests of the state, the state came to serve the army."[80] Though those interests were framed as a righteous struggle to free downtrodden peoples from Western depredation and colonization, among the occupied peoples, "Japanese rule ... its harshness, sheer brutality, and rapaciousness ensured that the Japanese could never make any genuine, broad-based appeal to the majority of the

[76] Ibid., 173.
[77] Sharon Toci Lacey, *Pacific Blitzkrieg: World War II and the Central Pacific* (Denton, TX, 2013), 151.
[78] Allison, *The Columbia Guide to Modern Japanese History*, 227.
[79] Drea, *Japan's Imperial Army*, 231.   [80] Ibid., 256.

population."[81] The IJA that impressed the world with the upright discipline of its soldiers during the Boxer Expedition, the Russo-Japanese War, and World War I, irretrievably permitted a breakdown in that discipline – harsh as it was – which allowed radicalization and murder in Japan and appalling cruelty abroad.[82] As Historian Edward Drea writes, "War crimes may afflict all armies, but the scope of Japan's atrocities was so excessive and the punishments so disproportionate that no appeal to moral equivalency can excuse their barbarity."[83] The IJA's organizational culture produced tough, proficient, and courageous soldiers, but also allowed them to become the enemies of those they should have protected. The Rescript to Soldiers and Sailors, written to under-gird a continuing, professionalizing organizational culture, offers a fitting epitaph, "If you affect valor and act with violence, the world will in the end detest you, and look upon you as wild beasts. Of this you should take heed."[84]

[81] Harno Tohmatsu and H. P. Willmott, *A Gathering Darkness: The Coming of War in the Far East and the Pacific, 1941–1942* (Lanham, MD, 2004), xvii.
[82] Iritani, *Group Psychology of the Japanese in Wartime*, 22.
[83] Drea, *Japan's Imperial Army*, 259.
[84] Allison, *The Columbia Guide to Modern Japanese History*, 227.

10   Military Culture, Military Efficiency, and the Red Army, 1917–1945

Reina Pennington

The Red Army's military culture from 1917 to 1945 shows selective continuity with centuries of Russian military tradition, as well as dramatic innovation and discontinuity. The Bolshevik Party set out to create a new kind of state, a new kind of army, even a new kind of human being, the New Soviet Man. It never achieved the total transformation it envisioned, but the attempt shaped a unique military culture that blended new ideals with old traditions.

For all the discontinuities in the Red Army, one cannot consider the military culture of the Soviet era sui generis; continuities with the old imperial army were also in evidence.[1] Despite the dramatic transformations of the Soviet era, there were "persistent factors" in the culture of the Red Army.[2] Continuity was evident in many areas: the officer corps, conscription, a hierarchical rank structure, and military discipline. However, it was not the intention of the new Soviet state to allow such continuity; in fact, the state had intended just the opposite.

Revolution

Russia underwent a dramatic shift after the 1917 revolutions in every cultural sphere: political, social, and economic. A concurrent, intentional transformation of military culture that began with the February Revolution reflected these changes. Although the Provisional Government retained a traditional relationship to the imperial army, the newly formed "soviets" or committees had a powerful impact on military culture, striking at the heart of command structure and military professionalism. In March 1917, the Petrograd Soviet, a non-

---

[1] Roger R. Reese, *The Soviet Military Experience: A History of the Soviet Army, 1917–1991* (London, 2000), 1.

[2] Mikhail Tsypkin, "Soviet Military Culture and the Legacy of the Second World War," in Frank Biess and Robert G. Moelle, eds., *Histories of the Aftermath: The Legacies of the Second World War in Europe* (New York, 2010), 269–286, 271.

Bolshevik but socialist-minded committee formed during the February Revolution, issued Order Number One, which directed soldiers to elect committees in every unit. The committees could decide whether to accept or veto the orders of officers.[3] The Order also called for greater equality between officers and enlisted in forms of address and behavior. In the hectic days of 1917, its greatest effect was to create confusion and slow things down, as soldiers waited for committees to rule on the orders of their officers.

Some historians have viewed Order Number One as accelerating the breakdown of military discipline, or even as a Bolshevik plot. They have probably exaggerated its effects, but it did reflect the socialist view that military hierarchy should be transformed and the military itself should become democratic and egalitarian. This idealistic view continued to inform military culture after the Bolsheviks took power in October. With their arrival in power, the Bolsheviks aimed to destroy and remake all the institutions of the old state. The military symbolized the abuses of the old regime more than any other institution. The Bolsheviks reviled the oppressive features of the imperial army, especially the hierarchical rank structure, with socially elite officers who abused and neglected conscripts.

In 1917, the transformation of military culture seemed entirely possible. If the Bolsheviks had not already planned to create a new kind of army, events would have forced them to do so anyway. The army was destabilized, demoralized, and almost demobilized during the upheavals of the war. Although the Tsarist Army had achieved some tactical and operational successes, at the strategic level, failure was nearly total. Massive casualties, futile offensives, and rapidly deteriorating logistics led to mutiny and desertion.

The Bolsheviks had used few army units in their seizure of power in the October Revolution of 1917. A few military units supported the coup, but primarily the party relied on Red Guards for armed support.[4] Red Guards were a manifestation of the socialist view: armed and ideologically committed volunteers, mostly from the urban working class. The Red Guards were useful in seizing control of facilities from bureaucrats, but had practically no military training or skill that would prepare them for actual combat. There were particularly embarrassing defeats in military clashes in February 1918.[5] The Red Guards could not be expected to take the field and act as infantry. Even Nikolai Krylenko, the supreme commander in chief at that time and an advocate of democratizing the rank structure, had to admit that the Red Guards did

---

[3] Reese, *The Soviet Military Experience*, 2, and www.marxists.org/history/ussr/government/1917/03/01.htm. Some socialist parties advocated that military officers should be elected, although that was not part of Order Number One.

[4] Rex Wade, *Red Guards and Worker's Militias in the Russian Revolution* (Stanford, CA, 1984), 142.

[5] Reese, *The Soviet Military Experience*, 8.

not perform as hoped. He commented that when they encountered the German Army, "the Red Guard units are brushed aside like flies."[6]

Lenin negotiated for a truce and then a separate peace. The Bolsheviks signed the Treaty of Brest-Litovsk in March 1918. Lenin surrendered Poland, Ukraine, the Baltics, and other territories, but he gained peace. The soldiers of the old army took this as a sign and, feeling no obligation to an army now viewed as an anachronism, simply went home. The old army effectively ceased to exist.[7]

The Bolsheviks were already debating the future form of the army. In late 1917, they created the People's Commissariat for Military and Naval Affairs, which formed a collegium to oversee the creation of a new army. The writings of Marx and Engels did not provide specific guidance on army organization.[8] Was the purpose of the army to defend the nation, or to promote world revolution? Could it do both?[9] In January 1918, the Party called for "transformation of the standing army into a force deriving its strength from a nation in arms."[10] The Bolsheviks retained the "soviet" principle, wherein soldiers elected committees to represent their interests and would even elect their own commanders.[11] They formally designated the new army "The Workers' and Peasants' Red Army," or Raboche Krest'ianskaia Krasnaia Armiia (RKKA) in February 1918 – "the Red Army" in popular parlance. The name was changed to "Soviet Army" only in 1946.

Trotsky and the Russian Civil War

The RKKA was born in the Russian Civil War, which was larger, more brutal, and even more devastating to Russians than the First World War had been. The Bolsheviks viewed their political opponents as potential counterrevolutionaries; former generals began to foment armed opposition; and the former allies of the empire, with troops on the periphery, declared their support of the "White" armies against the "Reds." There was a clear and present danger of a military overthrow of the new Soviet state.

---

[6] Cited in Erich Wollenberg, *The Red Army: A Study of the Growth of Soviet Imperialism*, trans. Claud W. Sykes (Westport, CT, 1973) 63; https://en.wikipedia.org/wiki/Red_Army#cite_note-marxistsfr.org-6.

[7] Reese, *The Soviet Military Experience*, 9.

[8] David R. Stone, "Ideology and the Rise of the Red Army, 1917–1929," in Robin D. S. Higham and Frederick W. Kagan, eds., *The Military History of the Soviet Union* (New York, 2002), 51–63, 53.

[9] Joshua A. Sanborn, *Drafting the Russian Nation: Military Conscription, Total War, and Mass Politics, 1905–1925* (DeKalb, IL, 2003), 42.

[10] www.marxistsfr.org/history/ussr/government/red-army/1937/wollenberg-red-army/append01.htm

[11] Reese, *The Soviet Military Experience*, 8. Sanborn, *Drafting the Russian Nation*, 39.

In the crucible of war, Lenin and Trotsky "created a fortress state that Stalin inherited and managed as his sacred trust."[12] The disintegration of key institutions in 1917–1918 required desperate, innovative and ad hoc solutions to mobilizing and supplying troops. On top of that, the new state had to create a new structure, from a different kind of command hierarchy. Troops had to be organized, trained, and led. Military leadership was not resident among party activists or militia; it was only to be found among Russia's military professionals. Nevertheless, those professionals, the officer corps of the old army, represented in the Party's eyes class enemies of the worst sort.

The Treaty of Brest-Litovsk provided breathing space to reassess the form of the new army. In March 1918, Lenin appointed Leon Trotsky the people's commissar for the army and navy with the responsibility for forming an army to defend the new state. Trotsky's seven-year tenure had a major impact on the Red Army's military culture. Despite his total lack of military experience, the former journalist and political activist adopted a pragmatic and utilitarian approach to reforming the army. His policy led to the acceptance of some continuity with the old military culture, judiciously melded with an entirely new kind of army. It produced victory in the civil war for the state, but defeat for Trotsky as a party leader.

The new military culture had already produced failures. The first and most obvious failure was the concept of a volunteer, militia-style, democratically organized people's army. This concept would have entailed the complete erasure of the imperial military culture, at least in terms of mobilization, rank structures, and discipline. The Bolsheviks greatly overestimated the willingness of such volunteers to appear in anything like the numbers required, and they had to conscript soldiers, just like the imperial state.[13] In April 1918, Lenin's regime decreed conscription and compulsory military training.

From its birth until its death in 1991, "the Red Army would be the party's army."[14] But it would rely on many elements of traditional military culture to ensure that the party's army was an effective military force. Conscription was one such element. Efficient and smooth conscription required "a set of institutions … that simply did not exist" any longer. Conscription was achieved in the civil war through impressment and coercion.[15] Between March and October 1919, the Red Army became a regular army.

One of Trotsky's first actions was to eliminate the inefficient soviets in the army. Soldiers' committees were ordered to stand down; officers would no longer be elected. A mix of party activists ("Red Commanders") and former

---

[12] Robin D. S. Higham and Frederick W. Kagan, "Introduction," in Higham and Kagan, eds., *The Military History of the Soviet Union*, 1–10, 4.

[13] David R. Stone, "The Russian Civil War, 1917–1921," in Higham and Kagan, eds., *The Military History of the Soviet Union*, 13–33, 21.

[14] Reese, *The Soviet Military Experience*, 11.   [15] Sanborn, *Drafting the Russian Nation*, 47.

tsarist officers ("military specialists") would exercise command. In May 1918, the regime created the position of commander in chief of the army. Three former officers, all colonels or lieutenant colonels, held the post in the first year. But the army was not left to run things unsupervised. The new Soviet state had parallel structures of Party and government, with Party organs reigning supreme. The army was no exception, and became subject to layers of political and governmental oversight.

A system of dual command would ensure the political reliability of the military specialists and adherence to Party principles; political commissars were assigned at the regiment, brigade, and division levels, and three-man councils operated at the army and front levels. Only at the company and battalion levels did military commanders exercise sole command, and even then, their actions were subject to Party oversight.[16] In July 1918, at the Fifth Congress of Soviets, the Bolsheviks designated political commissars who would countersign the orders of military commanders.[17]

The Crucible of War

The brutality of the civil war seared a generation of Soviet soldiers, leaders, and civilians. "Utter viciousness" and atrocities marked military operations. Mass executions, torture, and crimes against civilians were common on all sides. At great cost – approximately 1 million military and 6 million or more civilian deaths – the Red Army achieved victory.[18]

The 1920 war against Poland was a different matter. After 123 years of partition and annexation by its neighbors, Poland had been reestablished as an independent state at the end of the First World War. Russia and Poland had contested large areas of western borderlands, from Lithuania through Belarus and the Ukraine, over the centuries. As the Germans withdrew in 1919, Polish and Soviet forces both sought to gain control of the contested areas. The Poles launched an offensive in Soviet Ukraine in 1920.[19] The Bolsheviks then counterattacked. The Red Army was seasoned but battered after years of civil war, and its strained logistics failed to provide supplies and reinforcements.[20] At the gates of Warsaw, the Red Army suffered a humiliating defeat. The two powers signed a peace treaty in 1921, but the Soviets thereafter regarded Poland "as a hostile neighbor."[21]

[16] Reese, *The Soviet Military Experience*, 11–12.   [17] Ibid.
[18] Stone, "The Russian Civil War, 1917–1921," 31.
[19] Robert Ponichtera and David R. Stone, "The Russo-Polish War," in Higham and Kagan, eds., *The Military History of the Soviet Union*, 35–50, 39–40.
[20] Ponichtera and Stone, "The Russo-Polish War," 42.   [21] Ibid., 47.

The new army reached a strength of 5 million by 1920. It had defeated the enemies of the new state, although it had lost much territory in the process. The new Soviet state was much smaller and the new borders were uncomfortably close to the heartland. The economy was in ruins, and the army had to be reduced to a tenth of its size – inadequate to defend against any serious threat, but all the new state could support.[22]

Interwar: 1922–1941

The Red Army largely demobilized in the early 1920s. The question of what kind of army the new state needed reappeared. Some idealists suggested that a socialist state did not need a conventional army with all its trappings of hierarchy and oppression. Some abhorred formal rank structure, drill, discipline, and even uniforms.[23] Many Party leaders argued that the Party should revisit creating an entirely new kind of army, based on ideological correctness and unconventional in every regard. A people's militia, guided by Red Commanders, would represent a truly socialist army.

However, Trotsky and others argued that victory in the civil war was largely the result of traditional military methods: conscription, strict discipline, and the leadership and knowledge provided by officers of the old army.[24] If the old military culture provided competence and efficiency, then the new army should incorporate those aspects as well. But leadership would not rest on privilege, as in the old army; Trotsky argued that the army should be a meritocracy, and merit should be assessed in terms of military performance. The concept of a meritocracy was well established in other European states, originating in the armies of the French Revolution. It constituted a break with traditional Russian military culture, but some Bolsheviks resisted such an approach because it conflicted with socialist values.

After much debate, the regime created a compromise army for peacetime, with a small professional standing army supported by a territorial militia.[25] The hybrid army was an acceptable compromise to the politically opposed factions in the Party and an interim solution to the inability of the state to maintain a large military force. Territorial militia were an economical means of maintaining a reserve force, but everyone recognized that such a force not only had a low skill level but was also politically less than reliable.[26] Territorial militia units were necessarily based in rural peasant communities, which were not strong supporters of the revolution. Ideologically driven Party functionaries viewed peasant conscripts with nearly the same political skepticism as they

[22] Stone, "Ideology and the Rise of the Red Army, 1917–1929," 54.   [23] Ibid., 51.
[24] Ibid., 52.   [25] Reese, *The Soviet Military Experience*, 3.
[26] Stone, "Ideology and the Rise of the Red Army, 1917–1929," 55.

viewed former tsarist officers. The idealists hoped that the standing army would wither away, but in the end it was the militia that proved ineffective. The debate continued throughout the 1920s, but the Tenth Party Congress settled the issue in 1931 in favor of a regular army.

Political changes also affected the army. Lenin's health failed and his death in early 1924 threw the Party into uncertainty. Without Lenin's protection, Leon Trotsky found himself marginalized and he resigned as the people's commissar for the army and navy in 1925. Mikhail Frunze, a respected Bolshevik who had demonstrated military skill in the civil war – one of the best of the Red Commanders – succeeded Trotsky. Frunze argued that with sufficient political oversight, a standing army could be reliable and was the only kind of army that could protect the state against its likely enemies. A militia, however loyal, could not prevail against the modern sophisticated armies of the imperialist powers.[27] Frunze died in 1925, but his tenure had a powerful effect on the transforming Red Army. Despite his feud with Trotsky, Frunze stressed the need for military discipline along with a hierarchical command structure and even sanctioned the abolition of the system of dual command.[28] The "Frunze Reforms" were the most important transformation that molded the Red Army for a decade following the civil war.[29]

In 1925, the regime enacted a new military service law; in 229 articles, the law clarified and codified the functioning of the Red Army. The law addressed persistent questions such as who should be conscripted and for how long. Lengthy debates over proper terminology were typical of the Bolsheviks. Initial drafts stressed that the purpose of the army was to defend both the revolution and the state; in the final version, references to worldwide revolution vanished. All citizens had a responsibility to defend the Union of Soviet Socialist Republics (USSR), although only "laborers" could be trusted to bear arms.[30]

Soviet military culture reflected the Bolshevik distrust of class enemies, but otherwise the purpose of the army and the obligation of citizens was precisely that of other national armies. In that sense, there was a "snap back" to the old military culture defined in Russia in 1874 with its focus on a national army. The "snap back" did not occur through tradition or force of the old military culture; the decision emanated from individuals who had little contact with the old culture. The concept of a citizen army that had a duty to defend the state was a practical one, shared by most states since the French Revolution. The Bolshevik dream of an army that would march under the banner of world revolution had proven impractical; defeat in Poland showed that reality. The

---

[27] Ibid., 55. Comparisons can be made with the decisions of the United States during the American Revolutionary War.
[28] Ibid.   [29] Sanborn, *Drafting the Russian Nation*, 58.
[30] Ibid., 60, www.rkka.ru/docs/all/z180925.htm.

world was not ready for a socialist revolution, so the important thing was to protect the new Soviet state until that moment arrived. The military law of 1925 reflected bitter disputes within the Party over Marxist idealism and what would eventually become Soviet policy: socialism in one country. In terms of military culture, "socialism in one country" meshed with a traditional national army. The new law created a stable military culture that brought "a sense of normality" to the army after years of debate, argument, and ad hoc solutions.[31] It combined elements of the old military culture with the new. It constituted a dramatic transformation, but one that owed more to the experience of total war than to Bolshevik ideology.

Kliment Voroshilov, generally regarded as far less capable than either Trotsky or Frunze, succeeded Frunze in 1925. One historian describes Voroshilov as "not especially bright."[32] His loyalty to Stalin outweighed his lack of skill. The attention of the Party shifted from the form of the army to the state of its modernization. Decisions were taken to focus on modern weapons while limiting the size of the army.[33] The first Five-Year Plan (1928–1932) sought to transform the Soviet Union into a modern state, which needed a modern army on a par with its European neighbors. Industrialization of the country would allow for the production of modern tools of war, especially tanks and aircraft.

The Soviets implemented the Five-Year Plans at great cost, particularly to the peasantry that provided the economic base for industrialization. Nevertheless, one can consider the plans "a proper grand-strategic tool" that were the mark of bold and innovative leadership.[34] The army was a major beneficiary of the breakneck industrialization and modernization achieved in the interwar years. It grew like an abused child that was force-fed (resulting in excessively rapid growth rates), interrogated and smacked around (through the use of commissars and purges), and both loved and abused by a state that was, at first, deeply ambivalent about having such a child at all.

From 1937 to 1941, the Red Army engaged in a series of small wars – "dress rehearsals" – in Spain, Finland, Poland, and the Far East.[35] Unfortunately, misreading of the applicability of these asymmetrical experiences produced many incorrect lessons. Commanders were punished for failures and purged for reasons known only to the Party, leaving an army that was "younger, less willing to take chances, and saddled with outmoded ideas about warfare" that

[31] Reese, *The Soviet Military Experience*, 5.
[32] David R. Stone, "Industry and the Soviet Army, 1929–1941," in Higham and Kagan, eds., *The Military History of the Soviet Union*, 65–78, 67.
[33] Ibid., 68.   [34] Higham and Kagan, *The Military History of the Soviet Union*, 4.
[35] Mary R. Habeck, "Dress Rehearsals, 1937–1941," in Higham and Kagan, eds., *The Military History of the Soviet Union*, 93–108, 93.

would prove disastrous in 1941.[36] But some positive changes began to occur as well. Voroshilov was succeeded in 1940 by Timoshenko, who had helped to salvage a Soviet victory against Finland and who focused on revamping Red Army training to be "more realistic and effective."[37]

The Great Patriotic War

From 1939 to 1945, the Red Army continued to combine shifting elements of the old military culture with the new.[38] Things did not begin well. The Red Army of 1941 was a force that was "unable either to attack or defend" and the Soviet Union was "a state without a functioning war machine, lacking a high command, bereft of operational plans."[39] It is no surprise that the Germans kicked in the door; the only surprise is that "the whole rotten structure" of the Soviet state did not come crashing down, as Hitler predicted. The Red Army was a precarious structure indeed, but rebounded in one of the most remarkable reversals in history. The resilience of the Soviet military was due at least in part to its military culture.

The military effectiveness of the Red Army was initially poor, but sufficient to prevent defeat. John Erickson notes that "this war-waging system worked indifferently, badly, disconcertingly, surprisingly, callously, and wastefully, but it worked finally."[40] Efficiency improved throughout the war as part of a "continuous struggle to produce effective commanders, suitable organization, superior weapons and appropriate tactics."[41] In wartime, the shock of near defeat swept away many aspects of military culture that might otherwise have led to even worse disaster. The events of 1941 blasted away many of the regime's assumptions about the nature of war, sweeping the slate clean for innovation and transformation.

Aspects of Russian Military Culture

One recent study of postwar Soviet military culture by Mikhail Tsypkin identified three key characteristics: a stress on the importance of geographic space to provide buffer zones and the option of trading space for time, an emphasis on mass, and an "ambiguous attitude to military professionalism."[42]

---

[36] Ibid., 95.   [37] Stone, "Industry and the Rise of the Red Army, 1929–1941," 76.

[38] Tsypkin, "Soviet Military Culture and the Legacy of the Second World War," 273.

[39] John Erickson, "The Great Patriotic War, Barbarossa to Stalingrad," in Robin D. S. Higham and Frederick W. Kagan, eds., *The Military History of the Soviet Union* (New York, 2002), 109–136, 109.

[40] Ibid., 133.   [41] Ibid.

[42] Tsypkin, "Soviet Military Culture and the Legacy of the Second World War," 269.

These characteristics are equally useful in examining Red Army military culture between 1917 and 1945.

Geographic Reality, or Trading Space for Time

Tsypkin emphasizes the importance of Russia's geography as one element of continuity in its military culture. The largest country in the world possessed few natural borders and consequently suffered repeated invasion. The only protection could be military forces sufficiently large to garrison the far-flung reaches of the empire.[43] The peace of 1919 deprived the Soviet state of some of the traditional peripheral territories; it sought to restore those regions, such as the Baltic and Caucasian Republics, into the Soviet sphere by signing the Nazi-Soviet Non-Aggression Pact of August 1939.[44]

Over the centuries, the trading of space for time was a strategy of necessity and not preference. The giving up of territory in order to buy time came at a punishing cost: it allowed the enemy occupation of the periphery. It surrendered resources in the land Russia's enemies captured, and it cost resources in recapturing the lost territories. Nevertheless, it allowed Russia to survive invasion by much-superior enemies like the Swedes and French, and the Soviet Union survived invasion by the largest occupation force in history. The price paid for survival was costly indeed, but the time gained by trading space allowed Russian and Soviet armies to rebuild, change strategies, and recover from errors. The Russian Army, and later the Red Army, shared the characteristic of near-miraculous, phoenix-like recovery from disaster that was made possible by trading space for time.

The willingness to trade space for time was understood as an effective past strategy, but not one desired for any future war. That is evident in the fact that in 1941, there was no plan for strategic withdrawal.[45] Only in the summer of 1942 were army units allowed to carry out fighting retreats as the Germans pushed forward on the southern steppe in Operation Blau. Even then, Stalin would set limits on how much space the Red Army would surrender, and that limit was the Volga River. In July 1942, Order 227 demanded "not another step back."

Mass: Quantity versus Quality?

Many historians commonly perceive the Russian state as favoring quantity over quality, and winning mainly by overwhelming its opponents with hordes of poorly trained soldiers. Joseph Stalin supposedly claimed that "quantity has a quality all its own," justifying a cannon-fodder mentality and immense

[43] Ibid., 271. [44] Ibid., 272.
[45] John Erickson, *The Soviet High Command, 1918–1941* (New York, 1962), 666.

casualties. The stereotype of "Russian hordes" has become the first and often the only explanation for Russian military victories. Admittedly, Russia historically tried to offset its weaknesses in quality (technological and professional) with quantity, by relying on the one resource it did have: a larger population than most of its opponents. The population was by no means a bottomless well, but it did allow Russia (and later the Soviet Union) to create large armies, absorb casualties, and generate replacements at a higher rate than its enemies.

Relying on quantity entailed costs, however: raising and supplying a large army, even if poorly equipped, was expensive. Maintaining and fighting with a large army often impaired quality; large forces could rarely be trained to the same standard as small forces. An army that expanded rapidly (as during the civil war and the Great Patriotic War) "also diluted the professionalism of the officer corps," which was spread thin, hastily promoted, or both.[46] At many points, although not continuously, Russia and later the Soviet Union maintained the largest army in Europe. A large army imposes heavy demands on the state, especially economic ones.

German sources and popular histories claimed the Soviets outnumbered the Wehrmacht by ten or even twenty to one. The numbers give a different picture. The Red Army, not the Wehrmacht, fought outnumbered in 1941 on the Eastern Front. For example, during Operation Typhoon, the Germans fielded 1.9 million troops against 1.25 million Soviet soldiers. Soviet mobilization efforts and steady German losses began to change the force ratios in 1942, but the Red Army only managed about a two to one advantage from February 1943 until mid-1944, maxing out at a little more than four to one by the war's end. The Red Army in the field actually peaked in size in mid-1943, but the *ratios* continued to shift in its favor due to Germany's inability to replace its losses.

Russia's quantitative strength derived more from its ability to mobilize than from a supposedly bottomless pool of recruits. At the end of the Second World War, the Red Army was not much larger than the American Army. However, the Soviets mobilized more troops; they fought longer and had to replace many more casualties. With fewer people available (due to the German occupation of large areas of Soviet territory), the Soviet Union mobilized nearly twice as many soldiers. It did so by stripping the civilian and agricultural workforces, which dropped by 40–60 percent. Although the Red Army often had quantity on its side, its numerical advantages were rarely overwhelming. Russian armies have relied more on quality and less on quantity than is generally recognized, despite the prevalence of a stress on mass in military culture.

---

[46] Tsypkin, "Soviet Military Culture and the Legacy of the Second World War," 275.

Military Professionalism

Military professionalism encompasses many key aspects of military culture – most notable, the skill of military leaders, both officers and senior enlisted, to perform their duties and to lead and train their subordinates. Both the old and new military cultures of Russia and the Soviet Union presented serious challenges to military professionalism. The imperial army often favored social status and personal connections over skill, while the Soviet state prioritized political reliability. John Erickson views the professionalism of the Soviet officer corps as "an extraordinary graft of the Prussian by imitation and the Imperial Russian by the force of unexpected circumstance," suggesting that professionalism owed more to traditional military culture than to any socialist transformation.[47] Every change that improved professionalism – especially command rank and privilege and the restoration of single command – was a change that reflected a return to the old military culture.

The first issue was officer-enlisted relations and rank structure, which were influenced by the Marxist ideology of social class relationships. The old military culture was one of social hierarchy as well as rank hierarchy. Officers were primarily members of privileged social classes with the aristocracy dominating the highest positions. Enlisted troops had to demonstrate awareness of their lower social status, which was inherent in military conduct. They were forbidden to use public transportation or attend public entertainments, and generally were "shunned by all levels of society." One historian has compared them to the "untouchables" of India.[48] Soldiers rankled at the humiliating treatment they received, and their desire for respect was one motivation in their support of the soldiers' committees of 1917.[49]

But how could soldiers and commanders share the egalitarian relationship demanded in a classless society, where rank was no longer supposed to have privileges, and still effectively carry out the work of an army? This challenge was at the heart of pendulum swings in Soviet military culture between egalitarianism and hierarchy. Generating conscripts required the Bolsheviks to abandon their ideal of a volunteer army. Generating leadership for the new army required them to abandon their ideal of a democratic and egalitarian army.

Military Specialists

Capable commanders could not be produced from thin air. Recruits might be turned into soldiers with a minimum of basic training, but leaders needed much more training than that. The only experienced military leaders available were the officer corps of the imperial army. The army required organizers who

---

[47] Erickson, *The Soviet High Command, 1918–1941*, 667.
[48] Sanborn, *Drafting the Russian Nation*, 62.   [49] Ibid.

understood how to conduct training and administer the day-to-day activities of the army, as well as lead it in battle. Only the old tsarist officers had that expertise.[50]

The most obvious example of how imperial organizational culture was transmitted in the Red Army was the use of former officers. The Bolsheviks viewed them as a transitory wartime expedient, a necessary evil, but they came to have a powerful influence on Red Army military culture. Many imperial army officers stayed in the field in 1918, even as the soldiers went home. Several thousand officers, motivated by patriotism, continued to defend the motherland regardless of political change. They tried to maintain defensive screens against the Germans and Austrians, using whatever troops remained to them as well as scattered groups of Red Guards.[51] In 1918, Trotsky promoted some former tsarist noncommissioned officers (NCOs) who were on active service to platoon commanders. Future leaders like Georgii Zhukov and Semion Budenny were among these former NCOs promoted to officer rank.[52]

The idea of allowing former tsarist officers to lead the new army was anathema to most Bolsheviks. Most officers were, by Bolshevik definition, class enemies. There were bitter disputes within the Party between those who saw the former officers as a necessary evil (Lenin and Trotsky) and those who opposed both the form and function of the traditional army. This was, in essence, a battle over military culture. Eventually, the civil war proved the effectiveness of the "military specialists." The question was whether new Red Army Commanders could become equally capable military professionals without embracing the aspects of the old military culture that were unacceptable to a socialist state.

Ironically, Stalin (who had opposed Trotsky's support of elements of old military culture) reintroduced traditional military ranks in 1935. The Red Army once more formally designated officers as captains, majors, etc. Yet the title of "general" was still unacceptable until 1940, although Stalin created the highest rank of "Marshal of the Soviet Union."[53] This represented a period of what John Erickson has described as "a brief triumph" for military efficiency.[54] Professionalization of the military leadership improved.[55] The political purges of 1937–1941 would soon undo much of this stab at professionalism.

The Party's Army

The Communist Party "shaped virtually every facet" of the development of the Red Army, including recruitment, promotion, and, most important, its values.[56]

---

[50] Reese, *The Soviet Military Experience*, 22.   [51] Ibid., 9.   [52] Ibid., 23.
[53] Stone, "Industry and the Rise of the Red Army, 1929–1941," 72.
[54] Erickson, *The Soviet High Command, 1918–1941*, 366, 371.   [55] Ibid., 402.
[56] Reese, *The Soviet Military Experience*, 11.

The Red Army became the "world's first political army" in which party values (which were not static) always took priority.[57] Erickson notes that "the purity and simplicity of military efficiency had been a constant loser since the Red Army had first come into existence" due to the prioritizing of political relia-bility over military skill.[58] Political oversight occurred "in pursuit of an objective in no particular way connected with improving the efficiency of the army as a combat instrument."[59] While the state desired an effective military force, it desired loyalty even more.

Suspicion is often identified as an inherent part of Russian culture, linked to the tendency of isolated and self-sufficient peasant communities to distrust outsiders.[60] Distrust of outsiders is not uniquely Russian, of course; isolation-ism and xenophobia have been characteristic of many cultures. Nevertheless, it is still fair to say that suspicion is a major characteristic of Soviet military culture, with deep roots in the imperial era. The Party demonstrated its suspi-cion of its own army in a variety of ways, most notably through its imposition of dual command and through the purges of the 1930s. Both aimed at securing the political reliability of the military.

Dual Command versus Single Command

The system of dual command by political commissars aimed at ensuring the loyalty of the army. The Party greatly feared that military professionals might feel a greater loyalty to their organization than to the regime – or worse, to the old regime or some other enemy.[61] It was a major shift in military culture, experienced by only a few other cultures such as that of the French Revolutionary army. Party representatives with varying degrees of military experience scrutinized and second-guessed commanders' orders. Commissars questioned the loyalty and skill of the commander every time they questioned an order. When commissars vetoed an order, it was equivalent to accusing the commander of sabotage or treason. Even when commissars took a more hands-off approach and rubber-stamped most or all orders, the review process slowed things down. Although dual command seemed to offer a solution to political reliability, it had a negative effect on morale (especially of the commanders) and military effectiveness.

The military hated the system of dual command and favored a traditional system of single command (*edinonachalie*). As the number of military specia-lists declined and Red Commanders increased, many argued that the inefficient system was no longer necessary. Commanders who were Party members could

---

[57] Ibid., 4.   [58] Erickson, *The Soviet High Command, 1918–1941*, 367.   [59] Ibid., 401.
[60] Higham and Kagan, *The Military History of the Soviet Union*, 7–8.
[61] Reese, *The Soviet Military Experience*, 11.

act as their own commissar, and more and more commanders were Party members.[62] In 1925, the Party ended the system of dual command, but not political oversight of the army. Commissars became "political officers" or *politruki* who no longer held command responsibilities or countersigned orders, but were still responsible for indoctrinating the troops in socialist consciousness and awareness of Party values.

Stalin briefly resurrected dual command in 1937–1940 and again in 1941–1942. The military purges that began in 1937 led the Party to reinstate commissars, then to withdraw them again in August 1940. The Winter War with Finland had revealed serious deficiencies in military effectiveness, and the regime restored single command as part of the effort to address those deficiencies. In less than a year, however, dual command returned in a knee-jerk panic response to the defeats during the German invasion. Commissars once more appeared in July 1941, this time to vocal opposition among military leaders, who felt that commanders needed freedom of action in wartime. One historian notes that the reintroduction of commissars was "a sign as always that the officer corps needed a touch of the Party whip."[63] Commissars were to assess the "worthiness" of military commanders and to "wage a relentless struggle with cowards, the creators of panic, and deserters."[64] The Party believed that ideological oversight could produce military effectiveness, despite repeated evidence that it negatively affected morale, initiative, and an effective command structure. In August 1942, Stalin again removed commissars from the chain of command, this time for good. Political officers remained with responsibilities for education and morale, but without responsibility for reviewing commanders' orders and without the authority to veto those orders.

The Purges

If there had been a precarious balance between political reliability and military efficiency in the first two decades of the Red Army's existence, that balance "was tipped deliberately but disastrously towards political reliability" by the purges of 1937–1941.[65] Despite the commissar system and ongoing suspicion of military loyalty, the army had enjoyed a "remarkable immunity" in the purges of 1929–1930 and 1933–1934.[66] It was not so lucky in 1937. The reasons are complex, but a leading historian warns us not to seek "too rational an explanation of the military purge."[67]

The military purges of 1937–1941 produced an immediate and deleterious effect on Soviet military culture. Political suspicion erupted in a volcanic flow

---

[62] Stone, "Ideology and the Rise of the Red Army, 1917–1929," 61.
[63] Erickson, *The Soviet High Command, 1918–1941*, 603.   [64] Ibid.   [65] Ibid., 509.
[66] Ibid., 374.   [67] Ibid., 472.

that burned all in its path and destroyed much of the creativity and innovation of the Red Army. In 1937, Tukhachevsky was arrested, charged with treason on trumped-up accusations of collusion with Germany, and executed. Anything associated with Tukhachevsky became anathema and even the term "deep battle" was forbidden.[68]

The most profound effect of the purges was on military professionalism, which left the officer corps "with its talent diminished and its ranks visibly thinned."[69] The purges targeted officers who had served in Spain and Finland with the best and most recent combat experience. The lower ranks were more fortunate than the colonels and generals. Many young officers who managed to fly under the radar of the purges later proved their value in the Great Patriotic War; future marshals such as Rokossovsky, Konev, Malinovsky, and Voronov all had experience in Spain, for example.[70]

Recent studies indicate that the military purges more often took the form of arrest, imprisonment, transfers, and demobilization than the form of execution. The goal was to ensure that "no military command group existed which might be of mind to seize this opportunity to undo Stalin's dictatorship. The sacrifice of a command was worth this security."[71] The high command "was not so much destroyed as neutralized."[72] At the lower ranks, "there was little continuity in the command staff for lessons learned by officers in one conflict to be passed on to other officers."[73]

Innovation: Operational Art, Deep Battle, and Deep Operations

The development of the concept of operational art and its incorporation into military organization and planning is a hallmark of Soviet military culture. Operational art represents a sophisticated theory that was uniquely Soviet, though subsequently adopted in one way or another by most other military cultures. The concept was developed in the 1920s and 1930s, was rejected for political reasons in the late 1930s, and then was resurrected in the Great Patriotic War.

After the First World War, most participants studied what all saw as the "fundamental problem of war": how to avoid a repeat of trench warfare and endless stalemate, and how to ensure that future war would be a war of maneuver.[74] In Germany, the emphasis was on *Bewegungskrieg*, a "war of

---

[68] Frederick W. Kagan, "The Rise and Fall of Soviet Operational Art, 1917–1941," in Higham and Kagan, eds., *The Military History of the Soviet Union*, 79–92, 80.
[69] Erickson, *The Soviet High Command, 1918–1941*, 666.
[70] Habeck, "Dress Rehearsals, 1937–1941," 98.
[71] Erickson, *The Soviet High Command, 1918–1941*, 509.   [72] Ibid., 472.
[73] Habeck, "Dress Rehearsals, 1937–1941," 102.
[74] Kagan, "The Rise and Fall of Soviet Operational Art, 1917–1941," 79.

242   *Reina Pennington*

movement" (later labeled by some observers as *Blitzkrieg*). In the Soviet Union, the focus was on "deep operations" and "deep battle," which the Red Army would conduct at the operational level. Some historians dismiss these Soviet concepts as derivative of developments in armored warfare theory in Germany and England, but as one historian notes, the bulk of Soviet theoretical thinking appeared in the 1920s, before Guderian, Liddell Hart, and Fuller publicized their ideas. The theory was defined in the 1920s and by the mid-1930s became part of official doctrine, which "changed dramatically to encompass the most sophisticated aspects" of the new operational art.[75] Some have dubbed this transformation a "revolution in military affairs."[76] It was certainly revolutionary.

Strategist Vladimir Triandafillov appears to have coined the term "deep battle," while Mikhail Tukhachevsky advocated its adoption. A dashing "military specialist" who had transformed himself into a revolutionary, Tukhachevsky was from a minor noble family, attended military academies before the First World War, and then fought with the Semyenovsky Guards as a young lieutenant. Captured by the Germans in 1915 and after four escape attempts, Tukhachevsky found himself in a high-security prison in Bavaria where he reportedly shared a cell with Charles de Gaulle. Tukhachevsky eventually succeeded in escaping the Germans and making his way back to Russia just before the October Revolution. He joined the Red Army and became one of the most successful young commanders during the civil war. Among his successes was the suppression of the Kronstadt Rebellion. However, Stalin blamed him for the Russian defeat in Poland and their relationship was thereafter one of hostility. Nevertheless, Tukhachevsky was a rising star: he became chief of staff of the Red Army (1925–1928) and then served in high staff positions in the People's Commissariat of Military and Naval Affairs. He was promoted to marshal of the Soviet Union in 1935.

Tukhachevsky became the primary advocate for changes in army doctrine, especially the adoption of "deep battle" and "deep operations." Deep battle called for a breakthrough by armored forces to be followed by exploitation forces in a series of "successive operations" that would never give the enemy time to regroup. Aviation would be responsible for disrupting enemy reserve forces.[77] A series of official publications codified the new concepts of operational art, including the *Field Regulations* of 1929, the *Instructions on Deep Battle* of 1935, and the *Provisional Field Regulations* of 1936. According to historian Fred Kagan, "the theory of deep battle and successive operations was light-years ahead of the armored warfare doctrine of any other state" in the

---

[75] Ibid., 80.   [76] Ibid., 79.
[77] Frederick W. Kagan, "The Great Patriotic War, Rediscovering Operational Art," in Higham and Frederick, eds., *The Military History of the Soviet Union*, 137–151, 140.

1930s.[78] But the military purges that began in 1937 with Tukhachevsky's trial and execution inhibited further discussion and development of deep battle.

The military purges of 1937–1941 interrupted the development of operational art precisely at the moment when the Red Army was testing the theory and was entering it into the realm of practice. Tukhachevsky's execution meant that anything associated with him became anathema. Even the term "deep battle" was unofficially forbidden.[79] This "triumph of ideological stupidity ... set Soviet thinking back 20 years."[80]

The experience of the Spanish Civil War caused a reevaluation of armor and aviation doctrine. Those surviving the purges saw armor and aviation as most effective when distributed to infantry commanders and used in direct support of ground operations. Instead of being viewed as an anomaly unlikely to fore-shadow large-scale war, these "lessons" of Spain served to confirm that the recently purged Tukhachevsky had advocated a flawed understanding of mobile war. The analysis of events in Spain further discredited the concept of deep operations.[81] Similarly, the poor performance of the Red Army against the Japanese at Lake Khasan in 1938 provided additional confirmation that large mechanized corps represented an incorrect way to use tanks. As a result, Stalin ordered the commander, Vasilii Bliukher, purged and executed for treason.[82] However, the Soviet victory over Japan at Khalkhin-Gol in 1939, which was largely due to Georgii Zhukov's utilization of deep battle tactics, was ignored. Even though Zhukov achieved an impressive surprise encirclement that destroyed a Japanese division, analysis in Moscow suggested that the victory was not the result of deep operations. Army analysts concluded that a "slow methodical advance by masses of foot soldiers" would have succeeded even better.[83] Studies of the German invasion of Poland in 1939 led, astonishingly, to the decision to disband Soviet tank corps altogether and distribute armor to infantry units.[84] However, Soviet analysis recognized the technological short-comings of Soviet tanks and aircraft relative to German equivalents, which led to the production of the T-34 and Il-2, among other weapons systems that would prove their worth in the coming war. Technology was not tainted by politics to a similar degree as were operational art and strategy.

The humiliating experience of the Red Army in Finland in 1939–1940 represented a wake-up call that even Stalin could not ignore. The continued catastrophes of poor leadership, misuse of frontal assaults, and mass casualties finally created willingness to reform.[85] Changes occurred in the senior leader-ship, and the army conducted studies that were more intensive and honest and that proposed detailed solutions. In June 1940, the army reestablished mechan-ized corps. Most importantly, in December 1940, a conference of the key

[78] Ibid., 137. [79] Ibid., 80. [80] Ibid., 139. [81] Habeck, "Dress Rehearsals, 1937–1941," 97. [82] Ibid., 99. [83] Ibid., 101–102. [84] Ibid., 104. [85] Ibid., 106.

military leaders featured a reevaluation of operational art. Without naming Tukhachevsky or deep battle, most of the leaders recognized that it was time to recover the innovative theories of Soviet operational art that would transform maneuver warfare.[86] It was a start, but the Germans invaded before the necessary restructuring and retraining could occur. Deep battle would only seep back into Red Army practice after the disastrous defeats of 1941.

There was a profound regression of Red Army operations, so that instead of countering the German invasion in 1941 not just with modernized technology but with modernized doctrine, the Soviets instead reverted to "an almost completely wrongheaded understanding of armored warfare."[87] As in France, although for different reasons, the most innovative military thinkers ran up against a recalcitrant military culture; in both cases, the result was failure to counter effectively the German invasion. Even so, the Red Army did not simply forget the promising new ideas of operational art. One can view the Red Army's victory over the Japanese at the Battle of Khalkhin-Gol in 1939 (where Georgii Zhukov was a corps commander) as the first implementation of deep battle in practice, if not in name. Zhukov continued his "discreet revival of the principles of 'deep battle'" at Stalingrad, in Operation Uranus. Although the counteroffensive was a great success, the victory was "precarious enough not to tempt the Soviet command to repeat it," in terms of creating a massive double envelopment.[88] Soviet forces were barely able to cope with the tens of thousands of Germans trapped in the cauldron.

Refinements to deep battle would lead to even greater successes. The Soviets transformed their doctrine in the period from 1943 to 1944, when they resurrected theories of operational art, which played a significant role in the pattern of successful offensives (and greatly reduced casualties) and contributed to victory in the war. By 1943, the Soviets were able to implement deep battle doctrine and by 1944, "they had surpassed their pre-war doctrine both theoretically and practically."[89] The Belgorod-Kharkov operation (August 1943) demonstrated the evolution of deep battle; "rather than frittering away operational maneuver forces in scattered groups in the enemy's rear, the Soviets concentrated two massive tank armies for the exploitation of a breakthrough," and "those armies were strong enough and fast enough to beat off or crush any German attempt to stop them."[90] Breakthrough was achieved the first day, and exploitation units functioned as desired, without getting bogged down in the breakthrough. Further refinements to deep operations followed, especially in improvements in echeloning forces at all levels: tactical, operational, and

---

[86] Ibid., 104.   [87] Kagan, "The Rise and Fall of Soviet Operational Art, 1917–1941," 80.
[88] Erickson, "The Great Patriotic War, Barbarossa to Stalingrad," 132.
[89] Kagan, "The Great Patriotic War, Rediscovering Operational Art," 150.   [90] Ibid., 145.

strategic.[91] Sequential and successive attacks forced the Germans "to shuttle their inadequate reserves and reinforcements hopelessly from one catastrophe to another."[92] In 1944 and 1945, Operation Bagration and the attack on Japanese forces in Manchuria continued to demonstrate the sophistication and efficiency of Soviet maneuver warfare. The ability of the Red Army to restore operational maneuver doctrine in wartime, quite literally under fire, was, according to Kagan, "a testimony to the surprising professionalism and flexibility of the senior Red Army command."[93]

Conclusion

Red Army military effectiveness was poor throughout most of this period. However, in wartime, when political oversight was relaxed, the Red Army demonstrated impressive flexibility. While the Germans continued to use the same methods in their major offensives, always exceeding their logistical capabilities, the Red Army continually changed and improved its operations. Historian Roger Reese has noted that "by 1941 the Red Army in many ways, both intentionally and unintentionally, resembled the reviled and much maligned imperial army."[94] And in John Erickson's view, "for its twenty-three years of existence before the Soviet-German War, the Workers and Peasants Red Army failed to evolve a tradition" at all, implying that there was no real transformation of military culture.[95] In many ways, the Red Army looked much like any other large European army. Bolshevik ideals about egalitarianism and elected officers were not absorbed into Red Army culture, and the postwar army would come to resemble "the tsarist army of the 19th century more than it did the Soviet Army of the 1920s."[96]

But the Red Army did not simply "snap back" to the old model. Many aspects of the imperial army disappeared, and the Soviet state permanently changed other aspects of military culture. The army that won the civil war and defeated the Germans in the Great Patriotic War was, on the whole, quite different from the old imperial army. The Red Army was a political army in which the "Communist Party's values became so intertwined with those of the military that the two became virtually indistinguishable." The result was a "union of party and army" that "was never seriously challenged by the army" even when it impaired military effectiveness.[97]

Military culture in the Soviet period was dynamic. There were attempts to "change everything" with dramatic pendulum shifts from one end of the spectrum to the other, in terms of organization, recruitment, hierarchies, and

---

[91] Ibid., 147.   [92] Ibid., 149.   [93] Ibid., 139.   [94] Reese, *The Soviet Military Experience*, 4.
[95] Erickson, *The Soviet High Command, 1918–1941*, 667.
[96] Reese, *The Soviet Military Experience*, 4.   [97] Ibid.

political oversight. Most of those efforts settled somewhere in the middle through a long process of debate and compromise. Idealists and pragmatists battled over matters of principle and questions of effectiveness. Due to its political subordination, the Red Army was indeed the "Party's army." In wartime, political control usually gave way to the need for military effectiveness on the battlefield. This produced a unique dialectic that distinguished Soviet military culture in 1917–1945 from any other.

11 An Army Like No Other
The Origins of the IDF's Military Culture

Gil-li Vardi

Where do organizational cultures come from? Scholars of military organizations rarely confront this question. Because they conceive military culture as an organization's DNA, an intricate and immutable patchwork hardwired into the army's collective psyche, and because militaries are among the most ancient forms of formal human organization, military scholars tend to eschew the question of cultural origins. But not all military organizations have their roots in centuries-old history; therefore, not all military cultures evolved organically over generations. In some instances, culture can be consciously manufactured ex nihilo. This chapter focuses on such a case: the Israeli Defense Force (IDF). Drawing on archival data, it demonstrates that the leadership of the newly established IDF imprinted, early on, a set of beliefs and values that continued to shape the organization for decades afterward.

Scholars often understand organizational culture as a set of collectively shared assumptions that shape how members of the organization derive meaning from their experiences. These assumptions also circumscribe the range of appropriate reactions to the various challenges these individuals confront.[1] As time progresses, lessons learned from these experiences become organizational knowledge. Soon after, they are mythologized as organizational truths; eventually, they transform into truisms, so self-evident and banal they hardly require explanation.[2]

Cultural evolution, in other words, is a slow and cumulative process, whereby habits gradually and organically transform. This is partly why revolutions in military affairs are so hard to achieve and implement; tradition is a

---

[1] See the discussion of military organization in Chapter 1. Also see Ann Swidler, "Culture in Action: Symbols and Strategies," *American Sociological Review* 51 (1986), 273–286, and Edgar Schein, *Organizational Culture and Leadership* (San Francisco, CA, 2010).

[2] See, for instance, Elizabeth Kier, *Imagining War: French and British Military Doctrine between the Wars* (Princeton, NJ, 1997), and Isabel Hull, *Absolute Destruction: Military Culture and the Practices of War in Imperial Germany* (New York, 2005).

powerful force that resists even the strongest pressures of renewal and innovation. Military organizations are particularly slow to evolve culturally. For organizations involved in armed conflicts, radical change is potentially dangerous and always costly.[3] We therefore assume that, with the exception of revolutionary circumstances or other unusual pressures such as political revolution, acute economic crisis, or colossal defeat in conflict, organizational culture is a resilient and even sluggish creature that operates on cumulative knowledge organically embedded into a coherent, powerful, and highly restrictive mind-set.

Yet if this is true, then where do organizational cultures come from? If "tradition" is the key to understanding organizational behavior, then what predates it? For something must have preceded it, something that eventually turned into tradition, or was abandoned as ineffective, useless, or otherwise undesirable, thus clearing the stage for the emergence of new lessons and traditions. The question addressed by this chapter, therefore, points us away from the dynamics shaping the evolution of military organizations, and back into the prehistory of armed forces. Paraphrasing Darwin, what is the origin of military species, and was it by means of natural selection that they evolved? What made any given armed force think and act in ways that later survived for decades, and what can the dynamics of the early beginning, of the time before tradition, tell us about armed forces and change today?

Most of the military organizations operating today cannot offer an answer to this question. Their archival collections cannot facilitate the necessary research. Either the origins of their traditions are shrouded in an undocumented or insufficiently documented distant past, or their modern, well-documented establishment is a mere recent incarnation of a primordial organization that preceded it, more often than not, a colonial force (for instance, the Indian or Jordanian Armed Forces), from which the current organization inherited a tradition and a past. Of course, there are ample examples of modern militaries going through the process of forming or reforming their culture, but most had some sort of former and formal organizational experience. The IDF, however, offers an interesting example of an army that has a relatively well-documented "big bang" beginning, that was not significantly affected by preexisting predecessors, and that was self-consciously fashioned. The IDF is an appealing case study of a military organization for two reasons: its forming and molding

---

[3] Clifford J. Rogers, "'Military Revolutions' and 'Revolutions in Military Affairs,'" in Thierry Gongora and Harald von Riekhoff, eds., *Toward a Revolution in Military Affairs? Defence and Security at the Dawn of the 21st Century* (Westport, CT, 2000); Williamson Murray and MacGregor Knox, "Thinking about Revolutions in Warfare," *The Dynamics of Military Revolutions* (Cambridge, 2001); Dima Adamsky, *The Culture of Military Innovation: The Impact of Cultural Factors on the Revolution in Military Affairs in Russia, the US, and Israel* (Stanford, CA, 2010), 15–23.

process is readily available to scholars, and it represents an armed force with little organizational history to guide it in the process of its forming.

The IDF was officially established in May 1948. A hastily organized, ragtag army, it was mostly comprised of former Haganah and Palmach members – the Yishuv's paramilitary organizations. Smaller armed groups of more right-wing political orientation, the Irgun Zvai Leumi (IZL) and Lehi, also joined the IDF. Other individuals in the early IDF had histories of military service and varying degrees of military experience, mostly as a result of their wartime service in the British armed forces. But all this experience represented less than thirty years of organized activity by paramilitary forces, none of which hitherto exclusively controlled organized violence. The majority of those who served in the new armed forces had also never before engaged in any kind of warfare beyond militia fighting, and had no experience in conventional wars. Neither did the newly forming IDF have the arms or military formations necessary for carrying out conventional warfare. The IDF was, therefore, an entirely new creation, and whatever organizational experiences or memories its members had were wholly inadequate and utterly irrelevant to its new status as the army of a fledgling sovereign state. The IDF thus offers a sort of "military history lab" of organizational culture: a well-documented military organization in the process of exploring desirable patterns of action, before formalizing its past experiences into a written doctrine.

This chapter begins with an examination of the IDF's efforts at "self-fashioning" into a new military organization, with its own marked and idiosyncratic patterns of behavior. It briefly surveys the IDF's cultural characteristics during the 1950s and 1960s, and then returns to explore the period between 1949 and 1952 in detail, in order to examine the origins of these behaviors. The analysis focuses on operational thought and planning, the cultivation of desirable personality traits, and early manifestations of the IDF leadership's perceptions of civil-military relations. The chapter concludes with an assessment of the potential contribution that the reexamination of the IDF's early history offers to scholars of military organizations.

Self-Fashioning: Shaping the IDF, 1948–1953

What can the IDF's birth teach us about organizational habits, how they are formed, and by whom? What are the dynamics that turn such habits into a lasting organizational mind-set? Scholars studying early IDF history have so far largely focused on its institutional history, emerging doctrine, and early buildup.[4] But what were the ideas that informed and ultimately shaped these

---

[4] For previous studies of the early IDF that focus on the technicalities of forces buildup and structure, the evolution of combined-arms doctrine and the execution of reprisal policy of anti-

three dimensions? What were the shared assumptions of Israel's military leadership about the armed forces that it was building, its objectives, the threats it faced, and the best ways to address these threats? And to what extent was the IDF able to exercise independence vis-à-vis the Israeli government and civil authorities in realizing this process of formalization?

Before examining the origins of IDF culture, it is worthwhile mentioning its traits when fully matured and widely practiced, from the late 1950s onward, until roughly 1982. The IDF's choices of policy and operational practices suggest an inherently offensive and eventually aggressive frame of mind; that is, the IDF leadership tended to emphasize the primacy of offense, regardless of – and oftentimes even against – political rationale and consequences.[5] The centrality of the offensive became intertwined with a tendency toward disobedience, which ran through all levels of command, from low- to high-ranking officers. In the 1950s, the general staff and most members of the government deliberately cultivated disobedience in the form of free reinterpretations of orders in the name of tactical excellence and battlefield successes. Last, since its establishment, the IDF exercised higher levels of political independence than previously assumed, mostly in agreement with governmental objectives (again, freely reinterpreting government policies and wishes), but oftentimes as an organization representing, first and foremost, its own interests.[6]

These patterns-to-be expressed themselves clearly and consistently in the form of values and assumptions debated in a series of general staff meetings

terror operations, as well as the contribution of different groups and individuals to the shaping of doctrine and structure, see Yoav Gelber, *A Nucleus for a Regular Hebrew Army* [in Hebrew] (Jerusalem, 1986); David Rodman, *Defense and Diplomacy in Israel's National Security Experience* (Sussex, 2005); Avner Yaniv, *Politics and Strategy in Israel* [in Hebrew] (Tel Aviv, 1994); Orna Ostfeld, *An Army Is Born: Main Stages in the Buildup of the Army under the Leadership of David Ben-Gurion*, vols. 1, 2 (Tel Aviv, 1994); Ze'ev Drory, *Israel's Reprisal Policy 1953–1956: The Dynamics of Military Retaliation* (London, 2005); Benny Morris, *1948: The First Arab-Israel War* (New Haven, CT, 2008); Benny Morris, *Israel's Border Wars, 1949–1956: Arab Infiltration, Israeli Retaliation, and the Countdown to the Suez War* [in Hebrew] (Jerusalem, 2003); Amiad Berzner, *Wild Broncos: The Development and the Changes of the IDF Armour 1949–1956* [in Hebrew] (Tel Aviv, 1999). For state and social mechanisms that prescribed Israeli strategic choices, see Yagil Levi, *The Other Army of Israel: Materialist Militarism in Israel* [in Hebrew] (Tel Aviv, 2003); and Yagil Levi, *Trial and Error: Israel's Route from War to De-escalation* (Albany, NY, 1999).

5 See, for instance, Dayan's suggestions in late 1955 to seize the Sinai, and the general staff's (GS) reprimand of Prime Minister Levi Eshkol for his "lobbying" efforts vis-à-vis the United States in May 1967. Motti Golani, *There Will Be War Next Summer: The Road to the Sinai War, 1955–1956* [in Hebrew] (Tel Aviv, 1997), 98–100, and Special General Staff Discussion with the Security Committee, June 2, IDFA 3/46/1980.

6 For a discussion of these patterns of behavior, see Gil-li Vardi, "Pounding Their Feet: Israeli Military Culture As Reflected in Early IDF Combat History," *Journal of Strategic Studies* 31(2) (2008), 295–324, and Gil-li Vardi, "Learning without Reference: The Israeli Defence Forces in Its First Twenty Years," *Military History Circle, Royal United Services Institute* (September 2009), https://rusi.org/commentary/learning-without-reference-israeli-defence-forces-its-first-twenty-years.

devoted to the questions and challenges of planning the IDF's structure, composition, buildup, and desirable character. These meetings, which took place frequently (regularly once or twice a week, but sometimes more often) and which were transcribed from January 1949 on, provided a space for honest, often heated, discussions about the kind of army the young military leadership aspired to design. They touched on various topics, from discipline, manners, physical appearance, and dressing code; through training, desired levels of operational and tactical readiness, strategic defensive and offensive planning and the future buildup of forces; to whose responsibility it was to prioritize all of these issues and to set official procedures. They discussed financial and manpower constraints as well as international and political limitations and opportunities.[7] In short, they covered it all – from core to miscellaneous – and in so doing, they provide us a unique glimpse into the self-understandings, expectations, and collective mind-set that shaped the Israeli armed forces at their beginning.

Early IDF discussions offer a surprising answer to the origins of its military culture. At first glance, two possible answers might appear highly plausible in pursuing the roots of culture: first, that organizational culture takes years to form and settle; and second, that a new army will consciously attempt to emulate other armed forces in the process. Indeed, scholars who study the IDF's early years tend to emphasize (to different degrees) a group of officers within the military's early leadership who graduated from and tried to mimic the British Army. This group of officers allegedly aspired, and in many ways succeeded, to instill order, discipline, and structure based on past service experiences.[8]

Yet a closer look at general staff discussions reveals a far more complex and nuanced picture. The personal service histories of general staff members do not always agree with their actual suggestions regarding the character and nature of the army they envisioned. More importantly, their shared assumptions about the future army were heavily affected and inspired by idiosyncratic local, Jewish, Zionist aspirations and a sense of cultural and historical uniqueness. The IDF's young military leadership, regardless of personal past experiences (in the British Army, the Haganah Forces, or other fighting organizations), wished to create an entirely new military organization that would respond to what it perceived as Israel's unprecedented and unparalleled security challenges. They gave special emphasis to creative ideas that were at times what the general staff itself

---

[7] This chapter is based on general staff discussions and operation directorate plans, appearing in the following IDF archive files, spanning from late 1948 to roughly 1954: IDFA 104/11/1955; 27/488/1955; 259/488/1955; 261/488/1955; 30/637/1956; 103/645/1956; 39/157/1959; 9/847/1962; 10/847/1962; 11/847/1962; 12/847/1962; 13/847/1962; 14/847/1962; 21/847/1962; 22/847/1962; 26/847/1962; 32/847/1962; 109/1034/1965; 15/678/1967.

[8] Gelber, *A Nucleus for a Regular Hebrew Army*. See also Morris, *1948*, 88, and Eliot Cohen, *Supreme Command* (New York, 2002), 147–148, 150–151.

conceded were mere "fantasies," but designs that young officers nevertheless believed they would be able to realize. Finally, the process of self-fashioning was speedy; in a matter of months, and no more than two years, the newly established IDF already formed the core of ideas and initial operational habits that characterized it for decades. The IDF of 1949 was eager to become an original military organization, was willing to study from all armies but emulated none, and was intentionally designed to fit the constraints, limitations, great challenges, and most of all emerging self-perceptions of the young Israeli state.

"For a year," said Maj. Gen. Yigael Yadin in April 1949, "we were unable to build an army, and what we did manage ... was practically a miracle. But we didn't have a chance to build an army as one should build an army. Other countries went step by step in building theirs."[9] Yadin and the rest of the general staff took 1949 as an opportunity to do just that: to build the army they imagined the Israeli armed forces should be. Their official assumption as of August 1949 was that Israel was not facing an imminent threat of war against its neighbors in the coming twelve to eighteen months, and that it was now time to organize the army.[10]

What kind of an army should the young Jewish state have? The military leadership had no time to deal with such theoretical questions; it faced looming security threats varying from sub-conventional conflicts to an all-out coordinated attack by Israel's neighbors. So it addressed practical questions. The values that guided these military leaders are easily identifiable from their straightforward approach. Yadin commented to his colleagues in the spring of 1949:

> A year and a half ago, when we made Plan D [the Haganah's offensive plan that marked the second phase of the War of Independence], we made some far-reaching suggestions that seemed like fantasies, but eventually, they were realized. And we know that if we will go to Jericho or Damia as a first response to any attack against us, we'll save ourselves and finish off with the enemy [Syria] in a week's time. And if we'll go to El-Arish in response to an Egyptian attack, we'll finish the war in two days.[11]

Yadin's words offer a perfect example of the mixture between lessons drawn from the War of Independence (fighting must be carried on to enemy territory as soon as possible), values (IDF actions as focused on initiative, daring, and offense), desirable mind-set (dare to dream, realize the most fantastic plans), and, finally, appropriate operational habits (offensive-oriented and even aggressive). This mixture evolved into the IDF's organizational culture, a sort of natural way for IDF officers to think about and understand military actions.

Fantasies, in other words, were welcomed. Yet they had to be anchored in reality, which was grim in 1949. David Ben-Gurion, Israel's first prime minister

[9] Maj. Gen. Yigael Yadin, GS Meeting, April 16, 1949, IDFA 10/847/1962.
[10] Chief of Staff, Lt. Gen. Yaakov Dori, GS Meeting, August 1, 1949, IDFA 11/847/1962.
[11] Yadin, GS Meeting, March 12, 1949, IDFA 9/847/1962.

and one of the chief architects of Israel's security doctrine, made that clear enough. The IDF, as he repeatedly emphasized, faced new challenges and had to become more organized, systematic, and professional. Many of the advantages available to the pre-1948 semi-guerrilla force had become irrelevant; daunting disadvantages had replaced them. These were mostly financial challenges and shortcomings related to manpower shortages.[12]

The basic assumptions, which later birthed Israel's security doctrine, were clear from the beginning to the military leadership. Israel's resources and manpower were scarce, and in the face of armed conflict, it would be necessary to mobilize as many reserve forces as possible, as quickly as possible, while Israel's standing army prevented the enemy from making progress. Such a military strategy necessitated superb intelligence and an extremely efficient and effective army.[13] The military leadership debated long and hard how to make these ends meet given the IDF's limited manpower and meager budget. The Israeli government denied most of its requests (for instance, the general staff issued a minimum requirement for six brigades, but had to contend with only four). On top of Israel's and the IDF's shortfalls on all fronts, general staff members were also painfully aware of the fact that neighboring countries' armed forces were drawing the lessons from their defeat in the War of Independence, while vigorously rearming.[14] They hoped to do the same and did not mince words about the necessity to do so. "We need to know the truth," said Deputy Defense Minister Shaul Avigur. "We succeeded [in the War of Independence] because our enemies were such military losers, and even so, we succeeded only after making a huge effort ... but we can't build on this happening again next time round."[15] Ben-Gurion fully supported this view.[16]

The Primacy of the Offense

How, then, was the IDF to compensate for its debilitating budgetary constraints? Though previous work emphasizes the IDF's early focus on its "defensive-offensive" strategy, this chapter argues that, from its inception, it

[12] David Ben-Gurion, GS Meeting, April 16, 1949, IDFA 10/847/1962. Also see Zvi Schreiber's words, in a similar spirit, in a general staff meeting on May 9, 1949, IDFA 10/847/1962. Schreiber was the chief of staff's financial advisor.
[13] Lt. Col. Shalom Eshet, GS Meeting, April 16, 1949, IDFA 10/847/1962. Eshet served in the Austrian Army (a service he mentioned in this meeting), and spent the meeting calling for the adoption of a force focused on training, unburdened with border defense missions.
[14] Lt. Col. Vivian Hertzog, GS Meeting, May 9, 1949, IDFA 10/847/1962.
[15] Shaul Avigur, GS Meeting, April 24, 1949, IDFA 10/847/1962. Also see Dori's words concerning the Arabs' learning of lessons and future attempts to force a decisive blow in GS Meeting, March 6, 1949, IDFA 9/847/1962.
[16] "Let's face the truth: we won not because our army is a miracle-maker, but because the Arab armies were rotten. Must this rot persist?" Elchanan Oren, ed., *David Ben-Gurion: War Diary*, 3 vols. (Tel Aviv, 1983), 2:853.

was a highly offensive-minded army. It partially outsourced territorial defense – that is, blocking the advance of various enemy forces – consciously and intentionally to frontier settlements designed and located for this purpose.[17] This allowed the IDF to focus on training and establishing itself as a cadre force rather than a stationary force guarding the borders. From its inception, the IDF rejected the idea of stretching itself along Israel's challenging borders as unfeasible and undesirable. Israel's sovereign territory was already awash with infiltrators and refugees trying to return to their villages or trying to terrorize Israeli civil populations; there were simply not enough forces to stop them.

Received wisdom attributes the birth of an official, doctrinal offensive approach – with regard to conventional threats as well as to daily or ongoing security challenges of a sub-conventional nature (*bitachon-shotef*) – to changes that took place in 1953. A shift from a "defensive-offensive" to a "offensive-defensive" strategy, and the launching of the Retaliation Policy, while establishing commando units (101 and later 202 and 890), served as a model for and a lesson on the kind and character of warfare IDF leaders wished to instill among their soldiers.[18]

The early official defensive-offensive approach requires clarification. That declared organizational values do not always fully agree with practiced values and patterns of thought and action is not unusual.[19] Unlike other, more institutionalized, and tradition-based armies, the IDF was still in the process of shaping its operational assumptions, planning, and basic mind-set, and, accordingly, its official doctrine. In this case, in 1953, the IDF fit its declared values (i.e., its doctrine) to a behavior that was already practiced and that was also more desirable in terms of self-perception. This is the reason for the small bureaucratic footprint this supposedly highly meaningful change left as a trace. This is also the reason why the government accepted the alleged shift so smoothly;[20] the offensive mind-set, contingency plans, and, when it came to sub-conventional warfare, retalia-

---

[17] Maj. Gen. Yigael Yadin, ibid., Lt. Gen. Yaakov Dori and other, GS Meeting, March 6, 1949, IDFA 9/847/1962, April 24, 1949, IDFA 10/847/1962 and August 15, 1949, IDFA 11/847/1962. For the various problems that followed this practice, see "Staff Meeting with Representatives of Settlements Organizations," September 20, 1949, IDFA 11/847/1962.

[18] See especially Amiram Oren, Oren Barak, and Assaf Shapira, "How the Mouse Got His Roar: The Shift to an Offensive-Defensive Military Strategy in Israel in 1953 and Its Implications," *International History Review* 35(2) (2013), 356–376. On a more general "defensive ethos" as a Yishuv and later Israeli public self-perception, see Anita Shapira, *Land and Power* (Stanford, CA, 1999), 353–370.

[19] Schein, *Organizational Culture and Leadership*, 7–72.

[20] "How the Mouse Got His Roar" offers a different explanation and a dismissive approach toward the "all-offensive strategy" claim. However, when focused on the IDF alone (unrelated to various government members, security agencies, and former Haganah leaders and their strategic preferences), an early offensive-offensive approach becomes clear. See also pages 257–258.

tion practices, were already there.[21] Only the official name of the doctrine changed, to reflect more clearly IDF practices. More than anything, this change was cosmetic.

The Offensive Approach to Sub-Conventional Conflict

The spirit of Unit 101 (established in 1953) – ruthlessness, eagerness for battle, blindness to the possible political implications of undermining international borders and therefore Israel's very security – did not come out of thin air. In effect, the same offensive approach was quite apparent in ongoing security operations as early as 1949, when Yigael Yadin expressed the general staff's interest in creating "fists": well-trained, concentrated forces that would operate at will and against specific targets, rather than thinly spread border forces operating defensively.[22] The "fists" expressed a natural extension of a small militia mind-set. They allowed small IDF forces to practice an offensively oriented approach as much as possible, given the reality of a chronic shortage of manpower and constant low-intensity challenges. The same concentrated forces would also be able to bear the initial brunt of a coordinated attack by conventional armed forces, while the reserve forces mobilized.

Yet the orientation of "fist"-like forces was meant to be, by definition, offensive and focused on answering constant border challenges. "We cannot hold the borders, so we'll have to be smarter and come up with actions that will guarantee our maximum security," commented the chief of staff, Lt. Gen. Yaakov Dori, in May 1949.[23] A few days earlier, when referring to defending Eilat and the southern border, Dori had noted that: "In our situation today, the action that can help [defend the border], namely retaliation acts against the Arabs east to the border are out of the question ... We're holding the line against the Egyptian only symbolically ... If Egypt won't attack that's fine, but we have to remember the roughly 150,000 refugees in the area."[24] This represented the embryonic form of the operational idea and logic behind the retaliation policy of the mid-1950s.[25] The assumption that the only answer was an offensive initiative (rather than static border defense) was already natural to

---

[21] Morris notes that retaliation as policy was evident since September 1949. Morris, *Israel's Border Wars, 1949–1956*, 210.

[22] See, for instance, Eshet and Yadin, GS Meeting, April 16, 1949, IDFA 10/847/1962; Lt. Col. Israel Bar, GS Meeting, May 9, 1949, IDFA 10/847/1962.

[23] Dori, GS Meeting, May 9, 1949, IDFA 10/847/1962.   [24] Ibid.

[25] The majority of retaliation operations in 1949–1951 were mortar shelling, aerial strafing, or laying of land mines against villagers considered either fedayeen or locals harboring them. Small raids, some of them executed by armed settlers, were rare; one such raid produced one of Sharett's earliest comments to Yadin on the possible severe diplomatic implications of a narrow, solely military perception of Israel's security policy and requirements. See Morris, *Israel's Border Wars, 1949–1956*, 213–223.

Dori in the spring of 1949, despite the fact that the IDF's forces on the southern front were so weak that Dori himself described them as "pathetic."

This embryonic offensive approach twinned with an utter indifference to international agreements and a tendency (shaped during the pre-state years and the War of Independence) to "create facts on the ground." Both tendencies were strongly evident in the IDF as early as the immediate aftermath of the 1948 war. Both rested on the imperative of armed action as a means of ensuring desirable outcomes. "Everybody thinks that the successful resolution of the [ceasefire] negotiations was a result of the territory we have under control, thanks to the military reality," commented Yigael Yadin in February 1949. "And I think we need to know this for the future too. How we manage the talks ... That's not the main thing ... I think too much importance is ascribed to political and diplomatic channels ... whereas the main reasons, the main motivations, are forgotten. The enemy really, objectively, had to negotiate for a ceasefire with us."[26] In other words, nothing but military success would determine Israel's future, and military success was therefore the ultimate – at times, the only – national goal. Ben-Gurion found himself compelled to remind the general staff that "military victories cannot become our goals in and of themselves." Yet in the same sentence, he acknowledged and thus reassured his officers that there are moments in which they do "constitute the only goal; they dictate our very existence."[27]

This approach became strongly entrenched among the veterans of the War of Independence and was consistently manifested from that moment onward. For example, consider Maj. Gen. Dori's informing of the general staff of an agreement reached with the Jordanian Legion regarding Jerusalem's territorial partitioning. The agreement was about to come into effect on May 1, 1949. Maj. Gen. Moshe Dayan wanted to ensure that Israel would have uninterrupted access to the railroad that passed through this territory. He recommended that the IDF make a move on that date and surprise the Jordanians by seizing all of Israel's allotted territory, and, regardless of the agreement, lay barbed wire and mines along the border. "There is another possibility, that we won't do it now, we'll do it some time, when we'll want it, but it'll be more difficult. Now it'll be easier, if we do it by surprise," explained Dori. The staff's reaction was quite revealing: offensive orientation and risk-taking were traits that both the general staff and the government understood to be characteristic of the IDF since its birth. Shaul Avigur replied: "Whatever is necessary that we do in order to take over the railroad, we need to do now, because we'll have to do it in any case in the future ... Our actions have always been attempts that were at risk of failure." To which Lt. Col. Eshet added, "After the previous few incidents

---

[26] Yadin, GS Meeting, February 25, 1949, IDFA 9/847/1962.
[27] Ben-Gurion, GS Meeting, March 16, 1949, IDFA 9/847/1962.

near Sdom and Beit-Jubrin, it is especially important that we carry comprehensive and strong military action ... Most important is what impression this
will leave on the Arabs."[28]

Offensive Approach and the 1950–1953 War Plans

Israel's strategic predicament and scarce resources translated immediately to an
all-embracing offensive approach, intended, if possible, to obviate an enemy
attack through preemptive strikes. This approach, a bitter lesson from the War
of Independence, was prevalent in the army from its inception. As mentioned, it
did not emerge organically in the early or mid-1950s; rather, the early 1950s
produced war plans that expressed a mind-set that had been consistently present
in every war plan since 1949. Prevailing arguments about an inherent shift in
IDF plans and operational practices from a "defensive-offensive" approach
toward an "offensive-defensive" orientation systematically disregard ample
earlier expressions of the latter. As Lt. Col. Shimon Avidan expressed in May
1949: "Our basic assumption is that our defensive plans all over the country
must be based on actions we initiate on enemy territory."[29] Yadin similarly
explained that the offensive is the IDF's "tool of defense," intended to disrupt
enemy initiative.[30]

Even the earliest IDF strategic contingency plans available are, therefore,
offensive-oriented, and even those dedicated specifically to defense call for
offensive action as soon as hostilities break out. For instance, a February 1950
directive ordering the operational planning of "Case North," a war against
Syria and Lebanon, drew a spectrum of contingencies and possibilities available to the IDF. These ranged from a preemptive strike followed by an
offensive aimed at the destruction of enemy forces, to first breaking an
enemy attack and immediately initiating an offensive. As early as 1950, planning orders emphasized nocturnal strikes, surprise attacks, and ambushes, as
well as leveraging advantages in the quality and quantity of arms.[31] Even more
telling is the Operations Directorate's recommendations for the actions and
goals that should follow the initial battle in the north, regardless of the nature of

[28] Dori, Avigur, and Eshet, GS Meeting, May 1949, IDFA 10/847/1962.
[29] Avidan, GS Meeting, May 9, 1949, IDFA 10/847/1962. Avidan was a Palmach company
commander; he also trained as a member of and commanded in Ord Wingate's night squad.
[30] Yadin, GS Meeting, March 6, 1949, IDFA 9/847/1962.
[31] Operations Directorate, Directive no. 2 of Operational Planning, Case North, February 6, 1950,
IDFA 259/488/1955. For the IDF, the possibility of an all-out war posed a grave danger to Israel,
but also an opportunity to redraw what it deemed as indefensible borders. A 1952 "Case All"
planning order issued by the Operations Directorate described the IDF's mission as "a.
Safeguarding the state and its borders in [the] face of aggression. b. Improving state borders
while striving to shorten the length of war." Case All, II – Non Surprise, Operations Directorate,
February 10, 1953, IDFA 109/1034/1965.

this battle (preemptive or defending against enemy attack). The second aim of the campaign, after completing the destruction of enemy forces and shortening the lines by taking Quneitra, was the seizure of Damascus.[32]

The Operations Directorate issued henceforth two sets of plans, defensive and offensive, for each front separately as well as for a "case all" – an all-out war against all of Israel's neighbors.[33] Yet these plans were not mutually exclusive; rather, they were meant to complement one another and to provide the general staff with latitude to adapt to shifting goals and real-time military developments. Even the decision as to which front to strike first remained flexible, but the general staff planned potential strikes with enthusiasm. As if almost religiously following the "best defense is good offense" dictum, the general staff persistently employed the method of pushing the battlefield away from Israeli settlements onto enemy territory. This central maxim was tirelessly handed down to future generations. "We need to move on to attack in [the Syrian town of] Quneitra in three days, not to fight inside [kibbutz] Deganya, otherwise we'll never realize our plans. And a classic defense plan against the Syrians should stipulate that within three days of launching their attack we are in Quneitra … If we don't have such defense plans, we don't have a plan to defend the state of Israel."[34] Likewise, Lt. Col. Israel Bar explained in October 1953 that "often times, defensive strategy must materialize by initiated operations … in most cases operational defense can only be realized by aggressive tactical actions."[35] Thus, the 1954 memo about Israel's security policy principles prepared for the minister of defense, and purportedly marking the birth of the IDF's "offensive-defensive" approach, merely echoed Yadin's words from 1949.[36]

The IDF Soldier and Officer: Creating a New Society

Who was to realize the daunting and demanding task of preparing and executing an "offensive-defensive" strategy? What did such an approach require from the organization and its members? The early IDF leadership was clear about this subject too. Its aspirations were lofty: to create the best soldiers possible, and in so doing, to produce an entirely new society that

---

[32] Ibid.

[33] See, for instance, "Case all" plans of February 1953 in IDFA 15/678/1967 and 109/1034/1965, 30/673/1956, and 27/488/1955; "Case all" Intelligence analysis of 1954 in IDFA 39/157/1959; combined cases, 1950, in IDFA 261/488/1955; "Case North," 1950, IDFA 259/488/1955.

[34] Yadin, GS Meeting, March 6, 1949, IDFA 9/847/1962. See earlier discussion of the alleged "shift" from a defensive-offensive doctrine toward an offensive-defensive one.

[35] Lt. Col. Israel Bar, *Ma'arachot* 80 (October 1953), 34.

[36] "Israel's Security Doctrine," Lt. Col. Yuval Ne'eman, Head of Planning Directorate, April 1954, IDFA 103/645/1956. Interesting, Ne'eman used the term in a general manner, yet his examples suggest he had mainly sub-conventional warfare in mind.

would maintain the qualitative superiority the IDF hitherto enjoyed vis-à-vis its neighbors. With this objective, the IDF's leadership fully aligned itself with the civil leadership's vision. Ben-Gurion in particular regarded the army as a national school of sorts, a true melting pot in which the army would forge all members of society into the new Israeli mold.[37] The general staff spent considerable time discussing the desirable character of its soldiers and especially of its officers. In effect, basic questions regarding the formal structure of military units (such as the brigade), doctrinal consistency, and the layout and number of training barracks were all considered in light of their future contribution toward the cultivation of the character of the Israeli officer.

The general staff envisioned this new, ideal officer as independent, self-confident, initiative-oriented, and always adapting to the reality of the battlefield with an open mind.[38] Its members saw open-mindedness and initiative as essential personal traits because they were essential for optimizing the performance of the army as a whole. The central objective was to produce cadres of officers that would be able to mobilize and operate rapidly at all levels of command, even those with which they had little experience. For this purpose, the general staff tried to strike a fine balance between a uniform doctrine and training procedure that celebrated flexibility and adaptability and hierarchical structures. In short, it was willing to bear the costs of chaos intentionally designed into the system in order to cultivate the kind of commanders and officers deemed appropriate and right for the mission. These officers, the general staff expected, would shape their subordinates in their mold.[39] An article devoted to the topic of "Initiative in Battle" recommended "educating combatants and their commanders, and shaping their image as daring, energetic, aggressive, active and flexible [minded], and maintaining a high-level unit spirit" as means of cultivating initiative.[40]

Dori and others did not separate the goals of building a state from building an army. The two were inseparable not only due to practical mobilization requirements but also as deeply entrenched beliefs about the nature of the IDF's mission. The Israelis were to be soldier-citizens and citizen-soldiers. Their military training was to accomplish much more than its immediate operational objectives. It was to fulfill what Dori described as "our Jewish and pioneering concepts," namely, the military leadership's version of Zionism.[41]

---

[37] Ben-Gurion, GS Meeting, September 18, 1949, IDFA 11/847/1962.
[38] See Ben-Gurion, CGS Dori, Maj. Gen. Moshe Carmel, and Maj. Gen. Elchanan Yishai, GS Meeting, September 18, 1949, IDFA 11/847/1962.
[39] Ibid.   [40] Lt. Col. Israel Bar, *Ma'arachot* 79 (July 1953).   [41] Dori, ibid.

Armies to Learn From: Other Models?

"[W]e are making all kinds of comparisons with other countries and such. I think we've gone through enough in this situation and we know exactly who is our enemy and where to find him, we know his attacking trends, and we can try and build our forces accordingly. But if we build them based on past events or based on other countries' successful experiences, we might end up seeing a collision between a beautiful theory and [our] reality, which will be different."[42] Yadin, a Haganah member from the age of fifteen, was not averse to learning from foreign armies and past experiences; indeed, he urged his colleagues to do just that, and to do it in a thorough and systematic manner.[43] Yadin and his colleagues in the general staff, regardless of personal backgrounds, were willing to learn from all relevant armies, but they decided to emulate none. Theirs was, in their eyes, a unique challenge, encumbered by an unprecedented and unusual set of constraints.

Each member of the general staff carried his own personal history of service, spoken languages, and cultural influences. As a group, they embodied a diverse set of personal and professional experiences. Consequently, they studied many different examples and considered a variety of candidate armies and military lessons as models for their emerging organization. Members of the general staff dedicated a considerable amount of time to discussing these influences. While their examples varied, the Swiss Army was most commonly drawn upon as a source of inspiration.[44] The Swiss system, a fighting cadre that relies heavily on reserves, was naturally an appealing military model. Yet they also examined an impressive variety of other armies, drawn from historically diverse periods. These included the Swedish Army and the Norwegian, Finnish, Latvian, Lithuanian, and Estonian prewar armies, all of which shared a reliance on reserves and cadres.[45] Finally, they also examined militia forces of several of the British Dominions, the French Army, the Czechoslovakian Army, the German territorial forces in East Prussia, and the US Army.[46]

Despite its availability as the most recent and accessible military example for general staff members, the British Army was rarely discussed among them. On the rare occasion that it was, most staff members were fully aware that the British military experiences were hardly applicable for addressing the

---

[42] Yadin, GS Meeting, February 25, 1949, IDFA 9/847/1962.
[43] See, for instance, Yadin, GS Meeting, February 25, 1949, IDFA 9/847/1962.
[44] See, for instance, GS Meeting, February 22, 1949, IDFA 9/847/1962; May 9, 1949, IDFA 10/847/1962; March 6, 1949, 9/847/1962. Also see Yitzhak Greenberg, "The Swiss Armed Forces As a Model for the IDF Reserve System – Indeed?" *Israel Studies* 18(3) (2013), 95–111.
[45] These discussions concluded that the reserve method can be effective only under certain geographic conditions.
[46] GS Meeting, April 4,1952, IDFA 21/847/1962; May 9, 1949, IDFA 10/847/1962; February 22, 1949, IDFA 9/847/1962; February 25, 1949, IDFA 9/847/1962; March 6, 1949, IDFA 9/847/1962, March 12, 1949, IDFA 9/847/1962.

challenges the IDF was facing. The only exception to that rule was the case of defending the home islands, but none of the general staff members had any direct experience with that effort.[47] Whatever the model eventually adopted, it was clear to the members of the general staff that there were significant benefits to studying and learning from other armies and foreign experts. Virtually all members of the IDF's early military leadership, particularly veterans of the Haganah, were eager to learn how to train and operate large formations, which they had no experience in managing.[48] Nevertheless, members of the IDF's general staff persistently adhered to the strategic imperatives, as they understood them, regardless of the model. "For us, a structure that does not allow us to hold assault forces which can act immediately is out of the question, even if we have reserve formations that can be [mobilized and] filled quickly ... We must always hold assault forces in full strength, ready and available for action."[49]

During the formative years of 1949 and 1950, there was surprising agreement between general staff members' visions, given their disparate backgrounds. Whether having served in the Haganah, the British Army, or other militaries in the past, these men exhibited only occasional and unsystematic differences regarding the IDF's desirable character, structure, buildup, and doctrine. Though one would expect such deliberations to be opinionated and potentially passionately divisive, no rifts emerged on fundamental topics such as basic discipline, strategic buildup, or planning. If anything, Haganah veterans were eager to instill order and disciplined planning, with a view to receiving governmental commitment to strengthening and growing the army. In so doing, they were honestly and openly self-reflective. "You talk a lot about purchases," said Shaul Avigur to Ben-Gurion, "but this thing is worthless unless it comes with first-rate organization of the force, and training."[50] Elsewhere Yadin noted that "we established the army without planning because from the first moment on we had to fight, we always faced operational pressures. Today ... all fronts are quiet ... we will have the time for ... planning, and not just on paper."[51] Later, he again joined Chief of Staff Dori

[47] As part of the discussion on territorial vs. non-territorial defense and formations, see Yadin, GS Meeting, February 25, 1949, IDFA 9/847/1962. British war experience was, however, widely discussed in *Ma'arachot*, the IDF's professional journal, from its first publication in 1939. A May 1955 volume offered an index of twenty years of publications; the index reveals *Ma'arachot*'s focus on British and American operational thought and experience. *Ma'arachot* 91–92 (May 1955).

[48] For calls for foreign experts, see GS Meeting, May 12, 1949, 10/847/1962; for Lt. Col. Yitzhak Rabin wishing to develop divisions rather than brigades as the largest formation, see GS Meeting, August 15, 1949, IDFA 11/847/1962.

[49] Lt. Col. Israel Bar, GS Meeting, May 9, 1949, IDFA 10/847/1962.

[50] Avigur, GS Meeting with Ben-Gurion, April 24, 1949, IDFA 10/847/1962.

[51] Yadin, GS Meeting, February 25, 1949, IDFA 9/847/1962.

and urged the general staff to organize the army using the most meticulous planning procedures possible.[52]

Likewise, Dori cautioned the general staff that in its attempt to build an army almost from scratch, it should not succumb to the assumption that things will eventually fall into place without detailed analysis and planning. "Improvisation saved us on more than several occasions," he reminded his audience, invoking what would remain a core IDF ideal. "But you should not always put your trust in improvisation, especially when you have the opportunity to think and analyze, to do things in a more scientific and structured way."[53] Like Dori, all of the aforementioned officers were Haganah veterans.

There was yet another nuance to the shared assumptions about the desired processes of learning and organizational dynamics. Dori himself succinctly summed up the narrow spectrum of learning options the IDF entertained: "We cannot simply copy the Swiss system as is. And we know our unique conditions are irrelevant to Switzerland. Even the best mobilization system cannot operate without a fist. The question is how powerful the fist needs to be."[54] While the general staff studied foreign models, it understood its strategic necessities and constraints through its unique and evolving cultural prism. This worldview prescribed certain choices that rendered all available "off-the-shelf" models inapplicable.

The IDF and the Government

Did the IDF's leadership exhibit similar levels of independence, introspection, and self-awareness when operating outside what one would consider a strictly military realm? Quite naturally, members of the Israeli government, as well as their presumed subordinates in the IDF high command, were concerned with the question of the nature and degree of political freedom enjoyed by the newly formed army.[55] The answer, not surprisingly, was subject to one's definition of political agency and interest. The IDF was consciously designed as an "apolitical army," intended to be uninvolved in party politics and serving as a tool for

---

[52] Yadin, GS Meeting, March 1, 1949, IDFA 9/847/1962. In effect, Dori had to cool Yadin off, claiming that the kind of planning he urged was not to stop the IDF from getting the organizing process started right away and learning "on the go."

[53] Dori, GS Meeting, August 1, 1949, IDFA 11/847/1962 (discussing the optimized structure of IDF brigades).

[54] Dori, GS Meeting, March 6, 1949, IDFA 9/847/1962.

[55] Ben-Gurion expressed his concerns over the "lack of civilian control" over the Haganah as early as October 1947. Since Ben-Gurion was the towering figure of Israeli politics, one can safely assume that the level of control he would have exerted over Israel's armed forces represented a historical peak of civilian control of military decision-making in Israel. Oren, *Ben-Gurion: War Diary*, 1:421, quote in Cohen, *Supreme Command*, 149. Cohen offers a useful account of Ben-Gurion's struggle to assert his control over the Palmach during the War of Independence and the Palmach's dismembering. Ibid., 163–172.

implementing governmental security policy.[56] Yet the IDF's leadership was not averse to expressing political, cultural, and economic interests, in actions more than in words. Indeed, the very meaning of an "apolitical" military was a source of political contention. Among the first battalions that demobilized in the aftermath of the War of Independence were those described as "politically unreliable," due to being comprised of former IZL and Lehi members, right-wing organizations opposing the political primacy of the leading Mapai Party.[57]

Previous work has thoroughly studied this form of political partisanship within the IDF. It would come as no surprise to readers familiar with Israel's political history that most members of the IDF's elite during its infancy considered the ruling Mapai Party their political home and unabashedly parti-cipated in enforcing its hegemony.[58] At the least, however, the IDF was successfully prevented from *direct* involvement in the political sphere.[59] Yet, when considering civil control over the military, the picture becomes more finely grained.[60]

The IDF exercised more independence than historians conventionally acknowledge. As Oren Barak and Gabi Shefer claim, the definitions and contours separating the "governmental" and "civil" domains from the "mili-tary" realm are at best blurry, designed in that fashion in the late 1940s and early 1950s. This allowed for extensive involvement by the IDF in building the Israeli state and society; however, as time went by, the civil and military arenas became interdependent and often inseparable.[61] An instructive example of the IDF's scope and magnitude of independence and involvement in nonmilitary and semi-military affairs is reflected in the ministers of transportation, agricul-ture, and especially the treasury's uneasiness about the IDF's actions in 1948

[56] Yoram Peri, *Between Battles and Ballots: Israeli Military Politics* (Cambridge, 1983), 38–45.
[57] All three Palmach brigades – the Haganah's striking forces – were, of course, disbanded too. This process marked "statism" (*mamlachtiut*) no less than it marked Mapai's control over the IDF. The Palmach was indeed the backbone of the IDF and it provided the majority of its low- and mid-ranking officers. However, while Ben-Gurion forced the disbandment of Palmach, the general staff itself enthusiastically forced the disbandment and political cleansing of the IZL and Lehi. See Lt. Col. Israel Bar, describing political affiliations of various brigades as a key factor affecting their future. GS Meeting, March 23, 1949, IDFA 9/847/1962.
[58] Ostfeld, *An Army Is Born*, 2:622–719.
[59] The IDF kept its loyalty to the Mapai Party, which led Israeli governments until 1977, yet avoided direct involvement in party politics. For an elaborate analysis of IDF early relations with Israeli party politics, see Peri, *Between Battles and Ballots*.
[60] A nuanced, sharp, and historically sound analysis of the changing nature of civil control over the IDF is to be found in Yagil Levi, *Who Governs the Military? Between Control of the Military and Control of Militarism* [in Hebrew] (Jerusalem, 2010).
[61] Oren Barak and Gabriel Shefer, "The 'Security Network' in Israel and Its Effect: A New Theoretical and Analytical Approach," in Gabriel Shefer, Oren Barak, and Amiram Oren, eds., *An Army That Has a State: New Approaches to Civil-Security Relations in Israel* (Jerusalem, 2008), 16–44. Also see Assaf David, "Civil-Military Relations in Israel," *Theory and Criticism* 41 (2003), 326–340 [in Hebrew].

and 1949. In complete defiance of these government agencies' authority, the
IDF built roads in service of its particular needs, trained its soldiers on
agricultural lands without seeking permission, and spent beyond its budget.[62]
Interesting, the early military leadership still saw itself as acting within the
boundaries of legitimate action in all these activities. For Maj. Gen. Yadin, the
IDF was "not outside its democratic authority" when "in contact" with civilian
authorities, "as long as it didn't deal with politics."[63] Just what the meaning was
of being "in contact" Yadin made clear earlier in the meeting. "I'll do my best to
affect security matters more ... when the [general] staff is doing it illegally – that
is a dangerous matter; but when it stops doing it, it will not be doing its job ...
there is no other choice ... the security problem must be interwoven to the
buildup of the country ... If the military stops applying pressure – whether
about [where to build] a port or ... [establishing a kibbutz in] Dan or Safia – it
is not doing its job." It is worthwhile stressing that, from its beginning, the IDF
itself, rather than any official civil authority, set the boundaries of its "job" and
duty. The IDF was to be as active as possible until told otherwise: "When the
Minister of Security will come and tell me not to grow vegetables or take care of
other businesses – I'll then know if I'm doing something against a set policy
[otherwise], I don't care about questions of popularity."[64] This state of mind
meant that the habit of independent action and the strength of personalities
involved (mainly the prime minister and the minister of security) would set the
future course of the IDF's "nonpolitical" involvement in state affairs.

Israel's military leadership also never shied away from direct involvement in
geopolitical decision-making. As early as 1949, high-ranking officers actively
participated in the armistice talks that shaped the postwar political order. This form
of involvement would turn into a habit. Generals and recent IDF emeriti would
play crucial roles in peace talks in 1973 and 1978 as well.[65] In July and August
1967, the general staff discussed a swift and intentional deployment of the IDF
into the newly occupied territories, partly as a means to prevent them from being
used as bargaining chips in future peace talks by creating facts on the ground.[66]

It is important to stress here that, despite the overall congruence between
state and military goals, the IDF's leadership realized, from the beginning, that
there were clear instances in which the army's and government's interests
would be inherently and potentially explosively misaligned. Budget and financial constraints were obvious points of friction.[67] The nature of the relationship

---

[62] Barak and Shefer, "The 'Security Network' in Israel and Its Effect."
[63] Yadin, "War Planning," GS Meeting, April 20, 1952, IDFA 21/842/1962.   [64] Ibid.
[65] Barak and Shefer, "The 'Security Network' in Israel and Its Effect."
[66] "Military Meanings of the New Borders," General Staff Operation Branch, July 2, 1967, IDFA
60/107/1970, and GS Meeting, August 7, 1967, IDFA 260/117/1970.
[67] Budget deficit and under-financing were the most obvious and impending constraints threatening the vast planning and build-up strategies the general staff discussed in the spring and
summer of 1949. They stood at the heart of virtually all the discussions the general staff held,

between military initiatives and their possible political ramifications was another, less obvious one. The early IDF's political independence was not manifest in overt disobedience.[68] But disobedience would eventually become a second behavioral nature. The behavioral tendency to act militarily regardless of civilian expectations, or even direct orders, did not originate in conscious and intentionally subversive resistance to civilian authority. Rather, it traces back to early instances in which overzealous military actors, who were engaging in action beyond their formal jurisdictional boundaries, amplified and radicalized civilian intentions. This tendency developed further as the military leadership grew more convinced of a self-diagnosed crisis in 1952 due to the perceived low quality of its available manpower, threatening both the IDF's spirit and its potency. Partly in an attempt to thwart a rapid deterioration, the IDF launched its policy (and units) of retaliation.[69] However, initiative quickly escalated into unintentional disobedience in the realm of political action, as it did on the operational level. To the same extent that the IDF freely interpreted orders in the early and mid-1950s to meet its emerging operational ethos, its officers tended to take action that carried political implications whenever and wherever it appeared to be aligned with governmental policy. Such actions were, almost without exception, distinctly radical and taken without awaiting authorization.

This pattern of independent action regardless of its political ramifications, however, did not emerge in the early 1950s. It is a clear legacy of the somewhat legal free-spirited origin from which the IDF stemmed, especially as it was tested and forged in war. A strong case in point was the IDF's actions vis-à-vis the Palestinian civilian population during the War of Independence. As the armed forces of the state, the IDF frequently enforced the expulsion of Palestinian villagers or terrorized them into "voluntary" exodus when such

and more than any other issue, exemplified and embodied the difference of interests between the IDF and the state, which faced a grim economic reality. See, for instance, general staff meetings on March 6, March 16, April 16, and April 24, 1949, IDFA 9/847/1962 and 10/847/1962.

[68] It was overt enough, though, for Ben-Gurion to write in his diary that "of all the deficiencies of our military, lack of discipline is the most severe, and above all at the highest level." Oren, *Ben-Gurion: War Diary*, 2:534, June 1948, quote from Cohen, *Supreme Command*. A year later, in October 1949, he again found himself explaining to CGS Yadin in a letter that the army is "unconditionally subordinate to the government." Yechud ve Ye'ud, quote from Amir Bar-Or, "The Link between the Government and the IDF during Israel's First 50 Years: The Shifting Role of the Defence Minister," in Daniel Maman, Eyal Ben-Ari, and Zeev Rosenhek, eds., *Military, State, and Society in Israel* (New Brunswick, NJ, 2001), 321–342, 323.

[69] See especially Yadin's concluding comments on the 1952 training exercise, IDFA 19/4/1955. Ben-Gurion, evidently, did not share the grim views on the IDF's capabilities, declaring its organizational and operational levels, as well as the commitment of its members, "very encouraging" in the fall of 1953. However, he did express concerns for the IDF's advantage in spirit, since the new immigrants lacked, according to him, the education, knowledge, and love of the country their local seniors exhibit. Ben-Gurion, "Armed Forces and the State, a Study," October 1953. Published in *Ma'arachot* 32 (May–June 1981), 2–11.

emigration did not emerge organically. That the IDF actively encouraged a Palestinian exodus using various means, and on a large scale, is today largely beyond doubt.[70] Yet received knowledge on the role the IDF played in creating the Palestinian refugee problem is that it functioned as the executioner of strategies emanating from local and at times national civilian authorities. Yet, in some cases on the southern front, reality was far more nuanced.

During the final months of 1948, David Ben-Gurion and Yosef Weitz (the director of the Land and Afforestation Department of the Jewish National Fund) agreed that driving out through intimidation Arab communities along the Faluja-Majdal axis would best serve the new state's interests. In late February 1949, shortly after the conclusion of the armistice agreement with Egypt, the local commander (later Maj. Gen.) Yigal Allon, asked the general staff for permission to evict the residents of Faluja and Iraq-al-Manshia for fear they might sustain infiltration efforts to Israel. The general staff apparently approved his request; a series of "incidents" to persuade the locals to leave ensued.[71] Was Allon's request known to and approved by the government, or was it a local initiative set in motion by the IDF's southern forces? If so, what were the motivations and justifications for such action? Documented approvals of expulsions are difficult to find and, to the extent that they exist, are even more difficult to declassify. A smoking gun in the form of a formal order or authorization from Ben-Gurion regarding the expulsion of Faluja and Iraq-al-

---

[70] Of the vast literature discussing the Palestinian flight – either forcefully or by self-decision – see especially Benny Morris, *The Birth of the Palestinian Refugee Problem Revisited* (Cambridge, 2004). It is important to note that the IDF still saw ethnic cleansing as part and parcel of its mission long after the War of Independence. Operations plan "Ben-Nun" from December 1951, intended to open and secure the routes to Jerusalem, clearly stated this objective: "Mission: Opening the way to Mt. Scopus, seizing the Latrun enclave and cleansing of the territory from enemy population [*sic*], and taking the demilitarized Governor's House area, while maintaining the state's borders." Operation Ben-Nun Order, December 1951, IDFA 109/1034/1965. "Ben-Nun" was also the name of two failed earlier operations during the War of Independence (May 1948) to capture Latrun and open a way to Jerusalem. The 1951 plan was prepared in the light of Jordanian king Abdullah's assassination a few months earlier and its possibly unfavorable political and strategic results. A later and more elaborate and ambitious version of Ben-Nun, now named "Nun," detailed its "mission: freeing the western part of land occupied by the Hashemite Jordanian Kingdom. Creating a defended line along the Jordan [River] and cleansing the territory from hostile population." The mission appeared again in relation to both Central Command and Southern Command. Central Command's mission was "seizing Jerusalem and the southern triangle, and cleansing the freed territories from hostile population." Southern Command's mission was "seizing Mt. Hebron ... cleansing the territory from hostile population not concomitantly with battle actions." The "territory" appendix discusses, among other things, the population of the Jordanian-occupied territories, ending with the sentence "the general state of mind of the residences after learning the lesson of the refugees [fate] is to stay where they are in case of military actions or an Israeli occupation." "Nun" Operation Order, Operations Directorate, April 1952, IDFA 109/1034/1965.

[71] Beatings, robberies, shootings, and various threats of future violence were all meant to persuade the locals to move to Hebron. Morris, *The Birth of the Palestinian Refugee Problem Revisited*, 522–525.

Manshia Palestinians has never been presented as evidence. Yet, if such a directive indeed occurred, Ben-Gurion's knowledge and control of the IDF's actions there were surprisingly minimal.

In a meeting that took place on March 16, 1949, formally intended to discuss "Personnel and Budget Cuts in the Army," the prime minister, in a sharp detour off topic, asked members of the general staff "whether it is true that the army in the south threatened the Arabs in Iraq-Manshia that it would unleash a Pogrom [*sic*] against them if they will not disappear? Is there any substance to this?" CGS Dori replied that "there was some of this. There were such thoughts, but people were told specifically not to do it. But still there was a campaign of 'whispering propaganda.'" Maj. Gen. Yadin interfered in the conversation and further explained: "There was a campaign of 'whispering propaganda' by all kinds of good people ... It's true that the army wants to revenge its dead, but the government keeps it from doing so."[72] The exchange suggests that Ben-Gurion had no knowledge of and certainly did not authorize the IDF's initiative to terrorize the inhabitants of Iraq-al-Manshia into leaving their village (if only due to Israel's official guaranteeing of the safety of civilians caught in the Faluja pocket in late February 1949, a promise the IDF obviously had no interest in or intention of keeping). While certainly not acting in defiance of the government or against the grain of its intentions, it is obvious that none of the practitioners awaited orders on the matter or volunteered information to the civilian authorities.[73]

The discussion that induced Ben-Gurion to ask about the whereabouts of the forces in Faluja and Iraq-al-Manshia sheds light on the IDF's motivations in pursuing the expulsions there. Maj. Gen. Yadin used the southern front as an example of the principles that should govern personnel cuts in the IDF. The logic was simple: the government should temporarily avoid cuts on fronts where large-scale actions might occur. The Egyptians are "a dormant volcano," Yadin commented, "but it's obvious that between Gaza and Rafah there is a volcano far greater than the Egyptians: 150 thousand local Arabs. The forces

---

[72] Ben-Gurion, Dori. and Yadin, GS Meeting, March 16, 1949, IDFA 9/847/1962. It is possible that Ben-Gurion, always aware of history's future verdict of his conduct, chose to ask his question despite knowing, if not the details, then the general trend of the IDF's actions in the Faluja pocket. This, however, does not negate the fact that the IDF took an independent action there, against the state's international commitment. More than Ben-Gurion's question, the answers that he received from Dori and Yadin attest to their indifference to this sort of diplomatic commitment and their subordination to it.

[73] In a letter to Dori, Moshe Sharett, Israel's foreign minister, bluntly referred to the IDF's "whispering propaganda" as an "unauthorized initiative by the local commander in a matter relating to Israeli government policy." Quoted by Morris, *The Birth of the Palestinian Refugee Problem Revisited*, 523. Sharett reminded the CGS that such actions may carry far-reaching political implications, such as staining Israel's name and sincerity in the United Nations and vis-à-vis the Egyptians, and might endanger the Jews of Egypt.

stirring restlessness there are many."[74] In other words, the IDF was in the difficult position of having to balance between its ability to respond to conventional and sub-conventional threats. Stretched to its limit, it was tempting to try to neutralize one threat so as to provide its forces with the necessary freedom to maneuver when challenged to fend off either an Egyptian or a Jordanian attack.[75]

The remaining residents of Iraq-al-Manshia left their village on April 21–22, 1949. Their expulsion was an IDF-initiated action, which was in accordance with government goals, yet it was also completely independent of governmental authorization. Most importantly, it was justified with operational and security necessities, which for the IDF clearly overruled civil authority. When examined through a tactical prism – local villagers might facilitate infiltration and terror missions – and fueled by feelings of revenge, nothing was considered outside the scope of the IDF's authority, as much as it was politically charged.

Iraq-al-Manshia is merely an early and by no means isolated example of the IDF creating "facts on the ground" without governmental approval. In this case, as would happen again in the future, it received ex post facto approval and support. Instances like this would eventually become habituated and normatively legitimated by the 1950s reprisal policy operations, culminating in the fateful political consequences of local IDF action during the Six Day War in 1967. All of these cases shared an underlying pattern set in 1949: the IDF would act as it saw fit whenever an operational opportunity (or threat) presented itself, regardless of the Israeli government's opinion, formal policy, and even explicit orders. Iraq-al-Manshia's story may sound banal and insignificant in the greater scheme of things. But it clearly embodies a disconnect between the IDF's officially espoused values and the underlying assumptions informing its actions. The same organization could, on one hand, pride itself on subordination to civil authorities and adherence to a strict policy of political noninvolvement. Yet at the same time, it could bluntly disregard those guiding principles when an opportunity to pursue its interests presented itself, regardless of the ramifications of such actions. No documents exist that unequivocally support this claim beyond the case of Iraq-el-Manshia. Yet, at least on the southern front, we can reasonably assume that such military initiative was hardly unique or infrequent.[76]

---

[74] Yadin, GS Meeting, March 16, 1949, IDFA 9/847/1962.

[75] Ibid. Referencing the pressing security problem posed by the 150,000 refugees, Dori again mentioned the volatile southern front and Arab successes there in clashes with small IDF forces in May. Dori, GS Meeting, May 1949, IDFA 10/847/1962.

[76] Morris too suggests that, at least in the case of Faluja, the IDF "set the policy in motion, with the civil and political authorities often giving approval after the fact." Ibid., 505. Morris included Iraq-al-Manshia in this trend; however, he claimed that Yosef Weitz and David Ben-Gurion ordered the IDF to initiate the terrorizing of the villagers. Ibid., 524.

Even in its infancy, the IDF was not an obedient creation of Ben-Gurion and other politicians. It was never an entity that acquiesced to the authority of others in the process of its own design, as well as in the formation of the state of Israel. The IDF's leadership determined from the beginning to have more than a mere say in policy matters. It was intent on setting and directing policy in matters deemed pertinent to the problem of "security." Above all, the IDF wanted to and was able to guarantee its freedom from governmental constraints on matters related to military operational necessity. Both "security" and "military operations," moreover, were definitions applied liberally. They were rarely understood as having political implications, and were therefore seldom acknowledged as the purview of governmental authority.

This pattern evolved during the War of Independence and continued between 1949 and 1953, when Israel initiated the reprisal policy. Contra previous accounts of the Israeli military in its infancy, the IDF's tendency to take independent action did not appear out of thin air in the 1950s. Matured in the mid-1950s and steadily escalating and entrenching itself since, the IDF's freedom of action peaked in 1982, before and during the Lebanon War.[77] Isra'el Tal noted in 1996 that "no one disputes the military command's subordination to political leadership, [yet] the IDF has become over the years a self-ruling, autonomous, dominating institution whose authority and responsibilities extend far beyond the limits defined in the early days of the state."[78] This pattern was clearly and self-consciously apparent in IDF practices from its birth.

Conclusion

The events shaping the IDF's early history are inherently interesting in their own right, but they also provide a useful key for explaining behavioral patterns and traditions of thought and practice in military organizations more generally. Even when such patterns were almost entirely absent, they would quickly emerge – possibly catalyzed into motion by a trauma of the magnitude of the War of Independence – and then rapidly become habituated into traditions and cemented into worldviews bequeathed from one generation to the next. The process was to a large extent self-conscious and reflective and in large part predesigned and forced from above. The young officers, who formed the majority of the Israeli military leadership for years to come, exemplified something unique and rare. They designed and then realized an almost ex

---

[77] For an analysis of distraught civil-military relations, including large-scale deception of the government by the minister of defense and military leadership before and during the Lebanon War, see Zeev Maoz, *Defending the Holy Land* (Ann Arbor, MI, 2006), 171–230, and Ze'ev Schiff and Ehud Ya'ari, *Israel's Lebanon War* (New York, 1984).

[78] Isra'el Tal, *National Security: The Few against the Many* [in Hebrew] (Tel Aviv, 1996), 108.

nihilo military culture, one that was not merely the sum or intersection of their collective pre-IDF histories as members of semi-guerrilla, militia, or established foreign armed forces. It was, as they intended it to be, a completely new concoction. And it reflected the values and spirit they deemed worthy and appropriate for the new Jewish state. Finally, it embodied the lessons from their formative experiences in the War of Independence.

This self-fashioning process is somewhat counterintuitive. But it is hardly surprising considering the environment and climate that birthed the state of Israel as well as its armed forces. The Zionist project was ultimately the product of a top-down process of nation building. It produced a new nation, one that required new institutions to serve its cause. As an ideology, Zionism emphatically rejected old and foreign notions of nationalism as obsolete or inappropriate for the "new Jew." This logic naturally extended to the IDF.

Yet the IDF's organizational climate was not a mere mindless reflection of the Zionist zeitgeist. The IDF was an army that, overall, exercised more agency in the process of its own making and shaping than was previously assumed. It was a self-conscious actor that did not limit its actions to the realm of military operations. From 1949 onward, it systematically impacted political, economic, and social processes. The IDF was never merely a silent golem or acquiescent creation of David Ben-Gurion and other politicians of the Yishuv and the young Israeli government; it was kicking and screaming from its birth.[79]

The seeds of the IDF's organizational culture – the offensive and aggressive spirit, the political shortsightedness, and the tendency toward disobedience to civil authority – appeared at its infancy. Yet this military culture was not, of course, fully matured by 1949; not even by the early 1950s had it matured. The emerging mind-set was initially shared predominantly by members of the military's leadership. It would take several years for it to congeal and propagate across the lower-ranking fighting forces.

This new culture was initially disseminated through various mechanisms: elite units, the education corps, concerted socialization of new cadres of officers, and ultimately the propagation of military myths through society at large. These would eventually facilitate the maturation of declared values into norms and habitual practices, while sometimes radicalizing them. The offensive spirit would turn, at times, into operational aggression and shortsightedness, as expressed in the crisis leading to the Six Day War. It would encourage disobedience in the name of success, as exhibited several times during the 1956 Sinai campaign. And it would lead to a chronic tendency toward liberally reinterpreting orders, at all levels, as overtly and repeatedly practiced at the

---

[79] For this view of Ben-Gurion's control of the IDF, see, for instance, Peri, *Between Battles and Ballots*, 59–61, and Cohen, *Supreme Command*, 133–172.

height of the mid-1950s retaliation policy.[80] The relations between the IDF and the government would ultimately become more nuanced as the military leadership gained experience and operational success and exercised greater self-confidence in light of its growing social prestige. The government for its part supported and amplified, both in word and in action, every single one of these organizational tendencies.[81]

While one would suspect that it took some time for the IDF's early hodge-podge of ideas to cement into a powerful system of normative assumptions, the process unfolded over a surprisingly short period. The rapid and self-conscious creation of an effective organizational culture is perhaps the founding generation's most groundbreaking achievement, one that exceeded its own expectations.

Yet there is more that we can learn from the IDF's example about the dynamics of cultural persistence and change. Once established, culture will quickly stabilize, even in the face of enormous pressures imposed by a highly challenging and changing external reality. The lessons learned from the myriad conflicts the IDF engaged in over the years consistently failed to leave a dent on its core cultural values. If anything, its cultural tendencies intensified and ossified, cataclysmically climaxing during the First Lebanon War of 1982. The crisis of confidence in the IDF that ensued forced the organization, for the first time in its history, to reflectively reevaluate the logic of its practice. The fast-forming and slow-evolving organizational culture of the IDF holds the key to understanding both its victories and its failures.

---

[80] Vardi, "Pounding Their Feet."

[81] For earlier expressions of independent military outlook and stance, see GS Meeting, April 4, 1952, "War Planning," especially the words of Chief of Staff Yadin. IDFA 21/847/62. Note, however, that in the early 1950s, the high command had to work long and hard to implement this spirit in the rest of the army.

12   The Weight of the Shadow of the Past

The Organizational Culture of the Iraqi Army, 1921–2003

Kevin M. Woods

This chapter explores the organizational culture of Iraq's army between its founding in 1921 and its collapse by the time of the American invasion in 2003. During this eighty-two-year history, the alignment of the organizational culture of the Iraqi Army moved from the face of a foreign occupation in the 1920s to a political tool of internal social and political coercion, to "probably the most potent military ever wielded by an Arab government."[1] However, by the time American troops pulled down the statue of Saddam Hussein in Baghdad's Firdos Square, the health of the army's organizational culture was well beneath its pinnacle and a mere echo of its historic norm.

Assessments of organizational cultures are often over-correlated with effectiveness; however, as Leonard Wong and others have argued, "organizational cultures are not good or bad, right or wrong; rather, they are either aligned or misaligned with the organization's environment."[2] The story of the creation, development, and devolution of a military's organizational culture provides a useful case study into the power of legacy and the potential for change under extraordinary circumstances, as well as the fragility of a misaligned organizational culture.

Any discussion of the organizational culture of Iraq's military is essentially a discussion about Iraq's army, and more specifically its officer corps. For

** This chapter does not represent the position of the Institute for Defense Analyses or the Department of Defense. The author would like to thank the participants in the Culture of Military Organizations Conference and the volume editors for comments and suggestions. Special thanks to my colleagues Dr. Peter Picucci, Dr. Alec Wahlman, and Carolyn Leonard for their thoughtful review comments. The title of this chapter is borrowed from Dan Reiter's argument that significant security decisions of minor powers "were determined mainly by lessons drawn from formative national experiences, and only marginally by variations in the levels of external threat." See " Learning, Realism, and Alliances: The Weight of the Shadow of the Past," *World Politics* 46 (July 1994), 490–526, 490.

[1] Kenneth M. Pollack, *Arabs at War: Military Effectiveness, 1948–1991* (Lincoln, NE, 2002), 552.
[2] Stephen J. Gerras, Leonard Wong, and Charles D. Allen, "Organizational Culture: Applying a Hybrid Model to the U.S. Army," Monograph, US Army War College (November 2008), 8.

most of Iraq's history, the army officer corps had an outsized impact on the political sphere. Fundamental and unresolved conflicts between the external and internal roles of the armed forces created and shaped the organizational culture of the Iraqi Army. Even when the organizational culture and operating environment were aligned, the effects of ruthless regime coup-proofing measures, which ironically enabled alignment, set the conditions for its inevitable collapse.

To explore the organizational culture of Iraq's army, this chapter considers the major factors that shaped its development. The first section examines some of the pre-Iraqi antecedents of culture, which in spite of the distance in time, influenced expectations of what a military raised in the land of Mesopotamia should do. The second section looks at the impact that two occupying powers, the Ottomans and the British, had on the development of Iraqi military culture. Next is an examination of the transformative impact that the Ba'ath Party, ruthless coup-proofing measures, and two major external wars had on the army's organizational culture. The fourth section discusses the impact of the military disaster in Kuwait and the subsequent decade of sanctions. The chapter concludes by assessing the arc of change during the Iraqi Army's eighty-two-year history and what it says about military culture after the fall of the Ba'ath Party from power.

The Long Shadow over Iraq's Military Culture

Mesopotamia, as the "cradle of civilization," holds the distinction of being among the first regions to produce many things considered bedrocks of human progress: writing, mathematics, astrology, law, and medicine, as well as organized warfare. Ancient Mesopotamian cultures cast long shadows over Iraq's modern military culture. Sumerian, Akkadian, Babylonian, Hittite, Hurrian, Kassite, and Assyrian cultures rose, expanded, and collapsed into dust, but all added to the myths and legends of great military prowess.

Saddam Hussein often used cultural references to the peoples, events, or lessons plundered from more than fifty centuries of recorded history. When he did not use these rhetorical images for self-glorification, he used them to erase sectarian or other social distinctions by harkening back to a mythic pre-Islamic unity of Arab peoples.[3] At other times, Saddam used the past to delineate racial or other divides. In the run-up to the Iran-Iraq War, for instance, he would often sprinkle references to the empire of the Elmaites

---

[3] See Amatzia Baram, *Saddam Husayn and Islam: Ba'thi Iraq from Secularism to Faith* (Baltimore, MD, 2014), 172–177, and Amatzia Baram, *Culture, History and Ideology in Ba'thist Iraq, 1968–1989* (London, 1991).

or to the threat of the "yellow snake," invoking distant memories of the Mongol invasion.[4]

Iraqi leaders often articulated and justified strategic aspirations with claims of an unbroken military culture stretching back through history. One historian identified the Sumerian concept of the "big man" or the cult of the "great man" as an enduring attribute of Iraqi culture. Such an individual could earn wealth, power, and status based on proving himself "more able than others."[5] Saddam, Iraq's last "great man," was quick to draw parallels to Nebuchadnezzar "to remind Iraqis of their [pre-Islamic] historical responsibilities" and to Saladin, a "great leader because he was able to make great use of the nation's spirit; he breathed life into it, united it, and gave it aim and purpose."[6] Another commentator noted of the region's ancient leaders: "If the Gods had transcendent powers, kings had armies."[7] The implicit legacy of this history, and the basis for Iraqi civil-military relations, was a military in service to the leader, not to the nation or the state.

While cultural legacies represent merely "part of the process of decision-making and behavior, but neither exhaustive of it nor a static element within it," they nevertheless matter.[8] Mesopotamia had an explicit concept of time that envisioned the past as something you watched as you moved through life. In effect, one walked backward into the future because the only reliable source of knowledge was the past. Under such a concept, the future was not only never far from the past, it was often subservient to it.[9]

Thirteenth-century historian Ibn Khaldun described the general organizational principle of Arabs as tribal.[10] Tribes across the ancient Arab world were essentially mini-states possessing autonomy over social, cultural, economic, political, and military issues. The agricultural or "urban" elites, also nominally tribal, both feared and admired the nomadic or Bedouin tribes. The mythic military superiority of the Bedouins was credited to the fact that all males were considered warriors, "free of government, and their very means of substance, based on camel or horse

[4] Jerry M. Long, *Saddam's War of Words: Politics, Religion, and the Iraqi Invasion of Kuwait* (Austin, TX, 2004), 69.
[5] William R. Polk, *Understanding Iraq* (New York, 2005), 20–21.
[6] Saddam Hussein, quoted in Fuad Matar, *Saddam Hussein: A Biography* (London: 1990), 235.
[7] Benjamin R. Foster, *The Age of Agade: Inventing Empire in Ancient Mesopotamia* (New York, 2016), 166.
[8] Patrick Porter, *Military Orientalism: Eastern War through Western Eyes* (Oxford, 2013), 81.
[9] Stefan M. Maul, "Walking Backwards into the Future: The Conception of Time in the Ancient Near East," in Tyrus Miller, ed., *Given World and Time: Temporalities in Context* (Budapest, 2008), 15–24, 15.
[10] Ibn Khaldun, *The Muqaddimah: An Introduction to History*, Nessim Joseph Dawood, ed., Franz Rosenthal, trans. (Princeton, NJ, 2009), 91–122.

breeding, are the very instruments of their mobile force backed by vast manpower."[11]

Tribes did not simply threaten notions of a centralized government; throughout the region's history, the tribes have always been an important, if unstable, source of "informal political power, mobilized manpower, and legitimacy.[12]" In the seventh century, armies marching under a banner of Islam conquered more territory than all the Middle Eastern empires that preceded them. These early Muslim armies defeated the Byzantine and Sasanian armies not with highly structured military forces, but by organizing men who "fought for their religion, the prospect of booty and because their friends and fellow tribesmen were doing it."[13] However, as external threat faded, even the binding power of Islam could not control the complex mix of tribal, sectarian, ethnic, and social groups.[14]

By the early twentieth century, most of these tribes had become increasingly large, sedentary, collective quasi-political organizations, but "the bulk of the settled population of the country, whether Arab or Kurd, was tribally organized and retained tribal mores and customs."[15] As Iraq's first king lamented, in the early 1930s, there was no Iraqi nation, but rather "[a] human mass devoid of any patriotic notion, full of traditions and religious nonsense and absurdities and there is nothing that is binding them together. They are quick to do mischief, inclined towards anarchy, ready to rise at any time against any government whatsoever."[16]

It is not surprising, then, that much of Iraq's modern military culture was the product of the interaction between emerging concepts of nationalism and much older social frameworks of tribalism. As a result, an organizational culture developed that extolled the virtues of the tribal warrior, while simultaneously worrying over the threat tribes presented to a unified state. For Saddam, history was the clearest indicator of things to come and the basis of his military outlook. Despite directing a modern military through two major wars, his "concept of war … did not adapt to modern times." As one of Iraq's corps

---

[11] Faleh Abdul-Jabar, "Sheiks and Ideologues: Deconstruction and Reconstruction of Tribes under Patrimonial Totalitarianism in Iraq, 1968–1998," in Faleh Abdul-Jabar and Hosham Dawod, eds., *Tribes and Power: Nationalism and Ethnicity in the Middle East* (London, 2003), 69–109, 72–73.

[12] Keiko Saki, "Tribalism As a Tool of State Control in Iraq: Observations on the Army, Cabinets, and the National Assembly," in Faleh Abdul-Jabar and Hosham Dawod, eds., *Tribes and Power: Nationalism and Ethnicity in the Middle East* (London, 2003), 136–159, 139–140.

[13] Hugh Kennedy, *The Armies of the Caliphs: Military Society in the Early Islamic State* (London, 2001), 6.

[14] For a succinct summary of the complex social milieu, see Bernard Lewis, "On Revolutions in Early Islam," *Studia Islamica* 32 (1970), 215–231.

[15] Phoebe Marr, *The Modern History of Iraq*, 3rd edn. (Boulder, CO, 2012), 19.

[16] Adeed Dawisha, *Iraq: A Political History from Independence to Occupation* (Princeton, NJ, 2009), 61.

commanders recalled, "Saddam could only imagine war as a tribal conflict or like the conflict between Alexander the Macedonian and the Persian King Darius or the conflict between Salahdin and the Crusades ... Saddam never realized there was a huge difference between modern war and ancient war."[17] In Saddam's version of the concept of the warrior king, rhetorical prowess and the will to control those with the means to remove him from power were adequate substitutes for demonstrated knowledge of military art and science.

External Sources of Iraqi Military Culture

In 1535, Ottoman ruler Sultan Suleiman the Magnificent marched into Baghdad and upended nearly 300 years of ruinous rule by Mongol chieftains and petty tyrants. During much of the next four centuries, competition between the predominately Shia Safavid Empire to the east and the Sunni Ottoman Empire to the west would determine events in Iraq. However, it would be the "Ottoman System," led by a small cadre of officials who exploited the natives for taxes while allowing a degree of local autonomy, which would frame the organizational culture of a future Iraqi military. This was the beginning of a professional military class in Iraq whose cultural touchstones were not the same as the population they nominally served.[18]

In the early nineteenth century, facing manpower shortages and increasing numbers of recalcitrant populations, the Ottoman Army instituted two policies that would influence the future organizational culture of the Iraqi military. First, it increasingly conscripted local Arabs, often from contending rural tribes, into a new army. This policy inculcated the peoples of Mesopotamia with the education, traditions, and outlook of a professional army. In addition, it offered yet another path to power for tribal leaders often at odds with each other as much as they were with the central authorities. Finally, it began a tradition where the army was seen as a "willing collaborator" with a foreign power.[19]

Arab officers of the late Ottoman Army were part of a distinct military culture that, while familiar, was unique to the still provincial nature of the future Iraq. Dysfunctional civil-military relations, a promotion system "largely based on favoritism and patron client relationships," and ineffective staff organizations above the battalion level characterized Ottoman military culture in the closing decades of the empire.[20]

---

[17] Ra'ad Hamdani, quoted in Kevin M. Woods, Williamson Murray, and Thomas Holaday with Mounir Elkhamri, *Saddam's War: An Iraqi Military Perspective of the Iran-Iraq War*, McNair Paper 70 (Washington, DC, 2009), 94.

[18] Bruce Masters, *The Arabs of the Ottoman Empire, 1516–1918: A Social and Cultural History* (Cambridge, 2013), 5.

[19] Ibid., 47.

[20] Mesut Uyar and Edward J. Erickson, *A Military History of the Ottomans: From Osman to Ataturk* (Santa Barbara, CA, 2009), 176–202.

Second, Ottoman governors increasingly commissioned auxiliary forces from among local tribes and through agreements with local religious leaders. Once created, however, these private militias became difficult to control, and at various times they challenged and even usurped the power of the local representatives of the Ottoman state.[21] For most of the last century of the empire's reign, Ottoman reformers tried to reclaim the authority that had devolved to the tribes through a policy of "divide and rule" designed to fragment increasingly powerful tribal confederations.

By the end of the nineteenth century, the Ottomans regarded the tribes of Mesopotamia as "a major obstacle to good government ... economic and social progress" as well as "a standing menace to law and order ... recalcitrant to taxation and conscription and an obstacle to the establishment of effective government authority."[22] It was clear, as one commentator argues, that "neither the devastating invasion of Hulaku Khan nor almost four centuries of Ottoman rule could eradicate" the Arab (tribal) influence.[23]

At the end of the First World War, British forces loosely occupied the three former Ottoman *vilayets* that now constitute Iraq.[24] During the next dozen years, a complex mix of domestic and foreign competitors vied for control of the state. In a cycle repeated throughout Mesopotamian history, perceived weakness of central political and military control (primarily in Baghdad) occasioned the resurgence of tribal authority, only to be resisted by a return to central control.

In 1920, a large southern (primarily Shia) tribal uprising began against British occupation, which soon gained support among others (including urban and rural Sunnis) who held anti-colonialist, nationalist, or nascent pan-Arabist beliefs. After four months and hundreds of causalities, British firepower succeeded in putting down the rebellion. Although it failed, the violence energized a new nationalism, forced London to pursue policies to put an Iraqi face on the occupation, and accelerated the creation of an independent state and army.[25]

The British quickly maneuvered their preferred candidate, Faisal ibn Husayn or Faisal I, onto the Iraqi throne.[26] The new king's attitude toward those who would serve in his new government was less than enlightened. Faisal I described the Kurdish and the Shia as unqualified to serve in government

---

[21] Virginia Aksan, *Ottoman Wars, 1700–1870: An Empire Besieged* (London, 2007), 44–75.
[22] Gokhan Cetinsaya, *Ottoman Administration of Iraq, 1890–1908* (London, 2006), 72–73.
[23] Mohammad Tarbush, *The Role of the Military in Politics: A Case Study of Iraq to 1941* (London, 1982), 8.
[24] The Ottoman *vilayets* were Mosul, Baghdad, and Basra.
[25] A contemporary British perspective on the uprising is well told in Sir Almer Haldane's *The Insurrection in Mesopotamia, 1920*, 2nd edn. (New York, 2005). Significant similarities exist between the dynamics and even the tactics of 1920 and those that began in the summer of 2003.
[26] Faisal was the son of the leader of the Arab revolt and Britain's First World War ally against the Ottoman Empire, the Sharif of Mecca Hussein ibn Ali'.

(including the military) owing to "the oppression they had under the Turkish rule," which "did not enable them to participate … or give them the training to do so."[27] Consequently, the Shia majority, who had led the 1920 revolt, found themselves omitted not only from the selection of a monarch but also from the very state they had helped to create.

In 1921, the British authorized the creation of an Iraqi national army, designed to be small, nonthreatening to the colonial system, and under the strict control of British forces occupying Iraq under a League of Nations mandate. The native army's primary purpose was to protect the new monarchy and to serve as a deterrent against the "more powerful than the well-armed tribes."[28] Given the state of relations between the ruling elites and the Shia and Kurdish populations, the army also had a requirement to be prepared to put down two revolts simultaneously.[29] This focus on internal control, whether inherited from the Ottomans or designed by the British, dominated the context in which the army's organizational culture would operate.

The officer corps for the new army came from Iraqis who had served in the Ottoman Army and had either defected to the Arab Revolt in 1915 (so-called Sharifians who were intensely loyal to the Ali family) or who were part of a later group of former Ottomans who joined after 1918.[30] Among the important social characteristics of these officers, especially the Sharifians, were that they were predominately long-time ex-patriots, Sunni, secular, not from noble (i.e., tribal) bloodlines, and prone to conspiratorial political activity. Many of the positions in the new Iraqi Army were held by Sharifian veterans, who were also members of the anti-Ottoman/pan-Arab secret society known as Al-'Ahd (The Covenant).[31]

In terms of professional outlook, this first generation of officers was raised in the German-influenced Ottoman military education and general staff system. Attributes of this modified Prussian model included preserving the established order, unifying the state, serving as the bastions of values and ideas, and embracing "the theory that [an aristocratic notion of] character in an officer mattered more than intellect." They possessed little patience for what they saw as political incompetence or waffling in national leaders. More

[27] Essay by Faisal I circulated among his closest advisors, cited in Abbas Kadhim, *Reclaiming Iraq: The 1920 Revolution and the Founding of the Modern State* (Austin, TX, 2012), 151.
[28] King Faisal I's confidential memorandum of March 1933, Hanna Batatu, *The Old Social Classes and the Revolutionary Movements of Iraq: A Study of Iraq's Landed and Commercial Classes and of Its Communists, Ba'thists, and Free Officers*, 3rd paperback printing (Princeton, NJ, 1989), 26.
[29] Eliezer Be'eri, *Army Officers in Arab Politics and Society* (New York, 1969), 327.
[30] This later group included Ottoman personnel who were released from British prisoner of war camps in India and shipped back to Iraq. Not surprising, some were reluctant to fight for their former captors against their former sovereign. Batatu, *The Old Social Classes*, 172, fn. 117.
[31] Ibid., 322.

important, they influenced the development of state institutions beyond the military. Most of the prime ministers and cabinet officials in the first few years of an independent Iraq had been Ottoman officers; more than 80 percent of officers commanding the early Iraqi Army were ex-Ottoman officers educated in Istanbul.[32] These men shared a common professional culture, as reformers and nationalists, and, more important, as the ultimate guarantors of the state and nation.

The Emergence of a Distinct Iraqi Military Culture

After Iraq achieved its independence in 1932, King Faisal's first priority was to continue to develop the army. Iraq, he wrote in March 1933, would never "progress toward genuine statehood" without a strong army. To that end, he established the army's second mission: to serve as the essential "spinal column for nation-forming."[33] As Faisal saw it, his problem was not the logic of his design, but the nature of the raw material. His assessment of the Iraqi population was that they were "prone to anarchy, and perpetually ready to rise against any government whatever."[34] Just after gaining independence, Faisal estimated that the restive tribes in Iraq were in possession of more than 100,000 rifles, while his army and police forces could muster no more than a fraction of that number.[35] The army's first test was just over the horizon.

In 1932, the Iraqi Assyrian minority, who had been a source of levies for the British military, clashed with Iraqi forces. Iraqi Army units, based in Mosul, ruthlessly put down the rebellion. A year later, a series of tribal rebellions began in the Middle Euphrates region of southern Iraq.[36] During the next several years, Iraqi troops and a nascent air force suppressed the southern tribes while "meting out savage punishment." Using a tactic that would become a routine tool of population control, the Iraqi Army executed a campaign of village destruction, mass incarceration, and summary executions with "corpses left hanging for all to see and ponder the unforgiving power of the state."[37] While

---

[32] Reeva Spector Simon, *Iraq between the Two World Wars: The Military Origins of Tyranny* (New York, 2004), 16.
[33] King Faisal, confidential memorandum dated March 1933, cited in Batatu, *The Old Social Classes*, 26. Under the terms of the Anglo-Iraqi Treaty of 1930, the British provided for the external defense of Iraq.
[34] Ibid., 25.   [35] Be'eri, *Army Officers in Arab Politics and Society*, 326–327.
[36] The causes of the revolts are complex and range from changes in land rights, general frustration at the lack of representation in Baghdad, and attempts by Arab Sunni politicians to "dissolve Shi'i particularism in a philosophy of secular Arab nationalism." Marr, *The Modern History of Iraq*, 42.
[37] Dawisha, *Iraq: A Political History*, 39.

these Arab tribes remained an ever-present source of power and dread, they shaped but did not threaten the stability of the state again until 1991.

The 1930s was also a period of rapid organizational development for the Iraqi Army. Between 1932 and 1941, Iraqi forces grew from eleven infantry battalions, two cavalry regiments, and five artillery batteries supported by a single squadron of aircraft to forty-five infantry battalions, twenty-four artillery batteries, and seven squadrons of aircraft.[38] A new generation of officers educated at the Royal Iraqi Military College (established just after the founding of the army) using translated British military texts manned the expanded force.[39] Most of the young officers were Sunni and hailed from urban areas of Iraq, while the conscripted force was tribal.

From the mid-1930s until the beginning of the Iran-Iraq War, the army underwent an uneven process of developing its organizational culture and an almost continuous engagement in the political life of the state. A wide range of political parties, beginning with Iraqi nationalist, pan-Arab nationalist, and Royalist factions, and later including Nasserist Free Officer Republicans, communists, and finally Ba'athists, co-opted, manipulated, supported, leveraged, or were victims of the military's willingness and ability to change or intimidate the political powers in Baghdad. External actors, primarily British, but also German and later American governments, would try to shape events by manipulating the structure or orientation of the Iraqi military. Rather than Faisal's "spinal column" around which a state could be built, the military quickly became like Iraq's great rivers, essential for survival but prone to destructive floods.

Beginning with the Bakir Sadiqi coup d'état of October 1936, military officers forced or attempted to force (sometimes violently) a change in government fifteen times between 1936 and 1968.[40] This propensity for military intervention in civil government created an environment in which political decisions regarding military effectiveness, base locations, and even under what circumstances the army could access ammunition constituted existential policy. Perhaps most problematic was the expectation among officers that as they rose in rank, they too would play a part of the game. Looking across this history, "one can say that the army featured more prominently in political bargaining than in military action."[41]

From its founding through the beginning of the Iran-Iraq War, Iraq's armed forces rarely engaged conventionally armed or organized opponents. During

[38] Pesach Malovany, *Wars of Modern Babylon: A History of the Iraqi Army from 1921 to 2003* (Lexington, KY, 2017), 15–16.
[39] Tarbush, *The Role of the Military in Politics*, 78–79.
[40] Be'eri, *Army Officers in Arab Politics and Society*, 246–250. See also Michael Eppel, *Iraq from Monarchy to Tyranny: From the Hashemites to the Rise of Saddam* (Gainesville, FL, 2004).
[41] Peter Sluglett quoted in Tarbush, *The Role of the Military in Politics*, 185.

those few occasions when they did operate outside of a counterinsurgency or punitive operation, the experience was generally negative. Beginning with the swift defeat of the pro-German Rashid Ali nationalist government at the hands of a small British expeditionary force in 1941, conventional military operations for the next thirty years were more "show-than-go." Before the Arab-Israeli wars of 1973, Iraqi forces made only token appearances on the battlefield.

During the 1948 war in Palestine, Iraq sent a small force (300 officers and 6,000 troops) to join the Arab forces assembled to stop the creation of Israel.[42] During the 1956 Suez Crisis, Iraqi armed forces did not participate beyond mobilizing a defensive show of force owing to the regime's political dependence on Britain. In the 1967 Arab-Israeli War, Iraq deployed a division to Jordan. One brigade participated in fighting near Jericho, but most of Iraq's forces did not arrive before the fighting was over.[43] Most of the delay was the result of logistical issues and the fear of Israeli air strikes during the long, exposed convoy operation.[44] In an anecdote indicative of a general willingness to sacrifice operational effectiveness for regime security, some Iraqi formations arrived without ammunition out of fear the deployment might provide cover for a military coup.[45]

From an organizational culture perspective, engagements against an external foe affected the institutional trajectory of Iraq's armed forces. On the heels of the Arab humiliation in the 1948 war Iraqi leaders decided to expand the army beyond that of a colonial constabulary force. The 1950s saw the addition of armored and engineering forces as well as a more robust general headquarters and logistical organizations.[46] Iraqi political leaders also deftly exploited Britain's desire to prop up its declining influence in the region and American desires to strengthen containment strategy to secure a steady stream of military arms from both nations until 1956.[47] In terms of organizational culture, this change expanded the army's range of missions but not the priorities of its officers.

The nationalist and pan-Arab fury over the 1956 Suez Crisis helped precipitate the end of the Iraqi royal regime by military coup two years later. The coup effectively put an end to significant Western support for and influence over the Iraqi military and opened the door to Soviet influence in Iraqi military culture. In October 1958, the Soviets agreed to train and equip three infantry

---

[42] See Pollack, *Arabs at War*, 743.

[43] The Iraqi air force did employ two Hawker Hunter fighter-bombers and a Tupolev-16 bomber against Israel.

[44] Malovany, *Wars of Modern Babylon*, 48–51, and Pollack, *Arabs at War*, 167.

[45] Malovany, *Wars of Modern Babylon*, 48.   [46] Ibid., 23.

[47] Daniel C. Williamson, "Exploiting Opportunities: Iraq Secures Military Aid from the West, 1953–56," *International Journal of Middle East Studies* 36(1) (February 2004), 89–102.

and one armored division with updated Warsaw Pact systems.[48] By the early 1960s, the Iraqi Army had grown to almost 70,000 troops, and while able to "maintain internal security," it was still judged as capable of offering "only minor harassing actions" against a major power.[49]

The disgrace of Arab forces in the 1967 Arab-Israeli War and Iraq's half-hearted involvement came at the end of what Phoebe Marr calls a "revolutionary decade" in Iraqi politics. Ethnic and sectarian struggles across the state occurred within a context of coups, plots, and a social shift back to localized and tribal roots. Communists, nationalists, and pan-Arabists battled over control of Iraqi politics in a shifting series of alliances. As was the case in decades past, the Iraq military was front and center of these struggles.

The Ba'ath Impact on Iraqi Military Culture

In 1968, a reenergized and savvy Ba'ath Party executed the so-called Ba'ath Revolution. As they briefly had in 1963, the Ba'athists came to power through a military-supported coup. This time, however, the Ba'athists were determined not to repeat their mistakes or those of their predecessors. In addition to a far-reaching social and economic agenda, the Ba'ath Party had a detailed conceptual plan for how it would transform the role of the military in the state. The primary reason was obvious. As Saddam noted in a 1971 interview, the military would be reformed so that "there is no chance for anyone who disagrees with us to jump on a couple of tanks and overthrow the government." The other reasons were, again according to Saddam, because military involvement in politics creates instability, inhibits military modernization, and weakens military effectiveness.[50]

In a process that would take a decade to unfold, the party, under the close supervision of Saddam Hussein, conducted the "Ba'athification" of the officer corps. The objective of Ba'athification, in addition to purging direct and even once-allied internal military threats, was to destroy the notion that military officers were "surrogates and guardians of national identity" and replace it with a comprehensive Ba'ath social organization.[51]

Through a ruthless system of carrots and sticks, political loyalty determined qualification for key military positions, while the party removed men with purely military backgrounds or dubious political leanings. It began at the top.

---

[48] Malovany, *Wars of Modern Babylon*, 25. This support quickly grew to include air forces and the beginnings of Iraq's navy with provisioning of Soviet coastal and riverine boats.

[49] CIA, RDO79S00427A000400060002-8, "The Arab-Israeli Situation (2050/61S) (6 December 1961, declassified 12 May 2000)," 25. Downloaded www.cia.gov/library/readingroom, July 10, 2017.

[50] Ahmed Hashim, "Saddam Husayn and Civil-Military Relations in Iraq: The Quest for Legitimacy and Power," *Middle East Journal* 57(1) (Winter 2003), 9–41, 18.

[51] Kanan Makiya, *Republic of Fear: The Politics of Modern Iraq* (Berkley, CA, 1998), 26–27.

Between the initial Revolutionary Command Council in 1968 and its second instantiation in 1971, military membership at the top of the revolutionary government went from 100 percent to only 5 percent. By the time Saddam consolidated power in 1979, that percentage had been effectively reduced to zero.[52] By the end of the decade, "the Ba'aths under Saddam Hussein had managed to do what no party had done in Iraq's history – it brought the military under civilian control."[53] Ironically and seemingly as an inadvertent by-product, by co-opting the senior officers, the Ba'ath Party created space among more junior officers to focus on the intellectual demands of their profession and less on state politics.

The 1973 Arab-Israeli War was initially an unwelcome test for the Ba'ath regime's transforming military. Unlike the token efforts during previous conflicts, however, this time Baghdad sent a large force of three-plus divisions totaling more than 60,000 troops to join the fight on the Golan Heights.[54] Once again, the Iraqi Army's impact on the battle remained limited owing in part to logistical challenges, piecemeal employment, and a lack of coordination across units and with its Syrian allies. A generous assessment of Iraq's performance was that "of the four Arab armies whose forces saw the lion's share of combat during the October War, Iraq's almost certainly performed the worst."[55] Despite Iraq's disappointing performance, the 1973 war was a strategic milestone in that it provided a glimpse of the kind of regionally relevant force Baghdad would need to build in order to fulfill both its self-described pan-Arab leadership role and, according to Saddam, its historic destiny.

The impact of the 1973 war on the Iraqi Army's culture was also significant. One Iraqi veteran of the war recalled that by "changing the objectives, the mentality of the military leaders, as well as the style of how we fought during the first [1967] war," the Iraqi military felt it was, for the first time, in a position to "challenge the Israeli Army."[56] The war provided the experience and confidence necessary to move more aggressively toward an integrated combined-arms maneuver force. The Iraqi Army had, in its losing effort, "acquired the greatest amount of battle experience since its foundation," especially on operational, logistical, and administrative issues.[57]

Between the 1973 Arab-Israeli War and the invasion of Iran seven years later, the Iraqi military was shaped by two other significant events. The first was a return to large-scale operations against the Kurds. Rebellious Kurdish

---

[52] Faleh Abdul-Jabar, "The Iraqi Army and Anti-Army: Some Reflections on the Role of the Military," in Toby Dodge, ed., *Iraq at the Crossroads*, Adelphi Paper 354 (London, 2007), 115–130, 117.
[53] Ibrahim al-Marashi and Sammy Salama, *Iraq's Armed Forces: An Analytical History* (London, 2008), 128.
[54] Pollack, *Arabs at War*, 167–176.   [55] Ibid., 173.
[56] Hamdani, quoted in Woods, Murray, and Holaday, *Saddam's War*, 22.
[57] Malovany, *Wars of Modern Babylon*, 62.

factions had been a nearly continuous military test for Bagdad. By the mid-1970s, temporary peace between Baghdad and the major Kurdish parties since the mid-1960s collapsed, and the Iraqi Army once again found itself in a major counterinsurgency campaign.[58] This time, the scale of the fighting caught the Iraqi military off guard, in part due to significant support for the Kurds from Iran.[59] In the end, Iraq curtailed what was becoming an expensive and potentially losing campaign by signing a humiliating deal with Iran to cede control to a strategic waterway in return for isolating the Kurds into another decade of relative peace.

The second significant event was a dramatic infusion of resources to the military toward the realization of the Ba'ath objective of becoming the most significant Arab military power in the Middle East. Thanks to Iraq's burgeoning oil production and a steep rise in global prices, the Iraqi military began to rapidly expand and modernize. In a few years, the army doubled in size, growing from six to twelve divisions. Most significantly, both the expansion and the modernization focused on armored units and associated supporting systems (like tank transporters) necessary to support a modern offensive campaign.[60]

The 1970s was considered a kind of intellectual golden age for officers of the Iran-Iraq War generation, especially those who were veterans of the 1967 and 1973 wars. While the effectiveness of Iraq's military left much to be desired, efforts to assess operations honestly, the creation of modern combined-arms forces, and the elevation of military education created a professionalizing environment. In effect, it was a two-tier system, one political and one professional.

Self-described professional officers came to dominate the army's tactical commands, even the occasional division- and corps-level commands. These officers, who were reaching their prime under the Ba'athification process initiated in 1968, nevertheless saw themselves as the vanguard of a new school of military Iraqi officer. Officers from this "reality school" drew sharp distinctions between "real leaders who were wise in thinking and speaking and those who just held high rank but were weak thinkers." The attitude, perhaps more felt than voiced, was "better a good soldier than a good Ba'ath."[61]

As the Iraqi Army grew in both size and technical quality, it also became more complex. After more than fifteen years of steady arms support from the

[58] On the ebb and flow of military operations between governments in Baghdad and Kurdish militias between the 1920s and the 1990s, see David McDowall, *A Modern History of the Kurds* (London, 2009).
[59] The Kurds also received covert support from Israel and the United States. See Douglas Little, "The United States and the Kurds: A Cold War Story," *Journal of Cold War Studies* 12(4) (Fall 2010), 63–98.
[60] Malovany, *Wars of Modern Babylon*, 32.
[61] Quoted in Woods, Murray, and Holaday, *Saddam's War*, 4 and 23.

Soviet Union, political disagreements with Moscow in the mid-1970s moved Iraq to seek diversity in weapons purchases. The preponderance of weapons systems, in the army especially, remained Soviet, but not exclusively so.[62] Supporting systems, everything from aircraft, artillery, transport, and communications, came from a variety of Eastern and Western Bloc sources.[63]

The Iraqi Army's doctrinal foundation was an equally complex mix of foreign influences. Legacy organization and tactical doctrine developed along a British infantry model began to take on Soviet characteristics by the 1970s. That Soviet trainers, advisors, and maintenance technicians influenced the Iraqi tactical forces was not surprising, but the shallowness of their impact, given the technical complexion of the force, was.[64] The barrier to greater influence was primarily the result of Iraq's increasingly well-developed officer education program, which served as a kind of "ideology free zone."

Iraqi officers conducting analyses of modern conventional wars, especially the Arab-Israeli Wars and the Second World War, developed an admiration for Western approaches to doctrine. Many of these officers likely hoped for a move toward a more Western organizational model. It was an uphill climb. In the mid-1970s, Saddam began to express a preference for more Soviet-style military doctrine, presumably because the Marxist undercurrent better aligned with his reading of Ba'ath ideology.[65] Nevertheless, the small professionalizing elements within the Iraqi Army quietly pushed back against "doctrine by political guidance."

The Iraq force that invaded Iran in 1979 was an eclectic one.[66] Intellectually, the officer corps was a mix of professionally educated and politically loyal officers, neither of whom had been tested. Organizationally, the army looked like a British unit employing tactical systems in a hybrid style with adapted

---

[62] Alexander J. Bennett, "Arms Transfer As an Instrument of Soviet Policy in the Middle East," *Middle East Journal* 39(4) (Autumn 1985), 745–774, 759–760.

[63] Iraq's primary arms suppliers through history were: 1920s–1950s (UK); 1960s (UK, USSR, France); 1968–1978 (USSR/France); 1979–1988 (USSR, France, Brazil, Czechoslovakia, Egypt, Germany, China, Austria, South Africa, Italy, and Switzerland). Rachel Schmidt, "Global Arms Exports to Iraq, 1960–1990," *A RAND NOTE* N-3248-USDP (1991), 3–10.

[64] The first Soviet military assistance groups arrived in Iraq in 1958. Iraq's battles with its domestic communist party made relations with Moscow an uneven affair for the next two decades. However, during the 1970s, Iraq received $4.9 billion in Soviet arms, including 2,100 tanks, 1,900 armored personnel carriers, 600 artillery pieces, Scud-B missiles, 190 advanced tactical fighters and other aircraft, helicopters, and missile boats. The Soviets also provided almost 50 percent of the weapons imported into Iraq during the Iran-Iraq War. William H. Mott IV, *Soviet Military Assistance: An Empirical Perspective* (Westport, CT, 2001), 93.

[65] Ra'ad Hamdani, quoted in Kevin M. Woods, Williamson Murray, Elizabeth A. Nathan, Laila Sabara, and Ana M. Venegas, *Saddam's Generals: Perspectives of the Iran-Iraq War* (Washington, DC, 2011), 44.

[66] See Michael Eisenstadt and Kenneth M. Pollack, "Armies of Snow and Sand: The Impact of Soviet Military Doctrine on Arab Militaries," *Middle East Journal* 55(4) (Autumn, 2001), 549–578.

Soviet tactical norms. It was also a tactical force led by officers who aspired to operate more like Western armies even as their political leaders planned for war through the lens of a mythologized past.

Saddam Hussein's consolidation of political power in 1979 was a milestone in Iraq's political history. It was, as one observer put it, "the end of the era of [the] soldier-politician."[67] Saddam and his closest advisors had refashioned the military into an instrument of party control and not a threat to it. Given almost a half-century of politics defined by military coups, this control went deeper than simply, as the leaders before him had arranged, a temporary truce. The institution of the military had fundamentally changed.

One of Saddam's most important tools of control in wielding that instrument was an iron grip on the senior officer corps. Ba'ath political control over the promotion system generally affected the most senior positions, never an optimal situation on the eve of a major war. But the older system of political patronage based on cutthroat political maneuvering might have delivered worse. It appears that below these senior appointments, the development of junior officers remained in the hands of the military, which since the early 1970s, had been increasingly developing and enforcing qualitative standards for training, education, and advancement.

Highly constrained selection at the top of the military hierarchy rested on political loyalty and, better yet, family loyalty. Saddam brought in close political confidants and fellow Tikritis to fill the senior military ranks. For example, he conferred general officer ranks on Izzat Ibrahim al-Duri (a military academy graduate with no service who became one of Saddam's longest-serving advisors), Husayn Kamil (a lieutenant before his promotion to general who ran Iraq's weapons development programs), and Ali Hasan al-Majid (a former corporal who earned the sobriquet "Chemical Ali" late in the Iran-Iraq War). Even Saddam acquired the rank of field marshal.

Other senior promotions went to men like Adnan Khairallah (an armor brigade commander and brother-in-law to Saddam), who was promoted from colonel to general and then appointed minister of defense. His peers considered Khairallah both tactically competent and politically ambitious. Despite some grumbling, many senior officers believed he could be helpful. He was, unlike many of the new instant generals, a soldier and seen as someone who "could protect the army from Ba'ath politics."[68]

A third archetype senior officer was embodied in men like General Abd al-Jabir Shanshal, chief of the Iraqi general staff from 1970 to 1984. Shanshal was respected for his longevity and perhaps even admired for his ability to avoid being on the wrong side of the political purges; however, his position seemed to

---

[67] Abdul-Jabar, "The Iraqi Army and Anti-Army," 118.
[68] Hamdani, quoted in Woods et al., *Saddam's Generals*, 42.

owe as much to a kind of nonthreatening incompetence as it did to Ba'ath Party loyalty. In the run-up to the war with Iran, he led a redesign of Iraq's military planning process, presumably to align it with Ba'ath principles. The result, aptly titled "Guidance for Political Planning of War," was seen by the professionals as "completely different" from what was taught in Iraq's military colleges.[69] Shanshal was to some officers a "logistician, not a leader ... the author of a 'school of thought' within the Iraqi military that refused to take responsibility."[70]

The other major tool of Ba'ath control over the military was the growth of security services designed to monitor not only the threats to the regime but also its guardians. The pervasive nature of Iraq's internal security system is well documented.[71] The corrosive effects on leadership and morale were an impediment to improvements in military effectiveness. Kanan Makiya's description in *Republic of Fear* captures well the impact the Ba'ath Party's violence-laden security apparatus had on society, including the military: "Nothing fragments group solidarity and self-confidence like the gnawing suspicion of having an informer in your midst."[72]

The other principle of coup-proofing in which the Ba'ath Party excelled was the development of parallel institutions. The idea was simple: never allow political power or influence to concentrate in any group with the means to change governments by force. Whether it was the development and growth of the popular army to offset the regular army or the Special Republican Guard to offset the potential risks of an elite Republican Guard, Iraqi resources, talent, and bureaucratic energy were often directed, from the standpoint of military effectiveness, in unproductive directions. The parallelism extended to the very top whereby "injecting kinship and clan groupings into every level of the army, the regime added a much stronger guarantee of loyalty ... [T]he end result was a two-tier system: the party controlled the military and the clan controlled the party."[73]

In fact, coup-proofing and not military effectiveness was the imperative in almost all institutional military decisions during Saddam's three-decade rule. This imperative permeated the organizational culture of Iraq's military from "promotion patterns, training regimes, command arrangements, and information management."[74] However, Saddam's aspirations for Iraq's military included more than keeping it out of politics. His determination to be a regional

---

[69] Ibid., 55.

[70] Interview with Maj. Gen. Aladdin Hussein Makki, in ibid., 114. After stepping down, Shanshal remained a senior military advisor to Saddam as minister of military affairs until 2003.

[71] For a concise organizational description of the security services and the military, see Central Intelligence Agency, "DCI Special Advisor Report on Iraq's WMD," *vol.* 1 (2004).

[72] Makiya, *Republic of Fear*, 63.   [73] Abdul-Jabar, "The Iraqi Army and Anti-Army," 116.

[74] Caitlin Talmadge, *The Dictator's Army: Battlefield Effectiveness in Authoritarian Regimes* (Ithaca, NY, 2015), 140.

and historic player as a military leader drove him to tolerate, albeit with extraordinary surveillance, a degree of independence in the organizational culture of Iraq's military. More important, the course of the Iran-Iraq War demanded it.

The Iran-Iraq War

In a case of political hubris meets untested military assumptions, a small group of trusted staff planned the invasion of Iran, focusing on the narrative value of the action rather than military requirements. The invasion would be Iraq's "historic chance" to elevate morale in the Arab world, and to push its military to "an elite level."[75] When the conflict began in 1980, a little more than a year after Saddam had consolidated his power, the Iraqi war effort lacked anything resembling a coherent strategy, a clear vision, or a realistic assessment of means and ways. Saddam apparently never considered what was required to achieve his "grandiose" goals. According to one observer, the regime's attitude, in a clear rebuttal to the military's reality school, was "as long as one was a Ba'ath he can always be a leader ... therefore there was no problem in a Ba'ath switching from being a politician to a military leader."[76] As a result, the early years of the war were, not surprisingly, disastrous.

The initial invasion unfolded in two major phases. First, the Iraqi Air Force sought to replicate Israeli successes in the 1967 war against Egypt and attempted to destroy the Iranian Air Force on the ground. It failed.[77] Second, the Iraqi Army launched a broad frontal attack into Iran from southeastern Iraq, the objective of which was more a matter of arbitrary distance than of an enemy force or a piece of terrain. A former senior Iraqi staff officer described the invasion plan as nine Iraqi divisions advancing along nine roads with "no main axis of advance, no secondary axis ... we were weak everywhere."[78] It was clear that Iraq could only realize the potential of the investments in equipment, training, and professional education during the 1970s if Saddam understood and recognized their value. He did not, and he would not do so for several war-torn, disillusioning years.

The dysfunctional civil-military relationship between Ba'ath leadership and senior members of the reality school began to change after Iraq's invasion bogged down and was rolled back by Iranian revolutionary and regular forces. Not surprising, the relationship among the military, the regime, and the nature

---

[75] Izzat al-Duri in a discussion with Saddam Hussein, September 16, 1980, quoted in Williamson Murray and Kevin M. Woods, *The Iran-Iraq War: A Military and Strategic History* (Cambridge, 2014), 94.

[76] Quoted in Woods, Murray, and Holaday *Saddam's War*, 25.

[77] Murray and Woods, *The Iran-Iraq War*, 100–104.

[78] Makki, in Woods et al., *Saddam's Generals*, 129.

of the threats facing the regime was a dynamic one. Where fear of a coup had suppressed certain aspects of military effectiveness, fear of losing a war allowed a degree of professionalism to reassert itself.[79] By 1984, a kind of bloody equilibrium had been reached. Recognizing the risk of a long-term campaign against a much larger foe, Saddam sought a way out by horizontally and vertically escalating the war.

First, the Iraqi Navy began to launch operations against Iranian forces in the Persian Gulf, preparing for what would become known as the "Tanker War" against the Iranian oil economy. Iraq then began a campaign that became known as the "War of the Cities" by employing Scud missiles as a psychological weapon against the Iranian population. Finally, Iraq used chemical weapons on the battlefield. The greatest utility of these horrible weapons was to terrorize the Iranian Revolutionary Guard, which lacked the training and equipment to survive on a chemical battlefield.[80] This last tactic spoke to both the ruthlessness and the desperation of an Iraqi regime struggling to adapt well-developed tools of internal coercion against the armed forces of a state adversary.

Failure and perceptions of failure in the first few years also led the regime to attempt to change the situation by applying Voltaire's "Admiral Byng Rule" whereby "it is good to kill an admiral from time to time, to encourage the others."[81] In Basra, the regime held a series of trials to judge any commander who had failed to hold territory. Under the supervision of Izzat al-Duri, one of Saddam's most trusted loyalists, the courts-martial were not "regular trials[s]," but were instead replete with "screaming, yelling and hurling of insults." As one officer at the time recalled, these and subsequent related drumhead courts-martial had a "great impact on the army ... from this point on, commanders chose to avoid responsibility." Fear of failure generated fear of responsibility and commanders simply learned to "wait for an order from higher up before executing any decision."[82]

Given the internal and external pressures on the officer corps at this time, it is somewhat surprising that it was at this moment that the organizational culture percolating just under the surface rose to the occasion. This emergence was also a sometimes counterintuitive result of other factors. A legacy of professional education dating back to the Ottoman era had been renewed and even invigorated in the 1970s. This provided a bubble for professional development

[79] Talmadge, *The Dictator's Army*, 10.
[80] For a discussion of the regime's assessments, analyses, and decisions on the initial employment of chemical weapons, see Murray and Woods, *The Iran-Iraq War*, 220–222.
[81] Voltaire, *Candide* (New York, 1918), 203.
[82] Woods et al., *Saddam's Generals*, 36. According to some reporting, more than 300 senior officers were executed for poor performance in this period. Efraim Karsh and Inari Rautsi, *Saddam Hussein: A Political Biography* (New York, 2002), 167.

generally free from the worst effects of the regime's coup-proofing efforts, and encouraged serious consideration of external threats and external military knowledge.

The Ba'ath regime began to accept the analytical judgments and professional military advice of officers from the reality school. This relatively small group of officers would likely not have existed, certainly not in any significant numbers, in an officer corps singularly obsessed with political manipulation and tribal revolts. Leveraging a small cadre of general officers with extensive operational experience and a wide-ranging military education, the regime began what were essentially two military transformations during the war.

The first was a serious effort to revamp the Iraqi Army's approach to training. Traditional Iraqi training was conducted as a centrally organized annual series of standard events. Early in the war with Iran, all training virtually stopped in order to stem the losses at the front. It soon became clear, however, that a more adaptable system was required. The new program "granted various headquarters complete freedom of action in carrying out their training activities." Commanders at the division level could now pull battalions out of the line to train "in accordance with the operational situation in its sector."[83] In support of the training mission, the Iraqi military instituted a lessons program. Driven by a series of formal "lessons learned" activities at the tactical through operational levels of war, the effort aimed to transmit practical lessons and experience quickly into training. The degree of organizational effort dedicated to this activity was a rarity in Arab armies. By the end of the war, research papers, training plans, conferences, and symposia dealing with lessons from the front were not only routine, but garnered the attention and patronage of Saddam himself.[84]

The second transformation came out of deliberately building a combat development system that could generate effective forces over the long term. The task of normalizing tactical and operational doctrine to match not only the needs of the battlefield but also the reality of Iraq's complex order of battle and the uneven nature of its human capital fell to the Combat Development Directorate (CDD).[85] In addition to developing doctrine, the CDD conducted campaign analyses in order to derive requirements for future military capabilities and updated organizations.

Rather than describe the specific work of the CDD, it is perhaps more informative to consider the background of its director for most of the Iran-Iraq War. General Aladdin Makki was considered a mentor to many of the officers of the realist school. His unusual background made him uniquely

---

[83] Malovany, *Wars of Modern Babylon*, 749.
[84] Makki, in Woods et al., *Saddam's Generals*, 134.
[85] Malovany, *Wars of Modern Babylon*, 741–742.

qualified for the task of blending the concepts underpinning Soviet, British, French, and American doctrine manuals in use at the time.[86] During a career that spanned 1957–1989, Makki alternated operational assignments with a diverse array of professional military education assignments. Before the Iran-Iraq War, he graduated or received a certificate from the British Royal Military Academy at Sandhurst, the British Infantry Platoon and Weapons courses, the British Armor School, the US Army Armor Advance Course, and the French War College.[87] Because he also taught at or commanded most of Iraq's military schools up through the war college, he was in a position to impact the thinking of a generation of officers, most notably in the realist school.[88]

Saddam's support endorsed the growing professionalism of his military not only for what it might do on the battlefield in the present but also for what it might do in the future. During this time, he told a group of senior officers:

> In all circumstances, no country can evaluate its arms or make any improvements to them unless it uses them in the war zone. Countries learn how to fight by fighting actual wars … all scientific advances in the world occurred during and after WWI and WWII. The Western countries use war to their advantage.[89]

The test of this new approach came in the wake of a devastating loss. In early 1986, Iran seized the al Faw Peninsula, which placed the southern flank of the Iraqi defense at risk. This disaster created an opportunity for the Iraqi military to demonstrate whether its efforts at transformation were successful. Despite the continued existence of unqualified Ba'ath generals, the tactical forces were increasingly competent and confident, were much more experienced, and had learned how to engage Saddam on military issues without appearing to pose a threat to the regime. Saddam's trust in the investments in training, education, and officer selection during the previous three years bore fruit: operations to retake the peninsula and then to roll back Iran's earlier gains were, compared to earlier operations, effective. From early 1987 through the end of the war in 1988, the reality school was ascendant in the organizational culture of the Iraqi military,

---

[86] In the end, the Iraqi Army blended doctrinal concepts from many sources, but preferred "American doctrine because we found it to be logical, detailed, and easy to apply." Makki, in Woods et al., *Saddam's Generals*, 134.

[87] Curriculum vitae of Maj. Gen. Aladdin Hussein Makki Khamas, in author's possession.

[88] Positions included an instructor at the Iraqi Military College (1958, 1968) and the Iraqi Staff College (1969, 1974), a professor of strategy at Al-Bakr University for Higher Military Studies (Iraq's war college) (1978), vice president of Al-Bakr University (1979–1981), and president of Al-Bakr University (1988–1989).

[89] Captured audiotape SH-SHTP-A-000-627, "Saddam and Senior Military Officials Discussing Arms Imports and Other Issues Related to the Iran-Iraq War (circa late 1983–early 1984)," cited in Kevin M. Woods, David D. Palkki, and Mark E. Stout, *The Saddam Tapes: The Inner Workings of a Tyrant's Regime 1978–2001* (Cambridge, 2011), 141–146.

even if the strategic decisions were still in the hands of men with questionable strategic and military abilities.

The Kuwait War

Shortly after the Iran-Iraq War, Saddam chose yet another high-risk military adventure. The decision to invade Kuwait in August 1990 stands as one of the worst, or at least the most ill-timed, strategic gambles in modern history. Saddam, aptly using a military analogy, would later tell his senior staff of the logic behind the decision. Iraq in 1990 was "like an army standing before a landmine ... when they stop, the artillery will finish them." The only solution for Iraq when faced with such an obstacle was to "pass it as quickly as possible ... if we were to stop, we could be exposed [and see] the death of our regime."[90]

The Iraqi Army was still the formidable force that had endured the Iran-Iraq War. Eight years of war and operational experience had expanded the pool of officers who operated under the reality school's banner. But the force was also exhausted. Cutbacks in training and maintenance accounts after 1988 had significantly affected the quality of the regular army forces that would occupy and have to defend Kuwait. Even the apparent ease with which Iraqi Republican Guard forces executed the invasion masked the real weaknesses of Iraq's most elite formations in terms of offensive operations that integrated air power and logistics.

The Iraqi leadership expressed confidence publicly and privately in its army's ability to withstand a Western counterattack. Some of the Ba'ath loyalists Saddam had elevated to general on the eve of the Iran-Iraq War had apparently learned little about warfare during eight bloody years, but they had not lost a step in playing to Saddam's preferences. Taha Ramadan told Saddam that he believed "war with America [will be] easier than the war with Iran ... it is going to be an ideal war."[91] Ba'ath military advice was not well supported by objective analysis.[92]

The chief of the general staff at the time of the Kuwait invasion was General Nizar al-Khazraji. Khazraji was considered a professional officer by his peers and, while not as educated as most, was seen as a member of the reality school. Makki described him as a hybrid, a "rare mix – he was a good Ba'ath but also a good, brave, professional soldier who was not afraid of consequences."[93] After the invasion, an operation about which he was purposely not consulted,

[90] Media file, Saddam Hussein in a national command meeting discussing the impact of the Gulf War on the Arab world, circa 1993, cited in Kevin M. Woods, *Mother of All Battles: Saddam Hussein's Strategic Plan for the Persian Gulf War* (Annapolis, MD, 2008), 48.
[91] Media file, State Command and Revolutionary Command Council Meeting (November 1990), cited in ibid., 160.
[92] See ibid., 124–171.   [93] Makki, in Woods et al., *Saddam's Generals*, 139.

Khazraji reportedly briefed Saddam that the qualitative and quantitative differences between Iraqi capabilities and those of the United States was deploying.
He assessed that if the war began, it could threaten the survival of the regime
and that Saddam should reconsider the occupation.[94] Khazraji had a reputation
as an officer who had, during the Iran-Iraq War, respectfully and successfully
convinced Saddam to change his mind with logical, "reality-based"
arguments.[95] The realists had reason to think he would succeed again, but
Saddam dismissed Khazraji from service. This response and the devastating
impact of the war and its aftermath marked the end of the reality school's
influence and the beginning of the descent from the high point of the Iraqi
military's organizational culture.

Iraq's defeat was devastating to the army as an institution, but it was the
aftermath of the war that pulled its army's organizational culture back to a
historical focus on internal control.[96] While successfully suppressed, the tribal
and deserter-supported uprisings in the south between March and May 1991 all
but destroyed the efforts dating back to Faisal I to use the army to build a nation.
Most prominently, the distinction between the "Persian threat" and Iraqi Shia
was lost in the violence, exacerbated by the regime's response, and exploited by
Tehran. The scale and savagery of the operations to suppress the rebellions not
only returned the army's culture to that of an earlier era but also shifted the
value of military advice. Gone were those officers whose education, training,
and operational experience had carved out what could be termed a survivable
niche within the context of a system obsessed with internal security. In came the
Ba'athists whom could be best described as ruthless purveyors of institutionalized violence outside of war.[97]

The Devolution of Iraqi Military Culture

After March 1991, those reality school officers who survived attempted to
return the force to the professional standards that had taken them to their
pinnacle in 1988. Two major factors made that effort futile. First, after 1991,
the military was physically a shadow of its former self. The defeat in 1991 had
only served to exacerbate the personnel and equipment losses from the Iran-
Iraq War. During the coming decade, cannibalizing resources to maintain
priority on specialized units like the Republican Guard destroyed most units'
operational coherence. Regular army units became the manpower, training, and

[94] Malovany, *Wars of Modern Babylon*, 522–523.
[95] Makki, in Woods et al., *Saddam's Generals*, 139–140.
[96] This is not to dismiss the almost continuous use of the army in suppressing internal resistance to the Ba'ath or central government, but these kinds of operations, after 1968, no longer provided the organizing logic of the force.
[97] See Makiya, *Republic of Fear*, 3–72.

support pools to a host of new paramilitary militias like the Fedayeen Saddam, a fanatical quasi-tribe designed to be "Brown Shirts" of a dying regime. Even Republican Guard units, while still the most loyal and best equipped, had reduced training to the point that armored vehicles were more useful as static guns than maneuver platforms.

The Ba'ath Party's harsh security tendencies and its coup-proofing policies returned with a vengeance after the 1991 war. The reasons are impossibly intertwined, but the regime realized that the image of the "infallible strongman" had taken a beating and with it the appeal of Ba'athism as an ideology. At a practical level, the precipitous decline in resources, already strained before Kuwait, made threats cheaper than bribes when it came to internal coercion. Finally, there was the realization that the most capable parts of the military, especially those that had proven themselves in the Iran-Iraq War, such as the Republican Guard, were viewed as a potential and rising threat.

Beginning with the end of the Iran-Iraq War and accelerating after the defeat in Kuwait, the threat of a military-led or -enabled coup returned to the forefront of regime concerns. Coup attempts began with the officers from the large and powerful Jubburi tribal clan in 1990, another in 1993 centered on officers from the well-connected Mukhlis tribal clan, and then a reportedly US-backed attempt occurred in 1996 through officers assigned to the Republican and Special Republican Guard. All failed and ended with the imprisonment and execution of many officers whose loyalty the regime had assumed was incorruptible.[98] Paranoia-driven logic of security sank deeply into every aspect of command, eating away at an already dysfunctional system. The overall loss of trust precipitated a loss of even the pretense of intellectual honesty and candor. What had been a professional highlight of the Iran-Iraq War, the effort to learn lessons, had become yet another vehicle in regime indoctrination in the 1990s. In a recording from a post-Kuwait lessons-learned conference, an Iraqi officer offered the following caveat to his peers, making perfectly clear that "reality" was once again only in the eyes of the Ba'ath: "I have discussed this with the chief of staff ... so that we can benefit from the positive lessons, which the command may allow us for example to teach in military institutions. And if there are any negative points, then according to the permission of the political or military leadership, we can also teach them."[99]

In the run-up to the 2003 war, simply manning the units of the Iraqi regular army was a challenge. Soldiers with any means whatsoever were routinely bribing their way out of service. Such hopelessness rippled upward: petty tyrants within the noncommissioned ranks enforced harsh discipline. The

---

[98] Amatzia Baram, "Saddam Husayn, the Ba'th Regime and the Iraqi Officer Corps," in Thomas Kearney and Barry Rubin, eds., *Armed Forces in the Middle East: Politics and Strategy* (Milton Park, 2004), 206–230, 221–222.

[99] Captured Iraqi document cited in Woods, *Mother of All Battles*, 269.

cost associated with poorly led, poorly treated, and unpaid draftees was a military prison population that exceeded capacity. Commanders, not wanting to explain the truth behind the depleted ranks, would release military prisoners in order to fill the ranks as a "cover for soldiers who had bribed [their commanders] to stay home."[100] For the rank and file, two of the historical pillars of their organizational culture had corroded into dust: a belief in their own military superiority and the confidence in the "strong man" leading them.

The regime's return to a military focus on internal survival was another factor in the resurgence of older, better-developed elements of organizational culture. In a postwar interview with the author, the regime's last minister of defense, Gen. Hashim Ahmed al-Hamed al-Tai, described how the regime prioritized threats after the 1991 war:

> Imagine a man beset by three mortal enemies. The first enemy is armed with a howitzer and is located within range but out of sight. The second adversary has a rifle and is situated on a hill overlooking your building. The third man is one whom you cannot see, [who] is in the house with you but is only armed with a small knife. Objectively, the artillery's firepower and the rifle's accuracy are the more worrisome challenges. However, when the lights go out in the house, the only threat that matters is the man closest to you.[101]

This logic drove choices from where army forces were based (focused on population control) and what they trained on (population control and survivability in the face of Western airpower).[102]

The tension between regime security and military effectiveness came to a head in the build-up to the last war. The security service had penetrated army units so deeply that all but the most routine forms of communication were not only monitored but also discouraged. Lt. Gen. Ra'ad al-Hamdani, a corps commander in the Republican Guard, described how official and "unofficial" spies on his staff competed to report back to the General Security Directorate or their patrons in the senior Ba'ath leadership or the family of the president. Responding to the suspicions and innuendo was a distracting and deadly serious task.

Coordination between commands all but ceased due to a lack of trust. Commanders of one unit were not allowed to contact the commanders of a unit on their flank without approval from higher headquarters and, even then, only under the eye of one of the ever-present security staffs. A healthy organizational culture relies on trust between leaders, led, and peers, but trust is a tightly controlled concept in authoritarian states. The necessities of coup-

---

[100] Amer Faris, *Red Flags: Memoir of an Iraqi Conscript Trapped between Enemy Lines in the 2003 Invasion* (London, 2009), 24–25.

[101] Discussion with the author, November 10, 2003, Baghdad.

[102] See Kevin M. Woods, *The Iraqi Perspectives Project: Saddam's Senior Leadership on Operation Iraqi Freedom* (Annapolis, MD, 2006), 39–48.

proofing after 1991 drove Iraq's governing regime to undercut trust across the military at every turn. Officers were not only under surveillance, but the regime and its spies actively tested them to see if they had a propensity to disloyalty. Using a "Trojan horse" technique, a security officer would instigate conversations critical of Saddam or the party. If the other participated, did not interject or, better yet, did not report the incident to the internal security office, he was "imprisoned or at least demoted and expelled from the army."[103]

Iraq's inability to maintain or develop an effective force through the sanctions era had a long-term, corrosive effect on what had been (only a decade before) a robust professional culture within the force. The new generation of officers entering the force in the late 1980s did not benefit from the golden age of the late 1970s and missed the transformation of the early Iran-Iraq War. Training was reduced to minimal individual skills maintenance and there was little if any of the collective or unit training so essential to combat readiness and developing the next generation of leaders.

The US-led invasion in 2003 was the final nail in the coffin of the Iraqi Army. Like so many things in the history of Iraq of this period, the health of the military's culture began and ended with Saddam. Lt. Gen. Hamdani once described the impact Saddam had on Iraqi military organizational culture: "The problem with Saddam was that he understood excellence in command as only a matter of courage. Therefore, he concentrated on courageous people, even if they were stupid and for the most part disregarded expertise and professionalism."[104] As the Iraqi military reconstitutes itself in the post-Saddam era, what remains to be seen are what elements of Iraqi military organizational culture will reassert themselves in the new incarnation of the Iraqi state.

Conclusion

Military culture is a reflection of a dynamic process of learning and adaption within the context of the parent society's culture, resting on the foundation of previous military culture and often idiosyncratic elements derived from a "competitive, iterative exchange" across states and over time.[105] Some elements of the process of generation, modification, and even devolution of a military organizational culture may be common across time periods and even societies, but most are not. The unique interactions of history, circumstance,

---

[103] Amatzia Baram, "Saddam's Power Structure: The Tikritis before, during and after the War," in Toby Dodge, ed., *Iraq at the Crossroads: State and Society in the Shadow of Regime Change* (London, 2003), 93–114, 102–103.

[104] Woods, Murray, and Holaday, *Saddam's War*, 37.

[105] Porter, *Military Orientalism*, 32. Porter describes the dynamic, pragmatic exchange or mimicry across military cultures as the "hybridity of war."

and political context create unique conditions in a military's organizational culture.

Three subthemes not addressed earlier in this chapter appear just under the surface in interviews with former senior officers of the Ba'ath regime. First, the organizational culture of the Iraqi military was framed around a long-standing challenge: trying to maintain power in Baghdad in the face of a more numerous and, at times, more militarily relevant tribal society, a society whose tribal characteristics increasingly cut across ethnic, social, and sectarian lines. Saddam often spoke of the tribal values of "communal spirit, honor, and manly valor" even as he worked to keep at bay their power.[106] The tribes lay at the heart of why there was an Iraqi military, and they remained relevant to that military's mission until the end of the Ba'ath regime. Indeed, they have reasserted their historic role in various national and regional power vacuums caused by the US invasion in 2003.

The second was the military appeal of the Ba'ath Party's philosophy. It provided a comprehensive set of institutional beliefs and premises that appealed to a military whose inclinations were toward "progressive" or modernizing political ideas. Emerging out of the pan-Arab nationalism movements around the First World War, it rejected many of the borrowed political philosophies that had failed the region, and it looked to a middle class of urban, salaried, and educated elites, including military officers, as its natural constituency. Moreover, the process of neutralizing the political ambitions of the senior army officers created a space for rapid military development in a way that the Iraqi Army had not seen since its creation by the British in the 1920s.

The final issue was the role of Islam. The senior leadership of the Iraqi military was, as a group, secular in its professional outlook. For most of Saddam's rule, the Ba'ath Party and Ba'ath officials were officially silent on the issue of Islam. Saddam wanted "to stop party members from being carried away by the Islamic wave, a development likely to have utterly unpredictable consequences." In addition, "he wanted to be seen in the tradition of Arab-Muslim rulers who combined religious authority, political power, and military command in a single person."[107] Some have argued that the transformation went even farther and that "when the party reached the end of its tether in 2003, Baghdad was ruled by a regime that tried to look Islamic even though it retained some of its secular traditions."[108] In the end, Saddam tried to combine Ba'ath secularism, tribalism, and Islam in the only vehicle he could trust: himself.

In a sometime confounding logic, Saddam's ability to create a coup-proofed regime and his ability to set external military missions while retaining control

[106] Amatzia Baram, "Neo-Tribalism in Iraq: Saddam Hussein's Tribal Policies 1991–96," *International Journal of Middle East Studies* 29(1) (February 1997), 1–31, 5.
[107] Ofra Bengio, *Saddam's Word: Political Discourse in Iraq* (Oxford, 1994), 182.
[108] Baram, *Saddam Husayn and Islam*, 399–442.

against the threat of the tribes empowered positive change in the organizational culture of the Iraqi military. Prior to Ba'athification, senior Iraqi military leaders spent an extraordinary amount of energy on internal political maneuvering and the closely related mission of controlling a fractious population. After Ba'athification, these issues did not disappear, but a new logic for developing effective military forces was added at the very time an external existential threat appeared.

The real break in the army's organizational culture came when it was subjected to ruthless coup-proofing at the very top and close security monitoring throughout the officer corps. The upside, for those below the most senior positions who could avoid the often arbitrary cruelty of such a system, was the chance to build an organizational culture oriented on rational efforts to generate effective forces.[109]

Reflecting on the fundamental question of Saddam's relationship with his military, Hamdani argued that Saddam could never reconcile the fundamental difference between what he called tribal and civilized (or state) warfare. In a conversation following the aborted threat to reinvade Kuwait in the fall of 1994, Saddam warned one of his best generals that "the problem is that you are too limited to military academic standards, but education has two sides. You are heading towards the more dangerous side. At the technical level, I consider you the best commander in our army, but at the moral and political level you are dangerous."[110]

According to Hamdani, Saddam was trapped between what he saw as two distinct sides of war. On one side, Saddam needed professional military officers competent in developing and employing a large, modern armed force. On the other side, Saddam sought men who could fight the battles that never end, those at the "moral and political level." At this level, Saddam employed an idiosyncratic doctrine combining Ba'ath, tribal, and criminal logic, which valued "violent and ignorant personalities."[111] The former group, in steady decline after 1988, was always walking a razor's edge as a most valued and most threatening resource. They saw themselves as the keepers of Iraq's military culture. However, it was the latter group, generally as ignorant of Iraq's military culture as they were of the profession of arms, which left its mark most indelibly on Iraq's military culture during this period, with bitter consequences for the regime.

---

[109] Effectiveness here is measured in comparison to its own previous performance and that of its adversaries.

[110] Saddam quote as recalled by Ra'ad Hamdani, in Woods et al., *Saddam's Generals*, 38.

[111] Ibid.

13   US Army Culture, 1973–2017

Peter R. Mansoor

On April 5, 2003, the tanks and infantry fighting vehicles of Col. Dave Perkins's 2nd Brigade Combat Team, 3rd Infantry Division, began the first of two "Thunder Runs" into the heart of Baghdad in an attempt to collapse Iraqi resistance and oust Saddam Hussein from power. When the task force reached the center of the Iraqi capital two days later during the second raid, it stayed. Soon the forces of Gen. James Mattis's First Marine Division along with the remainder of Maj. Gen. Buford "Buff" Blount's 3rd Infantry Division arrived. The regime collapsed. It had taken the joint forces of the United States and its coalition allies just three weeks to vanquish their enemy, a seeming validation of the effectiveness of US ground and air forces and their focus on major combat operations against the military forces of a modern nation-state.[1]

Beneath the veneer of a "mission accomplished" lay deep-seated problems that would torment the US Army in years to come.[2] In the run-up to the Iraq War, army leaders had focused on so-called rapid, decisive operations that would quickly collapse an opposing armed force at its center of gravity.[3] Information superiority, speed, and guided munitions would enable smaller, more high-tech forces to prevail against larger, less nimble enemy forces.[4] As the invasion of Iraq showed, the concept was valid in a discrete set of circumstances: an inferior opposing force established according to a modern, Western model; terrain that allowed for precise targeting; and incompetent enemy

[1] For an examination of the 2003 invasion of Iraq, see Michael R. Gordon and Gen. Bernard E. Trainor, *Cobra II: The Inside Story of the Invasion and Occupation of Iraq* (New York, 2006).

[2] On May 1, 2003, President George W. Bush landed on the aircraft carrier USS *Abraham Lincoln* under a banner declaring "Mission Accomplished." The hasty declaration of victory would haunt the Bush administration as Iraq descended into chaos.

[3] According to Prussian military philosopher Carl von Clausewitz, the center of gravity is "the hub of all power and movement, on which everything depends." *On War*, ed. and trans. Michael Howard and Peter Paret (Princeton, NJ, 1976), 595–596. The center of gravity may be the enemy's army or its capital; in the case of Iraq, the center of gravity was Saddam Hussein, his principal Ba'athist associates, and the Republican Guard forces that guarded the regime.

[4] For an overview of the concept of rapid, decisive operations (RDO), see US Joint Forces Command J9 Futures Lab, "A Concept for Rapid Decisive Operations," RDO Whitepaper version 2.0, www.globalsecurity.org/military/library/report/2001/RDO.doc.

leadership.[5] The invasion appeared so successful that the commander of US Central Command, US Army Gen. Tommy Franks, retired shortly after the fall of Baghdad, leaving the job of mopping up to others. It was up to his successor, US Army Gen. John Abizaid, to declare three months later that enemy forces "are conducting what I would describe as a classical guerrilla-type campaign against us. It's low-intensity conflict in our doctrinal terms, but it's war however you describe it."[6] The term "guerrilla" was the last thing the Bush administration and the US Army wanted to hear.

The seeds of failure in Iraq lay in the army's history. US Army culture rests on a deep-seated historical legacy that honors the massive land campaigns of the service's past. Its educational system teaches officers to venerate the Battles of Vicksburg and Gettysburg, Grant's 1864 Overland campaign, Sherman's seizure of Atlanta and subsequent March to the Sea, the Meuse-Argonne offensive in World War I, the campaigns for Leyte and Luzon in the Pacific War, and the Normandy invasion and drive across France and Germany in 1944–1945. The pacification of Native Americans, Filipino guerrillas, and military assistance missions to Greece and other countries? Not so much. Noted American military historian Russell Weigley has postulated that the strategy of annihilation represents an American "way of war."[7] When the United States goes to war, according to his thesis, it does so with overwhelming force to win decisive victories by smashing its opponents in conventional combat. The assumption was peace would presumably follow, but Weigley had little to say about how American forces would turn battlefield triumph into political success in war's aftermath.

Subsequent works have disputed this notion, in particular Brian Linn's *Journal of Military History* article "The American Way of War Revisited" and Antulio Echevarria's treatise *Reconsidering the American Way of War.*[8] Weigley's thesis, they note, is too constrained to take into account the wide variety of experiences the US Army has undergone in nearly 250 years of conflict. In his subsequent work, Linn suggested that a triad encapsulates the army's intellectual tradition: the Guardians (who see war as more science than art and homeland defense as the primary goal), Heroes (who view war as an art where military genius and human intangibles mean more than principles of war

---

[5] In this regard, Iraq was the perfect venue for RDO. As for the leadership of Saddam Hussein, who up to the day the war started maintained that the Bush administration's threat of invasion was a bluff, it was pathetic. See Kevin M. Woods, *Iraqi Perspectives Project: A View of Operation Iraqi Freedom from Saddam's Senior Leadership* (Norfolk, VA, 2006).

[6] Vernon Loeb, "'Guerrilla' War Acknowledged," *Washington Post*, July 17, 2003.

[7] Russell F. Weigley, *The American Way of War: A History of United States Military Strategy and Policy* (New York, 1973).

[8] Brian Linn, "The American Way of War Revisited," *Journal of Military History* 66(2) (April 2002), 501–533; Antulio J. Echevarria II, *Reconsidering the American Way of War: U.S. Military Practice from the Revolution to Afghanistan* (Washington, DC, 2014).

and other scientific theories), and Managers (whose focus on large-scale, industrialized warfare often left them unprepared for small wars or post-conflict operations).[9] Service culture, he notes, is honed "in peacetime, often over several decades, and is greatly influenced by the service's perception of its own martial traditions, its interpretations of lessons learned from recent conflicts, its understanding of current threats and opportunities, and its vision of future wars."[10]

In the post–World War II era, the Vietnam War represented a watershed for the army's culture. For a military service steeped in remembrance of battlefield triumphs at Saratoga, Yorktown, Chapultepec, Gettysburg, Vicksburg, San Juan Hill, Normandy, Okinawa, and Inchon, the sudden and wrenching defeat against a Third World nation caused anguish and much soul-searching. Furthermore, the rot of careerism that had set in during the Vietnam years was in danger of de-professionalizing the institution. In 1970, an Army War College study on military professionalism concluded that too many senior officers focused on personal advancement, or "ticket punching," at the expense of their integrity and the welfare of their subordinates. A "zero defects" mentality gripped the officer corps, making leaders risk averse and encouraging micromanagement.[11] The enlisted force fared no better; racial animosity, drug and alcohol use, and low morale beset the ranks.[12] By any accounting, the army was a deeply troubled institution as it emerged from defeat in Vietnam.[13]

The army did its best to put its Vietnam experiences behind it. Army leaders never embraced a holistic review of the army's performance in Vietnam. "Army involvement in counterinsurgency was first seen as an aberration and then as a mistake to be avoided," writes Conrad Crane, who was one of the lead authors of the army's 2006 rewriting of its counterinsurgency doctrine.[14] In the post-Vietnam period, army leaders not only relegated counterinsurgency doctrine to the ash heap of history but also adjusted the force structure to eliminate the types of capabilities needed to pursue such operations.[15] Instruction on counterinsurgency at the Command and General Staff College fell from forty

[9] Brian Linn, *The Echo of Battle: The Army's Way of War* (Cambridge, MA, 2007).
[10] Ibid., 3–4.
[11] US Army War College, "Study on Military Professionalism," June 30, 1970, 31, www.dtic.mil/cgi-bin/GetTRDoc?AD=ADA063748. Army leaders were concerned enough by the study's conclusions to classify the report as "For Official Use Only" for three years.
[12] The officer corps also drank heavily, a historical legacy from the frontier army that has waned over the years, but that has not completely disappeared even today.
[13] Officer-scholars of the period noted the crisis of professionalism in the army. See, for instance, William L. Hauser, *America's Army in Crisis: A Study in Civil-Military Relations* (Baltimore, MD, 1973).
[14] Conrad Crane, *Avoiding Vietnam: The U.S. Army's Response to Defeat in Southeast Asia* (Carlisle Barracks, PA, 2002), 2.
[15] David Fitzgerald, *Learning to Forget: U.S. Army Counterinsurgency Doctrine and Practice from Vietnam to Iraq* (Palo Alto, CA, 2003), 204.

hours in 1977 to just eight hours in 1979.[16] By the mid-1980s, counterinsurgency was part of an elective, no longer taught to every student. Instructors trying to create a syllabus for courses in low-intensity conflict at Fort Leavenworth decided to seek help from the US Army Special Operations School at Fort Bragg, North Carolina – the home of the Green Berets. They came away emptyhanded, informed by officers there that they "had been ordered to throw away their counterinsurgency files in the 1970s."[17]

The 1970s marked the nadir of the army as it transitioned to an all-volunteer force, adjusted the officer and enlisted personnel management systems, and attempted to regain lost competencies in conventional war fighting. With the American economy beset by stagflation, with high youth unemployment, and with entry-level military pay comparable to civilian pay, the transition to an all-volunteer force initially appeared to be a success. It was seen as an equal-opportunity employer and an avenue of upward mobility for minorities and women. As the decade wore on, low pay raises caused the purchasing power of the average soldier to decline. The G.I. Bill ended in 1976; simultaneously, the army instituted a flawed selection and classification test that made a large number of enlistees appear more capable than they really were. Recruit quality declined even as the army fell 16,000 soldiers short of its recruiting goal by the last year of the decade.[18] To make matters worse, drug problems and racial tensions infested the ranks. Lieutenants in Germany in the late 1970s had to patrol the barracks with loaded pistols to keep enlisted soldiers in line.[19] US Army Europe, having been used as a rotational pool for manpower for the Vietnam conflict, was in poor shape to defend against a Soviet offensive.[20] Gen. Edward "Shy" Meyer, the army's chief of staff, testified to Congress in 1979 that the army was a "hollow" force due to personnel shortages and lack of funds for readiness and training. How the army was expected to halt a determined Red Army attack through the Fulda Gap in Germany was anyone's guess.

The 1973 Arab-Israeli War provided a wake-up call, if one were needed, that the army was unready for a large-scale war involving massed armored forces. The lethality of the modern battlefield was on full display in this conflict, in which antitank guided missiles and other weapons destroyed 2,650 tanks – more than the army's inventory in Europe at the time.[21] The army's chief of

---

[16] Robert T. Davis II, "The Challenge of Adaptation: The U.S. Army in the Aftermath of Conflict, 1953–2000," The Long War Series Occasional Paper 27 (Fort Leavenworth, KS, 2008), 49.

[17] Crane, *Avoiding Vietnam*, 12.

[18] Thomas W. Evans, "The All-Volunteer Army after Twenty Years: Recruiting in the Modern Era," *Army History: The Professional Bulletin of Army History*, No. 27 (Summer 1993), 40–46.

[19] This fact has been confirmed to the author by a number of officers who served in Germany during that period.

[20] Davis, "The Challenge of Adaptation," 51.

[21] Richard W. Stewart, ed., *American Military History*, vol. 2 (Washington, DC, 2005), 377; www .history.army.mil/books/amh-v2/amh/0v2/chapter12.htm.

staff, Gen. Creighton Abrams, focused his efforts in part on restructuring combat organizations through greater integration of the National Guard and Reserves and the restoration of tactical excellence in conventional combat.[22] The newly created Training and Doctrine Command (TRADOC), under the command of Gen. William E. DePuy, launched into a rewrite of the army's basic war-fighting doctrine, Field Manual 100–5, *Operations*. The resulting doctrine of "active defense" featured a method of operations that could theoretically defeat a Red Army attack into West Germany.[23]

As war games showed, however, army units in Europe could only defeat the first wave of enemy forces; subsequent echelons would eventually arrive to overwhelm US and NATO forces. Army doctrine writers went back to the drawing board to develop doctrine to defeat echeloned Soviet forces in both time and space. While they worked on a new operating concept, the army began fielding a new generation of conventional weapons and revolutionized its training to make it more realistic.

Army leaders who survived the crucible of Vietnam reestablished the army's cultural foundations over the next two decades. Gen. Maxwell Thurman and others significantly improved Army recruiting and made the Volunteer Army work.[24] Drug testing significantly reduced drug use in the ranks, while the army slowly weeded out incompetent noncommissioned officers and professionalized those who remained through a newly instituted noncommissioned officer education system.[25] Pay raises and more successful advertising brought in higher-caliber recruits.[26] The army also successfully integrated women into the total force after the dissolution of the Women's Army Corps in 1978, although problems with sexual harassment plagued the institution and continue to do so today. The officer efficiency report was redesigned, compelling

[22] Suzanne C. Nielsen, "An Army Transformed: The U.S. Army's post-Vietnam Recovery and the Dynamic of Change in Military Organizations," Strategic Studies Institute (Carlisle Barracks, PA, 2010),40, https://ssi.armywarcollege.edu/pdffiles/PUB1020.pdf.

[23] Paul H. Herbert, *Deciding What Has to Be Done: General William E. DePuy and the 1976 Edition of FM 100–5, Operations* (Fort Leavenworth, KS, 1988).

[24] As head of US Army Recruiting Command from 1979 to 1981, Thurman successfully revamped the way the Army recruited soldiers. See Chapter 1 for details of his new approach to recruiting.

[25] Daniel K. Elder, "Educating Noncommissioned Officers: A Chronological Study on the Development of Educational Programs for U.S. Army Noncommissioned Officers," July 1999, http://ncohistory.com/files/Education.pdf. Alcohol abuse remains a significant problem, despite the army's best efforts at reducing alcohol use in the ranks. Genevieve Ames and Carol Cunradi, "Alcohol Use and Preventing Alcohol-Related Problems among Young Adults in the Military," National Institute on Alcohol Abuse and Alcoholism, https://pubs.niaaa.nih.gov/publications/arh284/252–257.htm.

[26] The 1980s were the heyday of the army's "Be all you can be" advertising blitz, selected by Advertising Age as number 18 of the top 100 advertising campaigns of the twentieth century. Tom Evans, "All We Could Be: How an Advertising Campaign Helped Remake the Army," *Army History* (January 20, 2015), https://armyhistory.org/all-we-could-be-how-an-advertising-campaign-helped-remake-the-army/.

supervisors to make more difficult choices when evaluating their subordinates. The system, which allowed senior raters to only rank one-third of their officers as "above center of mass" (the highest ranking), forced senior leaders to identify their best officers for promotion rather than lumping them all together with the same superlative reports and leaving the decision on whom to promote to centralized selection boards. The system still had its flaws; the lack of subordinate input into the evaluation process allowed some toxic leaders to thrive, a flaw still not fully resolved today.

Army training also significantly improved. Under the guidance of Maj. Gen. Paul Gorman, the deputy TRADOC commander for training, the army revolutionized its training system through the development of better assessment models and the creation of the National Training Center (NTC) at Fort Irwin, California. The Army Training and Evaluation Program, or ARTEP, established conditions and standards for war-fighting tasks and introduced more rigor into the evaluation of unit training.[27] The NTC provided the three pillars of modern training: an instrumented range, a corps of observer-controllers who could assess unit proficiency, and a dedicated opposing force trained in enemy doctrine and tactics. The newly designed Multiple Integrated Laser Engagement System, or MILES, provided a realistic method of scoring hits through an augmented system of "laser tag." The Opposing Force, or OPFOR, styled as the 32nd Guards Motorized Rifle Regiment, provided a tough opponent trained in Soviet-style doctrine and tactics to visiting units, or Blue Forces. A corps of observer-controllers provided feedback to unit leaders through after-action reviews, while the Center for Army Lessons Learned, established in 1985, collected best practices and disseminated them to the force.[28]

The Reagan defense build-up and associated intellectual ferment surrounding the creation of the National Training Center (1979), AirLand Battle doctrine (1982), and the School of Advanced Military Studies (1983) did much to restore the confidence of the army's officer corps. AirLand Battle was the product of innovative thinkers such as Gen. Donn Starry, commanding general of the Training and Doctrine Command; Lt. Gen. William R. Richardson, commanding general of the Combined Arms Center at Fort Leavenworth, Kansas; and Lt. Col. Huba Wass de Czege, Lt. Col. Leonard D. Holder, and Lt. Col. Richmond B. Henriques, who wrote the doctrine under the supervision of the director of the Department of Tactics at Fort Leavenworth, Col. Clyde J. Tate.[29] Using newly fielded weapons such as the "Big 5" (M1 Abrams main battle tank, M2 Bradley infantry fighting vehicle, AH-64 Apache attack helicopter, UH-60 Black Hawk utility helicopter, and

---

[27] Davis, "The Challenge of Adaptation," 56.   [28] Ibid., 57.
[29] The best history of the creation of AirLand Battle doctrine is John L. Romjue, *From Active Defense to AirLand Battle: The Development of Army Doctrine, 1973–1982* (Fort Monroe, VA, 1984).

the Patriot air defense missile system) along with a new generation of guided weapons (Hellfire and Maverick missiles, Copperhead artillery rounds, and forthcoming Multiple Launch Rocket and Army Tactical Missile systems), US ground and air forces would work together to disrupt a Soviet-style attack by attacking succeeding echelons in depth as the close battle was still raging. AirLand Battle returned a flexible, offensive attitude to an officer corps that had for too long been ensconced in a defensive mind-set. It also introduced the operational level of war to doctrinal discourse, a vital imperative to link tactical victories to strategic ends.

Wass de Czege went on to serve as the founding director of the US Army School of Advanced Military Studies (SAMS) at Fort Leavenworth, an organization he conceived and convinced Lt. Gen. Richardson to support. SAMS provided a second year of graduate-level education in the science and art of war to a select group of majors, who the army would then seed into key planning positions. Its first class graduated in June 1984 and soon showed their value to senior army leaders, who vied to get SAMS graduates placed on their staffs. Although not quite the "Jedi Knights" they were touted to be, SAMS graduates did much to improve operational-level planning.[30] In the same vein, the creation of the Combat Studies Institute at Fort Leavenworth and the Strategic Studies Institute at Carlisle Barracks established centers for military history and strategic analysis in the army, much-needed additions to the service's intellectual capital.[31]

Even as the army did its best to put the Vietnam experience behind it, the war was never far from its collective consciousness. The army staff initially turned over the analysis of lessons learned in Vietnam to a contractor, BDM Corporation. In June 1980, BDM finished its eight-volume "A Strategic Study of Lessons Learned in Vietnam," but the report never gained traction within the army.[32] The most influential work on Vietnam in army circles during the 1980s, rather, was Col. Harry Summers's *On Strategy*, written at the Army War College under the auspices of the army's vice chief of staff, Gen. Walter T. Kerwin Jr.[33] Summers contended that the army won all the battles in Vietnam at the tactical level, but lost the war in other realms. He did not contend that the Vietnam War was unwinnable, but rather that it was lost because the United States lacked a coherent national policy toward the war, employed a faulty strategy, and failed to maintain public support for its prosecution. To maintain public support, the US Congress should have declared war against North Vietnam. To win the war, the US military should have focused on what he

[30] Kevin C. M. Benson, "Educating the Army's Jedi: The School of Advanced Military Studies and the Introduction of Operational Art into U.S. Army Doctrine, 1983–1994," PhD Diss., University of Kansas, 2010.

[31] Davis, "The Challenge of Adaptation," 60–61.   [32] Ibid., 61.

[33] Harry G. Summers Jr., *On Strategy: A Critical Analysis of the Vietnam War* (Novato, CA, 1982).

viewed as the more lethal threat of a North Vietnamese invasion.[34] While US and allied forces created a strategic barrier across the demilitarized zone westward to Thailand, South Vietnamese troops could pacify their country with minimal US assistance. *On Strategy* was discussed by staff and war college classes and made successive versions of mandatory professional development reading lists for the next two decades.[35]

The point here is not to debate Summers's argument, but to acknowledge the impact it had on the psyche of the army's officer corps. His Jominian approach to Vietnam as a conventional conflict ignored its hybrid nature and allowed officers brought up in its shadow to focus on high-end combat operations at the expense of a more holistic approach to warfare.[36] The army could avoid educating or training its leaders for counterinsurgency warfare, stability and peacekeeping operations, and other "low-intensity conflict" missions in favor of fighting and winning the first battle of the next war. When the cadre at SAMS suggested that the army elevate "low-intensity conflict," the 1980s term for operations other than large-scale conventional combat, to the same status as conventional operations, army leaders rejected the notion outright.[37]

"No more Task Force Smiths" became the mantra, backed up by historical research into the first battles of American wars past.[38] Army leaders learned about the battles of the Ia Drang Valley, particularly those at Landing Zones X-Ray and Albany, but nothing about pacification, combined action platoons, or advisory duty. Tactics and operations dominated professional discourse, both in the professional military educational system and in the field army. US Army Europe was ordered to be ready to "fight tonight," a mind-set bolstered by a realistic mission against a defined enemy, including patrols of the East-West Inter-German border, the development of a general defense plan and associated battle books, and the maintenance of tactical forces on high-alert status.[39]

The renaissance of army culture in the 1980s paid dividends during the 1989 invasion of Panama, Operation Just Cause, and the Gulf War of 1991,

---

[34] This conclusion was disputed by other soldier-historians, who focused on the counterinsurgency fighting as the more important battleground. See, for instance, Andrew Krepinevich, *The Army and Vietnam* (Baltimore, MD, 1986).

[35] Richard Lock-Pullan, *U.S. Intervention Policy and Army Innovation: From Vietnam to Iraq* (New York, 2006), 119–120.

[36] For a more recent examination of Vietnam as a hybrid conflict, see Karl Lowe, "Hybrid War in Vietnam," in Williamson Murray and Peter Mansoor, eds., *Hybrid Warfare: Fighting Complex Opponents from the Ancient World to the Present* (New York, 2012), chapter 10.

[37] Fitzgerald, *Learning to Forget*, 204.

[38] Charles E. Heller and William A. Stofft, eds., *America's First Battles, 1776–1965* (Lawrence, KS, 1986). Task Force Smith was the first US Army unit to enter into combat with North Korean forces in 1950. Its defeat on the battlefield against a Third World adversary motivated the army to improve its readiness for combat in future years.

[39] The author experienced all of these realities firsthand as a company commander and plans officer in the 11th Armored Cavalry Regiment stationed in West Germany from 1987–1990. "Fight Tonight" is still the mantra of US Army forces in Korea.

Operation Desert Storm. Army leaders, staffs, and units performed superbly in both of these conflicts. Expeditionary forces flown thousands of miles from the United States along with locally based army units quickly dismembered the Panamanian Defense Forces and deposed Manuel Noriega from power.[40] In the Gulf War, army units sliced through the Iraqi Army and Republican Guards forces with ease, winning a decisive victory in just 100 hours. President George H. W. Bush stated what many army leaders believed: "It's a proud day for America. And, by God, we've kicked the Vietnam syndrome once and for all."[41] Historian Adrian Lewis concludes:

> Not since the reorganization and transformation of the Prussian Army, after its defeat at Jena in 1806 by the Grand Army of Napoleon, has an army gone through such extensive change. Ironically, in many ways, the transformation the Prussians sought was the exact opposite of what the US Army sought. The Prussians endeavored to produce a *national army* that was motivated by patriotism, out of the *professional army* of the old regime, the absolute monarch. The US Army endeavored to transform its *national army* into a *professional, long service Army* that was *not* reliant on patriotism and the will of the people: both succeeded.[42]

The post-Vietnam reforms had paid significant dividends, although they did not go far enough in educating army leaders to link tactical and operational virtuosity with strategic insight.[43]

The breakup of the Soviet Union in 1991 ended the threat against which the army had reorganized and trained its forces since the end of the Vietnam War. Army leaders struggled with conceptualizing what would come next, and in this regard, the decisive victory in the Gulf sowed the seeds of future failure. Desert Storm reinforced the belief in decisive battles at the expense of a more holistic view of war. Few paid attention to the messy aftermath of the conflict, during which Saddam Hussein cemented his grip on power with the brutal suppression of a Shi'a uprising in the south. He would have done the same in northern Iraq against the Kurds, were it not for the intervention of US military forces in Operation Provide Comfort.[44]

Army leaders also embraced the "Powell doctrine," a restrictive list of prerequisites established by the chairman of the Joint Chiefs of Staff, US

---

[40] Noriega was extradited to the United States, tried, and imprisoned on eight counts of drug trafficking, racketeering, and money laundering. He would die twenty-eight years later in an American prison.

[41] George Bush: "Remarks to the American Legislative Exchange Council," in Gerhard Peters and John T. Woolley, The American Presidency Project, March 1, 1991, www.presidency.ucsb.edu/ws/?pid=19351.

[42] Adrian R. Lewis, *The American Culture of War: The History of U.S. Military Force from World War II to Operation Iraqi Freedom* (New York, 2007), 304; emphasis in the original.

[43] Nielson, "An Army Transformed," 48.

[44] Gordon W. Rudd, *Humanitarian Intervention: Assisting the Kurds in Operation Provide Comfort, 1991* (Washington, DC, 2004).

Army Gen. Colin Powell, for embarking on military operations. The United
States, Powell believed, should only go to war under certain conditions: vital
national security interests were threatened, objectives were clearly attainable,
the risks and costs were fully and frankly analyzed, all other policy means were
exhausted, a plausible exit strategy existed, the consequences of action were
fully considered, the support of the American people was ensured, and broad
international support was realized.[45] The doctrine codified the lessons internalized by the Vietnam generation of military officers: a clear preference for
decisive conventional wars and a caution against using military force for more
limited, some might say nebulous, ends.

The 1993 version of FM 100–5, *Operations*, lumped every US Army mission aside from large-scale combat operations as "Operations Other than
War."[46] The manual did include an eight-page chapter on the topic, confirmation that these missions were not being entirely ignored. Nevertheless, in the
ensuing decade, operations such as Operation Provide Comfort in Iraq (1991–
1996), Operation Restore Hope in Somalia (1992–1993), Operation Uphold
Democracy in Haiti (1994–1995), Operation Joint Endeavor in Bosnia and
Herzegovina (1995–1996) and its successors, Operation Joint Guard (1996–
1998) and Operation Joint Forge (1998–2004), and the deployment of Task
Force Hawk to Albania during Operation Allied Force in Kosovo (1999) were
seen as lesser included missions to large-scale, conventional war fighting.
Army leaders placed some emphasis on joint operations, in particular army-
air force cooperation, but placed little thought on combined operations outside
of a NATO or Korean context.

After the Gulf War, army leaders embraced the notion of a revolution in
military affairs combining digital command and control systems, high-tech
intelligence, surveillance, and reconnaissance systems, and guided weapons.
They believed that better information and precision weaponry could replace
mass on the battlefield and enable the creation of lighter forces capable of rapid
deployment.[47] Used first in World War II, guided weapons had been part of the
army's inventory at least as early as 1981 when the Copperhead laser-guided
artillery round entered service, but army culture inhibited the conceptualization
of these cutting-edge technologies into a new war-fighting dynamic.[48] For a
decade, doctrine merely appended them to the existing war-fighting construct,

[45] Frank Hoffman, "A Second Look at the Powell Doctrine," War on the Rocks, February 20, 2014, https://warontherocks.com/2014/02/a-second-look-at-the-powell-doctrine/.
[46] Department of the Army, Field Manual 100–5, *Operations* (Washington, DC, 1993), Figure 2–1.
[47] The emphasis on rapid deployment was in part an outgrowth of the experience of Task Force Hawk during the Kosovo War. The task force had difficulties deploying from Germany to Albania and supporting itself once there, tarnishing the army's public image and leading some pundits to question its strategic relevance.
[48] Dima Adamsky, *The Culture of Military Innovation: The Impact of Cultural Factors on the Revolution in Military Affairs in Russia, the U.S., and Israel* (Palo Alto, CA, 2010).

while little discussion occurred in professional journals as to their potentially revolutionary impact on the battlefield.

During his tenure as army chief of staff from 1991 to 1995, Gen. Gordon Sullivan committed the army to leverage the power of the microprocessor and the ongoing revolution in information systems. Force XXI experimentation attempted to network tactical units and create a common operating picture to improve commanders' situational awareness.[49] The thinking was that superior command and control and intelligence would reduce the fog and friction of the battlefield and substitute information for massed firepower. Information age technologies would enable the execution of "rapid, decisive operations" that would overwhelm an adversary by attacking its center of gravity at the outset of military operations. The preference for the use of technologically sophisticated weapons to produce quick, decisive battles "had deep roots in American strategic culture."[50] Although the army conducted extensive experimentation with digitized forces at Fort Hood, Texas, and at the NTC, some aspects of emerging doctrine, such as deep attacks by rotary winged aircraft, relied primarily on computer models to determine their effectiveness. Army leaders' faith in these simulations would come back to haunt the force when it finally confronted a live enemy.

Ironically, the proliferation of digitized command and control systems amplified a culture of top-down control that had plagued the army since the Vietnam War. In that conflict, senior commanders flying in helicopters over the battlefield, often directing units on the ground without firsthand knowledge of what they faced, symbolized a culture of micromanagement that hampered the inculcation of a "mission command" mind-set that would free subordinate commanders to maneuver based on their analysis of the situation they faced. Digital systems would theoretically provide senior leaders needed information and free subordinate leaders from constantly updating their situation with higher headquarters, thereby enabling them to command without undue interference from above. In practice, as access to subordinate unit information grew, so too did the temptation to direct their operations. The army's current emphasis on instilling a mission command mind-set in its leaders is an attempt to reverse this trend and free subordinate commanders to take advantage of opportunities that might not be apparent just by staring at a computer screen or video feed.[51]

---

[49] US Army Training and Doctrine Command Pamphlet 525–5, *Force XXI Operations* (Fort Monroe, VA, 1994), 3–4 and 3–5.

[50] Fitzgerald, *Learning to Forget*, 205.

[51] Peter W. Singer, "Tactical Generals: Leaders, Technology, and the Perils," Brookings, July 7, 2009, www.brookings.edu/articles/tactical-generals-leaders-technology-and-the-perils/; Douglas A. Pryer, "Growing Leaders Who Practice Mission Command and Win the Peace," *Military Review* (November–December 2013), 31–41.

Despite the proliferation of contingency operations throughout the 1980s and 1990s, army culture remained firmly embedded in high-end war fighting. The chiefs of staff following Sullivan, Gen. Dennis Reimer and Gen. Eric Shinseki, were, in the view of one historian, "intelligent and dedicated officers," but "they were 'operators,' skilled executives steeped in the institutional culture who could be trusted to run the organization competently and pass it on to their successors."[52] Another perceptive academic notes: "The construction of the concept of 'operations other than war' to contain unmilitary activities and the Army's failure (or even acquiescence in the failure of higher authorities) to rigorously plan for events after the end of 'major combat operations' in Iraq are powerful examples of how institutional identity can obstruct organizational adaptation."[53] And, as Leonard Wong and Stephen Gerras note in Chapter 2, the army did its best to avoid uncertainty despite, or perhaps because of, its formal commitment to experimentation with digital systems. Unfortunately for the army, its culture failed to produce officers with the strategic vision necessary to chart a path to victory once the nation's civilian leaders committed the American military to a war in Iraq that violated just about every tenet of the Powell doctrine.

The rapid destruction of Iraqi forces in March and April 2003, highlighted by the "Thunder Runs" into the heart of Baghdad featured at the beginning of this chapter, seemed to validate the army's trajectory, but two incidents displayed cracks in its prewar cultural foundations. The first incident involved attacks by Iraqi militiamen, the Saddam Fedayeen, on American combat units and supply lines. As US soldiers fought off the fierce assaults, their commander, Lt. Gen. Scott Wallace, remarked, "The enemy we're fighting is a bit different than the one we war-gamed against, because of these paramilitary forces. We knew they were here, but we did not know how they would fight."[54] The remark landed Wallace in Secretary of Defense Donald Rumsfeld's doghouse, but it was an accurate assessment of the situation in which US forces found themselves. The second incident occurred on March 24, 2003, when the 11th Aviation Brigade conducted a deep attack against the Iraqi Republican Guards Corps's Medina Division. Iraqi antiaircraft artillery and small arms fire hammered the attacking Apache helicopters; enemy fire shot one helicopter down and damaged more than a dozen. The Medina Division escaped unscathed.[55] Faced with this reality, Wallace canceled all deep attack missions for the remainder of

---

[52] Linn, *The Echo of Battle*, 225.   [53] Fitzgerald, *Learning to Forget*, 206.

[54] Jim Dwyer, "A NATION AT WAR: IN THE FIELD – V CORPS COMMANDER; A Gulf Commander Sees a Longer Road," *New York Times*, March 28, 2003, www.nytimes.com/2003/03/28/world/nation-war-field-v-corps-commander-gulf-commander-sees-longer-road.html.

[55] Gordon and Trainor, *Cobra II*, 268–281.

the short conflict.[56] The army had spent the better part of a decade designing its forces and training to fight a mirror-imaged enemy; when the enemy refused to cooperate, officers and soldiers found themselves forced to adapt on the fly.

The aftermath of major combat operations illustrated more critical cultural shortcomings of the army's officer corps. Senior leaders who understood how to design and execute major combat operations were hard-pressed to develop an operational concept for stabilizing Iraq and preventing the outbreak of a virulent insurgency, or countering it once it did erupt, because an assumption had taken hold over time that "postwar" planning was not as important as combat operations. These deficiencies were reflective of an inability to understand how wars are won; not only by the outcome of great battles, important as they may be, but also by the establishment of effective governments in the aftermath of conflict.[57] Indeed, the job of stabilizing Iraq went to newly promoted Lt. Gen. Ricardo Sanchez, who not only lacked experience but also showed little aptitude for the task. He and the civilian head of the Coalition Provisional Authority (CPA), Ambassador L. Paul "Jerry" Bremer III, did not get along.[58] They "'literally hated each other,' an official in Washington said. 'Jerry thought Sanchez was an idiot, and Sanchez thought Jerry was a civilian micromanaging son of a bitch.'"[59] It is astonishing that arguably the most important military position in the US military in the summer of 2003 was filled by the most junior three-star in the army, an indictment of the lack of emphasis the service placed on the aftermath of major combat operations.

Preparation for "Phase IV" operations, or those tasks to be accomplished once major fighting ended, remained woefully incomplete and under-resourced.[60] Army leaders overlooked two decades of history by failing to prepare their troops for the chaos that would follow regime change, or provide them rules of engagement to prevent the massive looting that destroyed much of Iraq's infrastructure in a matter of days.[61] Then three disastrous political decisions – admittedly not the army's fault – precipitated a virulent insurgency

---

[56] Steve Liewer, "Iraq War: Tank-Killing Apache Copters Found New Task after Early Setbacks," *Stars and Stripes*, May 27, 2003, www.stripes.com/news/iraq-war-tank-killing-apache-copters-found-new-task-after-early-setbacks-1.6039#.WV18j-mQy70.

[57] Two recent works have explored the US Army's history with postwar stability operations and governance of occupied territory: Matthew Moten, ed., *Between War and Peace: How America Ends Its Wars* (New York, 2011), and Nadia Schadlow, *War and the Art of Governance: Consolidating Combat Success into Political Victory* (Washington, DC, 2017).

[58] Their backgrounds explain a great deal: Sanchez grew up on the streets of Los Angeles, while Bremer was a graduate of the 1963 class at Yale.

[59] George Packer, *The Assassins' Gate: America in Iraq* (New York, 2005), 325.

[60] For an examination of the planning for post-conflict operations in Iraq, see Gordon Rudd, *Reconstructing Iraq: Regime Change, Jay Garner, and the ORHA Story* (Lawrence, KS, 2011).

[61] Looting and chaos followed accompanied change in Panama in 1989, the L.A. riots in 1992, regime change in Haiti in 1994, and the Kosovo conflict in 1999.

against the coalition forces and their Iraqi counterparts. CPA Order 1 mandated extensive de-Ba'athification of Iraqi society, alienating a significant number of Sunni Arabs, while CPA Order 2 disbanded the Iraqi Army, throwing out of work hundreds of thousands of soldiers and disaffecting and dishonoring tens of thousands of officers. These "tragic mistakes," in the words of Lt. Gen. Jay Garner, head of the short-lived Office of Reconstruction and Humanitarian Affairs, motivated the Sunni Arab community in Iraq to oppose what they deemed to be an illegal occupation of their country.[62] The empowerment of highly sectarian Shi'a politicians in the Iraqi Governing Council completed the trifecta of political errors that energized a growing insurgency and eventually propelled Iraq into civil war.

With a few exceptions, army leaders were mentally unprepared for counter-insurgency operations and struggled to craft an appropriate tactical or operational response, much less assist political leaders in devising a strategy to stabilize Iraq. Commanders were encouraged to remain on the offensive against regime "dead enders" and do what they knew how to do best – hunt down insurgents and terrorists and kill or capture them.[63] Army leaders in Iraq put little thought into creating a more comprehensive counterinsurgency strategy and an operational concept to implement it.[64] The lack of strategic vision caused the "engine of change" to falter; units rotated into Iraq and learned a great deal during their tenure in country, but the army failed to disseminate the lessons across the force or systematize doctrine.[65]

Gen. John R. Galvin, a US Army general and former NATO commander, argues that service culture creates a "comfortable vision of [future] war ... one that fits our plans, our assumptions, our hopes, and our preconceived ideas." Most officers accept this vision broadly "until it comes under serious challenge as a result of some major event – usually a military disaster."[66] This dynamic played out once again in the Iraq War, which was merely the latest misfortune to shake the army officer corps. "Despite decades of personal experience to the contrary," historian Brian Linn contends, "army officers have consistently underestimated the difficulty of unconventional warfare, military occupation, and pacification. The price of this hubris has been high, in both the past and the present."[67] Part of the problem has been the army's selective use of history in preparing its doctrine and organizations for future conflict. "The Army's desire

[62] Bob Woodward, *State of Denial: Bush at War, Part III* (New York, 2006), 225.
[63] For an indictment of the first two years of occupation in Iraq, see Tom Ricks, *Fiasco: The American Military Adventure in Iraq, 2003 to 2005* (New York, 2006).
[64] Maj. Gen. David Petraeus devised a holistic counterinsurgency program for the 101st Airborne Division in northern Iraq, but other divisions did not follow suit and the strategy did not outlive the redeployment of his division back to the United States.
[65] For the experience of one brigade in Iraq in 2003–2004, see Peter R. Mansoor, *Baghdad at Sunrise: A Brigade Commander's War in Iraq* (New Haven, CT, 2008).
[66] Linn, *The Echo of Battle*, 4.   [67] Ibid., 237.

to turn away from its Korean War and Vietnam War experiences is symptomatic of this tendency to selectively use the past to look ahead," writes one historian. "If there has been a poverty of expectations, it is because the army forgets the full-range of its past experience."[68]

To make matters much worse, poor leadership and ethical breakdowns led to the abuse of Iraqi detainees at the Abu Ghraib prison, leading to the relief from command of Brig. Gen. Janis Karpinski, commander of the 800th Military Police Brigade.[69] Karpinski was one of the few general officers disciplined by the army for failures of leadership. In a scathing article published in May 2007, Lt. Col. Paul Yingling took the army's general officers to task for their failures in Iraq. "America's generals have repeated the mistakes of Vietnam in Iraq," Yingling wrote, raising the specter of the ghosts of wars past. Army leaders failed to organize or train their forces for the types of wars they would encounter after 9/11, failed to give appropriate strategic advice to civilian policy makers, failed to devise plans to stabilize Iraq in the wake of regime change, and failed to adapt to the type of war their troops confronted. Yingling boldly stated, "The intellectual and moral failures common to America's general officer corps in Vietnam and Iraq constitute a crisis in American generalship." He continued:

> The system that produces our generals does little to reward creativity and moral courage. Officers rise to flag rank by following remarkably similar career patterns. Senior generals, both active and retired, are the most important figures in determining an officer's potential for flag rank. The views of subordinates and peers play no role in an officer's advancement; to move up he must only please his superiors. In a system in which senior officers select for promotion those like themselves, there are powerful incentives for conformity. It is unreasonable to expect that an officer who spends 25 years conforming to institutional expectations will emerge as an innovator in his late forties.[70]

Nor were army generals being held to account. "As matters stand now," Yingling concluded, "a private who loses a rifle suffers far greater consequences than a general who loses a war."[71]

There were exceptions that proved the rule. Shunted off to Fort Leavenworth after two tours in Iraq, Lt. Gen. David Petraeus used his position as commander of the Combined Arms Center to rewrite the service's counterinsurgency doctrine. An accomplished leader with a Princeton PhD, Petraeus had the creativity

---

[68] Davis, "The Challenge of Adaptation," 111.

[69] The Article 15–6 investigation of abuses at Abu Ghraib by Maj. Gen. Antonio Taguba can be viewed at https://fas.org/irp/agency/dod/taguba.pdf.

[70] Paul Yingling, "A Failure in Generalship," *Armed Forces Journal*, May 1, 2007, http://armed forcesjournal.com/a-failure-in-generalship/.

[71] Ibid. Tom Ricks seconded the notion of lack of accountability in the army's general officers in his historical study, *The Generals: American Military Command from World War II to Today* (New York, 2012).

that all too many army officers lacked. He assembled an eclectic group of civilian and military intellectuals possessing a wide variety of backgrounds to provide input on the doctrine, which was written by a team headed by his West Point classmate Conrad Crane.[72] Many of the contributors to the doctrine, such as Lt. Col. John Nagl, had followed nontraditional career paths.[73] The resulting product, the December 2006 version of Field Manual 23–4, *Counterinsurgency*, conceptually retooled the army for counterinsurgency operations, albeit nearly four years after the start of the Iraq War.

The decision by the Bush administration to surge additional forces into Iraq and to put Petraeus in charge of the effort provided an opportunity to reverse the tide of a war almost lost. For eighteen months beginning in January 2007, Multi-National Force–Iraq implemented a fully resourced counterinsurgency campaign to destroy al-Qaeda in Iraq, defeat the Sunni insurgency, and co-opt various militia groups that had sprung up across the country. Petraeus and his field commander, Lt. Gen. Ray Odierno, mandated adherence to the new counterinsurgency doctrine that placed protection of the Iraqi people as the most important consideration in the design and execution of military operations. Petraeus took advantage of unforeseen opportunities such as the tribal awakening and the willingness of local communities to step up and defend themselves against insurgent and militia violence. By the end of the surge in July 2008, violence had dropped by more than 90 percent, creating the conditions for the resumption of political discourse in Iraqi society.[74]

After a belated start, the army began to train its forces in counterinsurgency scenarios at its combat training centers in Fort Irwin, California; Fort Polk, Louisiana; and Hohenfels, Germany. It also established a center for advisory training at Fort Riley, Kansas, to prepare personnel for service on military transition teams in Iraq and Afghanistan. In 2008, the Combined Arms Center refashioned the army's core operational doctrine, Field Manual 3–0, bringing it in line with post-2001 experience. The spectrum of conflict now ran from stable peace through unstable peace through insurgency all the way to general war. Military operations conducted along this spectrum included operational themes such as peacetime military engagement, limited intervention, peace operations,

---

[72] Conrad Crane, *Cassandra in Oz: Counterinsurgency and Future War* (Annapolis, MD, 2016); Fred Kaplan, *The Insurgents: David Petraeus and the Plot to Change the American Way of War* (New York, 2013).

[73] Nagl was a Rhodes Scholar with an Oxford DPhil and the author of a prescient book on counterinsurgency, *Learning to Eat Soup with a Knife: Counterinsurgency Lessons from Malaya and Vietnam* (New York, 2002).

[74] Peter R. Mansoor, *Surge: My Journey with General David Petraeus and the Remaking of the Iraq War* (New Haven, CT, 2013). Regrettably, decisions by the Obama administration to continue to support highly sectarian Prime Minister Nouri al-Maliki after he lost the election of 2010 and to withdraw US forces from Iraq in 2011 resulted in a downward spiral that reenergized opposition to the Iraqi government and paved the way for the 2014 invasion of Iraq by the Islamic State of Iraq and al-Sham, or ISIS.

and irregular warfare in addition to major combat operations. Most importantly, the army finally recognized that full spectrum operations included "combinations of offensive, defensive, and stability or civil support tasks."[75] Thirty-five years after the end of the Vietnam War, the army had finally decided to embrace the full range of military missions.[76]

However, the Officer Personnel Management System, the primary embedding mechanism in the US Army, continued to shape the army's officer corps according to industrial-age priorities. In the post–Cold War era, the army continued to promote officers based on their command efficiency reports, which were heavily dependent on success in branch-qualifying positions, performance at combat training center rotations, and time spent in the "muddy boots" army.[77] Army culture prized command over staff expertise and charismatic leadership over intellectual acumen; officers avoided service in the Pentagon and on higher-level staffs. Few officers sought so-called broadening assignments out of the mainstream of army service such as advanced civil schooling, instructor or teaching assignments, or think tank fellowships.[78] One study showed that over a two-year period (2011–2012), officers selected for infantry battalion command spent 80 percent of their careers within brigade combat teams, with service as an aide to a general officer as the most common broadening assignment.[79] Sadly, one must agree with the conclusion of retired army strategist Jason Warren, who argues that General of the Army Dwight D. Eisenhower and Chief of Staff of the US Army Gen. Omar Bradley would today have been non-selects for battalion command due to lack of World War I combat experience and would have ended their careers as majors or lieutenant colonels.[80] Yet Eisenhower possessed exactly the kind of broad education and experiences that made him indispensable as the senior ranking US commander in Europe in World War II. Instead of recognizing such unique talent, army culture in the post-Vietnam era created a generation of general officers superbly conditioned to replicate themselves with each promotion board.

Even more detrimental to the service's future was its attitude toward education. Army officers viewed school assignments as a break from operational duties and an opportunity to recharge their batteries and spend time with their

---

[75] Department of the Army, Field Manual 3–0, *Operations* (Washington, DC, 2008), 3–1, https://fas.org/irp/doddir/army/fm3-0.pdf.

[76] Not all army intellectuals embraced counterinsurgency warfare; see, for instance, Gian Gentile, *Wrong Turn: America's Deadly Embrace of Counterinsurgency* (New York, 2013).

[77] Branch-qualifying positions for combat arms officers include platoon leader, company commander, executive/operations officer, battalion commander, and brigade commander.

[78] Col. Thomas D. Boccardi, "Polyester Culture: The U.S. Army's Aversion to Broadening Assignments," US Army War College, Carlisle Barracks, PA, March 30, 2012, www.dtic.mil/get-tr-doc/pdf?AD=ADA568278, 7–12.

[79] Ibid., 12.

[80] Jason Warren, "The Centurion Mindset and the Army's Strategic Leader Paradigm," *Parameters* 45(3) (Autumn 2015), 27–38, quote on 29–30.

families. While most officers attained a master's degree, they have "become analogous to the Ranger Tab for the Infantry officer – something expected and necessary for career progression – and not evidence of a proclivity for serious thought about the military profession."[81] This attitude was exactly opposite of that of the interwar army, which viewed school assignments as more difficult than time in the field force. In that era, Command and General Staff School coursework took up five and a half days a week, with additional study in the evenings to prepare for lessons. At Fort Leavenworth, a chosen cohort of officers learned how to lead and manage large formations that did not exist in peacetime, engaged in intellectual debate, and honed the tactics and techniques of combined-arms warfare. The schoolhouse was essential for professional development due to the lack of properly organized, manned, trained, and equipped units in a force devastated by the austerity of the Great Depression. The top graduates often remained on the faculty to educate the next generation of field-grade officers.[82]

In the interwar army, officers selected for professional military education understood they were being advanced ahead of their peers. Competition at the staff college made them work even harder to study and learn their profession. In comparison, at the dawn of the twenty-first century, army leadership decided that every field-grade officer would attend the Command and General Staff College beginning in 2003.[83] This "no major left behind" policy encouraged average performance since there was no reward for outperforming one's peers. Furthermore, due to the personnel demands of the wars in Afghanistan and Iraq, attendance at the staff college lagged and a large backlog developed. To make matters worse, promotion rates to major increased to build an officer corps for a larger army. Promotion rates of nearly 100 percent resulted in little distinction among officers in a year group, driving out some high performers and instilling a zero defects, risk-averse culture of mediocrity in the remainder.[84]

The result of the army's promotion and professional military educational systems has been the selection of leaders based on tactical and technical competence rather than on strategic potential and the creation of an army that was supremely competent in operational matters, but whose senior leaders sometimes had difficulties thinking more broadly. In an essay on anti-

---

[81] First Lt. Anthony M. Formica, "Lost in Transmission: How the Army Has Garbled the Message about the Nature of Its Profession," *Military Review* 92 (March–April 2012), 44–52, quote on 47.
[82] Peter J. Schifferle, *America's School for War: Fort Leavenworth, Officer Education, and Victory in World War II* (Lawrence, KS, 2010).
[83] For the background to this decision, see Col. Brian D. Prosser, "Universal ILE Policy: Concept, Reality and Recommendations," US Army War College, Carlisle Barracks, PA, March 30, 2007, www.dtic.mil/get-tr-doc/pdf?AD=ADA468953.
[84] Tim Kane, "Why Our Best Officers Are Leaving," *The Atlantic*, January/February 2011, www.theatlantic.com/magazine/archive/2011/01/why-our-best-officers-are-leaving/308346/.

intellectualism in the army, retired US Army Col. Lloyd J. Matthews related a telling anecdote: "A distinguished Army four-star general, now retired, once boasted to me that he never read anything but the contents of his in-box. The Army culture that produced this sort of swaggering, know-nothing complacency simply has to give way to a tough insistence that our senior leaders be whole men and women."[85] More than a decade later, another officer commented that little had changed. "In some ways, the battlefield-dominant US Army created by these men has become a more ethical version of the Wehrmacht, which the institution intentionally sought to emulate in the 1970s and 1980s. The Army has developed a force capable of winning nearly every firefight, while simultaneously blunting its development of strategic leaders."[86] Retired colonels Charles Allen and George Woods write that "the cultural legacy of muddy boots, anti-intellectualism, and egalitarianism hinder the [US Army's] effective development of senior leaders."[87] Finally, in a recent, perceptive article on professionalism, First Lt. Anthony Formica writes, "In their strategic negotiations with other jurisdictional actors, [army officers] have demonstrated a clear preference for being seen as ground warfare experts, a title that implies more vocational occupation than professional domain."[88]

Notwithstanding these warnings, the army seems to be exiting its conflicts in Afghanistan and Iraq with more balance than it did its last cataclysm in Vietnam.[89] Despite a renewed emphasis on conventional combat operations and operational deployments in NATO to Poland and the Baltic States, the most recent army capstone doctrine continues to put emphasis on stability operations in the guise of "wide area security."[90] The last two chiefs of staff, Gen. Ray Odierno and Gen. Mark Milley, have put increased emphasis on building the army's intellectual capital. Odierno initiated the Strategic Broadening Seminars Program and the Advanced Strategic Planning and Policy Program, as well as including broadening assignments in professional development guidance in the latest version of the officer evaluation report.[91] The relatively

---

[85] Lloyd J. Matthews, "The Uniformed Intellectual and His Place in American Arms, Part II: The Effects of Anti-intellectualism on the Army Profession Today," *Army* 52(8) (August 2002), 31–40, quote on 34.

[86] Warren, "The Centurion Mindset," 28.

[87] Charles D. Allen and George J. Woods, "Developing Army Enterprise Leaders," *Military Review* (July–August 2015), 42–49, 44.

[88] Formica, "Lost in Transmission," 51.

[89] For a discussion of the future of US military operations, see David Barno, "Military Adaptation in Complex Operations," *Prism* 1(1) (December 2009), 27–36.

[90] "Army forces simultaneously and continuously combine offensive, defensive, and stability operations through a blend of combined arms maneuver and wide area security." Department of the Army, ADP 3–0, *Unified Land Operations* (Washington, DC, 2011), 2–3.

[91] Michael Shekleton, "Developing Strategic Leaders: An Option," The Strategy Bridge, December 6, 2016, https://thestrategybridge.org/the-bridge/2016/12/6/developing-strategic-leaders-an-option.

new career field of "strategist" includes education of selected officers at the Army War College's Basic and Advanced Strategic Arts Programs. In 2012, the army reinstated a competitive selection board for attendance at the Command and General Staff College, once again selecting less than half of each officer cohort for resident attendance at Fort Leavenworth. Operational fellowships are available to a select group of officers to earn master's and PhD degrees from civilian institutions, while the Army War College has introduced greater rigor into its curriculum.

The effects of these changes are uncertain and will take years to play out. Service culture must set expectations early in an officer's career or they likely will never take root. Lt. Gen. H. R. McMaster, who rose to serve as the national security advisor in the Trump administration, wrote his study of the failure of the Joint Chiefs of Staff to make their views heard as the Johnson administration committed the United States to a ground war in Vietnam as a senior captain and junior major.[92] Even then, McMaster was twice passed over for promotion to brigadier general before finally being selected due to the intervention of Gen. David Petraeus, hand-picked by Secretary of Defense Bob Gates to chair the army's promotion board in 2007 even though Petraeus had to return from the war zone in Baghdad to do it. McMaster's West Point classmate Bill Rapp, who earned a PhD in political science at Stanford University, was selected for promotion to brigadier general while serving as chief of Petraeus's commander's initiatives group in Iraq; Rapp would go on to serve as commandant at the US Army War College before retiring as a major general.[93] But the career paths of these general officers have largely been the exception; whether the army can change its culture to make their journey the norm is problematic. Culture evolves slowly; it remains to be seen whether the army can overcome its anti-intellectual, heroic mind-set in favor of a more balanced mentality. If it is able to do so, the army will finally create the strategic competence in its general officers to match their tactical and operational expertise. The army will then perhaps be able not just to win its first battles but also to connect those victories to political goals and win the nation's wars.

---

[92] H. R. McMaster, *Dereliction of Duty: Johnson, McNamara, the Joint Chiefs of Staff, and the Lies That Led to Vietnam* (New York, 1997). McMaster earned his PhD at the University of North Carolina en route to West Point to teach military history as a rotational faculty member.

[93] Rapp also wrote and lectured on the role of military leaders in the making of strategy. William E. Rapp, "Civil-Military Relations: The Role of Military Leaders in Strategy Making," *Parameters* 45(3) (Autumn 2015), 13–26.

Part III

Maritime Forces

14   The Royal Navy, 1900–1945

Learning from Disappointment

Corbin Williamson

On December 11, 1941, a squadron of British warships built around the battle-ship *Prince of Wales* and the battlecruiser *Repulse* sailed through the Gulf of Thailand in search of a Japanese invasion convoy.[1] There, a coordinated air attack by Japanese land-based bombers sank both capital ships in a matter of hours. One vein of historical scholarship views this defeat as emblematic of the failure of the Royal Navy to prepare adequately for the challenges of World War II.[2] According to this school of thought, the inconclusive results of the 1916 Battle of Jutland during World War I led the navy to obsess in its training and education over refighting the battle during the 1920s and 1930s. Due to this preoccupation, the fleet supposedly entered World War II "instinctively hostile to the modern world of incessant invention, innovation, and change" and "too little blessed with innovative imagination."[3] However, such a perspective fails to capture the navy's critical interwar reforms that flowed from Jutland.

The interwar Royal Navy did closely analyze Jutland and World War I at sea, but used this analysis, both formal and informal, to correct problems the battle revealed: over-centralization of authority, a reluctance to fight night actions, and an overly defensive use of destroyers. The profound dissatisfaction of the officer corps with the fleet's performance in World War I led to changes in doctrine, training, and professional military education that improved the navy's World War II performance. These interwar reforms reduced the service's previously held efforts to avoid uncertainty by encouraging commanders to take the initiative. Through these reforms, the Royal Navy reinvigorated the fleet's ability to take the tactical offensive, especially in surface warfare, which

---

[1] The views expressed in this chapter are those of the author and do not reflect the official policy or position of the US government, the Department of Defense, or Air University. The author wishes to offer heartfelt thanks to Ryan Peeks and Joseph Moretz for reviewing and commenting on this chapter.

[2] Correlli Barnett, *Engage the Enemy More Closely: The Royal Navy in the Second World War* (New York, 1991); Lisle Rose, *Power at Sea: The Breaking Storm, 1919–1945* (Columbia, MO, 2007), 103–105, 109.

[3] Rose, *Power at Sea, 1919–1945*, 115; Barnett, *Engage the Enemy More Closely*, 49.

is the focus of this chapter.[4] The interwar reforms reflected an organizational culture that pursued improvement and learning in response to its disappointing performance in World War I.

Any attempt to understand the Royal Navy's culture must begin with the recognition that organizational culture is "difficult to assess, since it depends on nods, winks, and general attitudes long past."[5] Furthermore, the navy consisted of a number of smaller navies that all enjoyed unique characteristics. The big ship navy comprised the fleet's largest warships: battleships, battlecruisers, and cruisers, and later aircraft carriers. Relations between officers and sailors tended to be more formal, a reflection of the hierarchy required for a crew of hundreds of men and the greater presence of senior officers on big ships. In contrast, the atmosphere on destroyers and other escorts was more relaxed, within limits, due to the greater familiarity inherent in a smaller crew. This phenomenon also occurred in the submarine force, which tended to view itself as the elite within an elite navy. Finally, the Fleet Air Arm often felt underappreciated by the rest of the fleet, which in turn found naval aviators insufficiently "naval" in their bearing and attitude. In addition to these formal subdivisions, informal networks connected officers into various subcultures, such as torpedo specialists with ties to the Royal Geographic Society and the royal family for the period before World War I.[6] Still, these various subcultures all drew upon the navy's common heritage and tradition.

The Royal Navy, 1900–1914

The Royal Navy rose to prominence in the seventeenth and eighteenth centuries fighting against European enemies such as the Dutch, French, and Spanish. A series of victories in the Napoleonic Wars culminating in the 1805 Battle of Trafalgar established the supremacy of the Royal Navy. Its ships guarded the expanding British Empire by protecting the sea lines of communication that linked Britain to the rest of the world. Deployed globally, British warships gave London a visible diplomatic and military presence that undergirded the *Pax Brittanica* throughout the nineteenth century. However, by 1900, the fleet lacked direct experience in major combat operations since the Crimean War (1853–1856). This dearth of experience led to internal disagreements over how to best employ the new equipment coming into service in the late nineteenth century.

---

[4] I am indebted to Rear Admiral James Goldrick, Royal Australian Navy for the concept of the tactical offensive. See James Goldrick, "Learning How to Do Over the Horizon Warfare at Sea: The Clash of Emergent Communications Technology and the Naval Culture of Command in the First World War" (US Naval War College, Newport, RI, October 6, 2016), www.youtube.com/watch?v=aVTZ3o7pspg&t=228s.

[5] Charles Hamilton, *The Making of the Modern Admiralty: British Naval Policy-Making, 1805–1927* (Cambridge, 2011), 285.

[6] Andrew Gordon, *The Rules of the Game: Jutland and British Naval Command* (Annapolis, MD, 1996).

During this period, a number of technological developments profoundly altered the character of war at sea. Steam power gradually replaced sails as the principal form of propulsion and provided electrical power to ships. Steel hulls with plate armor supplanted wood as a ship's basic structural foundation. Rifled guns encased in turrets increased a ship's effective range and the ability to concentrate fire. Wireless radio held out the promise of instant communications between admirals and their subordinates. Self-propelled torpedoes, mines, and submarines added new threats to traditional surface ships from under the sea.

While these material improvements changed the tools of naval warfare, they did not fundamentally alter the Royal Navy's confidence in its own superiority, or that of the British public. British sailors in 1900 believed they belonged to an elite fighting force and were the heirs of Nelson, Howe, Jervis, with a proud tradition of success and preeminence. In the language of organizational culture, the navy enjoyed a high level of in-group collectivism. The nation's population shared this confidence in the navy, often referred to as the senior service.

The foundation for this confidence lay in the priority given to seamanship in personnel policies. Enlisted sailors, ratings, were long-service professionals who joined as boys or young men. Following an initial term of twelve years, ratings could sign up for a further ten years and receive a pension upon completion of the full term. After promotion to petty officer and then chief petty officer, a rating might advance to warrant officer, experienced sailors who provided long-term technical and institutional knowledge.[7] The two largest categories of ratings were sailors, who operated the guns, communications, and shipboard equipment, and stokers, skilled workers who operated the engines.[8]

For officers, the Royal Naval College, Dartmouth, provided the principal gateway into the Royal Navy. The college, typically known simply as Dartmouth, opened in 1905, taking over officer preparation from an old sailing hulk.[9] From 1903 to 1921, officer cadets spent their first two years at Royal Naval College, Osborne, before transferring to Dartmouth. The navy opened this second school as a temporary measure to handle the growing numbers of officer cadets as the fleet expanded in the years before World War I.[10]

Cadets entered the navy approximately at the age of thirteen and spent four years at Dartmouth, or two at Osborne followed by two at Dartmouth until

[7] James Goldrick, *Before Jutland: The Naval War in Northern European Waters, August 1914–February 1915* (Annapolis, MD, 2015), 26–27.

[8] Mike Farquharson-Roberts, *A History of the Royal Navy: World War I* (New York, 2014), 18–19.

[9] John Winton, "Life and Education in a Technically Evolving Navy, 1815–1925," in John Richard Hill, ed., *The Oxford Illustrated History of the Royal Navy* (Oxford, 1995), 250–279, 266.

[10] Robert Davison, *The Challenges of Command: The Royal Navy's Executive Branch Officers, 1880–1919* (Burlington, VT, 2011), 13–14.

1921.[11] These schools instilled naval discipline and culture in the context of a math- and science-based secondary education.[12] At age seventeen, cadets went to sea in training ships for six to eight months followed by promotion to midshipmen and service with the fleet for a little over two years. The navy believed strongly in the value of extended time at sea for officers in training.[13] After passing required exams, midshipmen became acting sublieutenants at approximately twenty.[14] After more training courses and exams ashore, they became commissioned officers as sublieutenants and went to sea. There they pursued a watch-keeping certificate followed by promotion to lieutenant, near the age of twenty-two.[15] A watch-keeping certificate allowed an officer to stand watch on a ship's bridge as a fully fledged member of the officer corps.[16] Education prior to becoming a lieutenant focused on the skills and knowledge needed to stand watch, as this was the fleet's principal demand of junior officers.

Dartmouth occupied a prominent place in the officer corps's sense of itself, though the school's products remembered their experience in varied terms. A 1929 Dartmouth graduate later described the institution in the following terms:

> For the most part what emerged was a definite breed of fit, tough, highly trained, but sketchily educated professionals, ready for instant duty, for parades or tea parties, for catastrophes, for peace or war; confident leaders, alert seamen, fair administrators, poor delegators; officers of wide interest and narrow vision, strong on tactics, weak on strategy; an able, active, cheerful, monosyllabic elite.[17]

In contrast to the regimentation of early career education, upon becoming a lieutenant, officers could exercise greater free will. Lieutenants could specialize in a particular field such as gunnery, signals, navigation, or torpedoes, though this was not mandatory. The navy later added other specializations such as submarines and aviation. Specialists took additional courses in their chosen technical field and served in staff postings, which typically delayed their opportunity to obtain their first independent command.[18] By 1900, conventional wisdom held

---

[11] Ibid., 104.
[12] Elinor Romans, "Leadership Training for Midshipmen, c.1919–1939," in Helen Doe and Richard Harding, eds., *Naval Leadership and Management, 1650–1950: Essays in Honour of Michael Duffy* (Woodbridge, Suffolk, 2012), 173–192, 178.
[13] Ibid., 176.
[14] John Roberts, "Great Britain: The Royal Navy," in Vincent P. O'Hara, ed., *To Crown the Waves: The Great Navies of the First World War* (Annapolis, MD, 2013), 129–177, 149.
[15] Davison, *The Challenges of Command*, 104; Quintin Colville, "Jack Tar and the Gentleman Officer: The Role of Uniform in Shaping the Class- and Gender-Related Identities of British Naval Personnel, 1930–1939," *Transactions of the Royal Historical Society* 13 (2003), 105–129, 108.
[16] Brian Lavery, *Churchill's Navy: The Ships, Men, and Organization, 1939–1945* (London, 2006), 130.
[17] Charles Owen, *No More Heroes: The Royal Navy in the Twentieth Century* (London, 1956), 131.
[18] Romans, "Leadership Training for Midshipmen," 173.

that officers with specialization, especially in gunnery and torpedoes, enjoyed an advantage in achieving higher ranks. The senior leaders of World War I were almost all gunnery or torpedo specialists.[19]

Some officers chose not to specialize, often in pursuit of an early command, typically a destroyer. Andrew Cunningham took this route, becoming a general service officer, a "salt horse," and had only the barest exposure to staff work in the interwar years.[20] He went on to become First Sea Lord after a successful tour leading the Mediterranean Fleet in World War II. Another general service officer, John Tovey, commanded the Home Fleet for three years during World War II and oversaw the successful pursuit and destruction of the German battleship *Bismarck*. Their experiences demonstrate that, while many viewed specialization as the route to high command, this was not an absolute rule.[21] While service on smaller ships such as destroyers and submarines gave junior officers far more responsibility than their counterparts on cruisers and battleships, experience on a large ship could provide greater visibility to senior officers, which many thought necessary for promotion.[22]

After eight years as a lieutenant, an officer became a lieutenant commander through seniority after the navy introduced this rank in 1914.[23] In contrast, subsequent promotions to commander and captain required an officer to pass a competitive selection board.[24] Specialists reverted to general service status upon promotion to commander. Those who made captain had eleven years to make rear admiral to avoid forced retirement. As a result, the navy maintained a stable of retired captains who had advanced through two competitive promotions and who, in a crisis, could return to service.[25]

Prior to World War I, professional education such as specialization beyond lieutenant was voluntary. The navy tended to believe that admirals achieved success primarily through innate qualities rather than formal education and that officer training culminated in an independent command at sea.[26] Before World

[19] Davison, *The Challenges of Command*, 6; Nicholas A. M. Rodger, "Training or Education: A Naval Dilemma over Three Centuries," in Nicholas A. M. Rodger, *Essays in Naval History, from Medieval to Modern* (Burlington, VT, 2009), 1–34, 24.

[20] Mike Farquharson-Roberts, *Royal Navy Officers from War to War, 1918–1939* (New York, 2015), 90; Michael Coles, "The Warrior and the Strategist, Cunningham and King, Training for High Command: A Comparative Study," in William B. Cogar, ed., *New Interpretations in Naval History: Selected Papers from the Twelfth Naval History Symposium Held at the United States Naval Academy, 26–27 October 1995* (Annapolis, MD, 1997), 273–287, 278.

[21] Farquharson-Roberts, *Royal Navy Officers from War to War*, 221–222.   [22] Ibid., 28.

[23] Joseph Moretz, *Thinking Wisely, Planning Boldly: The Higher Education and Training of Royal Navy Officers, 1919–39* (West Midlands, 2014), 212.

[24] Lavery, *Churchill's Navy*, 130–131.

[25] Farquharson-Roberts, *Royal Navy Officers from War to War*, 224.

[26] Christopher Dandeker, "Bureaucracy Planning and War: The Royal Navy, 1880 to 1918," *Armed Forces and Society* 11(1) (Fall 1984), 130–146, 144; Andrew Lambert, "History As Process and Record: The Royal Navy and Officer Education," in Greg Kennedy and Keith Neilson, eds., *Military Education: Past, Present, and Future* (Westport, CT, 2002), 83–104, 83.

War I, senior officers received little education to prepare them for higher command. Early efforts to provide this instruction, such as the 1900 War Course and the 1912 Staff Course, had limited impact on the fleet's leadership before the war.

In the years before 1914, patronage played a diminishing, though still visible role in officer promotion.[27] As a result, socially well-connected officers, who formed a "select naval aristocracy," regularly received choice assignments up through the war.[28] Thus the service reflected the continuing presence and influence of class in British society.

Royal Navy officers tended to come from the professional middle-upper class, which included doctors, the clergy, bankers, the military services, civil servants, and businessmen, as well as a few titled nobles.[29] For financially secure parents, a naval career offered their sons a steady job, the potential for promotion, and a respectable profession.[30] The financial demands of supporting an officer cadet for roughly the first nine years of his career limited the pool of applicants to those with families who could provide such support, less than 10 percent of the population.[31] As late as the 1930s and 1940s, an accent that suggested a lower-class background could torpedo any chance of obtaining a commission.[32] To a considerable degree, the officer corps was a self-perpetuating class as the navy favored applicants with a naval background.[33]

Concerns about the limited pool of officer candidates led the navy in 1913 to establish a path for selected secondary school graduates to become officers. This Special Entry scheme sought to broaden the stream of officer cadets and enjoyed some success in making an officer's career available to a wider spectrum of society. Special Entry cadets entered the navy at age eighteen instead of thirteen and thus enjoyed a broader general education prior to joining the fleet.[34]

Special Entry officers provided the bulk of engineers, who operated and managed the fleet's propulsion but could not command warships. As technology and technical skill became ever more important in naval warfare, engineer officers felt the navy should expand their authority and promotion potential beyond the confines of the engine room. In 1902, the Selbourne-Fisher scheme sought to address

---

[27] Farquharson-Roberts, *Royal Navy Officers from War to War*, 91.

[28] Gordon, *The Rules of the Game*, 37–38.

[29] Colville, "Jack Tar and the Gentleman Officer," 106–107.

[30] Ibid., 106–107; Romans, "Leadership Training for Midshipmen," 177.

[31] Colville, "Jack Tar and the Gentleman Officer," 108; Brian Lavery, *In Which They Served: The Royal Navy Officer Experience in the Second World War* (London, 2009), 74; Arthur Marder, *From the Dreadnought to Scapa Flow, vol. 1: The Road to War, 1904–1914* (Annapolis, MD, 2013), 31.

[32] Lavery, *Churchill's Navy*, 10.

[33] Farquharson-Roberts, *Royal Navy Officers from War to War*, 44; Lavery, *In Which They Served*, 74.

[34] Lavery, *In Which They Served*, 74–75.

this tension by mandating that cadets in the executive (line officers), engineering, and marine branches train together at Osborne and Dartmouth.[35] Under this program, engineers would one day be able to compete for command positions once they reached the appropriate rank. While only partially implemented for the marines, engineers looked forward to possibly one day commanding a ship of their own, though the Admiralty removed this option after World War I.

The navy struggled to meet several sets of competing goals in preparing officers: imparting leadership and technical skills as well as balancing obedience with creativity. The surest method for giving young men leadership training, placing them in charge of a small boat or a department, required time at sea to develop confidence. At the same time, rapid technological developments in naval warfare such as longer-range guns, wireless radios, and submarines meant that officers also needed a solid education in math and science.[36] An officer's first years, both at Dartmouth and at sea, sought to balance these goals.

Furthermore, the Admiralty also sought to balance the current demands of manning ships with the requirement to develop the fleet's future leaders. In the short term, officer education had to provide large numbers of junior officers to stand watch on ships, a demanding routine that required obedience to the captain's orders and exercising judgment within relatively narrow confines. Early career preparation culminated in the ability to stand watch, which separated executive officers from their engineering counterparts.[37] From this sizable group of junior officers whose originality had been somewhat constrained, the navy needed to select a few future admirals who could take the initiative and command in the chaos of battle.[38] One noted scholar summarized the products of the navy's officer preparation policies thusly:

> In 1914 the navy was desperately short of first-class minds, because it had made no effort to locate and encourage them, nor prepared an educational system that would get the best from less-gifted men. The educational system, as it existed in 1914, lacked coherence and ambition. It had not been allowed to develop, and it had positively held back the development of staff and command skills, insight and understanding, in favor of high-level training. When the test came, the navy had very few officers capable of holding their own in interservice conferences or of dealing with politicians.[39]

The ability to stand watch was not the only divide between executive and engineering officers. The executive officer corps was socially conservative and

---

[35] Oliver Johnson, "Class Warfare and the Selborne Scheme: The Royal Navy's Battle over Technology and Social Hierarchy," *Mariner's Mirror* 100(4) (2014), 422–433.

[36] Davison, *The Challenges of Command*, 67–68.   [37] Lavery, *Churchill's Navy*, 41.

[38] Farquharson-Roberts, *Royal Navy Officers from War to War*, 27; Andrew Lambert, *Admirals: The Naval Commanders Who Made Britain Great* (London, 2008), 160–161.

[39] Lambert, "History As Process and Record," 95.

more often than not from the south and southwest of England.[40] In contrast, the industrial regions of England and Scotland produced more engineer officers, who tended to be more democratic and less Victorian in their social views.[41] In addition to these geographic and philosophical differences, executive officers largely believed that their profession required innate characteristics of leadership and was therefore not open to all. A substantial portion of executive officers did not believe engineers possessed the qualifications for command and preferred that they focus on simply keeping the engines running.[42] The executive branch tended to reject the argument that the increasing technological sophistication of warships meant that engineers and engineering must play a more prominent role in the navy.

Class distinctions not only influenced executive views toward engineers but also enlisted sailors who overwhelmingly came from working-class families. Officers largely rejected the idea that ratings would ever "be suitable to become naval officers."[43] While officially the navy provided a path for ratings to become commissioned officers, in practice only a handful made this leap.[44] American personnel operating with the Royal Navy in World War I were taken aback by British officers using ratings as personal servants, which reflected the clearer social hierarchy in the United Kingdom.[45] On average an officer's greater access to nutritious foods and healthier lifestyle also meant that officers tended to be taller than ratings, reinforcing a sense of superiority.

The demands of naval life created a degree of separation between officers and the rest of British society. The combination of a long apprenticeship for officer cadets, extended deployments at sea made possible by steel hulls and steam power, and the intense commitment demanded by the navy meant officers especially lived apart from their civilian counterparts.[46] The navy did not necessarily view itself as superior to the rest of the British populace, though sailors were convinced of their own superiority compared to other navies.[47] In return, the public broadly shared this perception of the navy as the world's premier fleet, fully capable of mastering its enemies.[48]

Throughout the nineteenth century, the Admiralty viewed France and Russia as the Royal Navy's most likely enemies, though the British allied with the French against the Russians in the Crimean War. However, Britain smoothed

[40] Davison, *The Challenges of Command*, 14; John Horsfield, *The Art of Leadership in War: The Royal Navy from the Age of Nelson to the End of World War II* (Westport, CT, 1980), 99.
[41] Horsfield, *The Art of Leadership in War*, 100; Christopher McKee, *Sober Men and True: Sailor Lives in the Royal Navy, 1900–1945* (Cambridge, 2002), 47.
[42] Lavery, *In Which They Served*, 171.   [43] Ibid., 77.
[44] Farquharson-Roberts, *Royal Navy Officers from War to War*, 69.
[45] Ronald Spector, *At War at Sea: Sailors and Naval Combat in the Twentieth Century* (New York, 2001), 134.
[46] Farquharson-Roberts, *Royal Navy Officers from War to War*, 44–46.   [47] Ibid., 228–229.
[48] Ibid., 229.

relations with former rivals Russia and France while signing an alliance with Japan between 1902 and 1905.[49] At the same time, the growing German naval threat strengthened long-standing British efforts to seek naval assistance from the empire. In particular, Whitehall repeatedly tried to get the Dominions of Canada, Australia, and New Zealand to expand their naval forces with modest success.[50] The Dominions wanted to train their naval forces to Royal Navy standards but refused to accept uncritically London's direction in defense matters.[51]

The navy's four overarching missions consisted of two defensive and two offensive roles. The service sought to protect Britain and the empire from invasion, while defending the sea lanes of trade and commerce that fueled the British economy. As an island nation, Britain relied heavily on imports, especially for food and raw materials, which in turn required secure maritime communication links.[52] Offensively, the fleet supported the army and sought to deny the enemy access to maritime trade.[53] These missions endured through Admiral John Fisher's strategic redeployment in the years before World War I.

The beginning of the twentieth century found the Royal Navy supporting the army's Boer War operations in South Africa and fighting the Boxer Rebellion in China.[54] In response to the growing threat posed by Germany, First Sea Lord Admiral John Fisher launched a comprehensive effort to reform the navy's strategic posture in 1904, while simultaneously reducing operating costs. Reorganized fleets based in Britain, Gibraltar, and the Mediterranean provided strategic flexibility, while squadrons of battlecruisers would protect trade routes. London could use the nation's commanding position in global financial, insurance, and shipping markets to torpedo the German economy as rapidly as possible in war.[55] Britain only partially implemented Fisher's vision, though he did succeed in concentrating warships in European waters.

Gathering the battleships in a small number of fleets highlighted the need for doctrine to coordinate the growing firepower of these fleets. However, the fleet lacked an agreed-upon doctrine for fleet engagements due to disagreements about how to incorporate recent technical advances and command styles.[56] Improvements in gunnery and fire control, the limitations of existing command and control capabilities, and the gradual replacement of pre-dreadnoughts with dreadnought battleships all combined to frustrate efforts to establish a common

[49] Duncan Redford and Philip Grove, *The Royal Navy: A History since 1900* (London, 2014), 21.
[50] David French, "The British Armed Forces, 1900–1939," in Chris Wrigley, ed., *A Companion to Early Twentieth-Century Britain* (Malden, MA, 2003), 167–181, 172.
[51] Moretz, *Thinking Wisely, Planning Boldly*, 105.
[52] French, "The British Armed Forces, 1900–1939," 177.
[53] Roberts, "Great Britain: The Royal Navy," 131–132.
[54] Redford and Grove, *The Royal Navy*, 7–9.   [55] Ibid., 25–31.
[56] Nicholas Lambert, *Sir John Fisher's Naval Revolution* (Columbia, MO, 1999), 211–214.

doctrine.[57] Furthermore, the concept of doctrine remained "anathema to many senior officers" brought up in the tradition of independent command at sea.[58]

Generally, commanders expected that a fleet action would comprise a gunnery duel between linear formations.[59] Up through 1910, the navy's senior leaders assumed that such battles would involve battleships, almost to the exclusion of other types. However, in 1910, the fleet began to experiment with large formations of battleships, cruisers, and destroyers. These additional ships could defend the battle line from enemy destroyers and their torpedoes, but complicated command and control for the admiral in command.[60] Admirals typically viewed destroyers in a defensive, rather than offensive, role, in part because of the challenges of coordinating a destroyer attack during a fleet action.[61]

As the Royal Navy concentrated in home waters, fleet commanders gained opportunities to exercise larger formations regularly. However, the uncertainty introduced by new technologies such as submarines, dreadnoughts, and battle-cruisers undermined efforts to develop doctrine from exercises.[62] Some exercises focused on lines of battleships engaged in a gunnery duel with destroyers relegated to defensive tasks, while others examined the threat posed by submarines.[63] The control challenges posed by large formations of disparate ship types only grew with the smoke from the fleet that obscured visual signal flags. In 1910, the commander in chief of the Home Fleet, Admiral William May, reviewed thirty-four recent tactical exercises and concluded that "it would be almost impossible to get a signal through, on account of the smoke from the funnels and the guns."[64] The cost of large-scale maneuvers limited their frequency. The fuel consumed in the 1913 fleet exercises cost nearly £200,000.[65] Financial limitations on exercise ammunition expenditure meant that important problems with British gunnery went undiscovered until 1914. Furthermore, exercises focused on daylight actions to the detriment of night fighting skills.[66] Pre–World War I exercises highlighted a number of issues that would trouble the navy during the coming conflict.

[57] Ibid.
[58] Joseph Moretz, "The Legacy of Jutland: Expectation, Reality, and Learning from the Experience of Battle in the Royal Navy, 1913–1939," in Greg Kennedy, ed., *Britain's War at Sea, 1914–1918: The War They Thought and the War They Fought* (London, 2016), 149–164, 150.
[59] Ibid., 151.   [60] Lambert, *Sir John Fisher's Naval Revolution*, 216–217.   [61] Ibid., 219–220.
[62] Ibid., 211–214.
[63] Duncan Redford, "Naval Culture and the Fleet Submarine, 1910–1917," in Don Leggett and Richard Dunn, eds., *Re-inventing the Ship: Science, Technology and the Maritime World, 1800–1918* (Burlington, VT, 2012), 157–172, 163; Edmund Poland, *The Torpedomen: HMS Vernon's Story, 1872–1986* (London, 1993), 82.
[64] Lambert, *Sir John Fisher's Naval Revolution*, 220; Gordon, *The Rules of the Game*, 355.
[65] James Goldrick, "The Impact of War: Matching Expectation with Reality in the Royal Navy in the First Months of World War I at Sea," in Michael Epkenhans, Jörg Hillmann, and Frank Nägler, eds., *Jutland: World War I's Greatest Naval Battle* (Lexington, KY, 2015), 63–78, 65.
[66] Stephen Roskill, *Admiral of the Fleet Earl Beatty: The Last Naval Hero, an Intimate Biography* (New York, 1981), 61, 72; Goldrick, "The Impact of War," 71.

The navy's approach to command tended toward centralization during this period. Victorian social values and naval tradition reinforced this trend. The navy's approach firmly reflected the Victorian ideals and values of British society. Victorians prized deference to superiors, obedience, and conformity; despised over-intellectualism; and often viewed scientific professionals with suspicion.[67] They also celebrated feats of bravery, even when these feats ended in tragedy such as Captain Robert Scott's failed 1912 expedition to the Antarctic.[68] Within the service, these values tended to emphasize housekeeping at sea and strict discipline while stifling displays of initiative in the presence of a superior officer.[69] The officer corps prized independent command at sea, where a captain exercised great authority over his ship and crew. A captain's ability to control almost every element of his environment magnified the influence of Victorian culture's deference to authority within the officer corps. In short, the "delegation of decision-making, even on minor matters, was not in the tradition of the service" by 1914.[70]

British leaders in the early twentieth century struggled to coordinate military and naval policy. The Committee on Imperial Defence, reorganized in 1904, sought to reduce interservice rivalry by bringing the prime minister, key ministers, and the uniformed heads of the army and navy together.[71] However, liaison between the services focused more on avoiding interference than on integrated operations, which occurred at lower levels if at all.[72] Efforts to create truly joint defense policy struggled until the development of the War Cabinet in World War I provided the appropriate administrative organ for such work.[73] The absence of a proper naval staff within the Admiralty and the navy's belief in its primacy in British strategy also served to hinder relations with the army.

Both Liberal and Conservative governments believed that the Royal Navy must be large enough to defeat any potential rival. The overall steady growth of the navy's pre–World War I budget reflected that conviction. Politicians firmly believed in the fleet's ability to cut off German trade in the event of war.[74] Despite this confidence in the navy, military and naval affairs were not central to British politics or the fabric of society. Although the nation's principal martial celebration pre–World War I was Trafalgar Day, "the British public liked bands and bright uniforms because they were entertainment, the exact

---

[67] Simon Schama, *A History of Britain, vol. 3: The Fate of Empire, 1776–2000* (New York, 2002), 346; Gordon, *The Rules of the Game*, 150; Coles, "The Warrior and the Strategist," 279–280; Colville, "Jack Tar and the Gentleman Officer," 107.

[68] Gordon, *The Rules of the Game*, 377–378.   [69] Rodger, "Training or Education," 14.

[70] Hamilton, *The Making of the Modern Admiralty*, 251.

[71] Geoffrey Searle, "The Politics of National Efficiency and of War, 1900–1918," in Chris Wrigley, ed., *A Companion to Early Twentieth-Century Britain* (Malden, MA, 2003), 56–71, 63.

[72] Hamilton, *The Making of the Modern Admiralty*, 236.   [73] Ibid., 227.

[74] French, "The British Armed Forces, 1900–1939," 170.

opposite of harbingers of war."[75] Large concentrations of warships such as fleet reviews and royal occasions kept the navy in the public consciousness due to their theatrical value.[76] For their part, British governments tended to view the armed forces as an "insurance policy" to protect British interests and project power.[77]

According to one noted author, British governments recognized that the nation needed armed forces, though "they regarded them as being at best a necessary evil."[78] Influenced by a classically liberal political culture that believed free trade could reduce the frequency of war, politicians tended to view military and naval spending like "an insurance policy," which never received absolute priority except in wartime.[79]

Despite this intellectual climate, the Royal Navy's budget in the years prior to World War I benefited from a standing political commitment to maintain a battleship fleet equal to Britain's two largest rivals, a policy designed to match or exceed the expanding shipbuilding programs of European nations, especially Germany.[80] Furthermore, the Admiralty enjoyed considerable administrative strength in the budget process as annual navy estimates were sent directly to the Cabinet for approval without first consulting Treasury officials.[81] Due to the Boer War (1899–1902), military spending dominated British government finances in 1901, accounting for 58 percent of government spending that year.[82] After the war, steady improvements in naval technology drove up construction costs and by 1903, rising warship prices resulted in the navy receiving a quarter of every pound spent by the government.[83] The navy's growing shipbuilding program meant that defense spending overshadowed the cost of social programs.[84] For example, in 1905, naval outlays were roughly double the

[75] Kenneth Morgan, *The Oxford Illustrated History of Britain* (Oxford, 1984), 522.
[76] Jan Rueger, *The Great Naval Game: Britain and Germany in the Age of Empire* (Cambridge, 2007), 27.
[77] French, "The British Armed Forces, 1900–1939," 168.   [78] Ibid.
[79] Ibid.; David Edgerton, "Liberal Militarism and the British State," *New Left Review* 185 (1991), 139–169.
[80] French, "The British Armed Forces, 1900–1939," 167–168.
[81] George Peden, "Financing Churchill's Army," in Keith Neilson and Greg Kennedy, eds., *The British Way in Warfare: Power and the International System, 1856–1956: Essays in Honour of David French* (Burlington, VT, 2010), 277–299, 279; Jon Sumida, *In Defence of Naval Supremacy: Finance, Technology, and British Naval Policy, 1889–1914* (Annapolis, MD, 1993), 25–26.
[82] Kathleen Burk, "Financing Kitchener's (and Everyone Else's) Armies," in Keith Neilson and Greg Kennedy, eds., *The British Way in Warfare: Power and the International System, 1856–1956: Essays in Honour of David French* (Burlington, VT, 2010), 257–276, 258.
[83] Ibid.
[84] Paul Kennedy, "The Influence of Sea Power upon Three Great Global Wars, 1793–1815, 1914–1948, 1939–1945: A Comparative Analysis," in Nicholas A. M. Rodger, J. Ross Dancy, Benjamin Darnell, and Evan Wilson, eds., *Strategy and the Sea: Essays in Honour of John B. Hattendorf* (Woodbridge, Suffolk, 2016), 109–137, 116–117.

national spending on social services such as education and pensions.[85] The introduction of the all-big gun HMS *Dreadnought* and new battlecruisers drove up the cost of the nation's naval construction program. Due to a cross-party consensus around battleship construction, spending on the Royal Navy grew from 56 percent of total defense spending in 1905 to 61 percent in 1911.[86] This growth in naval spending combined with the costs of the Boer War to significantly increase the national debt.[87] However, this increase in public debt paled in comparison with the costs of World War I.

The Service in World War I

In early August 1914, Britain declared war on Germany, plunging the nation into World War I. Offensively, the Royal Navy supported the army and sought to deny the enemy access to maritime trade.[88] Defensively, the navy sought to counter the German navy's triple challenge to British trade and sea power: German cruisers stationed overseas, the High Seas Fleet, and submarines.[89] Supporting the army involved securing the Channel and mounting overseas expeditions to seize German colonies and bases. To counter the High Seas Fleet, the navy abandoned its traditional reliance on a close blockade of the enemy's ports due to the threat posed to blockading ships by torpedoes and mines. Instead, the Grand Fleet waited in its base in Scapa Flow for an opportunity to crush the High Seas Fleet in the North Sea, while lines of older, smaller ships interdicted merchant ships bound for Germany using a distant blockade, which ultimately played an important role in Germany's defeat.

In response to the stalemated trench lines in France after fall 1914, London ordered an assault on the Dardanelles with the goal of knocking Turkey out of the war. Turkish defenses beat back a naval assault in March 1915 and held off Allied ground forces until London called off the fiasco in late 1915. In contrast, the navy enjoyed greater success hunting down German surface raiders seeking to attack Allied sea lines of communication. In particular, the December 1914 Battle of the Falklands destroyed a German squadron that had defeated a British force in November at the Battle of Coronel off the Chilean coast.

The Grand Fleet's commander, Admiral John Jellicoe, faced a serious challenge in 1914: how to control a massive collection of ships that poured smoke from funnels and turrets in action. The line of Grand Fleet battleships alone stretched for more than a dozen miles at standard spacing. This distance

---

[85] George Peden, *The Treasury and British Public Policy, 1906–1959* (Oxford, 2000), 32.
[86] Ibid.   [87] Schama, *A History of Britain*, 517–518.
[88] Roberts, "Great Britain: The Royal Navy," 131–132.
[89] Tim Benbow, *The History of World War I: Naval Warfare, 1914–1918: From Coronel to the Atlantic and Zeebrugge* (London, 2008), 31.

presented a daunting communications problem even without adding dozens of escorting cruisers and destroyers. The wireless radios and radio offices of the day could not support the deluge of messages produced by such a fleet in battle. Furthermore, smoke along with the typically dismal North Sea weather limited the utility of visual flag signals. In addition to these technical challenges, the Grand Fleet played a critical role in Allied strategy. Churchill later described Jellicoe as "the only man who could lose the war in an afternoon."[90]

In response, Jellicoe adopted a centralized command and control system through instructions that sought to cover every conceivable scenario, in keeping with his personal preference for centralization.[91] Doctrinally, the resulting Grand Fleet Battle Orders represented the culmination of a decades-long move toward centralization and deference to superiors throughout the fleet that reflected Victorian culture.[92] However, the Battle of Jutland demonstrated the limits and problems with this approach, which in turn led to calls for change.

After several minor actions in the North Sea, the Grand Fleet's opportunity to win a major victory came on May 31, 1916, at the Battle of Jutland. Admiral David Beatty's battlecruisers intercepted the German battlecruiser squadron and both sides brought the balance of their fleet into action, though poor contact reporting hampered Jellicoe's efforts to make sense of the tactical situation. After a brief engagement between the two fleets, Jellicoe chose not to attempt a night action and the Germans reached port the next day after passing through the rear of the British fleet during the night. While British losses exceeded German losses, the blockade and British control of the North Sea remained in place. Still, the inconclusive battle led to bitter recriminations within the navy over whether to blame Jellicoe or Beatty for missing an opportunity to repeat Nelson's crushing victory at Trafalgar, a damaging debate that continued into the 1920s. The battle revealed the limits of Jellicoe's belief in centralized command and control, which the Admiralty shared. For example, when Commodore Reginald Tyrwhitt received the first signals from the Battle of Jutland, he immediately put his force of destroyers to sea from Harwich. However, the Admiralty ordered him back to port.[93] Centralized control and the navy's deference to senior officers led to numerous missed opportunities in combat.[94]

In late 1916, Admiral David Beatty replaced Jellicoe and began to push the Grand Fleet toward decentralization and greater reliance on subordinates,

[90] Roy Jenkins, *Churchill: A Biography* (New York, 2001), 216.
[91] Hamilton, *The Making of the Modern Admiralty*, 241.
[92] For a more complete argument, see Gordon, *The Rules of the Game.*
[93] Andrew Gordon, "Operational Command at Sea," in John Reeve and David Stevens, eds., *The Face of Naval Battle: The Human Experience of Modern War at Sea* (Crows Nest, 2003), 38–52, 39.
[94] Goldrick, "Learning How to Do over the Horizon Warfare at Sea," pt. 13:40.

building upon more limited reforms instituted by Jellicoe after Jutland.[95] These shifts away from centralization continued and grew after the war.

Despite the attention focused on the German surface fleet, the greatest threat to Allied shipping came from German submarines. Germany began a campaign of unrestricted commerce raiding in February 1915, though American protests curtailed this initial effort. A second such campaign launched in February 1917 led to serious losses of merchant shipping and played a role in American entry into the conflict. Eventually in April 1917, under great pressure from the politicians, the navy introduced convoys, overcoming internal opposition. Convoys, along with American naval assistance, reduced losses to a manageable level.[96]

The Royal Navy led the Allied naval effort as the undisputed senior partner, though Allied fleets made major contributions to the war at sea. The French helped protect convoys arriving at French ports and patrolled the western Mediterranean. The Italian fleet kept the Austro-Hungarian surface fleet bottled up in the Adriatic, while Japanese forces seized German possessions in the Pacific and escorted Australian and New Zealand troop convoys. In 1917, the US Navy joined the war and provided destroyers to help combat German submarines in the Atlantic. An American battleship squadron also operated as a fully integrated part of the Grand Fleet, adopting British tactics, formations, and signals. This multinational formation represented a significant achievement for two navies "largely unacquainted" in 1914.[97] While each of these relations produced tension and conflict at some point, overall the Allied navies worked well together.

The Royal Navy largely succeeded in its principal wartime missions: guarding the British Army's movements and supply lines, protecting Britain's maritime lines of communication, and eventually cutting off German access to overseas resources. However, postwar commemorations produced jealous attitudes among some naval officers. As one author noted, British naval officers "had been brought up to think that sea power was absolutely crucial to the existence of Britain and its empire," yet the memorialization of the war favored the Western Front.[98] Furthermore, the cost of creating and sustaining the first mass army in modern British history contributed to the erosion of British financial strength in comparison with the United States.[99]

[95] Andrew Field, *Royal Navy Strategy in the Far East, 1919–1939: Planning for War against Japan* (New York, 2004), 124–125.
[96] Redford and Grove, *The Royal Navy*, chapter 3.
[97] Michael Simpson, ed., *Anglo-American Naval Relations, 1917–1919* (Aldershot, 1991), xi.
[98] Farquharson-Roberts, *Royal Navy Officers from War to War*, 41.
[99] Burk, "Financing Kitchener's (and Everyone Else's) Armies," 257.

The Interwar Period

The navy emerged from World War I disappointed and frustrated at the failure to win a second Trafalgar. This unmet expectation, however unrealistic, spurred a series of linked interwar reforms, principally in doctrine, training, and professional military education. Through these reforms, the navy reinvigorated an offensive ethos and placed a higher priority on subordinates taking the initiative based on an understanding of the admiral's intent, similar to modern "mission command." Perceived failure to achieve naval and national standards of victory created a determination to improve based on historical experience, which in turn led to the interwar rediscovery of the tactical offensive. In response to wartime experience, the navy instituted a number of doctrinal changes, which commanders tested, refined, and practiced in exercises. The resulting doctrine emphasized the need for initiative, independent action, and aggressiveness, which worked alongside an increased emphasis on strategy and tactics in interwar naval education.

Interwar exercises often featured a British fleet engaging Japanese forces near Singapore.[100] Interwar planners expected a war with Japan in which the navy relieved the forces stationed at and then operated from the naval base at Singapore. A fleet operating out of Singapore could protect British shipping in the Indian Ocean, threaten Japanese trade in the Pacific, and engage the Japanese fleet. However, in peace, most of the British fleet operated in British home or Mediterranean waters, so the first task would be to gather a force to relieve Singapore, which could take several weeks. Such exercises focused on fleet actions as this scenario "was the most testing" for elements across the fleet.[101] Safety restrictions introduced some artificial elements, though the concerns were valid enough. During training, the Royal Navy lost a submarine along with its crew over the course of exercises in 1921, 1922, 1924, and 1926.[102]

First and foremost, interwar doctrine prioritized subordinates understanding the commander's intentions and demonstrating initiative and judgment.[103] Exercises practiced squadrons operating detached or at a distance from the main body in order to decentralize command and control. Emphasizing aggressiveness and initiative in combat, doctrine called for warships to quickly close the range with the enemy and touted the benefits of opening fire first in surface actions.[104] This shift represented a return to an older Royal Navy expectation of aggressiveness in command, as demonstrated in the 1757 execution of Admiral

---

[100] Moretz, "The Legacy of Jutland," 160.
[101] Geoffrey Till, "Maritime Airpower in the Interwar Period: The Information Dimension," *Journal of Strategic Studies* 27(2) (2004), 298–323, 320.
[102] Thomas Hone and Trent Hone, *Battle Line: The United States Navy, 1919–1939* (Annapolis, MD, 2006), 120.
[103] Field, *Royal Navy Strategy in the Far East*, 140.   [104] Ibid., 129–130.

Byng for failing to "do his utmost" to relieve Minorca against the French. This execution helped to establish a "culture of aggressive determination" within the officer corps, according to one leading scholar.[105] By 1939, the fleet's fighting instructions firmly reflected this evolution, declaring that "divisional commanders have full authority to manoeuvre their divisions so as best to achieve the destruction of the enemy."[106]

At Jutland, Jellicoe had declined the opportunity to engage the German fleet at night. This decision reflected prewar thinking, which shied away from night actions and their tendency to undermine the benefits of numerical superiority. In contrast, the interwar navy faced the real prospect of fighting at a numerical disadvantage against the Japanese and now viewed night actions as a means of evening the odds.[107] Furthermore, Japanese and German capital ships enjoyed an advantage in long-range gunnery, which a night action would mitigate.[108] The fleet began practicing night fighting as early as the Atlantic/Mediterranean fleet exercises in February 1922.[109] Night drills gradually became more common and two exercises in the mid-1930s demonstrated the navy's progress. In a large March 1934 exercise, the Mediterranean Fleet, escorted by destroyers commanded by Cunningham, intercepted and defeated the Home Fleet at close range at night in atrocious weather.[110] Mediterranean exercises in 1935 practiced aerial reconnaissance and shadowing at night, culminating in a night surface action.[111] In a clear reversal of pre–World War I practice, instructions issued in 1939 declared that "night action between heavy ships ... must be regarded as a definite part of our policy."[112]

The navy also changed destroyer doctrine due to inconclusive destroyer attacks at Jutland. Whereas pre–World War I thinking viewed destroyers as defensive screens for the battle line, interwar practice called for destroyers to attack enemy formations aggressively on their own initiative with large torpedo salvos. Exercises involving decentralized, divided formations drilled this approach into destroyer captains.[113] Practice destroyer attacks involved prolific

---

[105] Nicholas A. M. Rodger, *Command of the Ocean: A Naval History of Britain, 1649–1815* (New York, 2006), 272.

[106] David MacGregor, "The Use, Misuse, and Non-Use of History: The Royal Navy and the Operational Lessons of the First World War," *Journal of Military History* 56(4) (1992), 603–616, 610.

[107] Field, *Royal Navy Strategy in the Far East*, 142; Joseph Moretz, *The Royal Navy and the Capital Ship in the Interwar Period: An Operational Perspective* (London, 2002), 225.

[108] Moretz, *The Royal Navy and the Capital Ship in the Interwar Period*, 226.

[109] Moretz, "The Legacy of Jutland," 160.

[110] Michael Simpson, *A Life of Admiral of the Fleet Andrew Cunningham: A Twentieth Century Naval Leader* (New York, 2004), 23; John Wells, *The Royal Navy: An Illustrated Social History, 1870–1982* (Dover, 1994), 157; Coles, "The Warrior and the Strategist," 281.

[111] Paul Halpern, ed., *The Mediterranean Fleet, 1930–1939* (London, 2016), 161.

[112] MacGregor, "The Use, Misuse, and Non-Use of History," 610.   [113] Ibid.

use of torpedoes to maximize the potential for damaging hits.[114] By the late 1930s, the fleet's doctrine provided for a number of types of destroyer assaults, reflecting an overall interwar focus on flexibility and initiative.[115] Finally, exercises emphasized contact reporting and maintaining contact, which had been inconsistent at Jutland.

The interwar fleet also sought to build upon the initials steps taken by British naval aviation in World War I. This effort suffered from the fact that for almost all the 1920s and 1930s, the Royal Air Force (RAF) controlled the navy's aviation arm, with damaging results. Without dedicated land-based air support, the interwar fleet relied heavily on aircraft carriers. Interwar exercises led commanders to the conclusion that defense against air attack should rely on antiaircraft armament and ship resiliency over defensive combat air patrols.[116] In 1934, the fleet's senior carrier admiral concluded that land-based aircraft posed a greater threat to ships than did enemy carrier planes.[117] In time, experience in World War II undermined both assumptions. Financial restrictions limited ammunition expenditure and the availability of aerial target drones, which contributed to overly optimistic views about the effectiveness of the fleet's defenses against air attack.[118] On the other hand, the navy also emphasized reconnaissance, navigation, and reporting by carrier aircraft, which paid dividends in World War II. Interwar doctrine called for carrier aircraft to scout for enemy formations and slow enemy ships with aerial attacks, especially using torpedoes.[119] Mediterranean exercises highlighted the danger of aerial-launched torpedoes to capital ships, which led the navy to emphasize the role of torpedo bombers in strike operations.[120]

In World War I, the introduction of convoys had effectively averted the growing success of German submarines. After the war, planning focused on a possible conflict with Japan, which in turn focused anti-submarine development on warship defense rather than trade protection, since Japanese submarine doctrine focused on attacking warships. The return of the German submarine threat in the mid-1930s refocused attention on trade defense and convoys. However, the interwar fleet placed too much faith in the ability of sonar (asdic) to locate submerged submarines through offensive patrols. When World War II showed the futility of these patrols, "the wider navy [tended] to overcorrect, concluding that asdic was largely useless." Still, the late 1930s

---

[114] Poland, *The Torpedomen*, 82, 91.

[115] MacGregor, "The Use, Misuse, and Non-Use of History," 610–611.

[116] Till, "Maritime Airpower in the Interwar Period," 314.

[117] Moretz, *The Royal Navy and the Capital Ship in the Interwar Period*, 128.

[118] Geoffrey Till, "Retrenchment, Rethinking, Revival, 1919–1939," in John Richard Hill, ed., *The Oxford Illustrated History of the Royal Navy* (Oxford, 1995), 319–347, 320.

[119] Moretz, *The Royal Navy and the Capital Ship in the Interwar Period*, 129–130, 232.

[120] Poland, *The Torpedomen*, 119.

focus on trade defense paid off when Britain introduced convoys shortly after war began in September 1939.[121]

Reforms in professional education played a critical role in the navy's interwar renaissance after World War I. An initial reform involved increased requirements for future captains. Beginning in 1921, officers had to take exams before commanding a destroyer and in 1930, prospective destroyer captains also had to have required tactical training. In 1931, the Admiralty extended this tactical training requirement to flotilla commanders and captains of cruisers and larger warships. These requirements served as primary embedding mechanisms designed to affect a change in the service's command culture.[122] The navy also recognized the need for more intensive officer education prior to taking an independent command.

As part of a growing emphasis on preparation for command, the interwar Admiralty reframed or launched four courses that helped better prepare the officer corps for future conflicts. The following table summarizes the four courses.

Royal Navy professional military education institutions[123]

Course (Date Began)	Topics	Students (Primary)	Duration	Location
Staff Course (1912)	Staff work, policy, strategy, operations	Lieutenant Commanders, Commanders	10 months	Royal Naval Staff College (Greenwich)[124]
Tactical Course (1925)	Tactics, employment of fleet in combat	Commanders, Captains	8–11 weeks	Tactical School, Portsmouth Dockyard
Senior Officers' Technical Course	Weapon and material capabilities, past operational experience	Commanders, Captains	8–12 weeks	Portsmouth Dockyard
Senior Officers' War Course (1900)	Policy, strategy, naval history, international law	Commanders, Captains	4 months	Royal Naval War College (Greenwich)[125]

---

[121] George Franklin, *Britain's Anti-Submarine Capability, 1919–1939* (London, 2003), 24, 186–190.

[122] See Chapter 1 for a survey of organizational culture theory and terminology.

[123] Moretz, *Thinking Wisely, Planning Boldly*, 21, 25, 27–28, 62–67, 104, 223, 215; Harry Dickinson, *Wisdom and War: The Royal Navy College Greenwich, 1873–1998* (Abingdon, 2012), 96; Winton, "Life and Education in a Technically Evolving Navy," 276–277; Marder, *From the Dreadnought to Scapa Flow*, 32–33; MacGregor, "The Use, Misuse, and Non-Use of History," 608; Lambert, "History As Process and Record," 83, 94–97; Hamilton, *The Making of the Modern Admiralty*, 244.

[124] Portsmouth until 1919, then Greenwich.

[125] Greenwich until 1906, then Portsmouth from 1906 to 1914, then Greenwich from 1920 to 1939. See Marder, *From the Dreadnought to Scapa Flow*, 32.

All four courses emphasized the need for commanders to encourage sub-ordinate initiative, which complemented the drive for decentralization written into doctrine and practiced in exercises. Several of these courses sought to analyze and understand the navy's World War I performance, including but not limited to Jutland. This interwar historical analysis benefited from student bodies with considerable operational experience. The massive size of the World War I Grand Fleet meant that a large percentage of the officer corps was present at Jutland. As a result, interwar discussions of Jutland at naval educational establishments could draw upon the direct experience of the students to enrich the discussion.

The creation of a naval staff led the navy to create a course in staff work in 1912, though World War I interrupted this effort. Reformed in 1919 at a new Royal Naval Staff College at Greenwich, the course sought to correct some of the staff problems the fleet encountered in the war. In particular the course emphasized subordinates taking the initiative.[126] In the interwar years, the course comprised roughly thirty lieutenant commanders and commanders with a few captains and marines.[127]

Concerns stemming from World War I also led the Admiralty to establish the Tactical School in 1924 at Portsmouth Dockyard. Each Tactical Course at the school lasted for eight weeks and involved approximately twenty officers, mostly captains, who were about to assume command of ships or flotillas.[128] The students studied tactics, analyzed fleet exercises, worked through tactical games, and helped prepare tactical publications for the fleet.[129] During the interwar years, the course emphasized initiative, the value of torpedo attacks, and the effectiveness of torpedo bombers.

The Senior Officers' Technical Course, held at Portsmouth, served as a refresher for commanders and captains on the latest technical developments. The students, fifteen to twenty commanders with a few captains, visited technical establishments such as the gunnery and signal schools to learn about recent advances and ongoing projects. The course existed prior to World War I, but the Admiralty recast it, along with the staff course, after the war. Together, the Tactical Course and the Senior Officers' Technical Course had considerable impact on the interwar officer corps since a large number of students completed these courses. Each course lasted roughly two months and the navy offered each four times a year.[130]

---

[126]   Moretz, "The Legacy of Jutland," 155–156.
[127]   Farquharson-Roberts, *Royal Navy Officers from War to War*, 62–63.
[128]   Moretz, "The Legacy of Jutland," 158; Farquharson-Roberts, *Royal Navy Officers from War to War*, 155.
[129]   Field, *Royal Navy Strategy in the Far East*, 130.
[130]   Moretz, *Thinking Wisely, Planning Boldly*, 67, 104, 213.

Along with the Tactical Course and the Senior Officers' Technical Course, the Senior Officers' War Course also helped prepare officers for future command positions. Established in 1900, the War Course lasted four months and covered national policy, strategy, naval history, international law, and, to a lesser degree, tactics. Students also examined strategic and tactical problems identified by naval intelligence.[131] Prior to World War I, the absence of preparatory education limited the War Course's impact.[132] The navy offered the course at various locations during the period but principally at the Royal Naval War College located in Greenwich near the Royal Naval Staff College.

The interwar Admiralty ordered that officers should attend the Senior Officers' Technical Course, followed by the Senior Officers' War Course, and finally the Tactical Course before taking command, though often this rule was inconsistently enforced.[133] All three courses accepted Royal Naval Reserve students, which helped keep up enrollments when the tight budgets of the 1920s limited the number of active duty students.[134] The interwar navy also used school attendance as a way to keep promising officers who lacked a follow-on assignment employed, which could result in an officer taking a course twice.[135]

The navy's educational reforms required comparatively low levels of funding, which aligned nicely with Britain's interwar political and fiscal climate. The carnage of World War I convinced British politicians of the 1920s of the need to avoid a major war. Through agreements such as the League of Nations, the 1925 Locarno Treaties, the 1928 Kellogg-Briand renunciation of war, and various naval disarmament treaties, Whitehall pursued peace through collective security, conciliation, and disarmament.[136] Domestically, this political perspective led to the 1919 Ten Year Rule, which stated that defense spending should be predicated on the assumption that the nation would not be involved in a major war for ten years.[137] Due in part to economic concerns, successive governments continued to follow the Ten Year Rule through to 1932.

In 1919, Britain's national debt was ten times greater than the prewar total, leading to widespread calls to curb spending.[138] Furthermore, beginning in 1919, the government began expanding pensions and unemployment insurance coverage.[139] The growth in debt combined with increased social spending

[131] Hamilton, *The Making of the Modern Admiralty*, 219.
[132] Lambert, "History As Process and Record," 97.
[133] Moretz, *Thinking Wisely, Planning Boldly*, 216.   [134] Ibid., 100.   [135] Ibid., 100–102.
[136] Brian Bond and Williamson Murray, "The British Armed Forces, 1918–39," in Allan Millett and Williamson Murray, eds., *Military Effectiveness, vol. 2: The Interwar Period* (New York, 2010), 98–130, 98–100.
[137] Donald Lisio, *British Naval Supremacy and Anglo-American Antagonisms, 1914–1930* (New York, 2014), 13–14.
[138] Morgan, *The Oxford Illustrated History of Britain*, 534–535.
[139] Schama, *A History of Britain*, 446.

created a restrictive financial climate that persisted throughout the 1920s and early 1930s. Even after the Washington Naval Treaty curtailed the navy's battleship construction program, a 1922 committee chaired by Sir Eric Geddes recommended further economies, which became known as the "Geddes Axe." The "Axe" led to defense spending cuts of 44 percent between the 1921–1922 and 1923–1924 budgets.[140] These cuts curtailed shipbuilding programs and reduced personnel salaries, which in turn damaged morale.[141]

Administrative and bureaucratic factors also served to limit naval spending in the 1920s. In a reversal of pre–World War I practice, the Admiralty could not propose spending increases to the Cabinet without first obtaining Treasury approval.[142] Furthermore, in 1924, the government's adoption of the Ten Year Rule gave the Treasury considerable influence over the Admiralty, leading to a series of delays and deferments in warship construction.[143] As Chancellor of the Exchequer in the late 1920s, former First Lord Winston Churchill pursued further reductions in spending that impacted shipbuilding and the Fleet Air Arm.[144]

In addition to Treasury demands, the navy suffered no shortage of public critics, such as the 1926 Colwyn Committee that coupled "highly publicized charges of waste and management" with calls for cuts in oil reserves, supplies, dockyards, and personnel.[145] Altogether, this wide array of pressure to limit naval spending led to tighter internal controls in that naval officials became less willing to spend money on anything "that might be seen as not strictly necessary, such as experiments with new equipment . . . or large-scale maneuvers."[146] As a result, the navy curtailed practice ammunition expenditure and training.[147]

In 1919, relations with the Americans became increasingly tense over a range of maritime and naval disputes such as freedom of the seas and the disposition of captured German warships. The American demand for naval parity with Britain became the principal point of contention, since the Admiralty proved reluctant to give up global naval superiority. Ultimately, the Washington Naval Conference (1921–1922) gave the Americans parity in

[140] Peden, *The Treasury and British Public Policy*, 170.
[141] Farquharson-Roberts, *Royal Navy Officers from War to War*, 126.
[142] Peden, "Financing Churchill's Army," 279.
[143] Peden, *The Treasury and British Public Policy*, 171; John Ferris, *Men, Money, and Diplomacy: The Evolution of British Strategic Policy, 1919–26* (Ithaca, NY, 1989), 187; Charles Hamilton, "British Naval Policy, Policy-Makers and Financial Control, 1860–1945," *War in History* 12 (4) (2005), 371–395, 383–384.
[144] Peden, *The Treasury and British Public Policy*, 213; David MacGregor, "Former Naval Cheapskate: Chancellor of the Exchequer Winston Churchill and the Royal Navy, 1924–1929," *Armed Forces and Society* 19(3) (1993), 319–333, 322.
[145] Lisio, *British Naval Supremacy and Anglo-American Antagonisms*, 90–93.
[146] Hamilton, "British Naval Policy, Policy-Makers and Financial Control, 1860–1945," 384; Hamilton, *The Making of the Modern Admiralty*, 294–296.
[147] Till, "Retrenchment, Rethinking, Revival, 1919–1939," 320.

exchange for cancelling most of their current shipbuilding program, which Britain could not afford to match.

In contrast, France found the Washington agreement insulting, as the treaty stipulated French equality with Italy in battleship tonnage in fourth place behind Britain, America, and Japan. By the 1930s, Mussolini's Italy appeared more threatening and French naval leaders began seeking a naval alliance with Britain to counter the Italians.[148] The French and British reached several agreements before 1939, including reciprocal port access, division of national areas of responsibility in the Mediterranean, and exchange of communication procedures.

Anglo-American naval ties took the opposite tack. Elements within the US Navy viewed the Royal Navy with distrust throughout the interwar years. These attitudes stemmed from tensions over naval arms limitation, American naval subordination in the First World War, and commercial rivalry, combined with traditional nineteenth-century American wariness of British motives. The two navies did pursue several joint planning ventures and shared limited technical data in the late 1930s, though with few immediate results.[149]

Concerned about growing German strength, Britain began to rearm in 1934, leading to an initial 21 percent increase in defense spending from 1934–1935 to 1935–1936. In 1937, the pace of rearmament picked up, leading to a 40 percent increase in 1937–1938 in the navy's budget.[150] The Admiralty translated this increased funding into a major shipbuilding program and by 1939, British shipyards physically could not lay down any new major warships. Still, the RAF fared better during rearmament as the navy's share of defense spending fell from just under half in 1932–1933 to a third by the end of the decade.[151]

Controversy and conflict dominated interwar relations with the RAF. During World War I, the navy built a large air arm, the Royal Naval Air Service, comprising more than 55,000 personnel and almost 3,000 planes by 1918. However, in April 1918, the newly created RAF absorbed the navy's air service as well as the army's Royal Flying Corps. This merger placed the fleet's aviation arm under RAF control and kicked off a generational struggle over control of naval aviation. The Admiralty argued that the RAF treated naval aviation as a second-class citizen, while the RAF insisted on the need for centralized control of all aviation assets. The ensuing bureaucratic and policy

---

[148] George Melton, *From Versailles to Mer El-Kébir: The Promise of Anglo-French Naval Cooperation, 1919–1940* (Annapolis, MD, 2015), 20.

[149] Greg Kennedy, *Anglo-American Strategic Relations and the Far East, 1933–1939: Imperial Crossroads* (London, 2002), 19–40; Lawrence Pratt, "The Anglo-American Naval Conversations on the Far East of January 1938," *International Affairs* 44(4) (1971), 745–763; Malcolm H. Murfett, *Fool-Proof Relations: The Search for Anglo-American Naval Cooperation during the Chamberlain Years, 1937–1940* (Singapore, 1984).

[150] Peden, *The Treasury and British Public Policy*, 294.

[151] Ibid.; Ferris, *Men, Money, and Diplomacy*, 187.

struggles damaged relations between the services for years to come. The flavor of navy-air force relations in the 1920s comes across clearly from the RAF index entry in Roskill's *Naval Policy between the Wars*: "controversy with Admiralty ..., Admiralty demand for ..., on Admiralty protests ..., dispute over control of Air Force with Admiralty ..., dispute with Admiralty re-opened."[152] In 1937, the RAF agreed to return control of the Fleet Air Arm, comprising ship-based aircraft, to the Royal Navy while retaining control of land-based naval aviation units such as maritime reconnaissance planes. The Admiralty and the RAF continued to argue over the employment of Coastal Command's land-based aircraft throughout most of World War II, though the navy gained operational, albeit not administrative, control of Coastal Command during the war.[153] While the Admiralty made several misjudgments about naval aviation in the interwar era, the navy's development of air power "appears to have been more sinned against than sinning."[154]

Within the navy, the disappointment of World War I led to a resurgence of traditional executive officer attitudes. In 1925, the Admiralty chose to restrict command positions to executive officers, taking that option away from engineer officers, who bitterly labeled the decision the "Great Betrayal."[155] Despite the uproar from engineers, the move had significant support among the navy's senior leaders. For example, the director of the Gunnery Division wrote in 1924 that the navy "should be well rid" of those who felt that engineers were victims.[156] In contrast, the US Navy had amalgamated its line and engineer officer corps in 1899.

Similarly, while the Special Entry scheme expanded, Dartmouth products retained the most senior positions. During the interwar years, Special Entry provided roughly 20 percent of the navy's officer cadets.[157] However, the overwhelming majority of officers in 1939, and almost all the flag officers, still came from Dartmouth.[158]

---

[152] Stephen Roskill, *Naval Policy between the Wars, vol. 1, The Period of Anglo-American Antagonism, 1919–1929* (London, 1968), 631.

[153] Christopher Bell, "Air Power and the Battle of the Atlantic: Very Long Range Aircraft and the Delay in the Atlantic 'Air Gap,'" *Journal of Military History* 79(3) (2015), 691–719, 695; Tim Benbow, "Brothers in Arms: The Admiralty, the Air Ministry, and the Battle of the Atlantic, 1940–1943," *Global War Studies* 11(1) (2014), 41–88.

[154] Geoffrey Till, "Airpower and the British Admiralty between the World Wars," in Robert Love, ed., *Changing Interpretations and New Sources in Naval History: Papers from the Third United States Naval Academy History Symposium* (Annapolis, MD, 1980), 340–351,350.

[155] Farquharson-Roberts, *Royal Navy Officers from War to War*, 122.

[156] Charles Hamilton, "Review of *The Challenges of Command: The Royal Navy's Executive Branch, 1880–1919* by Robert Davison," *International Journal of Maritime History* 24(1) (2012), 518–519, 519. The author was either Captain Bernard Collard, who was the director until April 1924, or Captain H. G. Walwyn, who took over from Collard.

[157] Farquharson-Roberts, *Royal Navy Officers from War to War*, 75.

[158] Horsfield, *The Art of Leadership in War*, 144; Rodger, "Training or Education," 24.

Immediately after World War I, the officer corps suffered a series of blows that damaged morale. In 1918, the RAF made off with a large number of talented, technically skilled officers by absorbing the navy's air arm.[159] By the 1920s, the fleet had too many lieutenant commanders, many of whom thought they had little chance of further promotion and "saw themselves as serving out their time until they could retire on a pension."[160] In response, the government and the navy instituted a series of personnel cuts including the aforementioned "Geddes Axe," which forced a number of officers to retire as an economy measure.[161] These cuts and retirements dashed the hopes of many volunteer officers who had joined the navy during the war and transferred to the regular force after the war in hopes of a naval career.[162] Budgetary cuts also impacted ratings. In September 1931, hundreds of Atlantic Fleet sailors mutinied at Invergordon in response to pay cuts perceived as regressive. Although resolved within days, the mutiny highlighted the impact of pay cuts on morale. In 1932, the Admiralty began putting senior officers on half pay or unemployed pay to allow promotions to continue for the large block of lieutenant commanders.[163] For the officer corps, these challenges hurt morale and the perception of the navy as a career.

In response to these personnel problems, the navy reformed promotions in 1933 by instituting a batch system. Previously, all officers up for promotion to commander or higher, those "in the zone," competed with everyone else in the zone.[164] This system favored those officers with more experience who were about to move out of the zone and those with higher-visibility assignments, such as on an admiral's staff. Under the batch system, the Admiralty grouped officers with seniority within a six-month range together to form a batch, which received a specific number of promotions as the batch entered the zone. As the batch moved through the zone, officers received these promotions at set intervals. As a result, officers competed for promotions only against the rest of their batch and not against the much larger group of officers who were in the zone.[165] This change, along with other reforms, helped improve morale in the officer corps in the 1930s.

After the disappointment of Jutland, the Royal Navy pursued a linked series of interwar reforms in doctrine, training, and officer education. Despite a restrictive fiscal climate and bruising policy battles with the RAF, the navy corrected a number of deficiencies identified in World War I, such as hesitancy to fight at

[159] Hamilton, *The Making of the Modern Admiralty*, 308.
[160] Farquharson-Roberts, *Royal Navy Officers from War to War*, 138.   [161] Ibid., 129.
[162] Lavery, *In Which They Served*, 75.
[163] Farquharson-Roberts, *Royal Navy Officers from War to War*, 169.
[164] Moretz, *Thinking Wisely, Planning Boldly*, 212.
[165] Farquharson-Roberts, *Royal Navy Officers from War to War*, 174.

night, overly centralized command and control, and insufficiently aggressive destroyer employment. These efforts paid off in World War II, particularly in surface warfare.

Fighting World War II

The demands of World War II stretched the fleet across the world's oceans, and the scale of the conflict precludes any effort at comprehensive examination. The navy's principal roles broadly involved defeating German air, surface, and especially subsurface efforts to cut the sea lines of communication that linked Britain with the resources of the empire and the world, securing command of the Mediterranean through a long, costly struggle with the Italian Navy and the Luftwaffe, providing naval support for evacuations and amphibious landings around the European continent, and in the war's final year employing long-range carrier strike warfare against the Japanese in the Pacific.

The navy's wartime operations repeatedly reflected the interwar effort to learn lessons from World War I, specifically skill in night actions, the offensive use of destroyers, divided formations, carrier-based torpedo attacks, and subordinates taking the initiative. In particular, operations against Axis surface ships demonstrated the fleet's improved performance. In December 1939, three British cruisers defeated the German pocket battleship *Graf Spee* off Uruguay using decentralized tactics. Admiral Cunningham's tenure with the Mediterranean Fleet exemplified the interwar emphasis on initiative. On July 19, 1940, Captain John Collins in the Australian light cruiser *Sydney* departed from his scheduled operation to provide support to five British destroyers moving west between Greece and Crete. In the resulting action off Cape Spada, *Sydney* heavily damaged an Italian light cruiser, which two British destroyers finished off with torpedoes. When Cunningham asked Collins how *Sydney* arrived at the action so quickly, Collins replied, "Providence guided me, sir." Cunningham concluded, "Well, you can continue to take your orders from providence."[166] As a primary embedding mechanism, the admiral's praise for Collins demonstrated the Mediterranean Fleet's commitment to initiative. Cunningham also commanded the November 1940 nighttime air strike that crippled the Italian fleet at Taranto, which highlighted the effectiveness of British aerial torpedo attacks, a focus of interwar exercises.

In May 1940, the German invasion of France put the future of the French fleet in doubt. At Churchill's insistence, on July 3, 1940, the Royal Navy attacked the French squadron located at Mer-el-Kébir in Algeria and seized a number of French warships in British ports. The attack stemmed from British doubts over the French Admiralty's commitment to keeping their ships out of

---

[166] Gordon, "Operational Command at Sea," 39–40.

German hands. Only marginally effective in sinking French ships, the Royal Navy killed almost 1,300 French sailors and poisoned Anglo-French naval relations for the rest of the war.[167] Nevertheless, the fall of France and Italian entrance into the war in the summer of 1940 destroyed the navy's prewar planning assumptions, stretching the service's resources thin.[168]

France's surrender in June 1940 also created doubt in Washington about Britain's ability to survive without American aid, which in turn convinced senior American admirals such as Chief of Naval Operations Admiral Harold Stark of the importance of aiding Britain. In July 1940, the British instituted a policy of open technical exchange with the Americans and began allowing large numbers of American observers on board their ships and aircraft. Spring 1941 staff talks in Washington, growing collaboration between British and American naval commanders in the western Pacific, and President Franklin Roosevelt's September 1941 decision to allow American ships to escort Atlantic convoys all strengthened Anglo-American naval relations.[169]

Operationally, the March 1941 Battle of Cape Matapan underlined the Mediterranean Fleet's skill in night fighting and the value of interwar torpedo and night training. During a daylight action, British carrier aircraft disabled the Italian heavy cruiser *Pola* with a torpedo, forcing the Italians to leave two additional heavy cruisers and a destroyer behind to assist the stricken vessel. That night, a British battle line of three battleships savaged the Italian formation with gunfire at close range while destroyer torpedo attacks compounded the damage. The Italians lost all three cruisers as well as two destroyers in the melee.

Two months later, the German battleship *Bismarck*, accompanied by the heavy cruiser *Prinz Eugen*, attempted to break out of the North Sea to attack North Atlantic convoy routes. British cruisers tracked the two German ships throughout the night of May 23, providing regular reports that allowed a British squadron to intercept the Germans the next morning. In this initial engagement, the Germans sank the British battlecruiser *Hood* and damaged the battleship *Prince of Wales*. On May 26, an evening carrier torpedo attack crippled the German battleship, allowing British battleships to intercept and sink the *Bismarck*. This use of carrier aircraft to slow the enemy so that the British battle line could engage reflected interwar doctrine, regularly practiced in exercises.[170] Furthermore, during the chase, Captain Philip Vian disregarded

---

[167] For a more thorough examination of this episode, see Melton, *From Versailles to Mer El-Kébir*.

[168] Andrew Boyd, *The Royal Navy in Eastern Waters: Linchpin of Victory, 1935–1942* (South Yorkshire, 2017), 55.

[169] David Reynolds, *The Creation of the Anglo-American Alliance, 1937–1941: A Study in Competitive Co-operation* (Chapel Hill, NC, 1982); James Leutze, *Bargaining for Supremacy: Anglo-American Naval Collaboration, 1937–1941* (Chapel Hill, NC, 1977).

[170] Till, "Maritime Airpower in the Interwar Period," 317.

his orders to find and escort a British battleship, instead launching a night torpedo attack on the *Bismarck* with his destroyers.[171] While the attack failed to register any hits, the episode clearly demonstrated personal initiative and an offensive use of destroyers. Furthermore, Vian went on to become the second in command of the British Pacific Fleet, a promotion earned in part because of his willingness to rely on his own judgment. In a more successful use of destroyers at the Battle of Cape Bon on December 13, 1941, four British destroyers intercepted a convoy of two Italian light cruisers at night and sank both, primarily with torpedoes.[172]

The navy also demonstrated the priority the service placed on aggressive leadership through disciplinary actions. The First Sea Lord tried to have several senior officers court-martialed during the war for failing to act more aggressively, including Captain John Leach of the battleship *Prince of Wales* after the May 1941 *Bismarck* engagement.[173] These efforts also served as primary embedding mechanisms that proved the Admiralty's commitment to officers taking risks in wartime.

Cunningham demonstrated this quality in the May–June 1941 evacuation of British and Commonwealth forces off the island of Crete. After evacuating British forces from Norway and France in 1940 and Greece earlier in 1941, the navy once again fought to spirit away soldiers from a potential life inside German prison camps. During the evacuation, the Mediterranean Fleet operated for extended periods well within range of German bombers with little air cover and suffered the results of interwar misjudgments about fleet air defense. Cunningham lost three cruisers and six destroyers, while more ships suffered serious damage under exacting conditions. However, Cunningham insisted, "we must not let them [the Army] down, at whatever cost to ourselves."[174] At the height of the evacuation when the army's senior commanders in the eastern Mediterranean told Cunningham that his ships need not make further trips to Crete, he noted that "the Navy had never failed the Army in such a situation."[175] Cunningham embodied the navy's leadership ethos and a sense of history when he argued that were the fleet to abandon the army at Crete, "our naval tradition would never survive such an action."[176] The admiral declared, "It takes the Navy three years to build a ship. It will take three hundred years to build a new tradition."[177] The evacuation from Crete stands as a seminal moment in the navy's support to the army.

[171] Gordon, "Operational Command at Sea," 40.   [172] Poland, *The Torpedomen*, 237.
[173] James P. Levy, *The Royal Navy's Home Fleet in World War II* (New York, 2003), 97–98.
[174] Michael Simpson, *The Cunningham Papers: vol. 1, The Mediterranean Fleet, 1939–1942* (Aldershot, 1999), 409.
[175] Spector, *At War at Sea*, 179.   [176] Ibid., 183.
[177] Winston Churchill, *The Second World War, vol. 3, The Grand Alliance* (New York, 1950), 265.

Forced to fight Germany and Italy in Europe, the prospects for sending a large fleet to Singapore at the end of 1941 appeared remote without external aid. Furthermore, the German bases on the French coast gave U-boats easy access to the Atlantic sea lanes, dramatically increasing their range and time on station. When Japan attacked in December 1941, the navy faced a three-ocean war with at most a one and a half ocean fleet. American assistance proved critical in the Allied effort to secure global sea lines of communication, with the British primarily responsible for the Indian Ocean, Mediterranean, and North Atlantic (the latter along with the Royal Canadian Navy).

By the end of 1942, a series of amphibious landings supported by the fleet began reversing the earlier pattern of evacuation. On beaches in North Africa in 1942, Sicily and Salerno in 1943, and Anzio, Normandy, and southern France in 1944, the navy landed the army and supported its operations ashore. Operations later in the war underlined the effectiveness of the navy's interwar reforms. In December 1943, torpedoes helped sink the German battleship *Scharnhorst*, damaged by battleship gunfire after dark. Also in 1943, the navy incorporated advances in radar technology into its destroyer torpedo doctrine. Centimetric radar allowed destroyer flotillas to attack simultaneously from multiple directions.[178] Captain Manley Power demonstrated this capability by sinking the Japanese cruiser *Haguro* in May 1945 with a night torpedo assault. Power also showed initiative by ignoring Vice Admiral Harold Walker's order cancelling the operation.[179]

By 1945, American naval expansion propelled the US Navy beyond the Royal Navy as the world's largest fleet, especially in naval aviation. The experience of the British Pacific Fleet (BPF) illuminated the impact of this transition. The BPF constituted the Royal Navy's strongest fleet of World War II, but it operated as part of an American carrier task force that alone was four times larger. Furthermore, the British adopted American procedures, a reversal of the 1917 Grand Fleet roles. This disparity extended to the two navies' evaluation of the BPF's six months of operations with the Americans. While the British felt that the BPF demonstrated their ability to conduct American-style long-range strike warfare, American naval aviators found British naval aviation subpar and dependent on American largesse.[180] Certainly relations with the US Navy in 1945 had improved since 1917, but the Royal Navy exchanged roles from senior to junior partner.

[178] Poland, *The Torpedomen*, 241.   [179] Ibid., 242–243.

[180] Jonathan Robb-Webb, *The British Pacific Fleet: Experience and Legacy, 1944–50* (Burlington, VT, 2013); Reminiscences of Admiral Felix Stump, USN, interview by John T. Mason Jr., 1963, 233–235, Columbia Oral History Archives, Rare Book & Manuscript Library, Columbia University; Reminiscences of Vice Admiral Herbert D. Riley, USN, interview by John T. Mason Jr., 2004, 162–163, US Naval Institute Library, Annapolis, MD; Reminiscences of Rear Admiral Harold B. Miller, USN, interview by John T. Mason Jr., 1995, 115–119, US Naval Institute Library, Annapolis, MD.

Conclusion

The Royal Navy as an organization changed due to widespread consensus within the officer corps on the need for reform and not primarily due to Admiralty edicts. Certainly, Admiral David Beatty's term as First Sea Lord in the 1920s witnessed the first steps of doctrinal, educational, and training improvements. However, impetus for change in each of these areas flowed from multiple sources. For example, officers such as Vice Admiral Herbert Richmond, the president of the Royal Naval War College at Greenwich in the early 1920s, and contributors to the *Naval Review* had been clamoring for more rigorous officer education and touting the benefits of such an approach for years. Similarly, the interwar Mediterranean Fleet's growing skill with night actions reflected a long-term commitment from consecutive exercise planners and fleet commanders.

The navy's historical sensibility provided critical support for the interwar reforms. Officers regularly described the move toward decentralization and a greater emphasis on the tactical offensive as recovering a "Nelsonic spirit."[181] The navy's emphasis on tradition and corporate memory of its past created a strong historical consciousness. Aware of and proud of the navy's strong traditions, officers sought to live up to their predecessors' standards. Many felt that their World War I performance, while victorious, had not met historical standards of success. The resulting determination to improve led to serious interwar analysis of the recent past, including but not limited to Jutland, which provided the basis for the interwar doctrinal, educational, and training changes.

The critical element of the interwar reforms lay within the generation of officers who served in the First World War and survived the 1920s budgetary pruning to fight, and, for some, to lead, in the next and larger conflict. This cadre commanded the interwar ships, schools, and fleets that produced the Second World War's junior officers. The determination of World War I veterans to avoid repeating the navy's mistakes, which they witnessed firsthand, meant that "a ground swell of doctrinal rebellion . . . rolled steadily up the flag list in the 1920s and 1930s."[182]

---

[181] Hamilton, *The Making of the Modern Admiralty*, 284–285.
[182] Gordon, *The Rules of the Game*, 571.

15   US Navy Cultural Transformations, 1945–2017
The Jury Is Still Out

John T. Kuehn

From the start of the United States' participation in World War II until the present day, the culture of the US Navy transformed significantly several times. All of these "cultural revolutions" – if we may call them that – influenced how the navy fought after World War II in both hot wars and cold. The result by 1991 was a heterogeneous mix of the old, pre–World War II culture and the postwar cultural transformations. Navy culture changed in response to organizational transformations as well as to sociological trends that operated in tandem, reflecting larger societal transformations in American culture.[1] However, because the US Navy has not fought another blue-water navy at sea since 1944, a comprehensive test of its combat effectiveness must wait on events.

Culture and the Navy

First one must address the issue of organizational culture in general as it relates to navies.[2] The US Navy has a lengthy history that confers upon it a unique, dynamic, and evolving organizational culture. Service organizations of this sort do not change at the whim of an individual or collective group choice, but rather are the culmination of choices often made when those cultures are first

---

[1] The author's memories are of post–World War II US Navy culture in Japan from 1958 to 1961. His father, a navy physician, remained in the reserves and every summer the family repaired to a nearby naval air station, first in Olathe, Kansas, and later in Pensacola, Florida, for a two-week "vacation." He can still remember his brother, a Navy ROTC midshipman at Tulane University, telling him about Admiral Elmo Zumwalt's "Z-grams" that attempted to align a conservative navy culture with the American society that emerged from the twin catharses of the 1960s–1970s counterculture revolution and Vietnam. The author joined the navy in 1981, specifically its naval aviation clan, and has experienced and observed all the cultural changes since. He continues a close relationship with the US naval officers who attend the US Army Command and General Staff College.

[2] This chapter follows the construct presented in Chapter 2, although the US Navy might alternatively be categorized as an *institutional* culture; see fn. 4 later in this chapter.

established, something scientists call initial conditions.[3] Moreover, service cultures of long duration are more stable, or more paradigmatic, to use Thomas Kuhn's phrasing. They encompass a much larger set of norms and rules, with a much broader mandate of functions, roles, missions, and capabilities for the larger societies that they ostensibly serve.[4] However, in the modern age, few societal organizations exist that are made from whole cloth. Most have their precedents, the government of the United States, for example, having the republics from classical antiquity, as templates from which they emerge.[5]

The US Navy sprang from the traditions of navies going back to the days of Themistocles, but especially from the traditions of the reigning navy for most of the American history until after World War I, Britain's Royal Navy. This cultural substrate remains today in the odd language that American sailors still employ: scuttlebutt, grog, goat locker, gun deck, and so on.[6] Unlike other human organizations, navies, especially their physical manifestation as fleets of warships, are shaped profoundly by the environment in which they operate – the sea. Foremost they are shaped by the lonely separateness that sea service confers. Ships exist to go from point A to point B, whether that point is along a coast or at sea. To accomplish this, they risk the dangers of storms, tides, currents, winds, and all that the "cruel sea" throws at them. At the same time, sailors on warships are separate in this endeavor from humans ashore, and until recently, from the company (mostly) of the female half of the species, since the function of war at sea was long a mostly male preserve.[7] For most of history, there were no cities, villages, or farms at sea, in what sailors call "blue water," those waters peopled mostly by men on ships.

This natural danger from the sea must be combined with the danger associated with the phenomenon of war.[8] Added to this is the attribute of ships being prisons that, until recently with the Internet, one immediately felt upon pulling out of port, matched by exhilaration at pulling safely into a friendly port. Thus,

---

[3] For an interesting take on initial conditions, see Alan Beyerchen, "Clausewitz, Non-linearity, and the Un-predictability of War," *International Security* 17(3) (Winter 1992), 59–90, 65.

[4] I am particularly indebted to Dr. Mark Mandeles for this characterization and quotation, which can be found in Norman Friedman, Thomas C. Hone, and Mark Mandeles, *America and British Aircraft Carrier Development, 1919–1941* (Annapolis, MD, 1999), 5–6. These authors cite Nobel Laureate Douglass C. North, *Institutions, Institutional Change, and Economic Performance* (New York, 1990). For paradigms, see Thomas Kuhn, *The Structure of Scientific Revolutions* (Chicago, IL, 1970), viii.

[5] See Gordon Wood, *The Creation of the American Republic, 1776–1787* (Chapel Hill, NC, 1998).

[6] See Admiral W. H. Smyth, *The Sailor's Lexicon* (New York, 1996), for explanations of these idiomatic terms.

[7] The author had the fortune, or the misfortune, of deploying aboard one of the last all-male-crewed aircraft carriers and airwings, the USS *America* (CV-66)/Airwing ONE, from 1995–1996, after which that ship was decommissioned. His next tour on an aircraft carrier in 1998 included a crew with more than 300 females present for duty.

[8] Carl von Clausewitz, *On War*, trans. and ed. Michael Howard and Peter Paret (Princeton, NJ, 1984), 113–114.

we see danger, isolation, loss of freedom, and loss of the basic amenities possible in a life ashore – things like a varied diet, regular bathing, sleep, and heterosexual sexual relations – combined into making for a culture of the sea; not easily shed once one goes ashore. All these things become exacerbated when the function of that ship and its crew is *readiness* for or deadly purpose in war. Navies, by virtue of the machines called ships, whether designed for wind or some other form of propulsion, tend to be focused on *technology* and use their own technological jargon about things nautical, so much so that sometimes sailors have conversations that are nearly incomprehensible when overheard by landlubbers. Roger Barnett, in his study on the navy's "strategic culture," characterizes it more viscerally. "Technology ... is more to mariners than life: it is home."[9] This technological mind-set is an organizational "artifact" of navy culture. We might establish the beginnings of a basic framework for *naval* culture, distinct from *military* culture, by observing how all these factors lead to a cohesive and unique social organization that tends to see itself as fundamentally different from other military organizations and society ashore. Human beings exist as two categories to sailors; to put it in the vernacular of the sea, as land-bound "pollywogs," or the trusty, crusty "shellbacks," who sail on the seven seas.[10]

Twentieth-century technology modified the culture of navies. Sailors began to plow the skies above and the depths below the surface of an already dangerous sea. More than the sea surface, the air and depths proved more inherently hostile to human life, taking it quickly in attempts to interlope through these mediums in airplanes and submarines. By World War II, most navies had two new subcultures residing within them: aviators and submariners. Both often claimed they were the "wave of the future," especially the aviators. Submariners proved most deadly during World War I. As these sailors cycled back into the "general population" of navy culture, they brought with them their own cultural norms. These in turn also transformed naval culture over time. The officers from these communities were even more prone to rapid decision-making under stress, and their tendency to indulge in the autocratic behavior of their surface brethren was more, not less, enhanced by their isolation.

[9] Roger W. Barnett, *Navy Strategic Culture: Why the Navy Thinks Differently* (Annapolis, MD, 2009), 74. The author recalls with great fondness his eighteen-month "home" underneath the port forward catapult on the aircraft carrier USS *America* (CV-66) in the 1990s. *USS America Cruise Book: The Final Chapter* (Norfolk, VA, 1996), 600. Cruise books are a wonderful resource to examine naval culture and the most complete collection of them can be found at the Washington Navy Yard in the Secretarial Library colocated with the Navy History and Heritage Command.

[10] John V. Noel Jr. and Edward L. Beach, *Naval Terms Dictionary*, 4th edn. (Annapolis, MD, 1983), 266, 227. Strictly speaking, pollywogs are people who have not "crossed the line" of the equator aboard a warship; trusty shellbacks are those who have, including the author. For an interesting depiction of crossing the line, one might refer to the film *The Bounty* (1984), where one scene portrays the ceremony aboard an eighteenth-century ship of the Royal Navy. www .imdb.com/title/tt0086993/ (accessed August 8, 2017).

Historical Context: World War II US Navy Culture

By the advent of the greatest war at sea in human history, the US Navy had a clearly formed identity based on these artifacts: the sea, cultural inheritance from the Royal Navy, and the US Navy's experiences as the navy of the American Republic. Henry Stimson's famous characterization of the navy applies: "the peculiar psychology of the Navy Department, which frequently seemed to retire from the realm of logic into a dim religious world in which Neptune was God, Mahan his prophet, and the United States Navy the only true Church."[11] However, naval officers view themselves as progressive and scientific in their approach to their profession, prizing efficiency above other virtues in solving their maritime problems.[12]

Historically, the navy was not composed, for the most part, of "the people." Only a limited and specialized seagoing demographic served as enlisted sailors until World War I. The officers came from an even narrower social background. A study of the navy's officer corps prior to World War II illustrates important points about navy culture. First, the prewar navy culture was predominately shaped by its officer corps.[13] It was the officer corps that managed the norms of naval culture. The US Naval Institute was not started by former enlisted rates, but by naval officers, active and retired.[14] Naval officers acted as the trend setters, although over the years, as military professionalism diffused to lower levels in the navy, this function has become more shared.[15]

---

[11] Henry Stimson, quoted in *Time*, February 9, 1948, http://content.time.com/time/magazine/article/0,9171,855981,00.html?iid=chix-sphere (accessed August 9, 2017).

[12] For a discussion of the US Navy officer corps's obsession with efficiency, see John T. Kuehn, *Agents of Innovation: The General Board and the Design of the Fleet That Defeated the Japanese Navy* (Annapolis, MD, 2008), 23–24; see also Harold Winton, *To Change an Army: General Sir John Burnett-Stuart and British Armored Doctrine, 1927–1938* (Lawrence, KS, 1988),27–30 for the definition of progressive. Thanks to Corbin Williamson for bringing this characterization to my attention in his as yet unpublished paper on the General Board of the Navy and naval aviation.

[13] Peter Karsten, *The Naval Aristocracy: The Golden Age of Annapolis and the Emergence of Modern American Navalism* (New York, 1972), 385. Karsten provides more evidence for the saying "familiarity breeds contempt," but he gets many things correct in between bouts of hyperbole. He served as a JAG officer and his familiarity with life at sea on a warship was limited. See www.history.pitt.edu/sites/default/files/Karsten%20CV.pdf (accessed July 20, 2017). Samuel Huntington claims that the modern officer corps establishes military professionalism; Samuel P. Huntington, *The Soldier and the State: The Theory and Politics of Civil-Military Relations* (Cambridge, 1957), 1–18, especially 7.

[14] See John T. Kuehn, "The Martial Spirit – Naval Style: The Naval Reform Movement and the Establishment of the General Board of the Navy, 1873–1900," *Northern Mariner/le marin du nord* 22(2) (April 2012), 121–140, 124–126. The Naval Institute's premier publication is its *Proceedings*, which remains the preeminent journal of professional US naval officers.

[15] One need only examine a current issue of the US Naval Institute *Proceedings*, for example October 2017, and note sections not included in those of thirty years ago such as "From the Deckplates" (16) and special articles by enlisted members (68), as well as the winning of Naval Institute competitions by enlisted entrants (4).

Second, the US naval officer population prior to World War II was over-whelmingly male, white, and a product of Annapolis. Karsten nicknames these men "Annapolites," and he is correct about their controlling the rules of their society's game.[16] However, these men saw themselves as progressives and scientific managers, and thus the door was open for new ideas, especially technological ones. Diffusion of new attitudes from the emerging subcultures of naval aviation and the submarine force also played a role in the transforma-tion of the navy into a more modern organizational culture.[17] But this culture has never abandoned its roots of fierce independence and ruthless decision-making. Roger Barnett writes that "discipline, fighting spirit, and self-reliance" constitute "the three cultural concepts of the US Navy." These enduring cultural artifacts existed before World War II and remain to the present.[18] Only *fighting spirit* has been somewhat changed and perhaps diminished, at least in the surface community, due to a lack of any major naval engagements since the battles off Okinawa in 1945, and even further back for surface battles with another surface fleet in 1944 at Leyte Gulf.[19]

This core culture went through at least three major "cultural revolutions" that led to the navy's culture of today: during and shortly after World War II, during the first half of the Cold War as influenced by admirals Arleigh Burke and Hyman Rickover with nuclear power and weapons, and during the period led by Adm. Elmo Zumwalt at the end of the Vietnam War. The establishment of the "nuke navy" inside the larger body during the second "cultural revolution" created a powerful subculture inside the navy that exists to this day. These revolutions' influence on the navy's culture has been profound and has perhaps most influenced its effectiveness as a military institution. This chapter closes with an epilogue that looks briefly at the "Tailhook" incident in 1991. Cultural changes that have occurred to the navy since the 1990s involve ongoing historical processes and must wait for analysis.

OpNav Culture

One can characterize navy culture on the eve of World War II as a progressive, elitist patriarchy. World War II changed this. The navy's officer corps grew

---

[16] Karsten, *The Naval Aristocracy*, 385.

[17] David W. Holden, doctoral dissertation, "Managing Men and Machines: U.S. Military Officers and the Intellectual Origins of Scientific Management in the Early Twentieth Century," unpub-lished doctoral dissertation (Lawrence, KS, 2016), 90–94, 114–115, 118; see also Bradley A. Fiske, *The Navy As a Fighting Machine* (New York, 1916).

[18] Barnett, *Navy Strategic Culture*, ix.

[19] This chapter refers to the aviation, submarine, and surface groups of officers as communities, which is how they are referred to inside the navy today. See also John T. Kuehn, "Is Mahan Dead?" *Historically Speaking* (January 2011), 30–32, for a discussion of the lack of major fleet engagement since 1944 and how that caused an identity crisis in the navy.

exponentially during the war. By 1944, there were more than 300,000 US naval officers.[20] They brought with them an egalitarianism and sense of mission not seen in the navy since the US Civil War. A young naval officer named William Appleman Williams found himself appalled by the racism he found in the navy. He had entered service in World War II, and as a result of his wartime experiences, he joined the National Association for the Advancement of Colored People (NAACP) to work in favor of better race relations, not just in the navy, but in the nation at large.[21]

However, the demobilization of the navy after the war saw many voices for change, especially those decrying institutionalized segregation in the navy, removed. In 1946 alone, the navy decreased by more than 7,000 vessels and 2 million personnel. Nevertheless, the vast majority of the senior officers (commander rank and above) remained dominated by the ranks of Annapolis graduates.[22] This helps to explain why the navy had so many problems in the 1960s and early 1970s, as well as the "disconnect" from the tide of change taking place in larger American society vis-à-vis civil rights for African-Americans. World War II changed the navy in other ways as well. One must remember that between the US Civil War and World War II, parts of the navy had really only engaged in sustained combat for less than a year against Spain in 1898 and eighteen months during World War I.

Peacetime navies have different habits than wartime navies. The navy produced by reformers such as Alfred Thayer Mahan, Stephen Luce, and Bradley Fiske focused on preparing *for* war more than it had on actually fighting *in* war. The prewar navy relied on technology to solve problems, but it also valued the study of history.[23] World War II emphasized the former, while diminishing the habits of the latter. The navy's transformation in World War II resulted in a culture that was ahistorical, preferring technological solutions for the emerging problems of the Cold War. The golden age of the Naval War College had passed, and despite the appointment of Raymond Spruance as president shortly after the war, the college focused on "lessons learned" from World War II in the context of a world perceived as radically changed by the advent of atomic weapons.[24] Newer submarines, radar, better munitions,

---

[20]   Fleet Admiral Ernest J. King, *U.S. Navy at War, 1941–1945* (Washington, DC, 1946), 152.

[21]   William G. Robbins, "William Appleman Williams 'Doing History Is Best of All, No Regrets,'" in Lloyd C. Gardner, ed., *Redefining the Past: Essays in Honor of William Appleman Williams* (Corvallis, OR, 1986), 3–20, 5.

[22]   Robert W. Love, *History of the U.S. Navy, vol. 2, 1942–1991* (Harrisburg, PA, 1992), 291.

[23]   For naval officers' valuation of history prior to World War II, see Dudley Knox, *21st Century Knox*, ed. David Kohnen (Annapolis, MD, 2016), 5–15; and for a good account of the navy's long-standing reliance and focus on new technology, see William McBride, *Technological Change and the United States Navy, 1865–1954* (Baltimore, MD, 2000).

[24]   Ronald H. Spector, *Professors at War: The Naval War College and the Development of the Naval Profession* (Newport, RI, 1977); Hal M. Friedman, *Digesting History: The U.S. Naval*

aircraft, and atomic bombs involved the future, not the past. World War II taught these officers that the American military-industrial machine would produce whatever they needed to solve their military problems.

The culture of the navy coming out of World War II became *presentist* and more technologically focused than its forbears, such that in less than two generations a service famed for its historians like Mahan, Dudley Knox, and H. H. Frost now lacked altogether in its body of leaders, with rare exceptions, those who valued honest study of the past.[25] This thinking was reflected organizationally by the preeminence of the staff of the Office of the Chief of Naval Operations, known as OpNav. Under Adm. Ernest King, OpNav had displaced and absorbed the powerful naval bureaus during the war. There was some attempt by James Forrestal and Adm. John Towers, president of the once-powerful General Board, to scale back the power of OpNav after the war. But the disestablishment of the General Board and the decline of the Naval War College saw OpNav reassert its postwar dominance of the navy and the navy's culture.[26] A self-perpetuating system was created, sustained by policies in the Bureau of Personnel that privileged "sea duty," especially that involving combat, over the study of past and service ashore (the latter had always been held in low regard). Thus, the "OpNav culture" emerged, composed of problem solvers who relied on technology for solutions. Also shaping the current operations focus of the OpNav was the forward deployment of the fleet on a regular basis in both Asia and Europe, a policy that remains in place to this day.[27]

Examining professional journals is one way to study an organization's cultural attributes. They reflect "culture talking to itself."[28] The mirrors of the navy's culture in this respect are the *United States Naval Institute Proceedings* (*Proceedings*) and the *Naval War College Review* (*NWCR*). Examining the February 1952 issue of *Proceedings* one finds ten articles. Four of the articles focus on technology or science, one on naval logistics,

War College, the Lessons of World War Two, Future Naval Warfare, 1945–1947 (Newport, RI, 2010), xxiii–xxv, 272.

[25] See Russell Weigley's discussion of the gifted Frost in *The American Way of War* (Bloomington, IN, 1973), 204–206. Frost passed away from a terminal disease while serving as the navy's liaison officer at Fort Leavenworth, Kansas, in the interwar period.

[26] This phenomenon is fully dealt with in my latest book, *America's First General Staff: A Short History of the Rise and Fall of the General Board of the Navy, 1900–1950* (Annapolis, MD, 2017), chapter 9, passim.

[27] The Bureau of Personnel replaced the older Bureau of Navigation, which had controlled the personnel policies of the navy. For the navy prior to the era of reform, see Charles O. Paullin, *Paullin's History of Naval Administration, 1775–1911* (Annapolis, MD, 1968). For the forward deployment of the fleet as a matter of policy, see Jeffrey G. Barlow, *From Hot War to Cold: The U.S. Navy and National Security Affairs, 1945–1955* (Stanford, CA, 2009), chapters 1–5, passim.

[28] The author first heard this characterization of culture come from Professor Susan Zeshoche of Kansas State University in 2002.

two on recollections of World War II experiences, one on "Excerpts from a Test Pilot's Diary," another on command of a ship going into "mothballs," and, finally, a de rigueur article by a marine on "Marines Afloat." One can lump the articles on logistics and the test pilot in with those on technology as being "technical." Thus, half the articles are of a technological or technical nature, and this does not include the technology reviewed later in the "Professional Notes." The articles that are historical were about the recent history of World War II.[29] The chief difference between *Proceedings* and the *NWCR* of that period lies in topical range. From September 1951 to March 1952, the latter mostly focuses on articles on Cold War foreign policy and the Soviet Union by the likes of Bernard Baruch and Edmund Walsh. Some articles discuss the "principles of war" and "Maritime Strategy," but still focus on confrontation with the USSR. There is not a single article on military or naval history other than an account of the rise of Soviet power developed from a lecture given in 1951.[30] These articles reflect a desire to come to grips with the strategic implications of the Cold War, but they also reflect a limited view as to what perspectives apply.

These trends in journals reflect navy culture as wrought by World War II. The developments during the Cold War, including wars in Korea and Vietnam, only served to reinforce the ascendency of the OpNav culture. It remains with us today and its efficacy in providing for efficient war fighting by the fleet has arguably declined over time. Admittedly, efficiency in war fighting *as a fleet* has been hard to judge because of the lack of a blue-water conflict that has tested the navy beyond power projection. Naval operations during the Iran-Iraq War such as "Earnest Will" and "Praying Mantis" (1997–1998) were a "pick-up" game and major US naval forces did not participate. Moreover, the wars in Iraq and Afghanistan provide no measure of fleet readiness for war at sea, since naval involvement in those conflicts remained limited to air power, some peripheral coastal operations, and (unwanted) riverine missions in Iraq. These operations reflect the OpNav cultural attitude of preparing for World War II–style fleet actions, while remaining ambivalent about "smaller wars" and operations often characterized as "short of war."[31]

A Manufacturing Culture

Culture molds military organizations' approaches to conflict. Similarly, conflict changes service cultures as dissonance develops between the perceptions of

[29] *United States Naval Institute Proceedings* 73(2) (February 1952).
[30] *U.S. Naval War College Information Service for Officers* 4(1) (September 1951) through 4(9) (March 1952). The name was later changed to the *Naval War College Review*.
[31] For a discussion of the Iran-Iraq operations, see David Crist, *The Twilight War: The Secret History of America's Thirty-Year Conflict with Iran* (New York, 2012), chapters 15–17, passim.

war in peacetime versus wartime reality.[32] Conflict and culture interact, and thus it is natural that the Cold War dynamic, and the early strategies that informed it, caused changes in the navy's organizational culture. Oddly, instead of naval aviation dominating a nuclear weapons–centered culture, it became the submarine component of the fleet that owned the balance of nuclear terror. After World War II, submarines seemed the least likely of the navy's "three great apes" – the surface, aviation, and submarine communities – to assume this role.[33]

Shortly after World War II, a variety of different groups inside and outside the navy looked at the delivery of atomic weapons and missile technology, much of it exploited from captured Nazi scientists, and concluded that ballistic missiles from land, long-range bombers, or carrier aircraft, or even atomic weapons on giant cruise missiles launched from battlecruisers, offered more promise.[34] But as the Truman administration slashed military end strength after World War II, budget battles resulted in the adoption of only one of these methods, especially after the departure (and death) of James Forrestal and the arrival of Louis Johnson as the second secretary of defense (SECDEF). This did not happen without conflict. Initially, because of a conference over roles and missions at Key West, it seemed the Truman administration would support both long-range bombers and a "super carrier" delivery option with the navy's SAVAGE aircraft.[35]

However, the suppression of the powerful naval aviation community during the "Revolt of the Admirals" resulted in its virtual "purge." At the height of the controversy in 1949, Johnson informed the vice chief of naval operations (CNO), Adm. Richard Connolly: "Admiral, the navy is on its way out ... the air force can do anything the navy can do nowadays, so that does away with the navy."[36] Luckily for the navy and the Marine Corps, the Korean War came less than a year later and saved both communities from extinction. Truman fired Johnson, reversed his policy, and approved plans to construct a new class of supercarriers.[37]

Hot war in Korea combined with the Cold War to open the door to a community also struggling in the postwar environment to establish its relevance, the submarine force. Studies by the General Board of the Navy prior to

---

[32] See John A. Lynn's model for this in *Battle: A History of Culture and Combat* (New York, 2004), xxi–xxii.

[33] See John Byron, "Three Great Apes," *Proceedings* 135(5) (May 2005), online at www.usni.org/magazines/proceedings/2005–05/three-great-apes (accessed November 6, 2017).

[34] Love, *History of the U.S. Navy*, 375.

[35] Barlow, *From Hot War to Cold*, 184–188; Kuehn, *America's First General Staff*, 213.

[36] Cited in George Baer, *One Hundred Years of Sea Power: The U.S. Navy, 1890–1990* (Stanford, CA, 1994), 310–318.

[37] Jeffrey G. Barlow, *Revolt of the Admirals* (Washington, DC, 1994), 288; Love, *History of the U.S. Navy*, 379.

its disestablishment at the end of 1950 had examined putting atomic warheads on cruise missiles aboard submarines. This had made perfect sense given that Adm. Louis Denfield was a submariner. Some of these studies had in fact been written by Capt. Arleigh Burke while he served as Adm. Towers's right-hand man on the board.[38]

Artifacts of navy culture after World War II – discipline, fighting spirit, and self-reliance – can also be used to characterize the officers of the submarine force. Submariners coming out of World War II possessed these attributes "on steroids." The cliché that they operated "alone and unafraid" captures this truth – one tempered by a draconian winnowing of their ranks early in the war.[39] Oddly, the submarine force was already experimenting with nuclear technology as a form of propulsion to realize a "true" submarine warship.[40]

This had come about because of one of the strangest career paths in navy history: that of innovative genius Hyman G. Rickover. Rickover's headstone at Arlington National Cemetery reads: "Father of the Nuclear Navy, 63 Years Active Duty." Rickover did not match the ideal type of naval officer described by Karsten. He was of Polish-Jewish descent and only avoided the Holocaust because his father had immigrated to the United States. Perhaps this contributed to Rickover's relentless hatred for totalitarianism, now represented by Soviet Russia, which had persecuted his ancestors in Poland and provided him a determination that saw its full flowering during the Cold War.[41]

Rickover's creation of a subculture of nuclear-trained officers occurred against the backdrop of a change in strategy after the Korean War fizzled out. President Dwight Eisenhower termed this strategy the "New Look," but it was more old than new. The president saw it as a means to "achieve both security and solvency."[42] The chairman of the Joint Chiefs of Staff (CJCS), Adm. Arthur Radford, supported Eisenhower enthusiastically. However, Radford also advocated a grand strategy based on massive retaliation. Containment of the Soviet Union was to be accomplished with thermonuclear blackmail using America's large inventory of hydrogen bombs. It was by this means that navy leaders found a way to justify the navy's existence in what appeared to be a fiscally constrained budget environment.[43]

[38] For the studies by Burke and others, see Kuehn, *America's First General Staff*, 211–213; the actual Burke Report can be found at the Naval Heritage and History Command Archives, Burke Papers, Boxes 5–7, "National Security and Navy Contributions Thereto for the Next Ten Years: A Study by the General Board," June 25, 1948, from Enclosure C ("Military"), GB study 425. This study was also known as serial 315.
[39] See John T. Kuehn, "Operational Requirements for Short Summary of World War II Submarine Ops," *Submarine Review* (Spring 2011), 113–124.
[40] As opposed to the submersible torpedo boats of the Second World War dependent on routine access to the surface for oxygen to charge their batteries.
[41] Francis Duncan, *Rickover: The Struggle for Excellence* (Annapolis, MD: Naval Institute Press, 2001), ix–xv.
[42] Love, *History of the U.S. Navy*, 372.   [43] Ibid., 373.

In the near term, however, it looked like both the army and the navy would lose budget share to the air force, which was to shoulder the balance of a nuclear retaliatory strike. The new CNO, Robert Carney, rejected an alliance with Gen. Matthew Ridgeway to oppose the "New Look" and instead decided to pursue navy programs that would enable it to participate, either in a lower-level atomic conflict or in a grand strategic thermonuclear exchange. Thus, Radford and Carney opened the door for Rickover and others to create the nuclear navy.[44] Perhaps Carney's actions reflected the existing fascination of navy leaders for new technology as well as their ahistorical bent.[45]

For most of the 1950s, the navy's primary means of delivery for nuclear weapons were its heavy aircraft carriers. This changed because of three revolutionary technologies: nuclear propulsion, ballistic missiles, and the decreasing size of nuclear warheads. The intersection of these technologies resulted in the Polaris ballistic submarine program, a revolution in military affairs (RMA) that was itself the intersection of four component RMAs: submarines, guided ballistic missiles, nuclear weapons, and nuclear propulsion.[46] Rickover had become involved in the nuclear propulsion RMA almost from the day nuclear power as an energy-generating source began. In 1947, Vice Adm. (VADM) Earle Mills, chief of the Bureau of Ships (which resided inside OpNav), appointed Capt. Rickover head of a liaison team with the Atomic Energy Commission (AEC). Mills also tasked Rickover to investigate building a small prototype reactor as a possible submarine propulsion system. Rickover convinced the AEC to make him head of its Naval Reactors Section, which eventually became the template organization around which he built the "nuke navy."[47]

At nearly the same time, Capt. Arleigh Burke, who later became one of Rickover's key allies as CNO, identified Soviet submarines as a primary naval threat in a key study for the General Board of the Navy. In fact, Mills got the General Board, in one of its last acts before disestablishment, to endorse BuShips's construction of a nuclear powered submarine in 1950; CNO Adm. Forrest Sherman secured congressional funding that same year. By 1951, Electric Boat contracted to build the first nuclear-powered submarine, the USS *Nautilus*. Rickover, of course, was placed in charge of the design of the reactor. On January 17, 1955, *Nautilus* put to sea, "underway on nuclear power."[48]

[44] Love, *History of the U.S. Navy*, 374–375.
[45] Carney was also involved in attempts by OpNav to disestablish the General Board of the Navy in 1946 and 1947; see Kuehn, *America's First General Staff*, 208–209.
[46] The term RMA here uses the definition in Williamson Murray and Macgregor Knox, eds., *The Dynamics of Military Revolution, 1300–2050* (Cambridge, 2001), 12–13.
[47] Duncan, *Rickover*, xviii, 98–101; Love, *History of the U.S. Navy*, 402–403.
[48] Duncan, *Rickover*, 139; Love, *History of the U.S. Navy*, 403–404.

Success breeds momentum and the Eisenhower administration authorized five more nuclear subs. These warships married Rickover's SW-2 reactor with an innovative teardrop design and a single screw (resulting in less noise). The submarines no longer needed to surface to charge their batteries and were 50 percent faster. The new CNO, Adm. Burke, was so impressed with the new designs (*Skate*-class) that he announced all further US submarines would be nuclear powered.[49] This key decision ensured that Rickover's ethos would dominate not only one type of submarine but also the entire community. A Rickover biographer described his ethos as: "inexhaustible energy, an insatiable appetite for work, an unswerving determination to define and reach his goal . . . and a gift for . . . trenchant, and ironic appraisals of his surroundings."[50] Many of these attributes became de rigueur inside the nuclear navy's culture.

Because of Rickover's acerbic personality, Raborn was picked as the Polaris program manager.[51] However, this left Rickover in charge of nuclear reactors and the accession, training, and education of officers to serve on nuclear-powered vessels. Unlike a program manager, whose job disappears with a successfully fielded program, Rickover was not going anywhere. Rickover understood that it was he who controlled the future because a system of his design would form the basis of the education of all officers in the nuclear navy. From this vantage point of training and education, Rickover slowly built a culture of nuclear-trained naval officers. With the decisions in the 1960s regarding nuclear-powered aircraft carriers and surface ships like USS *Bainbridge* and USS *Long Beach*, as well as improved SSBNs, Rickover's reach extended into all three major naval warfare communities. He had carte blanche over the selection of nuclear-trained officers and their initial eighteen months to two years of service in the navy. He personally interviewed each candidate for entry into the nuclear training "pipeline."[52] Rickover's antics in this regard became infamous, while the criteria for selection were often unfathomable.[53]

Rickover's expansion of nuclear propulsion into these other communities also gave him the ability to shape the leadership of the navy, and by the 1980s, two of his protégés, nuclear submariners Carlisle Trost and James Watkins, dominated the service.[54] For almost forty-five years, Rickover ran the nuclear program like a medieval fiefdom, and his tenure argues that continuity of

[49] Love, *History of the U.S. Navy*, 404.   [50] Duncan, *Rickover*, 98.
[51] Ibid., 152; Love, *History of the U.S. Navy*, 407.
[52] See the account of Zumwalt's interview in Larry Berman, *Zumwalt: The Life and Times of Admiral Elmo Russell "Bud" Zumwalt* (New York, 2012), 118–123.
[53] Robert B. Kuehn, to author dated 26 July 2017; Robert Kuehn was thrown out of his interview by Rickover twice – once for having long hair (with a trip to the barber) and once for "job shopping" – and then informed that same day he had been selected for the program.
[54] See Frederick H. Hartmann, *Naval Renaissance: The U.S. Navy in the 1980s* (Annapolis, MD, 1990), xi–xii, 79, 223, 264–267.

leadership is critical to the development of lasting institutions and can either stifle innovation or cause it to thrive. In Rickover's case it was mostly the latter. However, he had key allies in Burke, Raborn, and Mills, who helped him build the culture of the nuclear navy.

Even with Rickover's public relief by John Lehman in 1982, that culture continued to thrive, and still does today. Its attributes are a strange combination of obsessive "by the book" adherence to an almost holy writ publication entitled the *Reactor Plant Manual*, combined with an obsession that the nation is best served if a high-profile nuclear accident is avoided at all costs.[55] The submarine officers who dominate the nuclear component of the US Navy officer corps have "infected" the larger navy culture with cold-blooded risk-taking reflected in Cold War "tell-alls" like *Blind Man's Bluff*.[56] However, such risk-taking is often subordinate to the prime directive, the assurance of nuclear safety at all costs. However, even safety gives way to mission accomplishment on occasion, a tension between risk and safety being always present in this culture and consistent with the overarching OpNav culture of the navy aimed at mission accomplishment.[57]

Elmo Zumwalt, not long after his stint as the CNO, wrote of this culture and of Rickover in his memoir *On Watch*:

> I knew that [Rickover] would stop at nothing . . . to ensure that nuclear-powered ships received priority over vessels of any other kind . . . I knew that *his* Division of Nuclear Propulsion (now Naval Reactors) was *a totalitarian mini-state whose citizens – and that included not just his headquarters staff but anybody engaged in building, maintaining, or manning nuclear vessels – did what the Leader told them to* . . . or suffered condign punishment.[58]

This culture remains prevalent and powerful to the present, influencing navy organizational culture, especially as evidenced by the selection of the relatively junior Adm. John Richardson as CNO in 2016, not long after his appointment as chief of naval reactors. Intragroup commitment to nuclear power as the reigning "tribe" in the navy endures. The chief of naval reactors still interviews each nuclear program candidate, just as Rickover did.[59] With most of its

[55] This manual is now known as the *Engineering Department Manual for Nuclear Propulsion Plants* (EDM), OPNAV Instruction 9210.2c, June 30, 2015, located at www.navy.mil/ah_on line/archpdf/ah195706.pdf (accessed July 24, 2017).
[56] www.amazon.com/Blind-Mans-Bluff-Submarine-Espionage/dp/1610393589 (accessed July 17, 2017).
[57] Author interview with Robert B. Kuehn, former submariner, on July 28, 2017; on one occasion Kuehn skipped a step in the reactor shutdown checklist in order to accomplish the mission at the commanding officer's direction.
[58] Elmo R. Zumwalt, *On Watch: A Memoir* (New York, 1976), 85; emphases added. Zumwalt understood the importance of time in memoirs and the historical significance of his "report." This work is perhaps the best record of the Zumwalt "revolution" in existence.
[59] Author interview with Lt. Comr. Ryan Fickling, USN on July 27, 2017. LCDR Fickling is a fully qualified submarine officer recruited from NROTC at Vanderbilt University and served on fast-attack and nuclear cruise missile submarines (SSGN).

offensive punch in nuclear-powered fast-attack submarines (SSNs) and nuclear-powered aircraft carriers (CVNs), the smaller US Navy of today (currently about 280 warships) remains dominated by the "nuke" culture.[60]

The Zumwalt Revolution

The Cold War again went hot in Vietnam, with the navy playing a secondary role, going to war with the culture (and fleet) it had. Nuke officers did not yet dominate the navy's culture, which centered on the surface fleet and aviation. The non-nuclear officers in these communities found themselves in a shooting war that involved air strikes, shore bombardment, maritime interdiction, and something not seen since the US Civil War, riverine operations by sailors on small boats. Elmo "Bud" Zumwalt commanded US Naval Forces Vietnam from 1968 to 1970 (a two-star billet) during the most intense years of the fighting. Zumwalt's experience in the war and his sense of an identity crisis in the navy led to another cultural revolution.[61]

One historian considers Elmo Zumwalt and Hyman Rickover as "virtually opposites" in their temperament and style of leadership, devoting an entire chapter in a book to these "two men ... responsible for many of the funda-mental changes made in the US Navy during the post–World War II era."[62] Zumwalt and Rickover famously did not get along. Zumwalt was a surface warfare officer (SWO) and "political" admiral, having served as Assistant Secretary of Defense Paul Nitze's naval aide during the Kennedy administra-tion. Rickover was a perfectionist and engineer who cared little for political niceties. Rickover interviewed Zumwalt for the nuke program in 1959 for possible command of the nuclear-powered frigate USS *Bainbridge* or, alter-natively, as executive officer of the nuclear-guided missile cruiser *Long Beach.* Zumwalt set a record for being thrown out of Rickover's office (four times), but in the end Rickover selected him. However, the experience soured Zumwalt, who instead took command of the conventionally powered guided-missile warship USS *Dewey* (later classified as a guided missile destroyer, DDG). As far as Rickover was concerned, Zumwalt was missing the boat to the future, but he uncharacteristically tried again to pry Zumwalt away from Nitze to com-mand the *Long Beach.* Zumwalt almost succumbed; it was a prestigious command at sea and might help ensure that the nuclear clan would have "destroyer men" in it "to head out the submariners"; in other words, to ensure

[60] See "Status of the Navy," www.navy.mil/navydata/nav_legacy.asp?id=146 (accessed October 31, 2017).
[61] Berman, *Zumwalt*, 7–11.
[62] Edgar Puryear Jr., *American Admiralship: The Moral Imperative of Naval Command* (Annapolis, MD, 2005), 381–382, 399. Puryear's study includes lengthy passages of oral history interviews with contemporary admirals and officers close to both men.

the submarine community did not entirely dominate the nuclear navy. But Nitze would not hear of it and quashed Rickover's attempt to steal Zumwalt.[63]

Rickover later commented indirectly on Zumwalt, saying of his predecessor, aviator Adm. Thomas Moorer, "you could talk to [Moorer]," implying that Zumwalt was not good at listening.[64] Ironically, Rickover did not overtly contest the radical policies of Zumwalt, perhaps because on most of the building programs, with the exception of spending more on the non-nuclear surface fleet, the two men agreed. This applied especially to the nuclear-powered carriers and the Trident missile program, though personal relations between the two men remained strained. Zumwalt supported Rickover's promotion to four-star admiral, the first engineering duty officer to ever achieve that rank.[65]

On July 1, 1970, Elmo Zumwalt was appointed CNO at age forty-nine, the youngest man ever to hold the position. As a rear admiral, he was "deep-selected" over thirty-three other admirals because of the expectations of the liberal Republican Secretary of the Navy John Chaffee that Zumwalt could create a more "egalitarian navy." Outside the navy, the perception was of a service that was "behind the times."[66] Zumwalt's revolution had little to do with technology. Once selected as CNO, Zumwalt began a program of reforms that shook the navy to its core and caused a counterrevolution a few years later. Nonetheless, his reforms had a lasting impact on the navy, both in the officer corps, but more important, also among the enlisted rates, civilian dependents, and chief petty officers.

Zumwalt used his prestige and political top cover to implement social reform, commenting, "Whether or not [the reforms] were right can be argued ... I was ... chosen and the programs I had said I would initiate, I proceeded to initiate."[67] He was given sixty days to report on his proposed programs and their implementation to Chaffee, both to change the navy socially and to assess the future fleet architecture in the constrained budget environment as Vietnam wound down. Zumwalt formed a study group headed by his protégé, another "destroyer man," Capt. Stansfield Turner, to address the challenge. He named it Project Sixty.[68]

---

[63] See Zumwalt, *On Watch*, 88–95, for a complete transcript of the interview, which Zumwalt with his nearly photographic memory wrote down immediately afterward. Berman, *Zumwalt*, 117–125, 146–147.

[64] Duncan, *Rickover*, 228–229.   [65] Ibid., 231–235.

[66] Berman, *Zumwalt*, 11, 21. Duncan, *Rickover*, 228. Such an action had not been done inside a service since Zumwalt was a young officer in World War II, when Gen. George C. Marshall had been elevated to chief of staff of the army over a number of more senior officers.

[67] Cited in Berman, *Zumwalt*, 214.

[68] Zumwalt, *On Watch*, 66–80; Berman, *Zumwalt*, 230–232; Puryear, *Admiralship*, 428. Turner led the study group for the first forty days and then turned over the reins to Worth Bagley, Zumwalt's first choice for the job, who had been tied down in the Seventh Fleet helping prosecute the Vietnam War.

Project Sixty's recommendations, however, did not encompass a social revolution; instead they dealt with "fleet design" – that is the roles and missions for the navy in the near and long term to address threats to national security.[69] In an era of growing challenge by the Soviet navy, the study recommended moving the function of sea control up in priority above that of power projection. First priority remained Rickover's sine qua non, assured strategic retaliatory potential (the naval component of nuclear deterrence). However, Zumwalt's prioritization of sea control reflected his attitude that the fleet was inadequate to protect the sea lines of communication (SLOCs) across the North Atlantic. Zumwalt first focused on the design and structure of the navy to fight the type of war he thought most likely with the USSR, a conventional war.[70] However, this change in priorities resulted in little change in the navy's strategic culture, despite its realistic outlook. By the late 1970s, the OpNav navy vaulted power projection to priority over sea control due to the Carter doctrine and the Iranian hostage crisis.[71]

On the "people" issues, Zumwalt's impact was profound and lasting. His great concern was the abysmal reenlistment rate of 9.5 percent in 1970 and how this directly impacted the readiness of the navy as well as the fleet he wanted to build to fight the Soviets. Thus, military effectiveness, in addition to humanity, informed his actions. He dedicated his contemporary memoir "To the men and *women, enlisted* and commissioned, whose love of country, bravery in action, and *questioning minds* made it a duty and a pleasure for their service chief to try to *modernize and humanize the Navy*; I very respectfully submit this report."[72] The idea that a CNO sought, never mind lauded, questioning minds in the enlisted ranks had not been seen since the progressive era when the large seagoing navy had first been built and manned.[73]

Zumwalt promulgated his new personnel policies via correspondences that are now known to history as the "Z-grams." Zumwalt came up with the name, explaining, "policy or guidance emanating personally from the CNO . . . will be identified with a 'Zulu' series message designator immediately following the originator, e.g., 'fm CNO Z-01' . . . ." Z-01 was in fact Zumwalt's message to the fleet upon becoming the CNO, so the Z-grams began the first day of his

---

[69] For this definition of fleet design, see John M. Richardson, *A Design for Maintaining Maritime Superiority* (Washington, DC, 2016), www.navy.mil/cno/docs/cno_stg.pdf (accessed December 28, 2017).

[70] Zumwalt, *On Watch*, 60–63; Berman, *Zumwalt*, 233.

[71] For the hostage crisis and Carter doctrine, see Crist, *The Twilight War*, 8–12, 28–30; for the 1980s, see Hartmann, *Naval Renaissance*, chapter 4, passim. These events kept sea control distinctly secondary to the end of the Cold War and after.

[72] Zumwalt, *On Watch*, 167; emphases added.

[73] Writings from that period that indicate these attitudes had existed in earlier times include Rear Adm. Bradley Fiske, *From Midshipman to Rear-Admiral* (New York, 1919), and Fiske, *The Navy As a Fighting Machine*.

tenure as CNO. However, Zumwalt acknowledged that the first "real" Z-grams came out on July 20 as Z-04 and Z-05. They tell us much about his priorities. Z-04 gave to officers a benefit previously only allowed to enlisted sailors, automatic thirty days' leave in conjunction with permanent change of station orders. Conversely, Z-05 gave to enlisted sailors something officers and chief petty officers already had the ability to do, keep civilian clothes aboard ship for use on leave or liberty.[74] These two personnel actions made clear that the new egalitarianism Zumwalt intended to institutionalize would apply equally across all paygrades. In addition, a liberal policy toward civilian clothes for the lower enlisted ranks was another means to fight against the antimilitarism plaguing American society in the wake of Vietnam by demilitarizing the appearance of the lower enlisted ranks.[75] Officers could not complain that he was showing favoritism; he had made their lives easier too.

A complete review of Z-grams issued over the next four years is impractical for this study, but some of the most significant ones are worth addressing. Zumwalt believed that clothes made the man or woman and immediately sought to rationalize and simplify naval uniforms. Through a series of Z-grams he sought to ameliorate parochialism by eliminating the leather flight jackets and green uniforms of the aviation community. This was not done to punish aviators, but in some sense to bring them back into the navy. They would still have green flight jackets and flight suits, but otherwise they would dress just like their peers in submarines and surface ships.[76] Zumwalt also eliminated the dress khaki uniform that was something of clan garb for surface officers, a fact often forgotten by aviators. New enlisted uniforms in navy "working" blue were implemented and regulations put in place that briefly eliminated, then relaxed the requirement to wear the hard-to-maintain "crackerjack" uniforms. This led to some confusion, since the new uniforms for petty officers and above made it difficult for the layman to distinguish between a petty officer, a chief, and an officer when they were all dressed in a class "A" service dress uniform.[77]

Zumwalt's changes vis-à-vis women and minorities were even more countercultural. At a stroke he instituted equal rights for women, opening

[74] Zumwalt, *On Watch*, 172–173.   [75] Ibid., 167–168.

[76] When the author joined the navy in 1981, during his indoctrination at the Aviation Officer Candidate School in Pensacola, he was informed that "thanks to Zumwalt we are all black shoes now," referring to the fact that aviators were no longer authorized to wear brown shoes or boots and now wore black shoes and boots.

[77] See *Uniform Regulations of the United States Navy*, 1974, past versions available at Naval History and Heritage Command. See also Roger Worthington, "Saluting a Return to Navy Tradition," July 5, 1986, *Chicago Tribune* article discussing the changes by Zumwalt. During the period of his recruitment in 1981, the author visited a recruiting center in Cleveland and had a hard time distinguishing the various ranks from one another.

up previously closed programs at sea and flying aircraft to them.[78] The author was present as an officer candidate in Pensacola in the fall of 1981 when the first female aviation officer candidates (AOCs) graduated and proceeded to aviation and aviation intelligence training tracks in the fleet. Earlier, women had begun attending Annapolis. Under Zumwalt, the first female, Arlene Duerk, reached the rank of admiral.[79]

The fleet had traditionally been a bastion of racism and witnessed riots aboard its larger ships during the Vietnam War. Zumwalt put in place a system of minority rights advocates in commands throughout the navy, down to the unit (ship and squadron) level. He instituted a program of affirmative action, which on the whole allowed for the promotion and advancement of minorities previously held back by an informal system that one can only term as "naval Jim Crow."[80] Zumwalt ensured compliance with these reforms by creating "human relations councils" and then traveling throughout the fleet to attend their meetings. These councils blended officers and enlisted of all ranks and were accused of undermining "good order and discipline." Nevertheless, they got the message across that Zumwalt intended for change to occur. Some officers remembered these events as "mandatory rap sessions," but not all of them disapproved.[81]

Some of Zumwalt's most innovative reforms are ones that are familiar to sailors today: educational programs at sea (e.g., the Program for Afloat College Education [PACE]), the sailor of the year award, and his drug and rehabilitation programs. Also part of these reforms was his creation of formal career counseling and the forerunner of a human relations structure that became the pillars of personnel support in the navy. It had taken more than sixty years, but Josephus Daniels's idea of the navy as a giant at sea school where America's young could improve themselves had finally come into being. Zumwalt's was a successor to Daniels' vision of a virtuous, egalitarian navy.[82] One area where Zumwalt differed from Daniels was on the issue of alcohol. Although he did not bring alcohol back aboard ship, he did authorize beer in ashore barracks and even beer vending machines. Zumwalt also allowed "hard rock" music in enlisted

---

[78] See Puryear, *Admiralship*, 429–431, for a listing of the most important Z-gram reforms. Zumwalt was unable to open Annapolis to women since they were barred by federal law, but a year after he stepped down, Congress finally passed a law allowing females to attend the national service academies.

[79] Berman, *Zumwalt*, photo spread between pages 370 and 371.

[80] Puryear, *Admiralship*, 429–436.

[81] One of the first squadron operations officers the author worked for, a senior lieutenant commander, recalled Zumwalt's "rap sessions" had been more good than bad and credited them as being helpful in the long run with ridding the navy of class and race prejudice.

[82] See Lee A. Craig, *Josephus Daniels, His Life and Times* (Chapel Hill, NC, 2013), 244–245.

clubs and before long, this "new" type of music had migrated into the previously sacrosanct chiefs' and officers' clubs.[83]

Zumwalt's reforms are reminiscent of those that Marshal Philippe Petain took after the French Army munities of 1917, although more far reaching. But the intent was the same: if one takes care of one's troops and displays an interest in their welfare, they will serve more faithfully and honorably – and be more effective in combat.[84] Zumwalt extended the franchise of naval meritocracy beyond the "Annapolite" officer corps, or even the chief petty officer ranks, to everyone regardless of race, gender, or socioeconomic background. His critics lampooned his reforms as "beer, beards, and broads."[85] With the exception of the "broads," they seemed to focus on the peripherals, rather than the essentials, of his reforms. True, grooming standards grew more lax, sailors actually starting to look something like the young men and women in regular American society. Pictures of Zumwalt from the era show that he modeled what was acceptable; his own longish hair set the trend and would be astonishing in today's military, especially for a general officer. The words in a young sailor's letter to Zumwalt testify to the real value of his reforms: "Your Z-grams have had an electrifying effect upon those of us lacking in excesses of gold braid and upon the men with whom we work and live so closely. Even more than the printed Z-grams and their messages, the realization that 'The Man' cares for his men."[86]

Another area where Zumwalt played a role was the so-called Turner Revolution at the Naval War College (NWC). Zumwalt appointed his fellow "destroyer" admiral to the post of president of the college in 1972. Turner, a Rhodes Scholar, turned the curriculum on its head. Like Zumwalt, Turner believed in the efficacy of sea control and instituted a case study approach to teaching strategy as well as expanding the faculty base. Although Turner was there for only two years, his reforms were so well founded that the three-block curriculum he instituted remains in place today and is still regarded by many as the "gold standard" of American professional military education institutions.[87] Turner turned what had become a ticket-punching and moribund program into

[83] Puryear, *Admiralship*, 430. Alcohol would have to wait until the late 1970s with the authorization of beer, at the commanding officer's discretion, after forty-five continuous days at sea.

[84] The similarity of some of Zumwalt's reforms to those of Petain are remarkable. For comparison, see Puryear's list, 329–431, and Corelli Barnett, *The Swordbearers: Supreme Command in the First World War* (Bloomington, IN, 1975), 216–232.

[85] Berman, *Zumwalt*, 2. [86] Cited in ibid., 244.

[87] The author has taught NWC strategy and policy seminars since 2012. Vice Adm. Tim Barrett, RAN, "Mahan and Turner Restored: Naval Power and the Democratic States in the 21st Century," speech to the Sea, Air, and Space Conference, Maryland, April 14, 2015; "Another Crossroads? Professional Military Education Two Decades after the Goldwater-Nichols Act and the Skelton Panel," US House of Representatives, Committee on Armed Services (HASC), April 2010, 61.

the intellectual center of the navy once again. This intellectual revolution complemented Zumwalt's larger cultural one.[88]

Zumwalt faced numerous crises as he pushed these reforms. His most serious challenge came from Congress. In 1972, racial incidents occurred aboard the carriers *Kitty Hawk* and *Constellation. Kitty Hawk* had been deployed for a longer than normal period for Vietnam duty in support of the fierce fighting during the 1972 "Easter Offensive." *Constellation* was in the midst of intense work-ups to proceed to Vietnam to support the war. The incident on the *Kitty Hawk* was particularly violent and only defused because of the actions of the ship's minority executive officer, Cmdr. Ben Cloud, who convinced a rampaging mob to disperse.[89] When these incidents occurred, they caused a storm of media attention with critics arguing that Zumwalt's "permissiveness" had led to a breakdown in discipline. Zumwalt took quick action and used the occasion of a meeting of the Washington-area admirals, a group of more than eighty officers, to lay out a defense of his policies and explanations for how he handled these incidents.[90]

However, many of the admirals continued quietly to scheme against him. Shortly after Zumwalt's speech, the powerful chairman of the House Armed Services Committee, F. Edward Hebert of Louisiana, appointed a subcommittee to investigate the incidents, and indirectly Zumwalt's leadership. Representative Floyd Hicks of Washington headed the committee, which became known as the Hicks Committee. The last months of 1972 proved tense for Zumwalt and the navy. It seemed that the Hicks's committee, which even insiders in the Nixon administration agreed was a "hanging jury," might actually get Zumwalt fired and that a rollback of his reforms, especially those regarding race and women, might occur. As it turned out, the findings of subcommittee were so biased that they had no impact as the much larger scandal of Watergate pushed Zumwalt and his reforms back from the media limelight. Zumwalt wrote, "The giant torpedo that I had feared would blow my policies clear out of the water turned out to be a damp little squib."[91]

There were two types of officers: those who thought Zumwalt had done the navy a great service and those who thought he had ruined it.[92] In retrospect, the first group has the judgment of history on its side. Zumwalt brought the navy into line with the rest of the United States as to racial, sexual, and cultural norms that, on balance, made for a more cohesive US Navy. His impact, indirectly, on the navy in his appointment of Turner as president of NWC was also profound. Ships that have race riots cannot be effective instruments of

---

[88] Barrett, "Mahan and Turner Restored"; see also Hartmann, *Naval Renaissance*, 171–173.
[89] Berman, *Zumwalt*, 274–285.
[90] Zumwalt, *On Watch*, 235–239. The speech is on these pages.   [91] Ibid., 244–260.
[92] The author remembers entering the navy in 1981 and talking to older officers who had been through Zumwalt's reforms, and they generally adhered to these categorizations.

military power, and Zumwalt led the difficult fight for institutional change from the top down with grace and imagination in the face of bitter opposition from his fellow admirals and in Congress.

Counterrevolution or Renaissance?

Zumwalt retired after his term as CNO ended in 1974. Laird and others had wanted him to continue as CJCS to replace Moorer, but following a naval officer with another naval officer was simply not in the cards. Zumwalt's success in changing the navy had not been matched by his impact on maritime strategy. In the short term, his social reforms might have contributed to a decline in military effectiveness. Just as with the army in the post-Vietnam period, the navy became a "hollow force," although this was more the result of declining budgets. Moreover, making the navy look more like 1970s American society had its downsides. The Zumwalt reforms had affected good order and discipline, particularly given the normalization of marijuana use among young Americans whatever their race or gender. Adm. Thomas Hayward, another aviator, became the CNO in 1978. He credited Zumwalt for solving the racial problem, but also criticized his "relaxation of ... traditional military standards."[93] Critics often laid high-profile accidents involving drugs, especially on aircraft carriers, implicitly at the door of Zumwalt's liberalizing reforms.[94] However, Hayward practiced moderation in his approach, leaving most of Zumwalt's policies in effect. He addressed the drug problem and by December 1980, in anticipation of the incoming Reagan administration, had received approval to begin a revolutionary new urinalysis drug-testing program.[95] Rickover's insulated nuke culture also nurtured a limited agenda of rollback, especially as regards personal grooming and its normally "by the book" approach intolerant of too much personal initiative and flexibility of the type that Zumwalt had celebrated.

The moment for counterrevolution came with the appointment of a reserve naval aviator (and non-Annapolis graduate) from corporate America, John F. Lehman, as secretary of the navy in 1981. Lehman's charter was to create a "600-ship" navy and to reinvigorate the service from the perceived malaise and hollow force of the 1970s.[96] Lehman's actions speak to how one might roll back the clock, and how short such efforts often fall. He did bring back, much to

[93] Hartmann, *Naval Renaissance*, 34.
[94] See, for example, "Navy Reports 6 of 14 Killed Aboard *Nimitz* Had Used Marijuana," *New York Times*, June 18, 1981, www.nytimes.com/1981/06/19/us/navy-reports-6-of-14-killed-aboard-n imitz-had-used-marijuana.html (accessed August 10, 2017). Hartmann, *Naval Renaissance*, 20–23, 35–37.
[95] Hartmann, *Naval Renaissance*, 7.
[96] Norman Friedman, *The US Maritime Strategy* (Annapolis, MD, 1988), 6.

the naval aviation community's joy, brown shoes, leather flight jackets, and a cocky elitism. Several high profile films, chiefly *An Officer and a Gentleman* (1982) and the blockbuster *Top Gun* (1986) portrayed idealized views of naval aviation. These attracted some talented newcomers, mostly men, to the naval aviation ranks.[97] On top of this was the popular book *The Right Stuff* (subsequent film 1983) that granted de facto demigod status to naval aviators in American culture, especially the carrier-based fighter clan.[98] From this mix of internal changes and popular cultural influences was born the "Top Gun Culture."[99]

Meanwhile, the navy, now with a secretary committed to building up its strength, put its efforts toward readiness and designing a maritime strategy to match. One historian has characterized the initiatives that occurred under Lehman and CNOs James Watkins and Carlisle Trost as a "naval renaissance."[100] As Lehman worked with the president and Congress to get money for more ships, crews, and maintenance, the admirals worked on creating a "maritime strategy."[101] The new maritime strategy was published in 1984 and brought power projection back to priority in front of Zumwalt's more pedestrian sea control mission.[102]

The "600-ship" navy concept emphasized cultural attributes that reflected the effectiveness, or in naval terminology "efficiency," of the navy's ethos of the time. First was the attribute of "forward presence." The navy had been forward deployed since the beginning of World War II. However, forward presence does not equate automatically to readiness. A 600-warship fleet meant the problem of maintaining forward presence and the cultural artifact of readiness might be solved. This meant not just enough ships, but sufficiently trained crews and an ability to sortie when required for major war, as well as for ongoing crises. Zumwalt and his successor CNOs all recognized that it was not just new ships that were needed but also the readiness that goes with them. Six hundred ships would get the right number, but it would take time to man and train this force to achieve the readiness to meet a major crisis. Navy leaders believed that major crisis would be a conventional naval war with the Soviet fleet.

---

[97] See IMDB website for information on these films, e.g., http://m.imdb.com/title/tt0092099/ (accessed August 21, 2017); Friedman, *The US Maritime Strategy*, 2, also references the Top Gun advanced tactical training program for naval aviators.
[98] Tom Wolfe, *The Right Stuff* (New York, 1979).   [99] This is that author's nickname for it.
[100] Hartmann, *Naval Renaissance*, passim.
[101] For a complete account of the creation and content of the 1984 maritime strategy, see Friedman, *The US Maritime Strategy*.
[102] Hartmann, *Naval Renaissance*, xi–xiii. See also Peter D. Haynes, *Toward a New Maritime Strategy: American Naval Thinking in the Post–Cold War Era* (Annapolis, MD, 2015), 29, 31–33.

Lehman and President Ronald Reagan also turned their attention to the autocrat of the "totalitarian mini-state," Adm. Hyman Rickover. In the post-Zumwalt navy, it is rather astonishing that Rickover managed to survive for another eight years, continuing to advocate for his nuclear ships and submarines and personally tormenting every prospective officer prospect who contemplated joining his clan. However, Lehman was as ferocious a bureaucratic infighter as Rickover. Navy leaders had been discussing Rickover's successor for some time, trying to ensure that the organization that Rickover created would remain intact after he left. That was because most of those doing the discussing, such as Adm. James Watkins, were products of Rickover's cultural education. Watkins, later CNO (1982–1986), recalled "that Rickover invented his own navy so he could outwit the traditional one." Rickover's heart troubles and increasing short-term memory loss were also concerns. By early January 1982, the admiral's public testimony to the Senate led to a decision not to extend him in his job, since his existing congressional extension had come up for renewal. Rickover wanted to continue to serve to 1984, but subsequent meetings with Lehman, Reagan, and the cabinet all went poorly, and Rickover retired at the age of eighty-one.[103]

The OpNav culture that Zumwalt and Rickover had molded to meet Cold War challenges and social changes came into its own and experienced a period of consolidation and rebuilding with bigger budgets under the CNOs in the 1980s. Much of this was part of a larger "renaissance" in the armed services that saw the military rebuild and rearm after the malaise of Vietnam and the 1970s.[104] While the army created a new doctrine geared toward the Cold War entitled "AirLand Battle" (FM 100–5, 1982), so too did the navy publish the maritime strategy. As the army and air force reequipped with major weapons programs, known in the army as the "Big Five," the navy mirrored these efforts with its construction of the *Los Angeles* fast-attack submarines, *Aegis* cruisers, *Ohio* SSBNs, and new-generation aircraft for an increasing number of *Nimitz*-class nuclear-powered carriers.[105] The Carter administration had tried to slow down acquisition of these expensive aircraft carriers, but Lehman and Reagan made them the centerpiece of their 600-ship navy.[106]

---

[103] Hartmann, *Naval Renaissance*, 87–93; Duncan, *Rickover*, 277–290. Watkins's quotation is actually Hartmann's paraphrase.

[104] Hartmann, *Naval Renaissance*, 82; Love, *History of the U.S. Navy*, 670. Both authors specifically use the word "malaise" to describe the environment of the mid- to late 1970s.

[105] The navy's "renaissance" is covered in Hartmann's book, especially chapters 11 through 14; Friedman's *The Maritime Strategy*, as already noted, addresses the new strategy, see also fn. 88. For the story of the rejuvenation of army readiness, equipment, and doctrine, see John L. Romjue, *From Active Defense to AirLand Battle: The Development of Army Doctrine, 1973–1982*, TRADOC Historical Monograph Series (Fort Monroe, 1984); for the air force, see Robert Futrell, *Ideas, Concepts, Doctrine: Basic Thinking in the United States Air Force, 1961–1984, Volume II* (Maxwell, 1989), especially the later chapters to 1984.

[106] Love, *History of the U.S. Navy*, 707–710.

However, the culture that saw these programs and initiatives achieved had already been established. It was mission focused, geared toward an operational mind-set developed from World War II, and institutionalized as "OpNav" culture. Its nuclear component was a culture within a culture and more mission focused perhaps than any other component of the navy. Zumwalt had forced this institution to align with the times, and his successors were able to con-solidate these gains, especially when the public purse opened up during the Reagan administration. The fleet that was created aimed to fight a conventional or nuclear Cold War at sea. It had most of the tools it felt it needed, and it trained relentlessly in preparation to do so. Nuclear submarines plied the depths, either performing strategic deterrence or playing "blind man's bluff" with their Soviet counterparts. Fifteen carrier battle groups and associated amphibious readiness groups, with Marine Expeditionary Units (MEUs) embarked, deployed on a regular rotational basis to the Mediterranean Sea, Indian Ocean, and Western Pacific Ocean stations.

These force packages, as they were called, practiced for the big naval war that never came, but operated and maintained forward presence. They gained valuable experience in power projection from Grenada to the Gulf, although no one thought it worth putting aircraft carriers in the Gulf, especially after the frigate USS *Stark* was almost sunk in those waters by an Exocet anti-ship missile. At the same time, the MEUs aboard their ships cruised in tandem with these battle groups conducting what were then known as military operations other than war (MOOTW), such as noncombatant evacuation operations (NEO).[107]

A Valid Test of Sea Power?

Suddenly the Cold War ended, with the fleet at the peak of its readiness and effectiveness, untested in battle. Saddam Hussein's invasion of Kuwait the following year (1990) seemed tailor made to validate the expenses of the 1980s, the reforms of the 1970s, and the cultural artifacts of mission focus and forward presence. When Saddam made his ill-advised move, the United States had two aircraft carrier battle groups within range of Iraq, the *Eisenhower* aircraft carrier battle group in the Mediterranean and the *Independence* battle group in the North Arabian Sea. These naval forces formed the first critical elements of what became Operation Desert Shield, the defensive plan to hold Saudi Arabia, while the United States built up combat power for the First Gulf War (Operation Desert Storm).[108]

---

[107] Crist, *The Twilight War*, 220–229. The author personally participated in the NEO of the Beirut Embassy in 1989 while serving as embarked battle group staff on USS *Coral Sea* (CV 43).

[108] Edward J. Marolda and Robert J. Schneller Jr., *Shield and Sword: The United States Navy and the Persian Gulf War* (Annapolis, MD, 1998), 3–4.

The ability of the mature, Cold War navy to generate combat power on station and then augment it over time provided a lasting testament to the effectiveness of the navy that had come into being by the late 1980s. The ability to surge ready naval forces, in particular, was put to the test. A case in point was the *John F. Kennedy* (CV-67), which was the "ready" carrier battle group in the Atlantic and preparing to go into a period of extended maintenance for most of its ships when the invasion occurred. Adm. Riley Mixson, its commander, later wrote of the effort to deploy for the war:

> Carrier Group Two was heavily tasked ... Sailing orders and battle group ship assignments were provided with only five days' notice of deployment. Seven days were allotted for battle group workup ... Training continued during a seven-day transatlantic crossing enabling JFK (*John F. Kennedy*, CV-67) battle group to chop to CINCENT as a fully-ready battle group [CVBG]. On 1 January 1991 Carrier Group TWO [Rear Admiral Riley Mixson] was designated Commander, Task Force 155, in charge of three CVBG operations in Red Sea and commenced combat strike operations against Iraq on 17 January 1991.[109]

The excerpt reflects several key aspects of the reigning naval culture. First, navy culture remained dedicated to *readiness* – in this case, a readiness to deploy rapidly around the world at a moment's notice. Second, it emphasizes mission focus, not only being ready, but able to accomplish whatever mission might be assigned; in this case, the dominant mission of the navy in the post–World War II world, *power projection*, primarily with air and missile power. Barnett's three cultural components of "discipline, fighting spirit, and self-reliance" are also easily discernible in this excerpt. By the time combat operations began in January 1991, six carrier battle groups were in the Gulf and Red Sea ready to begin the campaign, which began, as noted earlier, on the night of January 17–18 with air operations.[110] However, power projection is only one element of sea power, broadly defined. The navy met the test in 1990–1991, but it had still not met the ultimate test of blue-water combat at sea with a near-peer or peer competitor fleet.

Tailhook and Beyond

The war in Iraq and Kuwait had barely ended when the "Top Gun" component of navy culture adjourned to Las Vegas for the annual "Tailhook" symposium in 1991. The previous year's gathering had been cancelled due to Saddam Hussein's invasion of Kuwait and the deployment of large numbers of naval

---

[109] Riley Mixson, Commander Carrier Group Two, Report on the Fitness of Officers, John T. Kuehn, NAVPERs 1611/1, January 31, 1991. FLEETEX stands for Fleet Exercise, CINCENT for Commander in Chief, Central Command.
[110] Marolda and Schneller, *Shield and Sword*, 139–140.

aviators, both navy and marine, who had deployed to support Desert Shield and, eventually, Desert Storm. Word inside the naval aviation community was that the 1991 version of "Tailhook" would be a "blow out," a party in naval aviation style to celebrate the nation's first major victory in a shooting war since World War II.[111] Ironically, the symposium was not far from its air force counterpart's tactical school at Nellis Air Force Base known as Red Flag. The Las Vegas Hilton hosted the convention in September 1991. Red Flag and Top Gun schools had increased the combat efficiency of both air force and navy pilots. The Desert Storm air campaign had offered validating evidence of the navy's effectiveness at power projection, including its acquisition of long-range land-attack cruise missiles.[112]

Culture is fickle. It can lead to triumph and to catastrophe, sometimes in the same year. On September 5, 1991, the Tailhook symposium began. By its end, the old adage that "what goes on in Vegas, stays in Vegas" was debunked. Eighty-three women and seven men eventually reported being assaulted or sexually harassed, mostly on the third floor of the Hilton on the night of September 7, where the so-called hospitality suites were located. When it appeared that senior navy officers were trying to cover up the complaints of Lt. Paula Coughlin, a female helicopter pilot, the scandal became public.[113]

What followed was not what anyone might have anticipated for the "Top Gun" culture. The navy, so recently the object of adulation and veneration following Desert Storm, became a pariah. The rest of the story is somewhat less well known. An excerpt from a *New Yorker* article following the suicide of CNO Adm. Jeremy Boorda in 1996 summarizes the cultural impact of subsequent events:

> Old hands measure [Tailhook '91] AGAINST Pearl Harbor in its devastating effect on the navy: the laxity and inattention that left the American fleet vulnerable in 1941 cost a single admiral his job; so far, the careers of fourteen admirals and nearly three hundred naval aviators have been ended or damaged by Tailhook. The scandal became the divide between the old navy, flawed but secure in its verities, and the new, conceived in the heat of the nation's culture wars.[114]

---

[111] Joslyn Ogden, "Tailhook '91 and the U.S. Navy," from Kenan Institute of Ethics, Duke University, at https://kenan.ethics.duke.edu/wp-content/uploads/2012/08/Tailhook&USNavy_Case2015.pdf (accessed August 29, 2017).
[112] For a complete analysis of the effectiveness of air power in Desert Storm, see Eliot A. Cohen and Thomas A. Keaney, *The Gulf War Air Power Summary (GWAP)* (Washington, DC, 1993).
[113] See Ogden, "Tailhook '91 and the U.S. Navy" (no page numbers, pages 1, 4, and 5 in my copy).
[114] Quoted from Peter J. Boyer, "Admiral Boorda's War," *New Yorker*, September 16, 1996, 68–69.

A female member of Congress, Representative Pat Schroeder, commented, "What you've got in the navy is a culture cracking." However, the scandalous behavior is remembered inside the navy alongside the perception that an undeserved "witch hunt" also occurred, one that saw two Gulf War navy commanding admirals, Riley Mixson and Stan Arthur, retire under less than ideal circumstances.[115]

The impact of Tailhook on navy culture and its effectiveness in combat awaits a lengthier treatment. However, naval aviation performed well enough in the "small wars" during the Clinton administration, Deliberate Force (1995) over Bosnia and Allied Force (1999) over Kosovo. Moreover, it participated in numerous no-fly zones, not just in the Balkans but also over northern and southern Iraq.[116] However, in all these operations, the US military has had command of the air over land; the "blue-water" test has yet to occur.

What remains today is a synthesis of the older artifacts and those from the "revolutions" discussed here. None of them has been "replaced" by the others in the strict sense of that word. The navy remains an OpNav-dominated culture, the primary artifacts of which center on sea service and technological solutions to operational challenges. It is peopled by senior leaders who tend to come from the ranks of the Rickover legacy system of nuclear officer selection but molded by new cultural mores wrought by Zumwalt and Tailhook '91.

Culture does not stand still, however, and a real maritime testing in non-permissive environments has not occurred since World War II. This in turn has prevented a means to more fully examine the influence of cultural changes in this period on naval combat effectiveness. As for the navy's combat effectiveness today, there are troubling signs. The recent collisions of USS *McCain*, USS *Fitzgerald*, and USS *Louisiana* are almost certainly due to poor readiness due to the ongoing high-tempo naval operations since 9/11.[117] Moreover, the navy routinely shortchanges the excellent professional education it and the other services can offer by failing to send officers to the services' colleges; for example, shorting its student quota at the US Army Command and General Staff College in 2017 by more than 50 percent.[118] The jury appears to be filing in on what these transformations have wrought, or not wrought, vis-à-vis the combat effectiveness of the navy today.

---

[115] Ibid., 69, 74–75; Anon., "I'm a Scapegoat, Admiral Says of Censure in Tailhook Case," *New York Times*, October 30, 1993, story on Rear Adm. Riley J. Mixson rebutting his censure by Secretary of the Navy John Dalton.

[116] The author participated in two of these three operations, flying combat missions over Bosnia and over southern Iraq in 1995.

[117] See Mary Salam, "Previous Collisions Involving U.S. Navy Vessels," *New York Times*, August 21, 2017. See also James Stavridis on the collisions as well as the "Fat Leonard" scandal at www.bloomberg.com/view/articles/2017-11-09/the-navy-s-crash-course-on-accountability (accessed November 9, 2017).

[118] The author was provided these numbers by the Navy Element of the US Army Command and General Staff College via e-mail from Captain Trenton Lennard, USN, October 17, 2017.

16 The US Marine Corps, 1973–2017

Cultural Preservation in Every Place and Clime

Allan R. Millett

In assessing Marine operations in Iraq's al-Anbar Province as the Sunni Awakening began to erode the insurgency against Iraq's Shi'ia government, Francis J. "Bing" West stressed that the Marines would win the support of the Sunni sheiks because they understood tribalism. West had the personal credentials to label Marine infantry companies as tribes; indeed, the strongest tribes. As a Marine infantry officer in Vietnam, West had been both a participant in and a historian of the combined action program, a III Marine Expeditionary Force (MEF) initiative in pacification at the village level. Marine squads assumed leadership of Vietnamese village self-defense platoons. Headquarters Military Assistance Command-Vietnam (MACV) had finally accepted the reality that Vietnamese villagers would have to be armed and led in the war between the Viet Cong and those few villagers who resisted the Ho Chi Minh version of forced communalism. West provided a stark picture of the perils faced by a combined-action platoon and the program's limited success. He believed that the Marine Corps produced warriors who could wage tribal warfare in Iraq and Afghanistan against the jihadist tribes.[1]

In addition to the formal notes throughout this chapter, my judgments are based on thirty years' service as a Marine reserve officer, 1959–1990, including three and a half years on continuous active duty, 1959–1962. As an infantry officer, I commanded three different kinds of platoons, served as the XO and CO of a rifle company, and commanded an infantry battalion. I served as a battalion staff officer in personnel, intelligence, and operations. I also spent nine years as an adjunct faculty member of the Marine Corps Command and Staff College as well as deputy director mobilization-designate, History and Museums Division, and assistant to the Commandant (Special Projects). My major writings on the Marine Corps are *Semper Fidelis: History of the U.S. Marine Corps* (two editions, New York, 1980 and 2000); *In Many a Strife: Gerald C. Thomas and the Marine Corps, 1917–1965* (Annapolis, MD, 1993); coeditor and author, *Commandants of the Marine Corps* (Annapolis, MD, 2004); "The U.S. Marine Corps: Adaptation in the Post-Vietnam Era," *Armed Forces and Society* 9 (Spring 1983), 363–392, and "The Marine Corps," in Sam C. Sarkesian and Robert E. Connor Jr., eds., *America's Armed Forces* (Westport, CT, 1996), 112–143.
[1] Bing West, *The Strongest Tribe: War, Politics, and the Endgame in Iraq* (New York, 2008) and *The Village* (New York, 1972). For an analysis of the post-Vietnam Marine Corps, see James L.

The Marine Corps is a complex organization of 183,647 officers and enlisted personnel striving to remain a tribe. It wants to be a community of "family" members bound by loyalties. It is really a complex military organization with the mission of preparing for and waging war against other military forces. Like members of any primary group, Marines insist that "outsiders" cannot possibly understand family behavior. For example, racial tensions, even violence, in the Marine Corps in the 1970s were met with disbelief, and then attacked by the assertion that there were no white, black, or brown Marines, only green Marines. Objective studies found that minority Marines did not feel quite as green as their white comrades. Another assault on the concept of tribalism has been the increased number of female Marines and their exclusion until 2017 from some military occupational specialties (MOS) because senior officers doubted whether women had the physical strength to serve in infantry, artillery, and armor units. This argument did not exhaust the objections of male Marines, who resented the intrusion of young women into a culture of adolescent male chauvinism. Already under challenge in the 1990s, the Middle Eastern wars blurred the MOS distinctions attached to combat since "improvised explosive devices" never distinguished victims by gender.[2]

Another challenge to Marine Corps tribal values has also been one of its unique strengths: the integration of fixed-wing attack aircraft with a combined-arms ground combat force. Although Marine aircraft are purchased as part of naval aviation, the aviation component is expensive to man, train, deploy, and employ. The Marine Corps, however, insists that it cannot perform its unique function of amphibious warfare without its own organic aviation. It is not the aircraft that challenge the ideal of one Corps. It is the value system of the men and women who fly, direct, and maintain the aircraft and their symbiotic relationship with the US Navy's aviation community. The relative advantages for women in Marine aviation, more than 200 in flight status, only add one more point of tension within the air-ground team.[3]

What is not arguable is that Marines believe they are part of an elite military organization that requires the willing embrace of a culture that demands heavy commitments. Some generals without embarrassment have claimed their Corps is an armed priesthood serving the United States with an unmatched commitment. Just how Marines keep the tribal ideal alive within a complex organization explains Marine culture.

George and Christopher John, eds., *The U.S. Marine Corps: The View from the Late 1980s* (Alexandria, VA, 1988).
[2] Capt. Lynn M. Stow, USMC, "Recruiting Enlisted Women," *MCG* 101 (March 2017), 31–34.
[3] Lt. Gen. Jon M. Davis, USMC, Deputy Commandant for Aviation, "Fight Tonight, Fight Tomorrow," *Marine Corps Gazette* 100 (May 2016), 10–25. The *Gazette* publishes an annual aviation review. Hereafter referred to as *MCG*.

The Operating Forces

The structure of the US Marine operating forces in the twenty-first century reflects a growing complexity that endangers tribal values by demanding much greater specializations than merely pulling a trigger. In the 1990s, three divisions should have had twenty-seven infantry battalions. The actual number was twenty-four, and in 2015, it was nineteen. Some of the infantry spaces went to reconnaissance units: three force companies and six divisional battalions of which three are mounted in light armored wheeled vehicles (LAV). The field artillery arm has a table of organization strength of twelve battalions, but actually has only eight battalions. The Marine armored force is 447 M1A1 tanks in two and a half regular battalions and two reserve battalions.[4] The greatest change, initiated by Commandant Alfred M. Gray Jr. in the late 1980s, has been the growing stress on intelligence, surveillance, and reconnaissance activities (ISR). The practitioners find themselves scattered throughout the operating forces and are difficult to count. What one can count are battalions with primary ISR missions, which have doubled from five to ten. This number will increase given the creation of the US Marine Corps Cyber Command in 2015. One example is suggestive. When USMC Headquarters formed a special air-ground task force for an African contingency mission, the initial ISR direct support team numbered nine and then grew to fifty-five.[5]

Since its emergence in World War II as a naval aviation force, Marine air has provided great operational effectiveness and nagging internal problems. Aviation and ground officers disagree with each other and naval aviation. Few deny the special advantages of single-service air support, essential in amphibious operations. The Marine Corps aviation establishment remains large, expensive, and critical to combat operations since Marine ground forces often work far from navy warships and carrier aviation. About 34,000 Marines man three aircraft wings, which, like the ground forces, deploy as composite groups that match the ground combat element. The Marine Corps has almost 1,000 planes and helicopters: 462 fixed-wing aircraft, 268 MV-22A Osprey vertical lift planes, and 267 helicopters. The service operates at least 100 drones of various types and functions, including ground attack. Officers with a new primary MOS (7315) control the two new unmanned aerial vehicle squadrons. The most divisive issue is the allocation of high-quality enlisted personnel. The

[4] "Marine Corps Organization," HQMC, *Marine Almanac 2017*, online at: https://MarineCorpsc onceptsandprograms.com/almanac. Some of the artillery and tanks are prepositioned in ships or overseas bases.
[5] Lt. Col. Brian Russell, USMC, "Cyberspace and Electronic Warfare Convergence," a three-part series in the *MCG* 101 (July, August, and September 2017), 36–41 and 67–71; Capt. Kelly Haycock, USMC, "Embracing the Net-Centric Paradigm," *MCG* 101 (January 2017), 42–50.

ground forces will have increasing needs for field-qualified technicians for all sorts of ISR missions, whose integration must deal with breaking down air-ground cultural divisions.[6]

Another issue that influences Corps organizational behavior is the partnership with the navy for the conduct of amphibious operations. Title 10 US Code makes the Marine Corps an amphibious force-in-readiness composed of ground combat, air combat, and service support elements. This landing force needs a ride. Navy ships provide air and surface transportation to and over shorelines. Originally conceived 100 years ago for a naval campaign against Imperial Japan in War Plan Orange, the amphibious assault mission does not have the compelling strategic rationale it once had. One effect is to make the "Gator Navy" smaller. Fifty years ago, an amphibious ready group (ARG) with an embarked battalion landing team (BLT) possessed at least 5 ships. Even when a BLT became part of an expeditionary unit that included a composite squadron of AV-8B Harrier jets and helicopters, the ARG still had 4 or 5 ships, including an amphibious assault carrier (LHA). In 2017, the "Gator Navy" numbered 31 ships, not the 44 of 2000 or the preferred 40 ships. All are capable of helicopter operations, although only 9 (1 LHA and 8 landing helicopter docks) can conduct true vertical envelopments with Ospreys and helicopters. The 10 landing platform docks and 12 landing ship docks conduct surface landings by infantry, artillery, armor, and engineers.

The cost issues are not trivial. The *America* (LHA-1), the first of three planned Super LHAs, cost an estimated $3.8 billion and has no well deck for amphibious landing craft or amphibian tractors. By default, the two-dimensional amphibious assault may become a vertical envelopment-only operation, dependent upon the element of surprise created by the range and speed of the MV-22A Osprey force and the effectiveness of naval close air support. In the meantime, the Marine Corps will stress amphibious training and contingency deployments to reestablish its naval warfare orientation.[7]

On the assumption that Marine forces in Iraq and Afghanistan would shrink as the United States reduced its CENTCOM ground forces, Commandant James T. Conway announced in "Expeditionary Force 21 (EF 21)," distributed in 2014, that Marine operating forces would return (again) to their maritime roots. The expeditionary forces would be "fast, austere and lethal." They would also be smaller with two Marine Expeditionary Brigades (MEBs) as the ready, deployable force, creating one MEF equivalent from three nominal divisions and three aircraft wings. One-third of Marine units would deploy outside the

[6] Lt. Gen. Jon M. Davis, USMC, Deputy Commandant for Aviation, "Art of Readiness," *MCG* 101 (May 2017), 9–16.
[7] Col. Doug King, USMC (Ret.) and Maj. Brett A. Friedman, USMCR, "Fighting Forward to Ensure Littoral Access," *USNIP* 1 (November 2017), 26–31.

United States. The forces described in EF 21 would need an amphibious force of forty ships, although the navy thinks thirty-eight might be sufficient.[8]

The most recent mission statement from Headquarters Marine Corps, MCO 2025, "Marine Corps Operating Concept 2025" (2016), envisions a future of widespread "dispersed operations" in every type of conflict or military mission short of general war. Even the smallest unit would have major firepower and ISR capabilities. An infantry company would have the target acquisition and information access now associated with a reinforced infantry battalion. The logistical challenges of such operations are novel, complex, and challenging. Many of the techniques and technologies are now under development by the Marine Special Operations Command (MARSOC), established in 2006. With echoes from World War II, MARSOC can deploy groups from the three battalions of the Marine Raider Regiment. There are three service battalions to support this force. The smallest unit, the logistical support team, numbers seventeen Marines with twelve different MOSs. A company might also receive a medical detachment of fifteen. The concept also resurrects the 1980s idea of sea-basing, which requires the conversion of prepositioned cargo, ammunition, and Petroleum Oil Lubricant (POL) ships to a combat-capable expeditionary sea base vessel.

For the generations of Marines who served before the Gulf War, the twenty-first-century Corps is a confusion of new acronyms and equipment that supposedly improve joint force integration and efficiency. The "rebranding," which began with studies initiated in 2010 by Commandant James F. Amos, aims at improving readiness for limited contingency operations (e.g., humanitarian interventions), but without compromising readiness for major contingency operations like the wars in Iraq and Afghanistan. The challenge remains deciding how much logistical structure the Marine Corps should devote to sustained operations ashore, a phenomenon that began in the Korean War and runs counter to the missions assigned in Title 10, US Code.[9]

Marines: The Many and the Few

The demographic statistics for 1995–2016 released by Headquarters Marine Corps suggest that the Marine Corps faces the same social changes as the nation. The enlisted force has marched down the road of multiculturalism and enlarged roles for female Marines. All Marines may be "green," but green can

---

[8] Maj. Mark Montgomery, USMC, "Expeditionary Force 21," *MCG* 100 (March 2016), 115–117; Lt. Gen. Michael G. Dana, USMC, "21st Century Logistics," *MCG* 101 (October 2017), 12–15; Lt. Col. Howard Marotto et al., USMC, "A Vision for Future 'Smart Logistics,'" *MCG* 101, 23–25; Col. Paul Bertof, USMC, "The MARSOC Lens," *MCG* 101, 40–43.

[9] Gen. James F. Amos, USMC, "Resourceful Force Design," *MCG* 97 (December 2013), 10–15.

come in many shades. The Marine Corps first became larger (204,846 in 2009), then smaller as the ground force commitments in Iraq and Afghanistan rose and then shrank.

Gender and ethnicity changes have challenged "Old Corps" cultural norms. The service has the lowest number of female members (14,233) of all the services, which is still twice as many female members as there were in 1990. Changes in ethnicity also raise intriguing issues. Marines may be warriors, but they are closer to "rainbow warriors" than the mix of recent European immigrants, urban Irish street toughs, and rural youths that composed the enlisted force of the world wars. The first challenge was racial integration, which began in the 1950s and continues sixty years later with modest success. Economic opportunity and enlistment disqualifications have combined to reduce the percentage of black Marines from 16 percent (1995) to 10.4 percent (2016). At the same time, the white component of the Marine Corps has declined to 64 percent. Hispanic Marines make up 17.4 percent of the Corps, up from 9 percent in 1995. Asian, Native American, and Pacific Islander participation is 8.3 percent, up from 4 percent in 1995. The inherent cultural challenges range from English language competency to regulating tattooing. One complication is the possible opposition to gender integration from nonwhite officers and senior noncommissioned officers (NCOs), given the masculine dominance values in these varied communities.[10]

The social issue that challenges the Marine Corps more than any other is the family, complicated by the ages of married Marines and the inevitable demands of deployments. The Marine Corps is still the youngest of all the services with an average enlisted age of twenty-two; 66 percent of Marines are twenty-five or younger. Forty-two percent of them are married, the lowest percentage in all the services. Thirty-nine percent of enlisted personnel hold the rank of lance corporal (E-3) or below and do not receive dependent subsidies. Marriage is only the starting point of a larger challenge, dependent children. In 2016, Marine families (70,000) had 92,415 dependent children. Ten years ago, there were more dependent wives and children than Marines. As of 2017, this was no longer the case. The 183,647 active duty Marines have *only* 162,451 family members. Almost 4,000 single Marines have custody of 5,786 dependent children. Preschool-age dependent children are almost half of the dependent child population. The trend lines offer some hope for reducing these numbers; the percentage of married Marines in all enlisted ranks has declined as it has for junior officers.[11] Family support programs now in place for almost twenty years have blunted the potential turmoil caused by the deployment of

---

[10] Demographics from *Marine Almanac 2017*, online at: https://Marineconceptsandprograms.com/almanac.

[11] "Marines and Families" section, *Marine Almanac 2017*.

Marine forces heavy with married junior officers and enlisted personnel. Another personnel issue has been the annual separation rate, which hovers around 30,000 Marines, of which 94.7 percent are enlisted personnel. Seventy-five percent are first-term enlistees. Most separations are honorable and reflect career choices, not rejection or punitive action. They also include retirements, either for disability or longevity. No doubt multiple deployments on combat missions have influenced voluntary separations, but it does not appear to be a general issue.

The Marine Corps reserve is supposed to mirror the active duty force, and it does by most demographic measures. Its most important number is its limited size: 103,894 men and women, of whom one-third (35,571) are on active duty or members of a drill-pay select reserve unit. These Marines are members of the 4th Marine Division, 4th Marine Aircraft Wing, and the 4th Service Support Group comprising the 4th Marine Corps Air-Ground Task Force. A smaller group of drill-pay reservists is individual mobilization augmentees (IMA) assigned to train and serve with active duty units. Two-thirds of the ready reserves are individuals who may or may not be paid but who can attend schools, train, and participate in other ways. The Marine Corps reserve serves as an agency to recruit and screen recruits for the active force, since reserve recruits attend boot camps and have a six-month initial training obligation in the active force.

The distribution of officers by MOS suggests a force of technological and operational sophistication and complexity. Infantry officers number 2,281 while the total number of artillery and mechanized vehicle officers is only 1,319. Logistics and supply specialists number 2,502. The fields that blend ISR and communications have 2,536 officers. The single largest officer MOS category remains pilot or naval flight officer: 5,233, or about twice the number of infantry officers. The number of aviation specialists is enlarged by another 1,735 officers who have anti-air missions and non-flying ground missions.

The distribution of enlisted MOSs likewise exposes the Marine Corps's technical complexity. It is no surprise that 28,619 enlisted men are infantrymen, working in concert with 4,312 artillerymen and 2,477 crewmen of tanks and amphibian assault vehicles. At this point, "the Sands of Iwo Jima" vision fades, despite the Marine Corps's insistence that "every Marine is a rifleman." If one aggregates all the troops in the MOS 60-category of aviation services, they number 29,287 aviation specialists.[12]

The MOS aggregation of ISR-cyberwar-communications personnel produces a total of 20,725 specialists. Another large MOS is the 35 field; 13,003 personnel are in motor transport as drivers or mechanics. When recruiters try to attract quality recruits by stressing the possibility of using their training as an

---

[12] Enlisted MOS distribution, *Marine Almanac 2017.*

entrée to a civilian occupation, they are not being deceptive. Marine infantry-men, on the other hand, may feel that their training does not transfer to any acceptable civilian occupation except being a SWAT team member. The recruiter can stress personal development in appearance, self-discipline, leader-ship, maturity, and work ethic, which are not empty promises but more unpre-dictable. Military occupationalism – devotion to a work specialty – is not necessarily antithetical to institutional socialization. It is, however, a tempta-tion to create subtribes in the name of high expertise and special membership requirements, a phenomenon common in the army as well.[13]

Age and rank distribution statistics provide a portrait of a Marine Corps of mature, experienced specialists distributed over many military functions. Although 7,309 officers are under thirty years of age, those over thirty number 13,617, which includes 4,263 officers over forty. By rank, the Corps has 5,489 lieutenants, but it also has 6,759 captains and 3,875 majors, so 51 percent of its officers are middle manager-specialists. Even the number of infantrymen and crewmen for armor, artillery, amphibian tractors, engineering, and logistical vehicles does not reverse the distribution of ages in the enlisted ranks. Only 25 percent of enlisted men are under twenty-one, and 57.6 percent are twenty-one to thirty. Senior NCOs (thirty-one and over) are only 14.7 percent of the enlisted force.[14]

The essence of Marine officership remains the experience of command, especially of units in one's military specialty in combat. For an infantry officer, the Holy Grail is command of an infantry battalion. Any command, however, is preferable to no command. The quickest way to earn peer disapproval and a shortened career is to refuse command, which is now board-determined as well as approved through the chain of command to the division level. Not being an effective commander is not career-enhancing, but not commanding is worse since it leaves an officer's ability untested. The expansion of intelligence, logistics, and communications functions through electronic and other sensing methods should not reduce command opportunities, but it requires the integra-tion of technical expertise and command skills at a higher level. The Marine Corps may have to promote and retain officers and NCOs who handle a laptop more deftly than a radio handset. The challenge is to fight smarter, not harder.[15]

There is also a potential cultural clash between part of the officer Corps and junior enlisted personnel. Within the statistics of officer age, technical MOSs, and rank there is a suggestion that an increasing numbers of officers are "mustangs" or former enlisted personnel. They are likely to feel strongly

[13] Charts on officer and enlisted rank and MOS distribution, *Marine Almanac 2017*.
[14] Data on correlation of age and ranks in *Marine Almanac 2017*.
[15] For examples, see MSgt William W. Hess and GySgt Robert M. Moore, USMC, "Cybersecurity for the Future," *MCG* 101 (March 2017), 72–75, and Maj. Carl Forsling, USMC (Ret.), "Investing in Marines," *MCG* 101 (May 2017), 56–60.

about traditional Corps values, both organizational and social. As a rule, "mustangs" are self-made. They must be successful senior NCOs (for instance, serving as a drill instructor [DI]) with scarce technical MOSs, complete a college degree of some sort, and exhibit the ability to lead by example. "Mustangs" are proud of their enlisted service and wear the Good Conduct Medal (four years of superior enlisted service) with pride. It is hard to estimate how many officers are "mustangs," but sources of commission statistics for 2004–2016 provide some data for reasonable estimates. Lieutenants commissioned by graduation from the Naval Academy, the Naval Reserve Officers' Training Corps (NROTC) program, and the Platoon Leaders Course (PLC) program are unlikely to be former NCOs unless they attended college as part of the Marine Enlisted Specialist Program (MESP). This means that 861 lieutenants in 2015 were unlikely to be "mustangs," but that 127 MESPs certainly were. The largest (and only remaining) group was 740 graduates of the Officer Candidate Course, the gate by which most qualified NCOs become officers. There is, however, another gate, to become a warrant officer (WO) (four grades), which changed the status of 179 NCOs in 2004 and 217 in 2016, and placed them in specialist billets.

A comparison of two officer acquisition years reveals a consistent pattern of distribution of commissions:

	FY2004	FY2016
USNA*	195	260
NROTC	185	209
PLC	293	392
OCC***	412	740
MESP**	180	127
WO	179	216
Other	9	3
	1,453	1,948

* Includes officers from other service academies, but not "military" colleges like Virginia Military Institute and The Citadel, who are NROTC members.
** Includes all specialist-based commissioning programs for NCOs.
*** Officer Candidate Course.

At a minimum, 359 ex-NCOs became officers or WOs in FY2004. The unknown number of "mustangs" that graduated from OCC is likely to push that number well past 400. Using the same estimating process, the number of "mustangs" for FY2016 officer acquisitions would be an estimated 423. In other words, one-quarter of the new lieutenants and WOs in these two years were probably "mustangs."[16]

While one can applaud the Marine Corps for opening the officer ranks to enlisted men, the Corps has rewarded NCOs who are likely to defend social values and resist the demographic and occupational changes in the enlisted force. The "mustang" officers will finish their careers with a likely service time of thirty years, but advance no higher than captain or major since promotion laws link age and rank for officers and in effect bar many "mustangs" from being promoted beyond major. In one sense this is a personnel management challenge, but the more important potential issue is a cultural clash among the Marines at the cutting edge of the Corps's technological transformation.[17]

The career patterns of the last ten commandants reveal the persistent institutional requirement that the inner elite of the Corps know about the realities of combat command. The ten commandants who were *not* World War II veterans first came to office when P. X. Kelley became commandant in 1983. Of his successors, only Alfred M. Gray Jr. had fought in Korea as a young sergeant. The next four commandants were also Vietnam veterans until James T. Conway became commandant in 2006. All but James F. Amos were infantry officers and saw combat inside infantry battalions as unit commanders and staff officers. The six Vietnam veterans received four Silver Stars, eleven Bronze Stars with "V" device for valor in combat, and five Purple Hearts. The "Vietnam Six" were all infantry officers, as were Conway and three of the four commandants who followed him. James F. Amos is the only naval aviator to hold the office (2010–2014). Only the current commandant, Robert Neller, served as a company grade officer in combat since Vietnam.[18]

The Once and Future Marine Corps

One window into the way the Marine Corps sees itself is the content of "coffee table" books designed for the public, but targeted as gifts to families, retirees, veterans, and active duty Marines. The quality of these books varies in text, photographs, and artwork. What is consistent is that the authors and editors are Marines with backgrounds in publishing, public affairs, and journalism. Another commonality is the stress on combat with special attention to the world wars. Marines know about Belleau Wood and the wheat fields. Few know that more Marines died on June 6, 1918, than had died up to that point since 1775. Fewer knew that the initial 4th Marine Brigade attacks had no

[16] Data on sources of commissions, *Marine Almanac 2017*.

[17] Sections on officer acquisitions in the *Marine Almanacs* of 2005 and 2017.

[18] Official biographies of the commandants prepared by the Historical Division, HQMC, and posted on Wikipedia. Maj. Gen. Marvin Ted Hopgood Jr., *My Commandants: Personal Reflections on the Commandants of the Marine Corps* (The author, 2010).

artillery support, unthinkable on the Western Front by 1918. Predictably, the flag-raising on Mount Suribachi, Iwo Jima, receives ample representation, but without mention that for the only time in the Pacific War, Marine casualties exceeded those of the Japanese.[19] As one would suspect of such books, there is no bad news, and they ignore or mute controversies. If, however, one wants a taste of how Marines see themselves and want to be remembered, these books are without peer. For the Marines themselves, the classic written guidance on their culture, traditions, and devotion to duty are two books of enduring appeal: Col. Christian Holiday, USMC (Ret.), *The Marine Officer's Guide*, 8th edn. (Annapolis, MD, 2017) and Lt. Col. Kenneth Estes, USMC (Ret.), *Handbook for Marine NCOs*, 5th edn. (Annapolis, MD, 2008). Both books are passed down through an apostolic succession of authors, whose essential mission is to preserve Corps traditions.[20]

The Marine Corps is also adept at projecting an image of meritocratic populism that suggests that any Marine can contribute to the effectiveness of the Corps and advance in rank and responsibility. This appeal is genuine. The call for Marines to attend a conference on innovation at Quantico, sponsored by the Marine Corps Combat Development Command, stressed this role as a duty, not just an opportunity:

> The USMC isn't Uber, Air-BnB, or Google. We are different by mission, organization, and infrastructure, but if we believe that our current way of doing things stands in the face of exponential enemies, then we are on the wrong side of history . . .
> To win in present and future conflicts, leadership must provide effective strategies and free our Marines to rapidly innovative new technology . . . we must experiment, acquire, train, and field at the pace of the current technological cycle faster than our enemies on a permanent basis.[21]

The problem is whether a military organization can ever work as if it is AT&T, Apple, or Amazon. It has enemies, not consumers, and its errors create useless deaths, not product returns and falling stock prices.

Is the soul of the Corps defined by the 400 contractors who exhibited their latest high-technology wares at the 2017 "Modern Day Marine Exhibition" at Quantico? They may not be "merchants of death," but contractors are certainly the carriers of technocratic values, which challenge the very concepts of family and community by which Marines define themselves. Newly empowered

---

[19] The difference in *deaths*, however, favored the Marines by four to one.

[20] For the most recent examples, see Chuck Lawless, *The Marine Book: A Portrait of America's Military Elite* (New York and London, 1988); Col. Jon T. Hoffman, USMCR (Ret.) and Col. John E. Greenwood, USMC (Ret.), eds., *USMC: A Complete History* (Quantico, VA, 2002); and Col. H. Avery Chenoweth, USMCR (Ret.) and Col. Brooke Nihart, USMC (Ret.), eds., *Semper Fi: The Definitive Illustrated History of the U.S. Marines* (New York, 2005).

[21] Editorial Staff, "Light Speed Snails Making the Marine Corps Future Proof," *MCG* 101 (May 2017), 5.

organizations, blessed with the greatest information technology (IT) capacity, may devalue the leadership responsibility of a junior officer and enlisted force ("the millennials") who have grown up in the decentralized, lateral universe of social media. The Internet makes its users believe that all opinions are insightful and empowered by feelings that conquer facts. The "Marines United" controversy pitted young serving Marines and recent veterans against each other on issues involving sexism, privacy, gender identification, and nudity.[22] There will always be social practices acceptable in some parts of society that will not contribute to the training, discipline, and cohesion of units because they promote individual withdrawal and illusions of skill and security.

The Marine Corps has conceded that after boot camp, young Marines will return to their smartphones and tablets and rejoin their social media world. Rather than try to regulate access to social media – a hopeless task – Headquarters Marine Corps in ALMAR 008/17 encouraged Marines to use social media to report good news to their family and friends. At the same time, units must conduct classes on "on-line misconduct," a concept that extends well beyond traditional classified information. The Marines United embarrassment certainly disclosed the public damage the thoughtless use of social media can create. Most Marines know that smartphones can be a fatal source of attention deficit disorder in a combat zone.[23]

Every tribe requires high priests, and two generations of the Krulak family have provided generals who have explained the Corps to Marines and the public. The late Lt. Gen. Victor H. "Brute" Krulak, in a letter to Commandant Randolph Pate in November 1957, struck a high note worthy of John A. Lejeune. Asked by Pate to explain why the United States needed a Marine Corps, Krulak asserted that the nation did not need a Corps. Instead, the American people wanted a Marine Corps because Marines had earned the public trust for their valor and fighting competence. In a book written years later, Krulak identified those aspects of Marine culture that had made Marines so useful and trustworthy. In *First to Fight*, Krulak argued that the twentieth-century Marine Corps had created officers and enlisted personnel noted for operational innovation, improvisation, teamwork that created a mystical brotherhood of warriors, an uncanny knack for working in spartan conditions and deprivation of resources, and a special competence in killing the nation's enemies without fear or favor.[24]

---

[22] "Marines United" was a Facebook group that shared nude and suggestive photos of servicewomen.

[23] HQMC, MCTP6-10B, "Marine Corps Values," 2016; Maj. Henry C. Flynn, USMC, "Full Corps Press," *MCG* 101 (August 2017) 63–64; Capt. Justin Gray et al., USMC, "Socializing the Network," *MCG* 101 (October 2017), 79–82.

[24] Lt. Gen. Victor H. Krulak, USMC (Ret.), *First to Fight: An Inside View of the U.S. Marine Corps* (Annapolis, MD, 1999). The letter to Gen. Pate is reprinted on pages xii–xvi.

In real life, the career of General Charles C. Krulak, one of "The Brute's" three officer sons, embodied many of the traits his father called organizational values. As an infantry officer in Vietnam, Chuck Krulak (USNA, 1964) commanded a rifle platoon and two infantry companies and received the Silver Star and two Purple Hearts. In a career that ended with a tour as commandant (1995–1999), Chuck Krulak commanded an infantry battalion, an infantry regiment, and Fleet Marine Force (FMF) Pacific. He specialized in personnel administration, operational planning, recruit training, and joint operations. His service as commander of FMF logistical units in the Gulf War (1990–1991) won him special recognition as a manager of complex support operations at the theater level. Krulak had a deep concern for recruit training and the preparation of enlisted Marines for counter-terrorism, counterinsurgency, population control, and pacification that predated the wars in Iraq and Afghanistan. A Marine enlisted man, "the universal corporal," had to train for a "three-block war" that demanded a combination of patience, caution, high skills in marksmanship and field craft, ISR technological competence, and teamwork because future wars would be fought amid urban populations against shadowy foes.

As commandant, Krulak introduced a week-long training experience that completed an expanded twelve-week recruit training cycle. Called the "Crucible," the experience mandated the recruits survive a grueling series of forced marches, obstacle course challenges, tactical problems, and simulated combat without much rest or food. Drill instructors contributed to the high level of anxiety and confusion by both criticizing and encouraging the boots. The other American armed services conduct similar training for special operations candidates, including escape, evasion, and prisoner-of-war survival courses for pilots and air crews, but do not conduct "Crucible" experiences for all recruits. The "Crucible" does not (except on rare occasions) "fail" recruits, but brings a sense of unique accomplishment when the recruits finish the training, for they can now be called Marines by the DIs. The whole experience, as Krulak admitted, smacks of medieval warrior apprenticeship, Asian martial arts cults, and English public school culture, but it is essential to creating a sense of organizational loyalty and comradeship that the Corps promises its members.[25]

Recruit Training

Young adults join the Marine Corps because it promises communal values of loyalty, integrity, physical fitness, maturity, disciplined appearance, and comradeship. Although it does not abandon these values, the Corps cannot avoid

[25] Official biographical summary, Gen. Charles C. Krulak, USMC (Ret.), Commandant reference files, Historical Division, MCDEC; Gen. Charles C. Krulak, USMC, "CRUCIBLE: Building Warriors for the 21st Century," an "All Hands" memo, 1997, republished in *MCG* 97 (December 2013), 22–24.

organizational priorities. The dilemmas of choice between interpersonal loyalties and organizational culture appear more often and have become more difficult to evade. The risks and effects of poor judgment have greater significance, especially in a combat environment where lives are at stake. Comradeship becomes more essential but more delicate when the bullets are flying. Because it stresses that its core values are battle-tested and immutable, the Marine Corps places a special burden on *all* of its members, regardless of place and time, to be Marines first and specialists second.

The Marine Corps knows that recruiting young men and women who will survive boot camp and become effective is an assignment of high importance. Every year, the recruiters have to find some 30,000 to 40,000 candidates who must be physically fit, be high school graduates, have average or above average mental test scores, and be in the top three intelligence categories. There are also quotas for women and minority groups. Although the Marine Corps will accept youths seventeen to nineteen years of age, only 10,268 Marines in 2015–2016 were under the age of nineteen. Few recruits did not have a high school diploma or GED certification. There are almost no concessions on criminal records and prior drug use. Finding a not-so-few good men and women requires far more friendly persuasion and cost-benefit analysis than other eras demanded. The single greatest influence is someone the recruit knows who was a Marine and whom the recruit admires. Behavior paragons are not an overcrowded group. Recruiters count on high youth unemployment and soaring college costs to bring youths to their offices, but that may not bring enough of the right people into the armed services. It is too easy to say a long war and a bad press are the cause of public indifference toward military service. Eager to portray the effects of service in terms of personal growth and the opportunity for maturing experiences, the Corps neglects to picture itself as a high-tech "first employer." A frank recruiter should stress that fewer than 25 percent of Marines go on for a second enlistment, let alone a twenty-year career, yet the benefits of service are lasting and tangible, provided one survives.[26]

The place where Marine Corps culture is created is at a Marine Corps Recruit Depot where "boots" are shorn of their hair, privacy, and any control over their lives for twelve weeks. It is wrong to think, as civilian critics do, that boot camp creates warriors. It does not. It finds out if young men and women want to be Marines. With the exception of rifle marksmanship qualification, little that

[26] Maj. Christopher S. Tsirlis, "Recruiting for the 21st Century Marine Corps," *MCG* 101 (February 2017), 68–73; Subcommittee on Military Personnel, Committee on Armed Services, US House of Representatives, 94th Congress, 2nd Session, Report: "Marine Corps Recruit Training and Recruiting Programs," September 29, 1976 (Washington, DC, 1976), 3–13; J. Walter Thompson, Inc., "Who Joins and Why" August 1981, a study for Headquarters Marine Corps; Lt. Col. William Gilfillan II and Lt. J. R. Brown, USMC, "Recruiting and an All-Volunteer Force," *MCG* 61 (November 1977), 81–84.

happens at boot camp mirrors combat. A great deal goes on that is designed to indoctrinate boots and to discover if they have enough physical ability, sense of social interdependence, emotional stability, and strength of character to survive three months of stress, physical exhaustion, and anxiety. The survivors then receive the hallowed EGA – the eagle, globe, and anchor of the Marine Corps – and the right to be called Marine. Only then does serious training follow, designed to make the new Marines minimally competent in a military occupational specialty. Whether elimination is done by staff evaluation or by recruit choice, annual boot camp attrition runs between 10 and 15 percent. The failed recruits either have incapacitating physical conditions or suffer from emotional and psychological flaws that make them a risk to themselves and their fellow comrades. Recruiters cannot predetermine many of the characteristics and conditions that eliminate boots; nevertheless, they receive no credit for making their quota unless the recruits complete boot camp.

The Marine Corps realized in World War I that its rapid expansion required recruit training to be the primary agent of institutional socialization. Such training required isolation and common instruction by the best NCOs. The former US Navy correctional barracks in the seaside tidal swamps and islands of South Carolina known as Parris Island proved perfect for isolated deprivation. Not until World War II did the Corps create a second recruit depot in San Diego, California. Since the Marine Corps recruits heavily on the West Coast, especially for minority recruits, the San Diego recruit depot has survived even though it is surrounded by a municipal airport and civilian neighborhoods. Some believe San Diego training is too soft and "Californian." Even though San Diego screens one-third of all recruits, Parris Island sets the standard for boot camp.

Of the 2,168 dedicated hours of recruit training, only 528 hours are reserved for formal instruction. The basic syllabus of boot camp has changed little since World War II. In addition to close-order drill, the recruits endure a wide variety of physical training, inspections, and long marches. Basic known-distance marksmanship training is a high point of recruit training. Otherwise, boot camp is a world of pressure, fatigue, sleeplessness, and anxiety. Marine history lessons remind the boots of their legacy of heroism and endurance. The message is simple: individual preferences are not Marine Corps concerns. The reward is also simple: a boot camp survivor is now a "real" Marine.[27]

Marine officer candidates do not attend boot camp. They go to an officer candidate course at the Marine Corps Combat Development and Education Command in Quantico, Virginia. Even enlisted men who have survived boot

---

[27] Eugene Alvarez and Leo J. Daugherty III, *Parris Island: "The Cradle of the Corps"* (Atlantic Beach, FL, 2016); Leo J. Daugherty III, "To Fight Our Country's Battles: An Institutional History of the United States Marine Corps during the Interwar Era, 1919–1935," PhD diss., The Ohio State University, 2001. Both of these authors completed boot camp.

camp must go through the screening course at Quantico and then attend the Basic School, where real officer training occurs. Officer candidates come from a variety of sources: meritorious NCOs, the Platoon Leaders Course (college undergraduates), the Officer Candidate Course (college graduates), and a screening course for the NROTC Marine options and prospective Naval Academy graduates who have chosen to become Marine officers. Senior officers believe that there is no substantial difference between the institutional socialization that occurs at the recruit depots and at Quantico. The result may be the same, but the process is not. At both places, senior NCOs have day-to-day supervision, but at Parris Island, these NCOs are DIs, wear traditional Montana peak field covers ("Smokey the Bear" hats), and have considerable latitude in how they treat platoons and individual recruits.

At Quantico, the sergeant-instructors function within much closer senior NCO and officer supervision. This does not mean that officer-candidates receive gentler treatment.[28] Like boot camp, the officer candidate courses are not risk free, but there have been fewer training deaths, and few linked to training officers and NCOs. Deaths among officer-candidates come from driving accidents off base, congenital physical defects, or unpredictable reactions to heat stroke or heat exhaustion. The same sorts of problems appear in the field forces too, so these cases are not unique. Boot camp incidents, especially those that involve deaths, are publicized because the Marine Corps claims so much for the boot camp experience. Recruits believe that boot camp changes their lives; many believe standards in the field are not as high. The recruit experience ensures that Marines understand duty and teamwork, but recruit abuse dogs the process and puts the Corps on the public defensive.

The role of the DI is critical in recruit training, and the Marine Corps does not take the assignment of DIs lightly. They go to a special ten-week school that offers courses in applied psychology taught by experts. Once an all-volunteer group, DIs are now selected by potential from the entire Marine Corps. Being a DI is like entering the priesthood. It is also career-enhancing, sure to bring accelerated promotion and choices of duty station. If a DI finds himself or herself inclined to extra-official "training," it occurs in the barracks at night or on an isolated part of the post like Ribbon Creek, where a DI on a night march drowned six recruits in 1956. Drill instructors seldom report fellow DIs for recruit abuse. Unlike their role in the rest of the Corps, officers are reluctant to intrude on DI activities, and after every recruit abuse scandal, one reform is always to order closer officer supervision.

Whatever his or her ascribed status, the DI is under heavy official and peer pressure to graduate as many boots as possible. Peer competition between DIs

---

[28] Statistics and analysis of officer procurement, Deputy for Programs and Resources. *Concepts and Issues*, 1989–1995, and annual *Marine Almanac*, 1989–2017.

is real. Individual recruits who are low scorers may become special targets for abuse or vigilante actions by other recruits, the infamous "Code Red." The growing diversity of recruits – by sexual preference, race, family origins, religion, and personal habits – increases the likelihood that a DI will find reasons to single out recruits for abuse. Noncommissioned officers are the products of a competitive system that rewards conformity to Corps values as much or more than occupational competence. Drill instructors may view recruits as economic opportunists rather than young men and women who want to be *Marines*. Recruiters know the demographic profile of successful boots: white, athletic, high school graduates or better, active Christians, children of strong two-parent families of multiple siblings, extended family members who are veterans, a strong sense of patriotism, and a desire to use the military experience as a portal to adulthood. Part of the attraction was that the boots could serve with young people just like themselves in motivation. Despite the lore that being a Marine requires the "death" of one personality and the emergence of a "new" personality, the reality is successful recruits start with personal characteristics that ease organizational socialization.[29]

Part of the self-inflicted difficulty with boot camp is the quaint conceit that the DIs are conducting combat "training." They are instead choosing boots to be prepared for training. They also create conditions for a small group of boots to choose failure or to be "dropped on request," which means a general discharge for unsuitability. Even with the periodic crises caused by recruit abuse, the Marine Corps is unlikely to change the boot camp experience because it has created the expectation that it will be unpleasant, demeaning, and dangerous, and recruits join on that basis. Whether boot camp is an attraction or a barrier to recruiting trainable millennials remains to be seen. Changing boot camp and officer candidate screening would bring on an institutional crisis that would endanger the very organizational culture Marines value.

The most recent recruit abuse crisis pales by comparison with the experiences of the 1970s. Recruiting in the all-volunteer, antimilitary environment of the time, the Marine Corps sent almost 50,000 recruits annually to the boot camps. The Corps tried to meet the requirement that high school graduates had to climb from 55 percent (1975) to 75 percent (1977). No more than 18 percent of recruits could be Category IVs in intelligence. Difficulties meeting these goals resulted in widespread recruiting fraud. The DIs decided to cleanse the stables of unfit boots and washed out 12,000 trainees annually and would have dropped more except that Headquarters capped attrition at 15 percent. The attrition rate at Parris Island was 24 percent; at San Diego 11.6 percent. In

---

[29] Aaron O'Connell, *Underdogs: The Making of the Modern Marine Corps* (Cambridge, MA, 2012); Thomas E. Ricks, *Making the Corps* (New York, 1997).

FY1975 and 1976, the Marines dealt with 234 incidents of recruit abuse, the US Army just 53 cases. In 1972–1976, twenty-one recruits died in abuse-related episodes: four in training "accidents," nine from physical collapse, one from hypothermia in the wheel well of an airliner while trying to escape San Diego, four in suicides, and four in drowning while attempting to escape Parris Island. Congress investigated and concluded that the deaths were unfortunate collateral damage and that the Corps was cleaning up the worst abuses.[30]

The latest recruit abuse incident involved the suicide of a Muslim recruit who seemed ready to meet the challenges of boot camp until he got to Parris Island and met his fellow boots. Like other young men, Raheel Siddiqui joined the Corps to earn educational benefits after a rocky start at a branch of the University of Michigan. Siddiqui thought he could learn a marketable skill as an aviation technician. Although he had worked out, he had no prior experience with the humiliation, pain, stress, and peer ridicule that might have steeled him for boot camp. It was one thing to be screamed at by DIs. It was quite another to have his fellow boots turn on him for being an "Ay-rab," even though he was born and raised in Detroit by Pakistani parents. Siddiqui came to Parris Island during a rise in recruit abuse incidents from 2005 to 2014. The DIs focused on driving Siddiqui out of Parris Island with verbal harassment and physical abuse. He responded by jumping four stories to his death. His suicide set off almost two years of investigations, reliefs for cause, reforms in supervision, courts-martial, and public recriminations.[31]

What makes boot camp so special is that all Marine enlisted personnel have to complete the experience. The officer candidate courses at Quantico do not impress some NCOs. Boot camp is for everybody, not elite subsets of other services like US Navy SEALs. Boots just get to be Marines, and that is enough. Some students of youth behavior think that millennials will not surrender their individuality and Facebook identities for military service of any kind. Such Cassandras have predicted empty ranks before, and they were wrong. The challenge today is to retain boot camp as "the Crucible" that Commandant Charles C. Krulak imagined as a way to provide an experience that reveals the physical and psychic endurance necessary for a new generation of techno-troopers.

The Source of Marine Culture

For all its stress on its history and combat valor, the Marine Corps has a Homeric past that was manufactured in the 1920s to exploit a new favorable

---

[30] Subcommittee on Military Personnel, Committee on Armed Services, US House of Representatives, 94th Congress, 2nd Session, Report: "Marine Corps Recruit Training and Recruiting Programs," 13–36.

[31] Janet Reitman, "The Making – and Breaking – of Marines," *New York Times Magazine* (July 9, 2017), 30–43, 52–57; O'Connell, *Underdogs*, previously cited.

public image won on the battlefields of France by the 4th Marine Brigade. World War I and its strategic aftermath transformed a small colonial expeditionary light infantry force into the amphibious assault force it is today. According to Title 10 US Code, it is also a force ready to perform any mission the president may assign it. The Marine Corps became a "force-in-readiness," deployed by sea to support a national strategy of forward, collective defense. Commandant John A. Lejeune (1920–1929) transformed the exploits of the 4th Marine Brigade in France into public and congressional support, encouraged by a broad recruiting and publicity program. The key victory in Washington was to convince the US Navy that it could not wage war with Japan as planned in War Plan Orange (as revised in 1921–1922) without seizing and defending forward operating bases across the Pacific. That wartime role became the Corps's principal mission by Lejeune's direction in July 1921. It became an official mission in a revision of *Joint Action of the Army and Navy* (1927), approved by the Army-Navy Joint Board, the predecessor of the Joint Chiefs of Staff.

Lejeune recognized that the "new" Marine Corps, which would create a Fleet Marine Force in 1933, needed to develop an elite status based on performance, not martial appearance and small numbers. He appointed Maj. Edwin N. McClellan to be the first Marine official historian. McClellan's histories, notable for what they omitted, lauded the combat heroics of the Corps in every place and clime since 1775. Lejeune and McClellan created a "Marine Corps Birthday" of November 10, 1775, out of pure imagination and made it an annual ritual wherever Marines may be. They claimed that a Continental Congressional directive to George Washington to form two Marine battalions for naval expeditionary duty is the foundation of the Marine Corps. McClellan ignored the fact that Washington did not form the battalions. Until the twentieth century, the Corps accepted a birthday of July 11, 1798, the day Congress approved a Marine Corps Act that authorized a permanent shipboard security force and barracks-based shore establishment that included a Headquarters Marine Corps and a commandant. Congress recognized the Marine Corps as a separate naval service within the Department of the Navy with additional legislation in 1834.

Lejeune and McClellan used a selective version of Marine Corps history to indoctrinate recruits and remind serving Marines that they had a holy mission to preserve a heritage of valiant service in combat, however small, insignificant, and forgettable the incident. The service of a miniscule, unimpressive Marine battalion in the seizure of Mexico City in 1847 is a perfect example. The first stanza of the Marines' Hymn memorializes combat in "the Halls of Montezuma," meaning Chapultepec Castle, seized by US Army infantry regiments. Marine standards of appearance and uniforms, plus other tribal practices, have origins lost in history but sanctified by Lejeune. Shipboard language became hallowed tribal communication. That Lejeune was a Naval Academy graduate made naval culture attractive. Lejeune certainly restored better relations with the US Navy without compromising the love affair with Congress.[32]

The Marine Corps has dealt with adversity time and again, and the experience of adaptation is deep in its memory. One recent traumatic experience was the purge of the Corps after Vietnam by two commandants, Gens. Louis H. Wilson (1975–1979) and Robert H. Barrow (1979–1983). During their terms of office, Wilson and Barrow, highly decorated veterans of World War II and Korea, acknowledged that their ranks harbored criminals, drug dealers and users, black militants, white supremacists, shirkers, alcoholics, sexual predators, and mental and physical incompetents. By 1975, the Marine Corps had the worst rates in the armed forces for incarceration, unauthorized absence, and courts-martial; only the navy had worse rates for drug use and alcohol abuse. In Vietnam and worldwide, Marines were victimizing each other. Wounded by the end of the draft and public dismay for the growing defeat in Vietnam, too many imperfect young men entered the Corps. To fill the officer ranks without a reserve mobilization, the Corps had commissioned 7,000 NCOs who had served well, but had low potential as field-grade officers. It had promoted enlisted men to NCO ranks beyond their skill, experience, and commitment. In addition to joining recruits of doubtful trainability, the Corps accepted young men from Project 100,000, a bit of social engineering dictated by Congress to the Department of Defense. The disadvantaged youth of this cohort presented serious challenges in training and group cohesion.

Before the Wilson-Barrow personnel housecleaning ended at the end of the decade, an estimated 15,000 Marines had left the Corps involuntarily. Wilson and Barrow also raised recruiting standards. In acts of moral courage and professional risk, they allowed the Corps to fall below its post-Vietnam reduced strength of 196,000. They also used the instrument of administrative discharge to avoid the time-consuming legal actions required by the Uniform Code of Military Justice (1951) for awarding bad conduct or dishonorable discharges, an act of unavoidable legal mercy for the worst disciplinary problems. By cultivating Congress, they saved personnel funds and spent them on training

---

[32] Lt. Col. Merrill L. Bartlett, USMC (Ret.), "John A. Lejeune," in Allan R. Millett and Jack Shulimson, eds., *Commandants of the Marine Corps* (Annapolis, MD, 2004), 194–213; Maj. Gen. Cmdt. John A. Lejeune, USMC, "The Marine Corps, 1926," *US Naval Institute Proceedings* 51 (October 1925), 1858–1870; John A. Lejeune, *The Reminiscences of a Marine* (Philadelphia, PA, 1930); Maj. Edwin N. McClellan, USMC, *The United States Marine Corps in the World War* (1920) reprinted by the Historical Division, MCDEC, 2014 and 2017 as a World War I commemorative edition with added charts and appendices.

and equipment. Planned end strength fell from 189,000 to almost 180,000 by 1980. An improved Corps now faced new crises in Iran, Panama, and Lebanon.[33]

The tumult of the 1970s included racial conflict in the ranks and questions about constrained opportunities for black officers. The Marine Corps had become an all-white service in the nineteenth century and was determined to remain so. In World War II, under pressure from the Roosevelt administration, the Corps with great reluctance created black antiaircraft and beach defense battalions as well as ammunition and pioneer companies. These units deployed to the Pacific, but saw little combat. Of the 19,168 African-Americans who served as Marines, only 12,738 went overseas. Of the some 20,000 Marines who died in World War II, only 9 were black. Integration came to the Corps in the 1950s and began in the Korean War, but not until the Vietnam War did black officers and senior NCOs appear in combat leadership roles. The Vietnam era, however, sent the Corps on a racial recruiting spree, and by the 1970s, the enlisted force had become 22.4 percent African-American, though black officers and senior NCOs remained underrepresented. White officers and senior NCOs faced militant de facto black leaders in a Corps that had doubled its African-American members. Real or imagined, the grievances mounted: discrimination in promotions, hairstyles, mess hall food, widespread institutional racism, unequal military justice, and white working-class culture in enlisted clubs. Racial violence became common at Camps Lejeune and Pendleton in the 1970s.[34]

The Wilson-Barrow personnel reforms attacked racial discord as a priority issue for commanders and manpower planners. By raising recruiting standards, the percentage of black Marines in the ranks had declined to 12 percent by the eve of the Iraq-Afghanistan wars, but the numbers of black officers and senior NCOs increased, as did their promotion and assignment possibilities. Racism did not disappear, but racists no longer enjoyed de facto institutional toleration. Racial incidents became an off-base problem in which the Marine Corps took the part of protecting black Marines from bigoted police and landlords. During the same era, roughly 1980–2000, the Marine Corps became far more diverse in the cultural and ethnic sense since it admitted more native-born Hispanics

[33] The Wilson-Barrow purges are described in Col. David H. White Jr., USMC (Ret.), "Louis H. Wilson," and Brig. Gen. Edwin H. Simmons, USMC (Ret.), "Robert Hilliard Barrow," in Millett and Shulimson, eds., *Commandants of the Marine Corps*, 427–436 and 437–456.

[34] Headquarters Marine Corps, "Report to the United States Senate Armed Services Committee on the Marine Corps Mission, Force Structure, Manpower Levels, and Personnel Quality" (1976); Henry I. Shaw and Ralph W. Donnelly, *Blacks in the Marine Corps* (Washington, DC, 1975); Brig. Gen. Bernard E. Trainor, USMC, "The Personnel Campaign Is No Longer in Doubt," *MCG* 62 (January 1978), 22–38, Col. Alphonse G. Davis, USMC, *Pride, Progress, and Prospects: The Marine Corps Efforts to Increase the Presence of African-American Officers, 1970–1995* (Washington, DC, 1997).

and expatriates from the Middle East, Eastern Europe, Africa, the Caribbean, Central America, Asia, and the Pacific Islands. By 2017, almost one-third of the enlisted force came from nonwhite, non-European cultures, and Marines of Hispanic origins outnumbered African-Americans, roughly 30,000 to 20,000. Minority officers (black or Hispanic) still remain underrepresented (2,500 of 22,000) for complex reasons that involve educational and occupational opportunities in civil life for minority college graduates. The effects on concepts of command and officer responsibility are obvious: issues of authority and competence can become more complex by a lack of cultural empathy.[35]

It is possible that the Corps's rush to advanced military technology will force all the "primitives" from its ranks after their first enlistment and draw the ground and aviation subtribes together for information-sharing and quick response "kinetic action," the dream of commanders since World War II. One sign of the times is whether drone operators should be trained and certified as forward air controllers, thus far an assignment that requires a pilot's rating. Another challenge is deciding how much information a ground commander can usefully use; will he or she have a face shield that serves as a heads-up display? The possibilities of new technology in the ISR/Comm/Cyber world have raced ahead of making lasers incapacitation or killing weapons in the hands of ground combat troops. The concept of "supporting arms" is eroding as the technology of target acquisition improves. The challenge facing the Marine Corps is whether its military culture, based on human qualities, e.g., loyalty, commitment, and skill, can adjust in a war dominated by microchips.

The most recent effort to blend operational complexity and cultural simplicity comes from Commandant Robert B. Neller, who believes he can borrow the ethos of the legendary "All Blacks" New Zealand football team to raise the Corps's physical fitness and training standards. Neller has stressed the personal reading program identified with Gray and the younger Krulak. Neller also intends to make sobriety a Corps value, a proven way to curb off-duty indiscipline and increase physical readiness for force-wide physical and combat readiness tests. He hopes that the stress of multiple deployments since 2001 will provide the cohesion essential to unit effectiveness.[36]

A related issue is whether the Marine Corps can blend two cultures, both important to its political existence and self-image. There is the world of public advertising, recruiting, boot camps, sunset parades, and dress blues. Then there is a life in the operating forces: dangerous, stressful, demanding, under-

---

[35] The statistics are from the *Marine Almanac 2017* and earlier demographic material published by the Marine Corps and Department of Defense, especially Headquarters Marine Corps, *Manpower Statistics for Manpower Managers* (1989).

[36] Col. Christopher Woodbridge, USMC (Ret.), ed., "Learning without Losing: A Conversation with Gen. Robert B. Neller, 37th Commandant of the Marine Corps," *MCG* 101 (November 2017), 6–8.

resourced, arbitrary, boring, and exhausting. Monetary rewards can never be enough. There must be feelings of comradeship, achievement, and meaning that are both personal and communal. That is the Marine Corps's social contract. For all its possibilities for abuse, the boot camp experience remains the key to Marine Corps occupational socialization and esprit de Corps. Boot camp methods can be adjusted, but the real burden is upon recruiters to attract recruits who seem most likely to succeed. Although the current efforts to portray Marines as "first responders with guns," a hybrid of Rambo and Bono, are not without some truth, Marines deserve a more accurate portrayal of their service. Commandant Gray repeatedly insisted that Marines needed to close the gap between what they said they could do and what they could really do. He succeeded in narrowing that gap, but it remains, in part because the Corps has distinct divisions between its warrior image and its growing technological reality. There are two Marine Corps cultures, and the Corps must balance and adjust them for Marines to be as effective as they think they are.[37]

---

[37] In addition to the sources cited, a key source for this chapter is Office of the Deputy Commandant (Programs and Resources), *Concepts and Programs*, an annual unclassified publication of Headquarters Marine Corps. In addition to *Concepts and Programs*, I consulted the International Institute of Strategic Studies, *Military Balance 2017* (London, 2017), 51–53, and Dakota L. Wood, ed., Davis Institute for National Security and Foreign Policy, *2016 Index of U.S. Military Strength* (Washington, DC, 2015), 253–258, 304–305.

Part IV

Air Forces

17   The Culture of the Royal Air Force, 1918–1945

David Stubbs

The Royal Air Force (RAF) became the world's first independent air force on April 1, 1918, but it was 1922 before the RAF published its first formal doctrine manual.[1] Thereafter, until the production of the War Manual, Air Publication 1300 in 1940, the RAF produced a number of memoranda and doctrine documents, covering topics as diverse as the plan for its permanent organization to its thinking about the roles it should play in war. These documents provide some insight into the evolution of the RAF's behavior and beliefs, but they do not explain why the RAF's culture developed the way it did. Indeed, in order to understand why the RAF expressed and vigorously reinforced its early beliefs in its training and education system, it is necessary to explore the manner in which the RAF sought to protect its status as an independent force by propagating questionable beliefs and leveraged the evolution of wider societal thinking about the potential of air power to influence government defense policy.

As is often the case, the influence of the RAF's most senior officers, especially those who attended the RAF Staff College, would dictate the direction the service would take when confronting the issues of the day. Indeed, among the rank and file and junior officers, there is little evidence to suggest an appetite to engage in discussions about strategy and doctrine, as their professional and technical training focused almost exclusively on the tactical level and was sufficiently complex to require most of their attention.

This chapter therefore explores the evolution of the RAF's behavior, beliefs, and values by examining the claims made by its early leaders and the influence they had on the maturation of the service's underlying basic assumptions. It examines how the selection and staff college education of its early leaders affected the RAF's quest for survival as an independent force. In so doing, it describes how the RAF unconsciously developed an institutionalized aversion

---

[1] Neville Parton, "The Development of Early RAF Doctrine," *Journal of Military History* 72(4) (2008), 1157–1164.

to an open conceptual debate on air warfare, and how that trait resulted in organizational intolerance of those who attempted to engage in constructive dissent from within. It focuses particular attention on the assertiveness of Air Chief Marshal Sir Hugh Montague Trenchard, who, without appropriate intellectual scrutiny, propagated questionable views about how the application of air power would affect enemy morale. Ultimately, these views significantly affected the service's conceptual development and caused wide-ranging consequences for government policy, airmen, and civilians.

Selection and Attitude

The type of officer the RAF chose to retain when it contracted in size after the First World War represented a particular cross-section of British society. Most had previously served as officers in the British Army, which at that time represented "a narrow closed society with its own set of values and standards of conduct."[2] In recruiting the next generation of officers, RAF leaders expressed a desire to select those with "good character" rather than those from a particular social background. Yet, those responsible for making the selection judgments genuinely believed the most suitable candidates to become RAF officers were those educated, like themselves, at fee-paying public schools and elite universities.[3] Essentially, in the 1920s and 1930s, the RAF selected officers on the basis of the social class to which they belonged, with the same traits, strengths and weaknesses, and shared values as the original officer cadre.[4]

At the time, however, the class distinctions in the RAF were less pronounced than they were in the British Army and Royal Navy (RN), because its dependence on technology required the interaction between officers and airmen to rest on bonds of intelligent cooperation, rather than unquestioning obedience to authority.[5] During the Second World War, a comparative lack of formality prevailed and, in the context of traditional military attitudes, discipline was relatively lax.[6] Nevertheless, the societal and class preferences the RAF

---

[2] Byron Farwell, *Queen Victoria's Little Wars* (Newton Abbot, 1974), xviii.

[3] Martin Francis, *The Flyer: British Culture and the Royal Air Force 1939–1945* (Oxford, 2008), 15, 47–52. Harold Balfour, *Wings over Westminster* (London, 1973), 197. MRAF Sir John Slessor, *The Central Blue: Recollections and Reflections* (London, 1956), 4. TNA AIR 29/603, Operations Record Book, Aviation Selection Board, Cardington, September 1939. Cyril Henry Ward-Jackson and Leighton Lucas, eds., *Airman's Song Book* (Edinburgh, 1967), 99. The "Song of the Cadet" described a First Termer as "a premier school young man, a varsity type young man." TNA AIR 6/59, May 27, 1940.

[4] Hugh C. T. Dowding, *Twelve Legions of Angels* (London, 1941), 55.

[5] Francis, *The Flyer*, 5, 49–53.

[6] Sir Michael Howard, "The Armed Forces and the Community," *RUSI Journal* 141(4) (1996), 9–12. MOA FR 569, February 8, 1941, 3–4. Laddie Lucas, *Malta: The Thorn in Rommel's Side* (London, 1992), 119. Douglas Bader, BBC TV interview with Denis Tuohy, September 17, 1965, www.bbc.co.uk/archive/battleofbritain/11406.shtml, accessed June 17, 2017.

had unconsciously perpetuated were ubiquitous in 1941, leading some airmen to conclude that "the ruling classes" had found a way "to reserve all the flying jobs for themselves."[7] The vast majority of the interaction between officers and airmen was at the working level, where challenges to the RAF's collective beliefs were unlikely to emerge. Most officers lived in officers' messes, which had the atmosphere of a gentleman pilots' club.[8] Many junior officers enjoyed being notorious for their carefree youthful exuberance, scruffy high living, reckless driving, and heavy drinking.[9] The clubby "team-player" atmosphere reinforced institutional collectivist attitudes and fostered disdain toward those displaying overt ambition and alternative thinking; except, that is, when anyone wanted to lead a flight or a squadron, as this behavior reflected a continuance of their adolescent years at fee-paying schools, where those who captained the schools' sports teams or were prefects were highly respected.[10] From this environment, those later selected for staff college, a prerequisite to reach higher rank, would become responsible for verifying and endorsing the RAF's espoused beliefs, adapting its organizational thinking and devising its operational methods to meet the challenges ahead.

Evolution of Underlying Basic Assumptions

In September 1916, Trenchard, then the officer commanding the Royal Flying Corps in France, released a memorandum that described the airplane as an inherently offensive weapon, best used relentlessly in operations. He speculated that the ubiquitous nature of air warfare would complicate the efforts of defenders to intercept attackers, enabling those with sufficient determination to press home their attacks.[11] He reiterated these claims in another memoranda, "The Battle for Air Supremacy over the Somme, 1 June–30 November 1916." One historian has suggested that in compiling his thoughts about air power, Trenchard might have come under the influence of the work of Frederick Lanchester, the co-inventor of operations research. Indeed, Trenchard's

---

[7] MOA FR 569, "Airmen: Morale and Attitudes," February 1941, 5. Francis, *The Flyer*, 11, 47–48, 50, 52. Stephen Bungay, *The Most Dangerous Enemy* (London, 2009), 85–86.

[8] James S. Corum, "The Spanish Civil War: Lessons Learned and Not Learned by the Great Powers," *Journal of Military History* 62(2) (1998), 313–334. Lucas, *Malta*, 94.

[9] Francis, *The Flyer*, 16–18, 22, 34–36. David Rosier, *Be Bold* (London, 2011), 20, 59, 63.

[10] Kenneth Cross, *Straight and Level* (London, 1993), 8–9. Lucas, *Malta*, 148–149, 159–160.

[11] Phillip S. Meilinger, "Trenchard, Slessor, and Royal Air Force Doctrine before World War II," in Col. Philip S. Meilinger, ed., *Paths of Heaven: The Evolution of Airpower Theory* (Maxwell, AL, 1997), 41–78, 44–45. Meilinger was referring to Trenchard's memo "Future Policy in the Air," dated September 22, 1916.

definition of air superiority bore a remarkable similarity to Lanchester's "Square Law" theory.[12]

In 1918, when Trenchard was given command of the RAF's "Independent Force," charged with bombing Germany, he had to choose between attacking targets that analysis predicted would significantly affect the German war effort, or adopting a coercive strategy to force the enemy into submission. The first option, proposed by Maj. Hardinge Goulburn Giffard, a Royal Naval Air Service officer (self-styled as Lord Tiverton), would have enabled an informed decision. Tiverton's analysis of the German war industry led him to conclude that strategic bombing against specific targets was likely to be the most effective way to defeat an industrialized enemy.[13] However, Trenchard knew that bombing these targets had caused little material damage to buildings or personnel and his diary entry for August 18, 1918, revealed his doubts about the likely success of such a campaign. Consequently, he chose to trust his instincts and believe that the "moral effect" of bombing was likely to have a greater effect on the progress of the war, although he acknowledged that this effect was likely to diminish as the reality of the material effect was recognized.[14]

In early 1919, three weeks before his second spell as the RAF's Chief of the Air Staff (CAS), Trenchard's official dispatch on his "Independent Force" claimed that "the moral effect of bombing stands undoubtedly to the material effect in a proportion of 20 to 1" and argued that it was "necessary to create the greatest moral effect possible."[15] His claims for maintaining the offensive against an enemy's morale appeared to be officially vindicated in the 1920 release of Air Publication 1225, which assessed the effectiveness of the air raids carried out by Trenchard's Independent Force on enemy morale. It is now clear, however, that the authors deliberately excluded contradictory evidence, found by the postwar survey team, when writing AP 1225.[16] The publication of AP 1225 marked another important chapter in the development of the RAF's organizational thinking: one where official publications endorsed unproven assumptions as part of the process to institutionalize them as codified beliefs. By January 1921, another Trenchard paper, "Air Power and National Security," argued that "in the offensive lies the surest defence."[17] By July 1923, Trenchard

---

[12] Robin Higham, *The Military Intellectuals in Britain: 1918–1939* (New Brunswick, NJ, 1996), 126.

[13] Tami Davis Biddle, *Rhetoric and Reality in Air Warfare: The Evolution of British and American Ideas about Strategic Bombing, 1914–1945* (Princeton, NJ, 2002). 38–39, 41–44.

[14] H. Montgomery Hyde, *British Air Policy between the Wars, 1918–1939* (London, 1976), 44. Vincent Orange, *Slessor, Bomber Champion* (London, 2006), 32.

[15] Henry Albert Jones, *The War in the Air*, vol. 6 (Eastbourne, 2009), 136.

[16] Biddle, *Rhetoric and Reality in Air Warfare*, 57–61. TNA AIR 1/2104/207/36. Air Publication 1225, "Results of Air Raids on Germany Carried out by the 8th Brigade and Independent Force," 3rd edn., January 1920.

[17] Biddle, *Rhetoric and Reality in Air Warfare*, 71.

had concluded that using fighters for air defense "would be rather like putting two teams to play each other at football, and telling one team they must only defend their own goal line and keep their men on that one point."[18] Three decades later, Marshal of the Royal Air Force Sir John Slessor wrote that "there is no more dangerous fallacy than the belief that fighters alone can protect us from destruction. We must have the essential minimum."[19] Fundamentally, the RAF's organizational thinking, until the 1950s, evolved to reflect Trenchard's preference for offensive action over security, in terms of the "Principles of War."[20]

In 1918, Britain's postwar economic difficulties threatened the survival of the RAF as an independent force because, at the time, many believed that the independent air arm was unduly expensive. Consequently, as well as driving the RAF's ethos in terms of organizational thinking, Trenchard needed to be active in advocating the necessity for economy, while simultaneously providing the RAF with solid structural foundations.[21] He did so in an environment of internecine distrust, in which the army and the RN constantly challenged the need for a separate air force. To defend the RAF's independence, the Air Staff produced a draft paper, "The Role of the Air Force in the System of Imperial Defence."[22] It provided an indication of the RAF's doctrinal thinking about the evolution of strategic air warfare and suggested that the RAF could perform some of the nation's defense responsibilities more economically than either of the other two services.

In order to strengthen political support for the RAF's retention, Trenchard briefed the Committee of Imperial Defence (CID) on his belief that the morale of the civilian population would be the crucial factor in future wars. He told the CID it was essential for the RAF to remain independent so that it could take the necessary action to respond to emerging threats in a timely manner.[23] To provide some substance to support Trenchard's claims about the impact of bombing on morale, the RAF began to speculate that an adversary would be able to drop between 50 and 150 tons of high explosives per day on London for an indefinite period, and that each ton of bombs dropped was likely to yield fifty

---

[18] TNA AIR 5/416, Minutes of a Conference held in C.A.S.'s Room, Air Ministry on 19 July 1923 at 11 AM, 5.

[19] Orange, *Slessor, Bomber Champion*, 210. Also in Royal Air Force War Manual – Part 1 Operations, Air Publication 1300, chapter 7, paragraph 12, 1940.

[20] Air Staff Memorandum, No. 43. S. 28279, "The War Aim of the Royal Air Force," An address given by the Chief of the Air Staff (Trenchard) to the Imperial Defence College on the war aim of the Air Force, October 1928, 6.

[21] Hugh M. Trenchard, Memorandum by the Chief of the Air Staff, Air Ministry, November 25, 1919.

[22] Hyde, *British Air Policy between the Wars*, 100.

[23] TNA CAB 2/3, CID Meeting 139, May 27, 1921.

civilian casualties.[24] Essentially, the RAF was suggesting that over a relatively short period, the unusually high casualties would induce a collapse of morale among any population subjected to air attack.

Eleven months later, in October 1922, however, a change of government reignited the threat to the RAF's existence, especially as the new prime minister, Bonar Law, was in favor of the reintegration of the RAF into the army and the RN. The Admiralty, which in July 1922 had circulated a paper to the CID claiming that it did not wish to "abolish the Air Ministry or to destroy the Royal Air Force," began a political and press campaign to do just that.[25] Soon after, an interim report by the Salisbury subcommittee, set up to question the place for air power in the field of national defense, quantified the rationale for the future organization and structure of the RAF. The upshot of the ensuing arguments, articulated through memoranda and papers between the service chiefs and within the CID, was that the government increasingly began to understand and agree with the RAF's claims and ideas, which it considered both apposite and economical.[26] Consequently, both the interim and final reports, delivered in June and November 1923, verified the RAF's asserted need for an Independent Striking Force, equal in strength to the strongest air force within striking distance of Britain, as well as a Home Defence Air Force comprising a mixture of regulars and volunteers or reservists.[27]

A month after the interim report, the Air Staff began to use selective evidence from the RAF's experience of the "air control" policy in Iraq to support its claims that punitive air action had achieved the desired moral effect on the recalcitrant Iraqis.[28] Significantly, the Air Staff also deduced that the same results could be achieved by bombing in Europe.[29] At the Air Ministry later that month, Trenchard made clear he preferred to have significantly more bombers than fighters. He also voiced his thinking in terms of another principle of war: selection and maintenance of the aim. "The French in a bombing duel," he mused, "would probably squeal before we did." He then added that "[t]he

---

[24] Meilinger, "Trenchard, Slessor, and Royal Air Force Doctrine," 50. Biddle, *Rhetoric and Reality in Air Warfare*, 109–110.

[25] TNA CAB/24/160, CP 294 (23), 296 (23). Viscount Templewood, *Empire of the Air: The Advent of the Air Age* (London, 1957), 54–71. TNA CAB/24/161, CP 310 (23) was the RAF's official response.

[26] Hyde, *British Air Policy between the Wars*, 100–104.

[27] TNA CAB 23/46 Cabinet Conclusions, June 20, 1923. CAB/24/162, CP 461 (23) The Salisbury Report, dated November 15, 1923.

[28] Vincent Orange, *Coningham* (London, 1990), 38. Yuki Tanaka, "British "Humane Bombing" in Iraq during the Interwar Era," in Yuki Tanaka and Marilyn B. Young, eds., *Bombing Civilians* (New York, 2009), 23–28. James S. Corum, "Air Control: Reassessing the History," *Air Power Review* 4(2) (2001), 20–21. Eric Ash, "Air Power and Leadership: A Study of Sykes and Trenchard," in John Jupp, ed., *Air Force Leadership: Changing Culture* (Sleaford, 2007) 169.

[29] TNA CAB 24/161, July 5, 1923, 3. A theory reinforced by TNA AIR 8/87, J. M. Spaight's "The Doctrine of Air Force Necessity," written in 1927, in which he extrapolated lessons from the bombing of tribesmen.

nation that would stand being bombed longest would win in the end."[30] As far as Trenchard was concerned, the will to win in war was encapsulated in an equation in which the intellectual and physical components of war fighting were subordinate to the influence of morale.[31] The combination of the RAF's pervasive anti-intellectual culture, together with the nuances of the selection system it maintained and Trenchard's assertiveness, ensured that his views on morale went unchallenged. Henceforward, the teaching at the RAF Staff College showed a tendency to accept and perpetuate this perceived wisdom.

Staff College, the RAF's Reinforcing Mechanism

Trenchard had conceived the creation of an RAF Staff College in 1919.[32] His vision was realized when the first course began at Andover in 1922. Trenchard became intimately involved in the selection of those attending the first course, and his oversight of what was taught at the staff college became ubiquitous.[33] Though some historians have suggested that the early staff college courses provided an opportunity for open debate on the effectiveness of air power, the evidence suggests that any influence the students had in informing policy did not endure beyond the first two courses. One historian claims that by publishing the best essays from the first course, in December 1923, the RAF began the process to produce a school of thought that underpinned the RAF's physical foundations with intellectual reasoning. But he also acknowledged Trenchard's tendency to interfere with and correct perceived errors in the work of both college staff and students.[34]

The essays described earlier, published and circulated as Air Publications 956 (1923), together with those published by the staff college until 1927, were screened to ensure they reflected orthodox opinion. Their most common theme was that though bombing often did relatively little physical damage, its "moral effect" could be significant.[35] From the third course onward, a document entitled "Notes for the Use of Officers Attending Courses" encapsulated the collated "thinking" from the first two courses, together with original documents relating to the operational

---

[30] TNA AIR 5/416, Minutes of a Conference held in C.A.S.'s Room, Air Ministry, 19 July 1923, at 11 AM, 5. Squadron Leader C. F. A. Portal had been seconded from the RAF Staff College to attend the meeting.

[31] Air Publication 1300, Royal Air Force War Manual, Part 1 – Operations, February 1940, chapter 3.

[32] Permanent Organization of the Royal Air Force, "Memorandum by the Chief of the Air Staff," November 25, 1919, 6.

[33] Wing Cdr. Richard Anthony Mason, *The Royal Air Force Staff College 1922–1972* (Bracknell, 1972). Among those on the first course were Gp. Capt. Freeman, Wing Cdr. Peirse, Sqn. Ldr. Douglas, Sqn. Ldr. Portal, and Sqn. Ldr. Park.

[34] Allan D. English, "The RAF Staff College and the Evolution of British Strategic Bombing Policy, 1922–1929," *Journal of Strategic Studies* 16(3) (1993), 416–419.

[35] Ibid., 418–419. The other Air Publications were AP 1097 (1924), AP 1152 (1925), AP 1223 (1926) and AP 1308 (1927).

conduct of the Royal Flying Corps and the RAF in the First World War. These were then taught as accepted wisdom in subsequent courses.[36] After his acolytes had verified his opinions, Trenchard expected the staff college to concentrate on instruction rather than reflection. To reinforce accepted thinking and avoid unnecessary and potentially damaging controversy with the army and the RN, Trenchard disliked officers having unscreened articles published in the public press.[37] Moreover, any desire among junior officers to engage in alternative organizational thinking was stymied by the way the institutionalized beliefs were reinforced in the competition for places at the RAF's Staff College, through the entrance examination process. The examiners who oversaw the 1923 and 1924 iterations of the staff college entrance examinations unquestionably accepted the policy of incessant offensive as both valid and peculiarly applicable to the correct use of air power.[38] When setting the examination questions, they configured them in a way that gave lower scores to "off message" answers.[39] There can be little doubt that prospective staff college students came to understand the type of questions posed in the entrance examination, and it is likely that they tailored their answers to elicit the highest marks possible.[40] Thereafter, the teaching at the staff college further reinforced Trenchard's beliefs.

For instance, on May 6, 1925, a lecture given on the nature of war, given by the staff college's first commandant, Air Vice-Marshal Robert Brooke-Popham, advised the students that "it is now the willpower of the enemy nation that has to be broken, and to do this is the object of any country that goes to war."[41] In February 1928, an "Air Warfare Lecture," given by Air Commodore Edgar Ludlow-Hewitt, Brooke-Popham's replacement, advised that the RAF should reduce defensive aircraft to a minimum and that "every ounce of force" should go to offensive bombers.[42] By 1928, the Air Ministry considered that civilian morale was "infinitely more susceptible to collapse than that of a disciplined army."[43] In October the same year in an address given to the Imperial Defence College, Trenchard defined air superiority in terms of

[36] Ibid., 412, 426.
[37] Royal Air Force Museum, Hendon, Private Papers of Marshal of the Royal Air Force Viscount Trenchard, MFC 76/1/140/5, Letter from Captain T. B. Marson to Air Commodore Robert Brooke-Popham, October 19, 1923.
[38] English, "The RAF Staff College," 415, 419–421.
[39] Biddle, *Rhetoric and Reality in Air Warfare*, 92.
[40] Ibid., 100. Philip Joubert de la Ferté, a staff college commandant, worried how its influence had created in the minds of senior officers and their junior subordinates overly simplistic and one-dimensional views on the use and utility of air power.
[41] Meilinger, "Trenchard, Slessor, and Royal Air Force Doctrine," 58–59.
[42] English, "The RAF Staff College," 415. Trenchard reiterated his view in a lecture to the Imperial Defence College, reproduced as Air Staff Memorandum, No. 43. S.28279, "The War Aim of the Royal Air Force," October 1928, paragraph 6.
[43] TNA AIR 9/8, May 17, 1928.

maintaining offensive action to force an enemy onto the defensive, rather than in terms of gaining control of the air.[44] Even in 1940, a decade after Trenchard had relinquished the post of chief of the air staff, the legacy of his organizational thinking could be seen in the RAF's War Manual, which claimed that "there must be reason to suppose that the persons engaged at the target are likely to be demoralized by bombing" and suggested that civilians were more susceptible to bombing than troops, or any other body of men professionally trained in discipline, as such men were "not easily demoralized by bombing unless their morale has already been lowered through other causes."[45] One historian questioned whether the doctrinal orthodoxy at the staff college was maintained because it was what everyone thought, but it is clear that the directing staff helped maintain it with their ever-present red ink, to keep the mavericks in line. Staff college students probably realized that attempts to question the legitimacy of the pronouncements of the directing staff on contentious issues might have an adverse impact on the way they were assessed for suitability for higher appointments.[46]

Intolerance of Dissent

In essence, the intellectual debate at the RAF Staff College about the options for air power was cosmetic and the RAF's dogmatic teaching created an oppressive atmosphere in which notions of "constructive dissent" or "disciplined disobedience" were unlikely to emerge. After sifting through thousands of papers that passed through government departments in the 1920s and 1930s, an official historian concluded that the fears about the likely collapse of morale did not rest on analysis of the evidence, only on often-repeated opinion, together with a narrow-minded human interpretation of events.[47] Some air power historians have been astounded at the extent to which unchallenged assumptions permeated RAF official thinking.[48] Such views, however, are not universal and other air power historians have questioned this portrayal of the staff college environment. One historian, for instance, claims that the staff college exposed students to a "catholic" variety of reading, which empowered them to develop and express alternative thinking.[49] At the time, however, few

---

[44] Lord Trenchard, Chief of the Air Staff, Air Staff Memorandum No. 43. S.28279, "The War Aim of the Royal Air Force," an address to the Imperial Defence College, October 1928, 5–6.

[45] AP 1300, Royal Air Force War Manual. Part 1, Operations, chapter 8, paragraph 42, 1940.

[46] English, "The RAF Staff College," 427.

[47] Biddle, Rhetoric and Reality in Air Warfare, 80.

[48] Irving B. Holley Jr., "Reflections on the Search for Air Power Theory," in Phillip S. Meilinger, ed., The Paths of Heaven: The Evolution of Airpower Theory (Maxwell, AL, 1997), 582.

[49] Air Commodore (Ret.) Peter William Gray, "The Strategic Leadership and Direction of the Royal Air Force Strategic Air Offensive against Germany from Inception to 1945," University of Birmingham MPhil thesis, 2014, 78.

air power theorists wrote in the English language and there is little in the way of evidence to support the claim that the students questioned accepted wisdom at the staff college.

Trenchard may have grumbled about the lack of an RAF air power thinker to rival Clausewitz, Hamley, or Mahan, but only a small number of practitioners, theorists, and novelists had enough knowledge to challenge the official view, and those who did tended to agree with it.[50] One such commentator, who had extensive knowledge about the legality of air warfare, was James Maloney Spaight, a lawyer with experience in the War Office. Spaight, who was on good terms with Trenchard, had been an influential air power thinker and writer since 1914.[51] Despite the strong organizational pressure to conform, one freethinking air power theorist who did emerge in the RAF in the 1920s was Squadron Leader Cyril Gordon Burge. His attempts to scrutinize the RAF's claims for air power had much in common with current notions of "double loop learning," where skeptical analysis of the prescriptive practice-orientated teaching is used to effect cultural change.[52]

Burge had served under Trenchard in the Independent Air Force as an officer commanding 100 Squadron. This experience may have fueled his skepticism about the potential success of bombing morale as a viable offensive strategy for independent air warfare. In July 1926, when writing *Basic Principles of Air Warfare: The Influence of Air Power on Sea and Land Strategy*, a peculiar twist of fate saw him posted to the position of Trenchard's personal assistant. His book, published in Aldershot in 1927, with the foreword written by General Ironside, was unlikely to garner Trenchard's favor and although Burge had chosen to adopt the pseudonym "Squadron Leader" to mask his identity, it is clear that Trenchard knew he had written it.

Burge's book challenged Trenchard's thinking and the way air power was taught at the RAF's Staff College. It even suggested that the RAF ought to engage in closer cooperation with the army and the RN. Unlike Spaight, whose work formed part of the syllabus for the staff college entrance examination, Burge thought it misleading to believe that attacking aircraft would be able to penetrate enemy airspace to deliver an effective bombardment without having to fight their way to their targets.[53] In addition, he argued that tactics that relied on avoiding the enemy would not work, particularly in an age when air forces were rapidly growing. Instead, he prophesied that an air battle would take place

---

[50] Air Marshal Sir Hugh M. Trenchard, "Aspects of Service Aviation," *The Aeroplane* 19(17) (October 27, 1920), 698. Philip Guedalla, *Middle East 1940–1942: A Study in Air Power* (London, 1944), 10.

[51] Peter Gray, *Air Warfare, History, Theory and Practice* (London, 2016), 53–54, 88–89.

[52] Chris Argyris, "Single-Loop and Double-Loop Models in Research on Decision Making," *Administrative Science Quarterly* 21(3) (1976), 363–375.

[53] Squadron Leader, Basic Principles of Air Warfare: The Influence of Air Power on Sea and Land Strategy (Aldershot, 1927), 59–60.

and that achieving air superiority, which he defined in terms of freedom and denial to operate, would become a prerequisite for success. He cautioned against dogmatic and unproven doctrine, and thought it absurd to believe that British politicians would consider it acceptable to minimize the nation's air defense in order to enable the RAF's conceptual commitment to wholehearted offensive action.[54] Such well-reasoned and logical thinking directly challenged the RAF's vision for independent warfare. In February 1927, Trenchard, who probably wished to avoid another round of internecine fighting between the services, told Basil Liddell Hart that he did not want any officer to write books and had tried to stop Burge's book from being published.[55]

Though Burge's book was subsequently published, it signally failed to influence the evolution of RAF doctrinal thinking. When the book was reviewed in the *Royal United Services Institute (RUSI) Journal*, the reviewer appeared to misunderstand the nature of Burge's belief in the necessity of the fight for air superiority, as well as his other challenges to the RAF's evolving underlying assumptions. Consequently, the reviewer considered the book backward rather than forward looking.[56] More recently, an historian has also misjudged the book's challenge to orthodoxy with the conclusion that it was little more than a second-rate reflection of what Burge had learned about the principles of air warfare, as understood by the Air Ministry in 1925 and 1926, when he was at the staff college.[57]

In fact, Burge did not go to the RAF's Staff College, but he did go to the RN College at Greenwich in 1925 and, after his book was published, attended the junior division of the Army Staff College at Camberley in 1928. With him at Camberley was the recently promoted Wing Commander Arthur Harris, whose views diametrically opposed those of Burge.[58] It is interesting to speculate whether Harris was sent to Camberley to counteract the influence Burge was likely to have there. After completing the junior division at Camberley, Burge retired from the RAF on December 1, 1928. Given that Burge was only thirty-five years old, it is possible that he became a victim of Trenchard's assertiveness. Although we will never know how many RAF officers read Burge's book, we do know that one who did was Philip Guedalla, the author of an official

---

[54] Ibid., 2–3, 5–6, 12–13, 29, 55–57. Burge thought that Spaight's belief in the moral effect of air attacks was based on far too simplistic "one size fits all" thinking.

[55] Neville Parton, "The Evolution of Royal Air Force Doctrine, 1919–1939," PhD thesis, University of Cambridge, 2009, 94. Ross Mahoney, "The Forgotten Career of Air Chief Marshal Sir Trafford Leigh-Mallory, 1892–1937: A Social and Cultural History of Leadership Development in the Inter-War Royal Air Force," University of Birmingham MPhil thesis, 2014, 256–257.

[56] *Royal United Services Institution Journal* 72(486) (1927), 466–472. English, "The RAF Staff College," 423–425.

[57] English, "The RAF Staff College," 424–425.

[58] Henry Probert, *Bomber Harris* (London, 2001), 59.

review of RAF air power in the Middle East between 1940 and 1942. Guedalla made a deliberate point of referencing Burge's book when highlighting the ridiculousness of prewar thinking that air warfare would "consist entirely of one-way traffic by massed bombers," before he chastised aeronautical publications for their support of such one-dimensional thinking.[59] Except for Guedalla, historians have only recently recognized the prescient quality of Burge's thinking.[60]

In marked contrast to Burge's subsequent anonymity, Slessor, one of Trenchard's acolytes, became renowned as an air power theorist. He based his book *Air Power and Armies*, published six years after Trenchard retired, on the lectures he had given when he was the RAF directing staff officer at Camberley between 1931 and 1934. Before going to Camberley, Slessor had spent two tours on the air staff, where he became intimately acquainted with Trenchard's direction and guidance when writing air staff memoranda.[61] One historian has suggested that Slessor really wanted to write a book on strategic air power but felt compelled to write about what he had recently been teaching. Whatever his motives, Slessor, like Burge, concluded that air power could not win wars independently but, in Slessor's case, this was because his book assumed that the government would commit the British Army to a land campaign. Slessor also agreed with Burge in believing that the first requirement in any campaign would be to achieve air superiority though, oddly, he did not believe air superiority should be considered an end in itself.[62]

Pragmatists, Theorists, and the Influence of Popular Fiction

The generalized disdain for conceptual thinking by RAF officers, together with their desire to minimize uncertainty, led Winston Churchill to conclude that aviation attracted pragmatists, rather than those more philosophically inclined.[63] In trusting their senses when responding to the issues confronting them, RAF officers of the time typified the British trait of the "practical man": the type of man who exhibits a natural preference for incremental improvement over radical reform. "Practical men" are often apt to discount evidence that runs contrary to

---

[59] Guedalla, *Middle East 1940–1942*, 58.

[60] "Book review of *Basic Principles of Air Warfare*, by Group Captain Neville Parton," *Air Power Review* 10(2) (2007), 94–98, 94.

[61] Imperial War Museum (IWM), Department of Sound (DoS), Interview with Marshal of the Royal Air Force Sir John Slessor, August 3, 1978.

[62] Meilinger, "Trenchard, Slessor, and Royal Air Force Doctrine before World War II," 61–65.

[63] Group Captain Alistair Byford, "Fair Stood the Wind for France? The Royal Air Force's Experience in 1940 as a Case Study of the Relationship between Policy, Strategy and Doctrine," *Air Power Review* 14(3) (2011), 35–60, 49–50. Air Publication 3000, *British Air Power Doctrine*, 3rd edn., 1999, Introduction to chapter 2. The assessment reflects an introductory quote, attributed to a Winston Churchill, though its provenance is open to question.

perceived wisdom and, instead, trust "evidence" that supports the status quo.[64] In this context, it becomes easier to understand how, in the 1930s, the RAF's practically inclined leaders evaluated the effectiveness of bombing in the wars in China and Spain to tally with the RAF's articulated preconceptions and espoused beliefs.[65] It would be unfair to adjudge them too harshly in this regard, as the imagination of the wider population had also become stimulated by the mixture of imagery and propaganda that led civilians to believe they were likely to be subjected to air attack, from which there was little effective defense.

Capt. B. H. Liddell Hart wrote his first commentary on future war in *Paris, or the Future of War* in 1925. It proposed that aircraft possessed boundless opportunities to dislocate the normal life of an enemy population and that this could subdue their morale.[66] A year later, Tiverton, now known as the Earl of Halsbury, published "1944." It described a future in which a gas attack could annihilate London's population.[67] Unfolding events suggested that these apocalyptic prophecies were increasingly likely. The Japanese air attack on Shanghai in 1932 was quickly followed in 1933 by H. G. Wells's vision of the future in his book *The Shape of Things to Come*, which was also made into a film and described a future in which cities were heavily bombed. In a BBC radio broadcast on November 16, 1934, Winston Churchill queried the delight authors and filmmakers appeared to take in in portraying the likely horrors of a future air war, before he described the air threat emerging from Germany.[68] The following year, a book by Spanish Civil War veteran Thomas Wintringham suggested that millions of people might die in London, Paris, and Berlin as a result of air attacks. Even military theorist J. F. C. Fuller, the author of *The Foundations of the Science of War*, succumbed to the mood of the time by predicting that a major bombing attack on London would lead the population to yield to atavistic fear, and that the subsequent pandemonium would result in the destruction of the government.[69]

---

[64] Correlli Barnett, *The Lost Victory: British Dreams and British Realities 1945–1950* (London, 1995), 12, 14. Correlli Barnett, *The Verdict of Peace: Britain between Her Yesterday and the Future* (London, 2001), 316–319, 321.

[65] Greg Kennedy, "The Royal Navy, Intelligence and the Spanish Civil War: Lessons in Air Power, 1936–39," *Intelligence and National Security* 20(2) (2005), 238–263, 245–246, 252. Greg Kennedy, "Anglo-American Strategic Relations and Intelligence Assessments of Japanese Air Power 1934–1941," *Journal of Military History* 74(3) (2010), 737–773, 741, 758–759, 773. Byford, "Fair Stood the Wind for France?" 52–53.

[66] Biddle, *Rhetoric and Reality in Air Warfare*, 24, 104, 139.

[67] *The Spectator*, May 1, 1926, 29.

[68] Winston Churchill, "We lie within a few minutes striking distance," Radio broadcast, November 16, 1934.

[69] Richard J. Overy, *The Bombing War: Europe, 1939–1945* (London, 2009), 25–27, 31. Tom Wintringham, *The Coming World War* (London, 1935), 38–39. Ian Patterson, *Guernica and Total War* (Cambridge, MA, 2007), 110.

The attack on Guernica during the Spanish Civil War in 1937 attracted significant comment by both the *Times of London* and the *New York Times*. Their reports of destruction and damage caused by air attack corresponded with the expectations of military theorists, authors, and filmmakers. The impression they generated helped to condition the British population to expect to be bombed in any future war. Moreover, the official casualty figures for the attack helped to cement the air staff's trust in its estimates of likely casualties from bombing.[70] Indeed, the impression of death and destruction generated after the air attack on Barcelona in 1938 was so strong that the British government increased its assessment of the likely casualty rate from fifty to seventy-two per ton of bombs dropped.[71] In this environment, it is not surprising that those who actually witnessed the reality of the Spanish Civil War found it expedient to go along with the growing consensus. Wing Commander R. V. Goddard, the chairman of the Joint Intelligence Sub-committee on Spain, undertook a fact-finding mission to Spain in 1938. His report on what he saw vindicated the RAF's belief that regular troops would be less likely to succumb to attacks by close air support aircraft than irregular troops. He also concluded that the reason the bombing had not demoralized the civilian population was because it had been sporadic and inaccurate, and that the outcome would have been different with concentrated and repeated bombings.[72] The way the evidence was interpreted, therefore, contrived to vindicate the Air Staff's rhetoric in the run-up to the Second World War and tallied with the messages delivered in popular fiction, papers, films, and the reports by those who had experienced real-world events.

Embracing Operational Research

Surprisingly, therefore, after Britain declared war on Germany on September 3, 1939, the RAF did not immediately embark on the type of bombing campaign in which it had come to believe. The reasons for this are complex, but an examination of Section D of Spaight's *International Law of the Air, 1939–1945*, which described the provenance of each evolution of the RAF's bombing campaign, indicates that unfounded assessments of the size of the Luftwaffe's bomber force led to significant political anxiety about the impact heavy Luftwaffe attacks on London might have. The fear of being over matched caused the government to place limits on the RAF's bombing of Germany. Rather conveniently, the timing of this decision coincided with the appeal made by US President Franklin D. Roosevelt, on September 1, 1939, to all the

---

[70] James S. Corum, *Inflated by Air: Common Perceptions of Civilian Casualties from Bombing* (Maxwell, AL, 1998), 7–10.

[71] Terence H. O'Brien, *Civil Defence* (London, 1955), 53.

[72] Biddle, *Rhetoric and Reality in Air Warfare*, 116–118.

potential belligerents to refrain from bombing civilians or unfortified cities.[73] Consequently, when RAF bombing of Germany began in earnest, between July 13, 1940, and June 27, 1941, the RAF's directives, priorities, and instructions did not focus on bombing the German population to undermine morale, but was instead heavily influenced by the analysis of the German economy, conducted by the Industrial Intelligence Centre (IIC) and the Ministry of Economic Warfare (MEW). The Foreign Countries subcommittee had established the IIC in March 1931, headed by Maj. Desmond Morton, an officer on loan from the Secret Service. The IIC became the intelligence nucleus of the MEW in September 1939[74]; it assessed that Germany's need for oil was a critical vulnerability that the RAF ought to attack as a military priority.[75]

Those indoctrinated by the RAF in the efficacy and utility of attacking enemy morale found the idea of targeting Germany's oil reserves and supplies confusing and irritating.[76] Similarly, the RAF's antipathy toward analyzing the reasons for the defeat it suffered at the hands of the Luftwaffe in France in May 1940, together with worries about what such an inquiry might reveal, caused the Air Ministry some discomfort when it was required to identify the lessons. The RAF's leaders had already concluded that they knew what was needed at the strategic level, so they decided that the report should only look at tactical-level lessons.[77] Their beliefs in this regard explain the Air Staff's reticence in coordinating aerial warfare plans with the analysis of the MEW's economic studies. Nevertheless, the RAF gradually embraced the opportunities afforded by operational research and the defensively focused Fighter Command, in particular, utilized quantitative methodology when developing radar.[78] That said, a propaganda statement issued by the Ministry of Information in December 1940 summarized more typical views about the impact of bombing. It bore more than a passing resemblance to Trenchard's opinion of French resolve in 1923 by claiming "that all the evidence goes to prove that the Germans, for all their present confidence and cockiness, will not stand a quarter of the bombing that the British have shown they can take."[79] This type of propaganda was highly effective: two months later, a Mass Observation report on morale and attitudes acknowledged that "it seems to be a universally

---

[73] Albeit immediately ignored by the Luftwaffe, which bombed Warsaw, killing upward of 20,000 civilians.

[74] Ibid., 159, 162, 180.

[75] Wesley K. Wark, *The Ultimate Enemy* (London, 1985), 177–178, 181.

[76] Peter Gray, "The Gloves Will Have to Come Off: A Reappraisal of the Legitimacy of the RAF Bomber Offensive against Germany," *Air Power Review* 13(3) (2010), 9–40, 22–25.

[77] Byford, "Fair Stood the Wind for France?" 50.

[78] Maurice Kirby and Rebecca Capey, "The Area Bombing of Germany in World War II: An Operational Research Perspective," *Journal of the Operational Research Society* 48(7) (1997), 661–677, 663.

[79] Charles Webster and Noble Frankland, *The Strategic Air Offensive against Germany, 1939–1945, vol. 1*, Preparations (London, 1961), 169.

accepted axiom that the Germans 'couldn't stand up to bombing like we can.'"[80]

Successful attacks on oil targets required the bombing to be accurate, but avoiding the Luftwaffe's fighters and navigating to the targets in daylight proved more difficult than expected. The tendency of the RAF's directing staff in the 1930s to disadvantage fighters in prewar daylight bombing exercises helps to explain why the Air Staff were astonished at the catastrophic loss rates suffered during these early daylight attacks.[81] Subsequently, in order to continue the RAF's bombing campaign, it became necessary for Bomber Command to transition to bombing by night, which made accurate bombing even less likely. Consequently, the deputy CAS, Air Vice-Marshal Arthur Harris became convinced that Bomber Command should target industrial areas as a whole in order to inflict serious damage on the enemy.[82] On April 29, 1941, Harris minuted Sir Archibald Sinclair, the secretary of state for air, to tell him that "bombing oil plants does not kill Boche." By July 9, 1941, the Air Ministry acknowledged that Bomber Command was struggling to hit the prioritized targets when bombing by night, and provided a new "Outline Plan of Attack on German Transportation and Morale."

An analytical report written by David Bensusan Butt, produced on August 18, 1941, corroborated the growing perception that night bombing had been ineffective, as did a subsequent review by Bomber Command staff, which found that only 15 percent of aircraft bombed within five miles of the target point.[83] Put simply, the bombing campaign was struggling to bomb cities at night, never mind hit the relatively small oil targets. The only way to improve the performance of Bomber Command, it was concluded, was to provide the bombers with navigational aids sufficient to achieve the desired degree of accuracy. The only alternative to this option was to protect the bombers with escort fighters so they could bomb in daylight.

The Escort Fighter Option

The RAF had considered a role for escort fighters as early as 1923, but had decided "not to provide long-distance bombing formations with an escort of fighters."[84] Thirteen years later in November 1936, the deputy director of

---

[80] MOA FR 569, "Airmen: Morale and Attitudes," 10. Reproduced with permission of Curtis Brown, London on behalf of the Trustees of the Mass Observation Archive © Trustees of the Mass Observation Archive.

[81] Vincent Orange, *Dowding of Fighter Command: Victor of the Battle of Britain* (London, 2008), 50. Biddle, *Rhetoric and Reality in Air Warfare*, 89–90, 99.

[82] Probert, *Bomber Harris*, 112–113.   [83] Overy, *The Bombing War*, 267–268.

[84] TNA CAB/24/161. Comments by the Air Staff on Cabinet Papers Nos. CP 294(23) and CP 296 (23), July 5, 1923. Charles Webster and Noble Frankland, *The Strategic Air Offensive against Germany, 1939–1945, vol.* 2 (London, 1961), appendix 1, 63–70.

operations and intelligence, Air Vice-Marshal Richard Peirse, sent a memorandum to Air Vice-Marshal Christopher Courtenay suggesting that it might be worthwhile to observe fighter escort operations in Spain and that "we ought to prepare for such an eventuality."[85] A week later, he received an answer from Air Commodore William Sholto Douglas, the director of staff duties, which adjudged that "the bombers should be able to look after themselves without the addition of an escort of fighters."[86] Douglas, one of those chosen by Trenchard to attend the first staff college course, chaired the air fighting committee the following June, and at that meeting he reiterated the argument by claiming that the "drawbacks of any system of employing distant escorts were considerable." He repeated this view again in 1940 in an Air Fighting Committee meeting, but this time he went further, claiming that the very concept of escort fighters was flawed and that high-performance and heavily armed bombers could defend other bombers.[87] In November 1940, Douglas replaced Air Chief Marshal Hugh Dowding as commander in chief of Fighter Command, so his strong inclination against the idea of modifying fighters to perform long-range missions in support of bombers are likely to have percolated down to his staff, and through them to his successor, Air Marshal Trafford Leigh-Mallory.[88] Accordingly, the RAF's practically inclined officers chose to sidestep the option of providing long-range fighters to escort bombers in daylight. Consequently, Bomber Command was denied the option of having fighters to escort the bombers to targets in daylight and had to adjust the current tactics by innovating new navigational technologies and electronic defense aids.

Theory Meets Practice

On February 14, 1942, eight days before Harris took up his appointment as commander in chief of Bomber Command, the Air Ministry defined a new primary objective to attack the morale of the civilian population and, in particular, the morale of the industrial workers. This change marked the beginning of what became known as the "area bombing" campaign. The target list had been selected to optimize the capabilities provided by the new TR. 1335 ("Gee") navigation aid. Only the I. G. Farben synthetic oil works at Merseburg featured on the target list.[89] Thereafter, until the end of the war, Harris viewed

---

[85] TNA AIR 2/2613, November 23, 1936. Memorandum (DDO–Peirse) to (DCAS–Courtney).
[86] TNA AIR 2/2613, November 30, 1936. Minute (DSD–Douglas) to (DCAS–Courtney).
[87] TNA AIR 20/3605, June 9, 1937, Minutes of the 9th Air Fighting Committee, held at the Air Ministry. AIR 16/1024, March 12, 1940. Minutes of the 20th Air Fighting Committee, held at the Air Ministry.
[88] David Stubbs, "A Blind Spot? The Royal Air Force (RAF) and Long-Range Fighters, 1936–1944," *Journal of Military History* 78(2) (2014), 673–702.
[89] Probert, *Bomber Harris*, 132. TNA AIR 41/5, TR.1335 and Bombing Targets. Air Ministry Letter No. S46368/D.C.A.S., February 14, 1942.

"panacea" targets as unwarrantable diversions from the strategic task allocated to his command.[90] Under Harris's leadership, Bomber Command embarked on the type of campaign the RAF had conditioned its senior officer cadre to believe would be decisive. In April 1942, typical of the hyperbole surrounding the new offensive focus, the interservices research bureau assessed that the German civilian population was, at that moment in time, peculiarly susceptible to "morale bombing."[91] Contrarily, Allied leaders remained unconvinced and, at the Casablanca Conference in January 1943, decided that the independent bombing campaign was unlikely to bring the war to an end on its own and concluded that it would be necessary for land armies to be involved as a central theme in Allied calculations.[92] Nevertheless, in May 1943, Harris attempted to convince the CAS, Air Chief Marshal Sir Charles Portal, that the bombing had been so successful that the tipping point of a collapse in German morale was imminent. Two months later, when that point had still not been reached, Harris remained convinced that the air offensive was causing catastrophic harm in Germany.[93]

Between these dates, the limitations of the RAF's bombing tactics became overtly apparent. On June 3, 1943, a draft of what became known as the Pointblank Directive was sent to the operational commanders for comment.[94] The draft envisioned the primary objective would focus attacks against "enemy fighters in the air and on the ground." However, when the directive emerged eleven days later, it had been adjusted in a way that placated Harris, by reiterating, with equal importance, the need to undermine the morale of the German people.[95] The revised directive effectively acknowledged that only the US Army Air Force (USAAF) was suitably configured to fly offensive bombing missions with fighter escort in daylight operations against targets protected by the Luftwaffe. In April 1944, the highly successful Pointblank campaign, carried out for the most part by the USAAF, had caused a significant weakening of the fighting power of the Luftwaffe's defensive fighter force. The threat posed by the Luftwaffe had diminished to such an extent that in September, it was safe enough for RAF bombers to resume daylight operations against Germany, after an interlude in which Bomber Command had successfully supported the invasion of Normandy.[96]

---

[90] Marshal of the Royal Air Force Sir Arthur "Bomber" Harris, *Bomber Offensive* (London, 1947), 75, 77, 220–221; Kirby and Capey, "The Area Bombing of Germany in World War II," 665.

[91] Ibid., 666.   [92] Richard J. Overy, *The Air War, 1939–1945* (London, 1980), 73.

[93] Probert, *Bomber Harris*, 252, 221.

[94] Charles Webster and Noble Frankland, *The Strategic Air Offensive against Germany, 1939–1945, vol. 4*, Appendices (London, 1961, appendix 8: [xxxi], Draft Directive, ACAS(Ops)/DCAS to C-in-C Bomber Command, June 3, 1943.

[95] Gray, "The Strategic Leadership and Direction," 265.

[96] Overy, *The Bombing War*, 373–374, 377–378.

In explaining how Harris came to conclude that German morale was often on the point of collapse, it appears that Bomber Command's Operational Research Section misapplied its analysis in a way that consistently reinforced, rather than challenged, Harris's belief in the policy of area bombing. Kirby and Capey have suggested that as far as the Air Staff was concerned, area bombing was only an interim measure until improved navigation aids enabled precise bombing at night. Yet Harris, supported by Lord Cherwell, the scientific advisor to Churchill, was sanctioned to continue the area campaign on the belief that the destruction caused would be so great that the combination of fear and economic distress would create a crisis of morale amongst the German civilian population and cause an unbearable strain on the German economy. It was a flawed belief because contrary evidence, from a quantitative study of the effect of air raids on Hull and Birmingham, noted that while the air raids caused alarm and anxiety, they did not produce panic or antiestablishment sentiment. Cherwell had cherry-picked elements of this evidence to further reinforce the arguments supporting the case that area bombing was an effective tool to break morale.[97]

Other contrary evidence also appears to have been ignored. The Axis bombing of Malta between January and April 1942, described by Portal in July as "the heaviest air attack in history," had seen 7,605 tons of bombs dropped on the little island, killing 1,486 people and causing massive destruction of the urban and port areas.[98] Yet the bombing did not induce a collapse of the morale among the Maltese civilian population. For whatever reason, this evidence does not appear to have influenced the thinking of Bomber Command's Operational Research Section, the air intelligence community, the Political Warfare Executive, or the branch of the Ministry of Home Security known as R.E.8. All of these organizations appeared to succumb to a serious case of groupthink in the way they continued to provide optimistic reports about the effect of bombing on German industry and morale. Their judgment appears to have been based on wishful thinking, together with the way they made questionable assumptions about likely outcomes, before using evidence selectively to support their analysis.[99] Harris believed the tipping point he desired was not far away, and to justify this opinion, he chose to judge the measure of success his bombers were achieving by the level of destruction they were causing to German cities. In persevering with this strategy, he produced large "blue books," which were updated after each mission to show the amount of damage caused to certain cities. Richard Overy has pointed out

---

[97] Kirby and Capey, "The Area Bombing of Germany in World War II," 663, 666.
[98] RAF Museum, Signal from Air Ministry to HQ RAF Middle East, July 19, 1942, CAS to Air Vice-Marshal Lloyd. Overy, *The Bombing War*, 504, 510.
[99] Overy, *The Bombing War*, 664–665, 668–669.

that this was a crude strategy, crudely explained.[100] After the war, Harris claimed that the successful campaign against oil targets, the majority of which were undertaken by the USAAF, had been like betting on an outsider that happened to win the race.[101] The Air Staff, however, acknowledged that oil and communications, which they deliberately described in Harris-type language as the "most valuable sinews of war," were outside the area bombing target set and, once severed, brought about the German collapse.[102]

RAF Culture and Organizational Theory

The interpretation of events described in this chapter provides an overview of the development of RAF culture until 1945. It is clear that during the period from 1918 to 1945, the RAF cultivated the thinking of its senior officer cadre who, because of their atypical societal roots, held typically Edwardian and Social Darwinist beliefs about the nature of people and warfare. In terms of the principles of war, their natural preference for the prioritization of "offensive action" and "selection and maintenance of the aim" became enshrined in the various iterations of doctrine, pamphlets, and memoranda. It is equally apparent that the RAF's articulated artifacts and beliefs tell only a small part of the story about its cultural evolution, and that an exploration of the provenance of its underlying basic assumptions was necessary for the RAF's early culture to be better understood. When the RAF came into existence on April 1, 1918, the stupendous cost of fighting the First World War had already toppled Britain from the dominant global position it had held at the turn of the century and turned it into a country indebted to the United States. The British government had to cash in many of its overseas investments to pay for the war. Many of the advantages believed to accrue from its huge empire were illusory, as the cost of running and defending imperial possessions was often greater than the benefit Britain received in return. In the postwar climate of austerity, Lord Douglas Weir, the air minister, thought Trenchard "could make do with little and won't have to be carried."[103]

Accordingly, in the 1920s, Trenchard made much of the RAF's financial efficiency in achieving operational requirements. His immediate priority was the survival of the RAF as an independent force and consequently his "future orientation" was necessarily low. Trenchard felt obliged to focus on the short-term savings the RAF could help deliver, while simultaneously promising future strategic impact. In doing so, he made unproven and unverifiable claims, institutionalizing his vision of offensive action in the RAF's organizational

---

[100] Ibid., 309, 310.   [101] Harris, *Bomber Offensive*, 220.
[102] Kirby and Capey, "The Area Bombing of Germany in World War II," 674.
[103] Hyde, *British Air Policy between the Wars*, 52.

thinking. To be successful, he needed to belittle alternative visions for air power from those such as Burge, who challenged accepted wisdom. But, in doing so, he inadvertently created an environment that promoted institutional collectivism and propagated the RAF's conceptual predilection for "high uncertainty" avoidance.

One thing is demonstrably clear: the ability of bombing to affect the morale of an enemy's civilian population became a core belief among the vast majority of the RAF's senior officers. Their assumptions, which were never properly verified, were based on an intuitive feeling about how people were likely to react when under stress. However, belief in this vision, outside the confines of the RAF, was never properly verified or universally shared. In 1917, in an especially prophetic analysis of the topic, Winston Churchill speculated that:

> It is improbable that any terrorization of the civil population, which could be achieved by air attack, would compel the Government of a great nation to surrender. Familiarity with bombardment, a good system of dug-outs or shelters, a strong control by police and military authorities, should be sufficient to preserve the national fighting power unimpaired. In our own case we have seen the combative spirit of the people roused, and not quelled, by the German air raids. Nothing that we have learned of the capacity of the German population to endure suffering justifies us in assuming that they could be cowed into submission by such methods, or indeed that they would not be rendered more desperately resolved by them.[104]

Of course, the rate of advance of air warfare capabilities in the 1920s and 1930s, together with the hysterical representation of bombardment by airmen, journalists, and novelists, appeared to render such thinking obsolete. Indeed, Churchill's belief in the ability of Bomber Command to deliver victory would wax and wane as the war unfolded, but between the wars, few writers and commentators were willing to challenge the apocalyptic vision of the future. Typically, one of the few who did was Burge, who in 1927 thought: "We are dominated too largely, I think, by some specially striking incidents, attributing to them an importance which on closer examination proves to be exaggerated. To dogmatize about the employment of aircraft in war is futile, inasmuch as we have comparatively little historical guidance to rely upon."[105]

Burge's thinking, however, was at odds with the vast majority of prevailing opinion. The anecdotal experience of airmen such as Slessor, who witnessed the behavior of the civilian population in the aftermath of a Zeppelin attack in the East End of London in 1916, and Goddard in Spain is likely to have had a much greater influence on RAF opinion as they both conflated perceptions about the impact of air bombardment on the morale of the civilian population.

---

[104] Winston Churchill, *The World Crisis, vol. 2, 1916–1918, Appendix N, Memorandum of 21 October 1917* (London, 2015), 431.
[105] Squadron Leader, *Basic Principles of Air Warfare*, 2–3.

Indeed, Slessor later acknowledged that he maintained an intuitive faith in the utility of the bomber.[106] Consequently, the RAF institutionalized its organizational thinking and beliefs by choosing to avoid undertaking an objective analysis of the effectiveness of bombing and, instead, codified its faith as though it were fact, before self-vindicating the "facts" at the RAF's Staff College where, from the third staff course onward, RAF officers were instructed about the likely effects of bombing on morale. In terms of the nine major attributes of the GLOBE methodology, this cadre of senior RAF officers was a mixed bag when it came to performance orientation. While they were encouraged to strive for excellence and innovate when necessary, they would have become aware that any challenge to the RAF's core beliefs was unlikely to be tolerated. Consequently, they avoided engaging in conceptual challenges to perceived wisdom, which in turn acted as a reinforcing mechanism to consolidate the wider acceptance of the RAF's underlying basic assumptions.

In the 1920s and 1930s, the criteria used to select the RAF's officer cadre inadvertently enabled this distinct mind-set to prevail. As early as 1941, Dowding articulated his concern that those who attended fee-paying "public" schools were molded by the prefect system and involvement in competitive games to develop a strong "team player" ethos and were likely to accept a taboo on constructive thinking whenever a challenge to the team's viewpoint emerged.[107] The necessary influx of officers from grammar and secondary schools during the war altered the RAF's character somewhat, but as late as 1956, Slessor was adamant that the reason he preferred officers to come from fee-paying public schools was because such schools were "the best known method of producing leaders of men."[108] Their schooling had conditioned them not to expect power to be distributed evenly and, in general, they were happy to accept a subordinate role, although they aspired to high office and the decision-making power that came with it, whenever promotion became a possibility.

However, the trust they had in their leaders' knowledge and judgment in applying air power led to problems of groupthink. The evidence about the limited and temporary effect on the morale of civilians caused by bombing was available to see in Spain, England, and Malta. It is clear, however, that those charged with conducting studies and operational research to assess the effectiveness of Bomber Command were not inclined to contradict their leaders' beliefs in the effectiveness of bombing on civilian morale and were, instead, complicit in finding evidence to support the long-held beliefs of their superiors.

Indeed, the chasm between original thinking and the innovation exercised by practical men became apparent when it became clear that night bombing had

[106] Orange, *Slessor, Bomber Champion*, 18. Slessor, *The Central Blue*, 204.
[107] Dowding, *Twelve Legions of Angels*, 55. Stubbs, "A Blind Spot?" 701.
[108] Slessor, *The Central Blue*, 4.

been inaccurate and ineffective. At that time the "in-group collectivist" attitudes by those then in charge of Fighter Command was so high that the options to extend the range of the RAF's Spitfire fighters to support deep-penetration daylight bombing missions were simply not considered appropriate. The absence of long-range fighters in the RAF was ascribed to design issues with the Spitfire but, as the USAAF proved, these could have easily been overcome. Indeed, the RAF's practically inclined officers thwarted attempts by the RN and the USAAF to prompt the RAF into significantly extending the aircraft's range by conflating worst case assumptions and presenting them to senior leaders' as a portrayal of likely outcomes. Their disinclination to accept the possibility of alternative options effectively denied the RAF's long-range bombers daylight fighter escort until late summer 1944.[109]

Trenchard's faith in the utility of bombing an enemy to undermine enemy morale held sway over the idea that one should scrutinize options to exercise air power through analysis in order to determine what really worked. The RAF's blind faith in the effectiveness of bombing was compounded by the assertiveness of Trenchard, in stifling internal criticism of the teaching at the RAF Staff College, and by the way these beliefs were codified in doctrine. Moreover, RAF culture was further affected by nuances of officer selection, which inadvertently reinforced collective opinions because of the tendency of those selected to accept perceived wisdom. Finally, the RAF's faith in bombing morale chimed particularly well with the mood of the time, in which British authors, journalists, and governments separately concluded that air power was likely to have a devastating effect in future wars. Ultimately, the combination of these factors significantly affected the RAF's ability to respond to the unfolding operational environment, when prewar expectations that the Germans would be held in France failed to materialize. Indeed, the RAF fell back into its conceptual comfort zone by ignoring the clear opportunity to develop long-range fighters to support daylight precision bombing and, instead, relied on the innovation of its practically inclined officers and men to continue night bombing of area targets until the USAAF had effectively cleared the skies over Germany of enemy fighters. The preference for practical operators over conceptual thinkers, as a key component of RAF culture, would continue after the Second World War.

---

[109] Stubbs, "A Blind Spot?"

18   US Air Force Culture, 1947–2017

Robert Farley

The US Air Force (USAF) came into existence in 1947, birthed from the US Army Air Forces (USAAF). The USAAF had waged war against Germany and Japan in the air, and against the US Army and the US Navy in the halls of government. This chapter argues that both of these wars structured and defined the organizational culture of the USAF, laying down foundational attitudes that have characterized how the organization has fought wars across its existence. These themes, primarily involving organizational concentrations on precision, technology, and decisive effect, developed out of the air force's quest for autonomy, and have subsequently structured how the USAF understands its purpose.

This chapter traces the prehistory of the US Air Force, beginning in the years before World War I. It examines how military aviators' quest for autonomy from the army coincided with and influenced the work of a transnational epistemic community of airpower theorists. The argument then turns to specific cultural attitudes that emerged during the prehistory, explaining why they emerged and what impact they had on the nature of the organization once it became independent. This includes a discussion of how the air force propagated, enforced, and reinforced these tropes across its history, taking into account that culture has shifted over time, and that the USAF consists of multiple internally coherent communities. Finally, the argument examines the impact of these tropes on the political, strategic, operational, and tactical effectiveness of the air force as a military organization.[1]

Prehistory of the USAF

The foundations of USAF culture were laid in the forty years prior to the birth of the organization.[2] In 1907, the US Army established the Aeronautical Division within the Signal Corps, a communications-focused organization,

---

[1] Allan R. Millett, Williamson Murray, and Kenneth H. Watman. "The Effectiveness of Military Organizations," *International Security* 11(1) (1986), 37–71, 38.

[2] Richard P. Hallion, "U.S. Air Power," in John Andreas Olsen, ed., *Global Air Power* (Washington, DC, 2011), Kindle, 63–136, 64.

which had previously managed some lighter-than-air aviation assets, including balloons.[3] American aircraft first saw combat in 1916, during the Punitive Expedition against Mexico.[4] But US military aviation trailed behind that of Europe, where World War I served as a cauldron for technical and doctrinal innovation. Some American aviators served with French and British forces, however, and the army sent observers to the Western Front to learn from the European examples.[5] The American aviation industry did not mature at the same rate as its European counterparts, and when the United States entered the war, it employed mostly European-designed aircraft built under license.[6] By 1918, however, American aviators were fully engaged in combat, flying against German aircraft over the Western Front with the title of the US Army Air Service (USAAS), established in May 1918.

The theoretical foundations of airpower emerged in tandem with the organizational development of the first air forces. From the latter half of World War I until the 1930s, a transnational epistemic community of airpower theorists developed across the United States and Europe. The most important contributors to this community came from Italy, the United Kingdom, and the United States.[7] The Royal Air Force (RAF) gained its independence in 1918, in the final year of World War I, on the grounds that the Royal Flying Corps and the Royal Navy Air Service could not sufficiently coordinate their activities in the realms of offensive, defensive, or industrial action. The 1917 Smuts Report, describing the effect of German strategic bombing on London and the potential for offensive action against German industry, played a pivotal a role in the creation of the RAF.[8]

In the American case, the quest for autonomy went hand in hand with the development of the foundations of airpower doctrine. The air service demobilized after the war with the rest of the army, but soon reorganized itself on a more permanent footing.[9] Training and organizational structure were regularized, although the USAAS remained largely subservient to the ground combat arms. In 1926, the US Army Air Corps (USAAC) would replace the USAAS, a

---

[3] Charles J. Gross, *American Military Aviation: The Indispensable Arm* (College Station, TX, 2002), 16.

[4] Jeffrey S. Underwood, "Presidential Statesmen and U.S. Airpower," in Robin Higham and Mark Parillo, eds., *The Influence of Airpower upon History: Statesmanship, Diplomacy, and Foreign Policy since 1916* (Lexington, TX, 2013), 177–208, 178.

[5] Thomas Wildenberg, *Billy Mitchell's War with the Navy: The Interwar Rivalry over Air Power* (Annapolis, MD, 2013), Kindle, loc. 387.

[6] Maurer Maurer, *Aviation in the U.S. Army 1919–1939* (Washington, DC, 1987), xxi.

[7] Brian D. Laslie, *Architect of Air Power: General Laurence S. Kuter and the Birth of the US Air Force* (Lexington, KY, 2017), 31–32.

[8] National Archive. "Note by the Air Staff on the Reasons for the Formation of the Royal Air Force, citing Curzon report of 1916," 4. AIR 9/5: Plans Archives, *vol.* 47, "Separate Air Force Controversy 1917–1936."

[9] Gross, *American Military Aviation*, 54.

designation that lasted until 1941, when it became the US Army Air Forces (USAAF).[10] American military aviators conceptualized the optimal mission of their organization in ways that would maximize the potential for independence from the army and (less so) the navy. By the early 1920s, evangelists of airpower in and around the US military had begun to argue for both the independence of an air force and the primacy of airpower.[11] Of these evangelists, General William "Billy" Mitchell had the highest profile.[12] As part of a series of tests designed to evaluate the effect of air bombardment on naval vessels, Mitchell engineered the sinking of the former German battleship *Ostfriesland* with bombers off the Virginia Capes in July 1921.[13]

Tensions between Mitchell's perspective and the more traditional components of the army and navy quickly became apparent. It is easy to caricature the debates between aviators and the older parts of the army, but they boiled down to questions over the autonomy that aircraft would have from the traditional arms such as infantry, cavalry, and artillery.[14] Many senior soldiers envisioned aircraft playing roles that committed them to direct and indirect support of ground forces. This included ground support (light artillery), interdiction (longer-range artillery), and reconnaissance. Aviators argued that these roles failed to recognize the revolutionary potential of the airplane.[15] Mitchell's arguments also challenged the existence of the navy; he and many other army aviators believed that carrier aviation would inevitably, and fatally, trail behind land-based aviation. That said, aviators in the United States had both the space and the resources to develop independent airpower doctrine.[16]

The primary institutional structure for developing and propagating a doctrine of decisive victory was the Air Service School, established in 1920 at Langley Field in Virginia, and subsequently moved to Maxwell, Alabama in 1931.[17] Renamed the Air Corps Tactical School (ACTS) in 1926, the school took as its mission the education of air service (and eventually other) officers in the operational and tactical methods for improving the effectiveness of army air

[10] Ibid., 16.   [11] Maurer, *Aviation in the US Army*, 44.

[12] Alfred F. Hurley, *Billy Mitchell: Crusader for Air Power* (Bloomington, IN, 2006), 75.

[13] Robert O'Connel, *Sacred Vessels* (Oxford, 1993), 257.

[14] For interesting commentary on this discussion, see Capt. Laurence S. Kuter, "Memorandum: Bombing Accuracy in Spain and in China," in Phil Haun, ed., *Lectures of the Air Corps Tactical School and American Strategic Bombing in World War II* (Lexington, KY, 2019), 133.

[15] Peter R. Faber, "Interwar US Army Aviation and the Air Corps Tactical School: Incubators of American Airpower," in Philip Meilinger, ed., *The Paths of Heaven: The Evolution of Airpower Theory* (Maxwell, AL, 1997), 183–238, 186.

[16] Williamson Murray, "Strategic Bombing: The British, German, and American Experiences," in Williamson Murray and Allan R. Millett, eds., *Military Innovation in the Interwar Period* (Cambridge, 1996), 96–143, 107.

[17] Laslie, *Architect of Air Power*, 32. See also Robert T. Finney, *History of the Air Corps Tactical School 1920–1940* (Washington, DC, 1998); Peter Faber, "Paradigm Lost: Airpower Theory and Its Historical Struggles," in John Andreas Olsen, ed., *Airpower Reborn: The Strategic Concepts of John Warden and John Boyd* (Annapolis, MD, 2015), 11–47, Kindle, loc. 625.Hi.

assets.[18] Although the school was initially ecumenical with regard to mission and aircraft type, over time, it increasingly came to adopt and promulgate the idea that long-range strategic bombing, conducted primarily by heavy bombers, could provide decisive victory in war.[19] The instructors at the ACTS argued this position with such enthusiasm that some aviators, including especially fighter (pursuit) pilots, believed that their concerns were intentionally sidelined in service of long-range strategic bombing.[20] However, the offensive orientation of bomber doctrine eventually enabled such innovations as the development of long-range escort fighters, which allowed the organization to bring the fight directly to the Luftwaffe.[21]

Despite strong advocacy for independence, the USAAF would remain part of the US Army through the Second World War. During that conflict, it undertook a variety of tactical and strategic roles, including support of army ground forces in Asia, Africa, and Europe, as well as strategic bombing campaigns against Germany and Japan. These last, the former waged in concert with the Royal Air Force under the aegis of the Combined Bomber Offensive, represented the primary wartime effort of the USAAF in terms of resources, preparation, and expected impact. Some commentators have seen the July 1943 publication of FM 100–20, *Command and Employment of Air Power*, as a "declaration of independence," although views differ on its effect.[22] However, the strategic bombing campaigns, in combination with an idiosyncratic interpretation of the Mediterranean campaign, provided the justification for the detachment of the USAAF from the army. As part of a general reorganization of the US national security state in 1947, the air force became independent from the army, and the Departments of War and the Navy were subsumed, along with a new Department of the Air Force, under the Department of Defense.

Air Force Culture

The inception of the independent air force in 1947 offers a useful opportunity for taking a snapshot of the contemporary state of air force culture. The USAF came into existence with deeply held, often instrumental cultural priorities that colored and structured its vision of warfighting. This section uses the framework established by Leonard Wong and Stephen J. Gerras to more closely investigate these cultural attitudes.[23] The rest of this chapter examines how these cultural elements affected air force effectiveness, and how they have changed over time.

---

[18] Laslie, *Architect of Air Power*, 33.   [19] Ibid., 34.

[20] Perry McCoy Smith, *The Air Force Plans for Peace, 1943–1945* (Baltimore, MD, 1970), 33–34.

[21] David Stubbs, "A Blind Spot? The Royal Air Force (RAF) and Long-Range Fighters, 1936–1944," *Journal of Military History* 78(2) (2014), 673–702, 689; Laslie, *Architect of Air Power*, 97.

[22] Laslie, *Architect of Air Power*, 90–91.   [23] See Chapter 1.

Precision: Piercing the Fog of War

In the prehistory of the USAF, the ACTS developed its theory of decisive strategic effect around the concept of high-altitude, precision bombing.[24] Unescorted bombers, using advanced bombsights during daylight hours, would approach targets at high speed and high altitude and then deliver payloads of ordnance to carefully selected industrial targets.[25] These attacks would concentrate on critical nodes of the industrial economy, seeking to induce paralysis without causing widespread destruction to enemy cities. As its economy ground to a halt, the enemy would lose the ability to supply its deployed forces, and would find itself forced to make peace on terms advantageous to the United States. The focus on daylight, precision attacks against industrial targets set American air doctrine apart from that of the larger community of airpower theorists. In the United Kingdom, for example, attacks against enemy morale (in the form of direct bombing of enemy population centers) loomed much larger than attacks on industry, in part because of skepticism over targeting and precision.[26]

The American approach required precision in two different facets. The first involved the technical problem of putting bombs onto targets, often somewhat small and hard to identify. The Air Corps believed that the Norden bomb sight, available from 1931, would allow its bombers to hit targets with precision, even at high altitude, during daytime bombing runs.[27] However, USAAC doctrine also required the precise identification of targets, both in terms of understanding the location of specific factories and manufacturing plants, and in understanding the relevance of particular industrial goods to the larger economy.[28] While the former represented a greater technical problem than the Air Corps appreciated at the time (the attrition rate for bombers attacking during daylight hours proved prohibitively high, and in any case pilots and bombardiers often misidentified targets, bombing the wrong buildings with considerable precision), the latter proved a more intractable long-term problem. Even the best economists (and

[24] Capt. L. S. Kuter, "Practical Bombing Probabilities: Conclusion," in Haun, *The Book of ACTS*, 179.
[25] Maj. Muir S. Fairchild, "National Economic Structure," in Haun, *The Book of ACTS*, 238.
[26] Philip Meilinger, "Trenchard, Slessor, and Royal Air Force Doctrine before World War II," in Philip Meilinger, ed., *The Paths of Heaven: The Evolution of Airpower Theory* (Maxwell, AL, 1997), 41–78, 50.
[27] Timothy Moy, "Transforming Technology in the Army Air Corps 1920–1940: Technology, Politics, and Culture for Strategic Bombing," in Dominick A. Pisano, ed., *The Airplane in American Culture* (Ann Arbor, MI, 2003), 299–332, 324.
[28] Michael J. Eula, "Giulio Douhet and Strategic Air Force Operations: A Study in the Limitations of Theoretical Warfare," *Air University Review* (September–October 1986), 1-5, www.air power.maxwell.af.mil/airchronicles/aureview/1986/sep-oct/eula.html; Gian Gentile, *How Effective Is Strategic Bombing?* (New York, 2001), Kindle, loc. 2993.

sociopolitical analysts) struggled to develop a full picture of the enemy economy, and industrial economies generally proved far more resilient to attack than airpower theorists had expected.

Technology

Technology constitutes one of the foundations of the fighting power of military organizations. Doctrine and technology interact with one another; doctrine can provide the logic for technological innovation, while new technologies can overturn existing doctrinal and organizational structures. A focus on technology is hardly specific to air forces in general, or to the US Air Force in particular. As one airpower historian argues in his *Ten Propositions Regarding Airpower*, "technology and airpower are integrally and synergistically related."[29] This has resulted from fundamentally structural causes. The core technologies associated with aviation are newer than those associated with naval or land warfare, even granting the remarkable advances over the past 150 years in both of those fields.

Nevertheless, the pursuit of technological innovation has played an unusually large role in the culture of the USAF for the course of its history and prehistory. In the early days of American military aviation, army aviators were criticized for concentrating on technology at the expense of doctrine and of personnel development.[30] Progress in aircraft technology advanced at a rapid pace after the invention of the aircraft, only slowing in the decades after World War II, when jet aircraft began to reach maturity.[31] Between 1944 and 1957, for example, three successive generations of fighter aircraft superseded one another, rendering earlier aircraft virtually obsolete.[32]

The concentration of the USAF on technology may also have specific societal sources. As numerous analysts have argued, American defense circles have historically evinced an unusually large degree of fascination with technology, sometimes at the expense of other components of military power.[33] The source of fascination with technology, which extends beyond the air force

---

[29] Phillip S. Meilinger, "Ten Propositions Regarding Airpower," *Air and Space Power Journal* (Spring 1996), www.airpower.au.af.mil/airchronicles/cc/meil.html.

[30] James P. Tate, *The Army and Its Air Corps: Army Policy toward Aviation, 1919–1941* (Maxwell, AL, 1998), 5; Moy, "Transforming Technology in the Army Air Corps," 308.

[31] Murray, "Strategic Bombing," 98.

[32] John A. Tirpak, "The Sixth Generation Fighter," *Air Force Magazine*, October 2009. www.airforcemag.com/MagazineArchive/Pages/2009/October%202009/1009fighter.aspx.

[33] Colin S. Gray, *Weapons Don't Make War: Policy, Strategy, and Military Technology* (Lawrence, KS, 1993).

specifically and the American military generally, may lie in certain long-standing cultural tropes peculiar to American social and economic realities.[34]

Decisive Effect

In the interwar period, US Army Air Corps officers worked extensively on the concept of daylight precision bombing, the full realization of which would enable a force of strategic bombers to target and destroy critical nodes of production, bringing a modern industrial economy to its knees.[35] At its core, "strategic" bombing theory is the idea that long-range bombing can disrupt enemy state, societal, and military organizations sufficiently to win decisive victories in war.[36] Historically, airpower theorists have linked this concept to the need for organizationally independent air forces. One historian concludes that "airpower is an inherently strategic force" in his "Ten Propositions Regarding Airpower," along with the assertion that "airpower's unique characteristics necessitate that it be centrally controlled by airmen."[37]

To be sure, the advocates of particular military organizations have long focused on the unique contributions that their service can make to the security of a nation. But since the second half of World War I, airpower advocates have argued that air forces can, when autonomous and sufficiently supplied with resources, have independent decisive effect.[38] This is to say that air forces can win wars without, or with only trivial, support from land and sea services.[39] These guiding concepts combined to provide the logical underpinnings of the USAAF's great strategic offensives during World War II, and its plans for a strategic air offensive against the Soviet Union in the early Cold War.

Autonomy

All US services make use of the air in some fashion, and it is unsurprising that questions about the control of air assets often lead to interservice conflict.

---

[34] For an empirical (and somewhat skeptical) take, see Jon D. Miller and Rafael Pardo, "Civic Scientific Literacy and Attitude to Science and Technology: A Comparative Analysis of the European Union, the United States, Japan, and Canada," in Meinolf Dierkes and Claudia von Grote, eds., *Between Understanding and Trust: The Public, Science and Technology* (New York, 2000), 54–88.

[35] Haywood Hansell, "The Aim in War," in Haun, *The Book of ACTS*, 108; Gentile, *How Effective Is Strategic Bombing?* 264–308.

[36] David E. Johnson, *Learning Large Lessons: The Evolving Roles of Ground Power and Air Power in the Post–Cold War Era* (Santa Monica, CA, 2007), 182.

[37] Meilinger, "Ten Propositions Regarding Airpower."

[38] Giulio Douhet, *The Command of the Air* (Washington, DC, 1998); Mark Clodfelter, *Beneficial Bombing: The Progressive Foundations of American Air Power, 1917–1945* (Lincoln, NE, 2010), 44.

[39] Carl Builder, *The Masks of War: American Military Styles in Strategy and Analysis* (Baltimore, MD, 1989), 67, 71.

Indeed, these disagreements tend to erupt around missions at the border between two services, such as close air support.[40] However, the interservice conflicts that inevitably stemmed from the creation of the USAF had a constitutive effect on air force culture. To a considerable extent, the need to develop compelling arguments for institutional autonomy drove doctrinal thinking and factional conflict. In the prehistory of the USAF, pursuit aviation was intentionally deemphasized in favor of long-range bombing, largely for political reasons.[41]

The commitment to autonomy manifests itself in the internal and external retelling of specific organizational myths. For example, "penny packets," usually invoked in service of an argument for centralized control of airpower, most often refers to the experience of tactical airpower in the North Africa campaign during 1942 and 1943.[42] According to the narrative, senior leadership in the US Army initially sought to link airpower assets to specific ground units, which led to hoarding by local commanders and ineffectual commitment of insufficient force to broader campaign objectives.[43] Instead of harnessing the overwhelming, concentrated power of the USAAF from an operational perspective, army generals doled out airpower in "penny packets" for low-level tactical objectives. To be sure, parts of the "penny packets" story are true; the army as a whole struggled with the management of ground, air, and logistical assets in the early part of the North Africa campaign, and repeatedly reformed command arrangements in light of combat and operational experience. Part of this reform included a degree of centralization over the command of tactical aviation assets.[44] The story serves as a ready cautionary tale for linking airpower assets to local ground commanders, who lack a full understanding of strategic and operational objectives.[45]

The creation of the USAF did not relieve tensions between the services. Indeed, several interservice crises ensued in the immediate wake of the 1947 National Security Act. In 1949, the air force and navy came into conflict over whether aircraft carriers or strategic bombers should receive priority in an era of limited defense spending. The resulting "Revolt of the Admirals" cost

---

[40] Douglas N. Campbell, *The Warthog and the Close Air Support Debate* (Annapolis, MD, 2003), 65.

[41] Smith, *Air Force Plans for Peace*, 32.

[42] J. A. Chamier and Wing-Commander Gossage, "The Use of the Air Force for Replacing Military Garrisons," *RUSI Journal* 66(462) (1921), 205–216; Christopher M. Rein, *The North African Air Campaign: US Army Air Forces from El Alamein to Salerno* (Lawrence, KS, 2012).

[43] Richard R. Muller, "Close Air Support: The German, British, and American Experiences 1918–1941," in Williamson Murray and Allan R. Millett, eds., *Military Innovation in the Interwar Period* (Cambridge, 1996), 144–190, 185.

[44] Rein, *The North African Air Campaign*, 195–198.

[45] For a modern perspective. see Rebecca Grant, "Penny Packets, Then and Now," *Air Force Magazine*, June 2010. www.airforcemag.com/MagazineArchive/Pages/2010/June%202010/0 610penny.aspx.

several senior officers their careers and delayed construction of the navy's first supercarriers.[46] The army and the air force came into conflict at several points in the 1950s over development and ownership of ballistic missiles, even as the navy pursued its own ballistic missile program.[47]

Dimensions of Military Organizational Culture

These attitudes resulted in a set of tendencies that impacted air force combat performance and war preparation, which can usefully be described through the GLOBE dimensions of military organizational culture. The early USAF was notable among military organizations for its high humane orientation, its predilection for uncertainty avoidance, its relatively low power-distance self-conception, its assertiveness, and its future orientation. The USAF had a strong conception of its own humane orientation. Technology, precision, and the focus on decisive impact all contribute to this humane orientation; technology enables precision and transparency, which allow the discrimination between civilian and military targets. This helped the USAF distinguish itself from its Royal Air Force partner, at least rhetorically. The pursuit of independent decisive effect sought to avoid the destructive attrition that characterized the Western Front in World War I, thus resulting in a shorter, more humane war.[48]

Although generally an innovative organization within specific parameters, the early air force exhibited strong tendencies toward uncertainty avoidance, stemming primarily from the significant values placed on planning, precision, and transparency. Early work from the ACTS demonstrated a strong predilection for careful planning (down to the prescribed use of specific formations and targeting procedures), along with a voracious appetite for information in order to reduce the parameters of uncertainty.

Air force assertiveness plays out less in terms of the individual aggressiveness of specific members of the service, but rather in how the organization as a whole views its relationships with partner services and with civilian authorities. In this sense, the history and culture of the early air force created an orientation toward assertiveness, in which personnel could make strong claims on missions and on resources, specifically in interactions with civilian and other military authorities. This made the USAF particularly assertive with respect to its understanding of its prerogatives.

With respect to power distance, the USAF has an unusually horizontal authority structure for a military organization, due largely to its focus on

[46] Steven L. Rearden, *History of the Office of the Secretary of Defense: The Formative Years 1947–1950* (Washington, DC, 1984), 410.

[47] Richard M. Leighton, *History of the Office of the Secretary of Defense, vol. 3: Strategy, Money, and the New Look 1953–1956* (Washington, DC, 2001), 16.

[48] Clodfelter, *Beneficial Bombing*, 238–240.

piloting as a craft. The sense of the organization as a community of pilots, even as the percentage of pilots as members of the organization has dropped over the decades, smooths and softens the hierarchical relationships typical to military organizations. This tendency sometimes forces value trade-offs between the maintenance of a sense of community and the pursuit of military effectiveness.

Even (perhaps especially) in its prehistory, the air force has been a thoroughly future-oriented organization, a facet that explains much of its focus on technology. The air force conceptualized capability in terms of technology, developed long-term plans for the acquisition and production of technology, and consistently pursued innovation within the frameworks established by mission and doctrine. Of course, innovation outside of these frameworks has proved more difficult to incorporate into USAF planning.

Impact of Cultural Attitudes and Dimensions on Military Effectiveness

Of the vast literature on military effectiveness, this study uses the framework developed in the well-known Military Effectiveness series.[49] That framework established four distinct levels of effectiveness: political, strategic, operational, and tactical. Political effectiveness concerns the ability of an organization to secure the resources it needs to fulfill its mission, and to secure its position within the national security framework. Strategic effectiveness involves an organization's ability to successfully engage in long-range planning, and particularly in its capacity to link organizational resources to a compelling campaign plan. Operational effectiveness requires an organization to coordinate resources around the achievement of specific, short-term campaign objectives, as well as to coordinate with other services, allies, and elements of the national security state. Finally, tactical effectiveness refers to an organization's ability to field units capable of fighting at a level of proficiency in operationally relevant ways.

The effectiveness of an organization may vary across all four of these metrics; some politically effective organizations perform poorly at the tactical level, and vice versa. Indeed, effectiveness can vary even within a specific analytical level, as different components of an organization (fighters vs. bombers, for example) may perform more or less competently in combat. Moreover, individual combat and noncombat arms within an organization may also have different organizational cultures, or manifest different facets of a broader organizational culture.[50] The connections between organizational culture and

---

[49] Millett, Murray, and Watman, "The Effectiveness of Military Organizations"; see also Allan R. Millett and Williamson Murray, eds., *Military Effectiveness*, *vols. 1–3* (London, 1988).

[50] Geert Hofstede, "Identifying Organizational Subcultures: An Empirical Approach," *Journal of Management Studies* 35(1) (1998), 1–12, 1.

organizational effectiveness depend on situational factors.[51] Different cultural elements may, depending on the vagaries of technological and geopolitical uncertainty, become appropriate or inappropriate to the specific tasks faced by a military organization.[52] For example, specific organizational assumptions might facilitate tactical and operational effectiveness against a peer competitor in a likely theater of operation, but the same assumptions might actively reduce effectiveness in a different situation against a different foe.

Culture and Military Effectiveness in USAF History

The cultural attitudes discussed earlier in this chapter provided the USAF with a compelling political argument for its existence, and even for its primacy among the services in the early Cold War.[53] Unfortunately, the same cultural logic, which made the air force politically effective, sometimes limited its effectiveness in strategic, operational, and tactical terms in the conflicts that embroiled the United States during and after the Cold War. Requirements of space prevent a full accounting of the performance of the USAF during this period. The campaign accounts discussed here do not generally detail the causes of the military engagements, or the course of the campaigns, except insofar as these campaigns either demonstrate the relevance of cultural attitudes, or had an impact on the ongoing development of air force culture.

The newly created USAF immediately faced two major technological problems. The first problem it needed to resolve was how to restructure itself for the delivery of nuclear weapons. It had a political advantage over the other two services by virtue of the fact that B-29s had delivered the first two atomic weapons, and because it could easily integrate nuclear weapons employment into its organizational culture. The nuclear turn required less of a change in airpower theory than is commonly understood. Early atomic weapons were extremely destructive, but not so much that they could revolutionize the doctrine of strategic bombing. Moreover, the concept of airpower as a "knock-out" weapon preceded the development of nuclear weapons.[54] Bomber advocates had believed that conventionally armed aircraft could deliver sufficiently devastating attacks against industrial targets to effectively destroy an enemy's war-making capacity. After the experience of the Combined Bomber Offensive demonstrated the resilience of industrial societies, nuclear weapons filled the conceptual gap through the promise of considerably greater devastation.

---

[51] Williamson Murray, "Does Military Culture Matter?" *Orbis* 43(1) (1999), 27–42.
[52] See, for example, Elizabeth Kier, *Imagining War: French and British Military Doctrine between the Wars* (Princeton, NJ, 1997), 27–28.
[53] Smith, *Air Force Plans for Peace*, 15.   [54] Ibid., 33.

The second problem facing the air force was the transition to jet technology, which effectively required the replacement of virtually the entire USAF fleet in a short period of time. The expensive B-29 had a front-line shelf life of about six years.[55] In 1949, the air force began to replace the B-29 with the B-36 Peacemaker, which could attack the USSR from bases in the United States.[56] However, the big, slow B-36 was also vulnerable to Soviet interceptors. Introduced in 1951 and designed to operate from bases around the Soviet periphery, jet-powered B-47 medium bombers could deliver both tactical and strategic nuclear weapons against Soviet targets.[57] In 1955, the air force would introduce the B-52 Stratofortress, which replaced most of the previous bombers.

The air force's technological fixation and its predilection toward decisive strategic warfare helped it win the political battles necessary to the development of a fleet of strategic jet bombers. Air force culture enabled it to foster the development of jet technology in the defense industrial base, integrate that technology into its existing doctrine, and make a political case for the resources necessary to recapitalize the fleet. Most notably, the air force prevailed in the aforementioned "Revolt of the Admirals," which pitted strategic bomber advocates against aircraft carrier advocates.

Although the focus on nuclear weapons rendered some of the problems of precision-targeting irrelevant, the air force remained interested in the avoidance of uncertainty. From 1947 on, its work on airpower theory advanced in conjunction with associated organizations, such as the RAND Corporation.[58] RAND received the task of developing the theoretical foundation for the USAF's postwar force structure. RAND's work fit easily into the air force's vision of warfare, especially in its use of advanced analytical techniques to pierce the fog of war.[59] Researchers at RAND included Albert Wohlstetter, Bernard Brodie, and others associated with the world of strategic theory in the 1950s and 1960s.[60]

The development of missile technology posed a more difficult problem for the air force. On one hand, fast, high-altitude antiaircraft missiles (fired from either interceptors or ground batteries) forced a rethinking of strategic bomber doctrine.[61] Bombers were repurposed for low-altitude penetration missions, or cancelled altogether, a process that extended into the early 1960s.[62] On the

[55] Richard Rhodes, *The Making of the Atomic Bomb* (New York, 1986), 605.
[56] L. Douglas Keeney, *15 Minutes: General Curtis LeMay and the Countdown to Nuclear Annihilation* (New York, 2011), 45–46.
[57] Ibid., 47.
[58] Alex Abella, *Soldiers of Reason: The RAND Corporation and the Rise of the American Empire* (New York, 2008), 14.
[59] Ibid., 18.   [60] Ibid., 44, 68.   [61] Keeney, *15 Minutes*, 221.
[62] Carl Builder, *The Icarus Syndrome: The Role of Air Power Theory in the Evolution and Fate of the U.S. Air Force* (London, 1994), 151; Gross, *American Military Aviation*, 189.

other hand, the development of the intercontinental ballistic missile (ICBM) seemed to offer a more secure way to strike Soviet targets than existing bomber aircraft. Because both the army and the navy threatened to take over the missile portfolio, the air force grudgingly fought for ICBM technology, while at the same time making the case for a strategic bomber fleet.[63]

The jet and nuclear revolutions also affected fighter procurement. Although F-86 Sabres had performed well in the Korean War against Soviet-built MiG-15s, the air force expected that fighter-to-fighter combat would not dominate a clash against the Soviet Union.[64] Rather, destruction of Soviet bombers at long range, as well as the delivery of nuclear payloads against Soviet tactical targets, would be the tactical fighter's most important mission. The former would lead to the production of a series of interceptor types well suited to shooting down Soviet bombers on their way to the United States.[65] The latter led Tactical Air Command (TAC), the USAF command tasked with planning for tactical operations, to invest heavily in fighter-bombers optimized for delivering tactical nuclear payloads.[66]

In sum, elements of organizational culture allowed the USAF to excel at certain aspects of managing the aerospace revolutions of the early Cold War. Uncertainty avoidance led to a strong emphasis on global military planning; future orientation opened the door for the inclusion of new technologies; assertiveness characterized the service's approach to its competition with the army and the navy over missiles and nuclear weapons. However, the commitment and cultural investment of the USAF in nuclear weapons would prove problematic when it again faced the problem of limited war in Asia.

Vietnam

As the United States gradually became embroiled in the Vietnam War, the impact of concentration on the strategic bombing mission had palpably negative effects on the ability of the air force to wage the conflict. In 1964, in response to civilian interest in more assertive responses to North Vietnamese aggression, the USAF offered a series of relatively optimistic assessments of the potential for a coercive air campaign against North Vietnam.[67] Designed to force Hanoi to end its support for South Vietnamese rebels, the Rolling

---

[63] Builder, *The Icarus Syndrome*, 33.
[64] Jim Cunningham, "Rediscovering Air Superiority: Vietnam, the F-X, and the 'Fighter Mafia,'" *Air and Space Power Journal* (August 25, 2011), www.airpower.maxwell.af.mil/airchronicles/cc/jim.html.
[65] Robert Frank Futrell, *Ideas, Concepts, Doctrine: Basic Thinking in the United States Air Force: 1907–1960* (Maxwell, AL, 1989), 529–531.
[66] Gross, *American Military Aviation*, 173.
[67] Mark Clodfelter, *The Limits of Air Power: The American Bombing of North Vietnam* (New York, 1989), 73.

Thunder campaign drew on concepts in accord with the air force's cultural priors. The campaign plan expected that gradually escalating attacks against North Vietnamese infrastructure and logistics could raise the cost of aggression to a point at which the Communist leadership would conclude that the costs of war outweighed the benefits.[68] The campaign began in March 1965, and lasted (with some interruptions) into late 1968.

Given its bureaucratic and cultural convictions, it was almost impossible for the air force not to offer a solution to the Vietnam conflict that involved coercive attacks against North Vietnamese targets. The USAF was politically effective in foregrounding itself among US military efforts in the region, but is almost universally regarded to have failed at the strategic level. Despite significant damage to military and economic infrastructure, North Vietnam did not waver in its commitment to overthrow the Saigon government, and the attacks did not substantially reduce its capability to do so.[69] The USAF's strategic plan (granting some interference from civilian authorities) was insufficient to solving the political problem posed by North Vietnamese intransigence.

Operationally the USAF record was mixed. Over time, North Vietnam developed a complex, interlocked set of air defenses that made strikes difficult and costly. Prewar procurement training, geared toward meeting the Soviet threat with nuclear weapons, was not well designed to penetrate North Vietnamese defenses.[70] American losses against an undercapitalized foe were high. However, the air force adapted well to the problems presented by surface-to-air missile installations, developing specialized aircraft ("Wild Weasels") for attacking them.[71] It developed complex, large-scale strike packages capable of managing the multifaceted threat and even explored the option of using B-58 bombers as "pathfinder" aircraft in strike packages.[72]

Tactically, the air force struggled to establish command of the air. The interceptors and fighter-bombers designed in the 1950s were not optimized for air-to-air combat against enemy fighters. A lack of good fighter doctrine compounded the problem, as a concentration on safety and readiness had limited training in air-to-air combat.[73] Even the air-to-air missiles carried by USAF fighters performed poorly against small, maneuverable aircraft. This left

---

[68] Thomas C. Schelling, *Arms and Influence* (New Haven, CT, 1966), 74–75.

[69] Clodfelter, *The Limits of Air Power*, 130.

[70] Douglas M. White, "Rolling Thunder to Linebacker: US Fixed Wing Survivability over North Vietnam," (MMAS thesis, US Army Command and General Staff College, 2014), 21.

[71] William A. Hewitt, *Planting the Seeds of SEAD the Wild Weasel in Vietnam* (Darby, PA, 1992), 11–12.

[72] Anonymous, "The B-58 and SEA Camouflage Story," TBOVerse, www.tboverse.us/HPCAF ORUM/phpBB3/viewtopic.php?f=11&t=63.

[73] C. R. Anderegg, *Sierra Hotel: Flying Air Force Fighters in the Decade after Vietnam* (Washington, DC, 2001), 33.

the fighters and pilots largely unprepared to deal with the threat of small, maneuverable enemy fighters such as the MiG-17 and MiG-21, which appeared over North Vietnam in numbers during the early days of Rolling Thunder and imposed unacceptable losses on American aircraft.[74] The air force initially viewed the problem through a technological lens; its aircraft could not detect MiGs approaching from behind and below, and its missiles were designed to track and kill sluggish bombers rather than agile fighters.[75] The navy, on the other hand, suspected that its combat air crews lacked sufficient experience in air-to-air combat.[76] Its effort to improve training became the "Top Gun" program, accompanied by more flexible tactical employment doctrine.[77] Over time, the US Navy kill ratio increased from 3.7:1 to 13:1. The air force kill ratio did not improve until much later in the war, when the air force began to train its pilots against dissimilar aircraft.[78] Air force personnel policies also contributed to the problem, as pilots better suited for bombers and transport aircraft found themselves forced into fighter combat.[79]

On the political, operational, and strategic levels, the USAF performed better in the late-war Linebacker I and II campaigns. In both cases, it offered capabilities that could resolve the strategic problem; in the former case, the need to defeat a North Vietnamese offensive into South Vietnam, and in the latter, the need to reassure Saigon and Hanoi of American credibility.[80] Operationally, Linebacker I resulted in a significant success, and Linebacker II a partial success. However, the USAF still struggled tactically with the problems presented by North Vietnamese air defenses, a problem that the next generation of air force leadership would try to address.

Post-Vietnam: Cultural Change and Generational Transition

In the wake of the Vietnam War, the air force saw both a generational and a conceptual transition. The "rise of the fighter generals" came on the heels of the retirement of a large number of senior officers who had served in World War II, and who in some cases had undergone training in the prewar Army Air Corps.[81] Officers whose experiences were more tactical in nature, primarily including fighter pilots, replaced these older generals. These pilots had grown concerned about technological and tactical stagnation during the Vietnam War, and sought major reforms that would redistribute resources and effort across the service.

[74] Marshall L. Michel III, *Clashes: Air Combat over North Vietnam 1965–1972* (Annapolis, MD, 1997), 232–233.
[75] Michel, *Clashes*, 181, 186; Anderegg, *Sierra Hotel*, 33.   [76] Michel, *Clashes*, 186.
[77] Ibid., 183.   [78] Cunningham, "Rediscovering Air Superiority"; Anderegg, *Sierra Hotel*, 33.
[79] Anderegg, *Sierra Hotel*, 14.   [80] White, "Rolling Thunder to Linebacker," 72–73.
[81] Michael Worden, *Rise of the Fighter Generals: The Problem of Air Force Leadership 1945–1982* (Maxwell, AL, 1998).

Technological changes (discussed earlier) also deemphasized the role of the bomber in both limited and strategic warfare.

Perhaps unsurprisingly, the rise of the fighter generals led to what many described as a crisis within the air force.[82] While pursuit of technology remained a key organizational precept, the concept of independent decisive effect waned as an underlying institutional assumption. This reduced USAF assertiveness, a trend that would continue until the 1991 Gulf War. In 1982, the air force effectively ceded tactical primacy to the army's AirLand Battle doctrine, which subjected the USAF's tactical assets to an army plan to defeat the deployed forces of the Warsaw Pact in Central Europe.[83] The rise of the fighter generals also helped to produce a more practical turn in airpower doctrine. Out of concern over the performance of fighter pilots in combat during the Vietnam War, the air force introduced the Red Flag exercises in 1975.[84] These exercises involved active training in realistic situations, often against expert opponents flying dissimilar (sometimes former Soviet) aircraft.[85] In contrast with pilot training from the 1950s and 1960s, the Red Flag exercises began to more effectively prepare USAF (and eventually USN and USMC) personnel for air superiority missions.

The USAF also began to reconsider precision. It had begun to use precision-guided munitions (PGMs) during the later stages of the Vietnam War, to good effect against North Vietnamese targets.[86] But the events of the 1973 Yom Kippur War sparked new thinking on the impact of PGMs. The effectiveness of such weapons made the conflict far more lethal than either side had expected. Attrition rates on both sides created serious questions about how armies and air forces would conduct conventional warfare in the future.[87] These developments fell into line with a body of theory in Soviet military circles about the emergence of the "reconnaissance strike complex." Soviet theorists suggested that future warfare would depend on a combination of long-range, precision munitions, advanced sensors and reconnaissance capabilities, and real-time command and control that could enable near-direct communication between reconnaissance and strike assets. The destruction (at least in terms of reducing the organizational capacity of an enemy force) would approach that previously estimated to require the use of tactical nuclear weapons.[88]

---

[82] Gross, *American Military Aviation*, 54.

[83] Harold R. Winton, "Partnership and Tension: The Army and Air Force between Vietnam and Desert Shield," *Parameters* (Spring 1996), 100–119, 100.

[84] Brian D. Laslie, *The Air Force Way of War: US Tactics and Training after Vietnam* (Lexington, KY, 2015).

[85] Steve Davies, *Red Eagles: America's Secret MiGs* (London, 2011).

[86] Anderegg, *Sierra Hotel*, 128.

[87] Abraham Rabinovich, *The Yom Kippur War: The Epic Encounter That Transformed the Middle East* (New York, 2007).

[88] Barry Watts, "The Evolution of Precision Strike," *Center for Strategic and Budgetary Assessments* 2 (2013), 5.

Neoclassical Airpower Theory

The post-Vietnam period witnessed the rise of neoclassical airpower theory, which repackaged traditional cultural elements in new ways. Neoclassical airpower theory recognized the myriad failures of the strategic campaigns in World War II and Vietnam, but still had faith in the idea that airpower could, with the appropriate technological foundation, provide independent, decisive effect. In lieu of a focus on macroeconomic or social theory, which (however clumsily) guided the thought of the interwar airpower theorists, the neoclassical school concentrated on organizational theory, and in particular on the problem of how to induce organizational failure.

As the focus of the air force became more tactical, theorists began to develop ways of linking tactical, operational, and strategic effect.[89] Col. John Boyd coined the term "OODA Loop," referring to a cyclical Observe-Orient-Decide-Act process of organizational activity. Precision weapons, utilizing real-time intelligence, could sufficiently disrupt this process so as to induce organizational paralysis.[90] Boyd argued that a full appreciation of the OODA Loop and the use of modern airpower technology could eliminate the need to disarm the enemy, at least in the traditional sense of the term.[91] Similarly, Col. John Warden contributed a deeply influential book, *The Air Campaign: Planning for Combat*, that sought to restore the centrality of airpower to the US defense establishment.[92] Warden rejected the idea of subordinating airpower to ground forces. Instead, he argued that direct attacks on enemy leadership could produce decisive outcomes.[93] Warden compared a target state to an organic system, arguing that by destroying the critical linkages in that system, airpower could shut down a government and its attendant military institutions.[94] He treated the target as consisting of five concentric "rings." The innermost ring included the command structure, the next key production capabilities, the third transport and logistical capability, the fourth the populations and its food sources, and the fifth the fielded military forces of the enemy.[95] Attacks on the outermost ring were the least efficient ways to win a war, with attacks on inner rings yielding progressively better results.[96] Warden was optimistic that intelligence, combined with social and economic analysis, would yield rich targeting data.

---

[89] John Andreas Olsen, *John Warden and the Renaissance of American Air Power* (Washington, DC, 2007), 103.

[90] Grant T. Hammond, *The Mind of War: John Boyd and American Security* (Washington, DC, 2001), Kindle, loc. 235.

[91] Ibid., loc. 2975.

[92] John A. Warden III, *The Air Campaign: Planning for Combat* (Washington, DC, 1988).

[93] Olsen, *John Warden and the Renaissance of American Air Power*, 66.

[94] Colonel John A. Warden III, "Employing Air Power in the Twenty-First Century," in Richard L. Shultz and Robert L. Pfaltzgraff Jr., eds. *Future of Air Power* (Washington, DC, 1992), 57–82, 64–66.

[95] Ibid., 65.   [96] Ibid.

The strategic implications of this framework were obvious: airpower could decisively win wars on its own. Warden's formulation of the potential for airpower helped reinvigorate the idea that airpower could have independent, decisive impact. Combined, Boyd and Warden's vision amounted to a reformulation of classical airpower theory, based on the idea of leveraging intelligence and precision for strategic effect. These concepts enabled air force theorists to envision decisive victory along lines analogous to the interwar theorists. Precision attacks, guided by real-time intelligence, would cause operational and strategic paralysis in an opposing force, and indeed in the target state. The destruction of communications would tear apart the sinews that enabled organizations to function. It would take time, however, for all of the pieces to come together.

The Gulf War

In contrast to how the Vietnam War produced difficult questions about how well the USAF's cultural assumptions could provide the foundations for organizational effectiveness, the Gulf War seemed to offer confirmation of the central tenets of neoclassical airpower theory, demonstrating the centrality of airpower to the future of military conflict.[97] Early planning for a campaign to evict the Iraqi Army from Kuwait evaluated a number of options, including an air-heavy campaign that would eschew extensive direct attacks on fielded Iraqi forces, and a more conventional combined arms campaign that would destroy Iraqi units occupying Kuwait. The former, formulated in large part by John Warden and David Deptula, posited that the large ground forces deployed in Operation Desert Shield and eventually for Operation Desert Storm were unnecessary to defeat Iraq.[98] Instead, an air campaign, focused on attacking the sinews of Saddam Hussein's government, would leave Iraqi Army forces intact, and enable them to take power from Hussein's Ba'ath Party.[99] In this formulation, the destruction of enemy ground forces was actively detrimental to the war effort.

However, the theater commander (Army Gen. H. Norman Schwarzkopf) decided upon an air campaign followed by a combined arms offensive, provided Iraq failed to evacuate Kuwait in a timely fashion. The air campaign began on January 16, 1991, and lasted for twenty-nine days. The Gulf War saw the first employment of the Joint Force Air Component Commander, a USAF officer with authority over the entirety of coalition airpower, tasked with organizing and executing the air component of the war.[100] American and coalition air forces

---

[97] Colin S. Gray, *Airpower for Strategic Effect* (Washington, DC, 2012), 212.
[98] Williamson Murray, "Part I: Operations," in Thomas A. Keaney and Eliot A. Cohen, eds., *Gulf War Air Power Survey, vol. 2* (Washington, DC, 1993), 25.
[99] Olsen, *John Warden and the Renaissance of American Air Power*, 150.
[100] Johnson, *Learning Large Lessons*, 35; Murray, "Operations," 39.

achieved air supremacy within the first few days of the conflict by destroying Iraqi air forces on the ground and in flight. In the ensuing bombing campaign, the USAF and its partners attacked a wide array of Iraqi targets along the front lines and in depth. The attacks, mostly carried out with non-precision "dumb" ordnance, caused heavy damage to Iraqi deployed forces, as well as to logistics, communications, and government infrastructure.[101] A ground offensive launched on February 17 overwhelmed remaining Iraqi forces, ejected them from Kuwait, and ended the war.

Airpower triumphalism initially carried the day.[102] Advocates claimed that airstrikes broke the back of Saddam Hussein's army, allowing coalition ground forces to defeat the rump Iraqi Army with very low casualties.[103] These advocates concentrated on the morale effects of bombing on Iraqi front-line troops, the destruction of Iraqi command and control networks, the interdiction of Iraqi logistics, and the attrition of Iraqi fielded forces. In effect, airpower advocates argued that the USAF in the Gulf War had decisive effect at the strategic level, even granting that the "strategic" attacks had failed to drive Saddam Hussein from power.[104]

Later assessments of battle damage raised questions about the decisiveness of the air campaign.[105] Despite the heavy damage inflicted on Iraqi forces, during the coalition ground offensive they maneuvered into blocking positions, retaining good order and staying in communication with Iraqi leadership. Although the USAF and its partners inflicted heavy damage on the Iraqi economy and on Iraqi government installations, the Iraqi regime did not collapse, and only temporarily lost control over certain portions of its territory. The USAF generally maintained good relations with the army, the navy, and coalition partners, but friction occasionally arose, especially in post-conflict assessments. Within the USAF, however, the campaign was generally seen as a vindication of the neoclassical airpower theory, at least in principle.[106]

---

[101] Barry Watts and Thomas A. Keaney, "Part II: Effects and Effectiveness," in Thomas A. Keaney and Eliot A. Cohen, eds., *Gulf War Air Power Survey, vol. 2* (Washington, DC, 1993).
[102] Edward Luttwak, "Airpower in US Military Strategy," in Richard H. Shultz Jr. and Robert L. Pfaltzgraff Jr., eds., *The Future of Airpower in the Aftermath of the Gulf War* (Washington, DC, 1992), 17–38, 20.
[103] Luttwak, "Airpower in US Military Strategy," 19.
[104] Ibid., 30; Watts and Keaney, "Effects and Effectiveness," 15.
[105] Daryl Press, "The Myth of Air Power in the Persian Gulf War and the Future of Warfare," *International Security* 26(2) (Fall 2001), 5–44, 7; Stephen Biddle, "Victory Misunderstood: What the Gulf War Tells Us about the Future of Conflict," *International Security* 21(2) (Fall 1996), 139–179, 148. For an alternative interpretation and criticism of Biddle, see Thomas G. Mahnken and Barry D. Watts, "What the Gulf War Can (and Cannot) Tell Us about the Future of Warfare," *International Security* 22(2) (Autumn 1997), 151–162.
[106] Colin S. Gray, *Airpower for Strategic Effect* (Maxwell, AL, 2012), 212.

Effects-Based Operations and the Wars on Terror

The air force made clear its interpretation of the implications of the Gulf War in *Global Reach-Global Power*, a white paper arguing that the USAF could uniquely provide for the global projection of American power.[107] However, some within the air force remained less than satisfied with the success of the Gulf War and the later Kosovo campaign, in which US-led airpower helped coerce the Serbian government into relinquishing its rogue province.[108] In the wake of Kosovo, a body of thought emerged that came to embrace "effects based operations" (EBO).[109] Advocates of EBO argued for PGM attacks throughout the depth of enemy formations. Attacks on enemy front lines, reinforcements, and logistics would become part of the same operation, with the objective to paralyze the enemy military organization and prevent it from conducting its own operations. A radical increase in information-processing and communications technology, combined with the expansion of intelligence collection and aggregation capabilities into the upper atmosphere, would render the battle space more intelligible (and more plastic) than ever before, making the identification of critical targets possible.[110]

Hints of the ability of modern airpower to collaborate effectively with small-scale, "proxy" ground forces emerged during the Kosovo War, when KLA attacks enhanced the effectiveness of NATO airstrikes against the Serbian Army.[111] The collaborative concept came to maturity as the "Afghan Model," a form of ground-air cooperation developed in the early stages of Operation Enduring Freedom. The Afghan Model involves the combination of special forces, allied proxy fighting forces, and precision airpower to defeat the fielded forces of an enemy state.[112] Proxies screen the special operators from attack, fix enemy positions, and exploit tactical attacks by seizing ground. Special operators identify targets and coordinate precision strikes to support ground assaults. Precision attacks from aircraft and naval vessels either destroy enemy targets or sufficiently suppress them to allow proxy forces to overrun their positions. Modern communications and reconnaissance technology, supported by space-based assets, enable close collaboration between forces. When successful, the

---

[107] Olsen, *John Warden and the Renaissance of American Air Power*, 135.

[108] Andrew L. Stigler, "A Clear Victory for Air Power: NATO's Empty Threat to Invade Kosovo," *International Security* 27(3) (Winter 2002–2003), 124–157, 125; Benjamin Lambeth, *NATO's Air War for Kosovo: A Strategic and Operational Assessment* (Santa Monica, CA, 2001), 219.

[109] Paul K. Davis, *Effects-Based Operations: A Grand Challenge for the Analytical Community* (Santa Monica, CA, 2001), 3.

[110] Watts, "The Evolution of Precision Strike," 8.

[111] Ivo Daalder and Michael O'Hanlon, *Winning Ugly: NATO's War to Save Kosovo* (Washington, DC, 2000), 150–151.

[112] Stephen Biddle, "Allies, Airpower, and Modern Warfare: The Afghan Model in Afghanistan and Iraq," *International Security* 30(3), 161–176, 161–163.

model allows for the toppling of a government with minimal commitment of US or allied ground forces.

While the neoclassical vision of strategic airpower involved inducing a regime to concede or collapse by attacking "strategic" targets such as communication nodes, command complexes, and leadership concentrations, the Afghan Model focuses on the destruction and disruption of enemy forces in the field. The distinction between the Afghan Model and the more traditional understanding of decisive strategic airpower is subtle, but important. As conceived by classical and neoclassical theorists, airpower has decisive strategic effect because of its ability to defeat an enemy without the need to defeat fielded enemy forces. In other words, the enemy can be defeated without being disarmed. The Afghan Model rejects this, instead accepting the need for disarming the enemy (although this may not always mean the complete destruction of fielded forces). However, the Afghan Model is as much a political as a military concept, as it minimizes domestic opposition in the intervening country, nationalist reaction in the target country, and international disapproval.[113]

Conclusion

This chapter has treated organizational culture in constitutive fashion as an active, intentional means of managing reality, and also as an impersonal structure that enabled and limited particular choices. The pre-founders and founders of the USAF created a set of institutions with cultural precepts designed to win the wars that the United States would choose to fight, and to produce a military organization capable of managing American airpower independent from the existing military services. These founders did not view these two goals as contradictory, and indeed believed them to be necessary to one another.

These efforts boiled down to a fundamental belief: technology would enable aircraft to destroy targets that would force the enemy to end its armed struggle and concede America's political objectives. This depended on a further belief: that the enemy's economic, social, and political structures would be sufficiently transparent to enable the accurate targeting of specific critical sinews, the destruction of which would force (or at least incline) the opponent to sue for peace. This resulted in an organizational culture heavily focused on values of technological supremacy, precision, and transparency, all in the service of achieving independent, decisive victories.

---

[113] Chris Rawley, "Libya Lessons: Supremacy of the SOF-Airpower Team . . . Or Why Do We Still Need a Huge Army?" *Information Dissemination*, September 15, 2011, www.informationdis semination.net/2011/08/libya-lessons-supremacy-of-sof-airpower.html.

The air force retained a close relationship with mathematicians and game theorists developing nuclear weapons employment strategy.[114] One commentator notes that "American airmen have tended to be overzealous in their enthusiasm for pat formulas and engineering-type calculations seems hard to deny." He adds that these tendencies persist across generations, and that this represents a "bedrock error" in American airpower doctrine.[115] There is no question that neoclassical airpower theory prominently reproduced the traditional USAF focus on precision and transparency.

These ideas provided clear, long-term guidance for the air force as an organization, in both its history and its prehistory. Faith in strategic bombing provided clarity regarding procurement and innovation in the interwar and immediate postwar periods. A belief in the efficacy of technology helped to create productive ties with industry, allowing long-term innovation in airframes, weapons, and communications equipment. A recommitment to precision was finally realized in the advent of the precision-guided munitions of the 1970s and 1980s, which have legitimately revolutionized many aspects of modern warfare.

Finally, the overwhelming commitment to autonomy helped the organization develop a strategy for pursuing resources from the US government and for managing relations with the other two services. It provided a ready-made logic for fights over appropriations, strategic orientation, and prominence in foreign policy problem-solving. The appeal of decisive effect, combined with precision (offering the appearance of minimal cost) and technological impressiveness, made the use of the air force, often detached from the other two services, particularly appealing to civilian officials. In short, these cultural elements have enabled considerable political effectiveness on the part of the air force, while causing difficulties at the strategic, operational, and tactical levels.

Advocates of the "air force way of war" can reasonably argue that the long-term cultural foundation of the USAF will prove ever more productive as technology catches up with the visions of airpower established by the early theorists. Critics, on the other hand, may insist that technological dynamism is more complex than simply increasing the ability to hit targets with precision, and that in any case the social landscape of war is vastly more complicated than airpower theorists allow, making successful coercion a tricky business.

Despite its long pedigree, the culture of the air force may yet change in response to generational shifts and outside stimuli. Changes in communications technology have already altered one of the USAF's long-term cultural norms, the primacy of the officer-pilot, by allowing operators to conduct attacks from

[114] Lynn Eden, *Whole World on Fire: Organizations, Knowledge, and Nuclear Weapons Devastation* (Ithaca, NY, 2004), 74–75.
[115] Barry D. Watts, *The Foundations of U.S. Air Doctrine: The Problem of Friction in War* (Maxwell, AL, 1984), 106–107, 110.

remote locations using unmanned aerial vehicles. Moreover, the generational shift that put the "fighter generals" in charge of the organization has already changed.[116] Finally, the nature of the wars in the post-9/11 period has only occasionally allowed the air force to pursue its autonomy freely, and in fact has produced new avenues of collaboration with the other services, especially in the employment of special operations forces.

[116] Bruce Danskine, *Fall of the Fighter Generals: The Future of USAF Leadership* (Maxwell, AL, 2001).

Conclusion

Peter R. Mansoor and Williamson Murray

As the foregoing examinations of various armies, navies, and air forces have illustrated, culture is a key determinant in organizational effectiveness and plays an enormous role in the birth, life, and death of military organizations. Yet ironically, given its outsized importance to the success of militaries, the impact of their organizational culture often remains hidden from those most affected by it. Cultural biases often result in unstated assumptions that have a deep impact on the making of strategy, operational planning, doctrinal creation, and the organization and training of armed forces. For good or for ill, culture also forms the lens through which civilian and military policy makers view national security and consider the utility of force in achieving strategic goals. To make matters even more difficult to comprehend, the impact of culture on military affairs often remains opaque for years, if not decades, after the events it has affected.

Importance of Leadership in Establishing Organizational Culture

As with most human endeavors, leadership is essential to creating and maintaining organizational culture. Few leaders ever get the opportunity to shape an organization's culture from its inception, but those who do often have an outsized influence on its future orientation. As Gil-li Vardi notes in Chapter 11, Israeli military leaders consciously infused a spirit of offensive mindedness (as well as a somewhat less-consciously infused spirit of "cultivated disobedience") in the Israeli Defense Force (IDF) from the beginning of the state, which became the foundation of its culture until at least the 1982 Lebanon War, if not longer. This culture enabled the IDF to achieve significant tactical and operational victories against less competent opponents, but created difficulties for Israeli forces when they ran into better-prepared opposition, as happened in the 1973 Yom Kippur War, or into hybrid opponents that fused conventional and irregular military capabilities, as was the case in Lebanon. Leaders, therefore, must be discriminating when establishing the initial culture of an organization, for once embedded, that culture will prove extraordinarily difficult to change.

War magnifies the importance of leadership in establishing organizational culture. Examples from the US Civil War bear out this assertion. As Mark Grimsley discusses in Chapter 4, Robert E. Lee assumed command of the Confederate Army near Richmond during the fighting on the Peninsula in spring 1862, and in a period of just four months instilled in it his ethos of aggressive risk-taking. By the end of the Battle of Second Manassas (Second Bull Run, August 28–30, 1862), Lee had shaped the newly christened Army of Northern Virginia according to his vision and molded it into "the beating heart of the Confederacy." The various commanders of the Union Army of the Potomac, but principally Maj. Gen. George B. McClellan, also succeeded in creating an organizational culture in that army, but one that, in the words of Wayne Hsieh, was "sluggish, passive, and incapable of the aggressive decisiveness needed for success in offensive military operations."[1] While the rank and file of the Army of the Potomac were brave and skilled enough, their commanders all too often took counsel of their fears, resulting in battlefield defeats or the inability to follow up on fleeting opportunities when presented. Indeed, the difficulty historians confront in understanding the very different performances of US Civil War armies lies in the failure to recognize that each one of the major armies (the Army of Northern Virginia, the Army of the Potomac, the Army of the Tennessee, the Confederate Army of the Tennessee, and the Army of the Cumberland) developed quite different cultures of leadership, which affected their performance on the battlefield.

One Union commander who refused to take counsel of his fears was Ulysses S. Grant, founder of the Army of the Tennessee. After his first "encounter" with Confederate forces, in which Grant led the 21st Illinois Regiment against a small Confederate force located on the Salt River south of Palmyra, Missouri, Grant confessed his pre-battle jitters. But finding the enemy encampment abandoned, Grant reassessed the situation. "It occurred to me at once that Harris [the Confederate commander] had been as much afraid of me as I had been of him. This was a view of the question I had never taken before; but it was one I never forgot afterwards."[2] Indeed, from his first combat at Belmont, Missouri, on November 7, 1861, to the final surrender of Lee's Army of Northern Virginia at Appomattox Court House on April 9, 1865, Grant took the initiative and pressed the offensive – and mandated his commanders do the same if they wanted to retain their commands. Grant's seizure of Forts Henry and Donelson in February 1862, perhaps the most important strategic development in the first year of the US Civil War, instilled in his army a culture of aggressive movement and determination to succeed that was all too often absent in other armies. Even the near disaster at Shiloh furthered this war-

---

[1] Chapter 3, p. 55.
[2] Ulysses S. Grant, *Personal Memoirs* (1885; reprint, New York, 1982), 127.

fighting culture. After Union troops barely repulsed the initial Confederate attack on April 6, 1862, Maj. Gen. William T. Sherman found Grant in the darkness after midnight, sheltering himself under a tree from the drenching rain, a cigar clenched in his teeth. "'Well, Grant," said Sherman, "we've had the devil's own day, haven't we?" Grant's reply gave no credit to the enemy, but instead looked forward: "Yes, lick 'em tomorrow, though."[3] The message was clear and it resonated throughout the ranks; part of the culture of the Army of the Tennessee was one of unbounded confidence in its abilities, despite the odds.

Lee and Grant were outliers in quickly changing the culture of the armies they commanded. There are a few reasons for this: the urgency of war, their ability to select the leaders who would serve under them, and the malleable nature of the armies they commanded. Of these factors, the temporary nature of these organizations in the first months of the US Civil War is the most important. The armies Lee and Grant commanded were only recently established; their previous commanders were unwilling or unable to inculcate culture within them. What culture existed, therefore, was more easily altered by strong leadership. Lee and Grant changed the culture of the Army of Northern Virginia and the Army of the Tennessee in months rather than years, but this is clearly an exception to the norm that organizational culture changes slowly. The inability of Field Marshal Bernard L. Montgomery to change the culture of the British Eighth Army illustrates how even first-rate military leaders find it difficult to alter an organizational culture that has become deeply embedded. Leadership is crucial to instilling organizational culture, but there are clearly limits on what even superb military leaders can accomplish in this regard.

World War II has its share of examples of commanders instilling in their forces a culture that creates the soul of an organization. Field Marshal William Slim turned defeat into victory by reshaping the culture of the British Fourteenth Army in the Burma campaign. Between a devastating defeat in 1942 and a crushing victory in 1945 over the same opponent, Slim retrained his defeated forces and taught them to lose their fear of both the Japanese and the jungle. Like soldiers and officers in Grant's Army of the Tennessee, confidence in their abilities became the hallmark of Slim's troops, aided greatly by his outstanding battlefield leadership.[4] Likewise, Lucian Truscott molded the US

---

[3] Bruce Catton, *Grant Moves South* (New York, 1960), 141. When Gen. David Petraeus took command of Multi-National Force–Iraq during the surge of US forces in 2007, he used "lick 'em tomorrow" as his rallying cry. One of the coeditors, serving as Gen. Petraeus's executive officer at the time, witnessed the power of those words to inspire the troops.

[4] William Slim, *Defeat into Victory: Battling Japan in Burma and India, 1942–1945* (London, 1956); Daniel P. Marston, *Phoenix from the Ashes: The Indian Army in the Burma Campaign* (Santa Barbara, CA, 2003); George MacDonald Fraser, *Quartered Safe Out Here: A Recollection of the War in Burma* (Pleasantville, NY, 2001).

3rd Infantry Division from a subpar organization to one of the elite units in the
Army of the United States by instilling in it a culture of excellence, demanding
that his soldiers live up to the marching standards of their US Civil War
forbearers, and creating the most devastating fire support system in World
War II. The "Truscott Trot," a marching rate of four miles per hour, proved
its worth in the Sicily campaign, while Truscott's fire support system saved the
Anzio beachhead from disaster in the winter of 1944.[5] Truscott put a great deal
of effort into enhancing the confidence of his infantrymen, which boosted the
culture of excellence in the "Rock of the Marne" division. In time, one of his
suggestions, the creation of a distinctive insignia for combat infantrymen,
would become the much-coveted Combat Infantry Badge.[6]

These examples aside, even superb leaders are limited in what they can do to
change deep-seated organizational culture. As Williamson Murray notes in
Chapter 8, Field Marshal Bernard L. Montgomery could not change the culture
in the British Eighth Army in the two months between his assumption of
command and the Battle of El Alamein in October 1942. Nor could he do
much to create a culture of combined-arms harmony in the British forces in the
home islands prior to the June 1944 invasion of Normandy. As a result,
Montgomery relied on much more centrally planned and tightly controlled
battles, substituting prodigious amounts of resources and firepower for tactical
agility and effective use of combined-arms tactics, which his forces in most
cases lacked. The regimental culture of the British Army prized in-group
collectivism above all else; overcoming this deep-seated mind-set would take
more time than Montgomery had at his disposal.[7]

Perpetuating Organizational Culture

Selection of the right subordinate leaders is critical if an organization's culture
is to survive a leadership transition. Robert E. Lee and Ulysses S. Grant, while
working within the limitations of their respective political systems, both
selected key subordinates carefully. Although the Army of Northern Virginia
never underwent a change in senior leaders after Lee took command, the Army
of the Tennessee did. Despite several changes in command, the army the culture
of which Grant had fashioned remained a confident, aggressive military instrument in large part because Grant had chosen his successors wisely.

As Jorit Wintjes points out in Chapter 5, after World War I, the Reichswehr
leaders chose their officers carefully, leaning heavily on those who wore the red

[5] Lucian Truscott, *Command Missions: A Personal Story* (New York, 1954); Peter R. Mansoor,
The GI Offensive in Europe: The Triumph of American Infantry Divisions, 1941–1945
(Lawrence, KS, 1999), 103–104, 123–124.
[6] Mansoor, *The GI Offensive in Europe*, 116.
[7] See the GLOBE Dimensions of Military Organizational Culture in the Introduction.

stripe of the General Staff, along with proven battlefield commanders who also possessed great intellect – men such as future Field Marshal Erwin Rommel. This preserved the "Prussian" character of the army, for a time at least. But the massive expansion of the Wehrmacht from 1934 onward resulted in the induction of large numbers of officers imbued in larger German society and culture. For better or worse, by 1945, the Wehrmacht had become, in the words of historian Omer Bartov, "Hitler's Army."[8]

The US "nuclear" navy, as John Kuehn discusses in Chapter 15, retained a singular culture in large measure because it remained in the iron grip of one man, Adm. Hyman Rickover, for more than four decades. Rickover was idiosyncratic to say the least; he personally interviewed every officer who wished to enter the navy's nuclear program. Although these interviews were often strange affairs, they ensured that entrants embraced the culture that Rickover had created and maintained – which still exists today.[9] The experience of the nuclear navy under Rickover's control also carries within it a warning: the amount of control exerted by one person can be a dangerous thing depending on his or her character and competence. As Kuehn notes, Rickover's influence was largely for the better, but one wonders if the US Navy would have obtained a similar outcome through a succession of hand-picked leaders without giving so much power to a single individual.

Two other points on the perpetuation of organizational culture are worth mentioning. First, as Kevin Woods points out in Chapter 12 in the case of the Iraqi armed forces, "professional" military culture is difficult to sustain if political leaders are more interested in preventing the use of the military to launch a coup. This "coup-proofing" of armed forces creates brittle organizations under the control of regime loyalists, whose interests rarely include the creation of an organizational culture that would promote military effectiveness. For with military excellence comes power, and power in the wrong hands represents a threat to the regime. Only when faced with an existential crisis during the Iran-Iraq War was Saddam Hussein willing to allow his commanders the leeway to create effective forces, but this golden moment for the Iraqi military did not outlast defeat in the 1991 Gulf War.

The collapse of the new Iraqi Army in 2014 in Mosul when confronted by a few thousand fighters of the Islamic State of Iraq and al-Sham (ISIS) shows

[8] Omer Bartov, *Hitler's Army: Soldiers, Nazis, and War in the Third Reich* (New York, 1992).
[9] As an exchange cadet at the US Naval Academy in 1980, one of the coeditors roomed with two midshipmen who were studying nuclear engineering with the goal of joining the nuclear navy. They relayed to him a story, almost certainly apocryphal, about one such interview. The candidate was nervous and faring poorly. To shake him up, Rickover demanded that the candidate do something within thirty seconds to make him angry. The candidate picked up a large paperweight off of Rickover's desk and smashed to bits a large glass display case in his office. The admiral was indeed extremely upset; the candidate was also accepted into the nuclear navy.

the same dynamic in action. Iraqi Prime Minister Nouri al-Maliki, who spent most of his adult life examining Saddam's regime from exile, eviscerated the capabilities of his well-trained army after the withdrawal of US forces and advisors from Iraq at the end of 2011. In an attempt to ensure the army's loyalty, Maliki stripped it of its most competent leaders, putting in charge politically reliable officers who did little to ensure the training and combat effectiveness of their units. Maliki reaped what he sowed; the army was never a threat to his power. Regrettably for him, ISIS was.[10]

Continuity and Change

Military organizations have good reasons for their conservative natures. Changing proven war-fighting methods and reliable technology is risky business, in a business where failure can have catastrophic consequences – not just profit and loss, but death and destruction. Even when militaries are willing to experiment, as the British Army did with armored warfare on Salisbury Plain in 1927, their cultural biases often prevent wholesale changes to methods, organization, and equipment. Gil-li Vardi's assessment of cultural evolution illustrates the tension between continuity and change in military organizational culture:

> Cultural evolution, in other words, is a slow and cumulative process, whereby habits gradually and organically transform. This is partly why revolutions in military affairs are so hard to achieve and implement; tradition is a powerful force that resists even the strongest pressures of renewal and innovation. Military organizations are particularly slow to evolve culturally. For organizations involved in armed conflicts, radical change is potentially dangerous and always costly. We therefore assume that, with the exception of revolutionary circumstances or other unusual pressures such as political revolution, acute economic crisis, or colossal defeat in conflict, organizational culture is a resilient and even sluggish creature, which operates on cumulative knowledge organically embedded into a coherent, powerful, and highly restrictive mind-set.[11]

Militaries that have innovative, risk-taking cultures are therefore rare (albeit not unknown, as several examples from this volume illustrate), which makes rapid change difficult even when faced with the audit of combat. But organizations must change, or they will die; probably not in peacetime, when the penalties for failure to innovate are absent, but most certainly in war, when faced with existential crises. The Prussian Army lived off the reputation it had gained under the leadership of Frederick the Great until it was smashed at Jena-Auerstädt by Napoleon's Grande Armée; only then did reformers such as

---

[10] Peter R. Mansoor, *Surge: My Journey with General David Petraeus and the Remaking of the Iraq War* (New Haven, CT, 2013), Afterword.

[11] Gil-li Vardi, Chapter 11, this volume, p. 247–248.

Gerhard von Scharnhorst and August Neidhardt von Gneisenau succeed in changing the underlying culture from that of a long-serving professional force to a national army based on universal military service. The French Army in 1940 was less fortunate. Dismembered by the Wehrmacht in just six weeks, the old army's culture and reliance on top-down, centralized methodical battle died with it.[12]

Much of the existence of military organizations entails training and garrison activities as they prepare for war. In these sometimes long hiatuses between combat operations, cultural change is slow and gradual. Absent the harsh arbitration of combat, culture can become an insidious drain on readiness, especially if the officer corps focuses more on the perquisites of office than on the ultimate reason for its existence. One of the best examples in this regard is the Italian officer corps in the interwar period, which focused on just about anything other than war fighting. General Ubaldo Soddu, who would go on to command Italian forces (disastrously) in the war with Greece, summed up its attitude: "when you have a fine plate of *pasta* guaranteed for life, and a little music, you don't need anything more."[13]

Indeed, senior Italian officers were unworried about readying their forces for war, despite the manifest changes taking place in the military landscape in Europe in the 1930s. In a final meeting before his nation's entry into World War II, Italian chief of staff Marshal Rodolfo Graziani declared, "When the cannon sounds, everything will fall into place automatically."[14] Of course everything would not. As a result of this nonchalance, when Italian dictator Benito Mussolini took his nation into war with Greece in October 1940, Italian forces met with disaster. The commander of Italian forces in Albania and Greece, the aforementioned Soddu, lived up to his philosophy and spent his evenings composing film scores (presumably while enjoying a fine plate of pasta) as his forces suffered and nearly collapsed at the front. For his part Graziani, sent by Mussolini to take command of Italian forces in Libya and ordered to attack British forces in Egypt, absolved himself of responsibility in his diary. "And thus is accomplished what may well be recorded as a crime of historic proportions – against the commission of which I have fought with all my strength as long as I have been able ... For whatever evil may occur, I, before God and my soldiers, am not *responsible*."[15] The statement was a damning indictment of Italian military culture.

[12] For the best examination of French culture and military doctrine in the interwar period that led to disaster in 1940, see Robert Doughty, *Seeds of Disaster: The Development of French Army Doctrine, 1919–1939* (Hamden, CT, 1986).
[13] MacGregor Knox, *Mussolini Unleashed, 1939–1941: Politics and Strategy in Fascist Italy's Last War* (London, 1982), 57.
[14] Ibid., 121.   [15] Ibid., 163.

Yet some military organizations do change, assisted by cultures that embrace innovation and a reasonable degree of risk-taking. Aside from Stalin's purges (and granted that is a very large aside), the Red Army successfully innovated during the interwar period and again after its near defeat in 1941. The Reichswehr (aided by the Red Army) experimented with mobile, combined-arms warfare and set the stage for the combined-arms warfare revolution in military affairs that would lead Germany to victory over Poland, the Low Countries, and France in 1939 and 1940.[16] The US Navy and Marine Corps in the interwar period developed doctrine, equipment, and procedures for carrier and amphibious warfare, assisted by organizational cultures that valued professional military education and rigorous (and honest) experimentation with the limited available equipment and manpower.[17] As Allan Millett notes in Chapter 16, these same challenges of updating or adapting organizational culture continue to exist today, even as technological transformation accelerates.

Military Culture Is a Reflection of Societal Culture

It is a truism that militaries reflect the culture of the societies that create them. The warriors who manned Greek phalanxes and Roman legions reflected the martial character of their city-states. French infantry serving under the Republic and Napoleon found themselves inspired by very different motivations than the so-called scum of the earth serving under Wellington.[18] The Prussian and German officer corps came to reflect – and further – the militarism in German society as a whole.[19] The American officer corps reflects the democratic nature of American society.

Culture in newly established organizations is established by leaders, either deliberately (as in the case of the IDF) or more slowly through organic transformation (as in the Iraqi Army). But even newly established organizations must draw their culture from that of the wider society from which the military force originates. The IDF culture established between 1949 and 1952, for instance, would have failed in the Iraqi Army of 1980, 1991, or 2003 – or 2017 for that matter.

---

[16] MacGregor Knox and Williamson Murray, *The Dynamics of Military Revolution, 1300–2050* (Cambridge, 2001), chapter 9.

[17] Williamson Murray, "Transformation and Innovation: The Lessons of the 1920s and 1930s," Institute for Defense Analyses Paper P-3799, December 2002, www.dtic.mil/get-tr-doc/pdf?AD=ADA423507, 7–11, 14–16.

[18] For an analysis of British soldiers in the Napoleonic Wars, see Edward J. Coss, *All for the King's Shilling: The British Soldier under Wellington, 1808–1814* (Norman, OK, 2010), chapter 1.

[19] For a full accounting, see Gordon A. Craig, *The Politics of the Prussian Army, 1640–1945* (Oxford, 1955).

But when the military becomes a caste apart, believing itself to be superior to the wider society from which it emanates, the result could be military control of government or a degradation of the ethical foundations of the service. The Imperial German Army essentially ran the German government once Hindenburg and Ludendorff took charge of Germany's war effort in August 1916. They brought with them into office the German military culture of operationally focused decision-making, and ran the country into the ground. For instance, their curtailment of fertilizer manufacture in favor of increased munitions production resulted in massive malnourishment and starvation among the German people – one of the reasons for the popular revolt in 1918 that ended the kaiser's reign.[20] As David Hunter-Chester examines in Chapter 9, the Imperial Japanese Army was if anything even more shortsighted than the Germans, with relatively junior officers assassinating government officials who did not bend to their will and eventually dragging Japan into a war with China on the Asian mainland that it could not win.

Military Subcultures

Organizations often have subcultures with significant influence on the larger organization. Various German states, such as Bavaria, had a degree of influence on German military culture, however minor. As Allan Millett discusses in Chapter 16, even US military services such as the US Marine Corps have a number of "tribes," each with its own idiosyncrasies and subcultures. As Richard Sinnreich notes in Chapter 7, regimental soldiering can create a culture of its own, somewhat distinct from and at the same time part of the societal and military culture at large. The Victorian British Army was in essence a collection of regiments, each influenced by Victorian culture at large but with its own eccentricities. This amalgamation of subcultures works in imperial policing, but runs into difficulties when a military faces off against a near-peer competitor. Mobile, combined-arms warfare requires one culture, with all arms working together in harmony.

Culture and Strategy

An unchecked military culture can sometimes override governmental policy and strategy, creating a civil-military problem with significant consequences. This was the case with the Imperial Japanese Army in the interwar period and to a lesser extent with the IDF from 1948 to 1982. Both organizations wanted

[20] Jay Winter, "Some Paradoxes of the First World War," in Richard Wall and Jay Winter, eds., *The Upheaval of War: Family, Work and Welfare in Europe, 1914–1918* (Cambridge, 1988), 9–42, 39–40.

freedom from governmental constraints in what they viewed as operational matters. But as Prussian military philosopher Carl von Clausewitz cautioned, one cannot divorce military operations from the political contexts from which they arise.

Ironically, the Germany military set the gold standard in ignoring Clausewitz's dictum. German military culture had its roots in Prussian military thinking since the middle of the eighteenth century. Small, resource poor, and geographically positioned in the midst of more powerful neighbors, Prussian monarchs such as Frederick the Great relied on a relatively large, thoroughly trained, and militarily capable standing army to win quick, decisive victories over their opponents in order to forestall lengthy conflicts against superior adversaries.[21] This concept had a mixed record at best. Early victories in the Seven Years' War (1756–1763) did not prevent Prussia from nearly being overrun by a coalition of powerful adversaries. Napoleon's Grande Armée crushed Prussian forces at the battles of Jena-Auerstädt in 1806, leading to total defeat. On the other hand, Prussian victories at the Battle of Koniggratz in 1866 and at Sedan in 1870 led to triumph over the Austro-Hungarian Empire and France. A similar operational gamble by German military leaders in 1914, however, led to four years of costly war and ultimate defeat against a superior coalition of great powers. The Schlieffen Plan was an attempt to solve by brilliant maneuver the problem of a two-front war that had been created by poor policy and inappropriate grand strategy.

If this were the major strategic lesson that emerged from the ashes of World War I, it was lost on German military leaders. German military officers, steeped in Prussian and German military culture, went to great lengths to learn the tactical and operational lessons of World War I, which led to significant innovations in combined-arms warfare that resulted in victories over Poland, the Low Countries, and France in 1939 and 1940. But in failing to address more significant strategic issues, German leaders in World War II, admittedly with Hitler's strategic support, repeated every strategic mistake made by their imperial predecessors two decades earlier, resulting in a catastrophic war and the total destruction of the Third Reich.

The challenge of matching military strategy and organizational culture extends to the armed forces of democratic states as well. French and US military leaders emerged from World War II with armed forces and doctrinal concepts attuned to large conventional wars. Furthermore, the shuttering of professional military educational venues in both countries during the war years and the promotion of a generation of "muddy boots" soldiers resulted in a changing culture that produced a paucity of intellectual understanding of

---

[21] Robert Citino, *The German Way of War: From the Thirty Years' War to the Third Reich* (Lawrence, KS, 2005).

warfare and a lack of creativity in adapting doctrine and force structures to the conflicts faced by France and the United States in the post–World War II era. In Vietnam, the French and US armies failed to adapt quickly enough to succeed in the counterinsurgency conflicts in which they found themselves mired. After the US withdrawal from Vietnam in 1973, the US Army refocused its efforts on fighting and winning a conventional war in Europe against the Red Army. While arguably this was the most dangerous threat that had to be confronted during the final stages of the Cold War, it was not the most likely. Lack of preparation for "small wars" would continue to haunt US military leaders even after the Cold War had ended.

The impact of US military culture as it evolved after Vietnam was fully felt in the first years of the Iraq War. The US Army entered the war with a culture rooted in the belief that a revolution in military affairs based on precision guided munitions coupled with high-tech intelligence, surveillance, and reconnaissance systems had fundamentally changed the character of warfare in the post–Cold War period. Although this understanding of warfare might have been applicable in a conflict against a mirror-imaged enemy, it was thin gruel for the type of hybrid insurgency that soon developed in Iraq after the collapse of Saddam Hussein's regime in the spring of 2003. American leaders, steeped in a culture that privileged major combat operations and offensive warfare over more esoteric doctrinal subjects such as counterinsurgency warfare, struggled for several years to adapt to the war with which they were confronted. The army and the Marine Corps adapted to an extent during the surge of forces to Iraq in 2007 and 2008, but by then major strategic damage had already been done. The United States continues to live with the consequences today.

Culture in Technologically Focused Organizations

Technology-centric forces must take care not to allow a culture focused on technological excellence to turn into one centered on technological determinism. Air forces and navies especially rely on war-fighting platforms (fighters, bombers, aircraft carriers, surface ships, submarines, etc.) to accomplish their missions. But organizations that ignore the past, as the Royal Air Force did with respect to the lessons of strategic bombing in World War I, must regrettably learn in future conflict by expending blood and treasure while the enemy completes their education.

Air power enthusiasts decided to ignore the lessons of World War I in preparing for the next conflict; they consciously dismissed recent history as irrelevant. The airplane was a new technology and therefore history did not matter. Mostly as an institutional basis from which to justify their independence and partly because they really believed it, proponents of air power championed the idea of a bomber offensive that would leap over the stalemated carnage of the trenches, carry destruction directly to the enemy's homeland, and achieve victory without the messy carnage of trench warfare. Bombers would not even need fighters to accompany them to their targets; they would either escape detection or could defend themselves against enemy fighters rising to meet them.

Of course bomber proponents overlooked a number of factors that were apparent from the experience of World War I. They ignored the need for air superiority and disregarded the difficulty involved in getting bombers to their targets and then hitting those targets once located. Furthermore, civilian populations turned out to be less fragile than air power theorists believed. The level of destruction required to force a determined enemy to sue for peace was enormous, and the capabilities to inflict such damage simply did not exist when World War II began. As Williamson Murray notes, "Those military institutions in the 1920s and 1930s that attempted to leap into the future without reference to what had happened in the past ended up making mistakes that killed thousands of young men to no purpose. The succession of new gadgets notwithstanding, successful innovation in the past worked when it was tied in to a realistic appreciation of what was humanly possible."[22]

But there is some hope in the historical record as well. As Corbin Williamson explores in Chapter 14, the history of the Royal Navy between the world wars shows that a firm grip on history can assist military organizations in creating cultures that can explore the future and all its technological possibilities without jettisoning the hard-won lessons of the past.

The Criticality of Professional Military Education

Professional military education is critical in sustaining organizational culture. In the interwar period between World War I and World War II, the US Navy and Marine Corps possessed organizational cultures that encouraged forward thinking about warfare and rewarded those officers with the intellectual capacity to understand how to integrate improved technologies with new doctrine to create effective war-fighting organizations. This intellectual blossoming led to the development of effective strategies and the operational concepts required to implement them. Conceptual thinkers came to a deeper understanding of the nature of warfare in maritime theaters, including the importance of seaborne logistics over the vast expanses of the Pacific Ocean. Out of this thinking came the concepts of carrier battle groups and amphibious warfare, war-fighting concepts that either did not exist or were deemed as unworkable only twenty years earlier.

---

[22] Williamson Murray, "Clausewitz Out, Computer In: Military Culture and Technological Hubris," *National Interest* 48 (June 1, 1997), 57–64.

Furthermore, the navy and Marine Corps created opportunities for advancement in these new fields. US Navy policy mandated that only trained aviators could command aircraft carriers and naval air stations; thus, large numbers of naval officers sought flight training to maximize their chances for command. This policy meant that US naval officers had a thorough understanding of naval aviation even before the Japanese attack on December 7, 1941, sent most of the Pacific Fleet's battleships to the bottom of their anchorage at Pearl Harbor. Likewise, the creation of the Fleet Marine Force gave substance to Marine Corps thinking on amphibious warfare and command opportunities for officers intent on institutionalizing it. Navy and Marine officers were culturally attuned to the future of war fighting because service policies encouraged them along the way.

The Danger of Disconnect

For the US military today, one of the great dangers is the increasing self-selection of service personnel for entry into the armed forces and the distancing of US military culture from wider society.[23] Like the Victorian British Army, the US military today is becoming more physically and psychologically remote. Recruited and officered from a narrow and increasingly unrepresentative societal base, military service has become alien to most Americans, who are happy to tie yellow ribbons on their trees provided their sons and daughters are not sent into harm's way in messy wars in the Middle East and South Asia.

Self-selection and family history are producing provincialism among America's defenders. Maj. Gen. Jeffrey Snow, head of US Army Recruiting Command, writes:

> On top of the fact that only 29 percent of youth meet the qualifications for service, we are battling mounting misperceptions about service because of the extreme disconnect between the military and the American public. We are seeing that today's youth do not understand what service entails much less what leadership and educational benefits it provides. Unfortunately, they know only what they see on television, and they think life in the military will doom them to being mentally and physically broken, homeless, and unemployed.[24]

Citing surveys suggesting that as many as 80 percent of those who serve come from families with parents or siblings in uniform, a 2015 *Los Angeles Times* investigation reported that "Multigenerational military families ... form the heart of the all-volunteer Army, which increasingly is drawing its ranks from

---

[23] Richard Sinnreich provided the inspiration and much of the content for this section.

[24] Maj. Gen. Jeffrey Snow, "Army Recruiting Needs Your Support," *Army Echoes* (October 2017–January 2018), 6.

the relatively small pool of Americans with historic family, cultural or geo-graphic connections to military service."[25]

The American people hold their military in high regard, but this should not be reason for complacency. The fact is that American military culture is becoming a culture apart, with little sense of common values or shared sacrifice with the country at large. As James Fallows wrote not long ago about Americans' ambivalence toward those in uniform, "This reverent but disen-gaged attitude toward the military – we love the troops, but we'd rather not think about them – has become so familiar that we assume it is the American norm."[26] One serving officer grumbled that "many Americans, especially our elite classes, consider the military a bit like a guard dog. They are very thankful for our protection, but they probably wouldn't want to have it as a neighbor. And they certainly are not going to influence or inspire their own kids to join that pack of Rottweilers to protect America."[27]

For the British Army in 1914 and a previous generation of US Army troopers in 1941, combat against peer competitors brought them once again into align-ment with wider society, but at a very high price. While the British Expeditionary Force undoubtedly helped stave off not only Britain's own early defeat but also that of its French ally, and US forces on the Bataan Peninsula bought time for the Allied coalition in the Pacific to gather strength, they accomplished those feats only at the cost of their own near or total annihilation. There certainly is a better way of reconnecting America's military with the society that it serves and compelling it to adapt to the uncomfortable challenges of a changing battlefield landscape. Examining its culture, or cul-tures, and shaping them to conform to the most successful aspects of their historical counterparts would be a good place to start.

[25] David Zucchino and David S. Cloud, "U.S. Military and Civilians Are Increasingly Divided," *Los Angeles Times* (May 24, 2015).
[26] James Fallows, "The Tragedy of the American Military," *Atlantic* (January–February 2015), 18–21, 18.
[27] Quoted in Zucchino and Cloud, "U.S. Military and Civilians Are Increasingly Divided."

Index